B. P. Pratten

Hebrew-English Lexicon

Containing all the Hebrew and Chaldee Words in the Old Testament Scriptures

B. P. Pratten

Hebrew-English Lexicon
Containing all the Hebrew and Chaldee Words in the Old Testament Scriptures

ISBN/EAN: 9783337226091

Printed in Europe, USA, Canada, Australia, Japan

Cover: Foto ©Thomas Meinert / pixelio.de

More available books at **www.hansebooks.com**

HEBREW-ENGLISH LEXICON

CONTAINING

ALL THE HEBREW AND CHALDEE WORDS IN THE OLD TESTAMENT SCRIPTURES, WITH THEIR MEANINGS IN ENGLISH.

Multæ terricolis linguæ, cœlestibus una.

LONDON
SAMUEL BAGSTER AND SONS, LIMITED
NEW YORK: JAMES POTT & CO.
1898

PREFACE.

The best modern authorities have been consulted in the preparation of the present work; and we have endeavoured to give the results of their researches in as condensed and convenient a form for reference as possible.

The arrangement is that of Leopold's "Lexicon Manuale," which is itself taken altogether from the larger lexicons of Gesenius and Winer.

The valuable analytical Index which Leopold, from the same authorities, prints separately as an appendix, we have incorporated with the lexicon itself, in alphabetical order; thus making, it is hoped, a useful addition to his already copious collection of references.

To economise the student's time as far as possible, the meaning in English accompanies the reference wherever it has been found practicable to express it by a single word; in the hope of combining, in some degree, the advantages of the alphabetical with those of the radical arrangement, upon which the lexicon of Leopold is formed.

All fictitious roots have been discarded: i. e. words

occurring in no language, but which ought to be the roots whence certain Hebrew nouns have been derived, according to the analogy of the Hebrew grammar.

We are well aware of the advantage which these invented words afford to the arrangement under roots; but it is obvious, nevertheless, that nothing of this nature can compensate for the evil which arises from the presentation of a falsity to the mind of a beginner. The only words not occurring in the Bible which will be found in this lexicon are roots from the cognate languages, bearing a fair similarity of meaning to the Hebrew compounds which are arranged with them. In the many cases in which no such resemblance is to be found, the simplest form of the Hebrew compound has been printed in the larger character by which radical words are denoted.

The proper names are arranged as Leopold has given them, under the roots whence, according to the analogy of the Hebrew grammar, they would appear to be derived. This, however, is merely for the convenience of finding them in the lexicon. The derivations which he has added have been all but invariably discarded. A high authority in Hebrew lexicography having questioned the necessity, or even propriety, of inserting the proper names in the lexicon at all, it is right to explain that they have been retained in order to relieve the beginner in Hebrew from the necessity of resorting to the very expedient whereby that author proposes to dispense with them, namely, by referring him to an approved version. The compiler of the present work has found a frequent appeal to translations to interfere so fatally with his own progress in the acquisition of a language, that he has felt it his duty to bestow much care and pains upon them, making many additions to Leopold, so as to put the student in possession of the whole of the proper names that occur in the Hebrew Bible, even though in so many instances no better account of them can be given, than that they are names of persons or places.

As to the meanings (which form of course the really important part of the work), but very little use has been made of the Latin renderings of Leopold, which are only of any value when they repeat those of the authors upon whose labours his lexicon is founded. Leopold's authorities themselves, as well as others, to whose works he had probably no access, have been consulted upon every word. The concordances of Noldius and Fürst have also been appealed to in all cases of difficulty arising from variations of opinion among the authorities consulted; and thus from the passages themselves it has been endeavoured to form a judgment of the words which best expressed the sense of the sacred text. For this purpose, the racy idiomatic English of Professor Lee's renderings has been freely taken advantage of; this obligation to him is thankfully acknowledged.

The lexicon is specially designed to put into the hands of the English student, in a compressed and compendious form, the contributions of modern philology to the interpretation of the Hebrew Scriptures. There are many words the meaning of which the researches of the learned have not succeeded hitherto in elucidating. In such cases it has been deemed the best course to give the rendering in the Authorised English Version only. The speculations which may have been indulged in by interpreters, ancient or modern, as to their meaning, are of little value in themselves, while to the beginner they are worse than worthless; they are moreover known to the proficient, and the student will readily find them in the larger lexicons. We give a single instance. The word אַבְרֵךְ Gen. 41:43 is rendered by our translators "bow the knee," assuming it to be an anomalous Hiphil form of the denominative from בֶּרֶךְ "knee." This, though somewhat forced, is at any rate more feasible than the modern interpretation, which, assuming with considerable probability that it is an Egyptian word or phrase, declares that it is equivalent to ⲁⲡⲉⲣⲉⲕ, which is to be translated "bow the head." Such however is by no means the case The general meaning of the word ⲁⲡⲉ or ⲁⲫⲉ is "the top or summit of a thing." It does not appear to be used of the head at all in the Coptic Bible, but rather of the crown or scalp. The Egyptian word for the head, as a member of the body, is ϫⲱ. The word ⲣⲉⲕ means "to bow," but the construction of the supposed phrase is altogether foreign to the idiom of the language. Nor does it appear in any degree probable from the remains of it, which are very copious, that ⲁⲡⲉⲣⲉⲕ or ⲁⲫⲉⲣⲉⲕ would be a more intelligible direction to an Egyptian to bow the head than "crown bow" would be to an Englishman. The phrase repeatedly occurs in the Coptic Bible, and is written ⲣⲉⲕϫⲱ. It is to be regretted that biblical difficulties are too often dealt with in this loose unsatisfactory manner.

In the English meanings throughout, it has been endeavoured to counteract the blasphemous attempt of one of the great modern schools of sacred hermeneutics to vulgarise and debase the word of God by quaint and burlesque interpretations. On the other hand, it has been deemed expedient to avoid the equally fallacious principle of another class of interpreters, who elevate into authoritative glosses the renderings of writers confessedly ignorant of Hebrew, for no better reason than that they wrote some twelve or fifteen centuries ago.

We have striven to give the student the benefit of the labours of both schools, without leading him into the errors of either.

It is only needful further to explain that wherever a word or meaning is accompanied by one, or in some instances by two references, it is denoted that such word or meaning occurs in those places only in the Hebrew

ABBREVIATIONS OF GRAMMATICAL TERMS USED IN THE LEXICON.

m. masculine

f. feminine.

s. substantive.

pa particle.

part. participle.

denom. denominative; that is, a verb derived immediately from a noun (*de nomine*).

patron. patronymic: a proper name derived from that of the father of the individual.

sing. singular

pl. plural.

Niph. Niphal form of verb.

Hiph. Hiphil ,, ,,

Hith. Hithpael ,,

Pi. Piel ,, ,,

Pu. Pual ,, ,,

Po. Poel *or* Polel ,,

Hoth. Hothpael ,,

Ith. Ithpael ,, ,,

imp. imperative mood.

const. construct state of noun.

emph. emphatic state of noun.

LEXICON.

אָב m. (const. אֲבִי and אַב, Gen. 17:4, 5; with suff. אָבִי, אָבִיךָ, אֲבִיכֶם; pl. אָבוֹת).—I. *a father.*—II. *a progenitor, ancestor;* used generally for any senior male relative.—III. *an originator, inventor,* Gen. 10:21, &c.—IV. *a head, chief,* or *ruler;* applied to kings, prophets, priests, &c.; אָב לְפַרְעֹה *a father,* that is, a counsellor *to Pharaoh,* Gen. 45:8.

אַב m. Ch. (with suff. אֲבִי, אֲבוּךְ, אֲבוּהִי, pl. אֲבָהָן), *a father.*

אָבַב not used.

אֵב m., *greenness, freshness,* אִבִּים *green herbs.*

אֵב m., Ch. *fruit;* אִנְבֵּהּ for אִבֵּהּ, *his fruit.*

אָבִיב m.—I. *a green ear of corn,* Lev. 2:14.—II. *shooting into the ear;* spoken of barley, Ex. 9:31. Hence חֹדֶשׁ הָאָבִיב *the month Abib,* the name of the month in which the barley shoots into ear, corresponding partly with our March, partly with April, otherwise called נִיסָן.

אֲבַגְתָא p.n., one of the chamberlains of King Ahasuerus, Est. 1:10.

אָבַד (inf. אֲבֹד, אָבֹד, fut. יֹאבֵד and יֹאבַד).—I. *strayed, lost.*—II. *was ruined, perished* (const. with לְ or מִן); part. אֹבֵד *one about to perish, a wretch;* Pi. אִבַּד, and Hiph. הֶאֱבִיד *made to stray, dispersed, laid waste, ruined, destroyed.*

אֲבַד Ch. (fut. יֵאבַד), *perished;* Aph. הוֹבֵד *destroyed;* Hoph. הוּבַד *was destroyed.*

אֹבֵד m., *perishing, ruin.*

אֲבֵדָה f., *something lost, the grave;* see following word.

אֲבַדּוֹן *extermination, destruction, the grave,* the place where the body decays after death, opposed to שְׁאוֹל the place of the soul after death, Pro. 15:11, &c.; see the word.

וְאַאַבֶּדְךָ for וְאַבֶּדְךָ, אַבֶּדְךָ, Pi. fut. with suff.

אַבְדָן m., *extermination, ruin,* Est. 9:5; אָבְדָן the same, Est. 8:6.

אָבָה (fut. יֹאבֶה), in Kal only, *desirous, willing;* const. mostly with the neg. לֹא and with or without לְ.

אֵבֶה m., *a reed, rush;* אֳנִיּוֹת אֵבֶה *vessels made of reeds,* Job 9:26.

אָבוּא for אָבוּ pret. pl.

אֶבְיוֹן m., *wishing, desiring;* hence, *destitute, poor, miserable.*

אֲבִיּוֹנָה f., *desire,* Eccl. 12:5.

אֲבוֹי (lit. *misery*), *alas!* Pro. 23:29.

אֵבוֹשׁ fut.; see בּוֹשׁ.

אָבַח, אִבְחָה f.; אִבְחַת חֶרֶב, *the resting, descent of the sword;* according to others, *the threatening of the sword,* or, *the drawn sword.* Ezek. 21:20.

אֲבַטִּיחִים m. pl., *melons,* Nu. 11:5; see טבח.

אָבִי for אָבִיא Hiph. fut. 1 pers.; see בּוֹא, 1 Ki. 21:29; Mic. 1:15.

אֲבִי (*my father*), p. n., the mother of King Hezekiah, 2 Kings 18:2.

אֹבִידָה for אַאֲבִידָה Hiph. fut. 1. pers.; see אבד.

אֲבִיאֵל (*the divine Father*), p. n.—I. the grandfather of Saul, 1 Sa. 9:1.—II. one of David's generals.

אֶבְיָסָף, אֲבִיאָסָף (*father of gathering, collector*), p. n., one of the Korahites.

אֲבִיגַל, אֲבִיגַיִל (*she whose father rejoiceth,* or, *the dancer*), p. n.—I. the wife of Nabal, afterwards of David.—II. the sister of David, 1 Chron. 2:16.

אֲבִידָן (*the father of judgment, the judge*) p. n., one of the princes of Benjamin, Nu. 1:11, &c.

אֲבִיָּה, אֲבִיָּהוּ (*he whose father is Jehovah*), see אֲבִיָּם; p. n.—I. of a man. —II. of a woman

אֲבִיהוּא p. n., a son of Aaron.

אֲבִיהוּד (*the father of glory,* πατροκλος), p. n. of a man

אֲבִיחַיִל (*the father of artifices, he who is skilful*), p. n. of a man.

אֲבִיחַיִל (the same), p. n. of a woman.

אֲבִיטוּב (*father of goodness*), p. n. of a man.

אֲבִיטַל (*father of dew, rigorous*), p. n., a wife of David.

אֲבִיָּם (*the sailor*), p. n. of a man; the same as אֲבִיָּהוּ, and probably an error of some transcriber.

אֲבִימָאֵל p. n. of a man.

אֲבִימֶלֶךְ (*father of a king*), p. n.—I. a king of the Philistines, Gen. *c.* 20, perhaps the common name of the kings of that country.—II. name of a man, Jud. 8:31, &c.

אֲבִינָדָב (*father of willingness*), p. n. of a man.

אֲבִינֹעַם (*father of pleasantness*), p. n. of a man.

אַבְנֵר, אֲבִינֵר (*father of light*), p. n., one of Saul's generals.

אֲבִיעֶזֶר (*father of help*), p. n. of a man.

אֲבִי־עַלְבוֹן m. (*violator*), p. n. of a man.

אָבִיר, אַבִּיר *mighty;* see אבר.

אֲבִירָם m. (*father of pride, a proud one*), p. n. of a man.

אֲבִישַׁג f. p. n., one of David's concubines, 1 Kings 1:15, &c.

אֲבִישׁוּעַ (*father of salvation*), p. n. of a man.

אֲבִישׁוּר (*father of song, singer*), p. n. of a man, 1 Chron. 2:28.

אַבְשַׁי, אֲבִישַׁי (*father of gifts, generous*), p. n. of a man.

אֲבִישָׁלוֹם (*father of peace*), the grandfather of Abijam king of Judah, 1 Kings 15:2.

אֶבְיָתָר (*a father of excellence, he who excels*), *Abiathar*, the son of Ahimelech, a high priest in David's time, 1 Sa. 22:20.

יִתְאַבְּכוּ "they swell
; motion like volumes
sa. 9:17.

(יֶ), *mourned, lamented;*
לְ; Hiph. הֶאֱבִיל *made*
nourn; Hith. הִתְאַבֵּל
ok himself to mourn;
אֶ or עַל.

(אֲבֵלִים .pl ;אֲבֶל־, אֲבֵ),
rning; אֵבֶל m. (with
e same, *grief, howling.*
mourning of Egypt),
beyond Jordan, where
of Israel mourned for
when they carried him
urial, Gen. 50:11.

ed (Arab. *fresh, green,*

place, field; hence the
mes of places.—I. 'א
greater Abel, a district
tines, 1 Sa. 6:18.—II.
א a large city in the
ibe of Manasseh, called
Chron. 16:4.—III. 'א
ce in the land of Moab.
נ 'א a village of the
—V. א' מְחוֹלָה a village
f Issachar; hence the
מְחֹלָתִי; see the word.

certainly, but, indeed.
יבל.

one, rock (pl. אֲבָנִים,
like a stone; אֶבֶן יָד
h may be thrown with
(אֲבָנִים גְּדֹלוֹת) א' בַּר
—II. *precious stones,*
אַבְנֵי *shining stones.*

—III. *a weight;* אֶבֶן וָאֶבֶן *divers weights.*—IV. *a plummet.*

אֶבֶן עֶזֶר (*stone of help*), p. n. of a place, 1 Sa. 7:12.

אֶבֶן הָאֶזֶל (*stone of departure*), p. n. of a place.

אֶבֶן f. Ch. emph. state אַבְנָא; *a stone.*

אֹבֶן m., dual אָבְנַיִם.—I. "potter's wheel," Jer. 18:3.—II. "upon the stools," Ex. 1:16; Eng. Ver. The true meaning is uncertain.

אֲבָנָה p. n., a river of Damascus, 2 Ki. 5:12.

אַבְנֵט see בנט.

אַבְנֵר p. n. of a man; see אֲבִינֵר.

אָבַס, part. אָבוּס *fattened.*

אֵבוּס m. (pl. אֲבוּסִים) *a crib* or *stall* in which animals are fed; מַאֲבוּס m., *barn, granary,* Jer. 50:26.

אֲבַעְבֻּעוֹת *ulcers;* see בּוּעַ.

אֶבֶץ p.n. of a city in the tribe of Issachar.

אִבְצָן (*he who is shining, famous*), p. n., a judge of Israel.

אבק m., *fine dust, powder;* אֲבָקָה f., אַבְקַת רוֹכֵל *aromatic dust, powdered perfume;* "powder of the merchant," Cant. 3:6, Eng. Ver.; נֶאֱבַק Niph. *wrestled* (because the ancient wrestlers covered their bodies with dust before they began to wrestle).

אָבַר Kal, not used, *was strong;* Hiph. הֶאֱבִיר *flew, soared.*

אֵבֶר m., *quill, wing-feather.*

אֶבְרָה f., the same.

אָבִיר, אַבִּיר m.—I. *mighty* (an epithet of God).—II. *strong, valiant, noble;* אַבִּירִים *strong bulls,* or *horses;* אַבִּיר הָרֹעִים *the prince of the shepherds.*

אַבְרָם (*exalted father*), p. n., *Abram*; אַבְרָהָם (*father of a multitude*), p. n., the patriarch *Abraham*.
אַבְרֵךְ Gen. 41:43, "bow the knee," Eng. Ver. The true meaning is uncertain.
אֲבָרֶכְכָה Pi. fut. with suff.; see ברך.
אַבְשַׁי p. n., see אבישי.
אַבְשָׁלוֹם (*father of peace*), p. n., *Absalom*, the son of David.
אָגֵא (*fugitive*), p. n. of a man.
אֶגְאַלְתִּי Hith. pret. 1. pers. for הִגְאַלְתִּי; see גאל.
אֲגַג p. n., a king of the Amalekites.
אֲגָגִי *Agagite*, a title of Haman, Est. 3:1.
אָגַד not used (Ch. and Arab. *bound in a mass*).
אֲגֻדָּה f.—I. *a bunch* or *bundle* (*of hyssop*).—II. *a band* or *body of men*; אֲגֻדָּתוֹ *his church, people*, Am. 9:6. —III. *knots, bindings*, Isa. 58:6.
אֱגוֹז m., *a nut*, Cant. 6:11.
אָגוּר (*companion*), p. n. of a woman.
אֲגוֹרָה *wages*; see אגר.
אָגַל not used (Arab. *gathered together, collected*).
אֵגֶל m., אֶגְלֵי טָל *drops of dew*, Job 38:28.
אֶגְלַיִם (*two fountains*), p. n., a village of the Moabites, Isa. 15:8.
אָגַם not used (Arab. *was hot*).
אָגֵם Ch., *was stagnant* (of water); see עגם.
אֲגַם m. (pl. אַגְמֵי, אֲגַמִּים).—I. *a pool, pond, marsh*.—II. *flags, reeds*.
אָגֵם m., *sorrowful*.
אַגְמוֹן m.—I. *a reed, rush*.—II. *a rope of rushes*.—III. *a cauldron, kettle*, Job 41:12, this is however doubtful. See Lee in loco.
אָגַן (Arab. *a bason*); אַגָּן m., אַגָּנָה f., (pl. אַגָּנוֹת), *a bason* or *bowl*.
אֲגַף or אָגָף m., pl. אֲגַפִּים *hosts, armies* see גַּף.
אָגַר (fut. יֶאֱגֹר), *he laid up provision*.
אֲגוֹרָה f., *a small coin*; ὀβολός, 1 Sa 2:36; see גרה.
אִגְּרָא f. Ch. emph. state אִגַּרְתָּא; same as the following word.
אִגֶּרֶת f. (pl. אִגְּרוֹת), *letter, edict*.
אֲגַרְטָל *a dish* or *bason*, Ezr. 1:9.
אֶגְרוֹף *the fist*; see גרף.
אֵד *mist, vapour*; see אוד.
אָדַב Kal, not used, Hiph. *he languished was fatigued*; (לַאֲדִיב for לְהַאֲדִיב inf.).
אַדְבְּאֵל (*the finger of God*), p. n. of a man
אֲדַדֶּה for אֶתְדַּדֶּה Hith. fut.; with suff. אֲדַדֵּם; see דדה.
אֲדַד (*long-lived*), p. n. of a man.
אִדּוֹ p. n. of a man.
אֲדֹנָי, אָדוֹן *Lord*; see אֶדֶן.
אֲדוֹרַיִם (*two hills*), p. n., a city of Judah.
אֲדוֹרָם p. n. of a man.
אֱדַיִן Ch. adv., *then*; בֵּאדַיִן *at that very time*; מִן אֱדַיִן *from that time*.
אֲדִיקֵם Hiph. fut. with suff. for אֲדִקֵּם; see דקק.
אַדִּיר *great*; see אדר.
אֲדַלְיָה (*Jehovah's righteousness*), p. n. of a man.
אָדַם *was red, reddish brown*; Pu. part מְאָדָּם *growing, turning red*; Hiph *be red*; Hith. *grow red*.
דָּם m. (const. דַּם; with suff. דָּמוֹ, דִּמְכֶם; pl. דָּמִים, דְּמֵי).—I. *blood*; דָּם נָקִי

innocent blood; אִישׁ דָּמִים *a man of bloods,* i.e. *cruel.*—II. *slaughter, murder;* גֹּאֵל הַדָּם *avenger of blood;* אֵין לוֹ דָּם *blood is not on him,* i.e. *he has done no murder;* בֵּית הַדָּמִים *a bloody house.*—III. דַּם עֲנָבִים *blood of grapes, wine;* see דמה.

אָדָם m., *man* (in general); כָּל־אָדָם *all men;* אָדָם *a man,* as distinguished from a woman; בֶּן־אָדָם *mortal man.*

אָדָם p.n.—I. *Adam,* the first man.—II. a city on Jordan, Jos. 3:16.

אָדֹם, אָדוֹם m., אֲדֻמָּה f., *red, reddish brown.*

אֱדֹם (*red*), p.n., one of the names of Esau.

אֱדֹם p.n., *the land of Edom;* אֲדֹמִי *an Edomite.*

אֹדֶם m., *a ruby,* or *carnelion.*

אֵדֹם, וָאֵדֹּם Kal fut.; see דמם.

אֲדַמְדָּם m.; f. אֲדַמְדֶּמֶת; pl. אֲדַמְדַּמּוֹת *very red, glowing.*

אֲדָמָה f.—I. *ground, soil;* אֹהֵב א׳ *given to agriculture,* lit. *loving the ground.*—II. *fruit, produce.*—III. *region, country, the whole earth.*—IV. p.n., a city of the tribe of Naphtali.

אַדְמָה p.n., one of the cities of the plain.

אֶדַּמֶּה for אֶתְדַּמֶּה Hith. fut. 1. pers.; see דמה.

אֲדֻמִּים p.n. of a place.

אַדְמוֹנִי *red haired,* πυῤῥάκης.

אֲדָמִי p. n., a city of the tribe of Naphtali.

אַדְמָתָא (*land*), p. n. of a man.

אֶדֶן m. (pl. אֲדָנִים)—I. *the base of a column.*—II. *any foundation.*

אַדּוֹן, אַדָּן p. n. of a man.

אָדוֹן m. (from אדן, pl. אֲדוֹנִים), *proprietor, master, lord.*

אֲדֹנָי m., *the Lord,* exclusively applied to God.

אֲדֹנִי בֶזֶק (*lord of Bezek*), p. n., a king of the Canaanites, Jud. 1:5.

אֲדֹנִי צֶדֶק (*righteous lord*), p.n., Canaanitish king of Jerusalem, Jos. 10:1.

אֲדֹנִיָּה (*the Lord is my Lord*), p.n. of a m.

אֲדֹנִיָּהוּ p. n. of a man.

אֲדֹנִיקָם (*the Lord confirmeth*), p.n. of a m.

אֲדֹנִירָם (*the Lord exalteth*), p. n. of a man, 1 Ki. 4:6.

אָדַר does not occur in Kal; Niph. part. נֶאְדָּר, with Jod parag. נֶאְדָּרִי, *it hath become glorious;* Hiph. (fut. יַאְדִּיר) *he made glorious.*

אַדִּיר *great, powerful, glorious, majestic.*

אַדִּיר m., *a prince*

אֶדֶר m.—I. *a cloak;* see אַדֶּרֶת—II. *amplitude, splendour.*

אַדֶּרֶת f. (with suff. אַדַּרְתּוֹ).—I. *a cloak;* א׳ שִׁנְעָר *a Babylonish garment;* א׳ שֵׂעָר *a hair cloak.*—II. *magnificence.*

אֲדַרְגָּזְרִין Ch. pl., *officers of the court at Babylon,* Dan. 3:2, 3, the nature of their office unknown.

אַדָּר p n.—I. a place in the tribe of Judah.—II. of a man.

אִדַּר *threshing-floor;* see גדר.

אֲדָר m., the twelfth month of the Hebrew year, corresponding with our February and March.

אַדְרַזְדָּא Ch., *quickly, diligently.*

אֲדַרְכּוֹן, דַּרְכְּמוֹן, δαρεικὸς, a Persian gold coin.

אַדְרַמֶּלֶךְ (*the exalted Moloch*), p. n.—I. an idol of the Sepharvites, 2 Ki. 17:31.—II. a son of Sennacherib, Isa. 37:38, &c.

אֶזְרָע *arm;* see דרע.

אֶדְרֶעִי (*planting*), p. n.—I. the city of Og, Deu. 1:4.—II. a city of the tribe of Naphtali.

אִדְּרֹשׁ for הִדָּרֹשׁ Niph. inf. abs.; see דרשׁ.

אָדַשׁ (inf. אָדוֹשׁ the same as דּוּשׁ), *threshing*, beating out corn with the wheel, Isa. 28:28.

אָהַב, אָהֵב (inf. const. אַהֲבָה, אֱהֹב; imp. אֱהַב; fut. יֶאֱהַב; p. 1. אֹהַב and אֶהַב), *loved, desired, delighted in;* part. אֹהֵב (pl. אֹהֲבִים, f. אֹהֶבֶת) *a friend;* Niph. part. pl. נֶאֱהָבִים *loved, amiable;* Pi. part. מְאַהֵב *lover.*

אֶהַב Kal fut. 1. pers.

אַהֲבָה f., *love, beloved.*

אֲהָבִים m. pl. (sing. אַהַב), *amours, loves, love-gifts.*

אֳהָבִים m. pl. (sing. אֹהַב), the same.

אֹהַד (*strength*), p. n., one of the sons of Simeon.

אֲהָהּ *ah! alas!* an exclamation of sorrow.

אַהֲוָא p. n.—I. of a country.—II. of a river.

אֵהוּד (*he who is powerful*), p. n. of a man.

אֶהוֹדֶנּוּ (for אוֹדֶנּוּ) Hiph. fut. 1. pers. with suff.; see ידה.

אֱהִי the same as אֵי *where?*

אֱהִי probably for אַיֵּה *where?* which see: Hos. 13:10.

אֶהְיִ fut. apoc. 1. pers.; see היה.

אָהַל (fut. יֶאֱהַל), *pitched a tent, lived in tents;* Pi. fut. יַהֵל for יְאַהֵל the same; יַאֲהִיל *shone*, Job 25:5; see הלל *to shine.*

אֹהֶל m. (with ה parag. אֹהֱלָה; with suff. אָהֳלִי, אָהָלְךָ; Syr. אֹהֲלֶךָ; pl. אֳהָלִים; Syr. אֹהָלֵי, אֹהָלִים).—I. *tabernacle, tent, habitation.*—II. p. n. of a man, 1 Chron. 3:20.

אָהֳלָה (*her tent*), p.n., allegorical name of Samaria, Eze. 23:4.

אָהֳלִיאָב (*tent of her father*), p.n. of a m

אָהֳלִיבָה (*my tent with her*), p.n., allegorical name of Jerusalem, Eze. 23:4.

אָהֳלִיבָמָה (*my tent a high place*), p. n. of a wife of Esau.

אֲהָלִים m. pl., אֲהָלוֹת f., ξυλαλόη, ἀγάλλοχον, *lign-alocs*, a perfumed wood.

אֶהֱמָיָה fut. with ה parag. for אֶהֱמֶה, see המה.

אַהֲרֹן p. n., *Aaron*, the brother of Moses; בֵּית א׳, בְּנֵי א׳ *Aaronites.*

אוֹ conj.—I. *or, either;* יָמִים אוֹ עָשׂוֹר *ten days at least.*—II. *for;* אוֹ כִּי *but if.*—III. אוֹ....אוֹ, *whether....or.*

אַו *desire;* see אוה.

אוּאֵל p. n. of a man.

אוב not used.

אוֹב m. (pl. אוֹבוֹת).—I. *a spirit of divination*, or *necromancy.*—II. νεκρόμαντις, *a necromancer*, one who calls up spirits from the abyss to foretel future events.—III. *the art of necromancy.*

אוֹבוֹת I. *skins used as bottles for wine*, Job 32:19.—II. p. n. of a place in the wilderness.

אוֹבִיל (*he that causeth joy*), p. n. of a man, I Chron. 27:30.

אוֹבָל; see יבל

אוד not used (Arab. *bent, crooked; also wood*); etymology doubtful.

אֵד m., *smoke, mist*.

אוּד m., *smoking firebrand*.

אוֹדוֹת f. pl., *projects, means, cause*; עַל אוֹדוֹת (and אַל for אֶל) *because of*; עַל אֹדוֹתַי *on my account*; עַל אוֹדוֹתֶיךָ *because of thee*.

אוֹדְךָ, with נ epenth. אוֹדֶנְךָ Hiph. fut. 1. pers. with suff.; see ידה.

אֵיד m., *calamity, destruction*.

מְאֹד m.—I. *power, might, excess*; בְּכָל־מְאֹדֶךָ *with all thy might*; בִּמְאֹד מְאֹד *in great excess*; עַד מְאֹד, עַד לִמְאֹד *even to excess, exceedingly*.—II. adv. *exceedingly*.

אָוָה not used (Arab. *desired*); Pi. אִוָּה (fut. יְאַוֶּה), *desired, longed for*, const. with ב and ל; Hith. הִתְאַוָּה (fut. apoc. יִתְאָו), *desired, coveted, claimed*; וְהִתְאַוִּיתֶם לָכֶם *and claim for yourselves*, Nu.34:10.

אַו or אֵו m., *desire*, Pro. 31:4.

אַוָּה f.—I. *natural desire for food*.—II. *lust*.

מַאֲוַי m. (pl. מַאֲוַיִּים), *desires*, Ps. 140:9.

תַּאֲוָה f.—I. *desire, lust*.—II. *an object of desire*; see תאה.

אוחולה, Kri אוֹחִילָה Hiph. fut. 1. pers.; see חול.

אוֹי, אוֹיָה I. *alas!* expression of grief.—II. *ho!* expressing anger.

אוֹת com. (pl. אֹתוֹת).—I. *mark, memorial, warning*.—II. *sign, portent, miracle*.

אָת Ch. (pl. אָתִין), the same.

אִי m. (pl. אִיִּים).—I. *habitable land, continent, island*.—II. *shore, coast, countries on the coast*; אִיֵּי הַגּוֹיִם and אִיֵּי הַיָּם *isles of the Gentiles, isles of the West*, countries little known to the Hebrews.—III. אִיִּים *savage land animals*, Is. 13:22, hence:—IV. interj. *woe! horror!* see און.

אוֹיֵב *enemy*; see איב.

אוּזַי p. n. of a man.

אוּזָל p. n. of a city in Arabia; probably Senaar, the capital of Arabia Felix, Gen. 10:27.

אֱוִי p. n. of a king of Midian.

אוֹכִיל Hiph. fut. 1. pers.; see אכל.

אוֹכַל Kal fut. 1. pers.; see אכל.

אָוַל root not used; same as יאל.

אֱוִיל *a fool, an impious person*.

אֱוִיל־מְרֹדַךְ p. n., a king of Babylon, descendant of Nebuchadnezzar, 2 Ki. 25:27.

אֱוִילִי, same as אֱוִיל.

אִוֶּלֶת f. (with suff. אִוַּלְתִּי), *folly, sin*.

I. **אול** (Arab. *to dispose, govern aright*); root not used.

אוּל m.—I. *a prince*.—II. *administration*.—III. *body*, Ps. 73:4.

אוּלַי adv.—I. *perhaps, unless*.—II. p.n. of a river, Dan. 8:2.

אוּלָם, אֻלָם (pl. אֻלַמִּים).—I. m., *an entrance hall, vestibule*.—II. pa. *but, nevertheless*.—III. p. n. of a man.

II. **אול** (Arab. *grew thick*, of fluids); root not used.

אַיִל m. (const. אֵיל; pl. אֵילִים).—I. *a ram*.—II. *lintel, arch over a door or window*.

אֱיָל m., *strength, force.*

אֱיָלוּת f., the same.

אַיָּל com., *an antelope, gazelle.*

אַיָּלָה f. (pl. אַיָּלוֹת; const. אַיְלוֹת), *female antelope.*

אַיֶּלֶת f., the same; אַיֶּלֶת הַשַּׁחַר the name of the tune to which the Psalm is to be sung, Ps. 22.

אַיִל m. (pl. אֵילִים, אֵלִים).—I. *hero, mighty man.*—II. *the pine* or *terebinth* (a tall thick tree).

אֵילִם p.n. of one of the stations of the Israelites in the wilderness, Ex.*c.*15.

אֵל (with suff. אֵלִי; pl. אֵלִים, אֵלִם).—I. *hero, man of might.*—II. *power ;* יֶשׁ לְאֵל יָדִי *it is in the power of my hand,* i.e. I am able.—III. *God* (the true God); בְּנֵי אֵלִים *the sons of God,* i.e. *the angels.*—IV. an epithet denoting excellence; אַרְזֵי אֵל *cedars of God,* i.e. lofty, well grown.—V. *an idol, false god.*

אֵלָה f., *terebinth;* see אַיִל, אֵלָה, &c.

אֵלוֹן m.—I. *oak, lofty tree;* compare preceding word.—II. p.n. of a man. —III. of a city.

אֵלָם, אֵילָם m., *a lintel;* see אוּלָם I.

אִילָן m. Ch., *a tree.*

אוֹלִיךְ, וָאוֹלֵךְ Hiph. fut. 1. pers.; see הלך, ילך.

אוֹמָר p. n. of a man.

און or **אין** root not used; (Arab. *time, a fit time*).

אָוֶן m. (with suff. אוֹנִי, אוֹנְךָ, אוֹנָם; pl. אוֹנִים).—I. *vanity, falseness, that which is nothing,* hence:—II. *an idol;* בֵּית אָוֶן *house of idols;* בִּקְעַת אָוֶן *valley of idols* (a valley near Damascus, now *Un,* Am. 1:5). —III. *sin, wickedness.*—IV. *sorrow, distress;* בֶּן־אוֹנִי *the son of my sorrow;* לֶחֶם אוֹנִים *bread of affliction;* see אנן.

און m. (with suff. like אָוֶן).—I. *power.* —II. *manhood;* רֵאשִׁית הָאוֹן *firstborn.*—III. *wealth, riches.*

אַיִן const. אֵין I. *non-existence;* אֵין בַּבּוֹר *he was not in the pit;* אֵין יֹצֵא וְאֵין בָּא *there was neither going out nor coming in;* אֵין לִי *I have not,* lit. *there is nothing to me;* אֵין לָבוֹא "none might enter," Eng. Ver., Est. 4:2; אֵין דָּבָר, מְאוּמָה *nothing;* אֵין כֹּל *absolutely nothing;* אֵינֶנּוּ *it is not.*—II. with personal pronoun אֵינֶנִּי, אֵינְךָ, אֵינֵךְ, אֵינֶנּוּ, אֵינֶנָּה, אֵינְכֶם, אֵינָם and אֵינֵימוֹ *I am, was, not, shall not be, thou art not, &c.*—III. with prepositions, בְּאֵין *in not being, before, without,* כְּאַיִן *like not being, nearly,* Ps.73:2; לְאֵין *to him who has not,* Is. 40:29; מֵאַיִן (poetic only), *not,* absolute negation; מֵאֵין יוֹשֵׁב *no inhabitant,* Jer. 33:10.

אִין same as אַיִן, 1 Sa. 21:9.

אִי (perhaps from אַיִן), *not,* Job *c.* 22;

אִי־כָבוֹד (*ignoble*), p. n. of a man.

תְּאֵנָה f. (pl. תְּאֵנִים), *fig* (tree and fruit); יָשַׁב תַּחַת תְּאֵנָתוֹ *he sat under his fig-tree,* i. e. *he lived* peacefully and prosperously.

תְּאֻנִים m. pl., *vexation, vanity, falsehood,* Eze. 24:12.

אוֹן I. (*strength*), p. n. of a man.—II. אוֹן, אֹן *Heliopolis,* a city of Lower Egypt.

אוֹנוֹ (*strong*), p. n. of a city in the tribe of Benjamin.

אוֹנָם (the same), p. n. of a man.

אוֹ (*vigorous*), p. n., one of the sons of Judah.

אוּ p. n., a country where gold was found (perhaps the same as the following word).

אוֹפִ, אוֹפִר p. n., a country abounding in gold, gems, and perfumed wood.

אוֹ *a wheel*; see אפן.

אוּ *pressed, was urgent upon*; const. with בּ, לְ, מִן; Hiph. *pressed, hastened*; const. with בְּ, לְ.

אוֹצָ *treasure*; see אצר.

אוֹצְרָ Hiph. fut. 1. pers. with ה parag.; see רצא.

אוֹ I. *became light, shone, enlightened.* —II. *prospered*; imperat. אוֹרִי f. *shine thou*, Isa. 60:1. Niph. נָאוֹר (fut. יֵאוֹר, יֵאֹר), *become bright*; part. נָאוֹר *illustrious.* Hiph. הֵאִיר (fut. apoc. יָאֵר).—I. *enlighten, illuminate, kindle.*—II. ה׳ פְּנֵי, עֵינֵי פ׳ *cheer up, exhilarate*, lit. *enlighten the eyes*, or *face*; ה׳ פָּנָיו (const. with אֶל, אֶת, בְּ, לְ, עַל).—III. *instruct, inform* (illuminate the mind), Ps. 119:130.

אוֹר m. (f. Job 36:32).—I. *light, brightness, lightning, luminary*; אוֹר חַיִּים *the light of life* א׳ פָּנִים *light of the face*, i. e. cheerfulness, good will; pl. אוֹרִים *stars*, i. e. *luminaries*, Ps. 136:7.—II. metaph. *prosperity.*—III. *knowledge.*

אוּר I. *fire, the light of fire.*—II. p.n. of a man.—III. אוּרִים וְתֻמִּים (אֻרִים) LXX. δήλωσις καὶ ἀλήθεια, "Urim and Thummim," Eng. Ver., a part of the high-priest's breast-plate; meaning uncertain.—IV. אֻרִים (*lights*), p. n. of a country.—V. אוּר כַּשְׂדִּים p.n., *Ur of the Chaldeans*, a place in Mesopotamia.

אוֹרָה f. (pl. אוֹרוֹת).—I. *light*, Ps. 139:12.—II. *prosperity, joy*, Est. 8:16.—III. טַל אוֹרוֹת *light reflecting dew*, Isa. 26:19; אוֹרוֹת *herbs*, 2 Kings 4:39.

אוֹרוּ imp. pl.; see ארר.

מָאוֹר m.—I. *light*; מְאוֹרוֹת *stars*; *luminaries.*—II. *candlestick*; מְנֹרַת־הַמָּאוֹר *the candlestick in the tabernacle*, lit. *place of light.*

מְאוּרָה f., *den, hole, of a serpent*, Isa. 11:8.

אֻרוֹת *stables*; see ארה.

אוּרִי (*fiery*), p. n. of a man.

אוּרִיאֵל (*fire of God*), p. n. of a man.

אוּרִיָּה (the same), p. n.—I. the husband of Bathsheba.—II. a priest in the reign of Ahaz.

אות *sign*; see אָוָה.

אוּת or אוֹת; Niph. (fut. pl. p. 1. נֵאוֹת, p. 3. יֵאוֹתוּ), *consenting to, agreeing.*

אוֹתִיּוֹת part. f. pl.; see אתה.

אָז adv., *then, at that time* (used with either tense); מֵאָז (מִן־אָז).—I. *from that time, of old, before.*—II. *whence*; מֵאָז אַפֶּךָ *whence thine anger* (was kindled); מֵאָז בָּאתִי *whence I came*; with infin. מ׳ דַּבֶּרְךָ *whereof thou hast spoken.*

אֱזַי *then*, Ps. 124:3,4,5.

אֲזָא or אֲזָה Ch., *he kindled.*

אָזַב, root not used; Arab. the same meaning.

אֵזוֹב m., *hyssop.*

אֶזְבַּי p. n. of a man.

אֲזַד Ch., *went forth, departed.*

אֵזוֹר *belt*; see אזר.

אָזִין for אַאֲזִין Hiph. fut. 1. pers.; see אזן.

אַזְכָּרָה *memorial*; see זכר.

אָזַל *he went away, departed*; מְאוּזָּל *from* אוּזָל *Uzal* (see the word), Ez. 27:19, taken by mistake for Pu. part. of this verb. See Rosenmüller on the passage.

אֲזַל Ch., the same.

אֶזֶל m., *departure*, 1 Sa. 20:19, (some call it a p. n.).

אֱזֶל Ch. imp. for אֲזַל, Syr. for אֱזַל; see אזל.

אָזַן, Pi. אִזֵּן *attended to* and *investigated*, Ecc. 12:9. Hiph. הֶאֱזִין *heard, attended*; const. with אֶל, לְ, עַל, עַד: of God, *he hearkened, heard prayer*; of man, *he obeyed*.

מֹאזְנַיִם dual, *the balance*, lit. having two dishes, bilanx.

מֹאזְנַיִן Ch., the same.

אֹזֶן f. (with suff. אָזְנִי; dual אָזְנַיִם), *the ear*; בְּאָזְנֵי פ׳ *in the ears* (that is, the hearing), *of any one*.

אַזְנוֹת־תָּבוֹר p. n. of a city in the tribe of Naphtali.

אָזְנִי (*he who hearkens*), p. n. of a man, Nu. 26:16.

אֲזַנְיָה (*whom the Lord hears*), p. n. of a man.

אֻזֵּן שֶׁאֱרָה p. n. of a place.

אָזֵן m. (pl. אֲזֵנִים), "weapons," Deu. 23: 14, Eng. Ver.; meaning uncertain.

אֲזִקִּים *chains*; see זקק.

אָזַר (imp. אֱזֹר; fut. יֶאֱזֹר; with suff. יַאַזְרֵנִי), *bound, girt, clothed himself*; trop. אָזְרוּ חָיִל *they clothed themselves with strength*; const. with בְּ. Niph. part. נֶאְזָר *girded*; const. with בְּ. Pi. sense as Kal. Hith. *became bound, armed himself*.

אֵזוֹר m.—I. *a belt, girdle*.—II. *fetters*.

אֶזְרוֹעַ *arm*, same as זְרוֹעַ; see זרע.

אֶזְרָחִי, אֶזְרָח *native*; see זרח.

אָח m., (const. אֲחִי; with suff. אָחִי, אָחִינוּ, אָחִיךָ, אֲחִיכֶם; pl. אַחִים, אַחַי; with suff. אַחֵינוּ, אַחֶיךָ, אֶחָיו, אֲחֵיכֶם).—I. *a brother*.—II. *a relative*.—III. *a fellow countryman*.—IV. *a friend*.—V. any person or thing like another.—VI. a term of affection; אִישׁ מֵעַל אָחִיו *one from the other*; אִישׁ אֶל אָחִיו *one from the other*.

אַח Ch., *a brother*.

אַחֲוָה f., *fraternity*.

אָחוֹת f. (with suff. אֲחוֹתִי; pl. אֲחָיוֹת, with suff. אַחְיוֹתַי, אַחוֹתַיִךְ).—I. *sister*.—II. used as אָח V., which see; אִשָּׁה אֶל אֲחוֹתָהּ *one from the other* (of persons or things fem.).

אָח interj., *alas!* exclamation of grief.

אָחַח not used; οἰμώζειν, *to howl*; whence is derived:—

אֹחִים m. pl., *howlings*, or *howling animals* (it is uncertain which), Isa. 13:21.

אָח f., a pot filled with hot coals to warm rooms in winter, Jer. 36: 22, 23.

אַחְאָב (*brother of the father*), p.n., *Ahab*, king of Israel.

אֶחָב p. n. of the same king.

אַחְבָּן p. n. of a man.

אֶחָד const. אַחַד m., אַחַת with the pause, אֶחָת f.—I. *one*.—II. *the first* (used with days of the month); בְּאֶחָד לַחֹדֶשׁ *on the first day of the month;* שְׁנַת אַחַת *the first year.*—III. *alone, a single one;* לֹא, אֵין אֶחָד *not a single one, no one.*—IV. *a certain one* (τις); it has the power of the ind. article *a, an;* א׳ הָעָם *one of the people, a person;* נָבִיא א׳, *προφήτης τις, a certain prophet.*—V. *the same one, the same;* אַחַת, בְּאַחַת (פַּעַם), *at the same time, together;* כְּאִישׁ אֶחָד, כְּאֶחָד *as one man, together;* pl. אֲחָדִים *the same, united into one, a few.*

אָחַד Hith., *take hold of, unite thyself;* see יָחַד.

חַד Ch., *one, first, any one,* same as אֶחָד.

אָחוּ m., *the bulrush, reed,* an Egyptian word; Copt. *ᾱχι.*

אֵחוּד *(union),* p. n. of a man.

אַחֲוָה and אָחוֹת; see אָח.

אַחְוָה; see חוה.

אֲחִיָּה, אֲחוֹחַ p. n. of a man; patr. אֲחֹחִי.

אֲחַוֶּךָּ, with נ epenth. אֲחַוֶּנְּךָ, Pi. fut. 1. pers. with suff.; see חוה.

אֲחוּמַי p. n. of a man.

אָחוֹר *after;* see אחר.

אָחַז (inf. c. אֱחֹז; with pref. בֶּאֱחֹז; imper. אֱחֹז; fut. יֹאחֵז and יֶאֱחֹז).—I. *seized* (fear, terror); const. with בְּ.—II. *caught* (i.e. in hunting).—III. *took hold of, seized;* const. with בְּ of the part seized.—IV. *held, kept.*—V. *joined, united.*—VI. *locked up,* Neh. 7:3.—VII. *covered, overlaid, veneered,* 1 Ki. 6:10.—VIII. *drew by lot.* Niph.—I. *was caught,* Ecc. 9:12.—II. *was held,* Gen. 22:13. Pi. מְאַחֵז *shut up* (same as Kal VI.), Job 26:9. Hoph. מָאֳחָז *joined, united* (same as Kal V.), 2 Chron. 9:18.

אָחָז p.n.—I. *Ahaz,* king of Judah.—II. of a man.

אֶחַז fut. apoc. in pause for אֶחֱזֶה, אֶחַז; see חזה.

אֲחֻזָּה f., *possession, tenure.*

אַחְזַי p. n. of a man

אֲחַזְיָה and אֲחַזְיָהוּ p.n.—I. of the son of Ahab king of Israel.—II. of the son of Joram king of Judah.

אֲחֻזָּם p. n. of a man.

אֲחֻזַּת p. n. of a man.

אֲחַטֶּנָּה Pi. fut. 1. pers. with suff. for אֲחַטְּאֶנָּה; see חטא.

אֵחִי p. n. of a man.

אֲחִידָה; see חוד.

אֲחִיָּה *(friend of God),* p. n. of a man.

אֲחִיהוּד *(friend of the Jews),* p.n. of a m.

אַחְיוֹ p. n. of a man.

אֲחָיוֹת *sisters;* see אָחוֹת, in אָח.

אֲחִיחוּד and אֲחִיחֻד p. n. of a man.

אֲחִיטוּב *(loving good),* p. n. of a man.

אֲחִילוּד *(brother's son),* p. n. of a man.

אֲחִימוֹת *(brother of death),* p. n. of a m.

אֲחִימֶלֶךְ *(brother of a king),* p.n. of a m.

אֲחִימָן *(brother of gifts),* p. n. of a man.

אֲחִימַעַץ *(brother of anger),* p. n. of a m.

אַחְיָן *(brotherly)* p. n. of a man.

אֲחִינָדָב *(brother of good will),* p. n. of a man.

אֲחִינֹעַם *(brother of delight),* p.n. of a w.

אֲחִיסָמָךְ *(brother of defence),* p.n. of a m.

אֲחִיעֶזֶר *(brother of help),* p. n. of a man.

אֲחִיקָם *(brother of enmity),* p. n. of a m.

אֲחִירָם *(exalted brother),* p. n. of a m.

אֲחִירַע *(evil brother),* p. n. of a man.

אֲחִישַׁחַר (*brother of the morning*), p. n. of a man.

אֲחִישָׁר (*brother of song*), p. n. of a man.

אֲחִיתֹפֶל (*foolish brother*), p. n. of a m.

אָחֵל Hiph. fut. 1. pers., אָחֵל with dag. forte imp.; see חלל.

אַחְלָב (*fecundity*), p. n. of a place in the tribe of Asher.

אַחְלַי (*would that!*) p. n.—I. of a man.—II. of a woman.

אַחֲלַי, אַחֲלֵי *would that! I wish!* see חלה.

אַחְלָמָה *amethyst;* see חלם.

אֲחַסְבַּי p. n. of a man.

אַחְמְתָא p. n., *Ecbatana*, a city of Media, Ezr. 6:2.

אָחַר root not used; fut. 1. pers. pl. אֵחַר, Gen. 32:5. Pi. אִחַר (fut. יְאַחֵר), *delayed, waited, deferred* (Arab. the same); see יָחַר.

אָחוֹר m. (pl. אֲחֹרִים).—I. *the but-end of a spear*, 2 Sa. 2:23.—II. *the west, westward.* Adv. *behind, after;* מֵאָחוֹר, לְאָחוֹר, בְּאָחוֹר *behind;* לְאָחוֹר *hereafter*, Isa. 41:23.

אַחֵר m., אַחֶרֶת f. (pl. אֲחֵרִים, אֲחֵרוֹת). —I. *another;* אֱלֹהִים א׳ *other gods, idols.*—II. p. n. of a man.

אַחַר *the hinder part.* Adv. of time and place, *behind, afterwards.* Prep. *behind, after;* הָלַךְ א׳ *follow;* א׳ הַדְּבָרִים הָאֵלֶּה *after these things, afterwards;* א׳ דַּבֵּר פּ׳ *after he had spoken;* ... const. אַחֲרֵי (with suff. אַחֲרֶיךָ, אַחֲרָיו, אַחֲרַי), *behind, after;* א׳ כֵן אֲשֶׁר אַחֲרֵי כֵן *after;* *afterwards;* with prefixes מֵאַחַר, מֵאַחֲרֵי *after something past, after that;* מֵא׳ כֵן *afterwards;* מֵאַחֲרֶיהָ *behind him;* אֶל אַחֲרֵי *after;* עַל א׳ *behind.*

אֵחֲרוּ Pi. pret. pl. for אִחֲרוּ; see אחר.

אַחֲרוֹן m., אַחֲרוֹנָה f.—I. *the hinder part, the back part.*—II. *the latter day, or time.*—III. *the west;* יָם הָא׳ *the Mediterranean sea.*—IV *posterity;* דּוֹר א׳ *the generation to come;* אַחֲרֹנִים *successors;* לְאַחֲרוֹנָה, בָּאַחֲרוֹנָה *afterwards.*

אָחֳרִי Ch. adj. f., *another.*

עַד־אָחֳרִין Ch., *at last, at length.*

אַחֲרִית f.—I. *the last, the latter time;* א׳ הַיָּמִים *the latter days.*—II. *the end;* א׳ הַשָּׁנָה *end of the year.*—III. *posterity.*

אָחֳרָן Ch. m., *another.*

אֲחֹרַנִּית adv., *backwards.*

אַחְרַח (*after his brother?*) p. n. of a man.

אַחַרְחֵל (*behind a wall*), p. n. of a man.

אֲחַשְׁדַּרְפְּנִים m. pl., *chief satraps,* or *doorkeepers*, officers of the Persian court. ־ִין Ch., the same.

אֲחַשְׁוֵרוֹשׁ a title common to all the kings of Persia. It is spelt *Chosroes* by the later Greek and Latin historians.

אֲחַשְׁרֹשׁ the same.

אֲחַשְׁתָּרִי p. n. of a man; see next word.

אֲחַשְׁתְּרָנִים m. pl., *mules.*

אַחַת f., *one;* see אֶחָד.

אֲחֵת Ch. Aph. imp.; see נחת.

אֵחַתָּה Niph. fut. 1. pers. with ה parag.; see חתת.

אַט Hiph. fut. apoc. 1. pers. for אַטֶּה; see נטה.

אָטָד m., *black thorn;* rhamnus paliurus (Linn.).

אָטָד p. n., a place beyond Jordan, where was a threshing-floor; afterwards Abel-mizraim, Gen 50:10, 11.

אָטוּן m., *linen* (of Egypt) ὀθόνιον, probably an Egyptian word, Pro. 7:16.

אָטַט not used; (Arab. *uttered a low sound*).

אַט m. (pl. אִטִּים).—I. *necromancers, enchanters*.—II. *gentle, soft*. Adv. לְאַט, לְאַט, אַט אַט *softly, slowly*; לְאִטִּי *at my convenience*.

אָטַם *shut up, closed*. Hiph. the same; יַאְטֵם אֹזֶן *he closes* (his) *ear*.

אָטַר with עַל *shut*; fut. יֶאְטַר, Ps. 69:16.

אִטֵּר *maimed*; אִ׳ יַד יְמִינוֹ lit. *having his right hand bound* (left-handed).

אָטֵר (*he that halteth*), p. n. of a man.

אִי; see אָוָה and און.

אֵי *where?* with suff. אַיֶּכָּה *where art thou?* אַיּוֹ *where is he?* אַיָּם *where are they?* also with pronouns and adverbs, אֵי זֶה *who? what? where?* אֵי מִזֶּה *whence?* אֵי לָזֹאת *wherefore? why?* with ה demonst. אַיֵּה *where?*

אֵיכָה *where? how?*

אֵיךְ (apoc.) *how?*

אֵיכֹה (Kri אֵיכוֹ) *where?* 2 K. 6:13.

אֵיכָכָה *how?*

אַיִן always in comp.; מֵאַיִן *whence?* (for another meaning see און).

אֵיפֹה *where? how?*

אָן (contract. from אַיִן), *where? whither?* מֵאָן *whence?* עַד־אָן *until*; with the paragogic ה, אָנָה *whither? whereunto? where?* עַד־אָנָה *how long?* אָנֶה וָאָנָה *hither and thither*, 1 K. 2:36, 42.

אָיַב *hated, was an enemy*, Ex. 23:22.

אוֹיֵב m., *enemy*; אוֹיֶבֶת f., the same.

אֵיבָה f., *enmity*.

אֵיד *calamity*; see אוד.

אַיֵּה *where?* see אֵי.

אַיָּה f.—I. name of a bird of prey; "vulture, kite," Eng. Ver.; LXX. ἰκτίν; Vulg. *vultur*.—II. p. n. of a man.

אִיּוֹב (*miserable*), p.n., *Job*, the patriarch.

אִיזֶבֶל p. n., *Jezebel*, the wife of Ahab.

אֵיךְ, אֵיכָה; see אֵי.

אִי־כָבוֹד (*where is the glory?* i.e. without glory); p. n. of a man.

אַיֶּכָּה *where art thou?* אֵי with suff. and נ epenth.

אַיִל, אֵיל, אַיָּל, אַיָּל, &c.; see אול.

אֵילוֹן (*oak*), p. n.—I. of a city.—II. of a man.

אַיָּלוֹן (*place of hinds*), p. n. of a city.

אֵילְכָה for אֵלְכָה Kal fut. 1. pers. with ה parag.; see הלך, ילך.

אֵילִם (*grove of oaks*), p. n. of a place.

אֵילַת (*tree*), אֵילוֹת (*trees*), p. n., *Elath*, a city on the eastern gulf of the Red Sea, now Akabah.

אַיֶּלֶת *a gazelle*; see אול.

אָיַם root not used, *was terrible*; Ch. Pa. *frightened*.

אָיֹם, אֲיֻמָּה m., *terrible*, Hab. 1:7.

אֵימָה f. (pl. אֵימוֹת; with ה parag. אֵימָתָה) *terror*; pl. אֵימִים, אֵמִים.—I. *terrible things*.—II. *idols*, Jer. 50:38.—III. p.n. of one of the tribes of the Moabites.

אַיִן; see און and אֵי.

אֵינֵימוֹ *they are not*; see אַיִן with suff.

אִיעֶזֶר (*helpless*), p.n. of a man.

אֵיפָה, אֵפָה f., *Ephah*, a corn measure, capacity unknown; אֵיפָה וְאֵיפָה *divers measures*; אֵ׳ שְׁלֵמָה *just measure*.

אֵיפֹה; see אֵי.

אֵיפוֹא same as אֵפוֹא.

אִישׁ m. (pl. אַנְשֵׁי, אֲנָשִׁים; see אֱנוֹשׁ; three times אִישִׁים).—I. *a man*, as distinguished from a woman.—II. *a husband.*—III. *a male.*—IV. used collectively for the inhabitants of a country; אִישׁ יִשְׂרָאֵל *the Israelites.*—V. used to denote the qualifications of men; אִ׳ מִלְחָמָה *a warrior;* אִ׳ אֱמֶת *a faithful man;* אִ׳ שָׂדֶה *a husbandman.*—VI. *any one;* אִישׁ...אִישׁ *one...another.*—VII. *every man;* opposed to אָח, רֵעַ, עָמִית; וַיֵּלְכוּ אִישׁ לִמְקֹמוֹ *they went every one to his place;* כָּל-אִישׁ *every one.*—VIII. *every thing*, Ex. 25:20.—IX. impers., כֹּה אָמַר הָאִישׁ *thus it was said.*

אִישׁ, Hith. הִתְאוֹשֵׁשׁ (ἀνδρίζεσθαι, 1 Cor. 16:13); pl. הִתְאֹשָׁשׁוּ *become ye men*, i. e. be courageous, Isa. 46:8.

אִישׁוֹן m., lit. *little man*, i.e. the small image of one's self seen in the eye of another.—I. אִ׳ עַיִן, אִ׳ בַּת עַיִן *pupil of the eye;* hence:—II. אִ׳ חֹשֶׁךְ, לַיְלָה lit. *pupil*, i.e. middle, *of the night, midnight.*

אִשָּׁה or אֵשֶׁת f. (with suff. אִשְׁתִּי, אִשְׁתְּךָ and אֶשְׁתְּךָ), I.—*woman.*—II. *wife.*—III. *concubine.*—IV. opposed to אָחוֹת and רְעוּת, like אִישׁ.—V. *any one, every one.*—VI. applied to men by way of reproach.

אִישׁ־בֹּשֶׁת p. n. of a son of Saul.

אִישְׁהוֹד (*man of vigour*), p.n. of a man.

אִישַׁי (*manly*), p. n. of a man.

אִיתַי Ch., same as יֵשׁ *he is;* אִיתָךְ *thou art;* אִיתוֹהִי *he is;* אִיתָנָא *we are;* אִיתֵיכוֹן *ye are.*

אִיתַי p.n. of a man.

אִיתִיאֵל (*God with me*), p. n. of a man.

אִיתָם for אִתַּם Kal fut. 1. pers.; see תמם.

אִיתָמָר (*place of palm trees*), p. n. of one of the sons of Aaron.

אֵיתָן p. n. of a man; see יתן.

אַךְ adv., *only, alone, except;* אַךְ שָׂמֵחַ *only* (i.e. nothing else but) *rejoicing*, Deu. 16:15; אַךְ חֹשֶׁךְ *only* (nothing but) *darkness*, Ps. 139:11; אַךְ טָרֹף טֹרָף *he is only torn in pieces*, i.e. nothing else has happened to him, Gen. 44:28.

אַכַּד (*fortress*), p. n. of a city built by Nimrod, Gen. 10:10.

אֲכוּת Kal fut. 1. pers., see כתת.

אַכְזִיב p. n.—I. of a city in the tribe of Asher, Greek ἔκδιππα, now *Zib.*—II. of a city in the tribe of Judah.

אַכְזָר, אַכְזְרִיּוּת; see כזר.

אָכִישׁ (*Ethiopian*), p. n. of a king of the Philistines.

אָכַל (inf. אָכוֹל; const. אֱכֹל; with pref. לֶאֱכֹל; with suff. אָכְלְךָ, אָכְלוֹ; imper. אֱכֹל; with ה parag. אָכְלָה; fut. יֹאכַל and יֹאכֵל).—I. *ate.*—II. *devoured*, spoken of men or things; joined to the accusative with בְּ, מִן: אָכַל לֶחֶם *feasted;* אָכַל לֶחֶם פְּ׳ and בְּלֶחֶם, אִ׳ לֶחֶם עַל שֻׁלְחַן פְּ׳ *to be the guest inmate, of any one;* אָכַל לִפְנֵי יְהוָֹה *ate that which was offered in sacrifice;* אָכַל בְּשַׂר פְּ׳ *ate his flesh* i.e. injured him, Ps. 27:2; Niph. נֶאֱכַל, part. f. נֶאֱכֶלֶת *is, may be,* *eaten.* Pu. אֻכַּל *devoured, consumed.* Hiph. הֶאֱכִיל (fut. יַאֲכִיל; inf. הַאֲכִיל) *gave, made, caused, to eat, devour.*

אֲכַל Ch., the same.

אֹכֶל m., *food;* with suff. אָכְלוֹ.

אָכְלָה f., *meat, food,* Gen. 1:29, 30.

אֲכִילָה f., *meat, feast,* 1 K. 19:8.

מַאֲכָל m., *food,* that which may be eaten; עֵץ מַאֲכָל *fruit tree;* צֹאן מ׳ *cattle to be slaughtered for the table.*

מַאֲכֹלֶת, מַכֹּלֶת f., *food.*

מַאֲכֶלֶת f., *slaughtering knife,* lit. *devourer;* pl. מַאֲכָלוֹת.

אֻכָל *(eaten, consumed),* p. n. of a man.

וָאֲכַל, אֲכַל Pi. fut. apoc. 1. pers.; see כלה.

אֲכֶלְךָ Ex. 33:3, Pi. fut. 1. pers. with suff. for אֲכַלְּךָ; see כלה.

אָכֵן *truly;* see כון.

אַכֶּנּוּ Hiph. fut. 1. pers. with suff.; see נכה.

אָכַף *compel, bow down to,* Pro. 16:26.

אֶכֶף m. (with suff. אַכְפִּי), *palm of the hand,* Job 33:7.

אִכַּף for אֶכַּף Niph. fut. 1. pers.; see כפף.

אָכַר root not used; (Arab. *digged).*

אִכָּר m., *ploughman, husbandman.*

אַכְשָׁף *(city of magicians),* p. n. of a city in the tribe of Asher.

אַל *not, &c.;* see אלל.

אֵל *God;* see אול.

אֶל, אֶל־ prep. (with suff. אֵלַי, אֵלֶיךָ, אֵלַיִךְ, אֵלָיו, אֵלֶיהָ, אֵלֵינוּ, אֲלֵיכֶם, אֲלֵיהֶם, אֲלֵיהֶן; poet. אֵלֵימוֹ; pl. poet. אֱלֵי).—I. sign of the dative, like לְ.—II. *to, towards.*—III. *unto, at.*—IV. *of, concerning.*—V. *in, into*—VI. *among.*—VII. *by, through.*—VIII. *for, on account of;* the original meaning is *to; towards,* variously modified by the context; אֶל־פִּי יְהוָֹה *according to the command (mouth) of God;* אֶל־אַמָּה *a cubit,* i. e. according to the measure of a cubit, Gen. 6:16; וַיֹּאמֶר אֶל־שָׂרָה *he said concerning (relative to) Sarah;* וַיֵּלֶךְ אֶל־נַפְשׁוֹ *he went, having regard to his life,* i. e. to save his life; אֶל־בְּאֵר הַמַּיִם *near (i.e. towards) the well;* יָשַׁב אֶל־הַשֻּׁלְחָן *he sat at* (i.e. *to*) *the table.*—IX. used with other particles; אֶל־מִחוּץ לְ *without;* אֶל־אַחֲרֵי *behind me;* אֶל־תַּחַת a pleonasm, same as תַּחַת.

אֵל, with article הָאֵל, אֵלֶּה pron., *these, those;* אֵלֶּה־וְאֵלֶּה οἱ μὲν— οἱ δέ, *these—those;* Ch., the same.

אֵלָא *(terebinth),* p.n. of a man; see אֵלָה.

אֶלְגָּבִישׁ m., *hail;* see נבשׁ.

אַלְגּוּמִּים name of a tree; see אַלְמֻגִּים

אֶלְדָּד *(beloved of God),* p. n. of a man.

אֶלְדָּעָה *(called of God),* p.n. of a man.

אָלָה I. *lay under a curse, imprecate.*—II. *howl,* see אלל. Hiph. *swore, execrated, laid under a curse;* fut. apoc. וַיֹּאֶל.

אָלָה f.—I. *oath, imprecation;* בּוֹא בְּאָלָה *come into the terms of the oath,* agree by oath, Neh. 10:30; הֵבִיא בְּאָלָה *make one swear,* Eze. 17:13; נָשָׂא אָלָה בְּ *lay an oath upon any one.*—II. *curse, cursing;* הָיְתָה לְאָלָה *he was for a curse;* נָתַן לְאָלָה *he gave over unto cursing*

תַּאֲלָה f., *cursing.*

אֱלָהּ m. Ch., *God.*

אֱלוֹהַּ m., *God* (pl. אֱלֹהִים).—I. *God*, the true God.—II. *false gods*, idols; followed by the verb in the sing., very rarely in the pl.; אִישׁ אֱ׳ *a man of God;* בְּנֵי אֱ׳ *sons of God*, i. e. they that loved and served God; with pref. כֵּאלֹהִים, בֵּאלֹהִים, לֵאלֹהִים; const. אֱלֹהֵי.

אַיָּלָה *gazelle;* see אוּל.

אֵלָה *terebinth;* see אלל.

אֲלוּ Ch., *behold!* same as אֲרוּ.

אִלּוּ for אִם־לוּ, *otherwise, unless*, Ecc. 6:6, Est. 7:4.

אֱלוּל m.—I. *vanity;* same as אֱלִיל; see אלל.—II. *Elul*, the sixth month of the Hebrew year, answering nearly to our September, Neh. 6:15.

אֵלוֹן *oak;* see אוּל. אַלּוֹן the same; in אלל.

אַלּוּף *friend;* see אלף.

אָלוּשׁ (*lion's den*), p. n., one of the encampments of the Israelites.

אֶלְזָבָד (Θεόδωρος), p. n. of a man.

אָלַח, Niph. נֶאֱלַח *was corrupt, base.*

אֶלְחָנָן (*gift of God*), p.n. of a man.

אֱלִיאָב (*who has God for his father*), p.n. of a man.

אֱלִיאֵל (*strong in God*), p.n. of a man.

אֱלִיאָתָה or **אֱלִיָּתָה** (*to whom God comes*), p.n. of a man.

אֱלִידָד (*beloved of God*), p.n. of a prince of the Benjamites.

אֶלְיָדָע (*known of God*), p.n. of a man.

אַלְיָה f. (Arab. the same), the fat tail of the sheep in the East.

אֵלִיָּה, אֵלִיָּהוּ (*the Lord he* IS *God*), p.n., *Elijah* (Ἠλίας), the prophet.

אֱלִיהוּ, אֱלִיהוּא (the same), p.n. of one of Job's friends.

אֶלְיְהוֹעֵינַי, אֶלְיוֹעֵינַי (*mine eyes* ARE *unto the Lord*), p.n. of a man.

אֶלְיַחְבָּא (*hidden of God*), p.n. of one of David's generals.

אֱלִיחֹרֶף (*God* IS *his avenger*), p. n. of a man.

אֱלִיל *vanity;* see אלל.

אֱלִימֶלֶךְ (*God* IS *king*), p.n. of a man.

אִלֵּין, אִלֵּךְ pron. pl. Ch., *these, those.*

אֶלְיָסָף (*increased of God*), p. n. of a prince of the Gadites.

אֱלִיעֶזֶר (*holpen of God*), p.n. of a man.

אֱלִיעֵינַי (*God is mine eye*, i. e. directs me), p.n. of a man.

אֱלִיעָם (*people of God*), p. n. of a man.

אֱלִיפַז (*God is precious*), p.n.—I. of a son of Esau.—II. of one of Job's friends.

אֱלִיפַל (*my God* IS *strong*), p.n. of a man.

אֱלִיפְלֵהוּ (*whom God makes famous*), p.n. of a man.

אֱלִיפֶלֶט (*God* IS *his help*), p.n. of a m.

אֱלִיצוּר (*God* IS *his rock*), p.n. of a man.

אֱלִיצָפָן or **אֶלְצָפָן** (*whom God protects*), p. n. of a man

אֱלִיקָא p. n. of a man.

אֶלְיָקִים (*whom God makes strong*), p. n. —I. of the house-steward of Hezekiah.—II. of a king of Judah, afterwards changed to יְהוֹיָקִים (*Jehovah makes strong*).

אֱלִישֶׁבַע (*vowed to God*), p.n., *Elisheba* (Ἐλισάβετ), the wife of Aaron.

אֱלִישָׁה p. n. of a place on the shores of the Mediterranean.

אֱלִישׁוּעַ (*whose salvation is God*), p. n. of a son of David.

אֶלְיָשִׁיב (*whom God pardons*), p.n. of a man.

אֱלִישָׁמָע (*whom God hears*), p.n. of a m.

אֱלִישָׁע (*whose salvation is God*), p.n., *Elisha* (Ἐλισσαῖος), the prophet.

אֱלִישָׁפָט (*God is the judge*), p.n. of a m.

אֱלִיָּתָה p.n.; see אֱלִיאָתָה.

אֵלֶּךְ pron. m. pl. Ch.; same as Heb. אֵלֶּה *those*, Dan. 3:12, 13.

אֵלֵךְ with ה parag. אֵלְכָה, וְאֵלֵךְ Kal fut. 1. pers.; see ילך, הלך.

אָלַל root not used (Arab. *passed away quickly*).

אַל s., *nothing*, Job 24:25.; adv. *not*; with the fut. אַל־תִּירָאוּ *fear not*; אַל־נָא *do not* (I beseech you), Gen. 19:18.

אֱלִיל *vain things, vanity*; אֱלִילִים *idols*, lit. vain things.

אַלְלַי *woe is me!* see ילל.

אַלָּה f., *terebinth*, Jos. 24:26; see אול.

אַלּוֹן m.—I. *oak*.—II. p.n. of a man; see אול.

אָלַם not used in Kal either in Heb. or Arab. Niph. נֶאֱלַם *was dumb, silent*, lit. tongue-tied. Pi. *bound*, like sheaves of corn, Gen. 37:7.

אֵלֶם m., *silence*; אֵלֶם צֶדֶק *is justice silent?* Ps. 58:2; יוֹנַת אֵלֶם *the dove of silence*, title to Ps. 56.

אִלֵּם m., *dumb person*; pl. אִלְּמִים.

אֲלֻמָּה f. (pl. אֲלֻמִּים and אֲלֻמּוֹת), *a sheaf of corn*.

אַלְמֹן m., *widowhood*, Isa. 47:29.

אַלְמָן m., *a widower*, Jer. 51:5.

אַלְמָנָה f., *a widow*.

אַלְמְנוֹת for אַרְמְנוֹת *palaces*, Isa. 13:22.

אַלְמָנוּת f., *widowhood*; pl. אַלְמְנוּתִים.

אַלְמֹנִי m., *some one, a certain one*, lit. one not to be named; always joined with פְּלֹנִי, which see.

אֵלָם and אֻלָם; see אול.

אַלְמֻגִּים a resinous and odoriferous wood, not the produce of Canaan; perhaps *the red sandal-wood*, 1 Ki. 10:11, &c.; in 2 Chron. 2:7, it is transposed to אַלְגּוּמִּים.

אַלְמוֹדָד p.n. of one of the descendants of Shem, Gen. 10:26.

אַלַּמֶּלֶךְ (*the king's oak*), p.n. of a place in the tribe of Asher.

אַלְמֹנִי, אַלְמָנוּת, אַלְמָנָה, אַלְמֹן, אַלְמָן; see אלם.

אֶלְנַעַם (*God is his delight*), p.n. of a man

אֶלְנָתָן (*given of God*), p.n. of a man.

אֶלָּסָר p. n. of a city.

אֶלְעָד (*God is his help*), p.n. of a man.

אֶלְעָדָה (*whom God adorns*), p.n. of a m.

אֶלְעוּזַי (*God my strength*), p.n. of a m.

אֶלְעָזָר (*God is HIS helper*), p.n. of a m.

אֶלְעָלֵא, אֶלְעָלֵה p.n. of a town in the tribe of Reuben.

אֶלְעָשָׂה (*made of God*), p.n. of a man.

אָלַף *learnt*; fut. יֶאֱלַף. Pi. אִלֵּף *taught*. Hiph. part. f. מַאֲלִיפוֹת (from אֶלֶף), *producing a thousand*, Ps. 144:13.

אֶלֶף m., *a thousand*; dual אַלְפַּיִם *two thousand*; pl. אֲלָפִים *thousands*; שְׁלֹשֶׁת אֲלָפִים *three thousand*; אַרְבָּעִים אֶלֶף *forty thousand*; מֵאָה אֶלֶף *a hundred thousand*; אֶלֶף אֲלָפִים *a thousand thousands*; אַלְפֵי רְבָבָה 10,000,000; אֶלֶף s.—I. *a chiliad* (a troop of 1000 soldiers); שַׂר הָאֶלֶף, χιλίαρχος, *commander of a chiliad*.—II. *a nation*, *tribe* (i.e. *many persons*).—III. pl. אֲלָפִים *oxen*; see below.—IV. p.n. of a city in the tribe of Benjamin, Jos. 18:28.

אֲלַף, אֶלֶף Ch., *a thousand.*

אַלּוּף adj., *familiar, tame*, Jer. 11:19. s.—I. *a friend.*—II. *an ox (a tame animal).*—III. *head of a tribe* or *family*, φύλαρχος.

אֱלִפֶּלֶט (*God the deliverer*), p.n. of a m.

אֶלְפַּעַל (*God who performeth*), p.n. of a man.

אֶלְצָפָן p.n. of a man; see אֱלִיצָפָן.

אָלַץ (Syr. *he urged*). Pi. אִלֵּץ *pressed, urged on*, Jud. 16:16.

אַלְקוּם m., Prov. 30:31, מֶלֶךְ אַלְקוּם עִמּוֹ *a king who is irresistible;* "against whom there is no rising up," Eng. Ver.; meaning uncertain.

אֶלְקָנָה (*for whom God cared*), p. n. of a man.

אֶלְקֹשִׁי p.n. of a people.

אֶלְתּוֹלַד p.n. of a city; same as תּוֹלַד.

אֶלְתְּקֵא, אֶלְתְּקֵה p. n. of a city of the Levites in the tribe of Dan.

אֶלְתְּקֹן p.n. of a city in the tribe of Judah.

אֵם f. (with suff. אִמִּי; pl. אִמּוֹת).—I. *a mother.*—II. *a grand-mother.*—III. *a step-mother.*—IV. *metropolis, chief city;* אֵם הַדֶּרֶךְ *mother*, i.e. *head of two ways*, Ez. 21:26.—V *nation, entire people.*

אַמָּה f.—I. *fore arm*, hence:—II. *a cubit*, measure of 21·888 inches; dual אַמָּתַיִם *two cubits;* עֶשֶׂר אַמּוֹת *ten cubits;* שְׁלֹשׁ מֵאוֹת אַמָּה *three hundred cubits.*—III. *a basis* or *pedestal*, Isa. 6:4.—IV. p. n. of a hill, 2 Sa. 2:24.

אַמָּה f. Ch., *cubit.*

אֻמָּה f. (pl. אֻמּוֹת, אֻמִּים), *families tribes.*

אֻמָּה f. Ch., the same.

אִם cond. pa.—I. *surely, truly*, this is its radical meaning, hence:—II. *if;* אִם...אִם *whether...or;* עַד־אִם, עַד־אֲשֶׁר־אִם *whilst, until.*—III. *if? whether?* הַ...אִם, הַ...אִם...אִם, הֲ...וְאִם *whether?...or?*—IV. used as an asseveration אִם has the power of denial, אִם־לֹא of affirmation; אִם־אֶעֱשֶׂה *let me be accursed if I do it*, i.e. I will not do it.—V. in comp. הַאִם same as הֲלֹא *is not?* אִם־לֹא *unless.*

אֶמְאָסְאָךְ Hos. 4:6; perhaps for אֶמְאָסְאָךְ i. e. אֶמְאָסְךָ Kal fut. 1. pers. with suff.; see מאס.

אָמָה f. (with suff. אֲמָתִי; pl. אֲמָהוֹת; const. אַמְהוֹת), *maid-servant ;* בֶּן־אָמָה *servant.*

אֲמָהוֹת pl.; see אָמָה.

אַמָּה, אֻמָּה; see אֵם.

אָמוֹן, אָמוּן, אֱמוּנָה; see אמן.

אָמוֹץ (*strong*), p. n. of the father of Isaiah, Isa. 1:1.

אָמִי p. n. of a man.

אֵמִים p.n. of one of the giant races in Canaan.

אַמִּיץ *strong;* see אמץ.

אָמִיר *top;* see אמר.

אָמַל root not used; *was sick.* Pul. אֻמְלַל *sick, wasting, declining.*

אֲמֻלָה f., *pained, sick*, Eze. 16:30.

אֻמְלַל m., *wasting with disease*, Ps. 6:3.

אֲמֵלָל m. (pl. אֲמֵלָלִים), *wasted, feeble men*, Neh. 3:34.

אֲמָם p. n. of a city.

אָמַן I. *was true, faithful*; part. אֱמוּנִים *the faithful.*—II. *nursed, brought up*; part. אֹמֵן *foster-father, nurse.* Niph. נֶאֱמַן.—I. *was sure.*—II. *was enduring, durable*; בַּיִת נֶאֱמָן *an enduring house.*—III. *was faithful.*—IV. *was carried* (as a child), Isa. 60:4. Hiph. הֶאֱמִין *confided, entrusted, believed, relied on,* followed by בְּ, לְ with inf.

אֲמַן Ch. Aph. הֵימַן *entrusted.*

אָמָן m., *artificer*, Cant. 7:2.

אָמֵן m.—I. *a true thing, truth*; אֱלֹהֵי א׳ *the God of truth.*—II. formula of acquiescence, *Amen, so be it.*

אָמוֹן m.—I. *constant, unvarying*, Pro. 8:30.—II. same as הָמוֹן *the multitude*, Jer. 52:15.—III. p. n. of an Egyptian idol *Amoun* in נֹא אָמוֹן, which see.—IV. p. n. of a king of Judah.

אֵמוּן m.—I. *a faithful, true, sincere one.*—II. *educated, brought up*, Lam. 4:5.

אֹמֶן m., *faith*; adv. *truly.*

אֹמְנָה f., *beam, lintel*, 2 Kings 18:16.

אֱמוּנָה I. f. of אָמוֹן; וַיְהִי יָדָיו אֱמוּנָה *his hands were made steady, true.*—II. *faithfulness.*—III. *truth.* Pl. אֱמוּנוֹת.

אֲמָנָה f.—I. *covenant, contract*, Neh. 11:23.—II. p. n. of a river near Damascus.—III. of a region.

אָמְנָה I. adv., *truly, indeed.*—II. f., *education, nursing*, Est. 2:20.

אֻמְנָם, אָמְנָם adv., *certainly, verily*; הַאֻמְנָם *indeed?* 1 Kings 8:27.

אֱמֶת f. (with suff. אֲמִתּוֹ).—I. *permanency, durability.*—II. *truth*, especially religious truth; used for truthfulness in God, and piety in man.

אֲמִינוֹן, אַמְנוֹן (*faithful*), p. n. of a son of David.

אָמֵץ (imp. אֱמַץ; fut. יֶאֱמַץ), *was powerful, courageous*; with מִן *prevailed, was mightier than.*—Pi. I. *strengthen*, Job 4:1.—II. *repair* (a house), 2 Chro. 24:13.—III. *fasten, secure*, Pro. 8:28.—IV. *encourage.*—V. א׳ לֵב פ׳ *harden the heart.* Hiph. *strengthen, confirm.* Hith. *acquired power, took courage.*

אַמִּיץ *strong, prevailing.*

אֹמֶץ m., *vigour*, Job 17:9.

אָמֹץ m., *powerful, vigorous* (of horses) pl. אֲמֻצִּים Zec. 6:3.

אַמְצָה f., *strength*, Zec. 12:5.

אַמְצִי (*strong*), p. n. of a man.

אֲמַצְיָהוּ, אֲמַצְיָה (*strengthened of God*), p. n., *Amaziah* king of Judah.

מַאֲמַצִּים m. pl.; מַאֲמַצֵּי כֹחַ *confirmers of power*, Job 36:19.

אָמַר I. *he said* (to any one, with אֶל, לְ; of any one, with לְ and accus.); sometimes same as דִּבֶּר *he spoke*; inf. לֵאמֹר *saying.*—II. *commanded.*—III. *he thought*, lit. *he spake inwardly*, Gen. 44:28, Ex. 2:14, &c. &c. בִּלְבָבוֹ, בְּלִבּוֹ. Niph. *was said of* or *concerning any one* (with לְ); impers. יֵאָמֵר *it is said*; with לְ *it is said to some one.* Hiph. *made declared*, "avouched," Eng. Ver., Deu. 26:17, 18. Hith. *were declared, published, made famous.*

אֲמַר Ch., *he said, commanded.*

אֵמֶר m.—I. same as דָּבָר *a discourse*

speech; אִמְרֵי אֵל *the words of God.* —II. *an appointment, declaration,* Job 20:29; with suff. אִמְרִי; pl. אֲמָרִים.

אֹמֶר m., *enunciation, expression, saying;* same as דָּבָר *a thing, a matter.*

אִמֵּר (*tall*), p. n. of a man.

אִמַּר Ch., *a lamb,* Ezr. 6:9, 17, &c.

אִמְרָה f., *word, declaration, discourse;* pl. אֲמָרוֹת.

אֶמְרָה f., the same.

אָמִיר m., the pod which contains the fruit of the palm tree, Isa. 17:6.

מַאֲמָר m., *edict, command,* Ezr. 1:15, &c.

מֵאמַר m. Ch., the same.

אִמְרִי (*eloquent*), p. n. of a man.

אֱמֹרִי *the Amorite;* LXX. Ἀμοῤῥαῖος.

אֲמַרְיָה and אֲמַרְיָהוּ p. n. of a man.

אַמְרָפֶל p. n. of the king of Shinar, Gen. 14:1, 9.

אֶמֶשׁ *yesterday,* lit. the day before last night.

אֱמֶת *truth;* see אמן.

אַמְתַּחַת *sack;* see מתח.

אֲמִתַּי (*truth-teller*), p. n. of the father of the prophet Jonah, Jon. 1:1.

אָן, אָנָה, אָנֶה; see אַי.

אֹן *Heliopolis;* see און.

אֲנָא, אֲנָה Ch., pers. pron. *I.*

אָנָּא interj., *gently, I pray, &c.*

אִנְבֵּהּ Ch., for אִבֵּהּ; see אֵב in אבב.

אִנְדַּע; see יְנַדַּע.

אָנָה *he suffered,* Isa. 3:19. Pi. אִנָּה *he caused pain,* Ex. 21:13. Pu. *was made to suffer,* Pro. 12:21, Ps. 91:10. Hith. part. מִתְאַנֶּה *affecting irritation, seeming to be irritated,* followed by לְ.

אֲנָחֲרָה p. n. of a city.

אֲנִיָּה f., *suffering, pain,* Isa. 29:2.

תַּאֲנִיָּה f., the same, Lam. 2:5.

אֳנִי com., *a ship;* collectively, *a fleet*

אֳנִיָּה f., *a ship.*

תַּאֲנָה f., *sexual impulse,* Jer. 2:24.

תֹּאֲנָה f. *opportunity, revenge,* Jud. 14:4.

אֲנוּ com., *we,* Jer. 42:6; see אָנֹכִי.

אִנּוּן m., אִנִּין f. pron. pl. Ch., *these, those.*

אֱנוֹשׁ p. n.; see אנשׁ.

אָנַח. Niph. נֶאֱנַח *he sighed* (the things sighed for preceded by עַל, מִן).

אֲנָחָה f., *sighing, sobbing.*

אֲנִי *I;* see אָנֹכִי.

אֳנִי, אֳנִיָּה, אֲנִיָּה; see אנה.

אֲנִיעָם (*mourning of the people*), p. n. of a man.

אֲנָךְ m.—I. *lead.*—II. *a plummet,* Am. 7:7, 8.

אָנֹכִי (contr. אֲנִי; with the pause אָנִי), pers. pron. *I;* pl. אֲנַחְנוּ, sometimes נַחְנוּ (אֲנוּ Jer. 42:6), *we.*

אָנַן. Hith. הִתְאוֹנֵן *he groaned,* Nu. 11:1, Lam. 3:39.

אָנַס *urge, force,* Est. 1:8.

אֲנַס Ch., the same; *trouble,* Dan. 4:6.

אָנַף (fut. יֶאֱנַף), *breathe through the nose, snort;* hence *was irritated, angry* (with בְּ). Hith. הִתְאַנֵּף *became angry.*

אַף m. (with suff. אַפִּי).—I. *nose;* גֹּבַהּ אַף *disdainful, haughty,* lit. *turned up of nose,* Ps. 10:4.—II. *anger;* dual אַפַּיִם I. *nostrils* by synecd.—II. *face, countenance;* לְאַפֵּי same as לְפְנֵי *in the sight of, before;* מָנָה אַחַת אַפַּיִם *one of two persons,* i. e. a double portion, 1 Sa. 1:5.—III. *anger,* אֶרֶךְ א׳ *slow to anger;* קְצַר א׳ *quick to anger, hasty.*

אַן *also;* see in its place.

אֲנַף Ch., dual, *nostrils, face.*

אֲנָפָה f., name of an unclean bird, "heron," Eng. Ver.; LXX. χαραδριός; Lev. 11:19, Deu. 14:18.

אָנַק *cry out for pain;* inf. אֱנֹק; fut. יֶאֱנֹק. Niph. נֶאֱנַק *lament.*

אֲנָקָה const. אֶנְקַת f.—I. *crying out for pain.*—II. name of a reptile so called from its cry, Lev. 11:30.

אָנַשׁ root not used. (אֲנַס Ch., *compress, compel*). Part. אָנוּשׁ m., אֲנוּשָׁה f. *incurable* (of a wound), *grievous, mortal, unlucky* (of a day), *malignant* (of a disposition); Niph. *he became mortally sick,* 2 Sa. 12:15.

אֱנוֹשׁ m.—I. *man* (as mortal and miserable).—II. *mankind.*—III. *plebeian, low person;* pl. אֲנָשִׁים (const. אַנְשֵׁי; with suff. אֲנָשֶׁיךָ, אַנְשֵׁיהֶם), *man, men;* see אִישׁ.—IV. אֱנוֹשׁ p.n. of a son of Seth.

אֱנָשׁ, אֱנַשׁ Ch., *man.*

אַנְתְּ Ch., pers. pron. m., *thou.*

אָסָא (*healing*), p.n. of a king of Judah.

אָסוּ *cup;* see סוּךְ.

אֵסוּר, אָסִיר, אַסִּיר *bound;* see אסר.

אָסִי *harvest;* see אסף.

אָסָם m., pl. אֲסָמִים *store-houses, granaries;* LXX. ταμεῖα.

אָסַךְ root not used; (Arab. *death, destruction*).

אָסוֹן m., *injury, death by accident.*

אַסְנָה p. n. of a man.

אָסְנַפַּר p. n. of an Assyrian general.

אָסְנַת (*belonging to Neith*), p. n. of the wife of Joseph.

אֲסָעֲרֵם Syr. for אֲסָעֲרֵם Pi. fut. 1. pers. with suff.; see סער.

אָסַף (inf. אָסֹף; const. אֱסֹף; with suff. אָסְפְּךָ; fut. יֶאֱסֹף, with suff. יַאַסְפֵנִי; 1. pers. אֶאֱסֹף and אֹסֵף).—I. *collected, gathered* (with אֶל and עַל before the place in which).—II. *take away, take off, destroy;* א׳ נַפְשׁוֹ *he deprived himself of life.* Niph. נֶאֱסַף I. *was gathered, received.*—II. *was taken away, ceased.*—III. *perished,* Hos. 4:3, (with עַל, לְ, אֶל); נ׳ אֶל־עַמּוֹ, ־עַמָּיו, ־אֲבוֹתָיו, *was gathered to his people, fathers,* i.e. was buried; used in this sense alone נֶאֱסַף Nu. 20:26.—Pi. I. *gather, receive.*—II. *close the rear of a march,* Nu. 10:25, Jos. 6:9, 13. Pu. *was gathered.* Hith. הִתְאַסֵּף *gather themselves together,* Deu. 33:5.

אָסָף (*collector*), p. n. of a man.

אֹסֶף m., *ingathering, harvest of fruits.*

אָסִיף m., *harvest of apples.*

אֲסֵפָה f., *collection, gathering,* Isa. 24:22.

אֲסֻפִּים m. pl., *collection of stores or money, storehouses.*

אֲסֻפּוֹת f. pl., the same.

אֹסִפְךָ Kal fut. 1. pers. with suff. 1 Sa. 15:6; Kal part. with suff. 2 Ki. 22:20; see אסף.

אֲסַפְסֻף m., with the article הָאסַפְסֻף *mixed multitude,* Nu. 11:4.

אָסְפַּרְנָא Ch. adv., *exactly, carefully quickly.*

אַסְפָּתָא p. n. of a son of Haman.

אָסַר (fut. יֶאֱסֹר and יַאְסֹר).—I. *he tied, bound*, followed by לְ; א׳ הַמֶּרְכָּבָה *yoking the horses to the chariot*.—II. א׳ מִלְחָמָה *he kept together the battle*, i. e. made his troops attack closely and continuously. — III. אָסַר אִסָּר עַל־נַפְשׁוֹ *he bound himself by an oath*; part. אָסוּר *captive, prisoner*. Niph. *becoming bound*. Pu. *taken, reduced to bondage*.

אֵסוּר m., *chain*; pl. אֲסוּרִים; בֵּית הָאֵסוּר *prison*.

אֱסוּר Ch., the same.

אָסִיר m., *a captive*.

אַסִּיר m.—I. *captive*.—II. p. n. of a man.

אֱסָר m., *an obligation*.

אֱסָר m. Ch., the same.

אִסָּר m., the same.

מוֹסֵר m.; see in its place.

אֵסַר־חַדּוֹן p. n., *Esar-haddon* king of Assyria, the successor of Sennacherib; LXX. Ἀσορδάν.

אֶסָּרֵם Kal fut. 1. pers. with suff.; see יסר.

אֶסְתֵּר (*star*), p. n., *Esther* queen of Persia; her name before was הֲדַסָּה Est. 2:7.

אָע m. Ch., same as Heb. עֵץ *wood*.

אַף *nose*; see אנף.

אַף part., *also, moreover, nay, indeed*; אַף כִּי *indeed, truly*; אַף כִּי אָמַר *hath* (God) *indeed said*, Gen. 3:1.

אַף Ch., the same.

אַפְאֵיהֶם Hiph. fut. 1. pers. with suff.; see פאה.

אָפַד *he put on the Ephod*, Ex. 29:5, Lev. 8:7 (with לְ of the person, and בְּ of the thing).

אֵפוֹד m.—I. *Ephod*, a garment worn by the priesthood; נָשָׂא א׳ *he wore the ephod*, i. e. he fulfilled the priest's office.—II. perhaps the name of an idol, Jud. 8:27, &c.

אֲפֻדָּה f., *made like an ephod*; probably the dress of an idol.

אֵפֹד p. n. of a man.

אַפֶּדֶן *camp*; see פדן.

אָפָה *baking*. Niph. *baked*.

אֹפֶה m., *a baker*; pl. אֹפִים.

אֹפָה f., the same; pl. אֹפוֹת.

מַאֲפֶה m., *bakemeat*.

אֱפוֹ Syr. for אֱפוּ imp. pl. of the verb אפה.

אֵפוֹא, אֵפוֹ pa., οὖν, δή, *now, then*; אִם כֵּן א׳ *if then it be so*; אַיֵּה א׳ *where then?* מָה א׳ *what then?* דְּעוּ א׳ γινώσκετε οὖν! *know then!*

אֵפוֹד *ephod*; see אפד.

אֲפִיחַ p. n. of a man.

אַפַּיִם p. n. of a man.

אָפִיק *swelling*; see אפק.

אָפַל root not used (Arab. *set as the sun*).

אָפִיל m., אֲפִילָה f.—I. *concealed*.—II. *very dark*.

אָפֵל m., *obscure*.

אֹפֶל m., *thick darkness*; more intense than חֹשֶׁךְ.

אֲפֵלָה f., *darkness*; חֹשֶׁךְ א׳ *thick darkness*.

מַאֲפֵל m., *darkness*.

מַאְפֵּלְיָה f., *extreme darkness*, Jer. 2:31.

אֶפְלָל (*judgment*), p. n. of a man.

אָפַן root not used; same as פָּנָה *turn, roll*.

אוֹפָן m., *wheel*; const. אֹפַן; pl. אֹפַנִּים.

אֹפֶן *season* (περίοδος); דָּבָר עַל־אָפְנָיו *a word in season*, Pro. 25:11.

אֶפֶס m.—I. *termination, extremity;* אַפְסֵי אֶרֶץ *ends of the earth;* dual אָפְסַיִם *two extremities*, i.e. of both feet; *the soles* or *ankles*, Eze. 47:3. —II. *deficiency, wanting;* בְּאֶפֶס *without*, lit. *in there not being*, followed by the genitive of the thing; עַד א׳ *until there is none;* אַפְסִי *besides me;* בְּאֶפֶס *without;* מֵאֶפֶס *of, from nothing;* אֶפֶס כִּי *except, unless.*

אֶפֶס דַּמִּים p. n. of a town in the tribe of Judah, 1 Sa. 17:1; see פַּס דַּמִּים

אֶפַע m., *an adder*, Isa. 41:24; see פָּעָה.

אֶפְעֶה *adder;* see פָּעָה.

אָפַף *enclose, hem in;* pret. pl. אָפְפוּ; with suff. אֲפָפוּנִי.

אָפַק Kal, root not used; (Arab. *visited many countries*). Hith. הִתְאַפֵּק I. *went on, proceeded.*—II. *restrained himself from proceeding*, Gen. 45:1, &c.; LXX. ἀνέχομαι, ἐγκρατεύομαι.

אָפִיק m. adj.—I. *mighty, eminent man*, Job 12:21.—II. *river, torrent.*—III. *the bosses of a shield*, Job 41:7.—IV. *swellings of the sea.*—V. p.n. of a city in the tribe of Asher, Jud. 1:31, same as:—

אָפֵק p.n.—I. of a city in the tribe of Asher.—II. of a city in the tribe of Issachar.

אֲפֵקָה p. n. of a town in the mountains of Judah, Jos. 15:53.

אָפַר root not used; (Arab. *casting away*).

אֵפֶר m.—I. *ashes.*—II. *any thing worthless.*

אוֹפִיר p. n. of a kingdom; see in its place.

אֲפֵר m. (transpos. of פְּאֵר), *a tiara, crown*, 1 Ki. 20:38, 41.

אֶפְרֹחַ *chicken;* see פרח.

אַפִּרְיוֹן m., LXX. φορεῖον, *car, sedan*, Cant. 3:9, 10.

אֶפְרַיִם p.n.—I. *Ephraim*, the younger son of Joseph.—II. the tribe that descended from him.—III. afterwards, the kingdom formed by the ten tribes that revolted from the house of David.

אֶפְרָתָה, אֶפְרָת p.n.—I. of a city in the tribe of Judah: called also בֵּית־לֶחֶם.—II. same as אֶפְרַיִם, Ps. 132:6.

אֶפְרָתִי I. *an Ephraimite.*—II. an inhabitant of Ephratah.

אֲפָרְסָיֵא p. n. of an unknown people, Ezr. 4:9.

אֲפַרְסְכָיֵא p.n., as above, Ezr. 5:6.

אֲפַרְסַתְכָיֵא p. n. of the inhabitants of a city in Assyria, Ezr. 4:9.

וָאֶפַּת, אֶפַּת Niph. fut. apoc. 1. pers. for אֶפָּתֶה; see פתה.

אַפְּתֹם pa., *thus then, then moreover.* Ezr. 4:13.

אֶצְבּוֹן p. n. of a man.

אֶצְבַּע *finger;* see צבע.

אַצִּיעָה Hiph. fut. 1. pers. with ה parag., see יצע.

אָצַל I. *holding back, withholding*, with מִן.—II. *laying up with one's self*, with לְ. Niph. *contracted*, Eze. 42:6. Hiph. *withhold;* fut. וַיָּאצֶל, Nu. 11:25.

אָצִיל m. (Arab. *rooted, firm*).—I. *nobleman*, Eze. 24:11.—II. *end, extremity*, Isa. 41:9.

אַצִּיל m. *joint, suture*; אַצִּילֵי יָדַיִם *the wrists*.

אָצֵל p. n.—I. of a man.—II. of a place near Jerusalem, Zec. 14:5.

אֵצֶל prep., *near*; מֵאֵצֶל *near*; מֵאֶצְלוֹ *near him*.

אֲצַלְיָהוּ p. n. of a man.

אֹצֶם p. n. of a man.

אֶצְעָדָה *bracelet*; see צעד.

אֶצֹּק Kal fut. 1. pers. of the verb; see יצק.

אָצַר *treasured*. Niph. *laid up*, Isa. 23:1,18. Hiph. הוֹצַר *appoint as treasurer*, Neh. 13:13, with עַל; fut. with ה parag. אוֹצְרָה.

אוֹצָר m. (pl. אוֹצָרוֹת).—I. *treasury*. —II. *treasure*; בֵּית הָאֹ׳ I. *treasure-house*.—II. *warehouse*.

אֵצֶר p. n. of a man.

אֶצָּרְךָ Kri, Jer. 1:5, Kal fut. 1. pers. with suff.; see יצר.

אֶקְדָּח *carbuncle*; see קדח.

אַקּוֹ m., *gazelle*, Deu. 14:5.

אֶקַּח Kal fut. 1. pers. of the verb לקח.

אֶקְחֶה for אֶקְחָה Isa. 56:12, Kal fut. 1. pers. with ה parag., from לקח.

אֶקְרָאֶה Kal fut. 1. pers. with ה parag., from קרא.

אֹר *light*; see יְאֹר.

אֲרָא p. n. of a man.

אֵרֶא, וָאֵרֶא Niph. fut. apoc., from ראה.

אֲרִאֵל, אֲרִיאֵל name of Jerusalem; see ארה.

אָרַב *lying in wait, ambush*; with לְ, עַל; fut. יֶאֱרֹב, part. אוֹרֵב *ambuscader*. Pi. part. pl. מְאָרְבִים *lying in wait*. Hiph. *he places an ambush*, 1 Sa. 15:5.

אֲרָב p. n. of a town in the tribe of Judah.

אַרְבִּי a native of Arabia.

אֶרֶב m., *lying in wait, place of ambush*, Job 37:8, 38:40.

אֹרֶב m., the same; with suff. אָרְבּוֹ.

אָרְבָּה f., the same; pl. אֲרֻבּוֹת; const. אָרְבּוֹת.

אַרְבֶּה m., a species of *locust*, from רָבָה *was many*.

אֲרֻבָּה f.—I. *net* or *wicker work* to cover windows: hence,—II. *window*.—III. *pigeon-holes*, Isa. 60:8. IV. applied to the visible heavens, Gen. 7:11, 8:2.—V. *a chimney*, Hos. 13:3.

אֲרֻבּוֹת (*plots*), p. n. of a place in the tribe of Judah.

מַאֲרָב m., *ambush, ambuscade*.

אַרְבֵּאל p. n. of a place, Hos. 10:14; see בֵּית.

אַרְבַּע p. n. of a giant.

אַרְבַּע *four*; see רבע.

אָרַג I. *plaiting the hair*, Jud. 16:13. —II. *weaving*, Isa. 59:5; part. אֹרֵג *a weaver*, f. אֹרְגָה.

אֶרֶג m.—I. *texture, web*, Job 7:6.— II. *weaver's comb*, Jud. 16:14.

אַרְגֹּב p. n.—I. of the district of Og. —II. of a man.

אַרְגְּוָן Ch., *purple*, same as אַרְגָּמָן.

אַרְגַּז *bag*; see רגז.

אַרְגָּמָן m., *purple*.

אַרְדְּ p. n. *Ard*, a son of **Benjamin**; אַרְדִּי patronymic of Ard.

אַרְדּוֹן p. n. of a man.

אָרָה I. *pluck fruit*, Ps. 80:13.—II. *gather*.

אָרָה Nu. 22:6, imp. with ה parag.; see ארר.

אֻוֵרוֹת f. pl., *stables, stalls for beasts*, 2 Chron. 32:28.

אֻרְווֹת } f. pl., const. אֻרְוֹות.
אֻרָיוֹת } f. pl., const. אֻרְיוֹת.—I. *stalls*.—II. *stable*.

אֲרִי m., *a lion*; pl. אֲרָיִים and אֲרָיוֹת.

אַרְיֵה m., *a lion*.

אַרְיֵה m. Ch., *a lion*; pl. אַרְיָוָן.

אֲרַיֶּוְךָ Isa. 16:9, transpos. for אֲרַוֶּיְךָ or אֲרַיֶּוְךָ (same as רָיָה). Pi. fut. 1. pers. with suff.; see רוה.

אֲרִיאֵל, אֲרִאֵל (*lion of God*).—I. a name of the altar of burnt-offering.—II. a name for Jerusalem.—III. p. n. of a man.

אַרְאֵל (the same), p. n. of a man.

אַרְאֵלִי (the same), p. n. of a man.

אֶרְאֶלָּם m., "their valiant ones," Isa. 33:7, Eng. Ver.; probably for אֶרְאֶה לָהֶם *I will appear unto them* (Lee).

אָרוֹן com.—I. *ark, chest*; אֲרוֹן הַבְּרִית, אֱלֹהִים, הָעֵדוּת *the ark of the covenant*.—II. *coffin, mummy-case*, Gen. 50:26.

אֲרוּ Ch., *behold! see!*

אַרְוָד p. n., *Aradus*, a city and district on the coast of Phœnicia.

אֲרוֹד, אֲרוֹדִי p. n. of a man.

אֲרוּכָה *repairing*; see ארך.

אֲרוּמָה p. n. of a city.

אֲרוֹמִים *Syrians*; see אֲרַמִּי, ארם.

אֲרוֹמֵם for אֶתְרוֹמֵם Hith. fut. 1. pers.; see רום.

אָרַז *was firm, closely packed*; part אֲרֻזִים.

אֶרֶז m., *cedar*; pl. אֲרָזִים, const. אַרְזֵי.

אַרְזָה f., *cedar wainscot*, Zep. 2:14.

אָרַח *he goeth to herd with*, Job 34:8; part. אֹרֵחַ *traveller*.

אָרַח (*wanderer*), p. n. of a man.

אֹרַח com. (with suff. אָרְחִי; pl. אֳרָחוֹת; const. אָרְחוֹת; with suff. אָרְחֹתָם and 'אֹרְ).—I. *way, road, path*.—II. *mode* or *manner*; 'א יְהוָֹה *way of the Lord*, i. e. the way that pleases the Lord; א׳ חַיִּים *the way of life*, i. e. that leads to life; א׳ עוֹלָם *the old path*, i.e. the manners of ancient times.—III. *wayfaring man*.

אֹרַח m. Ch., the same; pl. אָרְחָן.

אֹרְחָה f.—I. *step, progress*.—II. *travelling company, caravan*.

אֲרֻחָה f.—I. *fixed portion, ration*.—II *portion generally*.

אֲרִיאֵל, אֲרָיוֹת, אַרְיֵה, אֲרִי; p. n.; see ארה.

אֲרִידַי p. n. of a son of Haman, Ἀριδαῖος

אֲרִידָתָא (*strong*), p. n. of a man.

אַרְיוֹךְ p. n.—I. of a king of Ellasar, Gen. 14:1.—II. of a Chaldean.

אֲרִיסַי p. n. of a son of Haman.

אָרַךְ (fut. יֶאֱרַךְ; pl. יַאַרְכוּ), *was long, became* or *was made long*; אָרְכוּ־לוֹ הַיָּמִים *he had tarried there many days*, Gen. 26:8. Hiph. הֶאֱרִיךְ trans. *make long, prolong*; ה׳ יָמָי פ׳ *lengthen his days, prolong life*; ה׳ אַפּוֹ, נַפְשׁוֹ *was long-suffering, patient*.

אֲרֻכָה, אֲרוּכָה f.—I. *lengthening out*.

3

—II. *repairing, restoring, healing;* (Arab. the same).

אֲרַךְ Ch. (part. אֲרִיךְ), *becoming, suitable.*

אָרֵךְ (const. אֶרֶךְ), *long;* א׳ הָאֵבֶר *with long pinions,* Ecc. 7:8; א׳ אַפַּיִם *slow to anger;* א׳ רוּחַ *μακρόθυμος, long-suffering.*

אֶרֶךְ p. n. of a city of Shinar, Gen. 10:10; hence אַרְכְּוָיֵא an inhabitant of Erech; אַרְכִּי the same.

אֹרֶךְ m., *length* (of time and space); with suff. אָרְכּוֹ.

אָרֹךְ m., אֲרֻכָּה f., *long, lasting long.*

אַרְכָה, אַרְכָא f. Ch., *time, duration.*

אַרְכֻּבָּה *the knee,* Dan. 5:6; see ברך.

אֲרָם f. (const. אֲרַם), p.n., *Aramea;* the region of Damascus and Syria to the Orontes and Mesopotamia; א׳ נַהֲרַיִם *Mesopotamia;* פַּדַּן אֲרָם *Padan Aram;* א׳ צוֹבָה part of *Syria;* א׳ דַּמֶּשֶׂק *Syria of Damascus;* א׳ מַעֲכָה the region beyond Jordan at the foot of Anti-Libanus; א׳ בֵּית־רְחוֹב part of *Syria;* see רָחַב.

אֲרַמִּי m., *Syrian* (f. אֲרַמִּיָּה; pl. אֲרַמִּים and אֲרוֹמִים).

אֲרָמִית adv., *in Syriac, in the language of Syria.*

אַרְמוֹן m. (pl. const. אַרְמְנוֹת), *palace.*

אַרְמֹנִי p.n. of one of the sons of Saul.

אֹרֶן m., *the mountain ash,* Isa. 44:14; LXX. *πίτυς;* Vulg. *pinus.*

אֲרָן p. n. of a man.

אֹרֶן p. n. of a man.

אַרְנֶבֶת f., *the hare,* Lev. 11:6, Deu. 14:17; (Arab. the same).

אַרְנוֹן (*sounding,* see רָנַן), p. n., *Arnon,* a river which bounded the land of Israel to the east.

אַרְנָן p. n. of a man.

אָרְנָן (אֲרַנְיָה 2 Sa. 24:15). p. n., *Araunah,* the Jebusite.

אֲרַע, אַרְעָא m. Ch.—I. *the earth.* —II. an epithet: *low, inferior,* followed by מִן.

אַרְעִית f. Ch., *low, mean.*

אַרְפָּד p. n. of a city of Syria.

אַרְפַּכְשַׁד p.n. of a son of Shem.

אֶרֶץ f., sometimes m. (with art. הָאָרֶץ; with suff. אַרְצוֹ; pl. אֲרָצוֹת).—I. *earth.*—II. *the world.*—III. *the ground;* אַרְצָה *on the ground.*—IV. *region, province.* Pl. אֲרָצוֹת I. *lands, countries.*—II. *heathen nations.*

אַרְצָא p. n. of a man.

אֲרַק f. Ch., *the earth,* Jer. 10:11.

אָרַר (imp. אָר; with ה parag. אָרָה; pl. אֹרוּ; fut. יָאֹר), *denounce, curse.* Niph. part. pl. נֵאָרִים *denounced, cursed.* Pi. אֵרַר *denounce, bring on a curse;* part. pl. מְאָרְרִים. Hoph. fut. יוּאַר *is made accursed.*

מְאֵרָה f., *cursing.*

אֲרָרָט p. n., *Ararat,* a mountain in Armenia.

אֲרָרִי same as הֲרָרִי *Ararite.*

אָרַשׂ. Pi. אֵרַשׂ, אֵרֵשׂ (with accusative אִשָּׁה) *espouse a wife* by entering into a contract under a fine; with בְּ of the sum mulcted. Pu. pret. f. אֹרָשָׂה *espoused;* part. f. מְאֹרָשָׂה.

אָרַשׁ root not used; (Arab. *he desired*)

אֲרֶשֶׁת f., *petition;* LXX. *δέησις,* Ps 21:3.

אַרְתַּחְשַׁשְׂתָּא, אַרְתַּחְשַׁסְתָּא, אַרְתַּחְשַׁשְׂתָּא } *Artaxerxes*, king of Persia.

אֲשַׂרְאֵל (same as אֲסַרְאֵל), p.n. of a m.

אֲשַׂרְיאֵל p.n. of a man; ־ִי patronymic of above.

אֵשׁ f., sometimes m. (with suff. אִשּׁוֹ, אִשְּׁכֶם, אִשָּׁם).—I. *fire.*—II. *lightning;* אֵשׁ אֱלֹהִים *lightning.*—III. *heat of the sun,* Joel 1:19, 20.—IV. *appearance of God.*—V. *God's fierce anger.*—VI. *ardour of mind.*—VII. *great tribulations.*

אֵשׁ com. Ch., emph. state אֶשָּׁא *fire.*

אִשֶּׁה m. (const. אִשֵּׁה; pl. אִשֵּׁי, אִשִּׁים).—I. *burnt-offering.* — II. *incense-offering.*

אֶשָּׁה f. (אֶשָּׁתָם Jer. 6:29), for אֵשׁ תַּם (*by*) *fire is consumed.*

אַשְׁבֵּל p. n. of a son of Benjamin; ־ִי patronymic of the same.

אֶשְׁבָּן p.n. of a man.

אֶשְׁבַּעַל p. n. of a son of Saul.

אֶשְׁבַּעַל p. n. of a son of Saul.

אָשַׁד root not used; (Arab. *he rushed*).

אֶשֶׁד m., *bed of a river* or *brook;* א׳ הַנְּחָלִים *bed of the torrents,* Nu. 21:15.

אֲשֵׁדָה *foot, base of a mountain;* pl. אַשְׁדוֹת; const. אַשְׁדוֹת.

אַשְׁדּוֹד (from שָׁדַד), p.n. *Ashdod* (Ἄζωτος), a city of the Philistines; אַשְׁדּוֹדִי *an Ashdodite;* ־ִית I. *a woman of Ashdod.*—II. *in the language of Ashdod.*

אִשָּׁה *woman;* see אנשׁ.

אָשְׁיָה f., *foundation,* Jer. 50:15; from שׁוּת.

אַשּׁוּר, אֲשׁוּרִי, אַשֻּׁר *footstep;* see אשר.

אַשְׁחוּר p. n. of a man.

אֲשִׁימָא p.n. of a god of the Hamathites.

אֲשֵׁירָה *erection;* see אֲשֵׁרָה.

אֲשִׁישׁ *foundation,* Isa. 16:7, see אשׁשׁ, perhaps for אִישֵׁי *men,* as Jer. 48:31.

אֲשִׁישָׁה, אֲשִׁין *food;* see אשׁשׁ.

אֶשֶׁךְ m., *testicles,* Lev. 21:20.

אֶשְׁכֹּל *Eshcol;* from שׁכל.

אַשְׁכֵּים Ch. Hiph. inf. abs.; from שׁכם.

אַשְׁכְּנַז p. n. of a people of North Asia.

אֶשְׁכָּר *a rich gift,* Eze. 27:15, Ps. 72:14; from שׁכר.

אֵשֶׁל m., *the tamarisk,* a middle-sized thorny tree; tamarix orientalis (Linn.).

אָשַׁם and **אָשֵׁם** (fut. יֶאְשַׁם).—I. *was guilty, sinned* (when against any one, with לְ; when in any thing, with בְּ and לְ).—II. *was conscious of guilt.*—III. *suffered for sin,* Ps. 34:22, &c. Niph. *suffered the consequences of sin,* Joel 1:18; Hiph. *bring on the consequences of guilt,* Ps. 5:11.

אָשֵׁם m., *guilty.*

אָשָׁם m.—I. *guilt,* i.e. the consequence of sin.—II. a sacrifice to expiate it.

אַשְׁמָה f.—I. (inf. of אָשַׁם), לְאַשְׁמָה בָהּ *to trespass therein,* Lev. 5:26; לְאַשְׁמַת הָעָם *so that the people trespass.*—II. *guilt, trespass.*—III. *a trespass-offering,* Lev. 6:5.

אַשְׁמַנִּים m., "desolate places," Eng. Ver., Isa. 59:10; meaning uncertain.

אַשְׁמֻרָה f., the three watches into which the night was divided; root שׁמר.

אֶשְׁנָב m., *a latticed window*, Jud. 5: 28, Pro. 7:6.

אַשְׁנָה p. n. of two cities in the tribe of Judah.

אֶשְׁעָן (*a prop*), p. n. of a city in the tribe of Judah.

אַשָּׁף m. Heb. and Ch. (pl. אַשָּׁפִים), *an enchanter*.

אַשְׁפָּה f., *quiver*; בְּנֵי א׳ *sons of the quiver, arrows*, Lam. 3:13.

אַשְׁפּוֹת f. pl., *dung, dung heap*.

אַשְׁפַּתּוֹת f. pl., the same.

אַשְׁפְּנַז p. n. of one of the eunuchs of Nebuchadnezzar.

אֶשְׁפָּר *measure, cup*, 2 Sa. 6:10, 1 Chron. 6:3.

אַשְׁקְלוֹן p. n. of a city of the Philistines.

אָשַׁר *went straight on, walked along*. —Pi. I. *guide, lead aright*.—II. *consider, pronounce good, happy*; Pu. אוּשַּׁר, אֻשַּׁר.—I. *was guided*.—II. *was esteemed happy*.

אָשֵׁר p.n. of one of the sons of Jacob; אָשֵׁרִי I. *an Asherite*.—II. p.n. of a city near Sichem, Jos. 17:7.

אֶשֶׁר m., *happiness*; only in the const. pl. as אַשְׁרֵי הָאִישׁ *blessed is the man*, Ps. 1:1; אַשְׁרֶיךָ *blessed art thou*, Deu. 33:29.

אֹשֶׁר m., *happiness*, Gen. 30:13; with suff. אָשְׁרִי.

אֲשׁוּר f.—I. *a step*.—II. *wood of the box tree*, Eze. 27:6.

אַשּׁוּר f.—I. *step*, Job 31:7.—II. p.n. f., *Assyria*, kingdom of; m., *an Assyrian*; אַשּׁוּרָה *into Assyria*; דֶּרֶךְ א׳ *the way of Assyria*.—III. אַשּׁוּרִים a race of Ishmaelites, Gen. 25:3.

אַשּׁוּרִי p. n. of a man.

אֻשַּׁרְנָא m. Ch., *wall, building*, Eze. 5:3.

תְּאַשּׁוּר m., *the box tree*, Isa. 41:19, 60:13.

אֲשֶׁר I. relat. pron. of every gender and number; *he who, she who, it which, &c.*—II. note of the relative when it comes before pronouns and adverbs; אֲשֶׁר הוּא חַי *he who lives*; א׳ אֶת־עָפָר *which is dust*; א׳ לוֹ, לָהּ *to whom*, sing.; א׳ לָהֶם, לָהֶן, *to whom, which*, pl.; א׳ אֹתוֹ, אֹתָהּ, *whom, which*, sing.; א׳ אֹתָם, אֹתָן, *whom, which*, pl.; אֲשֶׁר־לְשֹׁנוֹ *whose tongue*; א׳ בּוֹ, בָּהּ *in whom, which*; א׳ בְּאַרְצָם *in whose land*; א׳ מִמֶּנּוּ *from whom*; א׳ שָׁם *where*; א׳ מִשָּׁם *whence*; א׳ שָׁמָּה *whither*; א׳ תַּחַת כְּנָפָיו *under whose wings*.—III. precedes pron. of the 1. and 2. pers.; א׳ מְכַרְתֶּם אֹתִי *(ye) who have sold me*; א׳ בְּחַרְתִּיךָ *thee whom I have chosen*.—IV. compounded with preps.; אֶת־אֲשֶׁר *him whom*; בַּאֲשֶׁר *where*; כַּאֲשֶׁר *according to, as if, because, when*; מֵאֲשֶׁר *from thence, whence*.—V. preceded by adverbs; אַחַר, בַּעֲבוּר, תַּחַת, עַל, עַד, יַעַן connecting them with the following words.—VI. אֲשֶׁר לְ note of the genitive; הַצֹּאן א׳ לְאָבִיהָ *her father's cattle*; אֲשֶׁר conj. ὅτι, *because, that*; ἵνα with fut.; *since, when*, ὅτε; ὡς *as*, with כֵּן.

שֶׁ־ with dag. forte (sometimes שַׁ־) same as אֲשֶׁר relat. pron. and in its other significations; שֶׁשָּׁם *where*; שֶׁל *of, whose*; בְּשֶׁ־ *because*; כִּמְעַט שֶׁ־ *almost*; עַד־שֶׁ־ *until*. For אֲשֶׁר and שֶׁ; see Noldii Concordantiæ, and Prof. Lee's Grammar

בְּשֶׁל because, on account of; בְּשֶׁלִּי for my sake; בְּשֶׁלְּמִי on whose account? בְּשֶׁל אֲשֶׁר, whatever.

אֲשַׂרְאֵלָה (from אָשֵׁר and אֵל), p. n. of a man.

אֲשֵׁירָה, אֲשֵׁרָה (probably m. of עַשְׁתֹּרֶת), p. n. of a deity of the Syrians; pl. אֲשֵׁרִים and אֲשֵׁרוֹת images of this idol.

אֻשַּׁרְנָא *buildings*; see אשר.

אָשַׁשׁ root not used. Hith. הִתְאֹשָׁשׁוּ *be men*; see אִישׁ.

אָשִׁישׁ m. pl., const. אֲשִׁישֵׁי *foundations*; see in its place.

אֲשִׁישָׁה f., *cake, pancake*; pl. ים. and אֲשִׁישׁוֹת.

אֻשַּׁיִן m. pl. Ch., *foundations*.

אֵשֶׁת *woman*; see אנש.

אִשְׁתִּיו Ch. pret. pl. with א prosthet., from שתה.

אֶשְׁתָּאֹל p. n. of a town of the Danites.

אֶשְׁתַּדּוּר Hith. of שדר.

אֶשְׁתּוֹן p. n. of a man.

אֶשְׁתְּמֹה and אֶשְׁתְּמוֹעַ p. n. of a town in the tribe of Judah.

אֹת *sign*; see אוה.

I. **אֵת** m., *ploughshare*; pl. אִתִּים and אֵתִים 1 Sa. 13:21; with suff. אִתֵּיכֶם.

II **אֵת, אֶת־** note of:—I. the accus. —II. the nom. with verbs passive and neuter; יִקָּרֵא אֶת־שִׁמְךָ *thy name shall be called*; with suff. אוֹתִי, אֹתִי *me*; אוֹתְךָ, אֹתְךָ (with pause אוֹתָךְ; with ה parag. אוֹתְכָה, אֹתְכָה) m., אֹתָךְ f., *thee*; אֹתוֹ *him*; אֹתָהּ *her*; אֹתָנוּ *us*; אֶתְכֶם, אוֹתְכֶם *you*; אֹתָם, אֶתְהֶם, אוֹתְהֶם *them*, m.; אֹתָן with ה parag. אֹתָנָה, אֶתְהֶן *them*, f.

III. **אֵת, אֶת־** prep. *with, by, on, besides, towards*; אֶת־פְּנֵי פ׳ *before some one*; with suff. אִתִּי *with me*; אִתְּךָ (with pause אִתָּךְ) m., אִתָּךְ, אִתָּךְ f., *with thee*; אִתּוֹ *with him*; אִתָּהּ *with her*; אִתָּנוּ *with us*; אִתְּכֶם, אִתְּכֶן *with you*; אִתָּם *with them* (sometimes אֹתִי, אֹתוֹ, &c.); מֵאֵת denotes separation, *from*; מֵאִתִּי, מֵאוֹתִי *from me*; מֵאִתָּךְ, מֵאוֹתָךְ *from thee, &c.*

אֶתְבַּעַל p. n. of a king of Sidon.

אַתָּה (sometimes אַתְּ m.; אַתְּ, with pause אָתְּ, sometimes אַתִּי f.), pers. pron. *thou*; אַתֶּם m., אַתֵּן, אַתֵּנָה f., *ye*.

אָתָה (אָתָא Isa. 21:12), *came*; pret. pl. אָתָנוּ; imper. pl. אֵתָיוּ; fut. יֶאֱתֶה, תֵּאתֶה, וַיֵּתֵא, וַיֵּאת; pl. יֶאֱתָיוּ. Hiph. imper. pl. הֵתָיוּ *bring ye*.

אֲתָה Ch., *came*. Aph. הַיְתִי *brought*. Hoph. *was brought*.

אִיתוֹן m., *entrance*, Eze. 40:15.

אֶתְוַדַּע Hith. fut. 1. pers., from ידע.

אַתּוּן com. Ch., *furnace*, Dan. 3:6, 11, 15.

אַתִּיק, אַתּוּק m., *gallery*, Eze. 41: 3, 15.

אַתַּי p. n. of a man.

אֱתָיו Syr. for אֱתָיוּ which is for אֱתוּ imp. pl., from אתה.

אָתָיו for אָתָאנוּ pret. pl. 1. pers., from אָתָה. אָתָא.

אַתֶּם, אַתֵּן *you*; see אַתָּה.

אֵתָם p. n. of a place in the desert.

אִתְּמוֹל, אֶתְמוּל, אֶתְמוֹל *yesterday;* same as תְּמוֹל.

אָתַן root not used (Arab. *stepping shortly, she-ass*).

אָתוֹן f., *she-ass.*

אֶתְנָן, אֶתְנָה *gift;* see יתן.

אֶתְנִי (*gift*), p. n. of a man.

אַתִּקֶנְךָ Kal fut. 1. pers. with suff. and נ epenth., from נתק.

אֲתַר m. Ch., *place;* אֲתַר דִּי *in that place, where;* בָּאתַר *after;* בָּתְרָךְ *after thee.*

אֲתָרִים m., *places;* or p. n. according to others Nu. 21:1.

ב

בְּ prep.—I. of place: *in, among, with, near, before;* never motion either to or in a place.—II. of time: *in, within.*—III. used of the means or instrument: *by, with.*—IV. of the cause: *for, because.*—V. of the rule: *according to.*—VI. *by* (in an oath).—VII. often prefixed to the inf. of verbs, translated by *in* or *when;* with suff. בִּי; בְּךָ m. (with the pause בָּךְ); בָּךְ f.; בּוֹ, בָּהּ; בָּנוּ; בָּהֶן, בָּם, בָּהֶם and בָּכֶם.

בֹּאָה imp. with ה parag.; בָּאֵי, בָּאִים part. pl.; בֹּאֲכָה inf. with suff.; בָּאת and בָּאתְ pret. f. 2. pers., from בוא.

בִּאָה *entrance;* see בוא.

בָּאוּשׁ *wicked;* see באשׁ.

בָּאַר, Pi. בֵּאֵר.—I. *dig, cut upon* or *into, define well;* with עַל.—II. *make clear, publish,* Deu. 1:5.

בְּאֵר f. (pl. const. בְּאֵרוֹת).—I. *well, cistern.*—II. p. n. of one of the stations in the desert.—III. p. n. of a town in the tribe of Judah. בְּאֵר אֵלִים (*the well of heroes*), p. n. of a well. בְּאֵר לַחַי רֹאִי (*the well of the living God that seeth me*), p. n. of a well in the desert. בְּאֵר שֶׁבַע (*well of the oath*), p. n. of a city in the tribe of Simeon. בְּאֵרוֹת p. n. of a city in the tribe of Benjamin; בֵּרֹתִי בְּאֵרֹתִי, epithet of an inhabitant of *Beeroth.* בְּאֵרוֹת בְּנֵי יַעֲקָן (*wells of the sons of Iaachan*), p. n. of a station in the desert.

בֹּאר often, בּוֹר m.—I. *well of water; well of bitumen,* Gen. 14:10.—II. *pit* or *dungeon in which prisoners were kept;* בֵּית הַבּוֹר *prison house.*—III. *grave, sepulchre;* יוֹרְדֵי בוֹר *they that go down into the pit,* i. e. the dead; עַד בּוֹר *even to the grave;* with ה *den, place,* בֹּרָה. pl. בֹּארוֹת, בֹּרוֹת.

בְּאֵרָא p. n. of a man.

בְּאֵרָה p. n. of a man.

בְּאֵרִי p. n.—I. of the father of Hosea. —II. of the father-in-law of Esau.

בָּאַשׁ (fut. יִבְאַשׁ) *emitted an ill savour, stank.* Niph. *became fetid, in ill odour,* i. e. hateful; (with בְּ, אֵת). Hiph. הִבְאִישׁ *rendered, made bad,* i. e. *odious;* (with בְּ); int. *stank,* Ex. 16:24; *did wickedly, became bad;* (with עִם), 1 Chron. 19:6.

בְּאֵשׁ Ch., *was evil;* (with עַל), Dan. 6:15.

בְּאשׁ m.—I. *stench;* with suff. בָּאְשׁוֹ בָּאְשָׁם.—II. *evil, affliction.*

בָּאְשָׁה f., *poisonous herb,* probably hemlock, Job 31:40.

בְּאֻשִׁים m. pl., *wild, sour grapes,* Is 5:2, 4.

בְּאוּשׁ m. Ch., *bad, wicked;* f. emph. בְּאוּשְׁתָּא.

בָּאתַר *after;* see אֲתַר.

בָּבָה *pupil of the eye;* see בּוּב.

בֵּבַי p.n. of a man.

בָּבֶל p.n.f.—I. *Babylon;* with ה, signifying place, בָּבֶלָה.—II. *the kingdom of Babylon.*

בָּבְלַי Ch. *Babylonish;* pl. const. בָּבְלָיֵא.

בַּג *m.,* לְבַג, Eze. 23:7, a wrong reading; Kri לְבַז "for a spoil," Eng. Ver.

בָּגַד (fut. יִבְגֹּד, יִבְגַּד; inf. בָּגוֹד; const. בְּגוֹד; with suff. בִּגְדוֹ), *dissembled, acted perfidiously, cheated,* with בְּ and מִן; part. בֹּגֵד *a perfidious person.*

בֶּגֶד m. (f. Lev. 6:20; with suff. בִּגְדִי, בִּגְדוֹ; pl. בְּגָדִים; const. בִּגְדֵי, בִּגְדוֹתֶיךָ, Ps. 45:9).—I. *wrapper, coverlet.*—II. *cloak, garment.*—III. *dissimulation, perfidy.*—IV. *rapine, violence.*

בֹּגְדוֹת f. pl., *great perfidy,* Zep. 3:4.

בָּגוֹד m., בָּגוֹדָה f., *perfidious,* Jer. 3: 7, 10.

בִּגְוַי p. n. of a man.

בִּגְלַל *because;* see גלל.

בִּגְתָא p. n. of a eunuch of Ahasuerus.

בִּגְתָן p.n. of a eunuch of Ahasuerus.

בַּד m., *fine linen;* בַּדִּים *linen garments;* see also בַּד under בדד.

בָּדָא *originated, innovated;* part. with suff. בּדָאָם Syr. for בּוֹדְאָם.

בָּדַד, part. בּוֹדֵד *separate, solitary person.*

בַּד m., *being alone, separate, apart;* pl. בַּדִּים.—I. *shoots, branches.*—II. *staves of wood.*—III. *limbs, members of the body.*—IV. *defences,* i. e. *princes,* Hos. 11:6, &c.—V. *lies,* Is. 16:6, &c.

לְבַד adv., *alone, separate, only;* אָנֹכִי לְבַדִּי *I alone;* אַתָּה לְבַדְּךָ *thou alone;* לְבַדְּךָ *to thee alone;* לְבַדּוֹ *he alone;* לְבַד מִן and מִלְּבַד *besides;* מִלְּבַד אֲשֶׁר *beside that which;* לְבַד עַל the same.

בָּדָד m., *separate, alone, solitary;* לְבָדָד and בָּדָד adv. *apart, separate.*

בְּדַד p. n. of the father of Hadad king of Edom.

בְּדֵי same as בְּ; see דַּי.

בֵּדְיָה p. n. of a man.

בָּדַל Niph. *was separated;* with לְ it signifies, *unto something;* with מִן, *from something;* with אֶל, *he separated himself unto one thing alone.* Hiph. הִבְדִּיל I. *made, caused division,* const. with מִן and מֵעַל.—II. *distinguished, divided,* with בֵּין...לְ, בֵּין...לְבֵין, בֵּין...וּבֵין.—III. *designed,* with לְ.

בָּדָל m., בְּדַל אֹזֶן *portion of the ear,* Amos 3:12.

בְּדִיל m., *tin;* אֶבֶן הַבְּדִיל *the weight at the plumb-line, the plummet.*

מִבְדָּלוֹת f. pl., *separations, separate places,* Jos. 16:9.

בְּדֹלַח m. *bdellium,* a translucent and odoriferous gum; according to Lee, a precious stone, either *the crystal* or *the beryl,* Gen. 2:12, Num. 11:7.

בְּדָן p. n.—I. of a judge, perhaps the same as בָּרָק, 1 Sam. 12:11.—II. of another man, 1 Chron. 7:17.

בָּדַק (Arab. *tear, rend*); inf. בְּדוֹק

repairing injury, decay, 2 Chron. 34:10.

בֶּדֶק *injury, decay in a building;* with suff. בִּדְקֵךְ.

בִּדְקַר p. n. of a man.

בְּדַר Ch. same as Heb. בָּזַר; Pa. imper. בַּדַּרוּ *sprinkle.*

בָּהָה (Arab. *void*).

בֹּהוּ m., *emptiness, destitution.*

בַּהַט m., *marble,* Est. 1:6.

בָּהַל Niph. נִבְהַל.—I. *was terrified, astonished.*—II. *cast down, ruined,* with לְ *at,* מ *from.* Pi. בִּהֵל.—I. *cause to hurry, hasten.*—II. *astonish, confound, ruin;* fut. יְבַהֵל. Pu. part. מְבֹהָל *hurried, gotten too speedily.* Hiph. הִבְהִיל same as Pihel.

בְּהַל Ch., Pa. *affrighted.* Ithp. part. *alarmed.*

בֶּהָלָה f., *fear, terror, ruin;* pl. בֶּהָלוֹת.

בְּהִילוּ f. Ch., *hurry, haste,* Ezr. 4:23.

הִתְבְּהָלָה f. Ch., *haste.*

בָּהַם root not used; (Arab. *was dumb*).

בְּהֵמָה f. (const. בֶּהֱמַת; with suff. בְּהֶמְתֶּךָ).—I. *cattle.*—II. *wild beast;* בֶּהֱמַת יַעַר, הָאָרֶץ, הַשָּׂדֶה, *wild beasts;* pl. בְּהֵמוֹת; const. בַּהֲמוֹת, Job 40:15, name of some stupendous quadruped.

בֹּהֶן m.—I. *the thumb.*—II. *the great toe;* pl. בְּהֹנוֹת

בֹּהַן (*thumb*), p. n. of a son of Reuben; אֶבֶן בֹּהַן p. n. of a place in the tribe of Judah.

בָּהַק root not used; (Arab. *was shining*).

בֹּהַק m., LXX. ἀλφὸς, *a white scurf, cicatrix on the skin,* Lev. 13:39.

בָּהַר root not used; Ch. *he shone.*

בָּהִיר m., *breaking through the clouds* (of light), Job 37:21.

בַּהֶרֶת f., the *white spot* covered with hair which was the sure symptom of leprosy; pl. בֶּהָרוֹת, Lev. c. 13

בֶּהָרֵג for בְּהֵהָרֵג Niph. inf. with the pref. בְּ from הרג.

בָּהֲשַׁמָּה for בְּהָשַׁמָּה Hoph. inf. with suff. and pref. from שׁמם.

בּוֹא (fut. וַיָּבֹא, יָבוֹא; part. pl. בָּאִים, בָּאֵי), *entered, came* or *went in, to, for,* &c., with לְ, בְּ, אֶל; יָצָא וּבָא same as הָלַךְ, *he went in and out,* i. e. he lived familiarly; with לִפְנֵי הָעָם *to go before, lead the people;* בּוֹא בְּרִית *he entered into covenant;* בּוֹא אֶל with עַל אִשָּׁה *had connection with a woman;* שֶׁמֶשׁ בָּאָה *the sun was setting;* const. also with עַד, עַל, לְ, בְּ, אֶל; בּוֹא בַּיָּמִים *advanced in years;* with אֶת, עִם *went with, had intercourse with,* Ps. 26:4, Pro. 22:24. Hiph. הֵבִיא (with suff. הֱבִיאוֹ, imper. הָבִיא, הָבֵא, הָבִי; fut. יָבִיא, וַיָּבֵא) *caused, made, induced to enter, come in;* with אֶל, לְ, עַל. Hoph. הוּבָא *brought in.*

בִּאָה f., *entrance.*

מָבוֹא m., *entrance, porch;* מְבוֹא הַשֶּׁמֶשׁ *place of sunset.* Pl. מְבוֹאִים, const. מְבוֹאֵי and מְבוֹאוֹת.

מוּבָא m., *entrance,* 2 Sa. 3:25, Ez. 43:11.

תְּבוּאָה f.—I. *income.*—II. *store.*—III. *profit.*—IV. *produce;* pl. תְּבוּאוֹת.

תְּבוֹאָה f., Job 22:21; תְּבוֹאָתְךָ from בּוֹא, fut. Kal with ה parag.

בּוּב Niph. part. נָבוּב.—I. *proud, insolent*, Job 11:12.—II. *hollow*.

בָּבָה f., *apple of the eye, pupil*; בָּבַת עַיִן *pupil*, Zec. 2:12.

בּוּז (fut. יָבוּז), *despised, neglected*; with לְ comp. בזה, בזז.

בּוּז m.—I. *contempt*.—II. p. n. of a brother of Abraham, and of the nation he founded in Arabia Deserta; בּוּזִי *a Buzite*.—III. p. n. of a man, 1 Chron. 5:14.

בּוּזָה f., *contempt, contemptible thing*.

בַּוַּי p. n. of a man.

בּוּךְ Niph. נָבוֹךְ *confused, perplexed*, Ex. 14:3, Est. 3:15.

מְבוּכָה f., *confusion, perplexity*, Isa. 22:5; Mic. 7:4.

בּוֹכִיָּה Kal, part. from בכה.

בּוּל *increase*, same as יְבוּל; see יבל.

בּוּן and **בִּין**.—I. *distinguished, discerned*.—II. *perceived, understood*, with בְּ, אֶל, לְ, עַל; part. בָּנִים *prudent persons*; pret. בַּנְתָּ, בָּן and בִּינוֹתִי, בִּין; fut. יָבִין. Niph. נָבוֹן *became discerning*; part. נָבוֹן *wise*; נ׳ דָּבָר *wise in word, eloquent*. Pil. בּוֹנֵן *made him discerning*, Deu. 32:10. Hiph. הֵבִין.—I. *taught, explained*, with לְ, בְּ, אֶל.—II. *understood, was wise*; part. מֵבִין *skilful, learned*; imper. הָבֵן and הָבִין; with suff. הֲבִינֵנִי; fut. וַיָּבֶן, יָבִין. Hith. הִתְבּוֹנֵן same as Niph.; with בְּ, אֶל, עַל, עַד.

בַּיִן const. בֵּין s.—I. *interval, midst*; dual אִישׁ בֵּנַיִם *man of two intervals*, i. e. between the two armies, 1 Sam. 17:4.—II. prep. *between, among, within*; בֵּין...לְ, בֵּין...וּבֵין, בֵּין...לְבֵין *between...and* (*whether... or*, Lev. 27:12); with suff. בֵּינְךָ, בֵּינִי; with pause בֵּינוֹ, בֵּינֶךָ; with suff. pl. בֵּינֵיכֶם, בֵּנֵינוּ and בֵּינֵינוּ, בֵּינֶיךָ; בֵּינֵיהֶם; fem. אֶל־בֵּין־בֵּינוֹתָם; בֵּינוֹתֵינוּ *among*; אֶל־בֵּנוֹת לְ the same; מִבֵּין *from between*; מִבֵּינוֹת לְ the same; עַל־בֵּין *up among*; בְּבֵין *in the midst*.

בֵּין Ch., *among*; pl. with suff. בֵּינֵיהוֹן.

בִּינָה f., *intelligence, discernment, prudence*; Ch. the same.

תָּבוּן m., תְּבוּנָה f., *understanding, prudence*; pl. תְּבוּנוֹת.

בּוּנָה (*intelligence*), p.n. of a man.

בּוּנִּי from בָּנָה, p. n. of a man.

בּוּס (fut. יָבוּס and יָבוּס; part. pl. בּוֹסִים) *trampled, trod upon, despised*. Pil. בּוֹסֵס *trod down* (profaned holy place). Hoph. part. מוּבָס *trodden down*. Hith. part. f. מִתְבּוֹסֶסֶת *become trodden down*, Eze. 16:6, 22.

מְבוּסָה f., *treading upon*.

תְּבוּסָה f., *destruction*, 2 Chron. 22:7.

בּוּעַ root not used, Ch. *was boiling*.

אֲבַעְבֻּעוֹת f. pl., *spots on the skin*.

בּוּץ root not used; (Arab. *fine linen*).

בּוּץ, בֻּץ m., *βύσσος, linen, fine linen*

בֵּיץ m., or בֵּיצָה f., pl. בֵּיצִים *eggs*.

בּוֹצֵץ (*shining*), p. n. of a rock near Gibeah.

בּוּק root not used; (Arab. *heavy rain*; see בקק).

בּוּקָה f, *emptiness, devastation*, Neh 2:11.

מְבוּקָה f., *emptiness*; the same.

בּוּר *well*, same as בְּאֵר; see בָּאַר

בּוּר (same as בָּרַר), *explored.*

בּוֹשׁ (pret. בֹּשְׁנוּ, בֹּשׁוּ, בֹּשְׁתָּ, בּוֹשׁ; fut. אֵבוֹשׁ, יֵבוֹשׁ) *ashamed, put to shame, blushed,* with מִן and לְ; עַד־בּוֹשׁ *until they were ashamed.* Pil. בּוֹשֵׁשׁ *put to a stand, delayed,* Jud. 5:28, Ex. 32:30. Hiph. הֵבִישׁ and הוֹבִישׁ (from cognate יבשׁ) *brought to shame, confusion;* part. מֵבִישׁ *bringing, causing shame, wicked.* Hith. הִתְבֹּשֵׁשׁ *become ashamed,* Gen. 2:25.

בּוּשָׁה f., *shame, ignominy.*

בָּשְׁנָה f., the same, Hos. 10:6.

בֹּשֶׁת f.—I. *shame, blushing.*—II. *ignominy.*—III. *an idol.*

מָבוּשׁ m., pl. מְבֻשִׁים *secret parts,* Deu. 25:11.

בּוֹשַׁסְכֶם Po. inf. with suff. from בשׁם

בּוּת Ch.; בָּת *passed the night,* Dan. 6:19.

בַּיִת m. (const. בֵּית; with suff. בֵּיתְךָ, בֵּיתוֹ; pl. בָּתִּים, const. בָּתֵּי), *habitation.*—I. *temple* of God or idols. —II. *palace.*—III. *house, tent, cave;* (אֲשֶׁר עַל בַּיִת *mayor of the palace;* בֶּן יְלִיד, or בַּיִת *household-slave*).— IV. *sepulchre.* — V. receptacle of anything; בָּתֵּי נֶפֶשׁ *perfume boxes,* Isa. 3:20.—VI. *family, race.* With ה parag. בַּיְתָה, const. בֵּיתָה, adv. *inwards;* מִבַּיִת, מִבַּיִת לְ, בֵּית לְ *within;* מִבֵּיתָה, מִבֵּית לְ, לְמִבֵּית לְ *within.*

בַּיִת m. Ch., *house, palace, temple.*

בִּיתָן m., *great house, palace,* Est. 1: 5; 7:7, 8.

The p.n. of many towns are compounds of בַּיִת; בֵּית אָוֶן in the tribe of Benjamin; בֵּית־אֵל between Jerusalem and Sichem; בֵּית הָאֱלִי *a Bethelite;* בּ׳ אֵצֶל in Samaria; בּ׳ אַרְבֵּאל *Arbela* in Galilee; בַּעַל מְעוֹן, בּ׳ בַּעַל מְעוֹן and בֵּית מְעוֹן in the tribe of Reuben; בּ׳ בָּרָה (*ferry-house*) Βηθαβαρά, near Jordan; בּ׳ בִּרְאִי in the tribe of Simeon; בּ׳ גָּדֵר in the tribe of Judah; בּ׳ הַגִּלְגָּל same as גִּלְגָּל, see גָּלַל; בּ׳ גָּמוּל (see גָּמַל) in the land of Moab; בּ׳ דָּגוֹן; דִּבְלָתַיִם, see בּ׳ דִּבְלָתַיִם (*temple of Dagon*), in the tribe of Judah, also in the tribe of Asher; בּ׳ הָרָם and הָרָן in the tribe of Gad; בּ׳ חָגְלָה (*place of partridges*), town of the Benjamites in the tribe of Judah; בּ׳ חָנָן (*house of mercy*), in the tribe of Judah or Dan; בּ׳ חֹרוֹן two towns in the tribe of Ephraim; בּ׳ הַיְשִׁימוֹת town of the Reubenites on the shore of the Red Sea; בּ׳ כַּר a strong place of the Philistines in the tribe of Judah; בּ׳ הַכֶּרֶם (*house of vineyards*), in the tribe of Judah; בּ׳ לְבָאוֹת (*place of lionesses*), in the tribe of Simeon; בּ׳ לֶחֶם (*house of bread*) Βηθλεέμ, in the tribe of Judah, see אֶפְרָתָה; another town in the tribe of Zebulun; בּ׳ הַלַּחְמִי *a Bethlehemite;* בּ׳ מִלּוֹא; עָפְרָה, see בּ׳ לְעַפְרָה, see מִלּוֹא; בּ׳ מַעֲכָה a town at the foot of Hermon; בּ׳ הַמֶּרְחָק (from רָחַק), on the banks of Kedron; בּ׳ הַמַּרְכָּבוֹת (*house of chariots*), in the tribe of Simeon; בּ׳ נִמְרָה (*place of pure water*), in the tribe of Gad; בּ׳ עֶדֶן (*pleasant place*), a town near Damascus; בּ׳ עַזְמָוֶת, see עַזְמָוֶת; בּ׳ הָעֵמֶק (*house of the valley*), in the tribe of Asher; בּ׳ עֲנוֹת (*place of echo*), in the tribe of Judah; בּ׳ עֲנָת (the same), in the tribe of Naphtali; בּ׳ עֵקֶד הָרֹעִים (*place where shepherds bind their sheep*), near Samaria; בּ׳ הָעֲרָבָה (*place in the desert*), on the confines of Judah and Benjamin; בּ׳ פֶּלֶט (*place of flight*), in the tribe of Judah; בּ׳ פְּעוֹר (see פְּעוֹר), in the land of Moab, not far from Jordan; בּ׳ פַּצֵּץ (*place of dispersion*), in the tribe of Issachar; בּ׳ צוּר (*house of the rock*), in the mountains of Judah; בּ׳ רְחֹב (see רְחֹב, אֲרָם), a city of Syria; בּ׳ שַׁן, שְׁאָן (*house of sleep*), in the tribe of Manasseh, beyond Jordan; בּ׳ הַשִּׁטָּה (see שִׁטָּה), a town on Jordan; בּ׳ שֶׁמֶשׁ (*house of the sun*), name of several towns: *α*. of the Levites in the tribe of Judah; בֵּית־הַשִּׁמְשִׁי *inhabitant of....*; *β*. in the tribe of Naphtali; *γ*. in the tribe of Issachar or Zebulon; *δ*. same as אוֹן in Egypt; בּ׳ תַּפּוּחַ; תֹּגַרְמָה, see בּ׳ תּוֹגַרְמָה (*place of apple trees*), in the tribe of Judah.

from בָּזָה for בָּז, Zec. 4:10; see בּוּז.

, בִּזָּה *spoiled*; see בזז.

בָּזְאוּ, בָּזָא Isa. 18:2, *have spoiled.*

בָּזָה same as בּוּז *despised, spurned*; const. with לְ, עַל. Niph. part. נִבְזֶה *despised*; pl. נִבְזִים. Hiph. inf. הַבְזוֹת *make despised*, Est. 1:17.

בְּזֹה inf., *despised*, Isa. 49:7.

בִּזָּיוֹן m., *great contempt*, Est. 1:18.

בִּזְיוֹתְיָה (*despised of the Lord*), p. n of a town in the tribe of Judah.

נְמִבְזָה *contemptible*, 1 Sa. 15:9.

בָּזַז *took the spoil or prey*; part. pl. בֹּזְזִים *spoilers*; pret. pl. בָּזְזוּ, בָּזָזוּ and בַּזּוֹנוּ; inf. בֹּז; fut. יָבוֹז. Niph. נָבֹז, and Pu. בֻּזַּז *were spoiled*, Jer. 50:37.

בַּז m. (with suff. בִּזָּהּ), *spoil*; הָיָה לָבַז *was for a spoil*; נָתַן לָבַז *gave for a spoil.*

בִּזָּה f., *booty.*

בָּזָק m., *lightning*, Eze. 1:14.

בֶּזֶק p.n. of a town to the southward of Bethshan, Βεζέκ.

בָּזַר (fut. יִבְזוֹר), *dispersed*, Dan. 11:24; Pi. בִּזֵּר the same, Ps. 68:31.

בִּזְתָא p.n. of a eunuch of Ahasuerus.

בָּחַל *was greedy, niggard*; with בְּ, Zec. 11:8. Pu. part. f. מְבֹחֶלֶת *coveted, gotten by covetousness*, Pro. 20:21.

בָּחַן (imper. בְּחַן; with suff. בְּחָנֵנִי, בְּחָנוּנִי; fut. יִבְחַן).—I. *tried, tested* (metals with fire).—II. *tried* (men with affliction).—III. *tried* (God.... the heart). Niph. *be tried.*

בֹּחַן m., *examination, trial*, Isa. 28:16, Eze. 21:18.

בַּחַן m., *watch-tower*, Isa. 32:14.

בַּחוּן m., *mound, watch-tower*, Isa. 23:14.

בָּחוֹן m., *trial, experiment.*

בָּחַר (fut. יִבְחַר), *chose*; with בְּ, לְ, עַל; בָּחַר לוֹ *he chose for himself*; with מִן *preferred*; part. בָּחוּר

chosen, excellent. Niph. *chosen;* part. נִבְחָר *elect, excellent;* with מִן *better.*

בָּחִיר m., *elect;* (ἐκλεκτὸς τοῦ Θεοῦ *the elect of God*).

בָּחוּר m., *a youth;* pl. בַּחוּרִים *youths,* liable to be chosen (balloted) for military service.

בְּחוּרִים m. pl., *youth.*

בְּחוּרוֹת f. pl., the same.

בַּחֻרִים p. n. of a town in the tribe of Benjamin; בַּחֲרוּמִי and בַּרְחֻמִי an inhabitant of Bachurim.

מִבְחַר, מִבְחָר m.—I. *the choice, the best.*—II. p. n. of a man.

מִבְחוֹר m., the same, 2 Ki. 3:19; 19:23.

בָּטָא and בָּטָה *speaks wrongfully, falsely,* Pro. 12:18; part. בּוֹטֶה. Pi. בִּטֵּא *spake falsely.*

מִבְטָא m., *rashness in speaking;* מ׳ שְׂפָתַיִם, Nu. 30:7,9.

בָּטַח (inf. בְּטוֹחַ; with suff. בִּטְחֵךְ; imper. בְּטַח; fut. יִבְטַח; pl. f. תִּבְטַחְנָה), *trusted in, to, on;* with בְּ, אֶל, עַל, לְ, Job 6:20; impers. *was for a confidence;* part. בָּטוּחַ *trusted, was confident, incautious;* part. בּוֹטֵחַ *secure, confiding.* Hiph. הִבְטִיחַ *made to confide, trust;* with אֶל and עַל.

בֶּטַח m., *confidence, security;* בֶּטַח and לָבֶטַח adv. *confidently, securely, safely.*

בֶּטַח p. n. of a town of Aram Zobah, 2 Sam. 8:8.

בִּטְחָה f., *confidence,* Isa. 30:15.

בִּטָּחוֹן m., the same, Isa. 36:4, Ecc. 9:4.

בַּטֻּחָה f., the same; pl. בַּטֻּחוֹת, Job 12:6.

מִבְטָח m. (with suff. מִבְטַחִי, מִבְטַחָהּ, מִבְטֶחָם; pl. מִבְטָחִים), *trust, confidence;* metonym. *he in whom trust is reposed.*

אֲבַטִּיחִים see טבח.

בָּטַל *cease, fail,* Ecc. 12:3.

בְּטֵל Ch., *ceased,* Ezr. 4:24. Pa. בַּטֵּל *caused to cease, hindered.*

בֶּטֶן f. (with suff. בִּטְנִי).—I. *belly.*—II. *womb;* פְּרִי בֶטֶן *fruit of the womb, offspring;* מִבֶּטֶן, מִן־הַבֶּטֶן, מִבֶּטֶן אִמִּי ἐκ γαστρὸς, the same.—III. ἡ κοιλία *the inner man, seat of thought, feelings.*—IV. the projecting part of the chapiter of a column, 1 Ki. 7:20.—V. p. n. of a town in the tribe of Asher.

בָּטְנִים m. pl., *nuts,* Gen. 43:11. Pistachia vera (Lin.), a tree abounding in Palestine, but unknown in Egypt.

בְּטֹנִים p. n. of a town in the tribe of Gad.

בִּי pa. of supplication, (always with אֲדֹנָי or אֲדֹנִי), *Lord, I pray thee; ah, Lord!*

בִּין, בֵּין, בִּינָה *understand;* see בּוּן.

בֵּיצִים *eggs,* see בּוּץ.

בִּיקְּרוֹתֶיךָ f. pl., with suff., pref., and dag. euphon. see יָקַר.

בַּיִר *well;* same as בְּאֵר.

בִּירָה f.—I. *palace.*—II. *the temple.*

בִּירָה f. Ch., the same.

בִּירָנִיּוֹת f. pl., *palaces;* sing. never occurs.

בַּיִת, בִּיתָן, *house, &c.;* see בּוּת.

בָּכָה (fut. יִבְכֶּה, וַיֵּבְךְּ; inf. בָּכוֹ and בָּכֹה). —I. *wept.* — II. *mourned,* with אֶת, בְּ, עַל, לְ, אֶל. Pi. *deplored*, with עַל.

בָּכָא m.—I. *the Baka shrub*, Amyris Gileadensis (Linn.); pl. בְּכָאִים —II. עֵמֶק הַבָּכָא (*valley of weeping*), p.n. of a valley in Palestine, Ps. 84:7.

בֶּכֶה m., *weeping*, Eze. 10:1.

בָּכוֹ inf. abs. from בכה.

בָּכוּת and בְּכִית f., *weeping*, Gen. 50:4.

בְּכִי m. (with pause בֶּכִי; with suff. בִּכְיִי).—I. *weeping*.—II. *dropping of water in wells*, Job, 28:11.

בֹּכִים p. n. of a town near Gilgal.

בָּכַר Kal, root not used; (Arab. *early*). Pi. בִּכֵּר.—I. *brought forth early fruits*.—II. *was the first-born*, Deu. 21:16. Pu. passive of Pi., Lev. 27:26. Hiph. *brought forth her first-born*, Jer. 4:13.

בְּכוֹר m., *first-born*; בְּכֹרוֹת pl., *the first-born of brutes*, Gen. 4:4, Deu. 12:17. Trop. בְּכוֹר מָוֶת *the worm*, Job 18:13; בְּכוֹרֵי דַלִּים *the first-born of the poor, the poorest*.

בְּכוֹרָה f., *primogeniture*.

בְּכוֹרַת p.n. of a man, 1 Sa. 9:1.

בְּכִירָה f., *eldest, first-born daughter*.

בֹּכְרוּ (same as בֹּכֶר הוּא), p. n. of a man.

בִּכְרִי (*my first-born*), p.n. of a man.

בֶּכֶר m., *a young camel*, Isa. 60:6; f. בִּכְרָה *a young she-camel*, Jer. 2:23.

בֶּכֶר, בִּכְרִי p.n.—I. of a son of Ephraim.—II. of a son of Benjamin.

בִּכּוּר m, pl. בִּכּוּרִים and בִּכֻּרִים *first-fruits*; יוֹם הַבִּכּוּרִים *feast of first-fruits, Pentecost*, Nu. 28:26.

בִּכּוּרָה f., *the early fig*; תְּאֵנֵי בַּכֻּרוֹת *early figs*.

בְּכֹרַת p. n. of a man.

בַּל; see בלה.

בֵּל *Bel*, same as בַּעַל.

בְּלָא *destroy*; see בָּלָה.

בַּלְאֲדָן (*whose lord is Baal*), p.n. of a king of Babylon; see מְרֹדַךְ.

בָּלַג Kal, root not used (Arab. *opened, shone*).—Hiph. הִבְלִיג with עַל I. *made to rise*, Am. 5:9.—II. *made glad*, Ps. 39:14.

בִּלְגָּה (*joy*), p. n. of a priest.

מַבְלִיגִית f., *exhilaration*, Jer. 8:18.

בִּלְדַּד p. n. of one of Job's friends.

בָּלָה (fut. יִבְלֶה).—I. *grew old*.—II. *perished*; with מֵעַל *worn off*, spoken of clothes. Pi. בִּלָּה *made cold*

בְּלָא Ch. form. Pa. *destroy, make to disappear*, Dan. 7:25; see בלה Pi.

בָּלֶה m., בָּלָה f., *old, effete, worn out*, Jos. 9:4, 5, Eze. 23:43.

בָּלָה p.n. of a city.

בְּלוֹאִים and בְּלוֹיִם m. pl., *old, worn*, Jer. 38:11, 12.

בְּלוֹ m. Ch., *custom, tax*.

תַּבְלִית f., *destruction*, Isa. 10:26.

בָּל m. Ch., *the heart, mind*, Dan. 6:15.

בַּל (*wanting*); adv., *not, nothing*.

בְּלִי I. *loss, destruction*, Isa. 38:17.—II. *wanting, without* (written בִּבְלִי and בְּלִי); בִּ׳ דַעַת *without knowledge*; לִבְלִי *without*; מִבְּלִי *from want of*.—III. adv., same as לֹא *not*; הֲמִבְּלִי אֵין *is it not because there is not?* מִבְּלִי אֲשֶׁר לֹא *excepting that not*, Ecc. 3:11; עַד בְּלִי *until the ceasing of*, Mal. 3:10; עַל בְּלִי *because not*, Gen. 31:20

בְּלִימָה (compounded of בְּלִי and מָה), *nothing*, Job 26:7.

בְּלִיַּעַל (compounded of בְּלִי and יַעַל). —I. *uselessness.*— II. *wickedness, sin;* אִישׁ בְּ׳ *a wicked man.*—III. *injury, destruction;* נַחֲלֵי בְ׳ *destructive torrents,* i.e. overwhelming oppressions, Ps. 18:5.

בַּל and בִּלְעֲדֵי בַּלְעֲדֵי (compounded of בַּל and עֲדֵי).—I. *besides, without.*—II. *not concerning, nothing to;* בִּלְעָדַי *nothing to me;* מִבַּלְעֲדֵי the same.

בֶּלֶת *consumption;* used only with the parag. jod, בִּלְתִּי.—I. *without.* —II. *besides, except.*—III. adv., *not;* with suff. בִּלְתִּי *besides me,* בִּלְתֶּךָ *besides thee;* לְבִלְתִּי *not, that it may not,* with a verb; מִבִּלְתִּי with inf., *because it is not;* עַד־בִּלְתִּי *until it is not.*

בָּלָה. Pi. בִּלֵּה same as בָּהַל, *harassing*, Ezr. 4:4.

בַּלָּהָה f.—I. *terror.*—II. *calamity.*

בִּלְהָה p. n.—I. of the handmaid of Rachel.—II. of a town in the tribe of Simeon.

בִּלְהָן p. n. of a man.

בְּלוֹאִים, בְּלוֹ; see בָּלָה.

בֵּלְטְשַׁאצַּר p. n., Chaldee name of Daniel.

בְּלִיַּעַל, בְּלִימָה, בְּלִי; see בָּלָה.

בָּלַל (fut. יָבֹל).—I. *suffused,* Ps. 92:3. —II. *confounded,* const. with בְּ. Hith. *become confounded*, Hos. 7:8, with בְּ.—III. from בְּלִיל; *gave fodder,* Jud. 19:21. — IV. *fade, wither,* Isa. 64:5.

בְּלִיל m., *fodder for cattle*, lit. *mixture.*

תֶּבֶל m., *unnatural intercourse,* Lev. 18:23, 20:12.

תְּבַלֻּל m., *a disease in the eye.* Lev. 21:20; תְּ׳ בְּעֵינוֹ *confused* (i. e. indistinct for vision) *in his eye.*

בָּלַם *bound, bridled,* Ps. 32:8.

בָּלַס *pluck figs,* Am. 7:14.

בָּלַע I. *swallowed.* — II. *destroyed;* עַד־בִּלְעִי רֻקִּי *until I have swallowed my spittle;* i.e. in a moment, Job 7:19. Niph. *be swallowed up, lost;* with מִן הַיַּיִן *immersed in wine,* Isa. 28:7. Pi. as Kal; (כְּבַלַּע *as in a moment*). Pu. *was swallowed up.* Hith. as Niph., Ps. 107:27.

בֶּלַע m.—I. *swallowing up.*—II. *destruction;* with suff. בִּלְעוֹ.—III. p.n. of a town on the Dead Sea.—IV. of a man; בַּלְעִי m., *inhabitant of Bela.*

בַּלְעֲדֵי, בִּלְעֲדֵי *besides;* see בָּלָה.

בִּלְעָם (*stranger*).—I. p. n. of the prophet Balaam.—II. same as יִבְלְעָם.

בָּלַק *make waste,* Isa. 24:1. Pu. part. f. מְבֻלָּקָה *desolate,* Nah. 2:11.

בָּלָק p.n. of a king of Moab.

בֵּלְשַׁאצַּר and בֵּלְאשַׁצַּר p. n. of the last king of the Chaldees (Nabonnedus or Labynetus).

בִּלְשָׁן p.n of a man.

בִּלְתִּי *not;* see בֶּלֶת under בָּלָה.

בָּמָה f. (pl. בָּמוֹת, const. בָּמוֹתֵי [בָּמֳתֵי Kri] with suff. בָּמוֹתֶיךָ (בָּמוֹתַי).—I. *high place for idolatrous worship;* רָכַב עַל בָּמוֹתֵי אָרֶץ *he rode upon the high places of the earth,* i.e. he conquered. — II. *places for true worship.*—III. *fortresses, places of strength;* דָּרַךְ עַל בְּ׳ *he rode upon the high places,* i. e. he subdued.—IV. *waves of the sea*, Job 9:8.—V. *clouds*, Isa. 14:14.

בָּתֵּי הַבָּמוֹת same as בָּמוֹת *idol temples*; כֹּהֲנֵי הַבָּמוֹת *idolatrous priests*.

בָּמוֹת and בָּמוֹת בַּעַל p.n. of a town in Moab on the Arnon.

בִּמְהָל (*son of circumcision*), p.n. of a m.

בְּמוֹ same as בְּ; see מָה, מוֹ.

בָּמֳתֵי pl. const. from בָּמָה.

בָּנָה (inf. בָּנֹה; const. בְּנוֹת; fut. יִבְנֶה, וַיִּבֶן).—I. *built*, really.—II. *built*, metaphorically, i. e. raised, increased in family; const. with עַל, בְּ, לְ; בּ׳ אֶת־הָהָר *he built upon the hill*, 1 Ki. 16:24; בּ׳ בַּיִת לְ *he raised up a house to* —Niph. I. *was built*.—II. *was raised up*, as a house, family.

בְּנָה, בְּנָא Ch., *built*. Ithp. *was built*.

בֵּן m. (const. בֶּן, sometimes בִּן; with suff. בְּנִי, בִּנְךָ, בְּנוֹ; pl. בָּנִים, בְּנֵי). —I. *son*; בְּנֵי בָנִים *grandsons, posterity*; בְּנֵי עַמּוֹן *Ammonites*; אִישׁ מִבְּנֵי יִשְׂרָאֵל *an Israelite*; בְּנֵי צִיּוֹן *inhabitants of Zion*; בְּנֵי נְבִיאִים *sons*, i.e. *disciples of the prophets*.— II. used metaphorically; בֶּן־עַוְלָה *son of perverseness*, i. e. perverse person; בֶּן־מָוֶת *son of death*, i.e. a person guilty of a capital crime; בֶּן־קֶשֶׁת *son of the bow*, i.e. arrow, Job 41:20.—III. used with numerals; בֶּן־שְׁמֹנִים שָׁנָה *one eighty years old, octogenarian*; בֶּן־שָׁנָה *yearling*.—IV. *the young of brutes*; בֶּן־יוֹנָה *young dove*.—V. *young shoots of trees*; בֶּן־פֹּרָת *twig of a fruit tree*.

בֵּן p. n. of a Levite, 1 Chron. 15:18.

בַּר m. Ch., *son*; pl. בְּנִין, בְּנֵי.

בֶּן־אוֹנִי (*son of my sorrow*), p.n. given to Benjamin by his mother.

בֶּן־הֲדַד p.n. of the kings of Damascus.

בִּנּוּי p. n. of a man.

בֶּן־חַיִל (*strong*), p. n. of a man.

בֶּן־חָנָן (*son of mercy*), p.n. of a man.

בָּנִי (*built up*), p.n. of a man.

בֻּנִּי (*built up*), p. n. of two men.

בְּנֵי בְרַק p. n. of a town in the tribe of Dan.

בְּנֵי יַעֲקָן p.n. of a place.

בִּנְיָה f., *building*, Eze. 41:13.

בְּנָיָה (*built up of God*), p.n. of a man.

בְּנָיָהוּ the same.

בִּנְיָמִין (*son of my right hand*), p. n., *Benjamin*, the son of Jacob; אִישׁ־יְמִינִי, בֶּן־הַיְמִינִי, בֶּן־יְמִינִי and יְמִינִי *a Benjamite*; pl. בְּנֵי יְמִינִי; אֶרֶץ־יְמִינִי *land of the Benjamites*.

בֶּן־יָמִין I. same as בִּנְיָמִין.—II. p. n. of a man, 1 Sa. 9:1.

בִּנְיָן m., *building*, Eze. 40:5.

בְּנִינוּ (*our son*), p.n. of a man.

בָּנוּ for בָּאנוּ Kal pret. pl. I. pers., from בּוֹא.

בְּנוֹתֵיךְ for בְּנוֹתֵךְ Kal inf. with suff., from בנה.

בַּת f. (with suff. בִּתִּי; pl. בָּנוֹת; const. בְּנוֹת).—I. *daughter*.—II. *niece*.— III. the female inhabitants of any place; בְּנוֹת צִיּוֹן *the daughters of Zion*, Isa. 3:17; בְּנוֹת יִשְׂרָאֵל *daughters of Israel*.—IV. used for the inhabitants of any place collectively; בַּת צֹר *the Tyrians*, Ps. 45:12; בַּת מִצְרַיִם *the Egyptians*. —V. בְּנוֹת הָעִיר smaller cities dependent upon larger ones.—VI. used with numerals in the age of women: בַּת תִּשְׁעִים שָׁנָה *a woman of ninety* (see בֵּן III.).—VII. used metaph.: בְּנוֹת הַשִּׁיר *daughters of song*, i.e. singers; בַּת עַיִן *pupil of the eye* (see בֵּן II.).—VIII. applied to the produce of animals, trees, or places; בַּת הַיַּעֲנָה *female ostrich, &c.*

בַּת f. Ch., the same; pl. בָּתִּין.

בַּת־רַבִּים (*daughter of multitudes*), p. n. of the gate of Heshbon.

בַּת־שֶׁבַע (*daughter of an oath*), p. n. of the wife of Uriah.

בַּת־שׁוּעַ the same.

מִבְנֶה m., *building*, Eze. 40:2.

תַּבְנִית f.—I. *model*, πρωτότυπον.—II. *form, resemblance*.—III. *building*.

בָּנַט, Pers. *bando*; Sansc. *bandha*; Eng. *band*.

אַבְנֵט m., *a girdle* (a foreign word).

בְּנַס Ch., *was angry*, Dan. 2:12.

בְּנָעָה, בִּנְעָא p. n. of a man.

בְּסוֹדְיָה (*in the council of the Lord*), p. n. of a man.

בֵּסַי p. n. of a man.

בָּסַר root not used; (Arab. *unripe date*).

בֶּסֶר m., *unripe, sour grape*, Job 15:33.

בֹּסֶר m., the same.

בֹּעָא; see בעה.

בָּעַד root not used; (Arab. *after*).

בְּעַד prep., *after, behind*, as to time or place; with suff. בַּעֲדִי and בַּעֲדֵנִי, בַּעֲדֵינוּ, בַּעֲדֵנוּ, בַּעֲדוֹ, בַּעַדְךָ, בַּעַדְכֶם; מִבַּעַד לְ *behind*, Cant. 4:1, &c.

בָּעָה I. *pressed forward, ran over*, Isa. 64:1.—II. *requested, importuned*; fut. pl. תִּבְעָיוּן; imp. pl. בְּעָיוּ. Niph.—I. *become obtruded, swelled out*, Isa. 30:13.—II. *being sought*, Obad *v.* 6.

בְּעָה and בְּעָא Ch., *requested, prayed*, with מִן and מִן קֳדָם.

בָּעוּ f. Ch., *petition*, Dan. 6:8, 14.

בְּעִי m., *prayer*, Job 30:24.

בְּעוֹן *habitation*; same as מְעוֹן.

בְּעוֹר p. n. of the father of Balaam.

בֹּעַז p. n.—I. the husband of Ruth.—II. name of one of the pillars in Solomon's temple.

בָּעַט I. *trample upon, kick at*: hence,—II. *despise, reject*.

בְּעִי *building*; see בָּעָה.

בְּעָיוּ Kal imper. pl. with pause, from בעה.

בְּעִיר *beast*; see בער.

בָּעַל I. *possess, govern*.—II. *marry a wife*; part. pl. majest. בֹּעֲלַיִךְ *thy husband*; בְּעֻלַת־בַּעַל and בְּעוּלָה *married*.—III. (with בְּ) *despised*, Jer. 3:14; 31:32. Niph. *be married*.

בַּעַל m. (suff. בַּעְלִי, בַּעְלָהּ, בַּעְלֵיהֶם)—I. *lord*.—II. *husband*.—III. *owner, possessor*, that wherein any one excels; בַּעַל בַּ׳ הַחֲלֹמוֹת *dreamer*; בַּעֲלֵי שְׁכֶם *the Shechemites, &c.*; pl. בְּעָלִים (const. בַּעֲלֵי; with suff. בְּעָלָיו, בְּעָלֶיהָ) often used of one only.—IV. הַבַּעַל p. n., *Baal*, name of a Phenician god; הַבְּעָלִים *statues of Baal*.—V. p. n. of a man.—VI. compounded in the names of many towns: בַּעַל גָּד a town on the borders of Palestine, to the north; בַּ׳ הָמוֹן at the foot of Lebanon; בַּ׳ חָצוֹר in the tribe of Ephraim

בּ׳ חֶרְמוֹן one of the peaks of Mount Hermon; a town near it; בּ׳ מְעוֹן and בֵּת מְעוֹן in the tribe of Reuben; בּ׳ פְּרָצִים (*place of slaughter*) where the Philistines were routed by David; בּ׳ צְפוֹן in Egypt; בּ׳ שָׁלִשָׁה in Mount Ephraim; בּ׳ תָּמָר (*place of palms*) not far from Gibeah; בַּעֲלֵי יְהוּדָה Jews.

בְּעֵי m. Ch., *lord*.

בַּעֲלָה f.—I. *lady*.—II. used collectively (like בַּת) *a city*.—III. p. n. of a city in the north of Judah; otherwise קִרְיַת־בַּעַל and קִרְיַת יְעָרִים.—IV. another city in Judah; otherwise בָּלָה and בִּלְהָה.

בַּעֲלָה p. n. of a city in the tribe of Dan.

בְּעָלוֹת p.n. of a city in the tribe of Judah.

בְּעֶלְיָדָע (*whom Baal knows*), same as אֶלְיָדָע

בְּעַלְיָה (*in whom the Lord rules*), p.n. of a man.

בַּעַל־חָנָן (*the Lord of grace*), p. n. of a king of Edom.

בַּעֲלִיס p.n. of a king of the Ammonites.

בַּעֲנָא (*son of misery*), p. n. of a man.

בַּעֲנָה (the same), p.n. of a man.

בָּעַר *injure, consume.*—I. *by fire.*—II. *with anger.*—III. *burn.*—IV. *that which injures, is brutish* (from בְּעִיר); part. בֹּעֲרִים *cattle, beasts.* Niph. *become brutish.* Pi. בִּעֵר.—I. *injured, destroyed.*—II. *consumed with fire;* with בְּ, מִן and אַחֲרֵי. Pu. part. f. מְבֹעֶרֶת *burnt.* Hiph. same as Pi.

בְּעִיר m.—I. *beast, cattle* generally.—II. *beast of burden.*

בַּעַר m., *stupid, brutish.*

בְּעֵרָה f., *burning*, Ex. 22:5.

בַּעֲרָא p. n. of a man.

תַּבְעֵרָה p.n. of a place in the desert

בַּעֲשֵׂיָה (*work of God*), p.n. of a man.

בַּעְשָׁא p. n. of a king of Israel, son of Ahijah.

בְּעֶשְׁתְּרָה *an idol;* see עַשְׁתֹּרֶת.

בָּעַת. Niph. נִבְעַת *was terrified.* Pi. בִּעֵת.—I. *alarmed.*—II. *excited, came suddenly upon;* fut. יְבַעֵת; part. f. with suff. מְבַעַתֶּךָ.

בְּעָתָה f., *terror*, Jer. 8:15; 14:19.

בִּעוּתִים m. pl., *terrors*, Ps. 88:17.

בֹּץ, בִּצָּה *mud;* see בצץ.

בִּצֹּאתָו for בִּצּוֹתָיו pl. with suff. from בצץ or בִּצָּה.

בֵּצַי (same as בֵּסַי), p. n. of a man.

בָּצִיר *vintage;* see בצר.

בָּצָל m., *onion*, Nu. 11:5.

בַּצְלִית, בַּצְלוּת p.n. of a man.

בָּצַע I. *cut off parts, pieces.*—II. *acquire gain.* Pi. בִּצַּע I. *cutting off* (as the weaver his web from the loom): hence,—II. *finish, complete.*—III. *acquired filthy lucre*, Eze. 22:12.

בֶּצַע m. (with suff. בִּצְעָם).—I. *gain.*—II. *filthy lucre;* מַה־בֶּצַע *what gain?*

בָּצַץ root not used; (Arab. *run slowly*).

בֹּץ m., *mud, mire*, Jer. 38:22.

בִּצָּה f., the same; pl. with suff. בִּצֹּאתָו for בִּצּוֹתָיו.

בָּצֵק *swelled* (of the foot), Deu. 8:11, Neh. 9:21.

בָּצֵק m., *dough* (from its swelling in fermenting).

בָּצְקַת p. n. of a town in the tribe of Judah.

בָּצַר I. *cut, cropped off:* hence,—II. *pruned the vine.*—III. *gathered the vintage*, Ps. 76:13; part. בֹּצֵר *vintage-gatherer*; trop. *remorseless enemy*; part. בָּצוּר *inaccessible*, lit. *cut off from access;* בְּצֻרוֹת *hidden, incomprehensible*, Jer. 33:3. Niph. *cut off, prohibited*, with מִן. Pi. *fortified* (of cities).

בָּצִיר m., *vintage;* adj., same as בָּצוּר *fortified*, Zec. 11:2.

בְּצַר m., *gold;* perhaps *wealth*, Job 36:19.

בֶּצֶר m.—I. the same, Job 22:24, 25.—II. p. n. of a city in the tribe of Reuben.—III. p. n. of a man.

בָּצְרָה f.—I. *fold for cattle*, Mic. 2:12.—II. p. n. of a city of Edom, Βόστρα.—III. of a city of Moab.

בִּצָּרוֹן m., *fortified place*, Zec. 9:12.

בַּצֹּרֶת f., and pl. בַּצָּרוֹת *withholding of rain, drought*, Jer. 14:1; 17:8.

מִבְצָר m.—I. *fortification;* עִיר מ׳ *fortified town;* pl. מִבְצָרִים and מִבְצָרוֹת.—II. p. n. of a chief of the Edomites.

בַּקְבּוּק, בֻּקִּי, &c.; see בקק.

בָּקַע with בְּ.—I. *cut, cleft, divided.*—II. *laid open*, i. e. subdued, took (of fortified places).—III. *let go* (as young birds from eggs, or water from a dam).—Niph. I. *became cleft, destroyed.*—II. *laid open, subdued.*—III. *let go* (as young birds or water). Pi. same as Kal. Pu. pass. of Pi. Hiph. I. *cause to be subdued* —II. *sent forth*, with אֶל. Hoph. *was broken up*, Jer. 39:2. Hith. as Niph. I., Jos. 9:13, Mic. 1:4.

בְּקִיעַ m., *fissure*, Isa. 22:9, Am. 6:11.

בֶּקַע m. (*cutting*), half a shekel, Gen. 24:22, Ex. 38:26.

בִּקְעָה f., *valley, plain;* pl. בְּקָעוֹת; בִּקְעַת הַלְּבָנוֹן *valley of Lebanon*, between Anti-Libanus and Hermon, κοιλὴ Συρία, Cœle-Syria, Jos. 11:37, 12:7; בִּקְעַת אָוֶן, see אָוֶן.

בָּקַק I. *threw, cast off, out* (as fruit from a tree); with אֶת־עֵצָה *I will cast off (deprive of) counsel*, Jer. 19:7.—II. *make empty, void*, Isa. 24:1. Niph. נָבַק (inf. הִבּוֹק, fut. יִבּוֹק) *become void*, Isa. 19:3; 24:3. Pi. fut. יְבַקְקוּ *make empty, void*, Jer. 51:2.

בַּקְבּוּק I. *bottle, narrow-necked vase;* the word expresses the sound of a fluid issuing from it.—II. p. n. of a man.

בַּקְבֻּקְיָה p. n. of a man.

בַּקְבַּקַּר p. n. of a man.

בֻּקִּי p. n. of a man.

בֻּקִּיָּהוּ p. n. of a man.

בָּקַר *cut, laid open;* not in use: hence, Pi.—I. *look, inquire after.*—II. *observe.*—III. *care for*, with לְ and בֵּין...לְ.

בַּקַּר Pa. Ch., *inquired.* Ithpa. *was sought.*

בַּקָּרָה f., *inquiring after, seeking*, Ezr. 34:12.

בִּקֹּרֶת f., *observation, chastisement*, Lev. 19:20.

בָּקָר (from the plough which *cleaves* the earth).—I. *oxen* used in ploughing, Job. 1:14.—II. *oxen* generally; בּ׳ עָלוֹת *milch cows;* בֶּן בָּקָר *steer;* seldom pl. בְּקָרִים *oxen.*

בּוֹקֵר m., *herdsman,* Am. 7:14.

בֹּקֶר m. (pl. בְּקָרִים).—I. *dawn, morning;* לַבֹּקֶר, בַּבֹּקֶר, בֹּקֶר *in the morning;* לַבְּקָרִים, בַּבֹּקֶר בַּבֹּקֶר, לִבְקָרִים *every morning;* עַד הַבֹּקֶר *to-morrow morning.* — II. לַבֹּקֶר *early, soon,* Ps. 49:15, &c.

בָּקַשׁ. Pi. בִּקֵּשׁ *sought, sought out, after* or *into,* with עַל, מִן, לְ or בּ׳ אֶל according to the sense; בּ׳ אֶת־יְהוָֹה or אֶת־פְּנֵי יְהוָֹה *he sought the Lord;* בּ׳ נֶפֶשׁ פּ׳ *the soul, life of any one, to injure destroy it;* בּ׳ דַם פּ׳...*his blood.*

בַּקָּשָׁה f., *petition,* Est. 5:3; 7:3, Ezr. 7:6.

בַּר, בָּר, בֹּר *son, &c.;* see ברא and ברר.

בָּרָא (inf. בְּרֹא; with suff. בְּרַאֲךָ; imp. בְּרָא; fut. יִבְרָא).—I. *created, formed, made.*—II. same as בָּרָה *he ate.* Niph. *was created, born, produced.* Pi. בֵּרֵא. — I. *cut,* as with a sword or axe.—II. *make, form.* Hiph. הִבְרִיא *fatten,* 1 Sa. 2:29.

בְּרִיאָה f., *a wonderful, new thing.*

בַּר m., *son;* with suff. בְּרִי; another meaning, see in ברר.

בַּר m. Ch.—I. *son.*—II. *grandson;* with suff. בְּרֵהּ.

בְּרָאיָה (*created of God*), p. n. of a m.

בְּרֹאדַךְ; see מְרֹאדַךְ.

בַּרְבֻּרִים *fed beasts;* see ברר.

בָּרַד *hailed,* Isa. 32:19.

בָּרָד m., *hail.*

בָּרֹד m. (pl. בְּרֻדִּים), *spotted,* "grisled," Eng. Ver.

בֶּרֶד p. n.—I. of a place in the wilderness of Shur.—II. of a man.

בָּרָה I. *ate.*—II. same as בָּרַר *chose.* Pi. inf. בָּרוֹת *eating.* Hiph. *give food.*

בָּרִיא m., בְּרִיאָה f., *fat;* see another meaning above.

בָּרִי m., בְּרִיָּה f., *fat,* Eze. 34:20.

בִּרְיָה f., *food,* 2 Sa. 13:5, 7, 10.

בָּרוּת f. *food,* Ps. 69:22.

בְּרִית f.—I. *any agreement;* בַּעֲלֵי ב׳ *united in covenant,* Gen. 14:13.—II. the covenant made by God with the patriarchs, and ratified in the person of Jesus Christ.—III. the sign of that covenant (circumcision), Gen. 17:13; מַלְאַךְ הַבְּרִית *μεσίτης, the angel of the covenant, Messiah;* בַּעַל בְּרִית a name of Baal.

בָּרוּךְ *blessed;* see ברך.

בְּרוֹמִים *costly clothing;* see ברם.

בְּרוֹשׁ m.—I. *fir-tree;* עֲצֵי בְרוֹשִׁים *instruments of fir-wood,* 2 Sa. 6:5.—II. *staves of lances made of fir-wood,* Nah. 2:4.

בְּרוֹת m. the same, Cant. 1:17.

בֵּרוֹתָה, בֵּרוֹתַי p. n. of a city in Syria of Zobah.

בָּרוּת *eating;* see ברה.

בִּרְזָיִת p. n. of a woman.

בַּרְזֶל m. (with suff. בַּרְזִלּוֹ).—I. *iron.*—II. *hard as iron.*—III. *instrument of iron.*

בַּרְזִלַּי p. n. of a man.

בָּרַח (fut. יִבְרַח; part. m. בֹּרֵחַ, f. בֹּרַחַת).—I. *pass on.*—II. *fly,* with מִן,

בְּרַח לְךָ; imper. אַחֲרֵי, מִפְּנֵי, מֵאֵת *flee away.*—IV. *pass through*, Ex. 36:33. Hiph. *made to pass, fly.*

בָּרִחַ, בְּרִחַ m.—I. *a fugitive.*—II. p. n. of a man.

בְּרִיחַ m.—I. *transverse bar.*—II. *bars* or *bolts* for fastening the gates of a city; בְּרִיחֶהָ, Isa. 15:6, "her fugitives" as above, not "her princes" i. e. bars, defences.

מִבְרָח m., *fugitive*, Eze. 40:2.

בְּרִי, בָּרִיא, בְּרִיָּה; see ברה.

בֵּרִי (same as בְּאֵרִי *my well*), p. n. of a man.

בְּרִיאָה; see ברא.

בְּרִיעָה p. n. of a man.

בְּרִית *covenant;* see ברה.

בֹּרִית *soap;* see ברר.

בֶּרֶךְ f., *knee;* dual בִּרְכַּיִם *both knees.*

בֶּרֶךְ, בְּרַךְ f. Ch., the same.

בָּרַךְ (fut. יְבָרֵךְ; inf. abs. בָּרוֹךְ).—I. *knelt.*—II. *worshipped, blessed;* בָּרוּךְ לַיהוָֹה and בָּרוּךְ יְהוָֹה *blessed of the Lord;* בָּרוּךְ יְהוָֹה *blessed be the Lord.* Niph. *be blessed.* Pi. בֵּרַךְ, בֵּרֵךְ *pronounced, made, blessed*, with בְּשֵׁם יְהוָֹה, לְ. Pu. בֹּרַךְ *be* or *become blessed.* Hiph. הִבְרִיךְ *made kneel down*, Gen. 24:11. Hith. הִתְבָּרֵךְ *be made blessed*, Gen. 22:18, &c.; *account oneself blessed*, Deu. 29:18, &c.

בְּרַךְ Ch., *knelt.* Pa. *blessed.*

בָּרוּךְ p. n. of the friend of Jeremiah.

בָּרַכְאֵל (*blessed of God*), p. n. of a man.

בְּרָכָה f. (בְּרָכָה Gen. 27:38; const. בִּרְכַּת; pl. בְּרָכוֹת, const. בִּרְכוֹת).—I. *blessing*, ascription of praise to God.—II. the same received from God.—III. *favour, present* —IV. p. n. of a man.

בְּרֵכָה f., *pool, fish-pond.*

בֶּרֶכְיָה and בֶּרֶכְיָהוּ (*blessed of the Lord*), p. n. of a man.

אַבְרֵךְ; see in its place.

אַרְכֻּבָה f. Ch., *knee.*

בְּרַם Ch. pa. of confirmation, *but.*

בָּרַם root not used; (Arab. *garment adorned with gems*).

בְּרֹמִים m. pl., *costly raiment*, Eze. 27:24.

בָּרָם, לְבָרָם Kal inf. with pref. and suff., from ברר.

בַּרְנֵעַ (*fountain of delight*), p. n. of a place in the wilderness, written קָדֵשׁ־בּ׳, which see.

בֶּרַע p. n. of a king of Sodom.

בְּרִיעָה p. n. of a man.

בָּרַק *lightened*, Ps. 144:6.

בָּרָק m. (pl. בְּרָקִים).—I. *lightning.*—II. *glitter of a sword.*—III. p. n. of the captain who defeated the Canaanites, Jud. 4:6, &c.

בָּרֶקֶת f., *carbuncle.*

בַּרְקָנִים m. pl., *threshing waggons*, having sharp iron teeth, Jud. 8:7, 16.

בַּרְקוֹס p. n. of a man.

בָּרַר I. *examined, tested*, Ecc. 3:18.—II. *separated, selected, chose*, Eze. 20:38, with מִן and לְ; part. בָּרוּר *pure, chaste.* Niph. נָבַר *became pure;* part. נָבָר *pure* Pi. *purify*, Dan. 11:35. Hiph. *make clean, polish.* Hith. *become, appear pure.*

בַּר m., בָּרָה f.—I. *beloved*, Cant. 6:9. —II. *pure, clean.*—III. *empty, void*, Pro. 14:4.

בַּר, בָּר m.—I. *corn*, purified from the chaff.—II. *growing corn*; see another meaning in ברא.

בָּר m., *field, open plain*, Job 39:4.

בַּר m. Ch., the same.

בֹּר m.—I. *pureness.*—II. same as בֹּרִית.

בֹּרִית f., *soap*, Jer. 2:22, Mal. 3:2.

בַּרְבֻּרִים m., *stalled cattle*, 1 Ki. 5:3.

בִּרְשַׁע p. n. of king of Gomorrah.

בְּשׂוֹר, בְּשׂוֹרָה *good news*; see בשׂר.

בָּשָׂם m. (Anyrum opobalsamum), *the balsam tree*, an aromatic shrub.

בֶּשֶׂם and בֹּשֶׂם m. (pl. בְּשָׂמִים).—I. *the odour of perfumes.*—II. *the perfumes themselves.*

בָּשְׂמַת I. p. n. of the wife of Isaiah. —II. of the daughter of Solomon.

מִבְשָׂם p. n. of a man.

בָּשַׂר. Pi. בִּשֵּׂר I. *announce, declare.* —II. *tell glad tidings.* Hith. *was, became informed*, 2 Sa. 18:31.

בְּשׂרָה and בְּשׂוֹרָה f.—I. *good tidings*, 2 Sa. 18:22, 27.—II. the reward of good tidings, 2 Sa. 4:10.

בְּשׂוֹר p. n. of a river near Gaza.

בָּשָׂר m.—I. *flesh.*—II. *body.*—III. כָּל־בָּשָׂר *all living creatures.*—IV. עַצְמִי וּבְשָׂרִי *my bone and flesh, kinsman*; also בָּשָׂר *kinsman*, Lev. 15:2, &c.—V. *secret parts* (male).

בְּשַׂר m. Ch.—I. *flesh.*—II. *mankind.*

בָּשַׁל I. *ripened*, Joel 4:13.—II. *boiled, cooked*, Eze. 24:5. Pi. *boiled, cooked*; part. pl. מְבַשְּׁלִים *cooked*, Eze. 46:24. Pu. *was cooked.* Hiph. *matured, ripened*, Gen. 40:10.

בָּשֵׁל m., בְּשֵׁלָה f., *cooked.*

מְבַשְּׁלוֹת f. pl., *boilers*, Eze. 46:23.

בְּשֶׁלִּי, בְּשֶׁלְּמִי; see שֶׁל in אֲשֶׁר.

בִּשְׁלָם p. n. of a man.

בָּשָׁן p. n., *Batanea*, the region beyond Jordan, between Hermon and the brook of Jabbok.

בָּשְׁנָה *shame*; see בּוֹשׁ.

בָּשַׁס. Po. בּוֹשֵׁס same as בּוֹסֵס *trampling on, injuring*, Am. 5:11.

בֹּשֶׁת *shame*; see בּוֹשׁ.

בַּת *daughter*; see בנה.

בַּת *measure*; see בתת.

בָּתָּה and בַּתָּה; see בתת.

בְּתוּאֵל p. n.—I. of the father of Laban. —II. same as בְּתוּל name of a place.

בִּתְיָה p. n. of a man.

בָּתִּים *houses*; see בּוּת, בַּיִת.

בָּתַל root not used; (Arab. *separated*).

בְּתוּלָה f. (pl. בְּתוּלוֹת, בְּתֻלוֹת).—I. *a virgin.*—II. used for *nation, city, people*, like בַּת, which see.

בְּתוּלִים m. pl., *tokens of virginity.*

בָּתַק. Pi. בִּתֵּק *cut, pierce*, Eze. 16:40.

בָּתַר. Pi. בִּתֵּר *dissect, cut in two*, Gen. 15:10.

בֶּתֶר m. (with suff. בִּתְרוֹ).—I. *part, piece.*—II. *separation*, Cant. 2:17.

בָּתַר Ch., same as בָּאתַר *after*; see אַתַר.

בִּתְרוֹן p. n. of a place on Jordan.

בָּתַת root not used; (Arab. *cut, cleft*).

בַּת m. (f. Isa. 5:10), *Bath*; a liquid measure, the tenth part of a Homer.

בַּת m. Ch., the same.

בָּתָה f., *desolation, excision*, Isa. 5:6.

בַּתָּה f. (pl. בַּתּוֹת), Isa. 7:19, *clefts, fissures.*

ג

גָּאָה (fut. יִגְאֶה).—I. *grew high* (as a plant), Job 8:11; (as water,) Ezr. 47:5.—II. *becoming lofty, powerful, proud.*

גֵּא m., *proud*, Isa. 16:6.

גֵּאֶה m.—I. *elevated.*—II. *proud, arrogant;* pl. גֵּאִים.

גֵּאָה f., *pride, arrogance*, Pro. 8:13.

גַּאֲוָה f.—I. *excellency, majesty.*—II. *pride, arrogance.*

גְּאוּאֵל (*the divine majesty*), p. n. of a man.

גָּאוֹן m.—I. *excellency, glory.*—II. *pride;* pl. גְּאוֹנִים.

גֵּאוּת f.—I. *ascent*, Isa. 9:17.—II. *sublimity, excellency.*—III. *pride, arrogance.*

גַּאֲיוֹן m., *proud*, Ps. 123:4

גֵּוָה f. (for גַּאֲוָה).—I. *elevation, victory*, Job 22:29.—II. *pride*, Job 33:17.

גֵּוָה f. Ch., the same, Dan. 4:34.

גֵּאָיוֹת *valleys;* see גַּיְא.

גָּאַל (fut. יִגְאַל).—I. *redeem by paying value for.*—II. *retribute, avenge.*—III. *pollute;* part. גֹּאֵל *redeemer, avenger, relative*, to whom the duty of avenging the death of any one was assigned; part. pass. גְּאוּלֵי, גְּאוּלִים *redeemed, set at liberty.* Niph. נִגְאַל, נִגְאַל *was redeemed, liberated, polluted.* Pi. גֵּאֵל *polluted*, Mal. 1:7. Pu. *was polluted.* Hiph. אֶגְאַלְתִּי *contaminate*, Isa. 63:1. Hiph. *polluted himself*, Dan. 1:8.

גֹּאֶל m., *pollution;* pl. const. גָּאֳלֵי, Neh. 13:29.

גְּאֻלָּה f.—I. *relationship.*—II. *right, duty of redemption.*—III. *price of redemption.*—IV. *thing redeemed.*

מְגֹאֵל m., *next of kin after the Goel.*

גֵּב *locust;* see גּוֹב.

גָּבָא root not used; (Arab. *gathered together*).

גֶּבֶא m., *cistern, pit.*

גָּבַב root not used.

גַּב m. (with suff. גַּבִּי; pl. גַּבִּים, גַּבּוֹת).—I. *back.*—II. *defence, mound.*—III. *vaults.*—IV. *arch of the eyebrow*, Lev. 14:9; גַּב מָגֵן *the boss of a shield*, Job 15:26.

גַּב m. Ch., *back.*

גֹּב m. Ch., *well;* emph. גֻּבָּא.

גּוֹב m., *locust;* pl. גּוֹבַי.

גֵּב m. (pl. גֵּבִים), *locusts.*

גָּבַהּ (fut. יִגְבַּהּ; inf. גָּבְהָה).—I. *was high, lofty*, with עַל; when with מִן *was higher than.*—II. *exalted;* גָּבַהּ לִבּוֹ *his heart was lifted up;* or merely גָּבַהּ *lifted up.* Hiph. *raise, exalt.*

גָּבֹהַּ m. (const. גְּבֹהַּ; f. גְּבֹהָה).—I. *high, tall.*—II *haughty, proud.* Subst. *height*, 1 Sa. 16:7.

גָּבֵהַּ; const. גְּבַהּ m.—I. *high.*—II. *arrogant, proud.*

גֹּבַהּ m. (with suff. גָּבְהוֹ; pl. const. גָּבְהֵי).—I. *height.*—II. *majesty*, Job 40:10.—III. *arrogance;* גֹּבַהּ אַף *insolence*, Ps. 10:4.

גַּבְהוּת m., *pride*, Isa. 2:11, 17.

גְּבוּל, גְּבוּלָה *border;* see גבל.

גִּבּוֹר, גְּבוּרָה *mighty;* see גבר.

גִּבֵּחַ m., *bald*, Lev. 13:41.

גַּבַּחַת f.—I. *baldness.*—II. *loss of knap* (in cloth), Lev. 13:55.

גֵּבַי p. n. of a man.

גֵּבִים (see גֵּב), p. n. of a place not far from Jerusalem.

גְּבִינָה *cheese;* see גבן.

גָּבִיעַ *cup;* see גבע.

גְּבִיר, גְּבִירָה *master;* see גבר.

גָּבִישׁ; see גבשׁ.

גָּבַל *limited;* with בְּ and אֶת. Hiph. *set bounds to.*

גְּבַל p.n. of a Phenician city; גִּבְלִי an inhabitant of Gebal.

גְּבָל p. n. of a mountainous district beyond Jordan, Ps. 83:8.

גְּבֻל, גְּבוּל m.—I. *limit, boundary.*—II. *space* or *country limited.*

גְּבוּלָה, גְּבֻלָה f., pl. גְּבוּלוֹת *boundaries, lands.*

גַּבְלֻת f., *artificial work, device,* Ex. 28:22; 37:15.

מִגְבָּלָה f. (pl. מִגְבָּלוֹת), the same, Ex. 28:14.

גָּבַן root not used; (Syr. *curdled*).

גְּבִינָה f., *cheese,* 2 Sa. 16:2.

גִּבֵּן m., *hunchback,* Lev. 21:20.

גַּבְנֻנִּים m. pl., *risings, mounds;* הַר גַּ׳ *a hill of mounds,* i. e. made up of other hills.

גָּבִיעַ m. (with suff. גְּבִיעִי; pl. גְּבִיעִים). —I. *a cup* or *vase.*—II. *flower,* the calix of an artificial flower.

גֶּבַע p. n. of a town in the tribe of Benjamin.

גִּבְעָא p. n. of a man.

גִּבְעָה f., *a hill;* pl. גְּבָעוֹת.

גִּבְעַת אֱלֹהִים p.n. of a place.

גִּבְעַת בְּנֵי בִנְיָמִין p.n. of a city in the tribe of Benjamin.

גִּבְעַת פִּינְחָס p. n. of a city.

גִּבְעַת שָׁאוּל p. n. of a hill.

גִּבְעָתִי *inhabitant of Gibeah.*

גִּבְעוֹן p. n. of a city in the tribe of Benjamin.

מִגְבָּעָה f. (pl. מִגְבָּעוֹת), *the mitre* or *bonnet of the priests.*

גִּבְעֹל *flowering* (of flax), Ex. 9:31

גָּבַר and גָּבֵר (fut. יִגְבַּר).—I. *was powerful, mighty.*—II. *conquered,* (prevailed), with מִן or עַל. Pi. *made strong.* Hiph.—I. *was powerful,* Ps. 12:5.—II. *confirm,* Dan. 9:27. Hith. *became powerful, victorious.*

גֶּבֶר m.—I. *man, husband, hero;* pl. גְּבָרִים; לַגְּבָרִים *manfully.*—II. p. n. of a man, 1 Ki. 4:19.

גְּבַר m., Ch. the same; pl. גֻּבְרִין.

גְּבַר m. (same as Ch.), *man,* Ps. 18:26.

גְּבִיר m., *lord,* Gen. 27:29, 37.

גְּבִירָה f., *lady, queen.*

גְּבֶרֶת f. (with suff. גְּבִרְתִּי), the same.

גִּבֹּר, גִּבּוֹר m.—I. *mighty, brave.*—II. *renowned;* גִּבּוֹר חַיִל *renowned for wealth, rich.*

גִּבָּר m. Ch.—I. *brave, strong, heroic.* —II. p. n. same as גִּבְעוֹן, Ezr. 2:20.

גְּבוּרָה f.—I. *power.*—II. *courage.*—III. *acts of courage, power;* גְּבוּרוֹת יְהוָֹה *acts of God,* i.e. miracles.

גְּבוּרָה f. Ch. the same.

גַּבְרִיאֵל p.n. of an archangel.

גָּבַשׁ root not used; (Arab. *congelation*).

גָּבִישׁ m., *crystal* (lit. *ice*), Job 28:18.

גִּבְּתוֹן p. n. of a town of the Philistines in the tribe of Dan.

גָּג m. (with suff. גַּגּוֹ; pl. גַּגּוֹת).—I. *roof of a house.*—II. *covering, grate of the altar.*

גָּד, גַּד; see נדד.

גִּדְבְּרִין m. pl. Ch., *treasures*, Dan. 3: 2,3; same as גִּזְבָּר.

גִּדְגֹּדָה p. n. of a place in the Arabian desert.

גָּדַד *assault, attack* (as an army). Hith. הִתְגּוֹדֵד I. *cutting, making incisions.*—II. *attacking, assembling to attack.*

גְּדַד Ch., *cut down* (of a tree), Dan. 4:11, 20.

גְּדוּד m. (pl. גְּדוּדִים, גְּדֻדוֹת).—I. *cutting*, Jer. 48:37.—II. *furrow*, Ps. 65:11.—III. *section, detachment of an army.*

גַּד m., *coriander seed*, Ex. 16:31, Nu. 11:7.

גָּד m., *good fortune;* בְּגָד *prosperously*, Gen. 30:11.

גַּד nom., p. n. of an idol, Isa. 65:11.

גָּד p. n. *Gad.*—I. one of the sons of Jacob.—II. the tribe descended from him; גָּדִי *a Gadite.*

גַּדִּי p.n. of a man, Nu. 13:11.

גַּדִּיאֵל p. n. of a man.

גָּדָה root not used; (Syr. *leaping*).

גְּדִי m., *a kid;* pl. גְּדָיִים; const. גְּדָיֵי.

גְּדִיָּה f., pl. גְּדִיּוֹת *female kids*, Cant. 1:8.

גִּדָה f., const. pl. גְּדוֹת *banks of a river.*

גְּדוּד, גָּדִי; see נדד.

גָּדוֹל, גְּדוֹלָה, גְּדִילִים *great;* see נדל.

גִּדּוּף, גְּדוּפָה *reproach;* see נדף.

גְּדִי, גְּדִיָּה; see נדה.

גָּדִישׁ *heap;* see נדשׁ.

גָּדַל and **גָּדֵל** (fut. יִגְדַּל), *was* or *grew great* (in anything), with אֵת, בְּ, לְ, מִן, עַד. Pi. גִּדֵּל, גַּדֵּל I. *made* or *pronounced great:* hence, —II. *trained, educated.* Hiph. I. *became great.*—II. *made great, high;* הגו׳ אֵת פִּיו *he spake insolently.* Hith. *showed himself great.*

גָּדֵל m., pl. const. גִּדְלֵי, *great ones*, Eze. 16:26.

גָּדוֹל m. (const. גְּדוֹל and גְּדֹל; f. גְּדוֹלָה), *great* (in anything); גְּדוֹלִים *nobles;* גְּדוֹל חֶסֶד *great in mercy;* עוֹד הַיּוֹם גָּדוֹל *it is yet high day*, i. e. early, Gen. 29:7; pl. גְּדוֹלוֹת *great* (i. e. proud) *things*, Ps. 12:4.

גֹּדֶל m. (with suff. גָּדְלוֹ, גָּדְלוֹ), *greatness, magnificence, pride.*

גְּדֻלָּה, גְּדוּלָּה f.—I. *great* (act or deed). —II. *greatness;* pl. גְּדֻלּוֹת *great things.*

גְּדִילִים m. pl., *platted chain-work*, 1 Ki. 7:17.

גִּדֵּל p. n. of a man.

גְּדַלְיָה, גְּדַלְיָהוּ *Gedaliah*, p.n. of a man.

גִּדַּלְתִּי p. n. of a man, 1 Ch. 25:4, 29.

מִגְדָּל (pl. מִגְדָּלִים, מִגְדָּלוֹת).—I. *tower, castle.*—II. *pulpit*, Neh. 8:4.—III. artificial *mound*, in a garden covered with sweet flowers, Cant. 5:13.

מִגְדֹּל, מִגְדּוֹל p. n. of a city in Egypt.

מִגְדַּל־אֵל p.n. of a fortress in the tribe of Naphtali.

מִגְדַּל־גָּד p. n. of a place in the tribe of Judah.

מִגְדַּל עֵדֶר p.n. of a place near Beth lehem.

גָּדַע I. *cut off* or *down.*—II. *broke.* Niph. *became cut off, down.* Pi. *broke.* Pu. *was cut down*, Isa. 9:9.

גִּדְעֹם p. n. of a place in the tribe of Benjamin.

גִּדְעוֹן p.n. of a judge of Israel.

גִּדְעֹנִי p.n. of a man.

גָּדַף. Pi. גִּדֵּף *blasphemed.*

גִּדּוּף m., pl. גִּדּוּפִים, גִּדּוּפוֹת *reproaches,* Isa. 43:28; 51:7.

גִּדּוּפָה f., *reproach,* Zep. 2:8.

גָּדַר *walled, fenced up;* part. גֹּדֵר *fencer.*

גָּדֵר com. (const. גֶּדֶר; with suff. גְּדֵרוֹ; pl. גְּדֵרִים).—I. *wall, fence.* —II. *fenced place.*

גְּדֵרָה f.—I. *wall.*—II. *fence, hurdle.*— III. same as בֵּית גָּדֵר p.n. of a town in the tribe of Judah; גְּדֵרָתִי *a Gederite.*—IV. גְּדֵרוֹת and גְּדֵרוֹתַיִם p.n. of places in the tribe of Judah.

גְּדֶרֶת f., *a fence,* Eze. 42:12.

גֶּדֶר p.n. of a city of the Canaanites.

גְּדֹר p.n. of a town in the tribe of Judah.

גְּדֵרִי an inhabitant of בֵּית גָּדֵר.

גָּדַשׁ root not used; Ch. *heaped up.*

גָּדִישׁ m.—I. *sepulchral mound.*—II. *heap of corn.*

גֵּה for זֶה, Eze. 47:13.

גָּהָה *raise up,* Hos. 5:12.

גֵּהָה f., *relief, healing,* Pro. 17:22.

גָּהַר *bowed, bent downwards.*

גֵּו, גַּו, גּוֹא; see גוה.

גּוּב *cut, cleft;* part. גֹּבִים *ploughers.*

גֵּב m.—I. *board, plank.*—II. *well;* see another meaning in גָּבָה.

גּוֹב (*cistern*), p.n. of a place; see another meaning in גָּבָה.

גּוֹג p.n. of the king of Magog; see מָגוֹג.

גּוּד, יְגוּדֶנּוּ, see גָּדַד; *shall rush upon him,* Gen. 49:19; Hab. 3:16.

גָּוָה root not used.

גּוֹא, גּו m. Ch., *middle.*

גַּו m. Ch.—I. *middle;* with suff. גַּוָּהּ. —II. Heb. *back;* with suff. גַּוּוֹ.

גֵּו m.—I. *back.*—II. *middle;* with suff. גֵּוִי.

גֵּוָה f., *a body,* Job 20:25; see another meaning under גָּאָה.

גְּוִיָּה f.—I. *body, person.*—II. *dead body, carcase of men* or *animals.*

גּוֹי m. (with suff. גּוֹיִי; pl. גּוֹיִם, גּוֹיֵי, with suff. גּוֹיֵהֶם, גּוֹיֶךָ).—I. generally *people,* Israelites as well as foreigners.—II. specially, *foreign nations.*—III. multitudes of locusts, Joel 1:6; of animals, Zep. 2:14.

גַּיְא com. (const. גֵּיא; pl. גֵּאָיוֹת), *valley.*

גֵּיא, גַּיְא the same.

גַּי m. (const. גֵּי), the same.

גֵּאָיוֹת f. pl., *valleys.*

גּוּז *pass over,* Ps. 90:10; fut. apoc. וַיָּגָז, Nu. 11:31.

גּוֹזָל *young bird;* see גזל.

גּוֹזָן p.n., a district in North Mesopotamia, between the rivers Chaboras and Saocoras, the Γαυζανῖτις of Ptolemy.

גּוּחַ *break forth;* see גִּיחַ.

גּוֹי, גְּוִיָּה; see גוה.

גּוּל *rejoice;* see גִּיל.

גּוֹלָה, גּוֹלָן; see גלה.

גּוּמָּץ *pit;* see גמץ.

גּוּנִי p.n. of a man.

גָּוַע (fut. יִגְוַע; inf. גְּוֹעַ; const. גְּוַע and גְּוֹעַ), *expire, die.*

גּוּף Kal, root not used; (Arab. *shut up*). Hiph. fut. pl. יָגִיפוּ *let (them) shut,* Neh. 7:3.

גּוּפָה f., *dead body;* (Arab. the same).

גּוּר I. *sojourned, dwelt,* with בְּ, עִם,

אֵת; part. גָּר *dwelling with;* גָּרַת בֵּיתָהּ *her inmate.*—II. *avoided, feared,* with מִן and מִפְּנֵי.—III. *congregated, come together,* with עַל; see גָּרָה. Hith. הִתְגּוֹרֵר.—I. *withdraw.*—II. *dwell,* 1 Ki. 17:20. —III. *violent destroying,* Jer. 30:23.

גֵּר (גֵּיר, 2. Ch. 2:16), m., *sojourner, stranger.*

גֵּרוּת f., *sojourning, residing,* Jer. 41:17.

גּוּר m.—I. *lion's whelp;* גּוּר אַרְיֵה, Gen. 49:9, &c.—II. *jackall,* 2 Sa. 4:3.

גֹּר m. the same; f. pl. גֹּרוֹת.

גּוּר בַּעַל (*dwelling of Baal*), p. n. of a town in Arabia.

מָגוּר m.—I. *sojourning.*—II. *residence, habitation.*—III. *human life; sojourn on earth.*

מָגוֹר m., *fear, terror;* pl. מְגוּרִים.

מְגוֹרָה f., *fear;* pl. מְגוֹרוֹת.

מְגוּרָה f.—I. *granary.*—II. *fear, terror;* pl. מְגוּרוֹת.

מַמְּגוּרָה f. (pl. מַמְּגֻרוֹת), *granaries,* Joel 1:17.

גּוֹרָל *lot;* see גרל.

גּוּשׁ m., *clod,* Job 7:5.

גֵּישָׁן p. n. of a man.

גֵּז *fleece;* see גזז.

גִּזְבָּר *treasurer,* Ezr. 1:8; pl. גִּזַּבְרִין, Ezr. 7:21, and גְּדָבְרִין, Dan. 3:2, 3.

גָּזָה (Arab. *bring forth*); part. גּוֹזִי, lit. "*he who brought me forth,*" Ps. 71:6.

גָּזִית f.—I. lit. *cutting, hewing:* hence, —II. *hewn stones.*

גָּזַז (fut. יָגֹז; inf. גֹּז and גְּזֹז).—I. *shear, cut off hair, wool, &c.;* part. גֹּזְזִים *shavers.*—II. *drive away* (of quails), Nu. 11:31. Niph. pret. pl. נָגֹזּוּ *were cut off.*

גֵּז m. (pl. const. גִּזֵּי).—I. *shearing of sheep:* hence,—II. *the fleece.*—III. *young grass after mowing.*

גִּזָּה f., *fleece,* Jud. 6:39, 40.

גָּזֵז (*barber*), p. n. of a man.

גָּזַל I. *cut off.*—II. *snatch away, injure.* Niph. *was taken away,* Pro. 4:16.

גָּזֵל m., const. גְּזֶל *rapine, plunder.*

גְּזֵלָה f., the same.

גּוֹזָל m., *young pigeon,* Gen. 15:9; Deu. 32:11.

גָּזַם root not used; (Arab. *destruction*).

גָּזָם m., *a species of locust.*

גַּזָּם p. n. of a man.

גִּזֹנִי m., an inhabitant of Gizon.

גָּזַע root not used; (Arab. *cutting off*).

גֶּזַע m. (with suff. גִּזְעָם), *stock; trunk of a tree.*

גָּזַר I. *cut off, down.*—II. *in two parts divided.*—III. *decided,* as judgment. Niph. *was cut off,* with מִן; *was decided,* Est. 2:1.

גְּזַר Ch., *decided, determined* the fate of others by astrology; part. pl. גָּזְרִים *soothsayers.*

גֶּזֶר I. *division, section;* pl. גְּזָרִים.—II. p. n. of a city on the western frontier of the tribe of Ephraim, Γάζηρα.

גְּזֵרָה (גְּזִירָה) f., *place cut off, separated,* Lev. 16:22.

גְּזֵרָה f. Ch., *decision.* Dan. 4:14, 21

גִּזְרָה f.—I. *cut, polish* (of precious stones), Lam. 4:7.—II. *insulated, separated* (of a certain enclosure of the temple), Eze. 41:42.

מַגְזֵרָה f., *axe*, 2 Sa. 12:31.
גִּזְרִי inhabitant of *Gezer*.
גָּחוֹן *belly*; see גחן.
גֵּיחֲזִי, גֵּחֲזִי p. n. of a servant of the prophet Elisha.

גָּחַל root not used; (Arab. *to burn*).
גַּחַל m. (pl. גֶּחָלִים, גַּחֲלֵי).—I. *burning coals*.—II. *thunderbolts*.
גַּחֶלֶת f., the same; with suff. גַּחַלְתִּי.
גַּחַם p. n. of a man.

גָּחַן root not used; Ch. גְּחַן *bowed down*.
גָּחוֹן m., *belly of a serpent*, Lev. 11:42; with suff. גְּחֹנְךָ, Gen. 3:14.
גַּי, גֵּי, גַּיְא, גֵּיא; see גוה.
גַּחַר p. n. of a man.

גִּיד m., *sinew, nerve*.

גִּיחַ and גּוּחַ (fut. יָגִיחַ; part. גֹּחַ).—I. *drew out*.—II. *extended, elongated*. Hiph. *drew out*.
גִּיחַ or גּוּחַ Ch. Aph. *rushed forth*.
גִּיחַ p. n. of a place near Gibeon, 2 Sa. 2:24.
גִּיחוֹן I. p. n. of a river of Paradise, Gen. 2:13.—II. of an aqueduct near Jerusalem; otherwise שִׁלֹחַ.

גִּיל and גּוּל (fut. יָגִיל) *leap, exult, rejoice*, with בְּ, עַל, לְמַעַן.
גִּיל m., *exultation, rejoicing*.
גִּיל m. Ch., *equal in age, rank, &c.*, Dan. 1:10.
גִּילָה f., *exultation*.
גִּילֹנִי; see גִּלֹה in גלה.
גִּינַת; see גנן.

גִּיר (גִּר) m., *burnt lime-stone*, Isa. 27:9.
גִּיר m. Ch., *plaster of lime*, Dan. 5:5.
גֵּיו *stranger*, same as גֵּר; see גור.

גִּישׁ *clod*, same as גּוּשׁ.
גֵּישָׁן p. n. of a man.
גַּל for גֹּל Kal imper. from גָּלַל Ps. 119. 12. Pi. imper. apoc. from גָּלָה, Ps. 119:18.
גְּלָא Ch., *reveal*; see גלה.

גָּלַב root not used; (Arab. *drew, shaved*).
גַּלָּב m., *barber*, Eze. 5:1.
גִּלְבֹּעַ p. n., *Gilboa*, hills in the tribe of Issachar.
גִּלְגָּל, גַּלְגַּל, גֻּלְגֹּלֶת; see גלל.
גֶּלֶד m., *skin*; with suff. גִּלְדִּי *my skin*, Job 16:15.
גֻּלָּה *bowl*; see גלל.

גָּלָה (fut. יִגְלֶה, יִגֶל; inf. גְּלֹה, גְּלוֹת).—I. *laid bare, disclosed, opened*.—II. *depopulated a country*, i.e. *led into captivity, migrated*; part. m. גּוֹלֶה, f. גּוֹלָה *migrated, gone into captivity*; גָּלוּי *opened, proclaimed, published* (of an edict). Niph. נִגְלָה (fut. יִגָּלֶה, יִגָּל; inf. abs. נִגְלֹה, נִגְלוֹת).—I. *was uncovered, exposed, revealed*.—II. *migrated, went into captivity*, Isa. 38:12; part. f. pl. נִגְלֹת *revealed*, Deu. 29:29. Pi. גִּלָּה (fut. יְגַלֶּה, יְגַל).—I. *uncovered, made naked*.—II. *had carnal connexion with*, with אֶל and עַל. Pu. גֻּלָּה *was uncovered*; part. f. מְגֻלָּה *openly said*. Hiph. הִגְלָה, הֶגְלָה *led captive* (fut. וַיַּגְלֶה, וַיֶּגֶל). Hoph. הָגְלָה *was made captive*. Hithp. הִתְגַּלָּה *made himself naked*; fut. apoc. וַיִּתְגַּל, Gen. 9:21.
גְּלָא Ch., *revealed*. Piel גַּלִּי, גְּלִי *revealed*. Aph. הַגְלִי *carried captive*, Ezr. 4:10, 12.
גִּלֹה p. n. of a city in the mountains

of Judah; its inhabitants were styled גִּילֹנִי.

גֹּלָה, גּוֹלָה f.—I. *captivity.*—II. *captive, troop of captives.*

גּוֹלָן p.n. of a city of Batanea, Γαυλών.

גָּלוּת, גָּלֻת f., *captive;* as גּוֹלָה.

גָּלוּת f. Ch., the same.

גִּלָּיוֹן m., *tablet, book,* Isa. 8:1; pl. גִּלְיֹנִים *mirrors,* Isa. 3:23. Writing tablets and mirrors were both, in ancient times, plates of metal.

גָּלְיַת p. n., *Goliath,* the giant whom David slew.

גַּלִּים, גְּלִילָה, גָּלִיל, גִּלּוּלִים; see גלל.

גָּלוּם; see גלם.

גִּלַּח. Pi. גִּלַּח.—I. *shaved head* or *beard.* II. *devastated by war,* Isa. 7:20. Pu. *was shaven,* Ju. 16:17, 22; Jer. 41:5. Hithp. *shave himself.*

גִּלֹה p. n. of a city.

גָּלְיַת, גִּלָּיוֹן; see גלה.

גָּלַל (sing. p. 1. גַּלּוֹתִי, pl. גָּלֲלוּ; inf. גּוֹל, גֹּל; imp. גֹּל, גַּל).—I. *roll* (as a stone).—II. with מֵעַל *roll away,* used metaphorically of things morally heavy.—III. with עַל, אֶל, *commit to,* lit. *roll upon;* גּוֹל עַל יְיָ דַּרְכֶּךָ *commit thy way unto the Lord,* Ps. 37:5. Niph. נָגֹל *were rolled up,* Isa. 34:4; *rolled away,* Am. 5:24. Pil. גִּלְגֵּל *roll off,* Jer. 51:25. Hithpal. *roll, rush in violently,* Job 30:14. Hiph. הֵגֵל *roll,* Gen. 29:10. Po. גּוֹלֵל *roll about in,* Isa. 9:4. Hithpo. הִתְגּוֹלֵל *rolled in, weltered in,* 2 Sa. 20:12.—II. *fall upon,* with עַל, Gen. 43:18.

גָּלָל m.—I. *dung.*—II. בִּגְלַל *because, for the sake of;* בִּגְלָלְךָ *for thy sake.*—III. p. n. of a man.

גְּלָל m. Ch., *great, heavy,* (of stones).

גֵּלֶל m. (with suff. גֶּלְלוֹ; pl. גְּלָלִים; const. גֶּלְלֵי) *dung.*

גָּלָל, גִּלֲלַי p. n. of a man.

גִּלּוּלִים m. pl., *idols.*

גָּלִיל m.—I. *that which can be turned on hinges,* 1 Ki. 6:34.—II. *ring,* Cant. 5:14.—III. *circuit, tract of country;* הַגָּלִיל and הַגָּלִילָה p.n. of a region in the tribe of Naphtali, *Galilee.*

גְּלִילָה f. *circuit, region.*

גַּל m. (pl. גַּלִּים).—I. *a heap* (of stones, &c.).—II. *spring, fountain.*—III. pl. *waves, breakers.*

גַּלִּים p. n. of a town in the tribe of Benjamin; 1 Sa. c. 25; Jos. c. 10.

גֹּל m., *oil jar,* Zec. 4:2.

גֻּלָּה f.—I. same as גַּל (pl. גֻּלּוֹת) *well,* Jos. 15:10; Jud. 1:15.—II. const. גֻּלַּת *oil jar* or *vessel.*—III. vase-like ornaments, or flowers on the capitals of columns.

גַּלְגַּל m.—I. *wheel;* pl. גַּלְגַּלִּים.—II. *whirlwind.*—III. *chaff* (as driven by the wind).

גַּלְגַּל m. Ch., *wheel,* Dan. 7:9.

גִּלְגָּל m.—I. *cart wheel,* Isa. 28:28.—II. p. n. of a city between Jericho and Jordan.

גֻּלְגֹּלֶת f.—I. *skull.*—II. used in numbering men, as we say, *head of cattle;* with suff. גֻּלְגָּלְתּוֹ; pl. with suff. גֻּלְגְּלֹתָם.

מְגִלָּה f., *volume, roll, book.*

מְגִלָּה f. Ch., the same.

גָּלַם *wrapped together* (as a mantle), 2 Ki. 2:8.

גְּלוֹם m., *cloak, mantle,* Eze. 27:24.

גֹּלֶם m., *embryo, fœtus*, Ps. 139:16.

גַּלְמוּד m., *hard, barren, fruitless.*

גָּלַע. Hithp. הִתְגַּלַּע *intermeddle, be impudent.*

גִּלְעָד I. p.n., *Gilead*, the son of Machir, grandson of Manasseh: hence,—II. p.n. of a hill and town near Lebanon.—III. of a region beyond Jordan; גִּלְעָדִי *a Gileadite.*

גַּלְעֵד (*heap of witness*), p.n. of the heap of stones erected by Laban and Jacob, Gen. 31:47, 48.

גָּלַשׁ "appear," Cant. 4:1; 6:5, Eng. Ver.; meaning uncertain.

גַּם; see גמם.

גָּמָא. Pi. *drink in*, Job 29:24. Hiph. *give to drink*, Gen. 24:17.

גֹּמֶא m., *the paper reed;* תֵּבַת גֹּמֶא *an ark of reeds*, and כְּלִי גֹ׳ *a boat of reeds.*

גֹּמֶד m., *pruning knife, short-sword*, Ju 3:16.

גַּמָּדִים m. pl., *short-swordsmen*, Eze. 27:11.

גִּמְזוֹ p. n. of a town in the tribe of Judah.

גָּמַל (fut. יִגְמֹל).—I. *recompense, repay*, with לְ and עַל.—II. *mature, ripen.* — III. *wean as a child.* Niph. *was weaned.*

גְּמוּל *recompence, retribution*, either of good or bad actions.

גָּמוּל p. n. of a man.

גְּמוּלָה f., *recompence, retribution.*

גַּמְלִיאֵל (*God my restorer*), p.n. of a man.

תַּגְמוּל m., *retribution, kindness*, Ps. 116:12.

גָּמָל com., *camel;* pl. גְּמַלִּים.

גְּמַלִּי p. n. of a man.

גָּמַם (Arab. *filled up, desired*).

גַּם *moreover, also;* הֲגַם *is it not also?* גַּם...גַּם *and...also;* גַּם כִּי *but if, although.*

מְגַמָּה f., *desire, object*, Hab. 1:9.

גָּמַץ (Syr. *a well*).

גּוּמָּץ m., *a well* or *pit*, Ecc. 10:8.

גָּמַר (fut. יִגְמֹר).—I. *bring to pass.*—II. *finish, fail.*

גְּמַר Ch., *complete, learned*, Eze. 7:12.

גְּמַרְיָה and גְּמַרְיָהוּ p.n. of a man.

גֹּמֶר p. n.—I. of a northern race of people, perhaps the *Cymri.*—II. of the wife of Hosea.

גַּן *garden;* see גנן.

גָּנַב *he stole, with* or *without violence;* with לֵב, Gen. 31:20, 26, 27, "*stole away unawares.*" Niph. *stolen.* Pi. *secretly*, Ex. 22:11. Pu. *steals, was stolen.* Hith. *stole themselves away.*

גַּנָּב m., *a thief.*

גְּנֵבָה f., *stolen thing*, Ex. 22:2, 3.

גְּנֻבַת p. n. of a man.

גַּנָּה ,גִּנָּה; see גנן.

גָּנַז root not used; (Arab. *covered*).

גֶּנֶז m., pl. גְּנָזִים; const. גִּנְזֵי *treasures.*

גְּנַז or גֶּנֶז m. Ch., pl. גִּנְזִין *treasures.*

גַּנְזַךְ m., *treasury*, 2 Ch. 28:11.

גָּנַן *guard, protect*, with עַל ,אֶל. Hiph. the same.

גַּן com. (with suff. גַּנִּי, pl. גַּנִּים) *a garden.*

גַּנָּה f., *a garden;* pl. גַּנּוֹת.

גִּנָּה f., the same.

גִּינַת p. n. of a man.
גִּנְּתוֹן ,גִּנְּתוֹי p. n. of a man.
מָגֵן m. (suff. מָגִנִּי, pl. מָגִנִּים) *shield*, fig., *God the protector*, Gen. 15:10; מָגִנֵּי־אֶרֶץ *shields of the earth*, i.e. princes, Ps. 47:10., &c.
מְגִנָּה f., with לֵב *veiling, covering of heart*, Lam. 3:65.

גָּעָה *lowed* (as oxen), Job 6:5.
גֹּעָה p. n. of a place near Jerusalem.

גָּעַל *loathed, abhorred*. Niph. *was rejected, cast away*, 2 Sa. 1:21. Hiph. *cast* (brought forth prematurely), Job 21:10.
גֹּעַל m., *loathing*, Eze. 16:5.
גַּעַל p. n. of a man.

גָּעַר (fut. יִגְעַר) *rebuked, reproved*, with בְּ.
גְּעָרָה f., *chiding, reproof*.
מִגְעֶרֶת *rebuke, calamity*, Deu. 28:20.

גָּעַשׁ *shook, trembled*, Ps. 18:8. Pu. גֹּעַשׁ *was shaken*, Job 34:20. Hithp. *was moved*. Hithpo. the same,. Jer. 25:16.
גַּעַשׁ p. n. of a mountain in the tribe of Ephraim.
גַּעַת Kal. inf. const. from נגע.
גַּעְתָּם p.n. of the son of Eliphaz.
גַּף *body*; see גפף.
גֶּפֶן com.—I. *climbing plant*.—II. *vine*.

גָּפַף root not used; (Arab. *troop of men*).
גַּף m.—I. *person, self*; בְּגַפּוֹ *with himself only*, i.e. *alone*, Ex. 21:3,4.—II. *back*, i.e. *hillock*, Pro. 9:3.
גַּף m. Ch., pl. גַּפִּין *wings*.

גֹּפֶר m., name of a tree; probably, *the pitch-pine*, Gen. 6:14.
גָּפְרִית f., *brimstone*.
גָּר; see גָּרַר and גּוּר.
גֵּר ,גָּר; see גּוּר.
גֵּרָא (same as גֵּרָה), p. n. of a man.

גָּרַב root not used; like *scratch, scurf*, and many other words in all languages, an imitation of the noise made in *scratching*, &c.
גָּרָב m., *scurf, scurvy*.
גָּרֵב p. n. of one of David's generals.
גַּרְגְּרוֹת ,גַּרְגַּר; see גרר.
גִּרְגָּשִׁי p. n. of a nation of Canaanites.

גָּרַד Hithp. inf. הִתְגָּרֵד *scrape, scratch*, Job 2:8; see גָּרַב.

גָּרָה Pi. גֵּרָה *produce, kindle strife*. Hithp. *prepare to contend, contend with*; const. with בְּ.
תִּגְרָה f., *attack, stroke*, Ps. 39:11.
גָּרוֹן m., *throat*; see גרר.
גֵּרָה ,גָּרוֹן; see גרר.
גֵּרוּת *sojourning*; see גּוּר.

גָּרַז same as גָּזַר. Niph. pret. נִגְרַזְתִּי *I am cut off*, Ps. 31:23; 88:6.
גַּרְזֶן m., *axe*.
גִּרְזִי (גִּרְזִי) p. n. of a nation of Canaanites.
הַר גְּרִזִּים p n. of a mountain, *Gerizim*.

גָּרַל root not used; (Arab. *was gravelly, sandy*).
גּוֹרָל m. (pl. גּוֹרָלוֹת).—I. *lot*, lit. *the pebble* by which it was determined.—II. הִפִּיל, הִשְׁלִיךְ, יָדָה, יָדָה, נָתַן הַגּוֹרָל *determined by lot*; הָיָה לוֹ גּוֹרָל, עָלָה עָלָיו גּוֹרָל i. e. יָצָא *the lot fell*.—III. *the thing obtained by lot*.
גְּרֹל (const. גְּרֹל) Pro. 19:19; keri גְּדֹל *great*.

גֶּרֶם m. (pl. גְּרָמִים).—I. *bone.*—II. *powerful*, Gen. 49:14.—III. *framework, pulpit*, 2 Ki. 9:13.

גְּרֶם m. Ch., *bone.*

גָּרַם *cut, spoil*, Zep. 3:3. Pi. fut. יְגָרֵם *shall destroy.*

גַּרְמִי p. n. of a man.

גָּרַן root not used; (Arab. *place for drying dates*).

גֹּרֶן f. (pl. גְּרָנוֹת; const. גָּרְנוֹת).—I. *open place at the gate of a city, court of justice.*—II. *threshing-floor.*—III. *corn of the floor*, Job 39:12. גֹּרֶן הָאָטָד p. n. of a place beyond Jordan; see אָטָד.

גָּרַס *pained, overwhelmed*, Ps. 119:20. Hiph. fut. וַיַּגְרֵס *and brake, destroyed*, Lam. 3:16.

גֶּרֶשׂ m. (with suff. גִּרְשָׂהּ), *thrashed; perhaps, ground corn*, Lev. 2:14, 16.

גָּרַע I. *took away.*—II. *shaved, took away the beard*, Jer. 48:37. Niph. (fut. יִגָּרַע, יִגָּרֵעַ) *was taken away.* Pi. *draws off*; fut. יְגָרַע Job 36:27.

מִגְרָעוֹת f. pl., *ledges, steps in buildings*, 1 Ki. 6:6.

גָּרַף *swept away* (as a flood), Jud. 5:21.

אֶגְרוֹף m., *fist.*

מֶגְרָפָה f., *furrow*, Joel 1:17.

גָּרַר *he drew, dragged*; fut. יָגוֹר. Niph. fut. יִגַּר *chew the cud.* Po. *sawed*, 1 Ki. 7:9. Hithpo. *swept away*, Jer. 30:23.

גֵּרָה f.—I. *the cud.*—II. *Gerah*, a weight equal to the twentieth part of a shekel.

גַּרְגַּר m., *berry*, Isa. 17:6.

גַּרְגְּרָה f., *throat, front of the neck.*

גָּרוֹן m. (const. גְּרוֹן), *throat.*

מְגֵרָה f., *saw.*

גְּרָר p. n. of a city of the Philistines.

גֶּרֶשׂ *flower*; see גרס.

גָּרַשׁ *put forth, cast forth.* Niph. *was cast, driven, out.* Pi. גֵּרֵשׁ *expel.* Pu. גֹּרַשׁ *was expelled.*

גֶּרֶשׁ m., *produce, fruit*, Deu. 33:14.

גְּרֻשָׁה *expulsion.*

מִגְרָשׁ m.—I. *suburbs.*—II. *pastures, open places.*—III. *lands*, surrounding the cities of the Levites; pl. מִגְרְשׁוֹת, מִגְרָשִׁים.

גֵּרְשֹׁם p. n. of the son of Moses.

גֵּרְשׁוֹן (*Gershon*), p. n. of a man; גֵּרְשֻׁנִּי *a Gershonite.*

גַּשׁ, גֶּשׁ־, גְּשָׁה Kal imp., from נגשׁ.

גֹּשׁוּ Kal imp. pl., from נגשׁ.

גְּשׁוּר (*bridge*), p. n. of three places.—I. the country of the Canaanites to the east of Jordan.—II. of a district in South Palestine.—III. of a district in Syria. גְּשׁוּרִי *a Geshurite.*

גָּשַׁם Kal, root not used; (Arab. *fatness*). Hiph. part. pl. מַגְשִׁימִים *cause to rain*, Jer. 14:22.

גֶּשֶׁם m., *heavy shower*; pl. גְּשָׁמִים, גִּשְׁמֵי.

גֹּשֶׁם m., the same; with suff. גִּשְׁמָהּ.

גֶּשֶׁם m., *body.*

גֶּשֶׁם, גַּשְׁמוּ p. n. of a man.

גֹּשֶׁן (*Goshen*), p. n.—I. of the country bordering on Egypt, which was inhabited by the Israelites during the first captivity.—II. of a town in the tribe of Judah.

גִּשְׁפָּא p. n. of a man.

גָּשַׁשׁ Pi. fut. with ה parag. נְגַשְׁשָׁה *we feel, grope about*, Isa. 59:10.

גֶּשֶׁת Kal inf. with suff. גִּשְׁתּוֹ, from נגשׁ

גַּת f.—I. *the vat* in which grapes were trodden; pl. גִּתּוֹת.—II. p. n. of a city of the Philistines in the country of Goliath. גַּת הַחֵפֶר p.n. of a town in the tribe of Zebulun; גַּת רִמּוֹן p. n. of cities of the Levites in Dan and Manasseh; גִּתִּי *a Gittite*.

גִּתַּיִם p. n. of a town in the tribe of Benjamin.

גִּתִּית f., probably the name of a musical instrument; occurs in the titles of certain psalms.

גֶּתֶר p. n. of a people of Syria, Gen 10:23.

ד

דָּא pron. Ch. f. and neuter, *this*; דָּא לְדָא *together*.

דָּאַב same as דּוּב *was languid*.

דְּאָבָה f., *pining away*, Job 41:14.

דְּאָבוֹן m., *extreme languor, fainting*; const. דַּאֲבוֹן, Deu. 28:65.

דָּאג *fish*, same as דָּג; see דָּגָה.

דָּאַג I. *grieve, be anxious*, with לְ.—II. *fear*, with מִן.

דֹּאֵג (Syr. דּוֹיֵג), p. n. of a prince of the Edomites.

דְּאָגָה f., *anxiety, alarm*.

דָּאָה *flew*; fut. יִדְאֶה, וַיֵּדֶא.

דָּאָה f., name of a bird, *kite*, Lev. 11:14; LXX. γύψ; Vulg. milvus; corresponding passage, Deu. 14:13, רָאָה.

דֹּאר p. n., same as דּוֹר.

דֹּב *bear*; see דבב.

דָּבָא root not used; (Arab. *produced, multiplied*).

דֹּבֶא *riches, power*; LXX. ἰσχύς, Deu. 33:25; with suff. דָּבְאֶךָ.

דָּבַב *crept, flowed softly* (of wine), Cant. 7:10.

דּוֹב, דֹּב m. (pl. דֻּבִּים) *a bear*.

דֹּב m. Ch., the same.

דִּבָּה f.—I. *calumny*.—II. *calumniator*, Pro. 25:10.

דְּבוֹרָה *bee*; see דבר.

דְּבַח Ch., *sacrificed*, Ezr. 6:3; see זבח.

דְּבַח m. Ch., *sacrifice*, Ezr. 6:3.

מַדְבַּח m. Ch., *altar*, Ezr. 7:17.

דִּבְיוֹנִים m. pl., *pigeons' dung*, 2 Ki. 6:25.

דְּבִיר *oracle*; see דבר.

דָּבַל root not used; (Arab. *pressed together*).

דְּבֵלָה f. (const. דְּבֶלֶת; pl. דְּבֵלִים) *παλάθη, cake of dry figs*.

בֵּית ד׳, דִּבְלָתַיִם, דִּבְלָה p. n. of a city of the Moabites.

דִּבְלַיִם p.n. of a man.

דָּבַק and **דָּבֵק** (fut. יִדְבַּק; inf. דָּבְקָה). —I. *adhered, cleft to*.—II. *reached, attained*, with אֶל, לְ, בְּ. Pu. fut. pl. יְדֻבָּקוּ *made to adhere*. Hiph. (fut. יַדְבִּיק, וַיַּדְבֵּק) *joined, caused to stick, attained*. Hoph. part מֻדְבָּק *stuck to*, Ps. 22:16.

דְּבַק Ch., *adhered*, Dan. 2:43.

דָּבֵק m., *adhering*; pl. דְּבֵקִים.

דֶּבֶק m., *solder*, for joining metals; pl. דְּבָקִים *rivets* (for armour).

דָּבַר not used in the pres. pret.; part. דֹּבֵר *speaking;* דָּבָר *spoken;* inf. דַּבֶּרְךָ *thy speaking.* Piel דִּבֶּר, דִּבֶּר (fut. יְדַבֵּר) *he spoke, uttered words to* or *with any one,* with לְ, עַל, בְּ, אֵת, עִם, אֶל; *concerning any one,* with עַל, אֶל, בְּ; *against any one,* with עַל, בְּ; *by any one,* with בְּ, בְּיַד used idiomatically; דִּבֶּר דְּבָרִים לַעֲשׂוֹת *he threatened;* ד׳ *he uttered words;* ד׳ שָׁלוֹם, with אֵת or עִם *he spoke friendly with any one;* with בְּ the same; ד׳ לְאִשָּׁה *he asked her in marriage.* Pu. *was spoken.* Niph. *became,* i.e. *set about speaking,* with בְּ, עַל. Hiph. *subdued* (with his word); fut. וַיַּדְבֵּר. Hithp. part. מִדַּבֵּר *speaking.*

דָּבָר m. (const. דְּבַר; pl. דְּבָרִים, דִּבְרֵי).—I. *word;* בַּעַל אִישׁ דְּבָרִים *eloquent man.*—II. *thing.*—III. *thing, matter, subject in hand;* דְּבַר יוֹם בְּיוֹמוֹ *the thing* (duty) *of the day in its day;* אַחַר הַדְּבָרִים הָאֵלֶּה *after these things,* μετὰ ταῦτα: לֹא דָבָר *nothing;* אֵין ד׳ *there is nothing;* בַּעַל ד׳ *he who pleads a cause;* דְּבַר and עַל דִּבְרֵי *because;* עַל דְּבַר אֲשֶׁר *because of.*

דֶּבֶר m., *pestilence;* pl. דְּבָרִים.

דְּבִיר m.—I. *the oracle,* i. e. the place in the temple whence responses were given.—II. p. n. of a city in the tribe of Judah.

דֹּבֶר m., *fold, pasture,* Mic. 2:12.

דִּבְרָה f., *cause for adjudication;* עַל דִּבְרַת *because;* with שֶׁ־ *because that;* עַל דִּבְרָתִי *according to, after the order of,* Ps. 110:4.

דִּבְרָה f. Ch., *cause.*

דְּבוֹרָה f.—I. *a bee;* pl. דְּבֹרִים.—II. p. n. of a woman who judged Israel.

דֹּבְרוֹת f. pl., *floats, rafts,* 1 Ki. 5:23.

דַּבְּרוֹת f. pl., *sayings,* Deu. 33:3.

מִדְבָּר m.—I. any large plain used for pasture.—II. *a desert* or *wilderness;* הַמִּדְבָּר *the desert of Sinai.*—III. *speech, address,* Cant. 4:3.

דְּבַשׁ m. (with suff. דִּבְשִׁי).—I. *honey of bees.*—II. *honey dew,* collected in large quantities in Palestine.

דַּבֶּשֶׁת f.—I. *the hunch,* or more probably, *the pack-saddle of a camel.*—II. p.n. of a place, Jos. 19:11.

דָּגָה *multiplied,* Gen. 48:16.

דָּג (דָּאג) m., *fish;* pl. דָּגִים, דְּגֵי.

דָּגָה const. דְּגַת f., *a fish, fish* in general.

דָּגוֹן m., p. n. of an idol of the Philistines, probably in the form of a *fish.*

דָּגָן (const. דְּגַן) m.—I. *bread.*—II. *corn.*

דָּגַל part. דָּגוּל.—I. *marked, signalised,* Cant. 5:10.—II. fut. נִדְגֹּל *we will set up our banner,* Ps. 20:6. Niph. part. pl. נִדְגָּלוֹת *having banners,* i.e. *an army,* Cant. 6:4, 10; see next word.

דֶּגֶל m. (with suff. דִּגְלוֹ; pl. דְּגָלִים, דִּגְלֵי), *standard, banner.*

דָּגָן com.; see דגה.

דָּגַר *hatch, brood over eggs,* Isa. 34:15; Jer. 17:11.

דַּד m., dual דַּדִּים, דַּדֵּי *the two breasts of a woman.*

דָּדָה. Hith. fut. אֶדַּדֶּה *I will proceed gently, submissively, joyfully.*

דְּדָן (pl. דְּדָנִים), p. n. of the inhabitants of a district in the north of Arabia.

דֹּדָנִים m. pl., p. n. of a people.

דְּהַב m. Ch., *gold.*

מַדְהֵבָה f., an epithet of Babylon, lit. *place of gold,* Isa. 14:4.

דֶּהָיֵא p. n. of a people who were colonised in Samaria, Ezr. 4:9.

דָּהַם. Niph. part. נִדְהָם *reduced, impotent,* Jer. 14:9.

דָּהַר, part. דֹּהֵר *charging, attacking,* Nah. 3:2.

דַּהֲרָה f., *charge of cavalry;* pl. דַּהֲרוֹת, Jud. 5:22.

תִּדְהָר m., name of a tree; Vulg. ulnus; *the elm* or *box.*

דּוֹב same as דֹּב *bear;* see דבב.

דּוּב same as דָּאַב *wasting.* Hiph. part. pl. מְדִיבוֹת *things wasting,* Lev. 26:16.

דּוּג and דִּיג (from דָּג) *he shall fish,* Jer. 16:16.

דַּוָּג, דַּיָּג m., *a fisher.*

דּוּגָה f., *fishing,* Am. 4:2.

דּוּד I. root not used; Ch. *was agitated.*—II. same as יָדַד *he loved.*

דּוּד m.—I. *a pot* or *caldron;* pl. דְּוָדִים.—II. *basket;* pl. דּוּדִים.

דּוּדָאִים m. pl.—I. *baskets.*—II. *mandrakes,* plants used as philtres or love potions.

דּוֹד m. (pl. דּוֹדִים).—I. *love.*—II. *offices of love.*—III. *beloved.*—IV. *uncle.*

דּוֹדָה f., *aunt.*

דָּוִד, דָּוִיד p. n., *David* king of Israel

דָּוָה I. *was sick.*—II. *was unclean, polluted;* inf. דְּוֹתָהּ *her uncleanness* (i. e. the menses), Lev. 12:2.

דָּוֶה m., דָּוָה f., *sick, unclean.*

דְּוִי m., *sickness, disease,* Ps. 40:4.

דַּוָּי m., *habitual* (chronic) *disorder.*

דְּוֹת inf. of דָּוָה, which see.

מַדְוֶה m., *consuming disease.*

דּוּחַ. Hiph. הֵדִיחַ I. *expel,* Jer. 51:34.—II. *dispel,* i. e. scour clean.

דָּוִיד p.n., same as דָּוִד; see דּוּד.

דּוּךְ same as דָּכַךְ *beat, pounded,* Nu. 11:8.

מְדֹכָה f., *mortar,* Nu. 11:8.

דּוּכִיפַת f., LXX. ἔποψ; Vulg. upupa; *the hoopoe,* Lev. 11:19; Deu. 14:18.

דּוּם root not used, same as דָּמַם *was silent.*

דּוּמָה f.—I. *silent.*—II. *death.*—III. *the grave.*—IV. p. n. of a people of Arabia.

דּוּמִיָּה f.—I. *remaining, abiding.*—II. *quietness, silence.*

דּוּמָם m., *very quiet, silent.*

דּוּמֶּשֶׂק p. n., same as דַּמֶּשֶׂק.

דּוּן; see דִּין.

דּוֹנַג, דּוֹנָג m., *wax.*

דּוּץ (fut. יָדוּץ) *leaps, exults,* Job 41:14.

דּוּק Ch., *grind small,* Dan. 2:35.

דָּיֵק m., *entrenchment, foss, dyke,* used in sieges.

דּוּר I. *dwell, reside,* Ps. 84:11.—II *encircle, place round,* Eze. 24:5.

דּוּר Ch., *dwell.*

דּוּר m.—I. *a circle*, Isa 29:3.—II. *a ball*, Isa. 22:18.

דּוֹר, דֹּר m. (lit. *circle of years*).—I. *age, generation.*—II. *race of men;* עַד דֹּר, לְדֹר דֹּר, לְדֹר וָדֹר, דֹּר וָדֹר, כְּדֹר דֹּר וָדֹר *from generation to generation, for ever;* pl. דּוֹרִים *eternity;* דּוֹרוֹת *generations of men, posterity.*—III. *habitation* (see דּוּר); with אָבוֹת *sepulchre,* Ps. 49:20.

דָּר m. Ch., *age, generation.*

דּוֹר, דֹּאר, דּוֹר נָפָה and נָפוֹת דּ׳ p.n. of a city not far from Mount Carmel.

מְדוֹר m. Ch., *habitation.*

מְדָר m. Ch., the same.

מְדוּרָה f., *pile of fire.*

תְּדִירָא f. Ch., *a revolution;* בִּתְדִירָא *continually*, Dan. 6:17, 21.

דּוּרָא p.n. of a valley or plain in Babylonia.

דּוּשׁ and דִּישׁ (fut. יָדוּשׁ).—I. *tread, trample on.*—II. *tread out corn.*—III. metaphorically, *conquer enemies.* Niph. נָדוֹשׁ *was trampled down;* inf. abs. הִדּוֹשׁ. Hoph. fut. יוּדַשׁ *is trodden*, Isa. 28:27.

דּוּשׁ Ch., *is trodden*, Dan. 7:23.

דַּיִשׁ m., *time of treading out corn*, Lev. 26:5.

מְדוּשָׁה f., with suff. מְדֻשָׁתִי *my treading out*, Isa. 21:10.

דְּוִ see דָּוָה.

דָּחָה *drive, urge on to fall;* inf. abs. דָּחֹה; part. f. דְּחוּיָה *impelled.* Niph. *urged* or *impelled;* part. pl. נִדָּחִים, נִדְּחֵי. Pu. pl. דֹּחוּ *are driven.*

דְּחִי m. (with pause דֶּחִי), *impulse, being driven on.*

דַּחֲוָה Ch. f., pl. דַּחֲוָן Dan. 6:19. "instruments of music," Eng. Ver.; meaning uncertain.

מַדְחֶה m., *driving out, ruin*, Prov. 26:28.

דָּחַח Niph. fut. pl. יִדַּחוּ, same as דָּחָה Niph., *is urged, impelled.*

דְּחַל Ch., part. דְּחִיל *fearful.* Pa. *affright*, Dan. 4:2.

דֹּחַן m., *millet*, Eze. 4:9.

דָּחַף, part. pl. דְּחוּפִים *hurried, hastened.* Niph. *was hurried.*

מַדְחֵפוֹת f. pl.; לְמַדְ׳ *swiftly, hastily*, Ps. 140:12.

דָּחַק *press upon*, Joel 2:8; part. דֹּחֵק *oppressor*, Ju. 2:18.

דַּי m. (const. דֵּי, with suff. דַּיִּי), *a sufficiency, enough;* דֵּי הָשִׁיב *as much as shall restore*, Lev. 25:28; דַּיָּם *sufficient for them;* דֵּי חֲלֵב *enough of milk*, Pro. 27:27; בְּדֵי same as בְּ; כְּדֵי *as (it were) enough;* מִדֵּי same as מִן; מִדֵּי שָׁנָה בְּשָׁנָה *from year to year, yearly.*

דִּי Ch.—I. the relative pron. *who, which, what,* like אֲשֶׁר.—II. *of,* like the *de* of the modern European languages.—III. conj. like אֲשֶׁר *that.*—IV. same as כִּי, ὅτι. כְּדִי *when, as;* מִן דִּי *from the time when;* עַד דִּי *until.*

דִּי זָהָב (*enough of gold*); p.n. of a place in the desert near Sinai, Deut. 1:1.

דִּיבוֹן p.n.—I. of a town of the Moabites.—II. of a place in the tribe of Judah; same as דִּימוֹנָה.

דַּיָּג, דַּיָּג *fishermen;* see דּוּג.

דָּיָה root not used; Ch. דְּהָא *was black.*

דַּיָּה f., *black vulture, turkey buzzard;* LXX. ἴκτινος, Vulg. milvus, Deut. 14:13, &c.

דְּיוֹ m., *ink,* Jer. 36:18.

דִּימוֹן same as דִּיבוֹן p. n. of a town of Moab.

דִּימוֹנָה p. n. of a town in the tribe of Judah.

דִּין and דּוּן (pret. and part. דָּן; inf. and imper. דִּין; fut. יָדִין).—I. *judged.*—II *pleaded, defended.*—III. *punished,* with בְּ.—IV. *contend with one,* with עִם.—V. *govern,* with בְּ. Niph. part. נָדוֹן *contend,* 2 Sa. 19:10.

דִּין and דּוּן Ch., the same.

דִּין (דּוּן Job 19:29.) m.—I. *judgment.*—II. *cause for judgment* (דָּן and דִּין עָשָׂה *he pleaded a cause*).—III. *litigation, strife.*

דִּין m. Ch.—I. *judgment.*—II. *court of judgment.*—III. *punishment.*

דִּינָה p.n. of the daughter of Jacob.

דִּינָיֵא Ch., p.n. of a people of Assyria.

דַּיָּן m., *a judge;* Ch. pl. דַּיָּנִין *judges.*

דָּן p.n., *Dan.*—I. a son of Jacob and his tribe.—II. a city in the north of Palestine.

דָּנִיֵּאל ,דָּנִאֵל p.n., *Daniel.*

מָדוֹן m.—I. *dispute, contention;* pl. מְדוָנִים ,מִדְיָנִים.—II. אִישׁ מָדוֹן *man of height, stature* (see מדה), 2 Sa. 21:20.—III. p. n. of a city of the Canaanites.

מְדָן m. (pl. מְדָנִים).—I. *strifes, disputes.*—II. p.n. of the son of Abraham and Keturah.

מִדְיָנִי (pl. מִדְיָנִים) *Midianite;* see מִדְיָנִים.

מְדִינָה f., lit. *jurisdiction:* hence,—I *province.*—II. *region, country.*

מְדִינָה f. Ch., the same.

דּוֹדָנִים, see דּוֹדָנִים.

דִּיפַת p. n. of a son of Japhet, 1 Ch 1:6, a wrong reading for רִיפַת Gen. 10:3.

דָּיֵק *dyke;* see דּוּק.

דַּיִשׁ *tread;* see דּוּשׁ.

דִּישׁוֹן m.—I. a species of deer, Deut. 14:5.—II. p. n. of a son of Seir and of a district called after him.

דַּךְ *poor;* see דכך.

דָּךְ Ch. pron., *this, he;* fem. דָּךְ *she.*

דָּכָא. Pi. דִּכָּא.—I. *beat small, break.*—II. *trample on.*—Pu. *was broken, contrite.* Hith. fut. יִדַּכְּאוּ *shall be broken.* Niph. part., *beaten, oppressed,* Isa. 57:15.

דַּכָּא m.—I. *crushed.*—II. *humbled, dejected.*

דָּכָה *is broken,* Ps. 10:10. Niph. *broken, afflicted.* Pi. דִּכִּיתָ *thou hast broken.*

דֳּכִי m., with suff. דָּכְיָם, *their beating, dashing,* Ps. 93:3.

דָּכַךְ root not used, same as דָּכָה and דּוּךְ.

דַּךְ (with pause דָּךְ m.), *poor, mean, afflicted,* Pro. 26:28; יִשְׂנָא דַּכָּיו *makes hateful those whom it has afflicted.*

דַּכָּה f., *bruising,* θλάσις, Deu. 33:2.

דִּכֵּן Ch. pron., *this.*

דְּכַר Ch., same as זָכָר *male.*

דְּכַר m. Ch., *a ram;* pl. דִּכְרִין.

דִּכְרוֹן m. Ch. (emph. state דִּכְרוֹנָה), *memorial, record,* Ezr. 6:2.

דָּכְרָן m. Ch., the same, Ezr. 4:15.

דַּל *poor;* see דלה and דלל.

דָּלַג *leaping, skipping.* Pi. the same, with עַל.

דָּלָה I. *draw* (water from a well). Pi. *draw up* out of prison, Ps. 30:2. —II. *totter, vacillate, be lame;* דַּלְיוּ for דַּלּוּ, Pro. 26:7.

דַּל m. for דֶּלֶת *door,* Ps. 141:3.

דֶּלֶת *gate, door;* dual דַּלְתֵי, דְּלָתַיִם *folding, double doors* or *gates;* דַּלְתֵי שָׁמַיִם *the doors of heaven* (clouds?); דּ׳ פָּנִים *doors of the face* (jaws), Job 41:6; דּ׳ בֶּטֶן *doors of the womb.* Pl. דְּלָתוֹת; const. דַּלְתוֹת f. (m. Neh. 13:19). —I. *doors.*—II. *leaves, valves of gates.*—III. *leaves of a book,* Jer. 36:23.

דְּלִי m., *bucket,* Isa. 40:15.

דְּלִי m., dual דָּלְיַיִם (with suff. דָּלְיָו), *his drawings up* or *forth,* Nu. 24:7.

דָּלִית f., pl. דָּלִיּוֹת *boughs, branches.*

דְּלָיָהוּ, דְּלָיָה p. n. of a man.

דַּלָּה *poverty;* see דלל.

דָּלַח *disturb, render muddy* (of water), Eze. 32:2, 13.

דַּלְיוּ for דַּלּוּ Pi. imp. pl., from דלה.

דָּלַל *wasted, reduced, weakened.* Niph. (fut. וַיִּדַּל) *is wasted, reduced.*

דַּל m. (pl. דַּלִּים; f. דַּלָּה, pl. דַּלּוֹת), *poor, weak.*

דַּלָּה f.—I. *thin thread,* Isa. 38:12.—II. *smallness, poverty.*—III. *hair of the head,* Cant. 7:6; pl. דַּלּוֹת.

דְּלִילָה p. n. of the concubine of Samson.

דִּלְעָן p. n. of a town in the tribe of Judah.

דָּלַף I. *dropped.*—II. *shed tears.*

דֶּלֶף m., *rain drop.*

דַּלְפוֹן p. n. of the son of Haman.

דָּלַק (fut. יִדְלַק).—I. *burning, consuming.*—II. applied metaphorically to *strong mental affections,* with אַחֲרֵי. Hiph. *kindled, inflamed.*

דָּלֵק Ch., *burnt,* Dan. 7:9.

דַּלֶּקֶת f., *burning fever,* Deu. 28:22.

דֶּלֶת, דְּלָתַיִם, דְּלָתוֹת; see דלה.

דָּם; see אדם.

I. דָּמָה *was like to, resembled,* with אֶל, לְ. Niph. *was assimilated,* with כְּ. Pi. דִּמָּה.—I. *assimilated, compare,* with אֶל, לְ.—II. *imagined, thought, meditated.* Hithp. fut. אֶדַּמֶּה same as Niph., Isa. 14:14.

II. דָּמָה same as דָּמַם.—I. *silent, quiet.*—II. *ruined, destroyed.* Niph. *was silent, ruined.* Pi. *exterminate, destroy.*

דְּמָה Ch., *be similar, like.*

דְּמוּת f., *similitude, likeness;* כִּדְמוּת (also without כְּ) *as, like.*

דְּמִי m., *silence, rest.*

דֳּמִי m., the same.

דִּמְיוֹן m., same as דְּמוּת *likeness,* Ps. 17:12.

דָּמַם (pret. pl. דַּמּוּ; imp. and inf. דֹּם; fut. יִדֹּם; pl. יִדְּמוּ) *was dumb, quiet, inactive,* in consequence of some strong affection of the mind, with לְ; דּ׳ לַיהוָֹה *to wait silently upon the Lord.* Po. דּוֹמַמְתִּי *made silent,* Ps. 131:2. Hiph. הֵדַם *reduced to silence, ruined,* Jer. 8:14. Niph. נָדַם (fut. יִדַּמּוּ, תִּדֹּמִּי) *became silent, destroyed.*

דֻּמָּה f., *cut off, ruined,* Eze. 27:32.

דְּמָמָה f., *silence*, 1 Ki. 19:12.

דֹּמֶן m., *dung*.

דִּמְנָה p.n. of a town in the tribe of Zebulun.

מַדְמֵן p. n. of a town of Moab.

מַדְמֵנָה f.—I. *dung-hill*, Isa. 25:10.—II. p. n. of a town in the tribe of Benjamin.

מַדְמַנָּה p. n. of a town in the tribe of Judah, Jos. 15:31.

דֶּמַע m., lit. *tear* (with suff. דִּמְעֲךָ, Ex. 22:29), *juice of the grape, olive, &c.*

דִּמְעָה f. (pl. דְּמָעוֹת) — I. *tear.*—II. *weeping.*

דּוּמֶשֶׂק, דַּרְמֶשֶׂק, דַּמֶּשֶׂק p. n. —I. *Damascus*, a city of Syria.—II. *a Damascene* (supp. אִישׁ), Gen. 15:2.

דְּמֶשֶׁק or דְּמֶשֶׂק *damask*, silk cloth made at Damascus.

דָּן, see דִּין.

דֵּן Ch. pron., *this, that*; emph. דְּנָה; כִּדְנָה *thus*; עַל דְּנָה *thereupon*; אַחֲרֵי דְנָה *afterwards.*

דַּנָּה p. n. of a town in the tribe of Judah.

דִּנְהָבָה p. n. of a town in Edom.

דָּנִיֵּאל p.n.; see דִּין.

דָּנַנִּי Kal pret. with suff. and נ epenth., from דִּין.

דֵּעַ, דֵּעָה *knowledge;* see ידע.

דְּעֶה Kal imp. with ה parag., from ידע.

דְּעוּאֵל p. n. of a man.

דָּעַךְ.—I. *put out, extinguish.* — II. *made worse.* Niph. נִדְעֲכוּ *are extinguished*, Job 6:17. Pu. דֹּעֲכוּ the same, Ps. 118:12.

דַּעַת *knowledge*; see דע

דָּפָה root not used; (

דֳּפִי (with pause דֹּפִי *struction*, Ps. 50:2

דָּפַק.—I. *beat, drive* (33:13.—II. *knock* 5:2. Hith. *knocke*

דָּפְקָה p. n. of one of the Israelites in th

דַּק, דַּקָּה, דֹּק; see דקק.

דִּקְלָה p. n. of a distric Arabia, Gen. 10:27

דָּקַק (fut. יָדֹק, with suf *grind small.* Hiph suff. אֲדִיקֵם for קֵם also הָדֵק adv., *as* 30:36), *reduce to* fut. יוּדַק *is ground* 28:28.

דְּקַק Ch., *pounded.* A see דּוּק.

דַּק m., דַּקָּה f., *small, t*

דַּק s., *small dust.*

דֹּק m., *thin, fine cloth*

דָּקַר (fut. יִדְקֹר) *pierc* Niph. fut. יִדָּקֵר *through*, Isa. 13:1 מְדֻקָּרִים.—I. *they through.*—II. *slain* 4:9.

דֶּקֶר p. n. of a man.

מַדְקָרוֹת f. pl., *piercin* Pro. 12:18.

דַּר *marble;* see דרר.

דָּר, דֹּר *race;* see דּוּר.

דָּרָא root not used; (

דֵּרָאוֹן m., *abhorring*, 12:2.

דֵּרָאוֹן m. *abomination*, Isa. 66 : 24.

דָּרַב root not used ; (Arab. *point.*)

דָּרְבָן m. *goad ; βούκεντρον*, 1 Sa. 13 : 21.

דָּרְבוֹנוֹת f. pl. *goads*, Ecc. 12 : 11.

דָּרַג root not used ; (Arab. *step, stair*).

מַדְרֵגָה f. *steep place, precipice.*

דַּרְדַּע, דַּרְדַּר, דָּרוֹם, דְּרוֹר ; see דרר.

דָּרְיָוֶשׁ p. n. of the kings of Persia.—
—I. *Darius* the Median (Cyaxares II.).—II. *Darius* Hystaspes.—III. *Darius* Nothus.

דָּרַךְ I. *tread* (as grapes), with בְּ, עַל.
—II. *bend a bow*, by placing the left foot upon it; ד׳ חִצִּים *he shot arrows from the bent bow.*—III. *tread down, destroy.*—IV. *enter, pass in*, with בְּ, עַל.—V. *walk in state.*—Hiph. I. *caused to proceed, led.*—II. *bent as a bow.*—III. *trod down.*—IV. *took possession of.*

דֶּרֶךְ com. (with suff. דַּרְכִּי ; pl. דְּרָכִים, דַּרְכֵי ; dual דְּרָכַיִם).—I. *way, road;* ד׳ עֵץ *way to the tree;* ד׳ הַמֶּלֶךְ *king's highway.*—II. *journey;* ד׳ הַיּוֹם *a day's journey.*—III. *mode, manner, custom;* ד׳ יְהוָֹה *God's dealings.*—IV. *the fruits of one's ways*, Isa. 10: 24, &c.

מִדְרָךְ m., *foot-prints*, Deu. 2: 5.

דַּרְכְּמוֹן *drachm*, same as אֲדַרְכּוֹן.

דַּרְמֶשֶׂק *Damascus*, same as דַּמֶּשֶׂק.

דְּרָע com. Ch., *arm*, Dan. 2: 32.

אֶדְרָע com. Ch., *arm*, Ezr. 4: 23.

דַּרְקוֹן p.n. of a man.

דָּרַר root not used; (Arab. *flew, went, round*).

דְּרוֹר m.—I. *swallow* or *wild pigeon.*
—II. *spontaneously flowing myrrh*, Ex. 30: 23, hence:—III. *liberty;* קָרָא ד׳ לְ and בְּ *he proclaimed liberty to any one, he manumitted his slave;* שְׁנַת הַדְּרוֹר *the year of Jubilee*, in which all Hebrew slaves were free, Lev. 25: 10.

דַּר m., some unknown kind of *marble*, Ezr. 1: 6 ; LXX. *πίννινος λίθος.*

דַּרְדַּע p. n. of a man.

דַּרְדַּר m., *brambles.*

דָּרוֹם m., the country south of Judea

דָּרַשׁ I. *he sought, enquired for, into, &c.*, with בְּ, לְ, אֶל, אֶת.—II. *enquired about, concerning*, with עַל; used especially of asking supernatural counsel : with מֵעִם before the person asked; with בְּ, אֶל, לְ, before the being from whom the oracle is asked.—III. *demanded, asked, required:* with מִן before the person from whom the demand is made; דָּרַשׁ דָּם with מִן or מֵעִם or מִיַּד *required the blood of one slain*, i. e. avenge his death.—IV. *promoted, sought to accomplish;* ד׳ רָעַת פ׳ *sought to do him evil.*
—V ד׳ יְהוָֹה *sought the Lord*, in acts of worship.—VI. *cared for.* Niph. *was sought, enquired after.*

דַּרְיוֹשׁ m., *seeking*, Ezr. 10: 16.

מִדְרָשׁ m., *book, commentary*, 2 Chron. 13: 22.

דָּשָׁא *became grassy*, Joel 2: 22. Hiph. *sent forth grass*, Gen. 1: 11, 12.

דֶּשֶׁא m., *tender herb, first blades of grass.*

דָּשֵׁן *grew fat*, Deu. 31: 20.—Pi. דִּשֵּׁן

I. *made, considered fat.*—II. *anointed.*—III. from דִּשֵּׁן *removed ashes.* Pu. *was made fat, satisfied.* Hothpa. pret. הֻדַּשְּׁנָה *made fat* (of a sword), Isa. 34:6.

דָּשֵׁן m., *fat, fruitful.*

דֶּשֶׁן m. (with suff. דִּשְׁנִי).—I. *fatness of meat.*—II. *fertility.*—III. *ashes,* specially those of burnt-offerings, &c. which were used for manure.

דָּת f. (pl. דָּתִים, דָּתֵי), *edict, mandate, law.*

דָּת f. Ch., *law, edict.*

דְּתָבַר m. Ch., *judges* or *lawyers,* Dan. 4:12, 20.

דֶּתֶא emph. דִּתְאָה Ch. m., same as Heb. דֶּשֶׁא *grass.*

דֹּתַיִן p. n. of a place north of Samaria.

דָּתָן p. n. of one of the accomplices of Korah.

ה

הַ (הָ, הֶ).—I. def. art. ὁ, ἡ, τό *the.*—II. demon. pron. *this;* הַיּוֹם *this day.*—III. relat. pron. *who, which;* הֶהָלְכוּא *who went,* Jos. 10:24; הֶעָלֶיהָ *that which is above her.*—IV. sign of the vocative; הַמֶּלֶךְ *O King!* הַבַּעַל *O Baal!* 1 Ki. 18:26.

הֲ (הַ, הֶ) pref., sign of an interrogation; הֲשֹׁמֵר אָחִי אָנֹכִי *am I my brother's keeper,* Gen. 4:9.

הֵא (הָא Ch.) *behold!*

הֶאָח *aha!* exclamation of joy or scorn.

הֶאֶזְנִיחוּ for הִזְנִיחוּ Hiph. pret. pl., from זנח.

הַב with ה parag. הָבָה; pl. הָבוּ Kal imper., from יהב.

הָבֵא, הָבִיא Hiph. imper., from בּוֹא.

הֻבָאת Hoph. pret. f., from בּוֹא.

הֹבְאִישׁ for הוֹבִישׁ Hiph., from בּוֹשׁ.

הַבְהָבִים *gifts;* see יהב

הֵבוּ Hos. 4:18, pret. pl. for יָהֲבוּ, from יהב.

הִבּוֹק Niph. inf., from בקק.

הָבִי Ruth 3:15, Kal imp. f., from יהב, or Hiph. imp. f. for הָבִיא, from בּוֹא.

הָבַל (fut. יֶהְבַּל) *act vainly, sinfully.* Hiph. *cause to act vainly,* Jer. 23:16

הֶבֶל m. (with suff. הֶבְלִי; pl. הֲבָלִים, הַבְלֵי).—I. *vanity, instability, deception.*—II. *idols.*—III. *abortions,* Ecc. 6:4, and thence, *men* in general.—IV. adv., *vainly, in vain.*—V. p. n., *Abel,* the son of Adam.

הֲבֵל m., *vanity.*

הָבְנִים (הוֹבְנִים) *ebony,* Eze. 27:15.

הָבַר (Arab. *that which cuts*); הֹבְרֵי שָׁמַיִם *they who cut, divide the heavens, astrologers,* Isa. 47:13; Vulg. augures cœli; LXX. ἀστρολόγοι τοῦ οὐρανοῦ.

הָבַר Hiph. inf. from בּוּר.

הָגַג root not used; (Syr. *imagined*).

הָגִיג m., *deep, ardent meditation.*

הָגָה (fut. יֶהְגֶּה; inf. הָגֹה).—I. *murmur, coo, growl.*—II. *meditate.*—III. *declare one's meditations,* with בְּ.—IV. *discern, separate.* Po. inf. הֹגוֹ *utter, speak.* Hiph. part. pl. מַהְגִּים *mutterers,* i. e. *enchanters,* Isa. 8:19.

הֶגֶה m.—*murmur, whisper.*—II. *thunder.*

הָגוּת f., *meditation*, Ps. 49:4.

הִגָּיוֹן } m., *a musical stringed-instrument or the sound of one.*
הֶגְיוֹן }

הֹגָה 2 Sa. 20:13, for הוֹגָה Hiph. from יגה *he removed*

הָגוֹ Kal inf. abs. from II. הגה.

הֹגוֹ Po. inf. from הגה.

הָגִין m., הֲגִינָה f., *straight, commodious*, Eze. 42:12.

הָגְלָת (Syr. for הָגְלְתָה) Hoph. pret. f., from גלה.

הָגָר p.n. of the mother of Ishmael.

הַגְרִים, הַגְרִיאִים p. n. of a people castward of Gilead.

הֵד *shout;* see הדד.

הַדָּבְרִין m. pl. Ch., title of certain officers in the court of Babylon; "counsellors," Eng. Ver.

הָדַד root not used; (Arab. *shouting*).

הֵידָד *shouting* (of bodies of men).

הֵד m., *shouting*, Eze. 7:7.

הֲדַד p. n. of a king of Edom.

הֲדַדְעֶזֶר p.n. of a king of Syria.

הֲדַדְרִמּוֹן p. n. of a town not far from Megiddo.

הָדָה *guided* (his hand), Isa. 11:8.

הֹדוּ (for הִנְדּוּ Hindu), p. n. *Hindustan*, India.

הֲדוֹרָם p.n. of an Arab tribe, descended from Joktan, Gen. 10:27.

הִדַּי, חוּרַי p. n. of a man.

הָדַךְ *break down, overturn*, Job 40:12.

הָדַם root not used; (Arab. *destruction*).

הֲדֹם m., *footstool.*

הַדָּם m. Ch., *piece, fragment.*

הֲדַס m., *myrtle*; pl. הֲדַסִּים.

הֲדַסָּה p.n. the former name of Esther.

הָדַף (fut. יֶהְדֹּף), *thrust out, drive back.*

הָדַר (fut. יֶהְדַּר), *honoured, dignified* (in dress), Isa. 63:1; with פְּנֵי פ׳ *take the part of any one.* Niph *was honoured*, Lam. 5:12. Hith *was glorious*, Pro. 25:5.

הַדַּר Ch. Pa. *honoured.*

הָדָר m., *glorious, honourable, dignified.*

הֶדֶר m., *honour*, Dan. 11:20.

הֲדָרָה f. (const. הַדְרַת), *honourable* in apparel).

הֻדַּשְׁנָה Hothp. pret. f., from דשן.

הָהּ *ah!* exclamation of grief.

הוֹ same as הוֹי *alas!*

הוּא pers. pron. m.—I. *he, it.*—II *this, the same.*

הֲוָא Ch., *was;* same as הֲוָה.

הֱוֵא for הֱוֵה imp., from הוה.

הוּבַר Hoph. pret., from אבד.

הוֹבָדָה Ch. Aph. inf., from אבד.

הוֹבִישׁ Hiph., from בּוֹשׁ and יָבֵשׁ.

הוֹד *glory;* see with its comp. in נהד.

הוֹדָה Hiph. pret. הוֹדוּ; imp. pl. הוֹדוּת; inf. from ידה.

הָוָה.—I. *fell, descended.*—II. *existed, was;* part. הֹוֶה; imper. הֱוֵא, הֱוֵה, f. הֱוִי; fut. יְהוּא (for יְהוּ, יֶהֱוֶה).

הֲוָה, הֲוָא Ch., *was.*

הַוָּה f.—I. *intense desire, lust.*—II. *accident, injury, ruin.*

הֹוָה f., *accident, injury.*

הַיָּה f., same as הַוָּה *calamity.*

יְהֹוָה *Jehovah*, the name whereby God would be known to the Hebrews, Ex. 3:14. Written with prefixes (like אֲדֹנָי), מֵיְהוָֹה, לַיהוָֹה, בַּיְהוָֹה; with אֲדֹנָי it is written יֱהוִֹה (like אֱלֹהִים).

יָהּ an abbreviated form of יְהוָֹה.

יֵהוּא p. n.—I. *Jehu*, king of Israel.—II. of a man.

יוֹאָחָז, יְהוֹאָחָז p. n.—I. a king of Israel, the son of Jehu.—II. a king of Judah, the son of Josiah.

יוֹאָשׁ, יְהוֹאָשׁ p. n.—I. a king of Judah, the son of Ahaziah.—II. a king of Israel, the son of Joash.

יְהוֹזָבָד p. n. of a man.

יוֹחָנָן, יְהוֹחָנָן (*the Lord is merciful*), Ἰωάννης, p. n. of a man.

יוֹיָדָע, יְהוֹיָדָע p. n. of a man.

יְכָנְיָהוּ, יוֹיָכִין, יְהוֹיָכִין p. n. of a king of Judah, the son of Jehoiakim.

יוֹקִים, יוֹיָקִים, יְהוֹיָקִים (*the Lord confirmeth*), p. n. of a king of Judah, the son of Josiah.

יוֹיָרִיב, יְהוֹיָרִיב p. n. of a man.

יוֹנָדָב, יְהוֹנָדָב (*the Lord's gift*), p. n. of a man.

יוֹנָתָן, יְהוֹנָתָן (*the Lord giveth*, Θεόδωρος), p. n. of a man.

יְהוֹעַדָּה (*the Lord adorneth*), p. n. of a man.

יְהוֹעַדָּן p. n. of a woman.

יוֹצָדָק, יְהוֹצָדָק (*the Lord is righteous*), p. n. of a man.

יוֹרָם, יְהוֹרָם (*the Lord is exalted*), p. n.—I. a king of Judah, the son of Jehosaphat.—II. a king of Israel, the son of Ahab.

יְהוֹשֶׁבַע (*the Lord hath sworn*), p. n. of a son of king Joram.

יְהוֹשֻׁעַ, יְהוֹשׁוּעַ (*the Lord saveth*), p. n. of a man, *Joshua*.

יְהוֹשָׁפָט (*the Lord judgeth*), p. n.—I. of a king of Judah, the son of Asa.—II. of many men.

יוֹאָב p. n. of a man.

יוֹאָח p. n. of a man.

יוֹאֵל (*the Lord he is God*), p. n. of a man.

יוֹזָבָד p. n. of a man.

יוֹזָכָר p. n. of a man.

יוֹכֶבֶד p. n. of the mother of Moses.

יוֹעֵד (*the Lord is witness*), p. n. of a man.

יוֹעֶזֶר (*the Lord helpeth*), p. n. of a m.

יוֹעָשׁ p. n. of a man.

יוֹתָם p. n.—I. of a king of Judah, the son of Uzziah.—II. of a man.

הוֹהָם p. n. of a king.

הוֹ, הוֹי interj. of exhortation, threatening, grief, with אֶל, עַל and לְ.

הוּךְ Ch., *proceed, go*; fut. יְהָךְ; inf. מְהָךְ.

הוּכָּה for הֻכָּה Hoph., from נָכָה.

הֻלֶּדֶת, הוּלֶּדֶת Hoph. inf., from ילד.

הוּלְּלוּ for הֻלְּלוּ Pu. pret. pl., from הלל.

הוֹלֵלוֹת, הוֹלֵלוּת; see הלל.

הוּם pret. הָם *perturb, harass*, Deu. 7:23. Niph. *was moved, excited*; fut. f. וַתֵּהֹם. Hiph. *heave, swell, be tumultuous*.

מְהוּמָה f., *perturbation, tumult, vexation*.

תְּהוֹם com. (pl. תְּהוֹמוֹת), *the deep, the ocean*; from its tossing and roaring.

הוֹמִיָּה, הוֹמָה part. f., from המה.

הוֹמָם p. n. of a man.

הוּן Kal, root not used; (Arab. *was light*). Hiph. *made light of, despised*, with inf. and לְ.

הוֹן m.—I. *wealth, plenty.*—II. adv. *enough*, Pro. 30:15, 16.

הִין m., a liquid measure containing twelve logs (לֹג).

הוֹר, הֹ־עַד "thy progenitors," Eng. Ver., Gen. 49:26, from הרה.

הוֹשְׁבוֹתִים Zec. 10:6. Hiph. pret. 1. pers., with suff., for הוֹשַׁבְתִּים, from ישׁב.

הוֹשָׁמָע (*the Lord heareth*), p. n. of a m.

הוֹשֵׁעַ p.n., name of Joshua, afterwards changed to יְהוֹשֻׁעַ.

הוֹשַׁעְיָה (*the Lord saveth*), p.n. of a m.

הות Po. fut. תְּהוֹתְתוּ *attack unjustly*, Ps. 62:4.

הוּתַל Pu. or Hoph., from התל.

הָזָה *doze, sleep idly*, Isa. 56:10.

הֲזָדָה Ch. Aph. inf., from זוּד.

הִזְדַּמִּנְתּוּן Ch. Ithp., from זמן.

הִזִּילוּ Hiph. pret. pl., from זלל.

הִזַּכּוּ for הִתְזַכּוּ Hithp. imper. pl., from זכה.

הִזָּרוֹתֵיכֶם for הִזָּרוֹתְכֶם Niph. inf., with suff., from זרה.

הֶחְבְּאָתָה Jos. 6:17. Hiph. pret. fem., with ה parag., for הֶחְבִּיאָה, from חבא.

הֶחֳדַלְתִּי Jud. 9:9, 11, 13. for הֶחָדַלְתִּי Kal pret. 1. pers., with ה interrog., from חדל.

הֶחֱטִי Hiph. pret. for הֶחֱטִיא, הַחֲטִי inf. for הַחֲטִיא, from חטא.

הֵחֵל Hiph. pret., Eze. 20. Niph. inf, with suff. and pref. לְהֵחַלּוֹ, Lev. 21:4; see חלל.

הַט Hiph. imp. apoc., from נטה.

הֻטַּמָּא Hothp., from טמא.

הִטַּתּוּ Hiph. pret. 3. pers. fem. with suff., from נטה.

הַטֹּתָהּ Hiph. inf. with suff., from נטה.

הִי *lamentation*; see נהה.

הִיא pers. pron. f., *she, this*; see הוּא; with art. הַהִיא *the same, this very* (*woman, &c.*); Ch. the same.

הֻיְּדוֹת f. pl., Neh. 12:8; wrong reading for הוּדוֹת *dignities*; see in נָהַד.

הֵידָד *shouting*; see הדד.

הָיָה (inf. abs. הָיֹה; const. הֱיֹה, הֱיוֹת, with pref. בִּהְיוֹת; imper. הֱיֵה, f. הֲיִי, pl. הֱיוּ; fut. יִהְיֶה, apoc. יְהִי).—I. *came to pass* וַיְהִי, with כְּ and וְ *and it came to pass that.*—II. *was*, i.e. *existed*; never used as the logical copula, *is, was*; const. with לְ *there was to any one*, i.e. *he had*; with לְ and the inf. *was about to, intent upon*; with כְּ *was the same as*; with עִם *was, had communication with.* Niph. *came to be, took effect, had been*, Dan. 2:1; 8:27.

הַיָּה *ruin*; see הוה.

הֵיךְ Ch., same as אֵיךְ *how?*

הֵיכָל m. (pl. הֵיכָלוֹת, הֵיכָלִים).—I. *any great and splendid building, temple, palace*, &c.—II. *the temple of Jehovah built by Solomon.*

הֵיכַל m. Ch.—I. *palace.*—II. *temple.*

הֵילִיכִי Hiph. imp. f., from הלך, ילך.

הֵילֵל *glorious*; see הלל.

הִים *swell*; see הוּם.

הֵימָן p. n. of a man.

הֵימִן Ch. Aph. pret., from אמן.

הֵימִיר for הֵמִיר Hiph., from מוּר.

הִין *light*; see הוּן.

הַיְתִי Ch. Aph. pret.; הַיְתָיָה inf.; הֵיתָיִת Hoph. pret. f. 3. pers.; הֵיתָיוּ pl., from אתה.

הַךְ Hiph. imp. apoc., from נכה.

הִכּוּם Hiph. pret. pl., with suff., from נכה

הַכּוֹת Hiph. inf., from נכה.

הִכּוֹנֵן for הִתְכּוֹנֵן Hithpo., from כּוּן.

הָכִיל Eze. 21:33, for הַאֲכִיל Hiph. inf., from אכל (others make it Hiph., from כּוּל).

הַכֵּינִי Hiph imp., with suff. for הַכֵּנִי, from נכה.

הִכְּךָ Hiph. pret. with suff., from נכה.

הֶכְלַמְנוּ for הִכְלַמְנוּ Hiph. pret. pl. 1. pers., from כלם.

הִכָּם Hiph. pret. with suff., from נכה.

הֲכִנּוּ for הֲכִנֹּנוּ Hiph. pret. pl. 1. pers., from כּוּן.

הִכַּנִי Hiph. pret. with suff., from נכה.

הָכַר, fut. תַּהְכְּרוּ *ye contemn*, Job 19:3.

הַכָּרָה *astonishment;* see נכר.

הַל, the הֲ inter. and the pref. לְ written thus, for reverence sake, in the phrase הַל יְיָ Deu. 32:6.

הָלָא. Niph. part. f. נַהֲלָאָה *removed, cast away,* Mic. 4:7.

הָלְאָ *removed;* הָלְאָה pa., *thence, farther, onward;* denotes time and place.

הֶלְאָת for הֶלְאֲתָה Hiph. pret. f., from לאה.

הִלּוֹ Kal inf. with suff., from הלל.

הִלּוּלִים *great praise;* see הלל.

הַלָּזוּ, הַלָּזֶה, הַלָּז; see זֶה.

הָלַךְ and **יָלַךְ** (part. הוֹלֵךְ; pl. הֹלְכִים; f. הֹלֶכֶת, הֹלְכָה; inf. הָלוֹךְ; const. הֲלוֹךְ, לֶכֶת; with suff. לֶכְתְּךָ; imper. לֵךְ; with ה parag. לְכָה, לֵךְ; fut. יֵלֵךְ, וַיֵּלֶךְ; poet. יַהֲלֹךְ, אֶהֱלֹךְ, תְּהַלֵּךְ).—I. *walked, went, proceeded;* const. with many particles which modify the sense, e. g. with אַחֲרֵי *followed;* with אֵת, עִם *accompanied;* with בְּ *walked with,* i. e. brought, Hos. 5:6.—II. *made way, progress;* וַיֵּלֶךְ הָלֹךְ וְגָדֵל *increased continually.*—III. *proceeded, went on.*—IV. *went off, disappeared,* i. e. died, Gen. 15:2; Ps. 39:14. Niph. נֶהֱלָכְתִּי *I set about departing,* Ps. 109:23. Pi. הִלֵּךְ *went, proceeded.* Hiph. הוֹלִיךְ and הֵילִיךְ.—I. *cause to go, lead, conduct.*—II. *let perish,* Ps. 125:5. Hith. הִתְהַלֵּךְ *become walking, proceed, go on, go about.*

הֵלֶךְ m.—I. *going, travel,* 2 Sa. 12:4. —II. *a stream,* 1 Sa. 14:26.

הֲלַךְ Ch., *walked, proceeded.* Aph. the same.

הֲלָךְ m. Ch., *proceeds of the state, taxation.*

הֲלִיךְ m.; הֲלִיכָה f.; pl. הֲלִיכוֹת.—I *step.*—II. *way.*—III. *procedure.*

מַהֲלָךְ m.—I. *walk.*—II. *journey.*

תַּהֲלוּכָה f., *procession,* Neh. 12:31.

הֶהָלְכוּא, הָלְכוּא *who went,* Jos. 10:24. Kal pret. pl. with א parag. and ה relat., from הלך.

הָלַל *shone.* Pi. הִלֵּל.—I. *praised.* — II. *gloried.* — III. *pronounced vain-glorious, foolish, mad;* const. with לְ (הַלְלוּ־יָהּ [without dag. forte] *praise ye the Lord*). Pu. הֻלַּל *was praised;* part. מְהֻלָּל *praised, to be praised.* Hiph. הֵהֵל *shone.* Hith. *began to glory, boast.* Po. fut. יְהוֹלֵל *make a fool, shame.* Poal part. מְהוֹלָל *mad.* Hithpo. *became mad.*

הֵילֵל m., *Lucifer,* i.e. the morning star, Isa. 14:12.

הוֹלֵלָה f. (pl. הוֹלֵלוֹת), *glory, folly.*

הוֹלֵלוּת f., *folly*, Ecc. 10:13.

הִלּוּלִים m. pl.—I. *great praise, subject of praise*, Lev. 19:24.—II. *songs of, feasts of, joy*, Ju. 9:27.

הִלֵּל p.n. of a man.

מַהֲלָל m., *praising*, Pro. 27:21.

מַהֲלַלְאֵל (*the praise of God*), p.n. of a m.

תְּהִלָּה f.—I. *praise*.—II. *hymn of praise*; pl. תְּהִלּוֹת *praises*; pl. m. תְּהִלִּים *the book of Psalms*.

תָּהֳלָה f., *folly, emptiness*, Job 4:18

הָלַם *struck, beat*.

הֲלֹם adv., *hither*; עַד־הֲלֹם *thus far*.

הֶלֶם (*blow*), p.n. of a man.

הַלְמוּת f., *workman's hammer*, Jud. 5:26.

יַהֲלֹם m., name of a gem, *adamant*.

מַהֲלֻמוֹת f. pl., *beatings, stripes*.

הַם or הָם p.n. of an unknown place, Gen. 14:5.

הֵם, הֵמָּה pers. pron. m. pl., *these, they*; with the art. הָהֵם, הָהֵמָּה.

הִמּוֹן Ch., *these, they*.

הַמְּדָתָא p. n. of a man.

הָמָה (inf. const. הֲמוֹת; fut. יֶהֱמֶה; part. m. הֹמֶה; f. הוֹמָה).—I. *ferment* (as wine).—II. *moved* (as the bowels with mental emotions).—III. *roar, rage, murmur, moan*; part. f. pl. הוֹמִיּוֹת *noisy*, i.e. full of people, Pro. 1:21.

הֵם or הָם, pl. הָמִים; with suff. and pref. מֵהֱמֵהֶם *their riches*, Ezr. 7:11.

הֶמְיָה f., *sound of the lute*, Isa. 14:11.

הָמוֹן m. (f. Job 31:34).—I. *emotion*, lit. *moving the bowels*.—II. *musical sounds*.—III. *multitude of men, &c.*

הָמוֹן m., *abundance*; with suff. הֲמֹנְכֶם, Eze. 5:7.

הֲמוֹנָה the mystical name of a city, Eze. 39:16; see preceding verse.

הֵמִין for הֵימִין Hiph., from ימן.

הֲמִיתְתִּיו 1 Sa. 17:35, for הֲמִתְתִּיו, הֲמַתְתִּיו. Hiph. pret. 1. pers. with suff., from מות.

הֻמְּכוּ for הוּמְכוּ Hoph. pl., from מכך.

הָמַל root not used; (Arab. *rain continually*).

הֲמוּלָּה הֲמֻלָּה f., *commotion, rushing of wings*.

הָמַם (fut. וַיָּהָם, יָהֹם; inf. const. with suff. הֻמָּם).—I. *put in motion, agitated*.—II. *dispersed, put to the rout*.

הָמָן p.n. of a man.

הָמֹן *multitude*; see in הָמָה.

הַמְנִיךְ or הַמְנוּךְ Ch., *collar, bracelet*, Dan. *c*. 5.

הִמֵּס Niph. inf., from מסס.

הַמְסִיו Ch. for הַמְסוּ Hiph. pl., from מסה.

הֶמֶס m., pl. הֲמָסִים *slight noises*, Isa. 64:1.

הָמַר root not used; (Arab. *poured water*).

מַהֲמֹרוֹת f. pl., *torrents, floods*, Ps. 140:11.

הַמִּרוֹתָם Hiph. inf. with suff. and dag. euphon., from מרה.

הֵמַתָּה Hiph. 2. pers. with ה parag., הֵמַתִּי 1. pers., הֲמִתִּיהָ 1. pers. with suff., הֲמִתֶּם 2. pers. pl., from מות.

הֵן, הֵנָּה pers. pron. f. pl., *they, them*; with art. הָהֵנָּה; adv., *here, hither*; הֵנָּה וָהֵנָּה *hither and thither*, מִמְּךָ וָהֵנָּה *from thee hitherwards*, עַד הֵנָּה *thus far*.

הִנּוּן pers. pron. m. pl. Ch., *he*; f. הִנִּין *she*.

הֵן ,הֶן־ ,הִנֵּה ,הִנֶּה interj., *behold! lo!* with suff. הִנְנִי ,הִנֵּנִי ,הִנֶּנִּי *behold me! lo I am here!* הִנְּךָ *behold thou art, &c.*

הֵן Ch., *if, whether*; הֵן...הֵן *either... or.*

הַנַּח Hiph. imp., from ינח.

הִנִּיחַ Hiph. הֻנִּיחַ Hoph., from ינח.

הֲנָחָה *rest*; see נוּחַ.

הִנֹּם p. n.; גֵּי בֶן־הִנֹּם *the valley of the sons of Hinnom* (where Molech was worshipped).

הֵנַע p. n. of a city in Mesopotamia.

הַנְעֵל Ch. Aph. pret., הַנְעָלָה inf., from עלל.

הֲנָפָה Ch. for הָנִיף Hiph. inf., from נוּף.

הָסָה. Pi. imp. הַס; with pause הָס *hush! be silent!* pl. הַסּוּ. Hiph. (fut. apoc. וַיַּהַס), *made to be silent*, Nu. 13:30.

הִסִּית for הֵסִית Hiph., from סוּת.

הַעַל Hiph. imper. apoc., from עלה.

הֶעֱלָה for הֶעֱלָה Hiph., from עלה.

הָעֲלָה for הָעֳלָה Hoph., from עלה.

הֲפֻגוֹת *remission*; see פּוּג.

הַפֹּדְךָ part. with suff. and art., from פדה.

הָפַךְ (fut. יַהֲפֹךְ; inf. הָפוֹךְ; const. הֲפֹךְ; with suff. הָפְכִי).—I. *turn over.* — II. *subvert, ruin.* — III. *change, pervert, convert.* . Niph. נֶהְפַּךְ *was turned, &c.*; with עַל, לְ *to* or *into, was ruined.* Hoph. הָהְפַּךְ *turned upon, against*, Job 30:15. Hith. part. מִתְהַפֵּךְ *becomes turned about*; f. מִתְהַפֶּכֶת the same; fut. f. תִּתְהַפֵּךְ *becomes changed*, Job 38:14.

הֶפֶךְ ,הֹפֶךְ m., *perversion*, Eze. 16:34.

הֲפֵכָה f., *subversion*, Gen. 19:29.

הֲפַכְפַּךְ m., *turning, tortuous*, Pro. 21:8.

מַהְפֵּכָה f., *overthrow, subversion.*

מַהְפֶּכֶת f., *imprisonment, stocks*; בֵּית הַמַּהְפֶּכֶת *prison-house.*

תַּהְפּוּכָה f. (pl. תַּהְפּוּכוֹת), *perversion, perverseness.*

הַפְרְכֶם Hiph. inf. with suff., from פרר.

הִצְטַיֵּד Hith. denom., from צַיִד or צוּד.

הַצָּלָה *deliverance*; see נצל.

הֹצֶן m., *an armament, force*, Eze 23:24.

הַר m. (with art. הָהָר; pl. הָרִים; with art. הֶהָרִים), aff. הֲרָרִי ,הַרְרִי; pl. הֲרָרֶיהָ; also const. הַרְרֵיהָ, הָרֵי ,הֲרָרֵי.—I. *mountain.*—II. *mountainous district.* — III. *fastness, stronghold.*—IV. *strong men*, Isa. 41:15; with ה ָ— affix (הָרָה), *towards the mountain.*

הֲרָרִי *a mountaineer*, 2 Sa. 23:33.

הָרָרִי the same, *v.* 11, a title of Shammah.

הֹר p. n.—I. of the mountain in Edom where Aaron was buried.—II. of a mountain in Palestine.

הַר חֶרֶס p. n. of a mountain in the tribe of Dan, Jud. 1:35.

הָרָא p. n. of a region in Syria.

הַרְאֵל p. n. of the altar of burnt-offering, Eze. 43:15; elsewhere אֲרִיאֵל which see in ארה.

הֶרֶב Hiph. imp. apoc., from רבה.

הָרַג (fut. יַהֲרֹג; inf. הָרוֹג; const. הֲרֹג), with לְ, בְּ *kill, slay*, generally with violence. Niph. *was slain.* Pu. הֹרַג *slain.*

הֶרֶג m., } *slaughter, slaying.*
הֲרֵגָה f., }

הָרָה (inf. abs. הָרֹה, הָרוֹ; fut. f. תַּהַר, וַתַּהַר).—I. *conceived, became pregnant,* with לְ, אֶת; part. f. הוֹרָה; inf. הֹרוֹ *she that conceiveth.*—II. *conceive in the mind, devise.* Pu. הֹרָה *conceived,* Job 3:3.

הָרָה adj. f., *pregnant;* pl. הָרוֹת.

הָרִיָּה adj. f., pl. with suff. הָרִיּוֹתָיו *her pregnant women.*

הֵרוֹן } m., *conception.*
הֵרָיוֹן }

הַרְהֹר m. Ch., *imaginations,* Dan. 4:2, from Pa. Ch. הַרְהֵר.

הֹרָם p.n. of a king of Canaan.

הָרָם p. n. of a man.

הֵרֹמּוּ Niph. imp. pl., from רמם.

הַרְמוֹן m. (same as אַרְמוֹן) *palace,* Am. 4:3.

הָרָן p.n. of a man.

הֹרַנִי Hiph. pret. with suff., from ירה.

הָרַס (inf. הָרוֹס; fut. יֶהֱרֹס, יַהֲרֹס) *broke down.*—1. *houses, &c.*—2. *men,* i. e. *put down, reduced.*—3. *teeth,* Ps. 58:7. Niph. *was broken down.* Pi. *destroyed;* as Kal.

הֶרֶס m., עִיר הַהֶרֶס p. n. of an unknown city in Egypt, Isa. 19:18; "city of destruction," Eng. Ver.; some read חֶרֶס which see.

הֲרִיסָה f., *broken down,* Am. 9:11.

הֲרִיסוּת f., *ruin,* Isa. 49:19.

הֶרֶף Hiph. imp. apoc., from רפה.

הִרְצָת Ch. for הִרְצָתָה Hiph. pret. f. 3. pers., from רצה.

הָרָר, הָרֵר, הֲרָרִי; see הַר.

הָשֵׁב with pause for הָשֵׁב, הָשִׁיב Hiph imp. from שׁוּב.

הָשַּׁמָּה (in some editions הָשַּׁמּוֹה) Hoph. inf. with suff., from שׁמם.

הָשֵׁם p. n. of a man.

הַשְׁמָעוּת *hearing;* see שׁמע.

הָשַׁע Ps. 39:14, Hiph. imp., from שׁעה; Isa. 6:10, Hiph. imp., from שׁעע.

הִשְׁתַּחֲוָה Hithp., from שׁחה.

הִשְׁתַּעְשַׁע Hithpa., from שׁעע.

הִתְאֹשָׁשׁוּ Hithp., from אִישׁ.

הֲתָבוּתָךְ Ch. Aph. inf. with suff., from תּוּב.

הִתְגָּר Hithp. imp. apoc., from גרה.

הִתְוַדָּה Hithp., from ידה.

הִתְחַל Hithp. imp. apoc., from חלה.

הֵתָיוּ for הֶאֱתָיוּ which is for הַאֲתָיוּ Hiph. imp. pl., from אתה.

הֲתִימְךָ for הֲתִמְּךָ Hiph. inf. with suff., from תמם.

הִתּוּךְ *melting;* see נתך.

הֲתָךְ p. n. of a Persian eunuch.

הָתַל. Pi. הֵתֶל, הֵתֵל; (inf. הָתֵל; fut. יְהָתֵל; pl. יְהָתֵלּוּ, תְּהָתֵלּוּ) *deluded, deceived.* Hoph. הוּתַל *deceived.*

הֲתֻלִּים m. pl., *mockeries,* Job 17:2.

מַהֲתַלּוֹת f. pl., *delusions,* Isa. 30:10.

הֵתֵל Pi.; see התל.

הִתְנַבּוֹת Hithp. inf., from נבא.

הִתְנַבֵּיתָ Hithp. pret., from נָבָא.

ו

וְ, וּ, וָ, וַ conj., used to connect together words, phrases, sentences, &c.; it may be interpreted in modern languages by any of the particles which are applied to the same use: such as *and, but, if, moreover,* &c. according to the context.

וְדָן p.n. of a place in Arabia.

וָהֵב Num. 21:14, probably p. n. of a place or well.

וָו m., pl. וָוִים *hooks* or *pins* at the top of the pillars of the tabernacle.

וָזָר *loaded;* see יזר.

וַיְזָתָא p. n. of a son of Haman.

וָלָד, וֶלֶד; see ילד.

וַנְיָה p.n. of a man.

וָפְסִי p.n. of a man.

וַשְׁנִי p.n. of a man.

וַשְׁתִּי p.n. of the wife of Ahasuerus.

ז

זְאֵב m.—I. *a wolf.*—II. p. n. of one of the princes of Midian.

זֹאת demonst. pron. f. of זֶה *this, that.*

זֹה for זֹאת *this.*

זוֹ for זֶה relat. pron. *this,* Ps. 132:12.

זָבַב root not used; (Arab. *fly*).

זְבוּב m., *fly* or *bee;* בַּעַל זְבוּב (*fly-god*), p. n. *Baalzebub,* the idol of the Ekronites.

זָבַד *hath given, endowed,* Gen. 30:20.

זֶבֶד *a gift,* Gen. 30:20.

זָבָד p.n. of a man.

זַבְדִּי p.n. of a man.

זַבְדִּיאֵל (*gift of God*), p.n. of a man.

זְבַדְיָה (*given of the Lord*), p. n. of a man, Ζεβεδαῖος.

זְבַדְיָהוּ p.n. of a man.

זָבוּד p.n. of a man.

זַבּוּד p. n. of a man.

זְבִידָה, זְבוּדָה p. n. of a woman

זבב *fly;* see זְבוּב.

זבל ;see זְבוּלוּן, זְבֻל, זְבוּל.

זָבַח (inf. const. זְבֹחַ; fut. יִזְבַּח), *slaughtered for sacrifice.* Pi. זִבַּח *sacrificed.*

זֶבַח m. (with suff. זִבְחִי; pl. זְבָחִים [זְבָחוֹת], זִבְחֵי).—I. *slaughter of men or animals.*—II. *the thing slaughtered.*—III. *sacrifice.*—IV. *that which is offered in sacrifice.*—V. p. n. of a king of Midian.

מִזְבֵּחַ m. (const. מִזְבַּח; with suff. מִזְבְּחִי, מִזְבַּחֲךָ; pl. מִזְבְּחוֹת), *altar;* הַמִּזְבֵּחָה *toward the altar.*

זַבַּי p.n. of a man.

זָבַל, fut. with suff. יִזְבְּלֵנִי *he will dwell with me,* Gen. 30:20.

זְבֻל, זְבוּל m.—I. *habitation, place of residence.*—II. p. n. of a man.

זְבֻלוּן, זְבוּלֻן, זְבוּלוּן (*residence*), p. n. of a son of Jacob; זְבוּלֹנִי *a Zebulonite.*

זְבַן Ch., *gaining* (time), Dan. 2:8.

זְבִינָא p. n. of a man.

זָג m., *the transparent skin of the grape,* Nu. 6:4.

זֵד, זָדוֹן; see זוּד.

זֶה demonst. pron., *he, it, this, that;* with art. הַזֶּה *this;* זֶה...זֶה *the one...the other;* זֶה אֶל־זֶה *the one to the other;* כָּזֶה וְכָזֶה *thus and thus;* sometimes same as אֲשֶׁר *that;* זֶה פַּעֲמַיִם *these two times;* בָּזֶה *in this place, here, there;* מִזֶּה *hence;* מִזֶּה וּמִזֶּה *from this and that part;* מַה־זֶּה *what is this?* אֵי־זֶה *where?* לָמָּה־זֶּה *why?*

זוּ com., *this;* sometimes for אֲשֶׁר.

הַלָּזֶה m., הַלֵּזוּ f., הַלָּז com., } *this.*

זָהָב m. (const. זְהַב, זֲהַב).—I. *gold*; with a numeral preceding, supply שֶׁקֶל: עֲשָׂרָה זָהָב *ten shekels of gold.*—II. perhaps *fair weather*, Job 37:22.

זָהָה root not used; (Syr. *splendour*).

זִו m. (*beauty of flowers*), the second month of the Hebrew year, which probably began on the thirty-first day after the sun had entered Aries.

זִיו m. Ch., *majesty, splendour*.

זָהַם. Pi. זִהֵם *abhorred*, Job 33:20.

זַהַם p. n. of a man.

זָהַר. Hiph. הִזְהִיר I. *enlighten, give light.*—II. *admonish, warn*, with מִן of the thing to be avoided. Niph. נִזְהַר *was admonished.*

זְהַר Ch., part. זְהִירִין *admonished, cautioned.*

זֹהַר m., *brilliancy.*

זוֹ, זֹה *this;* see זאת.

זוּ the same; see זֶה.

זִו; see זהה.

זוּב.—I. *issue, flow*, as water, blood, &c. — II. *abound, overflow.* — III. *waste away, expire*; part. זָב; f. זָבָה; const. זָבַת.

זוֹב m., *issue, discharge of blood*, &c

זוּד, זִיד.—I. *boil, seethe*, Gen. 25:29. —II. *swell, behave* or *act insolently*, with אֶל or עַל (fut. with נ parag. יְזִידוּן), Deu. 17:13.

זוּד Ch. Aph., *was proud, haughty*, Dan. 5:20

זֵד m., *proud, haughty.*

זֵידוֹן m., *overflowing, overwhelming*, Ps. 124:5.

זָדוֹן const. זְדוֹן m., *pride, haughtiness, insolence.*

נָזִיד m. (part. Niph. for נָזוּד), any viand prepared by boiling.

זָוָה root not used; (Arab. *angle, corner*).

זָוִיָּה or זָוִית f. (pl. זָוִיּוֹת), *angle, corner of a building*, &c.

מֶזֶו m. (pl. מְזָוִים), *vault for corn, matadore*, Ps. 144:13.

זוּז, זִיז root not used; (Arab. *abundance, riches*).

זִיז m.—I. *abundance*, Isa. 66:11.—II. זִיז שָׂדַי *wealth* (i.e. cattle) *of the fields*, Ps. 50:11; 80:14.

זִיזָא p.n. of a man.

זִיזָה p.n. of a man.

מְזוּזָה f., *doorpost, jamb.*

זוּזִים p. n. of a race of giants.

זוֹחֵת p. n. of a man.

זוּל, part. זָלִים *removing, pouring forth, casting out*, Isa. 46:6.

זוּלָה const. זוּלַת f. (lit. *removal, rejection*), prep. *besides*; with suff. זוּלָתִי *besides me*; זוּלָתְךָ *besides thee, &c.*; with י parag. זוּלָתִי *besides.*

זוּן. Hoph. part. מוּזָנִים *fed, fattened*, Jer. 5:8.

זוּן Ch. Hithp. *nourished, fed*, Dan. 4:9.

מָזוֹן m., *food, meat.*

מָזוֹן m. Ch., *meat.*

זוֹנָה; see זנה.

זוּנָה, for זָנָה, Pu.; see זנה.

זוּעַ *moved, was agitated.* Pil. part. מְזַעְזַע *vexing*, Hab. 2:7.

זוּעַ Ch., part. pl. זָאעִין Dan. 5:19

(זַיְעִין) id. 6:27. *moving, in commotion.*

זְוָעָה f., *agitation, commotion.*

זַעֲיָה f., *vexation.*

זֵעָה f., *sweat* (as the result of *motion*), Gen. 3:19.

זַעֲוָן p.n. of a man.

זִיעַ p. n. of a man.

זוּר (pret. זָר, זֹר; fut. יָזוּר, וַיָּזַר).—I. *compressed, squeezed.*—II. (same as סוּר *departed*) *departed, receded, was strange, abominable, adulterous;* part. זָר *a stranger, a barbarian, an enemy;* f. זָרָה *strange woman, harlot.* Niph. נָזֹרוּ *been receding, falling off*, Isa. 1:4. Hoph. part. מוּזָר *made separate*, Ps. 69:9.

זוּרֶה m., *pressed together, broken*, Is. 59:5.

מָזוֹר m., *compression of a wound by bandages;* יָשִׂימוּ מ׳ *they make a binding* (wound), Obad. 7.

זָחַח. Niph. *be removed, separated;* fut. יִזַּח.

זָחַל *withdrew, hesitated, delayed*, Job 32:6; part. pl. זֹחֲלֵי עָפָר *fearful things (serpents of the dust).*

זִיד, זֵידוֹן *pride;* see זוּד.

זִיו *splendour;* see זהה.

זִיז, זִיזָה, זִיזָא; see זוּז.

זִיף p.n.—I. of a town and desert in the tribe of Judah; זִיפִי *a Ziphite.* —II. p. n. of a man.

זִיקוֹת *ornaments*, &c.; see זנק.

זַיִת const. זֵית m.—I. *olive tree.*—II. *olive;* הַר הַזֵּיתִים *Mount of Olives*, near Jerusalem.

זֵיתָן p. n. of a man.

זָכָה same as זָכַךְ *was pure.* Pi. זִכָּה *cleanse, purify.* Hitnp. imp. הִזַּכּוּ (for הִתְזַכּוּ) *be, become, clean*, Isa 1:16.

זָכוּ f. Ch., *purity, innocence*, Dan. 6: 23.

זָכַךְ *was pure, clean.* Hiph. הֵזַךְ *have cleansed*, Job 9:30.

זַךְ m., זַכָּה f.—I. *pure, free from dregs.*—II. *innocent, upright.*

זְכוּכִית f., *glass* or *crystal*, Job 28:17.

זַכַּי p. n. of a man.

זָכַר (fut. יִזְכֹּר).—I. *remember.*—II. *meditate upon, call to mind*, with בְּ, לְ; part. זָכוּר *remembered.* Niph. נִזְכַּר.—I. *be remembered, recollected.*—II. *be born a male*, from זָכָר, Ex. 34:19. -- Hiph. הִזְכִּיר *record, commemorate, make mention of;* part. מַזְכִּיר לְבֹנָה *bringing a memorial* or *praise-offering of frankincense*, Isa. 66:3; מַזְכִּיר s., *recorder*, ἱστοριογράφος.

זֵכֶר, זֶכֶר, m. (with suff. זִכְרוֹ).—I. *memory.*—II. *memorial.*

זָכָר m., *male.*

זָכוּר m., *male.*

זַכּוּר p.n. of a man.

זִכָּרוֹן m. (const. זִכְרוֹן; pl. זִכְרֹנִים, —וֹת) *memorial, record.*

זִכְרִי p.n. of a man.

זְכַרְיָה, זְכַרְיָהוּ (*whom the Lord remembers*), Ζαχαρίας, p. n. of a m.

אַזְכָּרָה f., *an offering for a memorial*, Lev. 2:2, &c.

זָלַג root not used.

מַזְלֵג m., *a fork with three teeth.*

מִזְלָגָה f., pl. מִזְלָגוֹת the same.

זָלַל, part. זוֹלֵל *acting basely, profligately, obscenely.* Hiph. הֵזִיל *debase, defile.* Niph. נָזֹל; pl. נָזֹלּוּ, נָזֹלוּ *were debased.*

זֻלּוּת f., *baseness, lightness,* Ps. 12:9.

זַלְזַלִּים m. pl., *tender branches,* Isa. 18:5.

זַלְעָפָה, זִלְעָפָה f.—I. *poisonous wind,* Simoon.—II. *great excitement.*—III. *hunger, famine.*

זִלְפָּה p.n. of the hand-maid of Leah.

זַמָּה, זִמָּה, זַמְזֻמִּים; see זמם.

זָמִיר, זְמִיר, זְמוֹרָה; see זמר.

זַמּוֹתִי, Ps. 17:3, for זַמֹּתִי; see זִמָּה or זמם.

זָמַם (pret. זַמּוֹתִי, זָמַמְתִּי; fut. pl. יָזֹמּוּ), *intended, determined;* part. זֹמֵם *determines, plots against.* Ps. 37:12.

זָמָם m., *determination, project,* Ps. 140:9.

זִמָּה f.—I. *intention, imagination.*—II. *sin,* specially adultery.—III. p.n. of a man.

זַמָּה f., pl. with suff. זַמּוֹתִי *my meditation* (Gesenius), Ps. 17:3.

זַמְזֻמִּים p. n. of a race of giants, same as זוּזִים, which see.

מְזִמָּה f., *thought, intention, purpose* (for good or evil).

זָמַן Kal, root not used; (Arab. *appointed time*). Pu. part. עִתִּים מְזֻמָּנִים, עִתִּים מְזֻמָּנוֹת *stated times.*

זְמַן Ch. Pa. *appointed, concerted,* or Hith. הִזְדְּמִן according to Ketib, Dan. 2:9.

זְמָן m., *appointed time;* pl. זְמַנִּים.

זְמָן, זְמַן m. Ch. (pl. זִמְנִין), *appointed time;* זִמְנִין תְּלָתָה *thrice, three times.*

זָמַר (fut. יִזְמֹר), *cut, prune.* Niph. *was cut.* Pi. זִמֵּר *he sang,* with בְּ; *celebrated the praises of,* with לְ.

זֶמֶר m., *mountain goat,* Deu. 14:5.

זָמִיר m., *pruning time,* Cant. 2:12.

זְמִיר m., *song, hymn;* pl. זְמִירוֹת.

זְמוֹרָה f., *branch, bough;* pl. זְמֹרִים.

זִמְרָה, זִמְרָת, const. זִמְרַת f., *song, praise, music;* זִמְרַת הָאָרֶץ *the cropping, gathering of the earth,* Gen. 43:11.

זִמְרִי p. n. of a man.

זִמְרָן p. n. of a son of Abraham.

זְמָר m. Ch., *sound* (of musical instruments).

זַמָּר m. Ch., *singer,* Ezr. 7:24.

מִזְמוֹר m., *psalm* or *hymn.*

מְזַמֶּרֶת f., pl. מְזַמְּרוֹת *psalteries.*

מַזְמֵרָה f., pl. מַזְמֵרוֹת *pruning instruments.*

זַן, with pause זָן m. (pl. זְנִים), *kind, species.*

זַן m. Ch., the same.

זָנָב m. (pl. זְנָבוֹת; const. זַנְבוֹת), *tail of an animal.*

זִנֵּב, Pi., *cut off, smite the rear of an army,* lit. *tail it.*

זָנָה I. *play the whore.*—II. *become, be idolatrous,* with אַחֲרֵי, בְּ, אֶל, מֵעַל, תַּחַת, מִתַּחַת, מֵאַחֲרֵי, מִן; part. f. זוֹנָה *harlot.* Pu. זוּנָּה *committed fornication.* Hiph. הִזְנָה *caused to commit whoredom.*

זְנוּן m., pl. זְנוּנִים.—I. *whoredom.*—II. *idolatry.*

זְנוּת f., *idolatry;* pl. זְנוּתִים.

תַּזְנוּת f., the same; pl. תַּזְנוּתִים.

זָנַח I. *stank,* Hos. 8:5.—II. *rejected, loathed.* Hiph. הִזְנִיחַ.—I. *stank* Isa. 19:6.—II. *rejected*

זָנוֹחַ p. n. of two towns in the tribe of Judah.

זָנַק. Pi. fut. יְזַנֵּק *strikes, restrains,* Deu. 33:22.

זֵק f., pl. זִקִּים Pro. 26:18, "fire-brands," Eng. Ver.; *arrows tipped with fire;* see זקק.

זִיקָה f., pl. זִיקוֹת Isa. 50:11, "sparks," Eng. Ver.; *sparkling ornaments,* (Lee); meaning uncertain.

זַעֲוָה, זַעֲוָן, זְוָעָה; see זוע.

זְעֵיר *little;* see זער.

זָעַךְ. Niph. נִזְעָכוּ "are extinct," Eng. Ver.; *are swift* (Lee).

זָעַם (imp. זָעֲמָה; fut. אֶזְעֹם), *was indignant, angry,* with עַל, אֶת. Niph. part. נִזְעָמִים *became indignant, angry,* Pro. 25:23.

זַעַם m. (with suff. זַעְמִי, זַעַמְךָ), *indignation, anger.*

זָעַף I. *was indignant, enraged,* with עַל, עִם.—II. part. pl. זֹעֲפִים *mentally excited, wretched,* σκυθρωποί.

זָעֵף m., *indignant.*

זַעַף m. (with suff. זַעְפּוֹ).—I. *anger.* —II. metaphorically, *the raging of the sea.*

זָעַק (fut. יִזְעַק; imp. זְעַק; inf. זְעֹק), *cry out, shout for help,* with לְ, אֶל of the person implored; with עַל, לְ, of the cause of suffering. Niph. *was crying out.* Hiph. הִזְעִיק *summoned, proclaimed.*

זְעִק Ch., *called to,* Dan. 6:21.

זַעַק m., } *a cry, shout for help.*
זְעָקָה f., }

זָעַר root not used; (Syr. *was little*).

זְעֵיר m., *a little.*

זְעֵירָה f. Ch., the same, Dan. 7:8.

מִזְעָר m., *a little* (of time or number,

זִפְרוֹן p. n. of a town in the north of Palestine, Nu. 34:9.

זֶפֶת f., *pitch.*

זֵק, זִקִּים; see זנק and זקק.

זָקָן com.—I. *the beard.*—II. *the chin.*

זָקֵן *was old;* fut. יִזְקַן. Hiph. *grew old.*

זָקֵן m. (const. זְקַן; pl. זְקֵנִים, זִקְנֵי), *old, aged,* with כִּי; pl. *heads of tribes* or *families;* f. pl. זְקֵנוֹת *old women,* Zec. 8:4.

זֹקֶן m., *age, old age,* Gen. 48:10

זִקְנָה f., *old.*

זְקֻנִים m. pl., the same.

זָקַף *erected, lifted up.*

זְקַף Ch. part. זְקִיף *lift up, hang a criminal.*

זָקַק *pour out, melt, fuse.* Pi. זִקֵּק *fuse as metals,* Mal. 3:3. Pu. *fused, purified.*

זֵק m., pl. זִקִּים *bonds, fetters;* see also in זנק.

אָזֵק m., pl. אֲזִקִּים *fetters,* Jer. 40:1, 4.

זָר, זָרָה; see זור.

זֵר; see זרר.

זָרָא part. from זור *strange, abominable,* Num. 11:20.

זָרַב. Pu. fut. יְזֹרְבוּ *they are bound, oppressed,* Job. 6:17.

זְרֻבָּבֶל p. n.; see זרה.

זֶרֶד p. n. of a valley in the land of Moab.

זָרָה *spread, disperse.* Niph. *was dispersed.* Pi. זֵרָה.—I. *disperse.*—II. *discern, sift.* Pu. זֹרָה *was dispersed, spread out.*

זְרֻבָּבֶל p. n. of the leader of the Jews on their return from Babylon.

זֶרֶת f., *a span*, a measure of 10·944 inches.

מִזְרֶה m., *winnowing fan.*

מְזָרִים m., Job 37:9, probably the name of some northern constellation.

מַזָּרוֹת Job 38:32, probably the same; but see more under נזל.

זֵרוּעַ, זֵרֹעַ *seed*; see זרע.

זַרְזִיף *shower*; see זרף.

זַרְזִיר *firm*; see זרר.

זָרַח (fut. יִזְרַח; inf. זְרֹחַ).—I. *rise as the sun.*—II. *give light, glory.*—III. *be white*; hence, *have leprosy.*

זֶרַח m.—I. *rising.*—II. p. n. of one of the sons of Judah, and others; זַרְחִי *a Zarchite.*

יִזְרַחְיָה, זְרַחְיָה p.n. of a man.

אֶזְרָח m., *indigenous, home born*, a tree not transplanted, Ps. 37:35.

אֶזְרָחִי (יִזְרָח) p.n., *an Ezrachite.*

מִזְרָח m., *the east*, the quarter of heaven whence the sun rises; מִזְרָחָה (and without ה affix) *towards the east.*

זָרַם *overwhelm*, Ps. 90:5. Po. זֹרֵם *made to pour down*, Ps. 77:18.

זֶרֶם m., *inundation*, of rain or otherwise.

זִרְמָה f., *effusion, emission*, Eze. 23:20.

זָרַם Pi. pret. with suff.; see זרה.

זָרַע (fut. יִזְרַע; inf. זְרֹעַ; imp. זְרַע). I. *sowing* (as seed, &c.).—II. *planting.*—III. metaphorically of righteousness, wickedness, &c. Niph. *was sown, was propagated, was dispersed*, Eze. 36:9. Pu. זֹרָעוּ *shall they be sown*, Isa 40:24. Hiph. part. מַזְרִיעַ *producing seed*; fut. תַּזְרִיעַ, Lev. 12:2.

זֶרַע m. (with suff. זַרְעֲךָ, זַרְעִי; pl. זַרְעֵי, זְרָעִים).—I. *seed.*—II. *seed time.*—III. *semen* (of animals).—IV. *issue, progeny.*

זְרַע m. Ch., the same.

זְרוֹעַ f., sometimes m. (pl. זְרֹעִים, זְרֹעֵי, זְרֹעוֹת).—I. *arm.*—II. *fore-leg of an animal.*—III. *strength, power, violence.*

זֵרוּעַ m., *seed corn*; pl. זֵרוּעִים.

זֵרְעִים and זֵרְעֹנִים m. pl., *legumes, vegetables.*

אֶזְרוֹעַ f., same as זְרוֹעַ *arm.*

יִזְרְעֶאל p. n.—I. of a town in the tribe of Issachar; m. יִזְרְעֶאלִי; f. יִזְרְעֵאלִית, יִזְרְעֵלִית *a Jezreelite.*—II. of a town in the tribe of Judah.—III. of a man.

מִזְרָע const. מִזְרַע m., *sown field*, Isa. 19:7.

זָרַף root not used.

זַרְזִיף m., *copiously raining*, Ps. 72:6.

זָרַק (fut. יִזְרֹק) *scatter, sprinkle*; with עַל *of grey hairs*, Hos. 7:9. Pu. זֹרַק *was sprinkled*, Nu. 19:13, 20.

מִזְרָק m., *bowl or cup*; pl. מִזְרָקִים, מִזְרָקוֹת.

זֵר m., *border, moulding.*

זַרְזִיר m., *firm, compact*, Pro. 30:31

זֶרֶשׁ p.n. of the wife of Haman.

זֶרֶת *span*; see זרה.

זַתּוּא p. n. of a man.

זֵתָם p. n. of a man.

זֵתַר p. n. of a eunuch of Ahasuerus.

ח

חָבָא Kal, root not used. Niph. נֶחְבָּא *became, was, hidden*; with

אֶל, בְּ followed by inf. with לְ
ἔλαθε, *in secret*; נַחְבֵּאתָ לִבְרֹחַ
thou fleddest secretly. Pu. חֻבָּא
same as Niph., Job 24:4. Hiph.
הֶחְבִּיא *hide, conceal*. Hoph.
הָחְבָּא same as Niph., Isa. 42:22.
Hithp. הִתְחַבֵּא *was, lay, hidden*.

מַחֲבֵא m., *hiding-place*, Isa. 32:2.

מַחֲבוֹא m., pl. מַחֲבֹאִים the same, 1 Sa. 23:23.

חָבַב part. חֹבֵב *loving, cherishing*, Deu. 33:3.

חֹב m., with suff. חֻבִּי *my bosom*, Job 31:33.

חֹבָב p. n. of the father-in-law of Moses.

חָבָה same as חָבָא *hide, be in concealment*; imp. f. חֲבִי. Niph. inf. הֵחָבֵה *lay hidden*.

חֲבָיָה p.n. of a man.

חֶבְיוֹן *covering, vail*, Hab. 3:4.

חוֹבָה p.n. of a place near Damascus, Gen. 14:15.

נַחְבִּי p. n. of a man.

חָבוֹר, חַבּוּרָה; see חבר.

חָבַט (fut. יַחְבֹּט) *beat off, threshed out*. Niph. *is beaten out*, Isa. 28:27.

I. חָבַל 1. *bind*; part. חֹבְלִים *binders, bands*, Zec. 11:7.—2. *bind by pledge, pledge*; inf. חֲבֹל; imp. חֲבֹל; fut. יַחְבֹּל, יַחֲבֹל. Pi. חִבֵּל *brought forth with pain*.

II. חָבַל *inflicting pain, oppressing*. Niph. *suffer pain, loss*, Pro. 13:13. Pi. *injure, corrupt*. Pu. חֻבַּל *injured, destroyed*.

חֲבַל Ch. Pa. *injure, destroy*. Ithp. *perish*.

חֵבֶל m.—I. *the throes of child-bearing*, ὠδίς.—II. *pains* generally, Job 21:17; pl. חֲבָלִים, חֶבְלֵי.

חֶבֶל m. (f. Zep. 2:6, with suff. חַבְלִי; pl. חֲבָלִים, חַבְלֵי, חֶבְלֵי)—I. *rope, cord*.— II. *measuring line*. — III. *tract of land, region, inheritance*. — IV. *snare, gin*.— V. *company, band of men*, I Sa. 10:5, 10.

חֲבֹל m., } *pledge, deposit*
חֲבֹלָה f., }

חֲבַל m. Ch., } *injury, hurt*
חֲבָל m. Ch., }

חֲבוּלָא f. Ch., *corrupt thing*, Dan 6:23.

חִבֵּל m., *mast of a ship*, Pro. 23:34.

חֹבֵל m., *sailor*.

תַּחְבֻּלוֹת, תַּחְבּוּלוֹת f. pl.—I. *guidance, direction*.—II. *rule of action*.—III. *wisdom*.

חֲבַצֶּלֶת f., bulbous-rooted flower, *lily*.

חֲבַצִּנְיָה p. n. of a man.

חָבַק *embrace, fold together*, with לְ. Pi. חִבֵּק *embraced*.

חִבֻּק m., *folding of the hands*.

חֲבַקּוּק p. n. of a prophet; LXX. Ἀμβακούμ.

חָבַר I. *joined, attached, assembled*, with אֶל.—II. *charm, bind with a spell*. Pi. חִבֵּר *bind, join*, with עִם. Pu. חֻבַּר *was joined*, with אֶל, לְ, Ps. 94:20. Hiph. fut. אַחְבִּירָה *I might compose, put together*, with עַל, Job. 16: 4. Hithp. *be joined*.

חָבֵר m., *companion*; pl. חֲבֵרִים, חַבְרֵי.

חֲבֶרֶת f., *associate*.

חֲבַר m. Ch., *companion*.

חַבְרָה f. Ch., the same.

חַבָּר m., pl., חַבָּרִים *associates*, Job 40:30.

חֶבֶר m.—I. *association.*—II. *incantation*, Isa. 47:9, 12; pl. חֲבָרִים.—III. p. n. of a man; חֶבְרִי *Heberite*, Nu. 26:45.

חֶבְרָה f., *association.*

חֹבֶרֶת f., *coupling*, Ex. 26:4, 10.

חָבוֹר p. n. of a river in Mesopotamia, *Chaboras.*

חַבּוּרָה, חֲבוּרָה f., *closing, seam, scar of a wound;* with suff. חַבֻּרָתִי; pl. חַבֻּרוֹת, with suff. חַבּוּרוֹתַי.

חֶבְרוֹן p. n.—I. of a town in the tribe of Judah.—II. of a man; חֶבְרֹנִי *a Hebronite.*

חֲבַרְבֻּרוֹת f. pl., *spots of the leopard*, Jer. 13:23.

מַחְבֶּרֶת f., *joining, seam;* with suff. מַחְבַּרְתּוֹ.

מְחַבְּרוֹת f. pl.—I. *binders, beams of timber*, 2 Chron. 34:11.—II. *iron cramps*, 1 Chron. 22:3.

הִתְחַבְּרוּת f., *league*, Dan. 11:23.

חָבַשׁ (inf. חֲבוֹשׁ; fut. יַחֲבֹשׁ, יֶחְבַּשׁ).—I. *bind, gird*, with עַל, לְ.—II. *govern, restrain.* Pi. חִבֵּשׁ *restrain*, Job 28:11, with מִן. Pu. חֻבַּשׁ *was bound up.*

חֲבִית m., pl. חֲבִתִּים *pancakes*, 1 Chron. 9:31.

מַחֲבַת f., *frying pan.*

חָגָב.—I. *locust.*—II. p. n. of a man.

חֲגָבָה p. n. of a man.

חָגַג (fut. יָחֹג), *feasting, revelling*, specially, keeping the festivals prescribed by law.

חַג m. (const. חַג; with art. הֶחָג; with suff. חַגֵּנוּ; pl. חַגִּים), *festival under the law.*

חָגָּא f., *refuge*, Isa. 19:17.

חַגַּי p. n. of the prophet *Haggai*; LXX. Ἀγγαῖος.

חַגִּי p. n. of a son of Gad.

חַגִּיָּה p. n. of a man.

חַגִּית p. n. of one of the wives of David

חָגָה root not used; (Syr. *a rock*).

חֲגָוִים, חַגְוֵי m. pl., *fastnesses, clefts.*

חָגוֹר, חֲגוֹרָה *girdle;* see חגר.

חָגְלָה p. n. of a woman.

חָגַר (fut. יַחְגֹּר).—I. *gird, attire;* with עַל of the part of the body attired; with בְּ of the object put on; part. חָגוּר *girt.*—II. *withhold, restrain.*

חָגוֹר m., } *girdle, belt;* pl. חֲגֹרוֹת.
חֲגוֹר m., }
חֲגוֹרָה f., }

מַחֲגֹרֶת f., *girding*, Isa. 3:24.

חַד Ch., *a, an, once;* see אֶחָד, also חדד.

חָדַד *are keen, fierce;* pret. חַדּוּ Hab. 1:8. Hiph. fut. יַחַד, יָחֵד *sharpens*, Pro. 27:17. Hoph. הוּחַד *sharpened*, Eze. 21:14—16.

חַד m., חַדָּה f., *sharp.*

חַדּוּדִים, חַדּוּדֵי m. pl., *very sharp*, Job 41:22.

חֲדַד p. n. of a son of Ishmael.

חָדִיד p. n. of a town of the Benjamites.

חָדָה (fut. apoc. יִחַדְּ), *rejoice*, Ex. 18:9. Pi. fut. with suff. תְּחַדֵּהוּ *make glad*, Ps. 21:7. Hiph. יַחַד *delight, make glad*, Pro. 27:17

חֶדְוָה f. Ch., *joy, gladness.*

חֲדִין m. pl. Ch., Dan. 2:32, same as Heb. חָזֶה *breast.*

חָדַל and חָדֵל (inf. חֲדֹל; imp. חֲדַל; fut. יֶחְדַּל) *cease, desist, forbear, fail,* with מִן.

חָדֵל m., *ceasing, wanting, failing.*

חֶדֶל with pause חָדֶל m., *leisure,* Isa. 38:11.

חָדֵלּוּ Jud. 5:7, with pause and with dag. euphon. for חָדְלוּ ,חָדֵלוּ pret. pl., from חדל.

חַדְלַי p. n. of a man.

חֲדַלְתִּי; see הֶחְדַלְתִּי.

חָדַק root not used; (Arab. *melongena spinosa,* a thorny shrub)

חֵדֶק and חֶדֶק, with pause חָדֶק m., *a species of thorn,* Pro. 15:19.

חִדֶּקֶל a river of Mesopotamia, perhaps *the Tigris.*

חָדַר, part. f. חֹדֶרֶת *enclosing, laying siege to,* Eze. 21:19.

חֶדֶר m. (const. חֲדַר; with suff. חֶדְרוֹ; pl. חֲדָרִים ,חַדְרֵי), *chamber, inner apartment;* fig. חַדְרֵי־תֵימָן *the chambers of the south,* i. e. *the south;* חַדְרֵי בֶטֶן *the inner parts of the body;* ח׳ מָוֶת *the tomb.*

חַדְרָךְ p. n. of a part of Syria, near Damascus, Zec. 9:1.

חָדַשׁ. Pi. חִדֵּשׁ *renew, restore.* Hith. *is renewed,* Ps. 103:5.

חָדָשׁ m., *new, recent, fresh;* f. חֲדָשָׁה (pl. חֲדָשׁוֹת).

חֹדֶשׁ m. (with suff. חָדְשׁוֹ; pl. חֳדָשִׁים, חָדְשֵׁי) —I. *new moon:* hence,—II. *certain feasts regulated by the moon.*—III. *month which began with the new moon;* חֹדֶשׁ יָמִים *a whole month.*—IV. p. n. of a woman; חָדְשִׁי the son of Hodash.

חֲדַת m. Ch., *new.*

חוּב. Pi. חַיֵּב *render due, forfeit,* Dan. 1:10.

חוֹב m., *debt,* Eze. 18:7.

חוֹבָה p. n.; see חָבָה.

חוּג *circumscribe,* Job 26:10.

חוּג m., *sphere, globe.*

מְחוּגָה f., *compasses,* Isa. 44:13

חוּד *propose a riddle, problem.*

חִידָה f., *parable, riddle.*

אֲחִידָה f. Ch., the same, Dan. 5:12.

חָוָה. Pi. חִוָּה *shew, declare.*

חַוֵּא ,חַוָּה ,חַוֵּי. Pa. Ch., *shew, declare.* Aph. the same.

אַחֲוָה f., *shewing, argument,* Job 13: 17.

אַחֲוָיָה f. Ch., the same, Dan. 5:12.

חַוָּה f., pl. חַוּוֹת *villages of huts;* see also under חיי.

חַיָּה f., *crowd of men,* 2 Sa. 23:11, 13; Ps. 68:11; see also under חיי.

חוּז root not used; (Arab. *shore, coast*).

מָחוֹז m., *haven, harbour,* Ps. 107:30.

חוּזַי p. n. of a man.

חוֹחַ m. (pl. חֲוָחִים ,חוֹחִים).—I. *thorn or bramble* generally.—II. *fish hook,* Job 40:26.—III. *a ring with spikes put round the necks of captives,* 2 Ch. 33:11.

חָח m.—I. *hook* or *ring put into the nose of animals,* e.g. the camel.—II. *a nose jewel,* worn as an ornament.

חוּט Ch. Aph., *join in one thread,* Ezr. 4:12.

חוּט m., *thread;* מִחוּט וְעַד שְׂרוֹךְ־נַעַל *from a thread to a shoe-latchet,* Gen. 14:23, i. e. nothing whatever.

חִוִּי p. n., *the Hivites,* a people of Canaan.

חֲוִילָה p. n. of an unknown district where there was gold.

חוּל and חִיל (fut. יָחִיל, יָחוּל; apoc. וַתָּחֹל, וַתָּחֶל, וַיָּחֶל; imp. f. חוּלִי; pl. חִילוּ).—I. *feel, be in pain.*—II. *tremble as a woman in labour.*—III. *bring forth,* Isa. 54:1. — IV. *precipitate, fall upon.*—V. *be strong, durable.*— VI. *waited;* see יָחַל. Hiph. fut. יָחִיל.—I. *shake,* Ps. 29:8. —II. *exult,* Job 20:21. Hoph. fut. יוּחַל *shall be brought forth,* Isa. 66:8. Pil. חוֹלֵל.—I. *dance in a circle,* Jud. 21:23. — II. *humble,* Job 26:5.— III. *bring forth.*—IV. *wait,* Job 35: 14. Pul. חוֹלַל *was born.* Hithpo. הִתְחוֹלֵל.— I. *was tormented.*—II. *fell upon.*— III. *waited,* Ps. 37:7. Hithpal. הִתְחַלְחַל *was pained,* Est. 4:4.

חוֹל m.—I. *sand.*—II. *measure, number,* Job 29:18.—III. *weight.*—IV. *abundance.*

חוּל p.n. of a son of Aram, Gen. 10: 23.

חַיִל m. (const. חֵיל; with suff. חֵילוֹ; pl. חֲיָלִים).— I. *strength, power;* עָשָׂה חַיִל *did valiantly.*— II. *an army;* בְּנֵי חַיִל or אַנְשֵׁי ח׳ *soldiers;* שַׂר הַחַיִל *general.* — III. *riches, wealth;* עָשָׂה חַיִל *acquired wealth.* — IV. *virtue, integrity.*— V. חַיִל הָעֵץ *strength* (i.e. fruit) *of the tree,* Joel 2:22.

חַיִל m. Ch.—I. *strength.*—II. *army.*

חֵיל and חֵל m.—I. *army.*—II. *outwork, space before a fortification.*

חִיל m. } —I. *pain.* —II. *trembling,*
חִילָה f. } *fear,* Ex. 15:14.

חֵילָה Ps. 48:14, same as חֵיל *fortification;* others read חֵילָהּ.

חַלְחָלָה f., *great, grievous pain.*

מָחוֹל m.—I. *dance, dancing.*—II. p. n. of a man.

מְחֹלָה f., *dance.*

חוּם root not used; (Arab. *was black*).

חוּם m., *black.*

חוֹמָה f., *a wall;* const. חוֹמַת; pl. חוֹמוֹת; dual הֹמֹתַיִם.

חוּס (fut. יָחוּס, יָחֹס; 1. pers. אָחוּס) *spare, pity, grieve for;* often with עַיִן *the eye.*

חוֹף *shore;* see חפף.

חֻפִּים, חוּפָם p.n. of a son of Benjamin; חוּפָמִי *a Chuphamite.*

חוּץ root not used; (Arab. *surrounded*).

חוּץ m. (pl. חוּצוֹת, חֻצוֹת).— I. *open place, court, garden.*—II. *out-fields, lands* (without a city). — Adv. I. *without,* opposed to *within;* חוּצָה, הַחוּצָה *without;* בַּחוּץ the same; לַחוּצָה, לַחוּץ the same; מִחוּץ the same; with לְ *besides;* מֵהַחוּץ *without,* Eze. 41:25; מִן הַחוּץ *without;* מִחוּצָה the same, Eze. 40:40, 44; אֶל־הַחוּץ, the same, Eze. 41:9; אֶל הַחוּצָה the same, Eze. 34:21; אֶל מִחוּץ לְ the same; חוּץ מִן *more than,* Ecc. 2:25.

חַיִץ m., *a wall,* Eze. 13:10.

חִיצוֹן m., חִיצוֹנָה f., *outer, exterior;* לַחִיצוֹן *without;* הַמְּלָאכָה הַחִיצוֹנָה *outward business,* i.e. civil, opposed to sacred, 1 Ch. 26:29.

חוּק, חוֹק same as חֵיק.

חָוַר, fut. pl. יֶחֱוָרוּ *shall be white, pale*, Isa. 29:22.

חוֹר, חוּר, חֹר m.—I. *white linen.*—II. *nobles.*—III. *cavern, aperture, hole;* pl. חוֹרִי, חֹרִים, חֹרֵי; see also חרר.

חִוָּר m. Ch., *white*, Dan. 7:9.

חֹרִי m., *white bread*, Gen. 40:16.

חֹרִי (τρωγλοδύτης) p. n., *a Horite*, i.e. *dweller in a cave*, a Canaanitish nation.—II. p. n. of a man.

חוּרִי p. n. of a man.

חוּרַי same as הִדַּי p. n. of a man.

חוּרָם, חִירָם p. n.—I. of a king of Tyre.—II. of a man.

חַוְרָן p. n. of a country beyond Jordan, Eze. 47:16, 18.

חֹרֹנַיִם p. n. of a city of the Moabites; חֹרֹנִי *a Horonite.*

חוֹרִים *white, &c.;* see חֹר in חרר.

חוּשׁ and **חִישׁ** (fut. יָחִישׁ; apoc. וַתָּחַשׁ; imp. חוּשָׁה).—I. *hasten* (part. חָשִׁים *hasting*).—II. *felt, enjoyed*, Ecc. 2:25, with לְ. Hiph. הֵחִישׁ.—I. *hasten, accelerate.*—II. *stumble, fail.*

חוּשָׁה p.n. of a man; חוּשָׁתִי *a Cushathite.*

חוּשַׁי p.n. of one of David's companions.

חוּשִׁים p. n. of a man.

חִישׁ adv., *hastily*, Ps. 90:10.

חוֹתָם *seal;* see חתם.

חָזָה (inf. חֲזוֹת; imp. חֲזֵה; fut. יֶחֱזֶה; apoc. אֶחֱז, תַּחַז).—I. *saw visions.*—II. *saw with pleasure.*—III. *look at, regard*, with בְּ; *look for, search out, choose*, with מִן; part. חֹזֶה; subst. const. חֹזֶה, חוֹזֶה; pl. חֹזִים.—I. *prophet, seer.*—II. *agreement*, Isa. 28:15.

חֲזָה, חֲזָא Ch., *he saw.*

חָזֶה m., *breast of an animal cut up;* const. חֲזֵה; pl. חָזוֹת.

חֱזוּ m. Ch., *vision.*

חֲזוֹ p. n. of a man.

חָזוֹן m., *vision, revelation.*

חָזוּת f.—I. *vision, revelation.*—II. *matter of vision.*—III. *agreement*, Isa. 28:18.

חָזוֹת f., *vision*, 2 Ch. 9:29.

חֲזוֹת f. Ch., *appearance*, Dan. 4:8, 17;

חִזָּיוֹן m. const. חֶזְיוֹן; pl. חֶזְיוֹנוֹת *dream, vision.*

חֶזְיוֹן p. n. of a man, 1 Ki. 15:18.

מַחֲזֶה m., *vision.*

מֶחֱזָה f., *window*, 1 Ki. 7:4, 5.

מַחֲזִיאוֹת p. n. of a man.

חֲזָאֵל p.n. of a king of Syria.

חֲזִיאֵל p.n. of a man.

חֲזָיָה p.n. of a man.

יַחֲזִיאֵל p.n. of a man.

יַחְזְיָה p.n. of a man.

חָזַז root not used; (Arab. *pierced*).

חָזִיז or חֲזִיז m., *thunder-bolt*, Zec. 10:1.

חֲזִיר m., *hog, swine.*

חֵזִיר p.n. of a man.

חָזַק (fut. יֶחֱזַק) *was strong, firm, powerful, unyielding*, applied to persons, mind, or things: const. with בְּ *in;* אֶל, עַל *on, to;* מִן *more than;* לְ *to, for.* Pi. חִזֵּק *made strong, firm.*—I. with יָד 1. *strengthened the hand.*—2. *supported.*—II. with לֵב 1. *hardened the heart.*—2. *restored, healed* Hiph. הֶחֱזִיק 1. *take fast* *hold of, obtain, retain,* with לְ, בְּ, עַל.—II. *applying strength to, repairing, confirming, prevailing.* Hith. הִתְחַזֵּק *became, waxed strong, received strength, &c.;* with לִפְנֵי *oppose, resist;* with בְּ or עִם *assist, aid.*

חָזֵק m., *becoming strong;* הוֹלֵךְ וְחָ׳ *waxing strong.*

חָזָק m., *strong, mighty, unyielding, prevailing,* used either in a good or bad sense.

חֵזֶק m., *strength;* with suff. חִזְקִי Ps. 18:2.

חֹזֶק m., the same; with suff. חָזְקִי.

חֶזְקָה f. (same as חֹזֶק inf., see חָזַק), כְּחֶזְקָתוֹ *when he gained strength,* with בְּ; בְּחֶזְקַת־הַיָּד *when the hand of God impelled.*

חָזְקָה f.—I. *force, vehemence;* בְּחָזְקָה *with power, vehemently.*—II. *repairing an edifice,* 2 Ki. 12:13.

חִזְקִי p.n. of a man.

חִזְקִיָּה, חִזְקִיָּהוּ, יְחִזְקִיָּה, יְחִזְקִיָּהוּ p.n., *Hezekiah,* king of Judah, and others; LXX. Ἐζεχίας.

יְחֶזְקֵאל (*the Lord strengthens*), p. n., *Ezekiel* the prophet; LXX. Ἰεζεκιήλ.

חַחִים, חָח *hook;* see חוח.

חָטָא (inf. חֲטוֹ, חֲטוֹא; fut. יֶחֱטָא).—I. *err, wander from.*—II. *sin;* with בְּ, לְ, or עַל *by, against.*—III. *miss the mark, fall short of,* with מִן; part. m. חוֹטֵא, חוֹטֶא; pl. חֹטְאִים; f. חֹטֵאת. Pi. חִטֵּא *expiate, cleanse, free from sin.* Hiph. הֶחֱטִיא I. *miss the mark.*—II. *cause to sin.* Hith. I. *be, become erring,* Job 41:17.—II. *be cleansed from sin.*

חֵטְא m. (with suff. חֶטְאִי; pl. חֲטָאִים, חֲטָאַי), *sin, wickedness.*

חֲטָי or חֲטָי m. Ch., *sin,* Dan. 4:24.

חֲטָאָה f., *sin.*

חַטָּא m., *sinner;* חַטָּאָה f., Am. 9:8

חֲטָאָה f., *sin,* Gen. 20:9.

חַטָּאָה f., *sin,* Ex. 34:7; Isa. 5:18.

חֶטְאָה f., *sin,* Nu. 15:28.

חַטָּאת f. (const. חַטַּאת; pl. חַטָּאוֹת; const. חַטֹּאת).—I. *sin.*—II. *sin-offering.*— III. *idol.*— IV. *punishment of sin,* Zec. 14:19; Pro. 10:16.

חַטָּאָה Ch. (Kri), חַטָּיָא (Ketib), *sin-offering,* Ezr. 6:17.

חָטָא, חֲטוֹ־ Kal inf. const., from חטא.

חָטַב (fut. יַחְטֹב) *cutting wood.* Pu. part. f. מְחֻטָּבוֹת *hewn stones,* Ps 144:12.

חֲטֻבוֹת f. pl., *striped, variegated,* Pro. 7:16.

חִטָּה f., *wheat;* pl. חִטִּים; Ch. חִטִּין and חִנְטִין *grains of wheat.*

חַטּוּשׁ p. n. of a man.

חֲטִיטָא p. n. of a man.

חַטִּיל p.n. of a man.

חָטַם (lit. *ring a camel through the nose,* which is the mode of bitting that animal); fut. אֶחֱטָם־לָךְ *I will restrain my anger against thee,* Isa. 48:9.

חָטַף (fut. יַחְטֹף) *rob, take by violence.*

חֲטִיפָא p. n. of a man.

חֹטֶר m., *stick, rod,* Pro. 14:3; Isa. 11:1.

חַי, חִיאֵל; see חיי.

חִידָה *riddle;* see חוד.

חָיָה (inf. חָיוֹ, חָיֹה; const. חֲיוֹת; imp. חֲיֵה; fut. יִחְיֶה; apoc. יְחִי) *he lived in health, safety, vigour, &c.;* with

מָן *recovered after sickness.* Pi. חִיָּה.—I. *giving, preserving, restoring life.*—II. *strengthen, make effectual;* חִיָּה זֶרַע *preserve seed,* Gen. 7:3. Hiph. הֶחֱיָה *give, preserve life.*

חֲיָה or חֲיָא Ch., *he lived;* imp. יֶחֱיֵי. Aph. part. מַחֵא *giving life.*

חָיֶה m., not used; f. חָיָה; pl. חָיוֹת *lively, strong,* Ex. 1:19.

יְחַוְאֵל p.n. of a man.

מִחְיָה f.—I. *means of living, food.*—II. *crude, raw,* i.e. *unsound, diseased,* Lev. 13:10, 24; see also in חוה.

חָיַי *lived;* pret. m. חַי, וָחַי; f. וָחָיָה, Ex. 1:16.

חַי m. (const. חֵי; pl. חַיִּים, חַיֵּי; with suff. חַיֶּיךָ), s. *living, alive;* חַי יְהוָֹה וְחֵי נַפְשְׁךָ *as the Lord liveth and thy soul liveth;* adj. (f. חַיָּה; pl. חַיּוֹת) *living, alive, safe, reviving;* כָּעֵת חַיָּה *according to the time of life;* metaphorically, *living* (i.e. springing) *water; living* (i.e. fresh) *meat.*

חַי m. Ch., *living;* pl. חַיִּין, חַיֵּי, s. *life.*

חַיָּה f. (const. חַיַּת, חַיְתוֹ; with suff. חַיָּתוֹ; pl. חַיּוֹת).—I. *life.*—II. *animal, wild beast;* see also in חוה.

חַוָּה (same as חַיָּה *life*), p. n. *Eve* the first woman; LXX. Ἔυα, Vulg. Heva; see also in הוה.

חֵיוָא f. Ch., *living creature.*

חַיּוּת f., *life.*

חַיְתוֹ const. state with ו parag. for חַיַּת from חַיָּה; see in חָיַי.

יְחִיאֵל p.n. of a man; יְחִיאֵלִי one of the family of Jehoel.

חִיאֵל p.n. of a man.

חִיל, חֵיל, חַיִל, חִילָה; see חול.

חֵילָם, חֵלְאָם p. n. of a city not far from the Euphrates.

חִילֵן same as חֹלֹן.

חִין; see חנן.

חַיִץ, חִיצוֹן, חִיצוֹנָה; see חוץ.

חֵיק and חֵק m., *the bosom.*—I. in a conjugal sense.—II. in a dishonest sense, Pro. 5:20.—III. in a moral sense, *the feelings, affections.*—IV. *bosom, lappet of a garment.*—V. *hollow place in a chariot,* 1 Ki. 22:35; *in the altar,* Eze. 43:13, &c.

חִירָה p. n. of a man.

חִישׁ *hastily;* see חוש.

חֵךְ, חִכָּה *palate;* see חנך.

חָכָה *waiting,* with לְ, Isa. 30:18. Pi. חִכָּה the same.

חַכֵּי for חַכֵּה Pi. inf. of חָכָה.

חַכְלִילִי m., *brightened with wine* (of the eyes), Gen. 49:12.

חַכְלִלוּת f., *fierceness of eyes,* Pro. 23:29.

חֲכִילָה p. n. of a hill in the wilderness of Ziph.

חֲכַלְיָה p.n. of a man.

חָכַם (fut. יֶחְכַּם) *was wise, intelligent, taught.* Pi. *made wise, taught.* Pu. part. מְחֻכָּם *made wise.* Hiph. part. f. מַחְכִּימַת *making wise,* Ps. 19:8. Hithp. *account oneself wise, cunning.*

חָכָם m. (f. חֲכָמָה).—I. *wise.*—II. *teacher of wisdom.*—III. *intelligent, clever;* חֲכָמִים *wise men* (of soothsayers, &c.); חֲכָמוֹת (i.e. קִינָה) *women skilled in lamenting at funerals,* Jer. 9:16.

חַכִּים m. Ch., *wise man, magician.*

חָכְמָה f., *wisdom.*

חָכְמָה f. Ch., *wisdom*.
חָכְמוֹת, חַכְמוֹת f., the same.
חַכְמֹנִי p.n. of a man.
חַל same as חִיל *pain*; see חוּל.
חֹל *profane*; see חלל.
חָלָא same as חָלָה *sick, weak, afflicted*.
חֶלְאָה f.—I. *refuse, filth, scum*, Eze. 24:6.—II. p. n. of a woman.
חֲלָאִים *diseases*; see חֳלִי in חלה.
חָלָב m. (const. חֲלֵב; with suff. חֲלָבִי), *new milk* or *cream*.
חֵלֶב and חֶלֶב m. (with suff. חֶלְבּוֹ; pl. חֶלְבֵי, חֲלָבִים).—I. *fat, fatness, the best of any thing*; ח׳ הָאָרֶץ *the fatness of the earth*; ח׳ חִטָּה *the best of the wheat*.—II. *hardness, impenitency*, Ps. 17:10, &c.—III. p. n. of a man.
חֶלְבָּה p. n. of a town in the tribe of Asher.
חֶלְבּוֹן p. n. of a city in Syria, Χαλυβών.
חֶלְבְּנָה f., *galbanum*, an odoriferous gum, Ex. 30:34.
חָלַד root not used; (Arab. *duration*).
חֶלֶד m. (with suff. חֶלְדִּי), *time, duration*; מְתִים מֵחֶלֶד *men of time*, i.e. of this world, Ps. 17:14.
חֹלֶד m., *a mole*.
חֻלְדָּה p. n. of a prophetess; LXX. Ὀλδά.
חֶלְדַּי p.n. of a man.
I. חָלָה (fut. apoc. וַיָּחַל), *was sick, weak, afflicted*, with עַל. Niph. נֶחֱלָה *became sick, weak, afflicted*; part. נַחְלָה (f. נַחְלָה), *diseased, infirm*. Pi. חִלָּה *afflicted*; with suff. חַלּוֹתִי *my sickness*. Pu. חֻלָּה *afflicted, infirm*, Isa. 14:10. Hiph. הֶחֱלִי (for הֶחֱלָה) *afflicted, made sick, infirm*. Hoph. הָחֳלָה *wounded*. Hith. *feigned sickness*; imper. apoc. הִתְחַל, fut. apoc. וַיִּתְחַל.
חַלּוֹתִי Ps. 77:11. Pi. inf. with suff., from I. חלה.
חֳלִי with pause חֹלִי m. (with suff. חָלְיוֹ; pl. חֳלָיִים). *disease, sickness, evil, inconvenience*.
חֲלִי m., *ornament, necklace*; pl חֲלָאִים.
חֶלְיָה f., the same.
אַחֲל m., *prayer*; אַחֲלֵי, אַחֲלַי *would that!*
מַחֲלֶה m., } *sickness, disease*
מַחֲלָה f., }
מַחֲלָה p. n. of a woman.
מַחְלוֹן p. n. of a man.
מַחְלִי p. n. of a man.
מַחֲלוּי m., pl. מַחֲלֻיִים *circumstances of disease*, 2 Chron. 24:25.
מָחֲלַת m., a title of Ps. 53 and 88; meaning uncertain
מָחֲלַת p. n. of a woman.
תַּחֲלוּא m., pl. תַּחֲלוּאִים, תַּחֲלֻאִים *diseases*.
II. חָלָה Kal not used; (Arab. *was sweet*). Pi. חִלָּה, with פְּנֵי *make propitious, conciliate favour, satisfy*; imp. apoc. חַל, fut. apoc. וַיְחַל.
חַלָּה, חַלּוֹן; see חלל.
חֲלוֹם *dream*; see חלם.
חֹלוֹן p. n. of a town in the land of Moab.
חֲלוֹף *passing away*; see חלף.
חֲלוּשָׁה *defeat*; see חלשׁ.
חֲלַח p.n. of a province in the kingdom of Assyria (Καλαχήνη).
חַלְחָלָה *pain*; see חוּל.

חָלַט. Hiph. fut. וַיַּחְלְטוּ, 1 Ki. 20:33, "did hastily catch," Eng. Ver.; "hasted greatly" (Lee).

חֳלִי, חֱלִי, חָלְיָה, חָלִי; see חלה.

חָלִיל *pipe*; see חלל.

חֲלִיפָה *change*; see חלף.

חֲלִיצָה *spoil*; see חלץ.

חָלַךְ root not used; (Arab. *intense blackness*).

חֵלְכָה with pause חֵלְכָה m., *very miserable*, Ps. 10:8, 14; pl. חֵלְכָאִים, *v.* 10.

חָלַל *pierced, wounded*, Ps. 109:22. Niph. נִחַל *profaned, became common, prostituted*; inf. הֵחֵל; fut. יֵחַל, תֵּחֵל. Pi. חִלֵּל.—I. *wounded*, Eze. 28:9. — II. *profaned, made common, violated* (a covenant). — III. *played upon the flute*, 1 Ki. 1:40, from חָלִיל. Pu. part. מְחֻלָּל *profaned*. Po. חוֹלֵל *wounding*. Poal. part. מְחוֹלָל *wounded*. Hiph. הֵחֵל. — I. *make profane, violate, loose, set free*.—II. *begin*; pret. 1. pers. הַחִלֹּתִי; inf. with suff. הַחִלָּם *their beginning*; fut. יָחֵל *shall begin*; יַחֵל *shall loose*. Hoph. הוּחַל *was begun*, Gen. 4:26.

חָלִיל m., *pipe*; pl. חֲלִילִים; חָלִילָה int. *profane! fie!* with לְ of the pers. and inf. with מִן; ח׳ לְךָ מֵעֲשׂוֹת *that be far from thee to do so*.

חָלָל (const. חֲלַל m.).—I. *pierced, wounded, slain*.—II. *profane, common*; f. חֲלָלָה *prostitute*, Lev. 21:7, 14.

חֹל m., *profane, common*.

חַלָּה const. חַלַּת f., *cake* (pierced with holes).

חַלּוֹן com., *window*, (i. e. *opening*); pl. חַלּוֹנִים.

מְחִלָּה f., pl. מְחִלּוֹת *caves, holes of the earth*, Isa. 2:19.

תְּחִלָּה f., *beginning*; בַּתְּחִלָּה *at first, formerly*.

חָלַם (fut. יַחֲלֹם).—I. *dream*.—II. *be fat*, Job 39:4. Hiph.—I. *make stout, strong*, Isa. 38:16.—II. part. מַחְלְמִים *causing to see visions*, Jer. 29:8.

חֲלוֹם m., *a dream*; pl. חֲלֹמוֹת.

חֵלֶם m. Ch.—I. *dream*.—II. p. n. of a man.

חַלָּמוּת f., Job 6:6, "egg," Eng. Ver.; *cheese*, (Lee).

חַלָּמִישׁ m., *flint, stone striking fire*.

אַחְלָמָה f., a precious stone; LXX. ἀμέθυστος.

חֹלֹן p. n.—I. of a town in the tribe of Judah; same as חִילֵן.—II. חֹלוֹן in the land of Moab; same as חֹרוֹן.

חָלַף (יַחֲלֹף).—I. *pass by, away*.—II. *put away*. Pi. חִלֵּף *change* (as clothes). Hiph. הֶחֱלִיף.—I. *change* (as clothes).—II. *renew*.

חֲלַף Ch., *pass by* or *away*.

חֵלֶף prep. *for, instead of*, Nu. 18:21, 31.

חֲלוֹף m.; בְּנֵי ח׳ *children of those passed away, orphans*, Pro. 31:8.

חֲלִיפָה f., *change, renewal* (of clothes, troops, &c.).

מַחֲלָף m., *knife for sacrifice*, Ezr. 1:9.

מַחְלָפוֹת pl. f., *locks of hair*, Jud. 16:13, 19.

חָלַץ (fut. יַחֲלִיץ).—I. *deliver, free*.—II. *give the breast*, Lam. 4:3.— III. *gird, arm for battle*, with מִן; חֲלוּץ הַנַּעַל *without sandals*. Niph. —I. *was delivered*.—II. *was armed*.

Pi. *deliver, set free*; חָלוּץ *girt, armed, ready*; חֲלוּץ צָבָא *host armed*; חֲלֻצֵי־מוֹאָב *warriors of Moab*. Hiph. יַחֲלִיץ *make strong*, Isa. 58:11.

חֲלִיצָה f., *spoil*, Jud. 14:19; 2 Sa. 2:21.

חָלָץ m., dual חֲלָצַיִם *loins*.

חֶלֶץ p. n. of a man.

מַחֲלָצוֹת f. pl., *dress of honour, mantle*.

חָלַק (fut. יַחֲלֹק).—I. *apportioned, divided land, wealth, spoil*.—II. *was smooth, fallacious*, with עִם. Niph. *was divided, distributed*. Pi.—I. *divided, distributed*, with אֵת.—II. *dispersed*, with לְ. Pu. *was divided*. Hiph. הֶחֱלִיק.—I. *make smooth, flattering*.—II. *taking portion*, Jer. 37:12. Hithp. *dividing, apportioning*, Jos. 18:5.

חָלָק m., *smooth, slippery, fallacious, flattering*.

חֵלֶק m. (with suff. חֶלְקִי; pl. חֲלָקִים).—I. *part, portion, lot of land, field*.—II. *portion of the sacrifice*.—III. *prey*; חַלְּקֵי נַחַל Isa. 57:6, "smooth stones;" Eng. Ver. *river gods* (Lee); לִי חֵלֶק with בְּ, עִם, אֵת *my portion is with, &c*.—IV. *smoothness*.—V. p. n. of a son of Gilead; חֶלְקִי son of *Chelek*.

חֲלָק m. Ch., *part, portion*.

חַלֻּק m., pl. חַלֻּקִים *smooth stones*, 1 Sa. 17:40.

חֶלְקָה f.—I. *slipperiness*.—II. *flattery*.—III. *portion*; pl. חֲלָקוֹת *slippery ways*, Ps. 73:18.

חֲלֻקָּה f., *division, divided part*, 2 Chron. 35:5.

חֲלַקּוֹת f. pl. Ch., *blandishments*, Dan. 11:32.

חַלְּקֵי pl. const. with dag. euphon., from חֵלֶק.

חֶלְקַי p. n. of a man.

חִלְקִיָּהוּ, חִלְקִיָּה p. n.—I. of a man.—II. the high priest in Josiah's reign.—III. the father of Jeremiah the prophet.—IV. the father of Eliakim.

חֲלַקְלַקּוֹת *very slippery ways, devices*

מַחֲלֹקֶת f. (with suff. מַחֲלֻקְתּוֹ; pl. מַחְלְקוֹת).—I. *appointment, distribution, order, course*.—II. p. n. of a place; סֶלַע הַמַּחְלְקוֹת.

מַחְלְקָה f. Ch., *distribution, order*, Ezr 6:18.

חָלַשׁ (fut. יַחֲלֹשׁ) *grow feeble*, Job 14:10; (fut. יַחֲלֹשׁ) *discomfit, reduce*, with עַל, Ex. 17:13.

חַלָּשׁ m., *weak person*, Joel 4:10.

חֲלוּשָׁה f., *discomfiture*, Ex. 32:18.

חָם m. (with suff. חָמִיךְ, חָמִיהָ) *father-in-law*; see also in חמם.

חָמוֹת f., *mother-in-law*.

חם *hot*; see חמם.

חָמָא root not used; (Arab. *curdled*, of milk).

חֶמְאָה (Syr. חֶמְּה) *cheese, curd*.

חֵמָה f., the same; see also in יחם.

מַחֲמָאוֹת f. pl., Ps. 55:22; read מֵחֶ׳ *than butter*.

חָמַד (fut. יַחְמֹד) *desired, coveted*; part. חָמוּד (pl. m. חֲמוּדִים, f. חֲמֻדוֹת) *desirable thing*. Niph. part. נֶחְמָד *desirable*. Pi. *greatly desired*, Cant. 2:3.

חֶמֶד m., חֶמְדָּה f., *desire, that which is desirable*; חֶמְדַּת כָּל גּוֹיִם *the desire of all nations*, i. e. Messiah Hag. 2:7.

חֲמֻדוֹת, חֲמוּדוֹת f. pl., *desirable things.*

חֶמְדָּן p.n. of a man.

מַחְמָד m. (pl. מַחְמַדִּים) *desirable, desirable things.*

מַחֲמֹדִים m. pl., the same, Lam. 1:7, 11.

חַמָּה, חַמּוּאֵל, חַמּוֹן; see חמם.

חֵמָה same as חֶמְאָה *butter;* see also in יחם.

חֲמוּטַל p. n. of the wife of Josiah.

חָמוּץ *sour;* see חמץ.

חַמּוּק *surround;* see חמק.

חֲמוֹר *ass;* see חמר.

חָמוֹת *mother-in-law;* see חָם.

חֹמֶט m., kind of *lizard,* Lev. 11:30; LXX. σαύρα.

חֲמִישִׁי *fifth;* see חָמֵשׁ.

חָמַל (fut. יַחְמֹל; inf. חֶמְלָה) *bear with, forbear with,* with עַל; *spare,* with אֶל, עַל.

חֶמְלָה f., *clemency.*

מַחְמָל *support, comfort,* Eze. 24:21.

חָמַם (fut. יָחֹם, וַיָּחָם; inf. חֹם, with suff. חַמּוֹ).—I. *be, grow hot;* כְּחֹם הַיּוֹם *in the heat of the day;* חַם לוֹ *he becomes warm.*—II. *hot with lust.* Niph. *became hot, inflamed;* fut. יֵחַם, יֵחַם; part. pl. נֵחָמִים. Pi. *warms, hatches,* Job 39:14. Hithp. *becomes warm,* Job 31:20.

חַם m.—I. *warm, growing hot;* pl. חַמִּים.—II. p. n. of a son of Noah. —III. perhaps Egypt (Copt. χημι), Ps. 78:51, &c.; see also חָם in its place.

חֹם m., *heat;* חֹם לֶחֶם *hot bread,* i.e. new.

חֵמָה f., const. חֲמַת *heat;* see in יחם.

חַמָּה f.—I. *heat, glow,* Ps. 19:7.—II *the sun.*

חַמּוּאֵל p.n. of a man.

חַמּוֹן p. n.—I. of a town in the tribe of Asher.—II. of a town in the tribe of Naphtali.

חַמָּן m., pl. חַמָּנִים *sun-images;* probably the *Amoun* of Egypt; Greek ἀμουν.

חָמַס (fut. יַחְמֹס), *doing violence, injury, wrong,* with עַל. Niph. *violated,* Jer. 13:22.

חָמָס m. (const. חֲמַס; with suff. חֲמָסִי; pl. חֲמָסִים), *violence, injury, that which is obtained by violence.*

תַּחְמָס m., *ostrich;* LXX. γλαῦξ; Vulg. noctua.

חָמֵץ (fut. יֶחְמַץ; with pause יֶחְמָץ; inf. חִמְצָה), *fermented, leavened;* part. חָמוּץ *scarlet;* part. חֹמֵץ. Hiph. part. f. מַחְמֶצֶת *fermented* Hith. *was excited, perturbed,* Ps 73:21.

חָמֵץ m., *leavened, fermented.*

חֹמֶץ m., *vinegar.*

חָמוֹץ m., *injured, oppressed,* Isa. 1:17.

חָמִיץ m., "clean provender," Isa. 30: 24, Eng. Ver.; "a salt, sour plant of the desert, much relished by the camel" (Lee).

חָמַק *withdrew, disappeared,* Cant. 5: 6. Hith. *loiter, act undecidedly,* Jer. 31:22.

חַמּוּק m., חַ׳ יְרֵכַיִךְ Cant. 7:2; probably *large beads,* strung together and worn as a girdle; such girdles are often represented in the tombs of Egypt.

חָמַר (fut. pl. יֶחְמְרוּ), *fermented, was excited.* Poal. חֳמַרְמַר *excited, become inflamed.* (From חֵמָר) Hiph. fut. with suff. וַתַּחְמְרָה *she cemented it with pitch*, Ex. 2:3.

חֵמָר m., *mineral pitch, ἄσφαλτος.*

חֶמֶר m., *wine.*

חֲמַר m., the same.

חֹמֶר m. (pl. חֳמָרִים).—I. *clay, earth, mire.*—II. *heap, mound of earth.* —III. *measure of capacity*, containing ten baths.

חֲמֹר, חֲמוֹר m.—I. *an ass.*—II. *a heap*, Jud. 15:16, same as חֹמֶר; dual חֲמוֹרָתַיִם.—III. p.n. of a man.

חֶמְדָּן, חַמְרָן p. n. of a man.

יַחְמוּר m., *goat* or *gazelle* of a brown colour.

חֹמֶשׁ m., *the abdomen;* see also in חָמֵשׁ

חָמֵשׁ const. חֲמֵשׁ f., חֲמִשָּׁה, חֲמֵשֶׁת m., *five;* pl. חֲמִשִּׁים *fifty;* with suff. חֲמִשָּׁיו, חֲמִשֶּׁיךָ; שַׂר חֲמִשִּׁים *captain of fifty.*

חִמֵּשׁ Pi. *divided into fifth part*, Gen. 41:34.

חֹמֶשׁ m., *fifth part*, Gen. 47:26.

חֲמִישִׁי, חֲמִשִׁי m., *fifth;* f. חֲמִישִׁית, חֲמִשִׁית; pl. with suff. חֲמִשִׁתָיו *the fifth part of it.*

חֲמֻשִׁים m. pl., *compact in battle array;* Aquila ἐνωπλισμένοι; Vulg. armati.

חֵמֶת m., *bottle, skin for holding liquids;* const. חֵמַת, חֵמֶת.

חֲמָת p. n., *Hamath* in Syria, north of Palestine; חֲמָתִי *a Hamathite.*

חַמּוֹת דֹּאר p. n. of a town in the tribe of Naphtali.

חֵן, חֵנָדָד; see חנן.

חָנָה (fut. יַחֲנֶה; apoc. וַיִּחַן).—I. *declined* (of the day), Jud. 19:9.—II. *pitch a tent, encamp;* with עַל *encamp against;* with לְ *defended.* —III. *dwell, reside*, Isa. 29:1.

חָנוּת f., pl. חֲנֻיוֹת *wells* used as dungeons, Jer. 37:16.

חֲנִית f., *spear, lance;* pl. חֲנִיתִים, חֲנִיתוֹת.

מַחֲנֶה m. (f. Gen. 32:9).—I. *camp.* —II. *army, body of people.*—III. *flock of cattle, locusts, &c.;* const. מַחֲנֵה; pl. מַחֲנִים (מַחֲנַיִם) מַחֲנוֹת.

מַחֲנֵה־דָן (*camp of the Danites*), p. n. of a place in the tribe of Judah.

מַחֲנַיִם (*two troops*), p. n. of a town in the tribe of Gad.

תַּחֲנוֹת f. pl., *camp*, 2 Ki. 6:8.

תַּחַן p. n. of a man; תַּחֲנִי *son of Tachan.*

חֲנִינָה, חֲנַנְאֵל, חָנוּן, חַנּוּן, חַנָּה; see חנן.

חָנוֹךְ, חָנִיךְ; see חנך.

חָנַט I. *ripened*, Cant. 2:13.—II. *embalmed, mummified*, Gen. 50:2, 2, 26.

חֲנֻטִים m. pl., *mummy, embalmed body.*

חִטָּה, חִטִּים, חִנְטִין *wheat;* see חִטָּה.

חָנַךְ *adapt, fit to certain ends.*—I. *teach a child*, Pro. 22:6.—II. *dedicate a temple.*

חֵךְ m. (with suff. חִכִּי).—I. *palate, taste.*—II. *moral perception*, Pro 8:7.

חַכָּה f., *fish-hook.*

חָנִיךְ m., *trained men*, Gen. 14:14.

חֲנוֹךְ p. n. of a man; חֲנֹכִי *the son of Chunoch.*

חֲנֻכָּה f., *dedication.*
חֲנֻכָּה Ch., the same.
חִנָּם *in vain;* see חנן.
חֲנַמְאֵל p. n. of a man.
חֲנָמָל m., *frost.*
חָנַן (fut. וַיָּחָן, יֶחֱנַן, יָחֹן; with suff. יְחָנְךָ, יְחָנֵּנוּ, תְּחָנֵּם; with נ epenth. יְחֻנֶּךָּ; inf. abs. חָנוֹן; const. חֲנַן; with suff. חֲנַנְכֶם, חֶנְנָהּ; imper. with suff. חָנֵּנוּ, חָנְנֵנִי, חָנֵּנִי; pl. חָנֻּנִי, חָנּוּנִי), *being, acting favourably, graciously, kindly.* Niph. נֵחַן *was pitiable,* Jer. 22:23. Pi. fut. יְחַנֵּן *be favourable, gracious to.* Po. חוֹנֵן the same, Pro. 14:21. Hoph. fut. יֻחַן *be favoured, find favour.* Hith. הִתְחַנֵּן *implore, supplicate favour,* with לְ, אֶל, לִפְנֵי; inf. with suff. הִתְחַנְנוֹ.
חֲנַן Ch., *show favour.* Hith. *implore favour.*
חֲנַנְאֵל p. n. of a fortress of Jerusalem.
חֲנָנִי p. n. of a man.
חֲנַנְיָה (Ἀνανίας), p. n. of a man.
חֵן m. (with suff. חִנּוֹ).—I. *grace, favour;* מָצָא חֵן בְּעֵינֵי פ׳ *found favour in his sight;* נָתַן חֵן בְּעֵינֵי פ׳ *gave favour in the sight of him.*—II. *elegance, grace of deportment.*—III. *worth, value.*—IV. *prayer for grace,* Zec. 12:10.—V. p.n. of a man.
חֵנָדָד p. n. of a man.
חִין m., *destructiveness,* Job 41:4.
חַנָּה f. (pl. חַנּוֹת).—I. *entreaty for favour, showing favour.*—II. p. n. of a woman, Ἄννα.
חָנוּן p. n. of a man.
חַנּוּן m., *very gracious.*
חַנִּיאֵל p. n. of a man.
חֲנִינָה f., *grace, favour,* Jer. 16:13.
חִנָּם adv.—I. *freely, for nothing.*—II. *in vain.*—III. *for nothing, undeservedly.*
תְּחִנָּה f.—I. *favour, mercy.*—II. *prayer for favour, prayer.*
תַּחֲנוּנִים m. pl., *prayers for mercy, supplications.*
תַּחֲנוּנוֹת f. pl., the same.
חָנֵס p. n. of a city in Egypt (Ἡρακλέους πόλις).
חָנֵף (fut. יֶחֱנַף), *was heathenish, profane, ungodly.* Hiph. הֶחֱנִיף the same.
חָנֵף m., *profane, ungodly;* חֲנֵפִים, חַנְפֵי.
חֹנֶף m., *heathenism,* Isa. 32:6.
חֲנֻפָּה f., the same, Jer. 23:15.
חָנַק. Niph. fut. וַיֵּחָנַק *hanged himself,* 2 Sa. 17:23. Pi. part. מְחַנֵּק *suffocating,* Nah. 2:13.
מַחֲנָק m., *suffocation,* Job 7:15.
חָסַד. Pi. חִסֵּד *accuse of baseness, impiety,* Pro. 25:10. Hith. (fut. תִּתְחַסָּד) *show thyself merciful,* 2 Sa. 22:26; Ps. 18:26.
חֶסֶד m. (with suff. חַסְדּוֹ; pl. חֲסָדִים, חַסְדֵי).—I. *favour, kindness, mercy;* עָשָׂה חֶסֶד with אֵת, עַל, לְ, עִם *he showed mercy to him.*—II. *goodness, benevolence.*—III. *shame, disgrace, incest,* Lev. 20:17.—IV. p. n. of a man.
חֲסַדְיָה p. n. of the son of Zerubbabel.
חָסִיד m., *gracious, confident;* חֲסִידֵי יְהוָֹה *they that trust in the Lord.*
חֲסִידָה f., *stork,* supposed by the ancients to be pious to its parents.

חָסָה (fut. אֶחְסֶה, אֶחֱסֶה), *trust, confide in*, with בְּ.

חֹסָה p. n. of a man.

חָסוּת f., *confidence*, Isa. 30:3.

חָסְיָה for חָסְתָה Kal pret. f.; pl. חָסָיוּ for חָסוּ, from חסה.

מַחְסֶה, מַחֲסֶה m. (with suff. מַחֲסִי), *refuge*.

מַחְסֵיָה p. n. of a man.

חָסַל *crop off, devour*, Deu. 28:38.

חָסִיל m., *kind of locust*, LXX. βροῦχος.

חָסַם (fut. יַחְסֹם), *bind, tie up, stop* (the mouth).

מַחְסוֹם m., *bridle, curb*, Ps. 39:2.

חָסַן. Niph. fut. יֵחָסֵן *was strong, powerful*, Isa. 23:18.

חֲסַן Ch. Aph. *confirm, make strong*.

חֱסֵן m. Ch., *might, power*.

חֹסֶן m., *strength, power, wealth*.

חָסוֹן m., *strong, powerful*.

חֲסִין m., *mighty*, Ps. 89:9.

חֲסַף m., *potter's clay*.

מְחֻסְפָּס m., *scaly, having scales*, Ex. 16:14.

חָסֵר (inf. חָסוֹר; fut. יֶחְסַר, יַחְסְרוּ) *want, lack, be in need*. Pi. *diminish, make to want*. Hiph. הֶחְסִיר *cause to fall short*.

חָסֵר m., *wanting, destitute of*, with מִן; חֲסַר־לֵב *without heart* (i. e. *sense*), *foolish*.

חֶסֶר m., *deficiency, want*.

חֹסֶר m., the same.

חַסְרָה (תַּרְחַס) p. n. of a man.

חֶסְרוֹן m., *much want*, Ecc. 1:15.

חַסִּיר m. Ch., *deficient*, Dan. 5:27.

מַחְסוֹר m. (with suff. מַחְסֹרוֹ; pl. מַחְסֹרִים) *want, lack, need*.

חָפָא same as חָפָה. Pi. *acted secretly, clandestinely*, 2 Ki. 17:9.

חָפָה *covered, veiled*. Pi. חִפָּה *overlaid, cased* (with gold). Pu. חֻפָּה "defence;" Eng. Ver., Isa. 4:5; see חָפַף. Niph. נֶחְפָּה *covered. overlaid*, with בְּ, Ps. 68:14.

חָפַז (fut. יַחְפֹּז).—I. *affright, alarm*.—II. *hurry*. Niph. נֶחְפַּז *was hurried*.

חִפָּזוֹן m., *haste, hurry*.

חָפַן root not used; (Arab. a measure containing two hands full).

חֹפֶן m., dual חָפְנַיִם, חָפְנֵי both hands closed so as to contain something.

חָפְנִי p.n. of the son of Eli.

חָפַף *cover, protect*, Deu. 33:12, with עַל.

חוֹף, חֹף m., *shore of the sea*.

חַף m., *pure, faultless*, Job 33:9 (lit. protected).

חֻפָּה f.—I. *defence*; see חפף.—II. *bridal chamber*.—III. p. n. of a man.

חֻפִּים p.n. of a man.

חָפֵץ (fut. יֶחְפַּץ, יַחְפֹּץ).—I. *delight, be pleased with*, with לְ and בְּ.—II. *bend, move*.

חָפֵץ m., *willing, delighting, acquiescing*; אִם ח׳ אַתָּה *if thou wilt*; ח׳ רֶשַׁע *delighting in wickedness*.

חֵפֶץ m. (with suff. חֶפְצִי).—I. *pleasure, delight*.—II. *wish, desire, will*.—III. *costly, precious*.—IV. *business, concern, affair*; pl. חֲפָצִים *precious things*.

חֶפְצִי־בָהּ *my delight* (*is*) *in her*.—I. a mystic title of Christ's true church, Isa. 62:4.—II. p. n. of the mother of Manasseh, 2 Ki. 21:1.

חָפַר (fut. יַחְפֹּר).—I. *dig* (as a well, &c). —II. *search out, investigate;* חָפֵר (fut. יֶחְפַּר) *blush, be ashamed, confounded.* Hiph. הֶחְפִּיר.—I. *blush.* —II. *cause to blush, put to shame.*

חֵפֶר p. n.—I. of a city of Canaan.— II. of a man; חֶפְרִי *a Hepherite.*

חֲפָרַיִם p. n. of a town in the tribe of Issachar.

חֲפַר־פֵּרוֹת (digger), *a mole,* Isa. 2:20; probably wrong reading for חֲפַרְפֵּרוֹת *moles.*

חָפְרַע p. n., *Pharaoh Hophra* king of Egypt; LXX. Οὐαφρῆ.

חָפַשׂ *search, investigate.* Niph. *shall be sought out,* Obad. *v.* 6. Pi. חִפֵּשׂ *search diligently.* Pu. חֻפַּשׂ *is searched.* Hithp. הִתְחַפֵּשׂ (from another root), *was clothed, bound, equipped, accoutred.*

חֵפֶשׂ m., *search, enquiry,* Ps. 64:7.

חָפַשׁ. Pu. חֻפָּשָׁה *she was freed,* Lev. 19:20.

חֹפֶשׁ m. בִּגְדֵי ח׳ *clothes of liberation,* i. e. *spread out to exhibit for sale,* Eze. 27:20.

חֻפְשָׁה f., *freedom,* Lev. 19:20.

חָפְשִׁי m. (pl. חָפְשִׁים), *free from servitude, evil, &c.;* בַּמֵּתִים ח׳ *free from the dead,* Ps. 88:6, i. e. free from the evils of life.

חָפְשׁוּת, חָפְשִׁית f., *freedom from business, servitude, &c.* בֵּית ח׳ *retreat, place of retirement,* 2 Ki. 15:5.

חֵץ *arrow;* see חצץ.

חָצַב and **חָצֵב** (fut. יַחְצֹב) *cut, hew out wood, stone, metal, &c.;* part. חֹצֵב s., *hewer;* applied to lightning, 1 Chron. 22:2, 15. Niph. *was engraven,* Job 19:24. Pu. *hewn,* Isa. 51:1. Hiph. *cause to cut to pieces.*

מַחְצֵב m., *hewing* (of stones).

חָצָה (fut. יֶחֱצֶה; apoc. וַיַּחַץ) *divide, apportion,* Ps. 55:24; לֹא־יֶחֱצוּ יְמֵיהֶם *shall not live out half their days.* Niph. *was divided.*

חָצוֹת const. חֲצוֹת f., *middle.*

חֲצִי with pause חֵצִי m. (with suff. חֶצְיוֹ) *half, part, portion of any thing;* see also in חצץ.

חֲצִי הַמְּנֻחוֹת p. n. of a man; patron. חֲצִי הַמָּנַחְתִּי.

מֶחֱצָה f., *half,* Nu. 31:36, 43.

מַחֲצִית f., the same.

חָצוֹר, חֲצוֹצְרָה, חָצִיר; see חצר.

חָצַן root not used; (Arab. *bosom*)

חֵצֶן m.—I. *bosom, chest.*—II. *bosom of garment,* perhaps, *girdle,* Neh. 5:13; with suff. חִצְנוֹ.

חֹצֶן m., the same; with suff. חָצְנִי.

חֲצַף Ch. Aph. *was urgent, pressing,* Dan. 2:15; 3:22.

חָצַץ, part. חֹצֵץ *rushing on,* Pro. 30:27. Pi. part. pl. מְחַצְצִים *persons taking part* (in conversation), Jud. 5:11. Pu. *are cut, decided,* Job 21:21.

חָצָץ m.—I. *gravel.*—II. *arrow,* i. e. lightning, Ps. 77:18.

חֵץ m. (with suff. חִצִּי; pl. חִצִּים, חִצֵּי).—I. *arrow;* בַּעֲלֵי־חִצִּים *bowmen.*—II. metaph. *lightning.*

חַצְצוֹן־תָּמָר and חַצֲצֹן־תָּמָר p. n. of a place in the tribe of Judah.

חֲצֹצְרָה *trumpet;* see חצר.

חָצַר root not used.—I. (Arab. *surrounding*).—II. (Arab. *field*).

חָצֵר com. (pl. חֲצֵרוֹת, חֲצֵרִים).—I. *enclosure, area, court.*—II. *village;* חֲצַר־אַדָּר (*threshing-floor of Addar*), p. n. of a town in the tribe of Judah; ח׳ סוּסִים, ה׳ סוּסָה p. n. of a town in the tribe of Simeon; ח׳ עֵינָן, ח׳ עֵינוֹן a town in the north of Palestine; ח׳ שׁוּעָל a town in the tribe of Simeon; חָצֵר הַתִּיכוֹן a town on the borders of Syria; חֲצֵרוֹת p. n. of a station in the desert.

חָצוֹר p. n.—I. of a town in the tribe of Naphtali.—II. of a town in the tribe of Benjamin.—III. of a region of Arabia.

חֶצְרוֹן p. n.—I. of a son of Reuben.—II. of a son of Perez; patron. חֶצְרוֹנִי.

חֶצְרַי p. n. of a man.

חֲצַרְמָוֶת (*court of death*), p. n. of a district in Arabia.

חָצִיר m.—I. *enclosure* (habitable place).—II. *grass;* see root II.

חֲצוֹצְרָה, חֲצֹצְרָה f., *trumpet;* from this word comes Pi. מְחַצְּרִים or Hiph. מַחְצְרִים (ketib מַחֲצֹצְרִים, מְחַצְּרִים) *persons blowing with trumpets.*

חֵק *bosom;* see חֵיק.

חֹק, חָק־, חֻקָּה; see חקק.

חָקָה. Pu. part. מְחֻקֶּה *engraven, carved.* Hith. with עַל *impressed, furrowed,* Job 13:27.

חֲקוּפָא p. n. of a man.

חָקַק *carve, engrave, inscribe;* part. חֹקֵק *legislator,* Jud. 5:9. Pu. part. מְחֻקָּק *statute,* Pro. 31:5. Po. *decide, decree,* Pro. 8:15; part. מְחֹקֵק *lawgiver.* Hoph. fut. יֻחָקוּ *engraven, inscribed,* Job 19:23

חֵקֶק m., pl. const. חִקְקֵי.—I. *impressions, imaginations,* Jud. 5:15.—II. *decrees,* Isa. 10:1.

חֹק, חָק־, חֹק m. (with suff. חֻקְּךָ, חָקְךָ; pl. חֻקִּים, חֻקֵּי, חֻקֵּי).—I. *statute, law.*—II. *custom, privilege.*

חֻקָּה f.—I. *statute.*—II. *custom.*

חָקַר (fut. יַחְקֹר; inf. חֲקֹר), *search, investigate, try.* Niph. נֶחְקַר *that may be searched.* Pi. חִקֵּר like Kal, Ecc. 12:9.

חֵקֶר m., *investigation, search, enquiry.*

מֶחְקָר m., pl. const. מֶחְקְרֵי *depths* (of the earth), Ps. 95:4.

חֹר, חֵר; see חָרַר חוּר.

חָרָא root not used; (Arab. *dung*).

חָרָא or **חֶרֶא** m., pl. חֲרָאִים *dung,* Isa. 36:12.

חַר or **חָר** m., the same; pl. const. חֲרֵי.

מַחֲרָאָה f., *draught-house,* 2 Ki. 10:27.

חָרֵב (fut. יֶחֱרַב, יֶחֱרַב).—I. *dry, be dry.*—II. *desolate, ruin.* Niph. נֶחֱרַב *was ruined.* Pu. חֹרַב *been dried.* Hiph. הֶחֱרִיב I. *dry up.*—II. *ruin.* Hoph. הָחֳרַב *was wasted, destroyed.*

חֲרֵב Ch. Hoph. f., הָחָרְבַת *is wasted,* Ezr. 4:15.

חָרֵב m.—I. *dry.*—II. *desolate, devastated;* f. חֲרֵבָה; pl. חֲרֵבוֹת.

חֶרֶב f. (with suff. חַרְבִּי; pl. חֲרָבוֹת). I. *sword.*—II. *sharp weapon* or *cutting instrument.*—III. *drought,* Deut. 28:22.

חֹרֶב m.—I. *drought.*—II. *heat.*—III *desolation.*

חֹרֵב, חוֹרֵב (*dry, desolate*), p. n. of one of the summits of Sinai.

חָרְבָּה f., pl. חֳרָבוֹת (const. חָרְבוֹת) *desolations.*

חָרָבָה f., *drought.*

חֲרָבוֹן m., pl. const. חַרְבֹנֵי *great droughts*, Ps. 32:4.

חַרְבוֹנָא p.n. of a Persian eunuch.

חָרַג *suffer pressure, trouble*, Ps. 18:46.

חַרְגֹּל m., *the larva of the locust*, Lev. 11:22.

חָרַד or חָרֵד (fut. יֶחֱרַד), *was timid, fearful, trembling*, with אֶל, לְ or מִן. Hiph. *affrighted.*

חָרֵד m.—I. *fearful, anxious*, with בְּ, אֶל, עַל.—II. *trembling.*

חֲרָדָה const. חֶרְדַּת f.—I. *fear.*—II. *trembling.*—III. p. n. of a station of the Israelites, Nu. 33:24.

חֲרוֹד p. n. of a place in the mountain of Gilboa, Ju. 7:1; חֲרֹדִי *a Harodite*, 2 Sa. 23:25.

חָרָה (inf. abs. חָרֹה; fut. יֶחֱרֶה; apoc. יִחַר), *was, became hot, angry*; חָרָה אַפּוֹ with בְּ, אֶל, עַל *his anger was kindled against*; חָרָה לוֹ *he was angry*; חָרָה בְּעֵינָיו *it grieved him*. Niph. נִחֲרוּ *were enraged, angry*; part. נֶחֱרִים *angry*. Hiph. הֶחֱרָה.—I. *made angry.*—II. *became warm, zealous*, Neh. 3:20. Hithp. fut. apoc. תִּתְחַר *be thou vexed.*

חָרוֹן m.—I. חֲ׳ אַף *heat of anger.*—II. *angry person*, Ps. 58:10.

חֳרִי m.; חֳ׳ אַף *heat, burning.*

תַּחְרָא m., "habergeon," Eng. Ver., Ex. 28:32, &c.; meaning uncertain.

תַּחֲרָה *contend with, emulate*, Jer 12:5; 22:15.

חָרוּז m., pl. חֲרוּזִים *necklace of precious stones*, Cant. 1:10.

חָרוּל m., *a thorny shrub*; pl. חֲרֻלִּים.

חָרוּץ *fine gold*; see חרץ.

חַרְחֻר *heat*; see חרר.

חָרַט (Arab. *engraver*).

חָרִיט m., pl. חֲרִיטִים *pockets, purses.*

חֶרֶט m.—I. *graving tool*, Ex. 32:4.—II. *writing style*, Isa. 8:1.

חַרְטֹם m., pl. חַרְטֻמִּים.—I. *the sacred scribes of Egypt who engraved hieroglyphics*, ἱερογραμματεῖς.—II. *the wise men of Babylon*, Dan. 1:20; 2:2.

חַרְטֻמִּין m. pl. Ch., same as חַרְטֻמִּים *wise men, magicians.*

חֳרִי *heat*; see חָרָה.

חֹרִי *bread*; see חָוַר.

חֲרֵי pl. const. from חַר *dung*; see חרא.

חָרִיץ *cutting*; see חרץ.

חָרִישׁ, חֲרִישִׁי; see חרשׁ.

חָרַךְ (fut. יַחֲרֹךְ), *roasts*, Pro. 12:27.

חֲרַךְ Ch. Hith. *was burnt*, Dan. 3:27.

חֲרַכִּים m. pl., *latticed windows*, LXX. δίκτυα, Cant. 2:9.

חָרַם. Kal not used; (Arab. *forbidden, sacred*). Hiph. הֶחֱרִים.—I. *devote to destruction.*—II. *apply to sacred uses*. Hoph. הָחֳרַם.—I. *was devoted to destruction, slain.*—II. *was consecrated.*

חֵרֶם m. (with suff. חֶרְמִי).—I. *devotion to destruction.*—II. *the thing so devoted.*

חֳרֵם p.n. of a town in the tribe of Naphtali.

חֵרֶם m. with suff. חֶרְמִי; (pl. חֲרָמִים). I. *a net.*— II. *allurements*, Ecc. 7:26.

חָרֻם m. (Arab. *cut off, tear*), *flat-nosed*, Lev. 21:18.

חָרִם p. n. of a man.

חָרְמָה p. n. of a town of the Canaanites.

חֶרְמוֹן p. n. of a range of hills in Anti-Libanus; חֶרְמֹנִים *Hermonites.*

חֶרְמֵשׁ m. (from חָרַם and חָרַשׁ), *sickle, reaping hook.*

חָרָן p. n.—I. of a city of Mesopotamia, Χαῤῥάν.—II. of a city of Arabia. —III. of a man.

חֹרֹנַיִם p. n. of a place; see חָוַר.

חַרְנֶפֶר p. n. of a man.

חָרַשׁ, חָרַם root not used; (Arab. *scratching*).

חֶרֶם m., *the itch*, Deu. 28:27.

חֶרֶם m. (with ה parag. חַרְסָה), *the sun*, Ju. 8:13; 14:18; עִיר הַהֶרֶס prophetic name of a city in Egypt, Isa. 19:18; see הֶרֶס.

חֶרֶשׂ m., *earthenware, potsherd;* כְּלִי חֶרֶשׂ *earthen vase.*

חַרְסוּת f., *pottery;* שַׁעַר הַחַרְסוּת *the potter's gate*, one of the gates of Jerusalem.

חָרַף (fut. יֶחֱרַף).—I. *pluck* (the fruit of), *eat up*, Isa. 18:6.—II. *strip of honour, value; reproach.* Pi. חֵרֵף I. *reproach, blaspheme.*—II. *expose to reproach*, Ju. 5:18. Niph. part. f. נֶחֱרֶפֶת *deprived of all right, espoused*, Lev. 19:20.

חֹרֶף m.—I. *autumn.*—II. *youth*, Job 29:4, (the year was supposed to begin in autumn).

חֶרְפָּה f. (pl. חֲרָפוֹת; const. חֶרְפּוֹת). —I. *reproach, contempt.*—II. *person* or *thing reproached.*

חָרִיף p. n. of a man; patron. חֲרִיפִי.

חָרֵף p. n. of a man.

חָרַץ (fut. יֶחֱרַץ).—I. *was sharp, active, courageous.*—II. *was decided, determined;* part. חָרוּץ.—I. *maimed, rent*, Lev. 22:22.—II. *decided, determined.*—III. *punishment.* Niph. part. f. נֶחֱרָצָה, נֶחֱרֶצֶת *decided, determined, decreed.*

חָרוּץ m.—I. *ditch, foss.*—II. *the sharp spikes of a thrashing dray;* pl. const. חֲרֻצוֹת.—III. *sharpened, instructed.*—IV. *gold.*—V. *decree;* pl. חָרוּצִים; see חרץ.—VI. p. n. of a man.

חָרִיץ m. (pl. const. חֲרִיצֵי).—I. *cuttings of cheese*, LXX. τρυφαλίς, 1 Sa. 17:18.—II. same as חָרוּץ *spikes, sharp points.*

חַרְצָן m., pl. חַרְצַנִּים *sour grapes*, Nu. 6:4.

חֲרַץ Ch., same as Heb. חָלָץ *loins*, Dan. 5:6.

חַרְצֻבּוֹת f. pl.—I. *bonds, bandages*, Ps. 73:4.—II. *grievous pains*, Isa. 58:6.

חָרַק (fut. יַחֲרֹק), *ground, gnashed the teeth;* (with שִׁנַּיִם, בְּשִׁנַּיִם and עַל *against*).

חָרַר.—I. *was hot.*—II. *was dry.* Niph. נִחַר, נָחַר (fut. יֵחַר), *was hot, dry;* נִחַר *became dry.* Pilp. inf. חַרְחַר *make hot, kindle*, as fire, Pro. 26:21.

חֲרֵרִים m. pl., *dry, parched places*, Jer. 17:6.

חֹר m., pl. חֹרִים, חוֹרִים *nobles, great men*; see also חָוַר.

חַרְחֻר m. — I. *inflammation, fever*, Deu. 28:22.—II p.n. of a man.

חֶרֶשׂ *potsherd*; see חרס.

חָרַשׁ (fut. יַחֲרֹשׁ).—I. *cut, plough the land.*—II. *engrave, sculpture*, with עַל (חֹרֵשׁ *ploughman*).—III. (fut. יֶחֱרַשׁ) *was dumb, silent, was deaf*, with מִן. Niph. *was ploughed*. Hiph.—I. *engrave, carve.*—II. *fabricate, devise evil*, 1 Sa. 23:9.—III. *be still, quiet*. Hith. fut. pl. יִתְחָרְשׁוּ *were silent*, Ju. 16:2.

חָרִישׁ m., *ploughing, tilling the land*; חֲרִישׁוֹ *his field.*

חֲרִישִׁי m., חֲרִישִׁית f., *very drying*, Jon. 4:8.

חָרָשׁ m. (const. חָרַשׁ; pl. חָרָשִׁים, חָרָשֵׁי), *worker, artificer*, in wood, stone, metal, &c.; חָרָשֵׁי מַשְׁחִית *forgers of destruction*, Eze. 21:36.

חֶרֶשׁ m.—I. *cunning work*; (גֵּי חֲרָשִׁים *valley of the mechanics*, near Jerusalem). — II. *silence, silently.*—III. p. n. of a man.

חֹרֶשׁ m. *wood, forest*; pl. חֳרָשִׁים; חֹרְשָׁה *into the wood*; בַּחֹרְשָׁה *in the wood.*

חֹרֵשׁ m., *artificer; cutting instrument* (Gesen.), Gen. 4:22.

חֵרֵשׁ m., *deaf*; pl. חֵרְשִׁים.

חַרְשָׁא p. n. of a man.

חֲרֹשֶׁת f.—I. *sculpture.*—II. p. n. of a place in North Palestine.

מַחֲרֵשָׁה f., *coulter*, 1 Sa. 13:21; pl. מַחֲרֵשׁוֹת.

מַחֲרֶשֶׁת f. (with suff. מַחֲרַשְׁתּוֹ), *ploughshare*, 1 Sa. 13:20.

חָרַת same as חָרַשׁ; part. חָרוּת *cut, engraven*, Ex. 32:16.

חֶרֶת (same as חֹרֶשׁ), p. n. of a wood in the tribe of Judah.

חָשִׂיף, חֲשׂוּפָא; see חשף.

חָשַׂךְ (fut. וָאֶחְשֹׂךְ, אֶחֱשׂךְ, תַּחְשֹׂךְ). I. *withhold, keep back.*—II. *save*, with מִן.—III. *refuse.*—IV. *spare*. חֹשֵׂךְ *sparing*, Pro. 13:24. Niph. fut. יֵחָשֵׂךְ *is restrained*, Job 16:6; יֵחָשֶׂךְ id. 21:30.

חָשַׂף (fut. יֶחֱשֹׂף), *make bare, denudate, expose.*—II. *draw* (as water)

חֲשׂוּפָא p.n. of a man.

חָשִׂיף m., *flock*, 1 Ki. 20:27.

מַחְשֹׂף m., *laying bare*, Gen. 30:37

חָשַׁב (fut. יַחְשֹׁב, יַחֲשָׁב־).—I. *think, devise, meditate.*— II. *consider, esteem, reckon, impute*, with inf. and לְ. חֹשֵׁב *artificer, deviser*; with לֹא *of no esteem*. Niph. נֶחְשַׁב (fut. יֵחָשֵׁב) *was thought, esteemed, computed, reckoned*, with לְ, כְּ, עִם, בְּ, עַל. Pi. חִשַּׁב *think, compute, esteem, reckon*, with אֶל. Hithp. *was accounted*, Nu. 23:9.

חֲשַׁב Ch., *considered, esteemed*, Dan. 4:32.

חֵשֶׁב m., *the belt, girdle of the ephod.*

חֶשְׁבּוֹן m.—I. *device, discovery.*— II. p. n. of a city of the Amorites, Ἑσβοῦς.

חִשָּׁבוֹן m. pl., חִשְּׁבוֹנוֹת *warlike machines*, 2 Chron. 26:15.

חַשַׁבְדָּנָה p. n. of a man.

חַשּׁוּב p. n. of a man.

חֲשֻׁבָה p. n. of a man.

חֲשַׁבְיָה, חֲשַׁבְיָהוּ p. n. of a man.

חֲשַׁבְנְיָה, חֲשַׁבְנָה p. n. of a man

מַחֲשָׁבָה, מַחֲשֶׁבֶת f. (pl. מַחֲשָׁבוֹת; const. מַחְשְׁבוֹת).—I. *thought, design, project.*—II. *work of art, ingenuity.*

חָשָׁה *was silent.* Hiph. הֶחֱשָׁה, part. מַחְשֶׁה *was* or *made silent.*

חֲשַׁח Ch., *persons, things wanting.*

חַשְׁחוּת f. Ch., *want, necessity,* Ezr. 7:20.

חֲשֵׁיכָה same as חֲשֵׁכָה *dark;* see חשך.

חָשַׁךְ (fut. יֶחְשַׁךְ) *be, become obscure, dark.* Hiph. הֶחֱשִׁיךְ *made dark, obscure;* fut. יַחְשִׁיךְ.

חָשֹׁךְ m., pl. חֲשֻׁכִּים *obscure persons,* Pro. 22:29.

חֹשֶׁךְ m. (with suff. חָשְׁכִּי).—I. *darkness.*—II. *ignorance.*—III *calamity, misery, destruction.*

חֲשׁוֹךְ m. Ch., *darkness.*

חָשֵׁךְ m., pl. חֲשֵׁכִים *obscured, darkened.*

חֲשֵׁכָה, חֲשֵׁיכָה f., *obscurity, darkness.*

חֶשְׁכָּה, חָשְׁכָה f., the same.

מַחְשָׁךְ m., I. *darkness.*—II. *adversity, trouble;* pl. מַחֲשַׁכִּים, מַחֲשַׁכֵּי.

חָשַׁל. Niph. part. נֶחֱשָׁלִים *debilitated, infirm persons,* Deu. 25:18.

חֲשַׁל Ch., *pounded to powder,* Dan. 2:40.

חַשְׁמַל some brilliant white or pale yellow metal; LXX. ἤλεκτρον.

חָשֻׁם p.n. of a man.

חֶשְׁמוֹן p.n. of a town in the tribe of Judah.

חַשְׁמוֹנָה p.n. of a station of the Israelites in the desert.

חַשְׁמַן m., pl. חַשְׁמַנִּים *rich, powerful men,* Ps. 68:32

חָשַׁן (Arab. *to adorn*).

חֹשֶׁן m., *breast-plate* of the high priest, called also ח׳ הַמִּשְׁפָּט.

חָשַׁק.—I. *desire, delight in,* with בְּ.—II. *it pleased, seemed good,* with לְ and inf. Pi. חִשֵּׁק *attached to,* Ex. 38:28. Pu. *was joined to,* Ex. 27:17.

חֵשֶׁק m. (with suff. חִשְׁקִי), *desire, delight.*

חֲשֻׁקִים, חֲשׁוּקִים m. pl.—the *tie-rods* or *poles* which passed through the upright pillars of the forecourt of the tabernacle.

חִשֻּׁקִים m. pl., *spokes of a wheel,* 1 Ki. 7:33.

חָשַׁר root not used; (Arab. *collected*).

חַשְׁרָה f., *collection of waters,* 2 Sam. 22:12.

חִשֻּׁרִים m. pl., *naves of wheels,* 1 Ki. 7:33.

חֲשַׁשׁ m., *dry grass, hay.*

חֵת, pl. חִתִּים p. n. of a people of Canaan.

חָתָה (fut. יַחְתֶּה), *take up* and *remove* (as fire, coals, &c.), *lay hold of;* fut. with suff. יַחְתְּךָ *he will lay hold on thee,* Ps. 52:7.

מַחְתָּה f.—I. *shovel* or *pan* for removing hot coals.—II. *censer.*—III. *dishes* for receiving the snuffs of the lamps; LXX. ὑπόθεμα.

חַת, חִתָּה, חַתְחַת, חִתִּית; see חתת.

חָתַךְ. Niph. נֶחְתַּךְ *has been determined,* Dan. 9:24.

חָתַל. Pu. and Hoph. חֻתַּלְתְּ, הָחְתֵּל לֹא, *thou wast not bandaged,* Eze. 16:4.

חִתּוּל m., *bandage for a wound,* Eze. 30:21.

חֲתֻלָּה f., *swaddling, bandage,* Job 38:9.

חֶתְלֹן p. n. of a place in Syria.

חָתַם (fut. יַחְתֹּם).—I. *seal, seal up.*—II. *conclude, finish,* with בְּ, בְּעַד. Niph. *was, became sealed.* Pi. *sealed, determined upon,* Job 24:16. Hiph. הֶחְתִּים *seal, shut up,* Lev. 15:3.

חֲתַם Ch., *sealed.*

חוֹתָם m. (with suff. חֹתָמְךָ).—I. *seal-ring.*— II. *seal.*— III. p. n. of a man.

חֹתֶמֶת f., *seal,* Gen. 38:25.

חָתַן, part. m. חֹתֵן *father-in-law, wife's father;* f. חֹתֶנֶת *mother-in-law, wife's mother;* with suff. חֹתַנְתּוֹ. Hith. הִתְחַתֵּן *became related by marriage,* specially with a daughter, with אֶת, בְּ, לְ.

חָתָן m. (const. חֲתַן; with suff. חֲתָנוֹ; pl. חֲתָנִים).—I. *relative.*—II. *son-in-law.*—III. *bridegroom.*—IV. *relative by blood,* i. e. circumcision, חֲתַן־דָּמִים Ex. 4:25, 26.

חֲתֻנָּה f., *marriage,* Cant. 3:11.

חָתַף same as חָטַף; (Arab. *destruction;*) fut. יַחְתֹּף *snatch away,* Job 9:12.

חֶתֶף m., אִישׁ ח׳ *man of rapine,* Pro. 23:28.

חָתַר (fut. יַחְתֹּר).—I. *dig, delve,* with בְּ *into.*—II. *row* (dig into water), Jon. 1:13.

מַחְתֶּרֶת f., *digging through,* i. e. breaking in.

חָתַת *be, become broken with shame, fear, &c.* Niph. נִחַת (fut. יֵחַת; pl. יֵחַתּוּ), same as Kal, with מִן, מִפְּנֵי. Pi. חִתֵּת I. *broken to pieces, shivered.*—II. *affrighted,* Job 7:14. Hiph. הֵחַת (pret. הַחִתֹּתָ, הַחְתַּתִּי), *break to pieces, ruin.*

חֲתַת m.—I. *ruin,* Job 6:21.—II. p.n. of a man.

חַת m. (with suff. חִתְּכֶם; pl. חַתִּים) *broken, spoiled,* applied to persons or things.

חִתָּה f.—I. the same.—II. *fear,* Gen. 35:5.

חִתִּית f., *fear, terror, dread.*

חַתְחַת m., pl. חַתְחַתִּים *broken down with fear,* Ecc. 12:5.

מְחִתָּה f.—I. *stroke, injury, ruin.*—II. *fear, terror.*

ט

טְאֵב Ch., *was glad,* Dan. 6:24.

טֵאטֵא *debase;* see טוא.

טָב, טָבְאֵל; see טוב.

טְבוּלִים m. pl. (Ethiop. טבלל *folded*) *turbans,* Eze. 23:15.

טַבּוּר m., *mountain, high place.*

טָבַח (inf. const. טְבֹחַ; imp. טְבַח) *slaughter,* specially animals for eating, also of men.

טַבָּח m.—I. *cook, butcher.*—II. *officer of state,* probably, executioner; שַׂר (רַב) טַבָּחִים *chief officer.*

טַבָּח m. Ch., *officer of state.*

טַבָּחָה f., *female cook.*

טֶבַח m. (with suff. טִבְחָהּ).—I. *slaughter of animals.* — II. *animals slaughtered.*—III. p. n. of a man.

טִבְחָה f., the same.

אֲבַטִּיחִים (trans.) m. pl., *melons,* Nu. 11:5.

מַטְבֵּחַ m., *slaughter*, Isa 14:21.

טִבְחַת (elsewhere בֶּטַח), p. n. of a city of Syria.

טָבַל I. *dip, plunge.* — II. *stain, dye.* Niph. *were dipped*, Jos. 3:15.

טְבוּלִים; see in its place.

טְבַלְיָהוּ p.n. of a man.

טָבַע *sunk down* (as into mud). Pu. טֻבַּע *sank in, were immerged*, Ex. 15:4. Hoph. הָטְבַּע *were let in* (as pillars in their bases, &c.).

טַבַּעַת f. (pl. טַבָּעוֹת; const. טַבְּעוֹת). —I. *seal ring.*—II. any *ring.*

טַבָּעוֹת p.n. of a man.

טַבְרִמּוֹן; see טוֹב.

טַבָּת p.n. of a town in the tribe of Ephraim.

טֵבֵת m., the tenth month of the Hebrew year, Est. 2:16.

טָהֵר (fut. יִטְהַר) *was, became, clean, pure*, from disease, from legal uncleanness, from moral impurity. Pi. טִהַר.—I. *cleanse, purify.*—II. *declare clean.* Pu. *was purified.* Hithp. הִטָּהֵר (pl. הִטֶּהָרוּ; imp. pl. הִטַּהֲרוּ) *was, became clean, purified.*

טָהוֹר (const. טְהוֹר, טְהָר־; f. טְהֹרָה; pl. טְהֹרוֹת) *clean, pure.*

טֹהַר m.— I. *brightness, glory.*— II. *purification.*

טֳהָר m., } the same.
טָהֳרָה f., }

טְוָא Ch., root not used; (Syr. *fasted*).

טְוָת f. Ch., *fasting*, Dan. 6:19.

טוּא or טוֹא. Pil. טֵאטֵא *humble, debase*; part. מְטַאֲטֵא *humbling, debasing*, Isa. 14:23.

טוֹב (pret. pl. טֹבוּ; fut. יִיטַב from יָטַב) *was good, agreeable*; טוֹב לִי *it pleases me*, Nu. 24:1; with בְּעֵינֵי the same. Hiph. הֵטִיב *do well, liberally, make good*, Hos. 10:1; *make happy*, Ecc. 11:9.

טוֹב m. טוֹבָה f.—I. *good.*—II. *happy, prosperous.* — III. *valuable.* — IV. *handsome* (goodlike).— V. *kind.*— VI. used adverbially, *well, rightly*; s. m. and f. טוֹבָה.— I. *goodness.* —II. *wealth.*—III. *prosperity, happiness*; לְטוֹבָה, לְטוֹב, with לְ *that it may be well with thee.*—IV. *beauty.* —V. p. n. of a country on the other side Jordan.

טָב m. Ch., *good, excellent.*

טָבְאֵל with pause טָבְאַל p. n. of a man, Syrian or Persian.

טַבְרִמּוֹן p. n., the father of Benhadad, king of Syria.

טוּב m.— I. *goodness.*— II. *wealth.*— III. *prosperity.*— IV. *beauty.*—V *goodness* (of discernment). — VI. *God*, as the source of all good. טוּב אֶרֶץ *the best part of the land*, Gen. 45:18.

טוֹב אֲדֹנִיָּהוּ p.n. of a man.

טוֹבִיָּהוּ, טוֹבִיָּה p.n. of a man.

טָוָה *spin* (lit. *twine*), Ex. 35:25, 26.

מַטְוֶה m., *yarn*, Ex. 35:25.

טוּחַ I. *plaister, paint.* — II. *overlay.* Niph. inf. הִטּוֹחַ *was covered, plastered*, Lev. 14:43, 48.

טִיחַ m., *plastering*, Eze. 13:12.

טֻחוֹת f. pl.—I. *inward parts, viscera*, Ps. 51:8.—II. *the motive power of the heavenly bodies*, Job 38:36.

טוֹטָפוֹת *bandages*; see טוּף.

טוּל. Hiph. הֵטִיל *cast forth, out, into*.

Hoph. הוּטַל *was, became cast out, forth, &c.* Pil. טִלְטֵל *cast out,* Isa. 22:17.

טַלְטֵלָה f., *entire casting out,* Isa. 22:17.

טוּף (Arab. *surrounded*).

טוֹטָפוֹת f. pl., *φυλακτήρια, frontlets;* probably jewels worn on the forehead.

טוּר see דּוּר and תּוּר.

טוּר m. (pl. טוּרִים, טֻרִים), *series, order, range.*

טִירָה f.—I. *any series of buildings.*—II. *palace.*—III. *certain chambers in the Temple.*

טוּר m. Ch., same as צוּר *mountain,* Dan. 2:35, 45.

טוּשׁ *fly swiftly,* Job 9:26.

טְוָת *fasting;* see טְוָא.

טָחָה (Arab. *expand*). Pil. part. מְטַחֲוֵי־קֶשֶׁת *archers,* Gen. 21:16.

טֻחוֹת *viscera;* see טוּחַ.

טְחוֹרִים *hæmorrhoids;* see טחר.

טָחַן (fut. יִטְחַן).—I. *grind with a hand-mill.*—II. *oppress.*

טְחוֹן m., *hand-mill,* Lam. 5:13.

טַחֲנָה f., the same, Ecc. 12:4.

טָחַר (Syr. *arms*).

טְחוֹרִים m. pl., *emerods* (hæmorrhoids).

טִיחַ *plaster;* see טוּחַ.

טִיט m., *mud, mire.*

טִין m. Ch., *clay, potter's clay.*

טִירָה *row;* see טוּר.

טַל *dew;* see טלל.

טָלָא, part. טָלוּא *patched,* having patches of various colours; pl. טְלֻאוֹת, טְלֻאִים. Pu. part. f. pl. מְטֻלָּאוֹת *patched* (of shoes), Jos 9:5.

טְלָאִים; see טֶלֶם, טְלִי.

טָלָה (Syr. *an infant*).

טָלֶה const. טְלֵה m., *young lamb.*

טְלִי m.—I. the same; pl. טְלָאִים.—II. p. n. of a town; see טֶלֶם.

טַלְטֵלָה, טִלְטֵל; see טוּל.

טָלַל. Pi. טִלֵּל *covered, roofed,* Neh. 3:15.

טְלַל Ch. Aph. אַטְלֵל *takes shade,* Dan. 4:9.

טַל m. (with pause טָל, with suff. טַלָּם), *dew.*

טַל m. Ch., *dew.*

טֶלֶם p. n. of a town in the tribe of Judah; also טְלָאִים.

טַלְמוֹן p. n. of a man.

טָמֵא (fut. יִטְמָא; inf. with ה parag. טָמְאָה), *was unclean, polluted,* with בְּ. Niph. נִטְמָא *was polluted,* with בְּ. Pi. טִמֵּא.—I. *polluted, defiled.*—II. *pronounced unclean.* Pu. part. f. מְטֻמָּאָה *polluted.* Hith. הִטַּמֵּא *polluted,* with לְ. Hothp. pret. f. הֻטַּמָּאָה the same, Deu. 24:4.

טָמֵא m., *unclean, polluted;* f. טְמֵאָה.

טֻמְאָה f. (pl. const. טֻמְאֹת), *polluted, defiled.*

טָמָה same as טָמֵא. Niph. pl. נִטְמִינוּ *we are unclean, despised.*

טָמַן *conceal, hide in the earth.* Niph. *was hidden.* Hiph. *hide,* 2 Ki. 7:8.

מַטְמוֹן m. (pl. מַטְמֻנִים), *treasure,* that which is laid up, hidden.

טֶנֶא (with suff. טַנְאֲךָ) m., *basket.*

טָנַף. Pi. *soil*, Cant. 5:3.

טָעָה same as תָּעָה. Hiph. הִטְעָה *made to err*, Eze. 13:10.

טָעַם (fut. יִטְעַם).—I. *taste.*—II. *discriminate, judge.*

טְעֵם Ch. Pa. *make to eat.*

טַעַם m.—I. *reason, judgment.*—II. *taste.*

טַעַם m. Ch., *edict.*

טְעֵם m. Ch.—I. *taste.*—II. *judgment.*—III. *edict.*

מַטְעַמִּים m., מַטְעַמּוֹת f. pl., *dainty meats.*

טָעַן.—I. *load* (of beasts of burden), Gen. 45:17.—II. Pu. טֹעַן *pierced through*, Isa. 14:19.

טַעַת Kal. inf.; see נטע.

טַף *infant*; see טפף.

טָפַח. Pi. טִפַּח *spread out, extend* (from טֶפַח), spec. with the hand.

טֶפַח m.—I. *palm, hand-breadth*, a measure of about three and-a-half inches; pl. טְפָחוֹת Ps. 39:6.—II. *coping stones of a building.*

טֹפַח m., *hand-breadth, measure.*

טִפֻּחִים m. pl., Lam. 2:20, *that which is stroked with the hand.*

מִטְפַּחַת f. (pl. מִטְפָּחוֹת), *upper garment, mantle.*

טָפַל.—I. *lay on* or *over.*—II. *cover, conceal.*

טִפְסַר m., *prince, general.*

טַפְסַר m., the same; pl. טַפְסְרִים.

טָפַף *tripping, mincing*, Isa. 3:16.

טַף m. (with pause טָף; with suff. טַפֵּנוּ), *child, infant.*

טְפַר m. Ch., *nails, claws.*

טָפַשׁ *fat, stupid*, Ps. 119:70.

טָפַת p. n. of a daughter of Solomon.

טָרַד *driving out*; part. טֹרֵד *perpetual, successive* (i. e. one driving out the other), Pro. 19:13; 27:15.

טְרַד Ch., *driving out, driven out.*

טָרָה root not used; (Arab. *was fresh*).

טָרִי m., טְרִיָּה f., *fresh, moist*, Jud. 15:15; Isa. 1:6.

טְרוֹם ketib, same as טֶרֶם.

טָרַח. Hiph. *stretches out*, Job 37:11.

טֹרַח m. (with suff. טָרְחֲכֶם), *pressure, wearying.*

טָרַם root not used; (Arab. *cut off*).

טֶרֶם adv., *not yet*; בְּטֶרֶם and טֶרֶם *before that*; מִטֶּרֶם the same.

טָרַף (fut. יִטְרֹף, יִטְרַף), *tear in pieces, wound, injure.* Niph. *be torn in pieces.* Pu. טֹרַף the same. Hiph. *feed, provide for.*

טֶרֶף m., *prey, provision, food.*

טָרָף m., *leaf* (that which is plucked), Gen. 8:11.

טְרֵפָה f.—I. *any thing torn.*—II. *animal torn by a wild beast.*

טַרְפְּלָיֵא Ch., p. n., a people so called, Ezr. 4:9; LXX. Ταρφαλαῖοι.

י

יָאַב *desired, longed for*, with לְ.

יָאָה with לְ *it becometh*, Jer. 10:7

יְאוֹר same as יְאֹר.

יֵאוֹתוּ Niph. fut. pl., from אות.

יַאֲזַנְיָה (*whom the Lord hears*), p. n of a man.

יַאֲזַנְיָהוּ (contr. יְזַנְיָה, יְזַנְיָהוּ), p. n. of a man.

יָאִיר (*the Lord enlightens*, Ἰάειρος), p. n. of a man; patron. יָאִירִי.

יָאַל I. same as אָוַל. Niph. נוֹאַל *was foolish*.—II. same as אוּל. Hiph. הוֹאִיל (fut. וַיּוֹאֶל.—1. *undertook, began*, with inf.—2. *was willing, contented*.

יֹאֶל, וַיֹּאֶל Hiph. fut. apoc., from אלה.

יֹאֶל, וַיֹּאֶל Hiph. fut. apoc., from II. יאל.

יָאֵר Hiph. fut. apoc., יֵאֹר Niph. fut., from אוֹר.

יָאֹר Kal fut., from ארר.

יְאֹר, יְאוֹר m., *a river*, specially the Nile; pl. יְאֹרִים *rivers*.

יָאַשׁ. Niph. נוֹאַשׁ *was hopeless, desperate*, with מִן; part. נוֹאָשׁ *desperate, in vain*. Pi. inf. יָאֵשׁ *rendered hopeless*, Ecc. 2:20.

יֹאשִׁיָּה p. n. of a man.

יֹאשִׁיָּהוּ (Ἰωσίας) p. n. of a man.

יֵאת, וַיֵּאת Kal fut. apoc., יֶאֱתָיוּ fut. pl., יֶאֱתָיֻנִי fut. with suff.; see אתה.

יְאַתְרַי p. n. of a man (same as אֶתְנִי).

יָבֵא Hiph. fut. apoc.; see בּוֹא.

יְבֹאֻנִי for יְבֹאוּנִי Kal fut. pl. with suff.; see בּוֹא.

יָבַב. Pi. יִבֵּב *cried out*, Jud. 5:28.

יוֹבָב p. n.—I. of a people in Arabia Felix.—II. of a king of Edom.—III. of a man.

יָבוֹ, וַיָּבוֹ 2 Ki. 12 : 12, for וַיָּבֹא Kal fut.; see בּוֹא.

יְבוּס p. n. of the Canaanitish inhabitants of Jerusalem; יְבוּסִי *Jebusite*.

יְבוּל *produce*; see יבל.

יֵבוֹשׁ Kal fut., from בּוֹשׁ.

יִבְחָר (*chosen of the Lord*), p. n. of a man.

יָבִין p. n. of two Canaanitish kings.

וַיֵּבְךְּ, יֵבְךְּ Kal fut. apoc.; see בכה.

יָבַל. Hiph. הוֹבִיל *bare, carried, led*. Hoph. הוּבַל *was borne, carried, led*.

יְבַל Ch. Aph. הֵיבֵל *bring*, Ez. 5:14; 6:5.

יְבוּל m. (with suff. יְבֻלָהּ, יְבוּלָהּ).—I. *produce* (of the earth, &c.)—II. *provision, wealth*.

בּוּל m.—I. *produce, increase*.—II. name of a month 1 Ki. 6:38, the eighth of the calendar, answering to our October.

מַבּוּל m. *flood* of Noah, *deluge*.

יָבָל m.—I. *stream of water*.—II. p. n of a son of Lamech.

יוֹבֵל com. (lit. *a protracted note* or *sound*), the *Jubilee*, a feast of the Jews announced by the sounding of horns; שְׁנַת הַיּוֹבֵל and יֹבֵל *the year of Jubilee*.

יוּבַל m.—I. *canal*, Jer. 17 : 8.—II. p. n. of a son of Lamech.

אֻבָל, אוּבָל m., *a river, canal*, Dan. 8 : 2, 3, 6.

יַבֶּלֶת f., *issue, running disease*, Lev. 22 : 22; Vulg. papulas habens.

תֵּבֵל f., same as אֶרֶץ.—I. *the world, the earth*, specially the inhabited part of it.—II. *the world's inhabitants, mankind*.

יִבְלְעָם p. n. of a town in the tribe of Manasseh.

יָבָם m. *husband's brother*; יִבֵּם. Pi. *marry the brother's wife*; see Deu. 25 : 5, 7.

יְבֶמֶת f. (with suff. יְבִמְתּוֹ) *brother's wife*; one married to her husband's brother.

יַבְנְאֵל p. n., two towns in the tribes of Judah and Naphtali.

יַבְנֶה p. n. of a town of the Philistines, Ἰαμνία, Ἰάμνεια.

יִבְנְיָה p. n. of a man.

יַבֹּק p. n. of a brook which runs into the river Jordan.

יְבֶרֶכְיָהוּ (*blessed of the Lord*), p. n. of a man.

יִבְשָׂם p. n. of a man.

יָבֵשׁ (inf. const. יְבשׁ; fut. יִיבַשׁ; pl. יִיבָשׁוּ) *was* or *became dry, arid.* Pi. יִבֵּשׁ *dry up.* Hiph. הוֹבִישׁ.—I. *dry up, make to wither.*—II. *was ashamed, confounded;* see בּוֹשׁ.

יָבֵשׁ m., יְבֵשָׁה f.—I. *dry.*—II. p. n. of a town in Gilead; called also יָבֵישׁ.—III. p. n. of a man.

יַבֶּשֶׁת, יַבָּשָׁה f., *dry land.*

יַבֶּשֶׁת f. Ch., the same.

יְבשֶׁת f., *dried,* Gen. 8:7.

וַיְּבַשְּׁהוּ, יַבְּשֵׁהוּ for וַיְיַבְּשֵׁהוּ Pi. fut. with suff.; see יבשׁ.

יְבשֶׁת Kal inf. const.; see יבשׁ.

יִגְאָל (*the Lord redeemeth*), p. n. of a man.

יָגַב same as גּוּב *ploughed;* part. יוֹגְבִים *ploughmen.*

יָגֵב m. pl., יְגֵבִים *ploughed lands,* Jer. 39:10.

יָגְבְּהָה with ה parag. יָגְבְּהָה p. n. of a town in the tribe of Gad.

יִגְדַּלְיָהוּ (*let the Lord be magnified*), p. n. of a man.

יָגָה. Niph. part. נוּגֶה *pained* (perhaps *cast out*). Pi. יִגָּה *afflict, pain,* Lam. 3:33. Hiph. הוֹגָה.—I. *afflicted.*— II. *removed,* 2 Sa. 20:13.

וַיַּגֶּה, יַגֶּה for וַיְיַגֶּה Pi. fut., from יגה.

יָגוֹן m., *affliction, grief.*

תּוּגָה f., *sorrow, grief.*

יָגוּר (*the Lord dwelleth there*), p. n. of a town in the tribe of Judah.

יָגְלִי p. n. of a man.

וַיֶּגֶל, יֶגֶל Hiph. fut. apoc.; see גלה.

יָגַע (fut. יִיגַע; pl. יִיגְעוּ), *labour to weariness;* with בְּ and לְ, *be wearied.* Pi. יִגַּע *fatigue, cause to labour to weariness.* Hiph. הוֹגִיעַ same as Pi. with בְּ.

יָגֵעַ m., *wearying, wearied.*

יָגִיעַ const. יְגִיעַ m.—I. *wearied, fatigued.*—II. *labour.*—III. *the fruit of labour, wealth.*

יָגָע m., *wealth,* Job 20:18.

יְגִיעָה f., *hard labour, exertion,* Ecc. 12:12.

יְגַר m. Ch., *heap of stones,* Gen. 31:47.

יִגַּר Niph. fut., from גרר.

יָגֹר (pret. יָגֹרְתִּי, יָגֹרְתָּ), *fear, be afraid of,* with מִפְּנֵי.

יָגֹר m., *fearing, afraid of.*

יָד com., generally f. (const. יַד; with suff. יָדִי, יֶדְכֶם; dual יָדַיִם, יָדַי, const. יְדֵי, with suff. יָדָיו, יְדֵיכֶם).—I. *hand;* with עִם, אֵת *assist, aid;* with בְּ, אֶל *hand against, afflicting, troubling;* with עַל *upon him, inspiring, strengthening.*—II. *power, spirit* or *word of God,* 1 Sa. 5:11, &c.—III. with prep. בְּיַד same as בְּ; לְיַד, עַל יַד, בְּעַד יַד, אֶל יַד, עַל יְדֵי *at hand, near.*—IV. *space, place;* אִישׁ עַל־יָדוֹ *every man in his place.*—V. *memorial, monument,* 1 Sa. 15:12;

2 Sa. 18:18.—VI. *by means of*. Pl. יָדוֹת; const. יְדוֹת.—I. *tenons of planks*.—II. *axletrees of wheels*, 1 Ki. 7:32, 33.—III. *arms of a throne*, 1 Ki. 10:19. Used with pref. בְּיַד with (בְּיָדוֹ *with him*), *by*, *before*, *against*; כְּיַד, מִיְּדֵי *from*, *out of*; יָד לְיָד *hand in hand*, as striking a bargain, Pro. 11:21.

יַד com. Ch., *hand*.

יְדָא *put forth*; see ידה.

וַיֵּרֶא, יֵרֶא fut. apoc.; see ראה.

יִדְאֲלָה p. n. of a place in the tribe of Zebulun.

יִדְבָּשׁ p. n. of a man.

יָדַד, same as דּוּד *loved*.

יָדִיד m., *beloved*, specially of God's children; pl. f., יְדִידוֹת.

יִדּוֹ p. n. of a man.

יְדִידָה p. n. of the mother of king Josiah.

יְדִידוּת f., *love*, Jer. 12:7.

יְדִידְיָה *beloved of the Lord*, a title of Solomon.

יָדָה.—I. *put forth* (as casting stones).—II. *uttering praise*; imp. pl. יְדוּ *they cast at her*, Jer. 50:14. Pi. *cast stones* or *lots*; fut. וַיַּדּוּ; inf. יַדּוֹת. Hiph. הוֹדָה (fut. יוֹדֶה, יְהוֹדֶה; with suff. אוֹדְךָ, אֲהוֹדֶנּוּ), *recount*, *commemorate* (God's mercies, with עַל); *praise*, *celebrate*, with לְ. Hith. הִתְוַדָּה *become known*, with עַל and לְ.

יְדָא Ch. Aph. *praise*, *celebrate*.

תּוֹדָה f.—I. *confession*.—II. *praise*, *thanksgiving*.—III. *company of persons giving thanks*.

יַדּוּ, וַיַּדּוּ for וַיְיַדּוּ. Pi. fut.; see ידה.

יֶדְכֶם, יֶדְכֶן; see יָד with suff.

יִדֹּם Kal fut.; pl. יִדְּמוּ; see דמם.

יְהוּדָה p. n.—I. the patriarch *Judah*.—II. Afterwards applied to the kingdom of the house of David.—III. Ultimately to the whole of Palestine.—IV. p. n. of a man.

יְהוּד Ch., *the Jews*, the kingdom of Judah.

יְהוּדִי (pl. יְהוּדִים, יְהוּדִיִּים).—I. *a Jew*; f. יְהֻדִיָּה *Jewess*; יְהוּדִית adv. *Hebrew*, the Hebrew tongue.—II. p. n. of a man.

הִתְיַהֵד. Hith. *became a Jew*.

יְהוּדָי Ch., *a Jew*.

יְהוּדִית; see יְהוּדִי p. n. of a wife of Esau.

יְהֻד p. n. of a town in the tribe of Dan.

הוֹדַוְיָה p. n. of a man.

הוֹדַוְיָהוּ p. n. of a man.

יָדוֹן p. n. of a man.

יַדּוּעַ p. n. of a man.

יְדוּתוּן, יְדֻתוּן, יְדִיתוּן p. n. of a Levite skilled in music; probably also a musical instrument invented by him.

יַדַּי p. n. of a man.

יָדִיד, יְדִידָה, יְדִידוּת, יְדִידְיָה; see ידד.

יְדָיָה p. n. of a man.

יְדִיעֲאֵל p. n. of a son of Benjamin.

יִדְלָף p. n. of a son of Nahor.

יָדַע (fut. יֵדַע, יֵידַע; inf. abs. יָדוֹעַ; const. דַּעַת; with suff. דַּעְתָּהּ; imp. דַּע, דְּעָה; part. יוֹדֵעַ, יָדֻעַ; f. יֹדַעַת).—I. *perceive*, *become informed*, *aware of*, *feel*.—II. *know carnally*.—III. *recognise*, *acknowledge*.—IV. *regard*; part. יָדֻעַ *wise*; יָדוּעַ *noted*, *illustrious*. Niph. נוֹדַע *known*, *apparent*, *recognised*. Pi

יֻדַּע *made to know*. Pu. part. מְיֻדָּע *known, familiar*. Po. יוֹדַע *declared, indicated*. Hiph. הוֹדִיעַ (imp. הוֹדַע; fut. יוֹדִיעַ; apoc. יוֹדַע), *make known, show, confess, inform, teach*. Hoph. הוּדַע *was, made known*. Hith. הִתְוַדַּע *made himself known*; with אֶל.

יְדַע Ch., *know, understand, perceive*; fut. יִנְדַּע. Hoph. הוּדַע *made known, taught*.

דֵּעַ m., pl. דֵּעִים } *knowledge, science, opinion*.
דֵּעָה f., pl. דֵּעוֹת }

דַּעַת f., *knowledge, science, opinion*.

יָדָע p.n. of a man.

יְדַעְיָה p. n. of a man.

יִדְּעֹנִי m. (pl. יִדְּעֹנִים), *false prophet, soothsayer*.

מַדַּע, מַדָּע m.—I. *knowledge, experience*.—II. *mind*.

מַדּוּעַ adv. interrog., *why then? why indeed?*

מַנְדַּע m. Ch.—I. *knowledge*.—II. *intelligence*.

מוֹדָע m., *familiar, friend*.

מוֹדַעַת f., the same.

יְדַשְּׁנֶה Pi. fut. with ה parag.; see דשן.

יָהּ one of the names of God; probably an abbreviation of יְהוָֹה.

יָהַב I. *give, allow*.—II. *appoint, place*; imper. הַב; with ה parag. הָבָה; f. הָבִי; pl. הָבוּ.

יְהַב Ch., *give, place*. Ith. *was given*

יְהָב m., *burden*; with suff. יְהָבְךָ Ps. 55:23.

הַבְהָבִים m. pl., *gifts*, Hos. 8:13.

יְהְדַּי p.n. of a man.

יֶהֱוּא for יְהוּ fut. apoc. pl., from הוה.

יֵהוּא p.n.; see הוה.

יְהוּבַד Ch. Aph. fut.; see אבד.

יְהוֹדֶה for יוֹדֶה Hiph. fut.; see ידה.

יְהוּדִית, יְהוּדִי, יְהוּדָה, יְהוּד; see ידה

יְהוָֹה the most sacred and unalienable name of God; see הוה.

יְהוֹשִׁיעַ for יוֹשִׁיעַ Hiph. fut.; see ישע.

וַיְהִי, יְהִי fut. apoc.; see היה.

יְהֵילִילוּ for יְיֵלִילוּ Hiph. fut.; see ילל.

יְהָךְ Ch. fut.; see הוך.

יַהֵל for יְאַהֵל Pi. fut.; see אהל.

יָהִיר m., *haughty, vain*.

יַהֲלֹם; see הלם.

יֶהֱמָיוּן fut. pl. with נ parag.; see המה.

יַהְצָה, יַהַץ p. n. of a city of Moab.

יִהְתַּלּוּ Pi. fut. pl. with dag. euphon. see התל.

יוֹב p. n. of a son of Issachar.

יוֹבָב; see יבב.

יוּבַל, יוֹבֵל; see יבל.

יוּכְלוּ Eze. 42:5, for יְאָכְלוּ, Hoph. fut.; see אכל.

יוֹלַדְתְּ for יוֹלֶדֶת part. f.; see ילד.

יוֹם m.—I. *day*; הַיּוֹם *this day, today, now*; בַּיּוֹם *this very day, immediately*; בְּיוֹם with inf. *on the day, when*; כַּיּוֹם *now, at present*; כַּיּוֹם הַזֶּה *as it is at this day*; מִיּוֹם *from the day since*; יוֹם יוֹם, יוֹם בְּיוֹם, כְּיוֹם בְּיוֹם *daily*; dual יוֹמַיִם *two days*; pl. יָמִים, const. יְמֵי, sometimes יְמוֹת *days, many days*; מִקֵּץ יָמִים, מִיָּמִים *after many days, some days, some time after*; חֹדֶשׁ יָמִים i. e. יֶרַח *an entire month*; שְׁנָתַיִם י׳ *two whole years*.—II. *duration, time*; מִיָּמֶיךָ *so long as thou livest*; כָּל־הַיָּמִים פ׳ *all his days*; בָּא בַּיָּמִים *advanced in years*.—III. *anniversary*; מִיָּמִים

לְיָמִים יָמִימָה *annually;* the same, Jud. 17:10; זֶבַח יָמִים *annual sacrifice.*

יוֹם m. Ch., *day, period.*

יוֹמָם adv., *by day.*

יָוָן p. n. *Javan* the founder of the Greeks, Ionians; בְּנֵי הַיְּוָנִים *Ionians, Greeks.*

יָוֵן *mire, clay.*

יַיִן m. (const. יֵין; with suff. יֵינִי).—I. *wine.*—II. *intoxication.*

יוֹנָה f. (pl. יוֹנִים).—I. *dove.*—II. p. n. of a prophet; see also in ינה.

יוֹנֵק, יוֹנֶקֶת; see ינק.

יוֹסֵף, יְהוֹסֵף (from אָסַף or יָסַף).—I. p. n. *Joseph,* the son of Israel, Ἰωσήφ.—II. given afterwards specially to the tribes of his sons, and generally to the kingdom of Israel. —III. p. n. of a man.

יוֹסִפְיָה p. n. of a man.

יוֹעֵאלָה p. n. of a man.

יוֹצֵת for יוֹצֵאת part. f.; see יצא.

יוֹר, וַיּוֹר Hiph. fut. apoc; see ירה.

יוֹרֶא Pro. 11:25 (*shall be watered*), for יְרָוֶה Hoph. fut., see רוה; or for יוֹרֶה Hoph. fut., see ירה.

יוֹרֶה, יוֹרֵי *teach;* see ירה.

יוּשַׁב חֶסֶד (*confirming mercy*), p. n. of a man.

יוֹשִׁבְיָה (*the Lord confirmeth*), p. n. of a man.

יוֹשָׁה p. n. of a man.

יוֹשַׁוְיָה p. n. of a man.

יוֹתֵר, יוֹתֶרֶת; see יתר.

יוֹשַׁבְתִּי Jer. 22:23, for יוֹשֶׁבֶת, part. f. with ׳ parag.; see ישב.

יַז, יֵז, וַיַּז, וַיֵּז Kal fut. apoc; see נזה.

יַז, וַיַּז Hiph. fut. apoc.; see נזה.

יַזִּיאֵל p. n. of a man.

יִזַּח Niph. fut.; see זחח.

יִזִּיָּה p. n. of a man.

יִזְלִיאָה p. n. of a man.

יָזֹמּוּ for יָזֹמּוּ Kal fut. pl.; see זמם.

יָזַן. (Arab. *weighed, was heavy*). Pu. part. מְיֻזָּנִים *appointed, accoutred for war* (of horses), Jer. 5:8, Kri.

יְזַנְיָה, יְזַנְיָהוּ; see יַאֲזַנְיָה

יִזְרָח, יִזְרַחְיָה; see זרח.

יֶזַע m., *sweat,* Eze. 44:18.

יָזֵר, וַיָּזַר Kal fut. apoc; see זור.

יִזְרְעֶאל p. n.; see זרע.

יָחַד (fut. יֵחַד) *unite, be as one,* with אֵת ,בְּ. Pi. יַחֵד *unite, make as one,* Ps. 86:11.

יָחִיד m., *solitary one, only one;* f. יְחִידָה.

יַחַד m., *union,* 1 Chron. 12:17; adv. —I. *as one.*— II. *singly, at once.* —III. *wholly, entirely, together;* יַחְדָּו ,יַחְדָּיו the same; the pron. is a pleonasm.

יִחַדְּ. וַיִּחַדְּ Kal fut. apoc.; see חדה.

יָחַד for יֵחַד Hiph. fut.; see חדד.

יַחְדּוֹ (*united*), p. n. of a man.

יַחְדִּיאֵל (*united with God*), p. n. of a man.

יֶחְדְּיָהוּ (*united to the Lord*), p.n. of a man.

יַחֲזִיאֵל ,יַחְזְיָה p. n.; see חזה.

יְחֶזְקֵאל ,יְחִזְקִיָּה ,יְחִזְקִיָּהוּ, p. n.; see חזק.

יֶחֱזָיוּן fut. pl. with נ parag.; see חזה

יַחְזֵרָה p. n. of a man.

יְחִיאֵל ,יַחְוְאֵל p.n.; see חיה ,חיי.

יְחִי ,וַיְחִי fut. apoc.; see חיה.

יְחִיתַן Hiph. fut. with suff. ןַ for ן because of the pause; see חתת

יָחִיד; see יחד

יָחַל Pi. יִחֵל.—I. *hope for, expect, wait.*—II. *cause to hope*, with לְ, אֶל. Hiph. הוֹחִיל same as Pi., with לִפְנֵי, לְ. Niph. נוֹחַל (fut. יִיָּחֵל) same as Pi.

יָחֵל *he will begin*; יָחֵל *he will play*, Hiph. fut.; see חלל.

יָחִיל m., *one waiting*, Lam. 3 : 26.

יַחְלְאֵל p. n. of one of the sons of Zebulon; patron. יַחְלְאֵלִי.

יִחֲלוּ Pi. pret. pl. with dag. euphon., from יחל.

תּוֹחֶלֶת f., *expectation, hope.*

יָחַם (fut. יֵחַם, יֵחַם; pl. וַיֵּחֲמוּ; f. וַיֵּחַמְנָה).—I. *be in heat* (for sexual intercourse): hence,—II. *conceive.* —III. *be hot with anger.* Niph. part. pl. m. נֵחָמִים *heated with idol worship*, Isa. 57 : 5. Pi. (inf. יַחֵם; pret. f. with suff. יֶחֱמַתְנִי) *conceived.*

יֶחֱמוּ for יֵחַמוּ Pi. pret. pl., from יחם.

יֵחַמְנָה, Gen. 30 : 38. for תֵּחַמְנָה Kal fut. pl. f., from יחם.

חֵמָה, const. חֲמַת f.—I. *heat.*—II. *anger, fury.*—III. *venom of noxious creatures*, Deut. 32 : 33.

חֵמָא, חֲמָא f. Ch., *heat, anger.*

יַחְמַי p.n. of a man.

יַחְמוּר *gazelle*; see חמר.

יֶחֱמַתְנִי for יִחֲמַתְנִי Pi. pret. f. with suff., see יחם.

וַיִּחַן, יִחַן Kal fut. apoc.; see חנה.

יְחָנְךָ for יָחְנְךָ Kal fut. with suff.; see חנן.

יֶחֱסָיוּן fut. pl. with נ parag.; see חסה.

יָחֵף m., *barefooted.*

יַחְצִיאֵל, יַחְצְאֵל p.n. of a man.; יַחְצְאֵלִי.

יָחַר same as אָחַר *tarrying*, 2 Sa. 20 : 5; fut. וַיִּיחַר; (וַיּוֹחֶר) Kri Hiph. fut. Ch.; see אָחַר).

וַיִּחַר, יִחַר Kal fut. apoc.; see חרה.

יַחַשׂ m., *generation, family*; סֵפֶר הַיַּחַשׂ *register of descent*, Neh. 7 : 5.

הִתְיַחֵשׂ. Hiph. *being, becoming registered* (as to pedigree); ἀπογράφεσθαι; inf. s., *registration.*

יֵחַת Kal fut. pl. יֵחַתּוּ with dag. euphon.; see נחת. Niph. fut.; see חתת.

וַיֵּט־, וַיֵּט, יֵט Kal. fut. apoc.; see נטה.

וַיַּט, יַט Hiph. fut. apoc.; see נטה.

יָטַב same as טוֹב (fut. יִיטַב, יָטַב, תִּיטְבִי) *be* or *seem, good, happy*; with לְ *it was well with him*; with לִפְנֵי, בְּעֵינֵי *it seemed good to him*; with לֵב *was glad* (did the heart good). Hiph. הֵיטִיב (fut. יֵיטִיב, יֵיטִיב, יֵטִיב) *do good, well to*; הֵיטַבְתָּ לִרְאוֹת *thou hast rightly seen*, Jer. 2 : 12; מֵיטִיב לְנַגֵּן *skilled in music*; with אֶל, לְ, עִם; inf. הֵיטֵב adv. *well, rightly.*

יְטַב Ch., *was good, happy*; with עַל *it pleased him.*

מֵיטָב m., *good, choice, best.*

יָטְבָה p.n. of a place.

יָטְבָתָה p. n. of a station of the Israelites in the desert.

יוּטָה, יֻטָּה p. n. of a city in the tribe of Judah.

יְטוּר p.n. of a son of Ishmael and of the people descended from him. *the Itureans.*

יֵיַדַע for יֵדַע Kal fut.; see ידע.

יֵיטִיב for יֵיטִיב Hiph. fut; see טב

יְיֵלִיל for יְיֵלִיל Hiph. fut.; see ילל.

יַיִן; see יָיִן.

יָמִימָה *annually*; לְיָמִים the same, Jud. 17:10; זֶבַח יָמִים *annual sacrifice*.

יוֹם m. Ch., *day, period*.

יוֹמָם adv., *by day*.

יָוָן p. n. *Javan* the founder of the Greeks, Ionians; בְּנֵי הַיְּוָנִים *Ionians, Greeks*.

יָוֵן *mire, clay*.

יַיִן m. (const. יֵין; with suff. יֵינִי).—I. *wine*.—II. *intoxication*.

יוֹנָה f. (pl. יוֹנִים).—I. *dove*.—II. p. n. of a prophet; see also in ינה.

יוֹנֵק, יוֹנֶקֶת; see ינק.

יוֹסֵף, יְהוֹסֵף (from אָסַף or יָסַף).—I. p. n. *Joseph*, the son of Israel, Ἰωσήφ.—II. given afterwards specially to the tribes of his sons, and generally to the kingdom of Israel. —III. p. n. of a man.

יוֹסִפְיָה p. n. of a man.

יוֹעֵאלָה p.n. of a man.

יוֹצֵת for יוֹצֵאת part. f.; see יצא.

יוֹר, וַיּוֹר Hiph. fut. apoc; see ירה.

יוֹרֶא Pro. 11:25 (*shall be watered*), for יֻרְוֶה Hoph. fut., see רוה; or for יוֹרֶה Hoph. fut., see ירה.

יוֹרֶה, יוֹרֵי *teach*; see ירה.

יוּשַׁב חֶסֶד (*confirming mercy*), p. n. of a man.

יוֹשִׁבְיָה (*the Lord confirmeth*), p.n. of a man.

יוֹשָׁה p. n. of a man.

יוֹשַׁוְיָה p.n. of a man.

יוֹתֵר, יוֹתֶרֶת; see יתר.

יוֹשַׁבְתְּ Jer. 22:23, for יוֹשֶׁבֶת, part. f. with י parag.; see ישב.

יַז, יֶז, וַיֵּז, וַיִּז Kal fut. apoc; see נזה.

יַז, וַיַּז Hiph. fut. apoc.; see נזה.

יְזִיאֵל p. n. of a man.

יִזַּח Niph. fut.; see זחח.

יִזִּיָּה p. n. of a man.

יִזְלִיאָה p. n. of a man.

יָזְמוּ for יָזֹמּוּ Kal fut. pl.; see זמם.

יָזַן. (Arab. *weighed, was heavy*). Pu part. מְיֻזָּנִים *appointed, accoutred for war* (of horses), Jer. 5:8, Kri.

יְזַנְיָה, יְזַנְיָהוּ; see יַאֲזַנְיָה.

יִזְרָח, יִזְרַחְיָה; see זרח.

יֶזַע m., *sweat*, Eze. 44:18.

יָזֵר, וַיָּזַר Kal fut. apoc; see זור.

יִזְרְעֶאל p. n.; see זרע.

יָחַד (fut. יֵחַד) *unite, be as one*, with אֵת, בְּ. Pi. יִחֵד *unite, make as one*, Ps. 86:11.

יָחִיד m., *solitary one, only one*; f. יְחִידָה.

יַחַד m., *union*, 1 Chron. 12:17; adv. —I. *as one*.— II. *singly, at once*. —III. *wholly, entirely, together*; יַחְדָּו, יַחְדָּיו the same; the pron. is a pleonasm.

יִחַדְּ, וַיִּחַדְּ Kal fut. apoc.; see חדה.

יַחֵד for יָחֵד Hiph. fut.; see חדד.

יַחְדּוֹ (*united*), p. n. of a man.

יַחְדִּיאֵל (*united with God*), p. n. of a man.

יֶחְדְּיָהוּ (*united to the Lord*), p.n. of a man.

יַחֲזִיאֵל, יַחְזְיָה p. n.; see חזה.

יְחֶזְקֵאל, יְחִזְקִיָּה, יְחִזְקִיָּהוּ, p. n.; see חזק.

יֶחֱזָיוּן fut. pl. with ן parag.; see חזה.

יַחְזֵרָה p. n. of a man.

יְחַוְאֵל, יְחִיאֵל p.n.; see חיה, חיי.

יְחִי, וַיְחִי fut. apoc.; see חיה.

יְחִיתַן Hiph. fut. with suff. ־ַן for ־ֵן because of the pause; see חתת.

יָחִיד; see יחד

יָחַל. Pi. יִחֵל.—I. *hope for, expect, wait.*—II. *cause to hope*, with לְ, אֶל. Hiph. הוֹחִיל same as Pi., with לִפְנֵי, לְ. Niph. נוֹחַל (fut. יִיָּחֵל) same as Pi.

יָחֵל *he will begin*; יָחֵל *he will play*, Hiph. fut.; see חלל.

יָחִיל m., *one waiting*, Lam. 3:26.

יַחְלְאֵל p. n. of one of the sons of Zebulon; patron. יַחְלְאֵלִי.

יִחֲלוּ Pi. pret. pl. with dag. euphon., from יחל.

תּוֹחֶלֶת f., *expectation, hope.*

יָחַם (fut. יֵחַם, יִחַם; pl. וַיֶּחֱמוּ; f. וַיֵּחַמְנָה).—I. *be in heat* (for sexual intercourse): hence,—II. *conceive.*—III. *be hot with anger.* Niph. part. pl. m. נֵחָמִים *heated with idol worship*, Isa. 57:5. Pi. (inf. יַחֵם; pret. f. with suff. יֶחֱמַתְנִי) *conceived.*

יֶחֱמוּ for יִחֲמוּ Pi. pret. pl., from יחם.

יֵחַמְנָה, Gen. 30:38. for תֵּחַמְנָה Kal fut. pl. f., from יחם.

חֵמָה, const. חֲמַת f.—I. *heat.*—II. *anger, fury.*—III. *venom of noxious creatures*, Deut. 32:33.

חֵמָא, חֲמָא f. Ch., *heat, anger.*

יַחְמַי p.n. of a man.

יַחְמוּר *gazelle;* see חמר.

יֶחֱמַתְנִי for יִחֲמַתְנִי Pi. pret. f. with suff., see יחם.

יִחַן, וַיִּחַן Kal fut. apoc.; see חנה.

יְחָנְךָ for יָחָנְךָ Kal fut. with suff.; see חנן.

יֶחֱסָיוּן fut. pl. with נ parag.; see חסה.

יָחֵף m., *barefooted.*

יַחְצְאֵל, יַחְצִיאֵל p.n. of a man.; יַחְצְאֵלִי.

יָחַר same as אָחַר *tarrying*, 2 Sa. 20: 5; fut. וַיִּיחַר; (וַיּוֹחֶר) Kri Hiph. fut. Ch.; see אָחַר.

יִחַר, וַיִּחַר Kal fut. apoc.; see חרה.

יַחַשׂ m., *generation, family;* סֵפֶר הַיַּחַשׂ *register of descent*, Neh. 7:5.

הִתְיַחֵשׂ. Hiph. *being, becoming registered* (as to pedigree); ἀπογράφεσθαι; inf. s., *registration.*

יֵחַת Kal fut. pl. יֵחַתּוּ with dag. euphon.; see נחת. Niph. fut.; see חתת.

יֵט, וַיֵּט, וַיֶּט־ Kal. fut. apoc.; see נטה.

יַט, וַיַּט Hiph. fut. apoc.; see נטה.

יָטַב same as טוֹב (fut. יִיטַב, יֵטַב, תֵּיטְבִי) *be or seem, good, happy;* with לְ *it was well with him;* with לִפְנֵי, בְּעֵינֵי *it seemed good to him;* with לֵב *was glad* (did the heart good). Hiph. הֵיטִיב (fut. יֵיטִיב, יֵטִיב, וַיֵּיטֶב) *do good, well to;* הֵיטַבְתְּ לִרְאוֹת *thou hast rightly seen*, Jer. 2:12; מֵיטִיב לְנַגֵּן *skilled in music;* with אֶל, לְ, עִם; inf. הֵיטֵב adv. *well, rightly.*

יְטַב Ch., *was good, happy;* with עַל *it pleased him.*

מֵיטָב m., *good, choice, best.*

יָטְבָה p.n. of a place.

יָטְבָתָה p. n. of a station of the Israelites in the desert.

יֻטָּה, יוּטָה p. n. of a city in the tribe of Judah.

יְטוּר p.n. of a son of Ishmael and of the people descended from him. *the Itureans.*

יֵידַע for יֵדַע Kal fut.; see ידע.

יֵיטִיב for יֵטִיב Hiph. fut; see טב

יְיֵלִיל for יְהֵילִיל Hiph. fut.; see ילל.

יַיִן; see יָנַן.

יָלַד, יָלֵד (fut. יֵלֵד, יֵלֶד; inf. abs לֵדָה, יָלֹד; const. לֶדֶת, לֵת; with suff. לִדְתָּהּ).—I. *bring forth.*—II. *beget* (part. יוֹלֶדֶת *mother*). Niph. נוֹלַד (fut. יִוָּלֵד), *was born.* Pi. יִלֵּד *aiding to bring forth,* Ex. 1:16; part. מְיַלֶּדֶת *midwife;* pl. מְיַלְּדוֹת. Pu. יֻלַּד, יוּלַד *was born.* Hiph. הוֹלִיד *cause to bring forth, produce, beget.* Hoph. inf. הֻלֶּדֶת, יוֹם הֻלֶּדֶת אֶת־ הוּלֶּדֶת *be born;* פַּרְעֹה *Pharaoh's birthday,* Gen. 40:20. Hith. הִתְיַלֵּד *recorded in the genealogies as begotten,* Nu. 1:18.

וָלָד m., *son, progeny.*

וֶלֶד m., the same.

יֶלֶד m.—I. *lad, youth, child.*—II. *young of beasts,* Isa. 11:7.

יָלִיד m., *offspring, son;* יְלִיד בַּיִת *household slave.*

יִלּוֹד m., *offspring, son.*

יַלְדָּה f., *girl, female child.*

יַלְדוּת f.—I. *birth,* Ps. 110:3.—II. *youth,* Ecc. 11:9, 10.

מוֹלָדָה p. n. of a town in the tribe of Judah.

מוֹלֶדֶת f. (pl. מוֹלְדוֹת).—I. *nativity, birth.*—II. *birth-place.*—III. *person born.*—IV. *relatives, members of the same family.*

מוֹלִיד p. n. of a man.

תּוֹלָד p. n. of a town in the tribe of Simeon; same as אֶלְתּוֹלַד.

תּוֹלְדוֹת f. pl.—I. *birth,* Ex. 28:10.—II. *posterity.*—III. *history;* סֵפֶר תּוֹלְדוֹת *genealogy,* Gen. 2:4; 6:9.

יָלוֹן p. n. of a man.

יַלִּיזוּ Rabbinical, for יָלִיזוּ, Hiph. fut. pl.; see לוּז.

יִיף Kal fut. apoc.; see יפה.

יַךְ, 1 Sa. 4:13. for יַד *hand.*

יַךְ, וַיַּךְ Hiph. fut. apoc.; see נכה.

יְכַבְּדָנְנִי Pi. fut. with suff. and נ epenth; see כבד.

יְכוֹנְנוּ for יְכוֹנְנֶנּוּ Pil. fut. with suff.; see כּוּן.

יָכַח. Hiph. הוֹכִיחַ.—I. *show, evince.*—II. *convince, chastise, punish,* with אֶת, אֶל, עִם. Hoph. הוּכַח *was reproved,* Job 33:19. Niph. נוֹכַח *be contending.* Hith. הִתְוַכַּח same as Niph., with עִם Mic. 6:2.

תּוֹכֵחָה f., *reproof, punishment.*

תּוֹכַחַת f. (with suff. תּוֹכַחְתִּי; pl. תּוֹכָחוֹת).—I. *argument.*—II. *reproof, punishment.*

יָכִין p. n.; see כּוּן.

יָכֹל (fut. יוּכַל; inf. abs. יָכוֹל; const. יְכֹלֶת) *capable of, equal to,* any action, so as *to succeed, prevail, overcome,* with לְ.

יְכֵל, יְכִל Ch. (part. יָכִיל, יָכִל; fut. יִכֻּל, יוּכַל, תִּכֻּל) *was able, prevailed, overcame.*

יְכָלְיָהוּ, יְכָלְיָה (*the Lord who prevaileth*), p. n., the mother of king Uzziah.

יְהוּכַל p. n. of a man.

יְכֶל Kal fut. apoc.; see כלה.

יִכֻּל Ch. fut.; see יכל.

יְכֹלֶת inf. const.; see יָכֹל.

יְכָנְיָה p. n.; see יְהוֹיָכִין in הוה.

יְכַסְיֻמוּ, Ex. 15:5, for יְכַסֻּמוּ, Pi. fut. with suff.; see כסה.

יֻכַּת, יֻכַּתּוּ for יוּכַת, יוּכְתוּ Hoph. fut.; see כתת.

יַכִּתּוּ for יַכְּתוּ, יָכֵתּוּ Hiph. fut. pl.; see כתת.

יַלִינוּ Hiph. fut. pl.; see II. לון.

יְלֵךְ *walk*; see הָלַךְ.

יָלַל Hiph. הֵילִיל (fut. יְיֵלִיל, יְיֵלִיל, יְהֵילִיל), *wail, howl, cry, mourn.*

יְלֵל m., *howling*, Deu. 32:10.

יְלָלָה const., יִלְלַת f., *wailing, lamenting.*

תּוֹלָלִים m. pl., *those who cause to lament*, Ps. 137:3.

יָלֵן Kal fut. apoc. in pause for יָלֵן; see לון.

יָלַע *retain, hold,* Pro. 20:25.

יַלֶּפֶת f., *itching scurvy*, Lev. 21:20; 22:22.

יֶלֶק m., *a hairy, winged locust.*

יַלְקוּט *bag*; see לקט.

יָם, const. יַם, יָם־ m.—I. *the sea.*—II. any great *lake.*—III. any large *river*; pl. יַמִּים; הַיָּם הַגָּדוֹל or הָאַחֲרוֹן *the Mediterranean*, i.e. Western Sea: hence יָם *the west*; רוּחַ יָם *the west wind*; יָמָּה *westward*; מִיָּם *from the west*; מִיָּם לְ *from the west of a district*; פְּאַת־יָם *sea* (that is *western*) *quarter*; יָם הַנְּחֹשֶׁת *brazen sea*, a large vessel for ablution in the temple of Solomon.

יְמוּאֵל p.n. of a son of Simeon.

יְמוֹת, יָמִים *days*; see יוֹם.

יִמַּח, וַיִּמַּח Kal fut. apoc.; see מחה.

יֵמִם m. pl., Gen. 36:24, perhaps *hot springs*; Vulg. aquæ calidæ.

יְמִימָה p. n. of one of Job's daughters.

יָמִין, יְמִינִי *right hand*; see ימן.

יִמְלָא, יִמְלָה p.n. of the father of Micaiah the prophet.

יְמַלֵּה for יְמַלֵּא Pi. fut.; see מלא.

יַמְלֵךְ p.n. of a prince of the Simeonites.

יָמַן. Hiph. הֵימִין *take the right hand or southward.*

יָמִין m.—I. *the right side, hand, leg, eye*; יַד יְמִינוֹ *his right hand*; מִימִין, מִיָּמִין, עַל יָמִין with לְ and suff., *at the right hand*; יָמִין, אֶל הַיָּמִין, לַיָּמִין *to, towards the right.*—II. *south*; מִימִין־ *southward* of any where.—III. p. n. of a man.

יִמְנָה p. n. of a son of Asher.

יְמָנִי m., יְמָנִית f., *right hand, side, &c.*

יְמִינִי *a Benjamin*; see בִּנְיָמִין in בָּנָה

תֵּימָן lit. *right* (because a man facing the rising of the sun would have his hand to the south).—I. *the south.*—II. *the south wind*; תֵּימָנָה *towards the south.*—III. p. n. of a city and district of the Edomites; תֵּימָנִי *a Temanite.*

יִמְנָע p. n. of a man.

יִמָּצוּ for יִמָּצְאוּ Niph. fut. pl.; see מצא.

יָמַר same as מוּר. Hiph. הֵימִיר *change, exchange*, Jer. 2:11. Hith. הִתְיַמֵּר *ye shall obtain rule*, Isa. 61:6 (like Arab. word for *commanded*; whence "Emir"—Lee).

יֵמַר for יִמְרַר (*was bitter*) fut.; see מרר.

יִמְרָה p. n. of a man.

יִמְרוּךָ for יֹאמְרוּךָ Kal fut. pl. with suff.; see אמר.

יָמַשׁ same as מָשַׁשׁ. Hiph. imp. הֲיִמִשֵׁנִי Kri, הֲמִשֵּׁנִי Ketib, *let me grope, feel*, Jud. 16:26.

יְנָאֵץ Syr. for יְנָאֵץ Hiph. fut.; see נאץ

wealth, treasure (acquired by fatigue).

יָעַץ (fut. יִיעַץ) *advise, admonish, counsel self* or *others*, with עַל, אֶל; part. יוֹעֵץ *counsellor*. Niph. נוֹעַץ *be advised, counselling, consulting*, with אֶת, אֶל, עִם. Hithp. יִתְיָעֲצוּ same as Niph.

עֵצָה const. עֲצַת f., *counsel*; בְּעֵצָה *deliberately*; see also עצה

מוֹעֵצָה f., pl. מוֹעֵצוֹת *counsels, devices*.

יַעֲקֹב, יַעֲקֹבָה p. n.; see עקב.

יַעֲקָן; see בְּנֵי־יַעֲקָן.

יַעַר m.—I. *honey-comb* (const. יַעֲרַת).—II. *wood, forest*; יַעְרָה *to the wood*; pl. יְעָרִים, יְעוֹרִים, יְעָרוֹת.—III. p.n.: יַעַר אֶפְרַיִם *grove of Ephraim*; קִרְיַת יְעָרִים a city in the tribe of Judah; יַעַר חָרֶת *the wood of Hereth* in the tribe of Judah.

וַיָּעַר, יָעַר Hiph. fut.; see עור.

יַעְרָה same as יְהוֹעַדָּה p.n. of a man.

יַעֲרֵי אֹרְגִים (*thickets*, perhaps abbreviated יָעִיר) p. n. of a man.

יַעֲרֶשְׁיָה p. n. of a man.

יַעֲשַׂי p.n. of a man.

יַעֲשִׂיאֵל p. n. of a man.

יִפְדְּיָה (*the Lord redeemeth*), p. n. of a man.

יָפָה (fut. יִיפֶה, וַיִּיף) *was fair, beautiful*. Pi. *beautified*, Jer. 10:4. Pul. יָפְיָפָה *was very beautiful*. Hith. *beautify oneself*.

יָפֶה const. יְפֵה m.; יָפָה const. יְפַת f., *beautiful, excellent*.

יָפוֹ, יָפוֹא p.n., *Joppa*, a celebrated port on the Mediterranean, Ἰόππη.

יְפִי m. (with pause יֳפִי; with suff. יָפְיוֹ), *beauty, excellence*.

יְפֵה־פִיָּה f., *very beautiful*, Jer. 46:20

יָפְיָפִיתָ Pul., Ps. 45:3, from יפה.

יָפַח same as פּוּחַ. Hith. *was panting in agony*, Jer. 4:31.

יָפֵחַ m.—I. *breathing out*.—II. *panting after, longing for*.

יַפְלֵט p.n. of a man; patron. יַפְלֵטִי.

יְפֻנֶּה p.n. of the father of Caleb and others.

יָפַע. Hiph. הוֹפִיעַ *exhibit brilliancy, shine forth*.

יִפְעָה f., *beauty, brilliancy*, Eze. 28:7, 17.

יָפִיעַ p. n.—I. of a town in the tribe of Zebulun.—II. of a man.

יֶפֶר Hiph. fut. apoc.; see פרה.

יַפְתְּ Hiph. fut apoc.; see פתה.

יָפַת root not used.

מוֹפֵת m.—I. *sign, wonder*.—II. *intimation, portent* (τύπος).

יֶפֶת p.n., *Japheth*, son of Noah; LXX. Ἰάφεθ.

יִפְתָּח p. n.—I. a town in the tribe of Judah.—II. a judge of Israel (Ἰεφθά).

יִפְתַּח־אֵל p. n., a valley in the tribes of Zebulun and Asher.

יָצָא (fut. יֵצֵא; inf. abs. יָצֹא; const. צֵאת; imp. צֵא; with ה parag צְאָה; part. m. יוֹצֵא, f. יֹצֵא, יֹצֵאת, יֹצֵת).—I. *go out, go forth*; with מִן, בְּ of the place whence; with of the place whither.—II. *issue* (from the womb), *be born*.—III. *descended*.—IV. *go forth* (from captivity or into captivity).—V. *shooting of a tree*, Isa. 11:1, also *grew, came forth* (of plants and flowers).—VI. *arose* (of the sun and stars).—VII. *issue a decree.* There are many similar usages, all modifications of the primary meaning *go forth.* Hiph. הוֹצִיא *cause to come out, bring out;* with דִּבָּה *brought up an evil report,* Nu. 14:36. Hoph. הוּצָא *was brought forth, out.*

יְצָא Ch., Shaph. שֵׁיצִיא *wrought out, finished,* Ezr. 6:15.

יָצִיא m., *issue, child,* 2 Chron. 32:21.

מוֹצָא m.—I. *outgoing.*—II. *time of outgoing.*—III. *place of outgoing.* —IV. *the east.*—V. *that which goeth out,* production, speech, &c. —VI. p. n. of a man.

מוֹצָאָה f.—I. *going forth,* Mic. 5:1.—II. *draught-house,* 2 Ki. 10:27.

תּוֹצָאוֹת f. pl.—I. *termination.*—II. *escape,* Ps. 68:21.—III. *result,* Pro. 4:23.

צֶאֱצָאִים m. pl.—I. *productions of the earth.*—II. *offspring.*

יָצַב same as נָצַב. Hith. הִתְיַצֵּב I. *was set up, stood fast,* with עַל, לִפְנֵי.—II. *stood up against,* with עַל.—III. *stood before, in presence of,* with לִפְנֵי, בִּפְנֵי, עִם.

יְצַב Ch. Pa. *certify.*

יַצִּיב m. Ch., *firm, fixed, settled;* כִּוָן יַצִּיב adv., *surely.*

יָצַג, הִצִּיג, יַצֵּג; see נצג.

יִצְהָר p.n.; see צהר.

יִצְחָק p. n.; see צחק.

יִצְטַבַּע Ch. Ithp. fut.; see צבע.

יִצְטַיָּרוּ Hith. fut. pl.; see ציר.

יָצַע, part. יָצוּעַ *laid, placed,* s. *bed.* Hiph. הִצִּיעַ *place, strew.* Hoph. הֻצַּע *spread* (as a couch), Isa. 14:11.

יָצִיעַ same as יָצוּעַ.

מַצָּע m., *bed* or *couch,* Isa. 28:20.

יָצַק (fut. וַיִּצֶק, יִצֹּק; inf. const. צֶקֶת; imp. צַק, יְצֹק).—I. *pour out.*—II. *fuse* (as metal), with עַל, בְּ; part. יָצוּק *hard* (like a cast of metal). Hiph. הִצִּיק *put down, place, lay out,* Jos. 7:23; 2 Sa. 15:24. Hoph. הוּצַק *be, become poured out;* part. מֻצָּק *firm,* Job 11:15.

וַיִּצֶק, יִצַּק Kal fut., from יצק.

יִצֹּק Kal fut., from יצק.

יְצֻקָה f., *casting, cast,* 1 Ki. 7:24.

מוּצָק, const. מֻצַּק m., *cast of brass;* see also in צוק.

מוּצָקָה f., pl. מוּצָקוֹת *funnels* for pouring the metal into moulds or casts, Zec. 4:2.

מוּצֶקֶת f., with suff. מֻצַקְתּוֹ *its being fused,* 2 Chron. 4:3.

I. יָצַר (fut. וַיִּצֶר, וַיִּיצֶר, יִצֹּר), *form, fashion, make;* part. יוֹצֵר *moulder, potter;* כְּלִי יוֹצֵר *fictile vases; creator.* Niph. נוֹצַר and Hoph. הוּצַר *was formed, made.* Pu. יֻצַּר the same.

יֵצֶר m. (with suff. יִצְרֵנוּ).—I. *figment, any thing formed.*—II. *thought, imagination.*—III. p. n. of a son of Naphtali; patron. יִצְרִי.

וַיִּצֶר, יִיצֶר Kal fut., Gen. 2:19, from I. יצר.

יְצֻרִים m. pl., *things formed, members,* Job 17:7.

II. יָצַר same as צוּר but intrans., *was straitened, distressed, anxious:* וַיֵּצֶר לוֹ *and he was in anxiety,* Gen. 32:8.

יִצְּרֶהוּ, יִצֹּר Kal fut. with suff., from II. יצר.

וַיֵּצֶר, יֵצֶר Kal fut., from II. יצר.

וַיָּצַר, יָצַר Kal fut. apoc.; see צור.

יָצַת (fut. יִצַּת, יִצַּתּוּ).—I. *burn*, Isa. 9:17, with בְּ.—II. *was on fire.* Niph. נִצַּת I. *was on fire, burnt.*—II. *burnt with anger*, with בְּ, 2 Ki. 22:13, 17. Hiph. הִצִּית, הוֹצִית *kindle, set fire to.*

יִצַּתּוּ Kal fut. pl. with dag. euphon., from יצת.

יָצָתִי for יָצָאתִי; see יצא.

יָקַב root not used; (Arab. *a tank*).

יֶקֶב m. (with suff. יִקְבֶךָ).—I. *wine* or *oil vat.*—II. the *trough* in which grapes are trodden, Job 24:11.

יְקַבְצְאֵל p.n., same as קַבְצְאֵל.

יָקַד (fut. יֵקַד, יִיקַד) *burnt* (as fire). Hoph. הוּקַד *became, was, burning.*

יְקַד Ch., *burning*, Dan. 3:6, &c.

יְקוֹד m., the same, *fire-brand*, Isa. 10:16.

יְקֵדָה f. Ch., the same. Dan. 7:11.

מוֹקֵד m.— I. *burning*, Isa. 33:14.—II. *fire-brand*, Ps. 102:4.

מוֹקְדָה f., *hearth* where the burnt-offerings were consumed, Lev. 6:2.

יָקְדְעָם p.n. of a city in the tribe of Judah.

יָקַה root not used; (Arab. *he obeyed*).

יְקָהָה or יִקְהָה, const. יִקְהַת f. *obedience.*

יָקֶה p.n. of a man.

יְקוּם whatever has been called into existence, Gen. 7:4, 23; Deut. 11:6, see קום.

יָקוּשׁ יְקוּשׁ; see יקשׁ.

יְקוּתִיאֵל p.n. of a man.

יִקַּח Kal fut.; יֻקַּח Hoph fut.; see לקח.

יָקְטָן p.n., a descendant of Shem, the son of Eber, Gen. 10:25, 26.

יָקִים p.n. of a man.

יְקַמְיָה p.n. of a man

יְקַמְעָם p.n. of a man.

יָקְמְעָם p.n., a city of the Levites in the tribe of Ephraim; see also קִבְצַיִם.

יָקְנְעָם p.n. of a city in the tribe of Zebulun.

יָקַע (fut. יֵקַע; pret. נָקַע which see).—I. *fell, became dislocated*, Gen. 32:26.—II. *fell away* (in mind, affection). Hiph. הוֹקִיעַ *suspend, hang, ἀνασκολοπίζειν.* Hoph. part. מוּקָעִים *hanged*, 2 Sa. 21:13.

יָקַץ (fut. וַיִּיקַץ, יִקַץ, יִיקַץ) *awake out of sleep*; see קוּץ.

יִקַץ Kal fut.; see יקץ.

יָקַר (fut. וַיִּיקַר, יֵקַר, יִיקַר) *became precious, prized, valued*, with לְ, בְּעֵינֵי. Hiph. הוֹקִיר (lit. *make precious*), *rare, scarce.*

יָקָר m. יְקָרָה f.— I. *precious, dear.*—II. *rare, scarce.* — III. *honorable, glorious.*

יְקָר m., *weight, value, honour, glory.*

יְקָר m. Ch. — I. *costly things*, Dan 2:6.—II. *honor, glory.*

יַקִּיר m., *precious, honored*, Jer. 31:20

יַקִּיר m. Ch., *honored, grave.*

יִקְּרֵךְ Kal. fut. with suff. and dag. euphon.; see קרה.

יָקֹשׁ, יָקֹשׁ (see נָקַשׁ, קוּשׁ) *snaring, taking by means of snares*; part. יוֹקֵשׁ *a fowler.* Niph. נוֹקַשׁ *was ensnared as a bird.*

יָקוּשׁ, יָקוּשׁ m., *fowler.*

יוֹקֵשׁ m., pl. יוֹקְשִׁים *snared*, Ecc. 9:12.

יָקְשָׁן p. n. of a son of Abraham.

מוֹקֵשׁ m. (pl. **מוֹקְשׁוֹת, מוֹקְשִׁים**) *snares* or *traps* for birds or beasts; mostly used metaphorically, as **מוֹקְשֵׁי מָוֶת** *snares of death, &c.*

וַיִּקֹשׁ, יָקֹשׁ Kal fut. apoc.; see **קשה**.

יַקְשׁ Hiph. fut. apoc.; see **קשה**.

יָקְתְאֵל p. n.—I. a town in the tribe of Judah.—II. a city in Arabia.

יָרֵא (fut. **יִירָא, יִרָא**; imp. **יְרָא**; inf. const. **יְרֹא**; with pref. **לְרֹא**; with ה parag. **יִרְאָה**), *feared* God, man, anything; with **מִן, לְ, בְּ, אֵת**. Niph. fut. **תִּוָּרֵא** *thou art to be feared,* Ps. 130:4; part. **נוֹרָא** *fearful, terrible, marvellous thing*; pl. **נוֹרָאוֹת**. Pi. **יֵרֵא** *alarm, cause to fear.*

יָרֵא, const. **יְרֵא** m. (**יְרֵאָה**, const. **יִרְאַת** f.), *fearing God* or *man*, with **מִפְּנֵי**.

יִרְאָה, const. **יִרְאַת** f., the same.

יִרְאוֹן p. n. of a city in the tribe of Naphtali.

מוֹרָא m.—I. *fear.*—II. *reverence,* Mal. 1:6.—III. *object of fear, reverence.*—IV. *fearful, stupendous act.*

מוֹרָה same as **מוֹרָא**; see also in **מָרָה**.

וַיַּרְא, יֵרֶא Kal fut. apoc.; see **ראה**.

יִרְאוּ for **יְראוּ** Ps. 34:10, imp. pl.; see **ירא**.

יִרְאוּ Kal fut. pl., see **ירא**; **יִרְאוּ** Kal fut. pl., see **ראה**.

יֹראוּ, וַיֹּראוּ 2 Sa. 11:24, for **וַיֹּרוּ**, Hiph. fut. pl. apoc.; see **ירה**.

יִרְאִיָּה p. n. of a man.

יָרֵב, יְרֻבַּעַל, יְרֻבֶּשֶׁת; see **ריב**.

יָרֵב, וַיָּרֶב, for **יַאֲרֵב**, Hiph. fut.; see **ארב**.

יִרְבְּיוּן Kal fut. pl. with נ parag.; see **רבה**.

יָרָבְעָם p. n., *Jeroboam*, the name of two of the kings of Israel.

יָרַד (fut. **יֵרֵד, וַיֵּרֶד, וַיֵּרַד**; imp. **רֵד, רְדָה, רֵד**; inf. abs. **יָרֹד**, const. **רֶדֶת**).—*descended, went down,* κατέβη (used both of men and things in a great variety of acceptations). Hiph. **הוֹרִיד** *make descend, bring down, cast down* (of men and things); *subdued*, with **תַּחַת**. Hoph. **הוּרַד** *brought down, lowered.*

יֶרֶד p. n. of a man, Ἰαρέδ.

יַרְדֵּן p. n. of the river *Jordan.*

מוֹרָד m., *descent, declivity*; **מַעֲשֵׂה מוֹרָד** *sloping*, perhaps *arched work*, 1 Ki. 7:29.

יִרַדֹּף Ps. 7:6, apparently a corruption, from **יִרְדֹּף** Kal fut. and **יְרַדֵּף** Pi. fut.; or possibly from two readings **יִרְדֹּף** and **יְרַדֵּף**.

יָרָה (fut. **יִירֶה**; inf. **יָרֹה**; const. **יְרוֹת, יְרוֹא**; imp. **יְרֵה**).—I. *cast out, shoot*, as arrows, &c.; part. **יוֹרִים** *archers*, Pro. 26:18.—II. *cast, lay a foundation*, see **יוֹרֶה**. Niph. fut. **יִיָּרֶה** *shall be shot*, Ex. 19:13. Hiph. **הוֹרָה** (fut. **יוֹרֶה, וַיּוֹר**).—I. *cast forth, shoot*, as arrows, rain, &c. (**מוֹרִים** *archers*); see **מוֹרֶה**.—II. *put forth*, as instruction, *teach*, with **מִן, אֶל, בְּ, לְ**.

יוֹרֶה m. (part. Kal).—I. *the former rain*, i. e. of the autumn.—II. p. n. of a man; same as **חָרִיף**.

יוֹרַי p. n. of a man.

מוֹרֶה m. (part. Hiph.).—I. *teacher, doctor.*—II. *arrow, archer.*—III. *former rain.*—IV. p. n. **אֵלוֹן** or

אֵלוֹנֵי מוֹרֶה *the oaks of Moreh*, near Sichem; גִּבְעַת־הַמּוֹרֶה *hill of Moreh* in the valley of Jezreel.

תּוֹרָה f.—I. *instruction, direction.*—II. *law, enactment.*—III. *the law*, as revealed to Moses and recorded in the Pentateuch.

יָרַה (fut. תִּרְהוּ), *was astounded with fear*, Isa. 44:8.

יֵרוּ, וַיֵּרוּ Hiph. fut. pl.; see ירה.

יְרוֹא, לִירוֹא for יְרוֹ Kal inf.; see ירה.

יְרוּאֵל p. n. of a desert.

יָרוֹחַ (same as יָרֵחַ), p. n. of a man.

יִרְוְיֻן Kal fut. pl. with נ parag.; see רוה.

יָרוּן Pro. 29:6, Kal fut.; see רנן. Others refer it to רון.

יָרוּץ for יָרֻץ Kal fut.; see רצץ.

יְרוּשָׁא, יְרוּשָׁה p. n. of the mother of king Jotham.

יְרוּשָׁלַיִם, יְרוּשָׁלֵם for יְרוּשָׁלֵם (*the habitation of peace*), p. n. of the principal city of Palestine, Ἱερουσαλήμ, Ἱεροσόλυμα.

יְרוּשְׁלֶם, יְרוּשְׁלֵם Ch., the same.

יָרֵחַ m., *the moon.*

יֶרַח m., (pl. יְרָחִים, יַרְחֵי).—I. *month*, one revolution of the moon round the earth.—II. p. n. of a people and country, Gen. 10:26.

יְרַח m. Ch., *month*.

יְרֵחוֹ, יְרִיחוֹ, יְרִיחֹה p.n., *Jericho*, a city in Palestine.

יְרֹחָם p. n. of a man.

יְרַחְמְאֵל p. n. of a man; patron. ־ִי.

יַרְחָע p. n. of a woman.

יָרַט *cast down to ruin, ruin.*

מוֹרָט m., "peeled" Eng. Ver.; "ruined" (Gesenius), Isa. 18:2, 7.

יְרִיאֵל p. n. of a man.

יָרִיב, יְרִיבַי; see ריב.

יְרִיָּה, יְרִיָּהוּ p. n. of a man.

יְרִיחֹה, יְרִיחוֹ p. n.; see יְרֵחוֹ.

יְרִיעָה, יְרִיעוֹת *shouting*; see ירע.

יָרֵךְ m. (const. יֶרֶךְ; with suff. יְרֵכוֹ).—I. *thigh*; שׁוֹק עַל־יָרֵךְ *hip and thigh*, i. e. *wholly*, Ju. 15:8; יֹצְאֵי יֶרֶךְ *offspring*, Ex. 1:5.—II. *stem* of the candlestick in the tabernacle; dual יְרֵכַיִם *both thighs*.

יַרְכָה f., *side, part, quarter*; dual יַרְכָתַיִם, const. יַרְכְּתֵי *the two sides.*

יַרְכָּה f. Ch., *thigh*.

יֵרַךְ Niph. fut., from רכך.

יַרְמוּת p. n. — I. a town in the tribe of Judah.—II. a town of Israel.

יְרֵמוֹת, יְרִימוֹת p. n. of a man.

יְרֵמַי p. n. of a man.

יִרְמְיָה, יִרְמְיָהוּ (*exalted of the Lord*), p. n. *Jeremiah*, the prophet.

יָרַע same as רוּעַ.—I. *was in evil condition*; fut. יֵרַע with לִי *I am in affliction*; with בְּעֵינֵי *it was evil in the eyes of.*—II. *was grieved, pained.*

1. יֵרַע Kal fut., from II. ירע Job 20:26; fut. apoc., from רעה.

יְרִיעָה f., *veil, curtain of a tent.*

יְרִיעוֹת (*veiled*), p. n. of a woman.

יִרְפְּאֵל p. n. of a place in the tribe of Benjamin.

יָרַק same as רָקַק *spit*.

יָרוֹק m., *green herb, shoot*, Job 39:8

יָרָק m., *green herb.*

יֶרֶק m., *freshness, green herbage.*

יֵרָקוֹן m.—I. *withering, wasting*; LXX. ὤχρα.—II. *the smut in corn.*

יְרַקְרַק m.—I. *gold colour*, Ps. 68:14. —II. *greenish* or *yellowish*; pl. f. יְרַקְרַקּוֹת.

יָרַשׁ, יָרֵשׁ, יְרֹשׁ (fut. יִירַשׁ, יִרַשׁ; inf. const. רֶשֶׁת; imp. רֵשׁ, רָשׁ, יְרַשׁ).—I. *possess, inherit.*—II. *dispossess others.* —III. *be, become poor*; יוֹרֵשׁ *heir.* Niph. *be, become poor.* Pi. יֵרֵשׁ *take into possession*, Deu. 28:42. Hiph. הוֹרִישׁ.—I. *cause to possess.* —II. *dispossess.*—III. *make poor, desolate.*

יְרֵשָׁה f., *possession*, Nu. 24:18.

יְרֻשָּׁה f., the same.

רֶשֶׁת f. (inf. *to take*; with suff. רִשְׁתּוֹ). —I. *net.* — II. *snare.* — III. *network.*

מוֹרָשׁ m. } *possession.*
מוֹרָשָׁה f. }

מוֹרֶשֶׁת גַּת p.n. of a district near Gath; מֹרַשְׁתִּי *a Moreshethite.*

תִּירֹשׁ, תִּירוֹשׁ m., *new wine, must.*

יִשְׂחָק same as יִצְחָק p. n.; see צחק.

יְשִׂימְאֵל p. n. of a man.

יָשַׂם same as שׂוּם intrans. *was set, laid*; fut. וַיִּישֶׂם, וָאִישְׂמָה.

יִשְׂרָאֵל (*a prince with God*), p. n., *Israel*, the new name given by God to Jacob, afterwards applied to his descendants; m. יִשְׂרְאֵלִי, f. יִשְׂרְאֵלִית *an Israelite.*

יִשָּׂשכָר p. n. *Issachar*, the son of Jacob, and the tribe that descended from him.

יֵשׁ - יֶשׁ (τὸ εἶναι), *is, are, was, were*; with suff. יֶשְׁךָ *thou art*; יֶשְׁנוֹ *he is*; יֶשְׁכֶם *ye are*; יֶשׁ לִי *I have*; יֵשׁ אֲשֶׁר *it is, because that*; יֵשׁ וָיֵשׁ *it is, yea it is*, 2 Ki. 10:15.

יָשַׁב (fut. יֵשֵׁב; inf. יָשֹׁב; const. שֶׁבֶת; with suff. שִׁבְתִּי; imp. שֵׁב, שְׁבָה). —I. *sit, sit down*, with בְּ, עַל.— II. *lie in wait for.*—III. *have intercourse with*, with עִם.—IV. *remain.*—V. *dwell in.*—VI. *was inhabited*, with בְּ, עַל. Niph. נוֹשַׁב *was inhabited.* Pi. יִשֵּׁב *cause to remain*, Eze. 26:4. Hiph. הוֹשִׁיב *cause to sit, dwell, reside in* or *with, inhabit.* Hoph. הוּשַׁב *made, caused to dwell.*

יֹשַׁבְתִּי; see יוֹשַׁבְתִּי.

שִׁיבָה f., *residing*, 2 Sa. 19:33; see in שׁוּב.

יֹשֵׁב בַּשֶּׁבֶת p. n. of one of David's generals.

יֶשֶׁבְאָב p. n. of a man.

יִשְׁבּוֹ בְנֹב p. n. of a man.

יָשְׁבְּקָשָׁה p. n. of a man.

מוֹשָׁב m. (pl. f. מוֹשָׁבוֹת; const. מוֹשְׁבֵי m.).—I. *residence.*—II. *seat.* — III. *time of residing*, Ex. 12:40.— IV. *act of sitting.*—V. *inhabitants.*

תּוֹשָׁב m., *settler, sojourner.*

יִשְׁבָּח p.n. of a man.

יָשֻׁבִי לֶחֶם p. n. of a man.

יָשָׁבְעָם p. n. of a man.

יִשְׁבָּק p. n. of a son of Abraham.

יָשׁוּב p. n. of a man; patron. יָשֻׁבִי.

יָשׁוּד for יָשֹׁד Kal fut.; see שׁדד.

יִשְׁוָה, יִשְׁוִי p. n. of a man.

יְשׁוֹחָיָה p. n. of a man.

יְשׁוּעָה, יֵשׁוּעַ *salvation*; see ישׁע.

יֶשַׁח m., *baseness, hypocrisy*, Mic. 6:14.

יִשְׁחוּ Niph fut.; see שחה.

יָשַׁט. Hiph. הוֹשִׁיט *extend, stretch out.*

יִשַׁי p. n., *Jesse*, the father of David; LXX. Ἰεσσαί.

יִשַּׁי for יַשִּׁיא Hiph. fut.; see נשא.

יִשִּׁיָּה, יִשִּׁיָּהוּ p. n. of a man.

יַשִּׂים for יָשֵׂם Hiph. fut.; see שׂמם.

יֵשֶׁל Kal. fut. apoc., from III. שׁלה.

יָשַׁם *was desolate, laid waste;* fut. תֶּשַׁם, תִּישַׁמְנָה; see שָׁמֵם.

יְשִׁימוֹן m.—I. any *great desert.*—II. specially, *the Desert of Sinai.*

יְשִׁימוֹת f., *desolations*, Ps. 55:16.

בֵּית־הַיְשִׁמוֹת p. n. of a place near the Dead Sea.

יִשֹּׁם for יָשֹׁם Kal. fut.; see שׁמם.

יַשְׁמֵם Hiph. fut.; see שׁמם.

יִשְׁמָא p. n. of a man.

יִשְׁמָעֵאל p. n.—I. *Ishmael*, the son of Abraham and Hagar. — II. of a man; יִשְׁמְעֵאלִים *Ishmaelites.*

יִשְׁמַעְיָה, יִשְׁמַעְיָהוּ p. n. of a man.

יִשְׁמְרַי p. n. of a man.

יָשֵׁן, יָשַׁן (fut. יִישַׁן) *slept, slumbered, dozed.* Niph. נוֹשַׁן *grew old, dry.* Pi. יִשֵּׁן *made to sleep*, Jud. 16:19.

יָשָׁן m., *old.*

יְשָׁנָה f.—I. the same.—II. p.n. of a town in the tribe of Judah.

יָשֵׁן m. יְשֵׁנָה f.—I. *sleepy.*—II. p. n. of a man.

שֵׁנָה f. — I. *sleep.* — II. *dream*, Ps. 90:5.

שֵׁנָא f., *sleep*, Ps. 127:2.

שְׁנָא or שְׁנָה f. Ch., the same.

שְׁנָת f., *sleep*, Ps. 132:4.

יֶשְׁנוֹ compounded of יֵשׁ and suff. וֹ with נ epenth.

יָשַׁע. Hiph. הוֹשִׁיעַ (fut. יוֹשִׁיעַ, יְהוֹשִׁיעַ; apoc. יוֹשַׁע) *deliver, set free, save*, with לְ, מִיַּד, מִן. Niph. נוֹשַׁע *was delivered*, with מִן; part. נוֹשָׁע *one saved*, Zec. 9:9.

יֶשַׁע, יֵשַׁע, יֶשַׁע m. (with suff. יִשְׁעִי, יִשְׁעֲךָ), *deliverance, freedom, safety, salvation.*

וַיִּשַׁע, יִשַׁע Kal fut. apoc., from שׁעה.

יוֹשַׁע Hiph. fut. apoc. יוֹשִׁעֲכֶם fut. with suff., from ישׁע.

יִשְׁעִי p. n. of a man.

יְשַׁעְיָהוּ p. n., *Isaiah* the prophet; LXX. Ἠσαΐας; Vulg. Isaias.

יְשַׁעְיָה p. n. of a man.

יֵשׁוּעַ (same as יְהוֹשֻׁעַ, Ἰησοῦς), p. n. of a man

יְשׁוּעָה f., *freedom, safety, salvation.*

מוֹשָׁעוֹת f. pl., *great salvation*, Ps. 68:21.

יָשְׁפֵה, יָשְׁפֶה *the jasper*, a variegated gem.

יִשְׁפָּה p.n. of a man.

יִשְׁפָּן p. n. of a man.

יָשַׁר (fut. יִישַׁר, יִשַׁר).—I. *proceed, go right*, i. e. directly onwards; יָשַׁר בְּדַרְכּוֹ *he went straight on his way.* —II. with בְּ, בְּעֵינֵי *he was right, upright, good.* Pi. יִשֵּׁר *make right, direct.* Pu. part. *made direct, plain, laid smooth*, 1 Ki. 6:35. Hiph. *made direct, straight forward*, Pro. 4:25.; (imp. הַיְשַׁר) *make direct*, Ps. 5:9.

יָשָׁר m., יְשָׁרָה f., *right, upright, righteous, true;* יָשָׁר s., *the book of right*, i. e. right things, Deu. 6:18.

יֵשֶׁר p. n. of a man.

יֹשֶׁר m., *rectitude, integrity.*

יִשְׁרָה f., the same.

יְשַׂרְאֵלָה p.n. of a man.

יְשֻׁרוּן m., a periphrastic title of Israel, applied to the whole people generally, lit. *entirely righteous.*

יִשַּׁרְנָה 1 Sa. 6:12, for תִּישַּׁרְנָה Kal fut. f. pl. 3. pers., from ישר.

מִישׁוֹר m.—I. *a plain.*—II. *truth, righteousness;* adv. *righteously, truly.*

מֵשָׁרִים, מֵישָׁרִים m. pl.—I. *true men.* —II. *truth, righteousness.*—III. לְמֵישָׁרִים, בְּמֵישָׁרִים *truly, righteously.*

יָשֵׁשׁ m., 2 Chron. 36:17, *aged, elderly person.*

יָשִׁישׁ m., the same.

יְשִׁישַׁי p.n. of a man.

וַיִּשְׁתַּחוּ, יִשְׁתַּחוּ Hith. fut. apoc. sing. for יִשְׁתַּחֲוֶה; see שחה.

יִשְׁתָּיוּן Kal fut. pl. with נ parag., from שתה.

יִשְׁתַּקְשְׁקוּן Hith. fut. pl., from שקק.

יַת Ch., same as Heb. אֵת.

וַיֵּתֵא, יֵתֵא Kal fut. apoc. for יֶאֱתֶה, יֵתֶה; see אתה.

יִתְאָו Hith. fut. apoc., from אוה.

יְתִב Ch., same as יָשַׁב *sit.* Aph. *reside,* Ezr. 4:17.

וַיִּתְגַּל, יִתְגַּל Hith. fut. apoc., from גלה.

יָתַד root not used; (Arab. *pin, nail*).

יָתֵד, const. יְתַד f. (pl. יְתֵדוֹת).—I. *pin, peg.*—II. *tent-pin;* hence *wise* (i. e. firmly fixed) *rulers,* Isa. 22:23, 25.—III. *dibble, to bore holes in the earth,* Deu. 23:14.

וַיְתָו, יְתָו Pi. fut. apoc., from תוה.

יִתְוַכַּח Hith. fut., from יכח.

יְתוּר *abundance;* see תּוּר.

יִתְזִין Ch. Ithp. fut., from זון.

יָתַח root not used; (Arab. *smote with a club*).

תּוֹתָח m., *club;* LXX. σφύρα, Job 41:21.

יִתְכַּס Hith fut. apoc., from כסה.

יִתְלָה p. n. of a city of the Danites.

יָתַם root not used; (Arab. *was an orphan*).

יָתוֹם m., *orphan.*

יִתֹּם, יִתְּמוּ, in pause יִתָּמוּ Kal fut., from תמם.

יִתַּמּוּ Niph. fut. pl., from תמם.

יִתְמָה p. n. of a man.

יָתַן root not used; (Arab. *was enduring*).

אֵתָן, אֵיתָן m.—I. *mighty, irresistible, violent;* יֶרַח הָאֵיתָנִים *the month of the powerful,* i. e. Tisri, 1 Ki. 8:2.—II. *might, irresistibleness.*—III. p. n., perhaps the author of Ps. 89.

יַתְנִיאֵל p. n. of a man.

יִתְנָן p. n. of a city in the tribe of Judah.

יָתַר, part. יוֹתֵר *exceeding, redundant.* Hiph. הוֹתִיר I. *cause to remain, leave.*—II. *abound, be wealthy.* Niph. נוֹתַר *be left, remain;* part. m. נוֹתָר, f. נוֹתֶרֶת *that which is left.*

יֶתֶר m.—I. *excellence, abundance,* עַל־יֶתֶר *unto abundance,* Ps. 31:24; adv., *abundantly, exceedingly.* —II. *residue, the rest of.*—III. *string* or *cord.*—IV. p. n. of a man; patron. יִתְרִי.

יִתְרָה f., *abundance, excess.*

יֹתֵר, יוֹתֵר (part. Kal).—I. *abundance, profit.*—II. adv., *more, further, moreover, excessively.*

יוֹתֶרֶת f.—I. *exceeding, redundant.*—II. *lobe,* i. e. excess *of the liver.*

יַתִּי־ m. Ch.—I. *excellent, extraordinary;* יַתִּירָה adv., *very, exceedingly.*—II. Heb. p. n., a town in the tribe of Judah.

יִתְרוֹ p. n., the father-in-law of Moses, who was also called יֶתֶר and חוֹבָב.

יִתְרוֹן m., *gain, profit, good.*

יִתְרְעָם p. n. of a man.

מוֹתָר m.—I. *increase.*—II. *excellence,* Ecc. 3:19.

מֵיתָר m.—I. *bow-string,* Ps. 21:13.—II. *tent-cord.*

יִתְּשָׂם Ch. Ithp. fut., from שׂוּם.

יְתֵת p. n. of a prince of Edom.

כ

כְּ, כָּ, כַּ pa. pref. signifying comparison, resemblance.—I. *as, as if, like;* כְּ...כְּ, כְּ...וּכְ, כְּ...כֵּן *as...so;* with suff. כָּכֶם, כָּהֶם; see כְּמוֹ.—II. *according to* (*κατά*).—III. *nearly, almost;* כַּיּוֹם הַזֶּה *as on this day;* כַּחֲצֹת הַלַּיְלָה *about midnight.*—IV. with inf. (sometimes with part.) *when, ὡς.*

כָּאַב (fut. יִכְאַב) *be pained.* Hiph. I. *cause pain,* Eze. 13:22.—II. *mar, ruin,* 2 Ki. 3:19.

כְּאֵב m., *pain.*

מַכְאוֹב m. (pl. ־ִים, ־וֹת).—I. *pain.*—II. *cause of pain.*—III. *sorrow.*

כָּאָה. Niph. *pained, enfeebled,* Dan. 11:30. Hiph. *pain, enfeeble the heart,* Eze. 13:22.

כָּאֶה m., *afflicted, helpless,* Ps. 10:10.

כָּאֹר Am. 8:8, for כַּיְאֹר.

כָּאֲרִי Ps. 22:17; see כּוּר.

כָּבֵד and כָּבַד (fut. יִכְבַּד.—I. *be heavy, grievous.*—II. *be grave, respectable, honorable,* with אֶל, עַל. Niph. *became honorable, glorious;* part. נִכְבָּדִים *nobles,* נִכְבָּדוֹת *made glorious,* with בְּ. Pi. כִּבֵּד I. *make heavy, sullen, unrelenting.*—II. *make honourable, honour,* with לְ, לְשֵׁם. Pu. כֻּבַּד *was honoured.* Hiph. I. *made heavy, grievous, sullen.*—II. *made honorable, glorious.*—Hith. מִתְכַּבֵּד *fancying himself honorable,* Pro. 12:9.

כָּבֵד const. כְּבַד, כְּבֵד, כָּבֵד m.—I. *heavy.*—II. *rich.*—III. *numerous.*—IV. *stupid, sullen.*—V. *grievous.*—VI. *dense.*—VII. *slow of utterance.*—VIII. *hard to be understood.*—IX. *the liver.*

כָּבוֹד m., lit. *heaviness:* hence,—I. *glory, splendour, majesty.*—II. *abundance, wealth.*—III. *multitude.*—IV. *mind, soul.*—V. *honour,* כְּבוֹד יְהוָה *the glory of God,* LXX. *δόξα Κυρίου.*

כָּבֹד, f. כְּבוּדָּה *glorious, precious.*

כֹּבֶד m.—I. *weight.*—II. *abundance.*

כְּבֵדֻת f., *heavily,* Ex. 14:25.

כָּבָה *was extinguished.* Pi. *extinguished.*

כָּבוּל p. n.—I. a district of Galilee.—II. a town in the tribe of Asher.

כַּבּוֹן p. n., a town in the tribe of Judah.

כַּבִּיר, כְּבִיר; see כבר.

כָּבַל root not used; (Arab. *iron fetter*)

כֶּבֶל m., *footlock of iron.*

כָּבַס part. כּוֹבֵס *fuller.* Pi. כִּבֵּס, כַּבֵּס *wash, cleanse* clothes and the like, not the body. Pu. כֻּבַּס *was washed.* Hothp. inf. הֻכַּבֵּס *to be washed,* Lev. 13:55, 56.

כָּבַע root not used; see גבע, קבע.

כּוֹבַע, כּוֹבַע m., *helmet.*

כָּבַר. Hiph. *multiplied,* Job 35:16; part. *abundance,* Job 36:31.

כְּבָר p. n. of a river in Mesopotamia, *the Chaboras.*

כְּבָר adv., *already, now.*

כַּבִּיר m., *mighty, powerful, great.*

כְּבִיר m., *cushion* or *pillow* cased with goat skin, 1 Sa. 19:13, 16.

כְּבָרָה f., *sieve,* Am. 9:9.

כִּבְרָה f., an unknown measure of length; LXX. ἱππόδρομος.

מִכְבָּר m., *brazen lattice-work.*

מַכְבֵּר m., *carpet, coarse cloth,* 2 Ki. 8:15.

כָּבַשׂ root not used; same as כָּבַשׁ *subdue.*

כֶּבֶשׂ m., *a lamb.*

כִּבְשָׂה, כַּבְשָׂה, כִּבְשָׂה f. (pl. כְּבָשׂוֹת const. כִּבְשׂת) *a she-lamb.*

כָּבַשׁ I. *trample, tread under foot;* metaph. *shall trample on sling stones,* i.e. not be harmed by them, Zec. 9:15.—II. *subdue, humble.*—III. *force,* Est. 7:8. Niph. *be subdued, humbled.* Pi. *subdued,* 2 Sa. 8:11.

כֶּבֶשׁ m., *footstool,* 2 Chron. 9:18.

כִּבְשָׁן m., *smelting furnace.*

כַּד *jar;* see כדד.

כְּדַב m., כִּדְבָה f. Ch., *lying, false,* Dan. 2:9.

כָּדַד root not used; (perhaps from Arab. *straitness*).

כַּד f. (with suff. כַּדֵּךְ; pl. m. כַּדִּים) *earthen jar, water vessel.*

כִּידוֹד m., *spark of fire,* Job 41:11.

כַּדְכֹּד m., *a precious stone,* perhaps *the ruby.*

כְּדֵי, see דַּי; כְּדִי, see דִּי; כִּדְנָה, see דֵּן.

כִּידוֹר m., *attack, onset,* Job 15:24.

כְּדָרְלָעֹמֶר p. n. of a king of Elam.

כֹּה pa.—I. *so, thus, in this form, manner, &c.;* בְּכֹה...בְּכֹה *on this manner and on that manner,* 1 Ki. 22:20.—II. *here, hither;* כֹּה...וְכֹה *hither and thither,* Ex. 2:12; עַד כֹּה *yonder,* Gen. 22:5.—III. *now;* עַד כֹּה *until now,* Ex. 7:16; עַד כֹּה וְעַד כֹּה *so and so long,* i.e. a very short time, 1 Ki. 18:45.

כָּה Ch., עַד כָּה *thus far,* Dan. 7:28.

כָּהָה (fut. יִכְהֶה; apoc. וַתֵּכַהּ).—I. *become weak, languid* (of the eyes). —II. of the mind or person, Isa. 42:4. Pi. כִּהָה, כֵּהָה *made weak, disheartened.*

כֵּהֶה f. כֵּהָה.—I. *expiring, fading* (of a lamp), Isa. 42:3.—II. of the eyes. — III. of a disease or eruption.— IV. אֵין כֵּהָה *not weak,* i. e. vigorous, Nah. 3:19.

כֵּהוֹת Pi. inf., from כהה.

כְּהַל Ch., *able, adequate.*

כָּהַן. Pi. כִּהֵן *act, officiate as priest.*

כֹּהֵן m. (pl. כֹּהֲנִים, כֹּהֲנֵי) *priest;* with הַגָּדוֹל or הָרֹאשׁ or הַמָּשִׁיחַ *the high priest.*

כָּהֵן m. Ch., *priest.*

כְּהֻנָּה f., *priesthood, office of the priest.*
כּוּב p. n., a country in the south, Eze. 30:5.
כּוֹבַע *helmet;* see כבע.
כָּוָה. Niph. תִּכָּוֶה *was, became burnt.*
כַּו m. Ch., pl. כַּוִּין *windows, casements,* Dan. 6:11.
כְּוִיָּה f., *burning, branding,* Ex. 21:25.
כִּי m. (for כְּוִי) *branding,* Isa. 3:24.
כִּי pa.; see further.
מִכְוָה f., *inflamed part* (of body), Lev. 13:24, 25, 28.

כּוּחַ root not used; (Arab. *conquer in battle*).
כֹּחַ, כּוֹחַ m.—I. *strength, vigour, power, ability.*—II. *wealth;* כֹּחַ הָאָרֶץ *fruit of the earth,* Gen. 4:12.—III. a kind of *lizard* (from its strength), Lev. 11:30.

כּוֹכָב m., *star, constellation.*

כּוּל *measured,* Isa. 40:12. Hiph. הֵכִיל I. *contain.*—II. *sustain.* Pil. כִּלְכֵּל I. *contain* (as a vessel).—II. *sustain* (with food).—III. *bear* (with firmness). Pu. כֻּלְכַּל *were sustained.*
כִּימָה *the constellation of the pleiades.*

כּוּמָז *bracelet of gold beads.*

כּוּן *fashioned, set in order,* Job 31:15. Pil. כּוֹנֵן *dispose, prepare, fix, establish,* with עַל, עַד, בְּ, אֶת. Pul. כּוֹנַן *established, confirmed.* Hiph. הֵכִין *dispose, prepare, fix, establish.* Hoph. הוּכַן *was disposed, prepared.* Niph. *be, become disposed, set in order, fixed, established* (of person or thing); part. נָכוֹן (f. נְכֹנָה) *firm, established, sure;* שַׁחַר נָכוֹן *the true dawn,* as opposed to the false, or premature twilight in the East, Hos. 6:3; אֶל־־נָכוֹן *certainly, for certain.* Hith. הִכּוֹנֵן, הִתְכּוֹנֵן same as Niph.
כֵּן adj.—I. *substantial, true;* pl. כֵּנִים —II. part. *really, truly:* whence, —III. *as, so, thus;* אַחֲרֵי־כֵן, אַחַר כֵּן *afterwards;* בְּכֵן *thus;* לָכֵן *therefore;* לָכֵן אֲשֶׁר *because;* עַל־כֵּן *because;* עַד־כֵּן *hitherto;* see also in כנן.
כֵּן Ch., *thus.*
אָכֵן pa. (for הָכֵן inf. abs. Hiph. *confirmed*), *surely, certainly, truly.*
כּוּן p. n., a Phenician city, 1 Chron. 18:8, called in 2 Sa. 8:8, בֵּרֹתַי *Berytus.*
כַּוָּן m., *small round cake,* Jer. 7:18; 44:19.
כִּיּוּן p.n. of an idol, Am. 5:26, called Ῥεμφαν, Acts 7:43, the planet Saturn.
יָכִין I. p. n. of a son of Simeon; patron. יָכִינִי.—II. one of the columns in the temple of Solomon.
מָכוֹן m.—I. *place, establishment.*—II. *foundation.*
מְכוֹנָה f.—I. *basis.*—II. p. n. of a town in the tribe of Judah.
מְכוּנָה f., *place,* Zec. 5:11.
תְּכוּנָה f.—I. *presence.*—II. *arrangement.*—III. *furniture, stores.*

כּוֹס f.—I. *drinking cup;* pl. כֹּסוֹת.—II. *rough-billed pelican,* Lev. 11:17; Deu. 14:16; Ps. 102:7.

כּוּר root not used; (Arab. *digging, piercing*); כָּאֲרִי *piercing,* Ps 22:17.

כַּר m., *camel's pack-saddle*, Gen. 31:34; see also כרר.

כָּרִי an officer of a certain rank, 2 Ki. 11:4, 19; כְּרֵתִי Kri, 2 Sa. 20:23.

כּוּר m., *furnace for melting metals.*

כּוּר עָשָׁן (*smoking furnace*), p. n. of a city in the tribe of Simeon.

כֹּר m., a measure of capacity, containing 10 baths.

כִּיּוֹר m. (pl. כִּיֹּרִים, כִּיּרוֹת).—I. *a pot* or *brazier* for fire, Zec. 12:6.—II. *laver of brass.*—III. *chafing dish*, 1 Sa. 2:14. — IV. *pulpit*, 2 Chron. 6:13.

כִּירַיִם m. dual, *pots* or *jars*, Lev. 11:35; LXX. χυτρόποδες.

כִּכָּר f. (for כִּרְכָּר).—I. *tract of country.*—II. כִּכַּר לֶחֶם *cake of bread*; pl. m. כִּכָּרוֹת *talent* (of gold or silver); dual כִּכָּרַיִם; const. כִּכְּרַיִם; pl. f. כִּכָּרִים, כִּכְּרֵי.

כַּכַּר f. Ch., pl. כַּכְּרִין the same.

מְכוּרָה, מְכוֹרָה f., *place of origin, birth*, lit. *digging*; see Isa. 51:1.

מְכֵרָה f., *sword*, Gen. 49:5.

כּוּשׁ p. n.—I. *Ethiopia.*—II. name of a man, Ps. 7:1.

כּוּשִׁי m. (pl. כּוּשִׁיִּים; f. כּוּשִׁית).—I. *an Ethiopian.*—II. p. n. of a man.

כּוּשָׁן f., Hab. 3:7, same as כּוּשׁ *Ethiopia.*

כּוּשַׁן רִשְׁעָתַיִם p. n. of a king of Mesopotamia.

כּוֹשָׁרָה f., *wealth*; see כשר.

כּוּת, כּוּתָה p. n. of a region whence the kingdom of Israel was colonised after its depopulation.

כָּזַב, part. כֹּזֵב *deficient, falling short*, Ps. 116:11. Pi. כִּזֵּב—I. *lie, deceive.*—II. *fail*, with לְ or בְּ. Hiph. *convict of falsehood*, Job 24:25. Niph. *was fallacious, false.*

כָּזָב m., *falling short of truth, lying, falsehood.*

כֹּזֵבָא p. n., same as כְּזִיב.

כָּזְבִּי p. n. of a Midianitish woman.

כְּזִיב p. n. of a town in the tribe of Judah.

אַכְזָב m., *deficient, deception, unstable.*

אַכְזִיב p. n.—I. a town in the tribe of Judah.—II. a town in the tribe of Asher, on the Mediterranean. Ἔκδιππα.

כָּזַר root not used; (Arab. *mudd turbid*).

אַכְזָר m., *untractable, cruel, fierce.*

אַכְזָרִי *very cruel.*

אַכְזְרִיּוּת f., *great cruelty*, Pro. 27:4.

כֹּחַ *strength*; see כּוֹחַ.

כָּחַד. Pi. כִּחֵד *keep back, conceal*, with מִן or לְ. Niph. I. *was concealed.*—II. *made useless, destroyed.* Hiph. I. *hold back.*—II. *bring to nought.*

כָּחַל *black* (the eyes) *with antimony*, Eze. 23:40.

כָּחַשׁ *fail, be deficient.* Pi. כִּחֵשׁ I. *withhold.*—II. *fail, deceive, deny, lie*, with בְּ and לְ. Niph. and Hith. *were, became liars*, with לְ.

כַּחַשׁ m.—I. *deficiency.*—II. *failure, falsehood.*

כֶּחָשׁ m., *lying*, Isa. 30:9.

כִּי pa.—I. *if, for*, at the beginning of a speech.—II. *because, therefore*, in the second member of a sentence: also,—III. *surely, without doubt.*

It connects the hypothesis and condition of an entire sentence, and may be translated by almost any particle that is so used; הֲכִי *whether? is not?* יַעַן כִּי ,עַל כִּי *because;* עַד כִּי *until;* כִּי עַל־כֵּן *therefore;* see also כָּוָה.

כִּי אִם I. *that.*—II. *if not*, with oaths. —III. *except*, after a negative.—IV. *but, only.*

כִּיד m., *ruin, destruction*, Job 21:20.

כִּידוֹן m.—I. *spear.*—II. גֹּרֶן כִּידוֹן (*the plain of spears*), p. n. of a district; see נָכוֹן.

כִּידוֹד *sparks;* see כדד.

כִּידוֹר *attack;* see כדר.

כִּיּוּן *an idol;* see כון.

כִּיּוֹר *pot;* see כור.

כִּילַי ,כֵּלַי *vessel;* see נכל.

כַּלַּפּוֹת *axes;* see כלף.

כִּימָה *Pleiades;* see כום.

כִּיס *bag;* see נכם.

כִּיר *pot;* see כור.

כִּיתְרוֹן Syr. for כִּיתְרוֹן.

כָּכָה same as כֹּה *thus;* אֵיכָכָה *how?* see אֵיךְ in אֵי.

כִּכָּר; see כור.

כֹּל ,כָּל־ *all;* see כלל.

כָּלָא *restrain, confine, withhold* (part. כָּלוּא ,כָּלֻא *shut up*), with מִן; fut. יִכְלֶה. Niph. *restrained, withholden.*

כֶּלֶא m. (with suff. כִּלְאוֹ), *prison;* בֵּית כֶּלֶא ,בֵּית הַכֶּלֶא the same; pl. בָּתֵּי כְלָאִים.

כֶּלָא ,כֻּלָּה f., *all that*, from כֹּל; see כלל.

כִּלְאַיִם dual, *of two sorts* or *kinds*, *ἑτερογενῆ.*

כְּלוּא (כְּלִיא) m., *prison.*

מִכְלָה f. (pl. מִכְלָאוֹת), *fold* or *pen for flocks.*

כִּלְאָב p. n. of a son of David.

כְּלוּב m.—I. *fruit-basket*, Am. 8:1,2. —II. *bird-cage*, Jer. 5:27.—III. p. n. of a man.

כֶּלֶב m.—I. *a dog.*—II. *bad, cruel man.*

כָּלֵב p. n. of a man, *Caleb;* patron. כָּלִבִּי.

כָּלָה (fut. יִכְלֶה ,תִּכְלֶה; apoc. יֵכֶל (וַתֵּכֶל).—I. *was completed, finished.* —II. *was wasted, ruined, decayed.* Pi. כִּלָּה I. *complete, determine.*—II. *waste, ruin, destroy*, with לְ. Pu. כֻּלָּה (fut. יְכֻלֶּה), *were completed.*

כָּלֶה, f. כָּלָה *consuming*, Deu. 28:32.

כָּלָה f., *completion, destruction;* עָשָׂה כָלָה *hath done even to destruction, altogether*, with אֶת ,בְּ; adv. כָּלָה, לְכָלָה *completely, entirely.*

כְּלִי m. (with pause כֶּלִי; pl. כֵּלִים, כְּלֵי).—I. *vessel.*—II. *boat*, Isa. 18: 2.—III. *musical instrument.*—IV. *arms, weapon.*—V. *implement of husbandry.*—VI. *clothing.*

כְּלָיוֹת const., כִּלְיוֹת f. pl., *the reins, kidneys*, metaph. as the seat of sense, the feeling.

כִּלָּיוֹן const., כִּלְיוֹן m.—I. *consumption*, Isa. 10:22.—II. *wasting of the eyes*, Deu. 28:65.

כִּלְיוֹן p. n. of a man.

מִכְלוֹת f. pl., with זָהָב, 2 Chron. 4: 21. *pure gold.*

תִּכְלָה f., *perfection;* LXX. *συντέλεια.*

תַּכְלִית f.—I. *extremity*, Neh. 3:21.—II. *boundary.* — III. *completeness perfection.*

כְּלוּלוֹת, כַּלָּה; see כלל.
כְּלוּהַי p.n. of a man.
כָּלְהֶם for כֻּלָּם, from כֹּל; see כלל.
כָּלְהֶנָה for כֻּלָּנָה, from כֹּל; see כלל.
כָּלוּ 1 Sa. 6:10, Kal pret. pl., from כלא.
כֶּלַח m.—I. *wealth.*—II. *insolence,* Job 30:2.
כֶּלַח p.n. of a city, Gen. 10:11.
כְּלִי, כִּלָּיוֹן, כְּלָיוֹת; see כלה.
כַּלְכֹּל p.n. of a man.
כָּלַל *perfected,* Eze. 27:4, 11.
כְּלַל Ch., *finished, completed;* Shaph. שַׁכְלֵל the same; passive אִשְׁתַּכְלַל *was completed.*
כָּלִיל m.—I. *whole, entire;* adv. *wholly, entirely;* כְּלִיל הָעִיר *the whole city.*—II. *whole burnt-offering,* i.e. offering entirely consumed, Deu. 33:10; Ps. 51:21.
כַּלָּה f.—I. *daughter-in-law.* — II. *spouse.*
כְּלוּלוֹת f. pl., *espousals,* Jer. 2:2.
כֹּל (כּוֹל Jer. 33:8) כָּל־.—I. *the whole, all.*—II. *complete, entire.*—III. *all, every.*—IV. *many, most of;* לֹא כֹל *none:* with suff. כֻּלָּנוּ *all we;* כֻּלְּכֶם *all ye;* כֻּלָּם, כֻּלְּהֶם *all they;* כֻּלָּנָה, כֻּלְּהֶנָה *all they,* f.; כֻּלּוֹ *all of it,* m.; כֻּלָּהּ the same, f.; with adv. כָּל־עוֹד *as long as,* כָּל־עֻמַּת שֶׁ־ *just as,* Ecc. 5:15.
כֹּל, כָּל־ Ch., the same; כְּלָא adv., *altogether, entirely.*
מִכְלָל m., *perfection,* Ps. 50:2.
מִכְלוֹל m., the same (of clothing), Eze. 23:12, &c.
מַכְלֻלִים m. pl., *splendid garments,* Eze. 27:24.
כָּלַם. Hiph. הִכְלִים, הֶכְלִים *put to shame, make ashamed, injure.* Hoph. *was ashamed, confounded.* Niph. *was ashamed, confounded*
כְּלִמָּה f., *shame, ignominy.*
כְּלִמּוּת *state of shame,* Jer. 23:40.
כִּלְמַד p. n. of a region or city.
כַּלְנֵה, כַּלְנֶה, כַּלְנוֹ p. n. of a city on the river Tigris (Ctesiphon?).
כָּלַף root not used; (Arab. *drove*).
כֵּלַפּוֹת f. pl., *axes* or *hammer,* Ps. 74:6; LXX. λαξευτήρια.
כִּלַּתּוּ Pi. pret. 3. pers. f. with suff., from כלה.
כְּלִתְנִי 1 Sa. 25:33, Kal pret. 2. pers. f with suff., from כלא.
כָּמַהּ *desired intensely* even to fainting.
כִּמְהָם p. n. of a man.
כְּמָה, כַּמָּה, כַּמֶּה; see מָה.
כְּמוֹ, כָּמוֹ pa., same as כְּ *thus, as, whether;* with suff. כָּמוֹנִי *as I am,* כָּמוֹךָ, כָּמֹכָה *as thou art;* כָּמוֹהוּ *as he is;* כָּמוֹהָ *as she is;* כָּמוֹנוּ *as we are,* sometimes for כָּכֶם, כְּמוֹכֶם, כְּמוֹהֶם; כָּהֶם *as ye, they, are;* כְּמוֹ...כְּמוֹ *as...so.*
כְּמוֹשׁ p. n., an idol of the children of Moab and Ammon; עַם כְּמוֹשׁ *the Moabites.*
כַּמֹּן m., the herb *cummin,* Isa. 28: 25, 27.
מִכְמַנִּים m. pl., *treasures,* Dan. 11:43.
כָּמַס *laid, treasured, up,* Deu. 32:34.
כָּמַר. Niph. נִכְמַר I. *was affected* (warmed with intense feeling, love, compassion).—II. *was black* with burning, Lam. 5:10.
כֹּמֶר m., pl. כְּמָרִים *idolatrous priests.*
כַּמְרִיר *blackest, gloomiest thing,* Job 3:5.

מִכְמָר, מַכְמוֹר m., pl. מַכְמֹרִים *net* used by fishermen.

מִכְמֶרֶת, מִכְמֹרֶת f., *net* used by fishermen.

כֵּן; see כּוּן and כָּנַן.

כָּנָה Kal not used; (Syr. *named*). Pi. כִּנָּה I. *call by name.*—II. *flatter.*

כְּנָת m. (man of the same name), *companion, associate*; pl. כְּנָוֺת (σύνδουλοι).

כְּנָת Ch., the same; pl. כְּנָוָן; with suff. כְּנָוָתְהוֹן, כְּנָוָתֵהּ.

כַּנֵּה; see כנן.

כַּנֵּה p. n. of a city (perhaps for כַּלְנֵה).

כִּנּוֹר m. (with suff. כִּנֹּרִי; pl. כִּנֹּרִים, כִּנֹּרוֹת), *harp* (κινύρα).

כְּנָווֹת, כְּנָוָן from כְּנָת; see כנה.

כָּנְיָהוּ p. n. of a king of Judah; same as יְהוֹיָכִין.

כַּנְּלֹתְךָ Hiph. inf. with pref. and suff. for כְּהַנְלוֹתְךָ; see נלה.

כִּנָּם; see כנן.

כִּנֵמָא Ch., "as it is said" (for כְּנְאֵמָא Lee).

כַּנָּה f., *stock, root,* Ps. 80:16.

כְּנָנִי p. n. of a man.

כְּנַנְיָה, כְּנַנְיָהוּ p.n. of a man.

כְּנַנְיָהוּ p. n. of a man.

כֵּן m. (with suff. כַּנּוֹ, כַּנֶּךָ.—I. *place, station.*—II. *base,* foot of the laver; see also כּוּן.

כֵּן m., *lice*; pl. כִּנִּים LXX. σκνίφες.

כִּנָּם for כִּנִּם same as כִּנִּים; see preceding word, Ex. 8:12.

כָּנַס *collect, gather together.* Pi. like Kal. Hith. *being collecting, comprehending,* Isa. 28:20.

מִכְנָס m., dual const. מִכְנְסֵי *drawers, breeches of linen* (for the priests).

כָּנַע. Hiph. הִכְנִיעַ *humble, debase, bring down.* Niph. נִכְנַע *was humbled, debased.*

כִּנְעָה f., *package, bale of merchandise,* Jer. 10:17.

כְּנַעַן I. p. n. of a son of Ham.—II. of the land inhabited by his posterity.—III. m., *a merchant.*

כְּנַעֲנִי (f. כְּנַעֲנִית; pl. כְּנַעֲנִים).—I. *a Canaanite.*—II. *a merchant.*

כְּנַעֲנָה p. n. of a man.

כִּנְעָנֶיהָ pl. with suff., from כְּנַעַן.

כָּנַף root not used; (Arab. *put away*). Niph. יִכָּנֵף *put away, remove,* Isa. 30:20.

כָּנָף f. (dual כְּנָפַיִם, כַּנְפֵי f.; pl. const. כַּנְפוֹת m. and f.).—I. *wing* (of a bird, &c.).—II. *wing* (of an army) —III. *skirt* (of a garment).—IV. *extreme part* (of the earth or land). —V. by meton. *person protected,* i. e. wife &c.

כִּנֶּרֶת, כִּנְּרוֹת, כִּנְּרוֹת p. n., a city in the tribe of Naphtali, near the sea of Galilee (Γεννησαρέτ); יָם כִּנֶּרֶת *the sea of Galilee.*

כְּנַשׁ Ch., *collect,* Dan. 3:2. Hith. *being assembled,* Dan. 3:3, 27.

כַּסְדַּי Ch., same as כַּשְׂדִּי *a Chaldean.*

כָּסָה, part. כֹּסֶה *covering, concealing,* Pro. 12:16, 23; כָּסוּי *covered,* Nu. 4:6, 14. Niph. נִכְסָה *being covered, concealed.* Pi. כִּסָּה *cover conceal,* with אֶל, אֵת, בְּ, לְ, עַל. Pu. כֻּסָּה, כֻּסָּה *covered, was covered,* with בְּ. Hith. same as Niph. Pu. with בְּ.

כֵּס m., כֵּ׳ יָהּ *the throne of Jehovah*, Ex. 17:16.

כֶּסֶא, כֶּסֶה m., *the new moon*, Ps. 81:4; Pro. 7:20.

כִּסֵּא, כִּסֵּה m. (with suff. כִּסְאִי; pl. כִּסְאוֹת), *regal chair, throne*.

כְּסוּת f.—I. *covering*.—II. *clothing*.

סוּת f., a false reading for כְּסוּת *garments*, Gen. 49:11.

כְּסָתוֹת f. pl., Eze. 13:18, 20, LXX. προσκεφάλαια, *cushions*, probably ornaments.

מִכְסֶה m., *covering*.

מְכַסֶּה m., *covering*, Isa. 14:11.

כָּסַח, part. כָּסוּחַ *cut off*.

כַּסּוּחָה *like filth*, Isa. 5:25; see סוּחַ.

כָּסַל *was a fool*; fut. יִכְסָלוּ Jer. 10:8.

כְּסִיל m.—I. *a fool*.—II. the constellation *Orion*.—III. p. n. of a city in the tribe of Judah.

כְּסִילוּת f., *foolish woman*, Pro. 9:13.

כֶּסֶל m.—I. *the loins*.—II. *the viscera*; pl. כְּסָלִים.—III. *expectation, confidence*.—IV. *foolishness*.

כִּסְלָה f.—I. *confidence*.—II. *folly*.

כִּסְלֵו m., the ninth month of the Hebrew year, answering to our November and December.

כְּסָלוֹן p. n. of a town on the borders of the tribe of Judah

כִּסְלוֹן p. n. of a man.

כְּסֻלּוֹת p. n. of a town in the tribe of Issachar.

כִּסְלוֹת־תָּבוֹר p. n. of a town at the foot of Mount Tabor.

כַּסְלֻחִים m. pl., p. n. a people so called.

כָּסַם *adorn*, Eze. 44:20.

כֻּסֶּמֶת f., a kind of corn, *spelt*, ζέα; pl. כֻּסְּמִים.

כָּסַס *apportion, divide out*, Ex. 12:4

מֶכֶס m., *fractional part, number*.

מִכְסָה f., *number*.

כָּסַף *desired intensely* (lit. grew pale with desire), with לְ. Niph. *become desirous, earnestly longing for*, with לְ.

כֶּסֶף m. (with suff. כַּסְפִּי; pl. כְּסָפִים).—I. *silver*.—II. *money*; with numerals, *the shekel of silver*; אֶלֶף כ׳ 1,000 *shekels*.

כְּסַף m. Ch., *silver*.

כָּסִפְיָא p. n. of a country.

כְּסָתוֹת *ornaments*; see כסה.

כִּסַּתְנִי Pi. pret. 3 pers. f. with suff., from כסה.

כְּעַן adv. Ch.—I. *so, therefore*.—II. *but*.—III. *now*; כְּעֶנֶת *so on*; see עתת.

כָּעַס (fut. יִכְעַס).—I. *was angry*.—II. *irritated*. Pi. כִּעֵס *irritate*. Hiph הִכְעִיס.—I. *was angry*.—II. *made angry, irritated*.

כַּעַס m.—I. *vexation, sadness*.—II. *anger*; pl. כְּעָסִים *excitements to anger*.

כַּעַשׂ m., the same, in Job only.

כַּף, כַּפּוֹת, כִּפָּה; see כפף.

כֵּף *rock*, Job 30:6; Jer. 4:29.

כָּפָה *avert, appease*, Pro. 21:14; see כבה.

כְּפוֹר, כְּפִיר, כְּפִירָה; see כפר.

כָּפַל *doubled*; part. כָּפוּל. Niph. *be repeated*, Eze. 21:19.

כֶּפֶל m., *doubling, twofold*; dual כִּפְלַיִם Job 11:6; Isa. 40:2.

כָּפַן *became languid*, Eze. 17:7.

כָּפָן m., *hunger*, Job 5:22; 30:3

כָּפַס (Syr. *tie, join*).

כָּפִיס m., *tie-beam;* "*tenon*" (Lee); LXX. κάνθαρος.

כָּפַף *bend, bow down*, with distress. Niph. *bow myself down*, with לְ *before*, Mic. 6:6.

כַּף f.—I. *palm of the hand.*—II. *hand* (with suff. כַּפִּי; dual כַּפַּיִם *both hands;* pl. כַּפּוֹת).—III. *sole of the foot.*—IV. *foot of a beast.*—V. *bason* or *phial.*—VI. *receptacle for the stone in a sling;* כַּף־הַקֶּלַע *cup of the sling*, 1 Sa. 25:29.—VII. *bent palm branches;* כַּפּוֹת תְּמָרִים *bent palm branches*, Lev. 23:40.—VIII. כַּף־הַיָּרֵךְ *cup of the thigh joint*, Gen. 32:26, &c.

כִּפָּה f., *curved branch, branch.*

כָּפַר.—I. generally *cover.*—II. specially, *pitch, smear with pitch*, Gen. 6:14, with בְּ. Pi. כִּפֶּר (fut. יְכַפֵּר) I. *cover, expiate for sin*, used of the sinner and the sin.—II. *appease anger.*—III. *avert calamity*, with אֶת, בְּעַד, לְ, עַל. Pu. כֻּפַּר—I. *was expiated.*—II. *was abolished.* Hith. *was expiated;* נִכַּפֵּר for נִתְכַּפֵּר Deu. 21:8.

כְּפוֹר m.—I. *vessel, covered cup.*—II. *hoar frost*, Ex. 16:14; Ps. 147:16.

כְּפִיר m.—I. *a young lion.*—II. metaph. *fierce, bold man.*—III. *village*, Neh. 6:2.

כָּפָר m., *village.*

כְּפִירָה p. n. of a city of the Hivites.

כְּפַר הָעַמּוֹנִי p. n., a town in the tribe of Benjamin.

כֹּפֶר m.—I. *pitch*, Gen. 6:14.—II. *a village*, 1 Sa. 6:18.—III. *expiation*, lit. *covering for sin*, λύτρον.—IV. *the cypress tree*, Cant. 1:14.

כִּפֻּרִים m. pl., *expiation.*

כַּפֹּרֶת f., *the covering of the ark; mercy-seat;* בֵּית הַכַּפֹּרֶת *the holy of holies.*

כָּפַשׁ. Hiph. *overwhelmed, covered*, Lam. 3:16.

כְּפַת Ch., *bound, tied.*

כַּפְתּוֹר p. n., a country of the Philistines; כַּפְתֹּרִים its inhabitants, Gen. 10:14.

כַּפְתֹּרִים m. pl.—I. *twisted capitals* or *columns.*—II. *ornamented bowls* of the golden candlestick, Ex. 25:36.

כֹּר, see כּוּר; כַּר, see כּוּר and כָּרַר.

כְּרָא or **כְּרָה** Ch. Ithp. *was pained, afflicted.*

כִּרְבֵּל. Pu. part. מְכֻרְבָּל *equipped clothed*, I Chron. 15:27.

כַּרְבְּלָא Ch., *a cloak*, Dan. 3:21.

כָּרָה *dig* (as a well, pit); with אָזְנַיִם *mine ears hast thou digged, opened*, Ps. 40:7. Niph. I. *was dug.*—II. *buy, purchase*, Deu. 2:6; Hos. 3:2.—III. *feast*, 2 Ki. 6:23.

כֵּרָה f.—I. *digging*, Zep. 2:6; pl. const. כְּרֹת.—II. *feast*, 2 Ki. 6:23.

מִכְרֶה m., *pit*, Zep. 2:9.

כְּרוּב m., pl. כְּרֻבִים, כְּרוּבִים.—I. *cherub;* a symbolical figure over the mercy-seat; described Eze. 4:6.—II. p. n. of a man, Ezr. c. 2; Neh. c. 7.

כְּרַז Ch. Aph. *proclaim*, κηρύσσειν, Dan. 5:29.

כָּרוֹז m. Ch., *herald*, Dan. 3:4.

sec כרת.

suff. כִּרְכֻּבוֹ) *brazier*
ting of the altar for
ne fire).

, Est. 8:15.

' a city on the Eu-
chemish (Κιρκήσιον).

m, Cant. 4:14.

rsian eunuch.

כ.

27:2, 3).—I. *vineyard.*
ard.—III. *orchard.*
resser.
man.

כֶּרֶם־אֵל; with suff.
well-cultivated plain, or-
-II. *Carmel*, a very fruit-
of Asher, near the Me-
כַּרְמְלִית m.; כַּרְמְלִי
lite.— III. גֶּרֶשׂ כַּרְמֶל
rst fruits (of the most
Lev. 2:14; 23:14.

ason.

in.

same as כִּסֵּא *throne.*

., *devoured*, Ps. 80:14.

his legs (as an animal
.—II. *bowed, lay down,*
ith לְ or לִפְנֵי before
III. *was weak.* Hiph.
v down, depress, afflict.
oth the legs or *leg bones.*

m cloth, calico, Est. 1:
he same).

כִּ *leap about, dance,*
16.

כַּר m. (pl. כָּרִים).—I. *fatted lamb.*—II. *the pasture where lambs feed.*—III. *battering ram.*

כִּרְכָּרוֹת f. pl., *dromedaries*, Isa. 66:20.

כְּרֵשׂ m., *belly*, Jer. 51:34.

כֹּרֶשׁ p. n., *Cyrus* king of Persia.

כַּרְשְׁנָא p. n., a Persian prince.

כָּרַת (imp. כְּרָת־; with ה parag כָּרְתָה; fut. יִכְרֹת).—I. *cut off, down*; כָּרוּת and כְּרוּת שָׁפְכָה *eunuch.* — II. with or without בְּרִית *make a covenant* (ὅρκια τέμνειν), (lit. strike a bargain), with אֵת, עִם, לְ.—III. *kill men*, Jer. 11:19. Niph. *was cut down, cut off.* Pu. כֹּרַת, כֻּרַת *cut off.* Hiph. הִכְרִית *cut off, destroy.* Hoph. הָכְרַת *was cut off*, Joel 1:9.

כְּרֻתוֹת f. pl., *beams* (things cut).

כְּרִית p. n. of the brook *Cherith*, which falls into the Jordan not far from Samaria.

כְּרִיתֻת, כְּרִיתוּת f., *divorce*; with סֵפֶר *bill of divorce.*

כְּרֵתִי p. n.—I. a tribe of the Philistines of the south west coast of Judea, derived from the Island of *Crete.*—II. title of certain brave soldiers in David's army.

כֶּשֶׂב m., same as כֶּבֶשׂ *lamb.*

כִּשְׂבָּה *female-lamb.*

כֶּשֶׂד p. n., a son of Nahor; the progenitor of the Chaldees.

כַּשְׂדִּים pl.—I. *Chaldees*, inhabitants of Babylon.—II. *astrologer.*

כַּשְׂדַּי m. Ch., *a Chaldee.*

כָּשָׂה *covered with fat*, Deu. 32:15

כָּשַׁל (fut. יִכְשׁוֹל).—I. *totter, stagger.* —II. *stumble.*—III. *stumble to fall* (part. כּוֹשֵׁל *weak, weary*), with בְּ. Niph. נִכְשַׁל *be tottering from weakness.* Pi. and Hiph. I. *cause to stumble.*—II. *fail, become weak.* Hoph. part. מֻכְשָׁלִים *made to stumble*, Jer. 18:23.

כַּשִּׁיל m., *an axe*, Ps. 74:6.

כִּשָּׁלוֹן m., *ruin*, Pro. 16:18.

מִכְשׁוֹל m.—I. *offence, delusion.*—II. *σκάνδαλον, cause of offence, place, instrument* or *cause of sin.*

מַכְשֵׁלָה f., *fall, ruin*, Isa. 3:6; Zep. 1:3.

כָּשַׁף. Pi. כִּשֵּׁף *used witchcraft*, 2 Ch. 33:6; part. מְכַשֵּׁף *magician, wizard;* מְכַשֵּׁפָה *witch.*

כַּשָּׁף m., *magician*, Jer. 27:9.

כְּשָׁפִים m. pl., *magical rites, incantations.*

כָּשֵׁר *do well, be acceptable*, Est. 8:5; Ecc. 11:6. Hiph. *give prosperity*, Ecc. 10:10.

כּוֹשָׁרָה f., pl. כּוֹשָׁרוֹת *great prosperity, wealth*, Ps. 68:7.

כִּשְׁרוֹן *prosperity, profit*, Ecc. 5:10.

כִּישׁוֹר m., *distaff*, Pro. 31:19.

כָּתַב I. *write, engrave*, with בְּ, עַל, אֶל before the material written upon; with לְ, אֶל, עַל before the person to whom the writing was addressed. Niph. *was written.* Pi. *wrote*, Isa. 10:1.

כְּתַב Ch., *he wrote.*

כְּתָב m.—I. *writing.*—II. *epistle.*—III. *record.*—IV. *Scripture.*

כְּתָב m. Ch., *writing, edict.*

כְּתֹבֶת f., *writing*, Lev. 19:28.

מִכְתָּב m.—I. *writing.*—II. *epistle ordinance* (thing written).

כִּתִּים, כִּתִּיִּים p.n. the *Chittim*, probably the inhabitants of Cyprus and of some part of Asia Minor.

כָּתִית *beaten small;* see כתה.

כֹּתֶל m., *wall*, Cant. 2:9.

כְּתַל m. Ch., *wall;* pl. emph. כְּתְלַיָּא Dan. 5:5.

כִּתְלִישׁ p. n. of a town in the tribe of Judah.

כָּתַם Kal not used; (Arab. *treasure up*). Niph נִכְתַּם *treasured up*, or as some interpret, *embroidered with gold;* see the next word, Jer. 2:22.

כֶּתֶם m., *the purest gold.*

מִכְתָּם m., *Michtam*, a word of uncertain meaning, occurring in the titles of Psalms 16, 56—60, probably the name of the tune or air to which they were sung.

כְּתֹנֶת, כֻּתֹּנֶת (with suff. כֻּתָּנְתִּי; pl. כָּתְּנוֹת; const. כָּתְנוֹת), *garment, shirt*, *χιτών.*

כָּתֵף const. כֶּתֶף f.—I. *shoulder* (with suff. כְּתֵפִי; pl. כְּתֵפִים).—II. *side* (of a building, the sea, a town); pl. כְּתֵפוֹת; const. כִּתְפוֹת; with suff. כְּתֵפָיו *sides, jambs of doors*, Eze. 41:2, 26.— III. *shoulders of axles, pivots*, 1 Ki. 7:30, 34.

כָּתַר. Pi. כִּתַּר *surround, encompass.* Hiph. I. *surround, come about.*—II. *comprehend.*

כֶּתֶר m., *diadem, crown.*

כּוֹתֶרֶת f. (pl. כֹּתָרוֹת), *cincture, capital of a column.*

כָּתַשׁ *break, bruise.*

מַכְתֵּשׁ m.—I. *mortar*, Pro. 27:22.—II. p. n. of a place, Jud. 15:19; Zep. 1:11.

כָּתַת (fut. יַכֹּת; imp. pl. כֹּתּוּ).—I. *break to pieces* (as a vessel, &c.).—II. *beat out* (as iron).—III. *beat down* (as enemies); part. כָּתוּת θλαδίας, *eunuch.* Pi. כִּתַּת same as Kal. Pu. *was broken.* Hiph. (fut. יַכְּתוּ) *defeat.* Hoph. (fut. יֻכַּתּוּ) *pounded to dust.*

כָּתִית m., *fine, pure oil.*

מְכִתָּה f., *breaking*, Isa. 30:14.

ל

לְ insep. pa.—I. *to, towards.*—II. *at, in.*—III. *till, until.*—IV. *in order to, for the purpose of.*—V. *for, belonging to, with respect to:* לָהֵן *therefore;* לָכֵן *so, thus, therefore;* לָמָּה *why?* When joined with subs. and adjs. it sometimes admits of being translated adverbially: לַשֶּׁקֶר *falsely;* לְצֶדֶק *justly.* It is also used in a sense allied to that of the Arab. لِ, and very foreign to the idiom of any European language: e.g. וַיִּקַּח לְיִרְמְיָהוּ *he took hold on Jeremiah*, Jer. 40:2, where it is equivalent to אֵת; probably it corroborates the meaning like the Arabic. With suff. לִי; לְךָ, (לְכָה), לָךְ (לָכִי); לוֹ, לָהּ; לָנוּ; לָכֶם, לָכֶנָה; לָהֶם, לָהֶן; לָכֵן, see מִן.

לְ Ch., *to, in order to, &c.*, like the Hebrew.

לֹא sometimes לוֹא *not, no;* לֹא כֹל *no one, none;* לֹא אִישׁ *no one;* לֹא דָבָר *nothing*, used for בְּלֹא *without*, and הֲלֹא *is it?* with pref. בְּלֹא *without, there is none;* הֲלֹא *is it not?* ἰδού; לְלֹא *without;* לֹא...גַּם *not even.*

לָא, לָה Ch., *not, nothing.*

לָהֵן Ch., *therefore, on that account* (see לְ), for לָא הֵן *unless.*

לָכֵן *therefore* (see לְ), for לָא כֵן *but if.*

לֹא דְבָר, לוֹ דְבָר p. n., a town in Gilead.

לֹא עַמִּי (*not my people*) mystic name given to the prophet Hosea, Hos 1:9.

לָאַב (Arab. *thirsted*).

תַּלְאֻבוֹת, תַּלְאוּבוֹת *thirst, drought*, Hos. 13:5.

לַאֲדִיב for לְהַאֲדִיב Hiph. inf. with pref., from אדב.

לָאָה I. *be weary, faint*, Job 4:2, 5.—II. *be vexed*, Gen. 19:11. Niph. נִלְאָה I. *become weary, faint.*—II. *was vexed.*—III. *dislike.* Hiph. הֶלְאָה I. *make weary.*—II. *vex.*—III. *ruin.*

לֵאָה p. n., *Leah*, one of Jacob's wives.

תְּלָאָה f., *weariness, trouble, vexation.*

לֵאוֹר for לְהֵאוֹר Niph. inf. with pref., from אור.

לָאַט same as לוּט *vail, cover the face*, 2 Sa. 19:5; see also לָאַט, לְאַט in אַט.

לָאט same as לָט, בַּלָּאט *secretly*, Jud. 4:21.

לָאַךְ root not used; (Ethiop. *he sent ministered*).

מַלְאָךְ m.—I. *messenger.*—II. *angel* (messenger of God).—III. *the Word of God*, Jesus Christ, Ex. 23:20, seq., &c.—IV. *prophet.*—V. *priest.*

מַלְאַךְ m. Ch., *angel.*

מְלָאכָה f. (const. מְלֶאכֶת; with suff. מְלַאכְתּוֹ; pl. const. מַלַאֲכוֹת).—I. *ministry.*—II. *work.*—III. *making, acquisition, wealth.*—IV. *flocks.*

מַלְאָכוּת f., *message, embassy*, Hag. 1:13.

מַלְאָכִי p. n., *Malachi*, the prophet, Μαλαχίας.

לָאֵל p. n. of a man.

לאם (Arab. *assemblage*).

לְאֹם m.(with suff. לְאֻמִּי; pl. לְאֻמִּים).—I. *family, tribe, nation.*—II. לְאֻמִּים p. n. of a people, Αλλουμαίωται, Gen. 25:3.

לֵב, לֶב־ (with suff. לִבִּי; pl. לִבּוֹת).

לֵבָב (const. לְבַב; with suff. לְבָבִי, לְבַבְכֶם; pl. לְבָבוֹת) m.—I. *the heart of man* or *beast.*—II. *the seat of thought, affection, &c.*, in man; בְּלֵב וָלֵב *with a double heart*, i.e. deceitful, Ps. 12:3.—III. *the middle* or *interior of any thing.*

לֵב, לְבַב m. Ch., *heart, mind*, as Heb.

לָבַב. Niph. *take heart, be bold, daring*, Job 11:12. Pi. לִבֵּב *give heart, encourage*, Cant. 4:9; see also in לְבִיבָה.

לִבָּה f., *heart, mind*, as לֵב.

לְבִיבָה f., pl. לְבִיבוֹת *pancakes* made of fine wheaten flour. Pi. לִבֵּב *he made such pancakes*, 2 Sa. 13:6—10, only.

לַבָּה for לֶהָבָה *flame*, Ex. 3:2.

לְבָאִים, לְבָאוֹת; see לָבִיא.

לְבַד *alone*; see בַּד, בדד.

לָבַט. Niph. נִלְבַּט *stumbled, fell*, Pro. 10:8, 10; Hos. 4:14.

לָבִיא *lioness*; perhaps also *lion*.

לְבִי m., pl. m. לְבָאִים.—I. *lions*; f. לְבָאוֹת *lionesses.*—II. p. n. of town in the tribe of Simeon.

לְבִיָּא f., *lioness.*

לְבִיבוֹת; see in לֵב.

לָבַן (from לְבֵנָה) *make bricks*, Gen. 11:3. Hiph.—I. *was white, pure.*—II. *made white, clean*, Dan. 11:35. Hithp. *shall become white, clean*, Dan. 12:10.

לָבָן m.—I. *white.*—II. p. n., *Laban*, the father-in-law of Jacob.—III. a place in the desert.

לְבָנָה f.—I. *the moon* (from her whiteness).—II. p. n. of a man.

לָבֶן, לְבֶן־ m., *white.*

לִבְנֶה m., *the white poplar.*

לִבְנָה f.—I. *whiteness, clearness*, Ex. 24:10.—II. p. n., a city in the tribe of Judah.—III. a station of Israel in the desert.

לְבֵנָה f. (pl. לְבֵנִים) *brick* or *tile.*

לְבֹנָה, לְבוֹנָה f.—I. *pure frankincense*, λίβανος.—II. p.n. of a town near Shiloh.

לְבָנוֹן, הַלְּבָנוֹן p. n., *Mount Lebanon*; so called from the whiteness of the snow on its eastern peak.

לִבְנִי p.n. of a man.

מַלְבֵּן m., *brick kiln.*

לָבַשׁ, לָבֵשׁ (fut. יִלְבַּשׁ).—I. *put on clothing, cloak*; part. לָבוּשׁ *clothed.*—II. used metaphorically for the possession of certain qualities, as *clothed with, glory, justice, &c.*,

covered with flocks (as a pasture); with many others. Pu. מְלֻבָּשִׁים *clothed.*—Hiph. I. *clothe, invest,* with עַל.—II. *cover* (as the sky with clouds).

לְבַשׁ Ch., *clothe.* Aph. the same.

לְבֻשׁ, לְבוּשׁ m., *upper* or *outer garment, cloak.*

מַלְבּוּשׁ m., the same.

תִּלְבֹּשֶׁת f., the same.

לַבַּת, Ex. 3:2, for לַהֶבֶת const., from לֶהָבָה.

לֹג m., *the log,* a liquid measure containing 24·3 solid inches.

לֹד p. n., a town in the tribe of Benjamin, *Lydda.*

לֵדָה Kal inf., from ילד.

לֶדֶת Kal inf., from ילד.

לִדְתָּנָה Kal inf. with suff. and ה parag., from ילד.

לָהַב. root not used; (Arab. *tongue of fire, flame*).

לַהַב m.—I. *flame.*—II. *glitter* of a sword or other weapon.—III. the weapon itself.

לֶהָבָה f., *flame;* pl. לֶהָבוֹת; const. לַהֲבוֹת; s. const. לַבַּת, Ex. 3:2.

לַהֶבֶת f., the same.

שַׁלְהֶבֶת *flame, destruction, fire.*

לְהָבִים same as לוּבִים *the Lybians,* Gen. 10:13.

לָהַג root not used; (Arab. *intense occupation*).

לַהַג m., *much study,* Ecc. 12:12.

לַהַד p. n. of a man.

לָהַהּ (fut. וַתֵּלַהּ) same as לָאָה *was faint, feeble,* Gen. 47:13.

לָהַהּ. Hithp. part. מִתְלַהְלֵהַּ *insane, mad person,* Pro. 26:18.

לָהַט *flaming,* Ps. 104:4; part. לֹהֲטִים *inflamed* (i.e. *furious*) *men,* Ps. 57:5. Pi. לִהֵט *set on fire, inflame.*

לַהַט m., *flame,* Gen. 3:24.

לְהָטִים lit. *flames:* hence, *dazzlings, delusions,* Ex. 7:11.

לָהַם. Hith. part. מִתְלַהֲמִים *enchanting, fascinating things, dainties,* Pro. 18:8; 26:22.

לֶהֱוֹן, f. לֶהֶוְיָן (*that they may be*) Ch. fut., the preformant dropped with the pref. לְ, from הוא, הוה.

לָהֵן; see לְ and לֹא.

לַהֲקָה (const. לַהֲקַת) trans. for קְהִלָּה *congregation,* 1 Sa. 19:20.

לוּ, לוּא I. *if, εἰ, ἐάν.*—II. *would that!* לוּלֵי, לוּלֵא (compound of לוּ, לֹא for לֹא) *unless.*

לֻבִים, לוּבִים p.n., *the Lybians,* inhabitants of the deserts west of Egypt.

לוּד p. n. of a people descended from Shem, Gen. 10:22; pl. לוּדִים; they inhabited some part of Africa, and probably Asia Minor.

לָוָה I. *borrow at usury.*—II. *get, obtain.* Niph. נִלְוָה *become turned, attached, joined,* with עַל, אֶל, עִם. Hiph. הִלְוָה.—I. *cause to borrow.* —II. *lend.*

לֵוִי p. n.—I. *Levi,* one of the sons of Jacob and Leah.—II. and לֵוִיִּי *a Levite;* pl. לְוִיִּם and בְּנֵי לֵוִי *Levites.*

לֵוִי Ch., *a Levite.*

לִוְיָה const. לִוְיַת *chaplet, garland,* Pro. 1:9, &c.

לָיָה for לִוְיָה, לוֹיָה f., pl. לֹיוֹת perhaps

architectural ornaments like *garlands*, 1 Ki. 7:29, 30, 36.

לִוְיָתָן m.—I. any *sea monster.*—II. *the sea serpent*, Isa. 27:1.—III. one of the carnivorous whales, Job 3:8, &c.

לְוָת Ch., *with*, Ezr. 4:12.

לוּז *escape, depart from*, Pro. 3:21. Niph. part. נָלוֹז *perverse, incorrigible.* Hiph. fut. יַלִּיזוּ *escape, flee from.*

לוּז m.—I. *almond tree*, Gen. 30:37. —II. p.n. of the town afterwards called בֵּית־אֵל, in the tribe of Benjamin.

לְזוּת f., *perverseness*, Pro. 4:24.

לוּחַ m.—I. *tablet of stone* or *wood.*—II. metaphorically, *of the heart.*—III. *leaf of a folding-door*, Cant. 8:9; לֻחֹת הָעֵדוּת, לוּחֹת הַבְּרִית *tables of the covenant, testimony*; dual לֻחֹתַיִם *benches* for the rowers of a ship, Eze. 27:5.

לוּחִית p.n. of a town in Moab.

לוֹחֵשׁ, הַלּוֹחֵשׁ p.n. of a man.

לוּט *cover, conceal*; part. לוֹט *covering*; לוּטָה f., *concealed.* Hiph. *hid.*

לָט m., *covert*; בַּלָּט *secretly*; pl. לָטִים *secret parts.*

לוֹט m.—I. *veil, covering*, Isa. 25:7. —II. p. n., *Lot*, the nephew of Abraham.

לֹט m., *gum-ladanum.*

לוֹטָן p. n. of a man.

לֵוִי, לִוְיָה, לִוְיָתָן; see לוה.

לוּלִים m. pl., *winding-stairs*, 1Ki. 6:8.

לֻלָאוֹת, const. לֻלְאֹת f. pl., *loops* or *eyes* for hooks.

לוּלֵי, לוּלֵא; see לוּ.

I. **לוּן** and **לִין** (fut. יָלִין; apoc. יָלֵן; with pause וַיָּלֶן, יָלֹן; imper. לִין).—I. *lodge, remain, pass the night*, with אֵת, בְּ. Hiph. הֵלִין *cause to remain*, Jer. 4:14. Hith. הִתְלוֹנֵן *lodge, remain*, Ps. 91:1; Job 39:28.

מָלוֹן m.—I. *lodging-house, inn.*—II. *quarters* (as of soldiers).—III. *tent, cot, hut*; f. מְלוּנָה.

II. **לוּן.** Niph. נָלוֹן *complain, murmur*; with עַל *against*; fut. pl. יִלֹּנוּ. Hiph. הֵלִין the same; fut. apoc. יַלִּינוּ, וַיָּלֶן; part. מַלִּינִים.

תְּלוּנוֹת f. pl. (with suff. תְּלֻנֹּתֵיכֶם), *murmurings.*

לוּעַ *swallow*, Obad. *v.*16.

לֹעַ m., *throat*, Pro. 23:2.

לוּץ *deride, scorn*, Pro. 9:12; part. לֵץ *scorner.* Hiph. הֵלִיץ *derided*; part. מֵלִיץ *interpreter, orator, ambassador.* Hith. הִתְלוֹצֵץ *was mocking*, Isa. 28:22.

לָצוֹן m., *derision*, Pro. 1:22.

מְלִיצָה f.—I. *interpretation.*—II. *saying, parable, enigma*, Pro. 1:6; Hab. 2:6.

לוּשׁ *knead dough.*

לוּשׁ p.n. of a man, same as לַיִשׁ.

לְוָת; see לוה.

לְזוּת; see לוּז.

לָחָה root not used; (Arab. *cheek-bone*).

לְחִי, with pause לֶחִי f. (dual לְחָיַיִם; const. לְחָיֵי).—I. *cheek, jaw.*—II. לְחִי and רָמַת לְחִי p.n., a place on the borders of Philistia.

לָחַח root not used; (Arab. *eyes wet with tears*).

לח m., *moist, green, fresh, new.*

לֵחַ m. (with suff. לֵחֹה Deu. 34:7), *vigour of youth.*

לָחַךְ (inf. לְחֹךְ) and Pi. לִחֵךְ *licked,* Nu. 22:4, *lapped up* (as a dog); with עָפָר *lick the dust.*

לָחַם (fut. יִלְחַם; inf. לְחֹם; imp. לְחַם). —I. *eat, feast upon, devour;* with בְּ *of;* לְחֻמֵי רֶשֶׁף *consumed of fever.* —II. *make, wage war,* with לְ, אֶת. Niph. נִלְחַם (inf. abs. נִלְחֹם; fut. pl. תִּלָּחֲמוּ).—I. *make war;* with בְּ, עַל, עִם, אֶל *against;* with לְ *for.*—II. with עַל, בְּ *besiege.*

לְחוּם m.—I. *eating, feasting* (with suff. לְחוּמוֹ).—II. *flesh* (with suff. לְחֻמָם Zep. 1:17).

לֶחֶם com.—I. *provision;* עֵץ בְּלַחְמוֹ *tree with its provision,* i. e. fruit, Jer. 11:19.—II. *feast.*—III. *bread.* — IV. *bread-corn,* Isa. 28:28; לֶחֶם הַפָּנִים (ἄρτος τοῦ προσώπου) *shew-bread,* lit. bread of the presence.

לְחֶם m. Ch., *a feast,* Dan. 5:1.

לָחֶם m. (inf. Pi.), const. לְחֶם *war,* Jud. 5:8.

לַחְמִי p. n. of a man, 1 Chron. 20:5.

מִלְחָמָה f.—I. *battle, war.*—II. *instruments of war,* Ps. 76:4; עָשָׂה מִלְחָמָה with אֶת, עִם *made war;* אִישׁ מ׳ *warrior, soldier;* עַם מ׳ the same.—III. *event of war, victory,* Ecc. 9:11.

מִלְחֶמֶת f., the same; with suff. מִלְחַמְתּוֹ.

לַחְמָס p. n. of a place in the tribe of Judah.

לְחֵנָה f. Ch., *concubine,* Dan. 5:2, 3, 23.

לָחַץ (יִלְחַץ) *oppress, afflict;* part. לֹחֲצִים *oppressors.* Niph. *was pressed, injured,* Nu. 22:25.

לַחַץ m. *oppression, affliction.*

לָחַשׁ. Pi. לִחֵשׁ; part. pl. מְלַחֲשִׁים *whisperers, pronouncers of charms.* Hith. *muse of, secretly consider, discuss.*

לַחַשׁ m.—I. *whisper.*—II. *incantation, charm.*—III. pl. לְחָשִׁים *amulets,* Isa. 3:20.

לָט, לַט; see לוט.

לָטָא (Arab. *cleave to the ground*).

לְטָאָה f., *a kind of lizard.*

לָטַשׁ *sharpen.* Pu. part. מְלֻטָּשׁ *sharpened,* Ps. 52:4.

לִוְיָתָן; see לוט.

לַיִל (const. לֵיל (לַיְלָה (pl. לֵילוֹת) m. —I. *night.*—II. *time of adversity;* adv. לַיְלָה, לֵילוֹת, בַּלַּיְלָה, בְּלֵילוֹת *by night;* יוֹמָם וָלַיְלָה *day and night.*

לֵיל m., *night,* Isa. 21:11.

לֵילְיָא m. Ch., *night.*

לִילִית f., *screech owl,* Isa. 34:14.

לִין; see לון.

לִיסּוֹד Kal inf. with pref. and dag. euphon., from יסד.

לִיקְהַת for לִיקְהַת; see יָקַהּ.

לַיִשׁ m.—I. *strong lion.*—II. p. n. of a man.—III. of a town in the north of Palestine.

לֵךְ, לְכָה, לְךָ imp., from הלך, ילך.

לָכַד I. *take,* (as a beast in toils, captives in war, &c.)—II *intercept*

Niph. *was taken.* Hith. *was, became adhering*, Job 41:9.

לֶכֶד m., *capture*, Pro. 3:26.

מַלְכֹּדֶת f., *snare, trap*, Job 18:10.

לְכָה imp. of יָלַךְ; לְכָה for לֵךְ; see לְ.

לֵכָה p. n. of a town in the tribe of Judah.

לָכִישׁ p. n. of a city in the tribe of Judah.

לָכֵן; see לְ, כֵּן, לֹא.

לֶכֶת Kal inf., from הלך, ילך.

לֻלָאוֹת; see לול.

לָמַד (fut. יִלְמַד).—I. *accustom to*, with אֶל.—II. *learn*, with acc. inf. Pi. לִמֵּד.—I. *accustom to.*—II. *teach*, with לְ of the person, and בְּ of the thing taught. Pu. לֻמַּד.—I. *was accustomed.*—II. *was taught.*

לִמֻּד, לִמּוּד m.—I. *accustomed.*—II. *trained, taught.*—III. *disciple.*

מַלְמָד m., *ox-goad*, Jud. 3:31.

תַּלְמִיד m., *learner*, 1 Ch. 25:8.

לָמָּה, לָמָה *why*; see מָה.

לָמוֹ; see לְ.

לְמוּאֵל, לְמוֹאֵל p. n. or title of king Solomon, Pro. *c.* 31.

לֶמֶךְ p. n. of a man, *Lamech.*

לְמַעַן; see ענה.

לָנֶה Zec. 5:4, for לָנָה Kal pret. f., from לון.

לַנּוּ for לַנְנוּ Kal pret. pl., from לון.

לָנִים Kal part. pl., from לון.

לֹעַ *throat*; see לוע.

לָעַב. Hiph. *ridiculing, deriding*, with בְּ, 2 Chron. 36:16.

לָעַג (fut. יִלְעַג) *mock, deride, scorn.* Niph. *stammer*, Isa. 33:19. Hiph. *mock*, with בְּ, לְ, עַל.

לַעַג m.—I. *derision, ridicule.*—II *cause of derision.*

לָעֵג m., *mocker*, Ps. 35:16.

לַעְדָּה p. n. of a man.

לַעְדָּן p. n. of a man.

לָעָה *was rash*, Job 6:3.

לָעַז *spoke barbarously*, Ps. 114:1.

לָעַט. Hiph. *feed, give to eat.*

לָעַן (Arab. *drove away*).

לַעֲנָה f.—I. *wormwood.*—II. metaph. *distress.*

לַפִּיד m., *lamp* or *torch.*

לַפִּידוֹת p. n., *Lapidoth* the husband of Deborah.

לִפְנֵי, לְפָנַי; see פָּנִים or פנה.

לָפַת *turned to, towards*, Jud. 16:29. Niph. *turned about.*

לַצְּבוֹת for לְהַצְּבוֹת Hiph. inf. with pref., from צבה.

לָצוֹן *scorn*; see לוץ.

לָצַץ, part. לֹצְצִים *scorners*, Hos. 7:5.

לַקּוּם p. n., a town in the tribe of Naphtali.

לָקַח (fut. יִקַּח; inf. abs. לָקוֹחַ; const. קַחַת; imp. קַח, לְקַח; with pause קָח; with ה parag. קְחָה).—I. *take*, with בְּ.—II. idiom, like the English *take* and *do.*—III. *take away.*—IV. *take possession of.*—V. *receive.* Niph. נִלְקַח *was taken.* Pu. לֻקַּח same as Niph. Hoph. (fut. יֻקַּח the same). Hith. part. f. מִתְלַקַּחַת *being taken with*, i. e. mixed, mingled with (of fire), Ex. 9:24, Eze. 1:4.

לֶקַח m., *taking, receiving*, specially instruction in religion.

לִקְחִי p. n. of a man.

מַלְקוֹחַ m., *capture, spoil;* dual מַלְקָחַיִם *the jaws.*

מֶלְקָחַיִם m. dual.—I. *tongs.*—II. *snuffers.*

מַלְקָחַיִם m. dual, the same.

מִקָּח m., *accepting* (of gifts), 2 Chron. 19:7.

מַקָּחוֹת f. pl., *merchandise,* Neh. 10:32.

לָקַט and Pi. לִקֵּט *collect, gather, glean.* Pu. and Hith. *was gathered.*

לֶקֶט m., *collecting, gleaning.*

יַלְקוּט m., *bag* or *purse,* 1 Sa. 17:40.

לָקַק *lick* (as dogs); fut. יָלֹק; pl. יָלֹקּוּ. Pi. part. מְלַקְקִים *licking.*

לָקַשׁ (Syr. *late*). Pi. *cut, crop,* Job 24:6.

לֶקֶשׁ m., *latter grass, aftermath,* Am. 7:1.

מַלְקוֹשׁ m., *the latter rain* (in March and April).

לֵרֹא for לִירֹא Kal inf. with pref., from ירא.

לָשַׁד (Arab. *sucking*).

לָשָׁד m. (with suff. לְשַׁדִּי) *moisture,* Ps. 32:4; לְשַׁד הַשָּׁמֶן perhaps *fluid oil,* Nu. 11:8.

לָשׁוֹן com.—I. *tongue;* אִישׁ לָשׁוֹן *calumniator.* —II. *language.* — III. *nation, community* (having one language).—IV. *tongue of flame,* Is. 5:24.—V. *tongue* (wedge) of *gold,* Jos. 7:21, 24.

לָשַׁן. Po. part. with י parag. מְלוֹשְׁנִי *calumniator,* Ps. 101:5. Hiph. the same, Pro. 30:10.

לִשָּׁן com. Ch., *tongue, language.*

לִשְׁכָּה f., *chamber,* specially those attached to the temple; with ה parag. לִשְׁכָּתָה *to the chamber:* pl. לְשָׁכוֹת.

לֶשֶׁם m.—I. *ligure,* a precious stone; LXX. λιγύριον.—II. p. n. of a city called also לַיִשׁ and דָּן.

לֶשַׁע p. n. of a city not far from Sodom

לַת for לֶדֶת with pref. לָלֶדֶת Kal inf., from ילד.

לֶתֶךְ m., *measure* (of capacity), *the half-homer,* Hos. 3:2.

לָתַע (Arab. *he bites*).

מַלְתָּעוֹת f. pl., *teeth,* Ps. 58:7.

מְתַלְּעוֹת f. pl. (trans.), *teeth.*

מ

מִ pref. prep.; see מִן.

מָא Ch., same as מה.

מַאֲבוּס m., *granary,* see אבס.

מְאֹד; see אוד.

מֵאָה const. f. — I. *a hundred;* dual מָאתַיִם *two hundred;* pl. מֵאוֹת *hundreds;* שֵׁשׁ מֵאוֹת *six hundred;* שְׁמֹנֶה מֵאוֹת *eight hundred.*—II. *a hundred-fold.* — III. *a hundredth part,* Neh. 5:11.—IV. p. n. of one of the towers of Jerusalem, Neh. 3:1.

מְאָה f. Ch., *a hundred;* dual מָאתַיִן *two hundred.*

מַאֲוַיִּים *desires;* see אוה.

מְאוּם; see מוּם.

מְאוּמָה; see מָה.

מְאֵרָה, מְאוֹרָה *curse;* see אור

מֹאזְנַיִם, מֹאזְנַיִן *balances;* see און.

מַאֲכֶלֶת, מַאֲכֹלֶת, מַאֲכָל; see אכל

מָאן m. Ch., *vessel.*

מָאֵן or **מָאֵן.** Pi. מֵאֵן (inf. מָאֵן; fut. יְמָאֵן) *refuse, be unwilling.*
מָאֵן m., *refusing.*
מֵאֵן m., pl. מֵאֲנִים *recusants.*

מָאַס (inf. מָאוֹס; const. with suff. מָאָסְם; fut. יִמְאַס).— I. *despise, reject.*— II. *set at nought, lightly esteem,* with בְּ. Niph. I. *was despised, rejected.* — II. same as מָסַס. Niph. *dissolve, waste,* Ps. 58:8; Job 7:5.

מַאֲפֶה *baked;* see אפה.
מַאֲפֵל, מַאְפֵּלְיָה; see אפל.

מָאַר (Arab. *irritate a wound*). Hiph. הַמְאִיר *irritated, pained;* צָרַעַת מַמְאֶרֶת *the inflamed leprosy.*

מַאֲרָב *ambush;* see ארב.
מְאֵרָה *curse,* see ארר.
מֵאֵת *from the;* see אֵת.
מִבְדָּלוֹת *separations;* see בדל
מָבוֹא *entry;* see בוֹא.
מְבוּכָה *confusion;* see בוּךְ.
מַבּוּל *deluge;* see יבל.
מְבוּסָה *treading down;* see בּוּס.
מְבוֹנִים *understanding;* see בּוּן.
מַבּוּעַ *spring;* see נבע.
מְבוּקָה *void;* see בּוּק.
מְבוּשִׁים, מְבֻשִׁים *prudence;* see בּוֹשׁ.
מִבְחוֹר, מִבְחָר *choice;* see בחר.
מַבָּט, מֶבָּט *hope;* see נבט.
מִבְטָא *rashness;* see בטא.
מִבְטָח *confidence;* see בטח.
מֵבִי for מֵבִיא Hiph. part., from בּוֹא.
מַבְלִיגִית *exhilaration;* see בלג.
מִבַּלְעֲדֵי *besides;* see בַּלְעֲדֵי in בלה.
מִבְנֶה *building;* see בנה.
מְבֻנַּי for סִבְּכַי, 2 Sa. 23:27.
מְבַעֲתֶךָ for מְבַעֲתְתֶךָ Pi. part. f. with suff., from בעת.

מִבְצָר *fortress;* see בצר.
מַבְּרָאשֹׁנָה comp. of בְּ, מָה and רִאשֹׁנָה

מָג m., *fire worshipper, magian,* Jer 39:3.

מַגְבִּישׁ p. n. of a place or person.
מִגְבָּלוֹת *devices;* see גבל.
מִגְבָּעָה *mitre;* see גבע.

מָגַד (Arab. *glory*).
מֶגֶד m., *excellence, glory.*
מְגִדּוֹ, מְגִדּוֹן p.n., a city of the Manassites in the tribe of Issachar; LXX. Μαγεδδώ; בִּקְעַת־מְגִדּוֹ *valley of Megiddo;* מֵי מְגִדּוֹ *brook Kishon.*
מִגְדָּנוֹת f. pl., *choice, precious things.*
מַגְדִּיאֵל p. n. of a prince of the Edomites.

מִגְדָּל, מִגְדּוֹל p. n.; see גדל.

מָגוֹג p. n. of a people and country, *Magog.*

מָגוֹר, מָגוּר, מְגוֹרָה, מְגוּרָה; see גּוּר.
מַגְזֵרָה *axes;* see גזר.
מַגָּל *sickle;* see נגל.
מְגִלָּה *mound;* see גלל.
מְגַמָּה *desire;* see גמם.

מָגַן. Pi. מִגֵּן *give, give freely.*

מָגֵן, מְגִנָּה; see גנן.
מִגְעֶרֶת *rebuke;* see גער.
מַגֵּפָה *plague;* see נגף.
מַגְפִּיעָשׁ p. n. of a man.

מָגַר, part. pl. const. מְגוּרֵי *fallen, delivered up,* Eze. 21:17. Pi. מִגֵּר *cast down.*
מְגַר Ch. Pa. מַגֵּר *cast down,* Ezr 6:12.
מִגְרוֹן p. n., a town in the tribe of Benjamin.

מְגֵרָה *saw;* see גרר.

מְגְרָפָה *furrow*; see גרף.
מִגְרָשׁ; see גרשׁ.
מִדְבָּר *wilderness*; see דבר.

מָדַד (pret. מַדֹּתִי, מָדְדוּ; fut. יָמֹד). —I. *extend a line.*—II. *measure.* —III. *apportion*, Isa. 65:7. Niph. (fut. יִמַּד) *be, can be, measured.* Pi. מִדַּד *measure* (see also in נדד). Po. מוֹדֵד the same, Hab. 3:6; "*viewed*" (Lee); see מוּד. Hith. הִתְמֹדֵד *extended, stretched out.*

מַד m.—I. *measure, extent*; with suff. מִדָּהּ; pl. מִדִּים.—II. *upper garment, tunic*, with suff. מַדּוֹ, מִדּוֹ; pl. מַדִּים, מִדִּין.—III. *hammercloth, covering for a throne*, Jud. 5:10.—IV. מִדִּין p.n., a city in the desert of Judah.

מִדָּה f. (m. Neh. 3:30).—I. *extent, measure*; אִישׁ מִדָּה *tall man*, 1 Chron. 11:23; בֵּית מִדּוֹת *spacious house*, Jer. 22:14; מִדַּת יָמַי *measure of my days.*—II. *tribute.* —III. *vesture*, Ps. 133:2.

מִדָּה, מִנְדָּה f. Ch., *tribute.*

מְמַדִּים m. pl., *extents, measure*, Job 38:5.

מֶדֶו m. (pl. with suff. מַדְוֵיהֶם), *garment.*

מָדוֹן m., *height, tallness*, 2 Sa. 21:20; see also in דין.

מַדְוֶה *disease*; see דָּוָה.
מַדּוּחִים *drivings out*; see נדח.
מַדּוּעַ *why*; see ידע.
מַדְחֵפוֹת; see דחף.
מָדַי f., *Media, the Medes*; מָדִי Ch. *a Median*, const. emph. מָדָאָה the same.
מַדַּי; see מָה. מִדֵּי; see דַּי.
מִדְיָן p.n., the son of Abraham and Keturah; מִדְיָנִי m., מִדְיָנִית f., *a Midianite.*
מִדִּין pl. for מַדִּים; see מַד in מדד.
מְדִינָה; see דִּין.
מְדֹכָה *mortar*; see דּוּךְ.
מַדְמֵן, מַדְמֵנָה, מַדְמַנָּה; see דמן.
מְדָן, מִדְיָנִים; see דִּין.
מַדָּע, מַדַּע; see ידע.
מְדָר Ch., same as מְדוֹר *habitation*; see דּוּר.
מַדְרָךְ; see דרך.
מְדָתָא with art. הַמְּדָתָא p. n. the father of Haman.

מָה, מַה־, מֶה inter. pron.—I. *what?* מַה־לָּךְ *what wilt thou?* מַה־לִּי וָלָךְ *what have I to do with thee?* —II. *how? how much?*—III. *for what? why?*—IV. *what? what sort?*—V. *something, anything, anything whatever*; מָה שֶׁ... *that which, the thing which* (in the book of Ecclesiastes only); מַה־ נּוֹרָא *how terrible*; מַזֶּה for מַה־זֶּה *what is this?* מַלָּכֶם *what mean ye?* Isa. 3:15; לְמַדַּי for לְמַה־דַּי *sufficiently*, 2 Chron. 30:3. Compounds: בַּמֶּה, בַּמָּה *why? how? wherefore?* כַּמֶּה, כַּמָּה *how many? how long? how much?* לָמָּה, לָמֶה *why?* לָמָּה זֶּה *why? wherefore?* לְמַבָּרִאשׁוֹנָה (לְמָה בּ׳ for) *because at first*, 1 Chron. 15:13; עַד־מָה *how long?* עַל־מָה, עַל־מֶה *wherefore?*

מָה (מָא) Ch., *why, wherefore?* מַה־שׁ *that which*, Dan. 2:28, 29; לְמָה, עַל־מָה *wherefore?* כְּמָה *how? how much? so much?* Dan. 3:33; מָה דִּי *that which.*

מְאוּמָה (comp. of מָה וּמָה or מָה אוֹ

מָה) *any thing*; with אַל, אֵין, לֹא *nothing*.

מָהַהּ. Hith. הִתְמַהְמַהּ *delay, tarry, wait.*

מְהוּמָה *tumult*; see הוּם.

מְהוּמָן p.n. of a Persian eunuch.

מְהֵיטַבְאֵל p. n.—I. of a man, Neh. 6:10.—II. of a woman, Gen. 36:39.

מְהֵימַן Ch., Aph. part. pass.; see אמן.

מְהַחֲתִין Ch. Aph. part.; see נחת.

מְהָךְ Ch. Pe. inf., from הוּךְ.

מָהַל, part. מָהוּל *debased, adulterated,* Isa. 1:22.

מֶהֱמֶהֶם Eze. 7:11, from הֵם; see המה.

מְהֻקְצָעוֹת for מֻקְצָעוֹת Hoph. part. f. pl., from קצע.

I. **מָהַר** *hasten, hurry,* Ps. 16:4. Pi. מִהַר *hasten, hurry*; used as an auxiliary, e. g. מִהֲרוּ שָׁכְחוּ *they soon forgot,* Ps. 106:13, &c. Niph. נִמְהַר *was hasty, hurried, rash.*

מָהִיר m., *ready, quick, skilful, hasty, speedy.*

מַהֵר m., מְהֵרָה f., *quick, ready, hasty, speedy, speed;* עַד־מְהֵרָה, בִּמְהֵרָה, מְהֵרָה adv., *quickly, readily, speedily.*

II. **מָהַר** *endow* (a wife with a dowry), Ex. 22:15; or *buy* (a wife with a dowry).

מֹהַר m., *gift* or *dower* (present made by a suitor to the parents of a damsel).

מַהֲרַי p. n., one of David's generals.

מוֹאָב p. n.—I. of a man, *Moab,* the descendant of Lot.—II. f., the land of *Moab,* situated between the Dead Sea and the river Arnon; m. מוֹאָבִי, f. מוֹאֲבִיָּה, מוֹאָבִית *a Moabite.*

מוֹאל same as מוּל *over against,* Neh. 12:38.

מוֹבָא *entrance;* see בּוֹא.

מוּג (fut. יָמוּג).—I. *flow.*—II. *dissolve, melt* (indicating weakness). Niph. נָמוֹג *were dissolved, undone.* Pil. מוֹגֵג I. *dissolve,* Ps. 65:11.—II. *waste away,* Job 30:22. Hith. *was dissolved, undone.*

מוּד Kal not used; see מוּט. Po. מוֹדֵד *moved,* Hab. 3:6.

תָּמִיד m.—I. *perpetuity.*—II. *perpetual.*—III. *continually;* עוֹלַת הַתָּמִיד *the continual,* i. e. *daily offering;* לֶחֶם הַתָּמִיד *the bread constantly placed in the temple.*

מוֹדָע, מֹדָע, מוֹדַעַת; see ידע.

מוּט (fut. יָמוּט) *totter* (to a fall), *fail.* Niph. נָמוֹט *be moved, tottering.* Hiph. fut. יָמִיטוּ *cause to fall, come down.* Hithpo. *be moved,* Isa. 24:19.

מוֹט m.—I. *tottering, vacillating.*—II. *pole, staff.*—III. *yoke* (for burdens), Nah. 1:12.

מוֹטָה f., *pole* or *staff.*

מוּךְ same as מָכַךְ *become indigent.*

מוּל *circumcise.* Niph. I. *was circumcised.*—II. *circumcise one's self.* Pil מוֹלֵל *cut off,* Ps. 90:6. Hiph. *cut off, down,* Ps. 118:10-12. Hithpo הִתְמוֹלֵל *is cut off, down,* Ps. 58:8.

מוּל (מוֹל Deu. 1:1, מוֹאל Neh. 12:38).—I. *near, with.*—II. *opposite, over against,* ἀντικρύ: compounds

אֶל־מוּל before, over against; אֶל־מוּל פְּנֵי in front of, before; מִמּוּל from before, opposite.

מוּלָה f. (pl. מוּלֹת), circumcisions, Ex. 4:26.

מוֹלָדָה, מוֹלֶדֶת, מוֹלִיד; see ילד.

מוּם (מאום) m., spot, blemish from disease.

מוּמָת Hoph. part., from מוּת.

מוּן; see מִין.

מוּסָב Hoph. part.; see סבב.

מוּסָד, מוּסָדָה, מוֹסָדוֹת; see יסד.

מוּסָךְ porch; see סכך.

מוֹסֵר (from אסר), pl. מוֹסְרִים and מוֹסֵרוֹת chains.

מוֹסֵר and ־וֹת p. n. of a place in the wilderness.

מוּסָר bonds; see יסר.

מוֹעֵד, מוֹעָדָה, מוֹעֲדָה, מוֹעָד; see יעד.

מוֹעֵד, מוֹעֶדֶת assembly; see מעד.

מוּעֶדֶת for מוֹעֶדֶת Kal part. f., from מעד.

מוּעָף darkness; see עוף.

מוֹעֵצָה counsel; see יעץ.

מוּעָקָה pain; see עוק.

מוֹפֵת sign; see יפת.

מוּץ, part. מֵץ oppressor, Isa. 16:4.

מוֹץ, מֹץ m., chaff.

מִיץ m., pressing, squeezing (cream to make butter), Pro. 30:33.

מוֹצָא, מוֹצָאָה; see יצא.

מוּצָא Hoph. part., from יצא.

מוּצָק, מוּצָקָה fused, cast; see יצק.

מוּצַק, מוּצָק; see צוק.

מוּק. Hiph. הֵמִיק mock, insult, Ps. 73:8.

מוֹקֵד, מוֹקְדָה burning; see יקד.

מוֹקֵשׁ snare; see יקשׁ.

מוּר Hiph. הֵמִיר.—I. change, alter, with בְּ.—II. exchange. Niph. נָמַר was changed, Jer. 48:11.

תְּמוּרָה f.—I. equivalent, recompense.—II. restitution, Job 20:18.—III. exchange, Ru. 4:7.

מוֹרָא; see ירא.

מוֹרָאִים for מוֹרִים Hiph. part. pl., from ירה.

מוֹרַג or מֹרַג m. (pl. מֹרִגִּים, מוֹרִינִים) threshing wain.

מוֹרָד descent, declivity; see ירד.

מוֹרָה, Ps. 9:21, same as מוֹרָא fear; see also in מָרָה; מוֹרֶה teacher; see יָרָה.

מוֹרָט ruin; see ירט.

מוֹרִיָּה p.n., same as מֹרִיָּה.

מוֹרִיגִים for מוֹרִגִּים pl., from מוֹרַג.

מוֹרָשׁ, מוֹרָשָׁה possession, inheritance see ירשׁ.

I. מוּשׁ I. move.—II. remove, Zec. 3:9. Hiph. הֵמִישׁ. I. move, depart.—II. remove, put away.—III. cease, desist, Jer. 17:8, with מִן.

II. מוּשׁ same as מָשַׁשׁ feel, Gen. 27:21, &c. Hiph. the same, Ps. 115:7, &c.

מוּשִׁי, מֻשִׁי p. n. of a man.

מוֹשָׁב dwelling, &c.; see ישׁב.

מוֹשְׁכוֹת; see משׁך.

מוֹשָׁעוֹת salvation; see ישׁע.

מוּת (pret. מֵת; 1. pers. מַתִּי; pl. מֵתוּ; part. מֵת; f. מֵתָה; inf. abs. מוֹת; const. מוּת; imp. מֻת; fut. יָמוּת; apoc. יָמֹת, וַיָּמָת) die (of man or beast). Pil. מוֹתֵת put to death, caused to die. Hiph. הֵמִית the same. Hoph. הוּמַת was caused to die.

מָוֶת m. (with ה parag. מָוְתָה; const.

מוֹת; with suff. מוֹתוֹ; pl. מוֹתִים). —I. *death;* מִשְׁפַּט מָוֶת *sentence of death*, Deut. 19:6; בֶּן־מָוֶת or אִישׁ־מ׳ *one guilty of a capital crime.*—II. *the grave;* שַׁעֲרֵי מָוֶת *gates of death.*—III. *person dead*, Isa. 38:18.—IV. *pestilence.*—V. *destruction, ruin.*

מוֹת m. Ch., *death.*

מָמוֹת m., pl. מְמוֹתִים *deaths*, Jer. 16:4; Eze. 28:8.

תְּמוּתָה f., *death;* בֶּן־תְּמוּתָה *condemned to death.*

מוֹתָר *abundance;* see יתר.

מֵזֵא, with suff. מֵזְיֵהּ Ch. Pe. inf., from אזא.

מִזְבֵּחַ *altar;* see זבח.

מָזַג (Arab. *mixture*); see מָסַךְ.

מֶזֶג m., *mixed wine*, Cant. 7:3.

מָזֶה *exhausted, reduced* (by famine), Deut. 32:24.

מַזֶּה for מַה־זֶּה, from מָה.

מִזָּה p. n. of a man.

מְזָוִים *cellar;* see זָוָה.

מְזוּזָה *door-post;* see זוז.

מָזוֹן *food;* see זון.

מָזוֹר *bandage;* see זור.

מֵזַח, מְזִיחַ m.—I. *a girdle.*—II. *pride*, Job 12:21.

מֵזִין for מְאַזִּין Hiph. part., from אזן.

מַזָּלוֹת; see נזל.

מַזְלֵג, מִזְלָגָה *fork;* see זלג.

מְזִמָּה *invention;* see זמם.

מִזְמוֹר, מְזַמְּרוֹת, מַזְמֵרוֹת; see זמר.

מְזָרִים, מִזְרֶה; see זרה.

מַזָּרוֹת; see נזל.

מִזְרָח *east;* see זרח.

מִזְרָק *cup;* see זרק.

מֵחַ, מֹחַ; see מחח.

מָחָא *smite, clap;* with יַד, כַּף *hands* Pi. the same, Eze. 25:6.

מְחָא Ch., *struck, smote.* Pa. *exult*, Dan. 4:32. Ithp. *was smitten*, Ezr. 6:11.

מַחֵא Ch. Aph. part., from חיא; see חיה.

מַחֲבֵא, מַחֲבֹאִים *hiding-place;* see חבא.

מַחְבֶּרֶת, מְחַבְּרוֹת; see חבר.

מַחֲבַת *frying-pan;* see חבת.

מָחָה I. *wipe away.*—II. *arrive at*, Nu. 34:11, with עַל. Niph. (fut. apoc. יִמַּח) *was blotted out.* Hiph. (fut. apoc. תֶּמַח) *blot out.*

מְחִי m., *striking*, Eze. 26:9.

מְחוּגָה *compasses;* see חוג.

מָחוֹז *harbour;* חוז.

מְחוּיָאֵל, מְחִיָּיאֵל p. n., a descendant of Cain.

מַחֲוִים p. n. of a place unknown.

מָחוֹל, מְחוֹלָה *dance;* see חול.

מַחֲזֶה, מֶחֱזָה, מַחֲזִיאוֹת; see חזה.

מָחַח (Arab. *marrow*).

מֵחַ m., *fat, rich.*

מֹחַ m., *marrow*, Job 21:24.

מְחִידָא p. n. of a man.

מִחְיָה; see חָיָה, חָוָה.

מְחִיר *price;* see מחר.

מַחֲלִי, מַחְלוֹן, מַחֲלֶה, מַחֲלָה, מַחְלָה, מַחֲלֻיִם; see חלה.

מְחִלָּה *hole;* see חלל.

מַחֲלָף, מַחְלְפוֹת; see חלף.

מַחֲלֹקֶת, מַחְלְקוֹת; see חלק.

מַחֲלַת, מָחֳלַת; see חלה.

מְחֹלָתִי *Meholathite;* see אבל.

מַחְמָאוֹת; see חמא.

מַחְמֶצֶת; see חמץ.

מִחַן Ch. Pe. inf., from חנן.

מַחֲנֶה, מַחֲנַיִם *camp*; see חנה.
מַחְסֶה, מַחֲסֶה, מַחְסֵיָה; see חסה.
מַחְסוֹם *curb*; see חסם.
מְחֻסְפָּס part. of the quadriliteral verb חִסְפֵּס; see חסף.
מָחַץ (fut. יִמְחַץ).—I. *dash violently* (the head to pieces)—(the foot into blood), Ps. 68:22.—II. *shoot arrows*, Nu. 24:8.
מַחַץ m., *contusion, bruise*, Isa. 30:26.
מֶחֱצָה, מַחֲצִית; see חצה.
מחצצרים; see in חצר.
מָחַק *destroyed*, Jud. 5:26.
מֶחְקָר; see חקר.
מָחַר same as מכר.
מְחִיר m.—I. *price*; בִּמְחִיר *with a price*.—II. p.n. of a man.
מָחָר m.—I. *morrow*, some *future day*; בְּיוֹם מָחָר לְמָחָר *to-morrow*; כָּעֵת מָחָר *for the morrow*; and מָחָר כָּעֵת הַזֹּאת *about this time to-morrow*; כָּעֵת מָחָר הַשְּׁלִישִׁית *this time the day after to-morrow*. —II. adv. *hereafter, henceforward*.
מָחֳרָת f., *to-morrow*; מִמָּחֳרָת, לְמָחֳרָת *the day after*; מִמָּחֳרַת הַשַּׁבָּת *the day after the sabbath*; עַד־מִמָּחֳרַת *until the next day*; לְמָחֳרָתָם adv. *the day after*.
מַחֲרֵשָׁה, מַחֲרֶשֶׁת; see חרש
מַחְשֹׂף; see חשף.
מַחֲשָׁבָה, מַחֲשֶׁבֶת; see חשב.
מַחְשָׁךְ *darkness*; see חשך.
מַחַת p. n. of a man.
מַחְתָּה *shovel, &c.*; see חתה.
מְחִתָּה *breaking, &c.*; see חתת.
מַחְתֶּרֶת *digging*; see חתר.

מְטָא Ch., *come on, to, arrive at*, with עַל.
מַטְאֲטֵא; see טוא.
מִטַּהֵר for מִתְטַהֵר Hith. part.; see טהר.
מַטֶּה, מַטָּה, מִטָּה, מִטָּה, מֻטּוֹת; see נטה.
מַטְוֶה *yarn*; see טָוָה.
מָטַל (Arab. *forged iron*): hence, the English word *metal*.
מְטִיל m., *iron bar*, Job 40:18.
מַטְמוֹן *treasure*; see טמן.
מַטָּע *plant*; see נטע.
מַטְעַמִּים *dainties*; see טעם.
מִטְפַּחַת *mantle*; see טפח.
מָטַר. Hiph. הִמְטִיר *rain, cause, give rain*; used also of *lightning, hail, fire and brimstone, manna, bread*. Niph. *was rained on*, Am. 4:7.
מָטָר m. (pl. מְטָרוֹת; const. מִטְרוֹת) *rain, shower*.
מַטְרִי p. n. of a man.
מַטְרֵד p. n. of a woman.
מַטָּרָא, מַטָּרָה; see נטר.
מִי interrog. pron.—I. *who?* בַּת־מִי *whose daughter?* לְמִי *to whom?* אֶת־מִי *whom?* בְּמִי *by whom?* מִי מָנָה *who can number?* מִי יִתֵּן וְהָיָה *would that it were!* מִי יִתֵּן עֶרֶב *would that it were evening!* —II. without interrog., *who, every one*; מִי אֲשֶׁר *whoever*.
מֵידְבָא p. n. of a city in the tribe of Reuben.
מֵידָד p. n. of a man.
מֵיטָב *good*; see יטב.
מִיכָא p. n. of a man, same as מִיכָיָא.
מִיכָאֵל (*who is like unto God?*) p. n.

—I. *Michael* the archangel.—II. of a man.

מִיכָה, מִיכָיָה p. n.—I. *Micah* the prophet.—II. also of other men.

מִיכָיָהוּ p. n.—I. of a man.—II. of a woman.

מִיכָה, מִיכָיְהוּ p. n. of a man.

מִיכָל p. n; see מכל.

מַיִם m. pl. (const. מֵי, מֵימֵי; with suff. מֵימֶיךָ; with ה loc. הַמַּיְמָה).—I. *water, waters,* used with pl. adj., with verb either pl. or sing.—II. *seed;* יָצָא מִמֵּי פ׳ *whose son, descendant he is,* Isa. 48:1.

מֵי־הַיַּרְקוֹן p. n., a city in the tribe of Dan.

מֵי־נֶפְתּוֹחַ p. n., a fountain near Jerusalem.

מוּן, מִין (Syr. *family*).

מִין m., *kind, species,* always with לְ pref.; פְּרִי לְמִינוֹ *fruit after his kind.*

תְּמוּנָה f., *resemblance, likeness.*

מֵינֶקֶת, מֵינִיקוֹת; see ינק.

מֵיפַעַת, מֵפַעַת p. n., a town of the Levites in the tribe of Reuben.

מִיץ *chaff;* see מוּץ.

מֵישָׁא p. n. of a man.

מִישָׁאֵל p. n. of a man.

מִישׁוֹר; see ישר.

מֵישַׁךְ p. n., *Meshach,* one of the captivity, called also מִישָׁאֵל.

מֵישַׁע p. n., a king of Moab.

מֵישָׁע p. n., a son of Caleb.

מֵישָׁרִים; see ישר.

מֵיתָר *cord;* see יתר.

מַכְאוֹב *pain;* see כאב.

מַכְבֵּנָא same as כַּבּוֹן.

מַכְבַּנַּי p. n. of a man.

מַכְבֵּר, מִכְבָּר *carpet;* see כבר

מַכָּה *stroke;* see נכה.

מִכְוָה *burning;* see כוה.

מָכוֹן, מְכוֹנָה, מְכוּנָה; see כּוּן.

מְכוּרָה; see כּוּר.

מָכִיר p. n., *Machir* the son of Manasseh, Gen. 50:23; perhaps for *a Manassite,* Jud. 5:14; patronymic מָכִירִי.

מָכַךְ. Niph. fut. יִמַּךְ *become weak,* Ecc. 10:18. Hoph. pl. הָמְכוּ for הֻמַּכּוּ *they perish,* Job 24:24.

מָכַל root not used; (Arab. *empty of water*).

מִיכָל m.; מִיכַל הַמַּיִם *brooks of water,* 2 Sa. 17:20.—II. p. n., *Michal,* the daughter of Saul and wife of David.

מִכְלָה, מִכְלָאוֹת, see כלא; מִכְלוֹת, see כלה.

מִכְלוֹל, מִכְלָל, מַכְלֻלִים; see כלל.

מַכֹּלֶת for מַאֲכֹלֶת *food;* see אכל.

מִכְמָס, מִכְמָשׂ, מִכְמַשׂ (see כָּמַס), p. n. a town in the tribe of Benjamin, Μαχμάς.

מִכְמָר, מַכְמֹר, מִכְמֶרֶת *net;* see כמר.

מִכְמְתָת p. n., a town on the borders of Ephraim and Manasseh.

מַכְנַדְבַי p. n. of a man.

מִכְנָס *breeches;* see כנס.

מֶכֶס, מִכְסָה *price;* see כסס.

מִכְסֶה, מְכַסֶּה; see כסה.

מַכְפֵּלָה p. n. of a district near Hebron.

מָכַר (fut. יִמְכֹּר; inf. with suff. מָכְרָהּ, מִכְרָם; imp. with ה parag. מִכְרָה). —I. *he sold,* with בְּ of the price. —II. *he gave a daughter in marriage* (in consideration of a gift). —III. *he gave up men* into the power of others. Niph. נִמְכַּר *was sold.* Hith. הִתְמַכֵּר I. *was sold.*—II. *was surrendered.*

מֶכֶר m. (with suff. מִכְרָם).—I. *value, price.*—II. *valuable article,* Neh. 13:16.

מִכְרִי p. n. of a man.

מִמְכָּר m., מִמְכֶּרֶת f.—I. *sale.*—II. *thing sold.*

מַכָּר *relative;* see נכר.

מִכְרֶה *pit of salt;* see כרה.

מְכֵרָה *sword;* see כּוּר.

מְכֵרָתִי *Macherathite,* patron. 1 Chron. 11:36.

מִכְשׁוֹל, מַכְשֵׁלָה; see כשל.

מִכְתָּב *writing;* see כתב.

מְכִתָּה *breaking;* see כתת.

מִכְתָּם; see כתם.

מַכְתֵּשׁ *mortar;* see כתשׁ.

מָלֵא, מָלָא (fut. יִמְלָא; inf. מְלֹאת).—I. *fill;* מִלְאוּ הַשְּׁלָטִים *fill the shields,* i. e. enlarge them so as to cover you, Jer. 51:11; מָלָא יָד *filled the hand,* i. e. conferred an office.—II. *fulfil, execute fully, thoroughly;* מָלְאָה צְבָאָהּ *her warfare is accomplished;* מְלָאָה נַפְשִׁי *my soul is full,* Ex. 15:9. Niph. נִמְלָא (fut. יִמָּלֵא) *is full, filled,* with לְ, מִן. Pi. מִלֵּא, מִלָּא (inf. מַלֵּא, מַלֹּאת; fut. יְמַלֵּא).—I. *fulfil* (of time, promise, &c.).—II. *fill the hand,* i. e. consecrate to the priest's office.—III. *fill as a vessel* (with accus. מִן), *insert,* i. e. *fill in,* of the stones in the breast-plate, Ex. 28:17.—IV. used with other verbs, &c., implying the completion of their action; מִ׳ יָדוֹ בַקֶּשֶׁת *he fully drew the bow,* lit. filled his hand with, 2 Ki. 9:24; קִרְאוּ מַלְאוּ *cry out strongly;* מִלֵּא אַחֲרֵי *fulfilled the followings,* i. e. followed fully. Pu. part. מְמֻלָּאִים *filled with gems,* Cant. 5:14. Hith. fut. יִתְמַלָּאוּן *they are fully set against me,* Job 16:10.

מְלָא Ch., *filled,* Dan. 2:35. Hith. *was filled,* Dan. 3:19.

מָלֵא m., מְלֵאָה f., *full* (used as מְלֹא, see above Pi. IV.); כֶּסֶף מָלֵא *full* (i. e. just), *money;* מֵי מָלֵא *waters of fulness* (i. e. ample), *abundant;* מְלֵא יָמִים *full of days,* Jer. 6:11.

מְלֹא, מְלוֹא, מְלוֹ m.—I. *filling, fulness;* מְלֹא כַף *the filling of the palm, palm full;* מ׳ חָפְנֵיכֶם פִּיחַ *both your closed hands full of ashes,* Ex. 9:8; מ׳ קוֹמָתוֹ *his full stature,* 1 Sam. 28:20.—II. *multitude,* Gen. 48:19.

מְלֵאָה f., *overplus,* excess of corn and wine which was to be offered to the Lord, Ex. 22:28; Nu. 18:27.

מְלֹאות for מְלֹאת Kal inf., from מלא.

מַלְאָכִים for מְלָכִים pl., from מֶלֶךְ.

מִלּוֹא m., p. n.—I. a certain part of the citadel of Jerusalem, called also בֵּית מִלּוֹא 2 Ki. 12:21.—II. a castle of the Sichemites, Jud. 9:6, 20.

מִלֻּאָה, מִלּוּאָה f., *insertion of gems* (see above מלא Pi. III.).

מִלֻּאִים m. pl.—I. *inauguration, consecration* (of priests).—II. אַבְנֵי מִלֻּאִים *set* (inserted jewels); see מִלֻּאָה.

מִלֵּאת f., Cant. 5:12, *fulness,* perhaps *prominency,* some peculiar mode of setting jewels.

מַלְאַךְ, מְלָאכָה, מְלָאכוּת, מַלְאָכִי; see לאך.

מַלְבּוּשׁ same as לְבוּשׁ *clothing*; see לבשׁ.

מַלְבֵּן *brick kiln*; see לבן.

מִלָּה *saying*; see מלל.

מָלוּ for מָלְאוּ Kal pret. pl., from מלא.

מָלוּךְ, מְלוּכָה *rule*; see מלך.

מָלוֹן, מְלוּנָה *inn*; see לון.

I. מָלַח. Niph. נִמְלַח *pass away, vanish*, Isa. 51:6.

מְלָחִים m. pl., *rolling, passing away*, Jer. 38:11, 12.

II. מָלַח (from מֶלַח), *salted*, Ex. 30:35. Pu. part. מְמֻלָּח. Hoph. *salted*, Eze. 16:4.

מֶלַח m., *salt*; יָם־הַמֶּלַח *the salt sea*, i. e. the Dead Sea; בְּרִית מֶלַח *covenant of salt*, i. e. perpetual, Nu. 18:19.

מְלַח m. Ch., *salt*.

מְלַח Ch., *eat salt*, Ezr. 4:14.

מַלּוּחַ m., ἅλιμος, *salt plant*, (halimus atriplex—Linn.).

מַלָּח m., pl. מַלָּחִים *sailors*.

מְלֵחָה f., *salt land, waste*.

מִלְחָמָה *war*; see לחם.

מָלַט. Pi. מִלֵּט, מִלֵּט.—I. *cause to escape, slip*.—II. *deliver, save*.—III. *hatch* (of eggs), Isa. 34:15. Hiph. same as Pi. Niph. *was delivered, set at liberty, saved*. Hith. same as Niph.

מֶלֶט m., *clay*.

מְלַטְיָה p.n. of a man.

מְלִילוֹת *ears of corn*; see מלל.

מְלִינִים Hiph. part. pl., from לון.

מְלִיצָה *saying*; see לוץ.

מָלַךְ *reigned*; with בְּ, עַל *was made a king*. Hiph. *make any one a king*, with לְ. Hoph. *was made king*, Dan. 9:1. Niph. *took, sought, counsel*.

מֶלֶךְ m. (with suff. מַלְכִּי; pl. מְלָכִים, מַלְכֵי) *king*, applied to God and also to idols; דֶּרֶךְ הַמֶּלֶךְ *royal way*.—II. p. n. of a man.—III. עֵמֶק הַמֶּלֶךְ p.n., a valley not far from the Dead Sea.

מֶלֶךְ m. Ch., *king*.

מְלַךְ m. Ch., *counsel*, Dan. 4:24.

מֹלֶךְ, with art. הַמֹּלֶךְ Μολόχ, *Moloch*, an idol of the Ammonites.

מַלְכָּה f., *queen*. Ch. the same.

מִלְכָּה p. n. of a daughter of Haran.

מְלֶכֶת f., מ׳ הַשָּׁמַיִם *the queen of Heaven, Ashtoreth, Astarte*, an idol of Canaan.

מֹלֶכֶת p. n. of a woman.

מַלּוּךְ (מְלִיכוּ, מַלּוּכִי) p. n. of a man.

מְלוּכָה f., *rule, government, royalty*.

מַלְכוּת f., *rule, kingdom, royal dignity*.

מַלְכוּת, מַלְכוּ f. Ch., the same.

מַלְכִּיאֵל p. n. of a man; ־ִי patron.

מַלְכִּיָּהוּ, מַלְכִּיָּה p.n. of a man.

מַלְכִּי־צֶדֶק p. n., *Melchizedek*, king of Salem.

מַלְכִּירָם p. n. of a man.

מַלְכִּי־שׁוּעַ p. n. of one of Saul's sons.

מַלְכָּם, מִלְכֹּם same as מֹלֶךְ.

מַלְכֶם for מַה־לָּכֶם; see מָה.

מַמְלָכָה f. (const. מַמְלֶכֶת; with suff. מַמְלַכְתּוֹ; pl. מַמְלָכוֹת *rule, regal government*; בֵּית מ׳ *seat of government*; עִיר מ׳ *capital city*; זֶרַע מ׳ *royal family*.

מַמְלָכוּת const. מַמְלְכוּת f., the same

מַלְכֹּדֶת *trap;* see לכד.

מָלַל *speaking.* Pi. מִלֵּל *announce, tell.*

מְלַל Ch. Pa. מַלֵּל *speak, announce.*

מִלָּה **f.** (pl. מִלִּים, מִלִּין).— I. *saying, argument.*—II. *thing spoken of.*

מִלָּה f. Ch. (pl. מִלִּין) *saying, decree.*

מִלֲלַי p. n. of a man.

מַלּוֹתִי p. n. of a man.

מְלִילָה f., pl. מְלִילוֹת *ears of corn,* Deu. 23:26.

מַלְמַד *goad;* see למד.

מָלַץ. Niph. נִמְלְצוּ *are become smooth, agreeable,* Ps. 119:103.

מֶלְצַר a certain office in the king of Babylon's palace; nature of the office unknown, Dan. 1:11, 16.

מָלַק *break, bruise,* Lev. 1:15; 5:8; LXX. ἀποκνίζειν.

מַלְקוֹחַ, מֶלְקָחַיִם, מַלְקָחַיִם; see לקח.

מַלְקוֹשׁ *latter rain;* see לקש.

מֶלְתָּחָה f., *wardrobe,* 2 Ki. 10:22.

מַלְתָּעוֹת *jaws;* see לתע.

מַמְּגֻרוֹת *granary;* see גור.

מְמַדִּים *measures;* see מדד.

מְמוּכָן p. n. of a prince of Persia.

מָמוֹת, מְמוֹתִים; see מות.

מַמְזֵר m.—I. *foreigner.*—II. *bastard.*

מִמְכָּר, מִמְכֶּרֶת *sale;* see מכר.

מַמְלָכָה, מַמְלְכוּת *kingdom;* see מלך.

מֶמֶר, מַמְּרֹרִים; see מרר.

מַמְרֵא p. n.; see מרא.

מִמְשָׁל, מֶמְשָׁלָה, מֶמְשֶׁלֶת; see משל.

מָן *manna;* מֵן, מִנִּים; see מנן.

מָן, מַן־ Ch. pron. — I. *who?* — II. *what?* מַן־דִּי *whoever.*

מִן, מִ־, מֵ, מִנֵּי, מִנֵּי (with suff. מִכֶּם, מִנֵּי, מִנִּי; מִנֵּהוּ, מִמֶּנּוּ; מֵהֶם or מֵהֶן, מֵהֶם; see מֵן in מנן) prep.—I. *from.*—II. *from out of.*—III. *of.*—IV. *by.*—V. *because of.* — VI. *besides.* — VII. *among;* תְּשַׁכֵּל מִנָּשִׁים *she shall be barren among women.*—VIII. *some of, part of.* — IX. *more than;* used also with inf.; הִשְׁחִיתוּ מֵאֲבוֹתָם *they are worse than the fathers;* מָתוֹק מִדְּבַשׁ *sweeter than honey;* אֶגְדַּל מִמֶּךָּ *I shall be greater than thee;* מִן...וְעַד; מִן...עַד *from ...unto;* לְמִן *from thence.*

מִן Ch., the same.

מְנָאוֹת; see מְנָת in מנה.

מִנְדָּה same as מִדָּה; see מדד.

מַנְדַּע *knowledge, &c.;* see ידע.

מָנָה I. *number.*— II. *appoint, constitute,* with לְ. Niph. נִמְנָה *was numbered,* with אֵת. Pi. מִנָּה *appoint, constitute,* with לְ, עַל. Pu. part. מְמֻנִּים *persons appointed,* 1 Chron. 9:29.

מְנָא, מְנָה Ch., *numbered, tried.* Pa. *constituted, appointed.*

מָנֶה m., a certain weight, perhaps of one hundred shekels.

מָנָה f. (pl. מָנוֹת) *part, portion.*

מְנָת f. (pl. מְנָאוֹת, מְנָיוֹת) *part, portion.*

מֹנִים m. pl., *times;* עֲשֶׂרֶת מ׳ *ten times,* Gen. 31:7, 41.

מְנִי m., *an idol,* Isa. 65:11.

מִנְיָן m. Ch., *number,* Ezr. 6:17.

מִנְהָרוֹת; see נהר.

מָנוֹד *refuge;* see נוד.

מָנוֹחַ, מְנוּחָה; see נוח.

מָנוֹן; see נוּן.

מְנוּסָה, מָנוֹס; see נוּס.

מָנוֹר; see נִיר.

מְנוֹרָה; see נוּר.

מִנְּזָרִים same as נְזִירִים.

מָנַח (Arab. *he gave*).

מִנְחָה f. (pl. מְנָחוֹת; with suff. מִנְחֹתֵיכֶם).— I. *gift to men.* — II. *to God, meat-offering.*

מִנְחָה f. Ch., *gift.*

מְנַחֵם p. n. of a man.

מָנַחַת p. n.—I. of a man.— II. of a place.

מִנִּי p. n. of a place, perhaps *Armenia*, Jer. 51:27; see also in מֵן, מִן, מנן.

מִנְיָן, מְנָיוֹת, מְנִי; see מנה.

מִיָּמִין, מִנְיָמִין p. n. of a man.

מָן m., *manna*, the food miraculously supplied to the Israelites in the wilderness.

מֵן m. with suff. מִנֵּהוּ *part of him*, with prep. מִן and suff.; מִמֶּנִּי *from me*; מִמְּךָ, מִמֵּךְ; f. מִמֵּךְ *from thee*; מִמֶּנּוּ *from him*; מִמֶּנָּה *from her*; see מִן.

מִנִּים, מִנִּי pl., *strings of an instrument*, Ps. 150:4; 45:9.

מִנִּית p. n., a place in Ammon.

מָנַע (fut. יִמְנַע) *keep back, withhold*, with מִן and לְ. Niph. נִמְנַע *was withholden, kept back.*

מְנָעֵל, מַנְעוּל; see נעל.

מַנְעַמִּים *delicacies*; see נעם.

מְנַעַנְעִים *cymbals*; see נוּעַ.

מְנַקִּיּוֹת *bowls*; see מְנַקִּית in נקה.

מֵנֶקֶת; see ינק.

מְנַשֶּׁה (*that which is forgotten*), p. n. — I. *Manasseh* the son of Joseph, Μανασσῆς; patron. מְנַשִּׁי, הַמְּנַשֶּׁה.— II. given also to other men.

מְנָת *part*; see מנה.

מַס, מִסִּים, מַס, מָס; see מסס.

מֵסַב, מְסִבֵּי, מְסִבּוֹת, מוּסַב; see סבב.

מַסְגֵּר, מִסְגֶּרֶת, מִסְגֶּרֶת; see סגר.

מַסַּד *foundation*; see יסד.

מִסְדְּרוֹן *portico*; see סדר.

מָסָה same as מָסַס. Hiph. הִמְסָה I. *dissolved, melted.*—II. *fainted.*

מַסָּה, see מסס; מַסָּה, see נסה.

מַסְוֶה m., *veil of Moses*, Ex. 34:33-35.

מְסוּכָה same as מְשׂוּכָה *hedge*; see שׂוּךְ.

מַסָּח; see נסח.

מִסְחָר *traffic*; see סחר.

מָסַךְ *mixed.*

מֶסֶךְ m., *mixture*, Ps. 75:9.

מִמְסָךְ *mixed wine.*

מְסֻכָּה, מָסָךְ; see סכך.

מַסֵּכָה, מַסֶּכֶת; see נסך.

מִסְכֵּן, מִסְכְּנוּת, מִסְכְּנוֹת; see סכן.

מְסִלָּה, מַסְלוּל; see סלל.

מַסְמְרִים, מַסְמְרוֹת, מִסְמְרִים; see סמר.

מָסַס I. *dissolve, melt.*—II. *faint.* Niph. נָמֵס, with pause נָמֵס (fut. יִמַּס; inf. הִמֵּס).—I. *was dissolved, melted.* — II. *enervated* by fear, grief, pain. Hiph. pl. הֵמַסּוּ *cause to faint*, Deu. 1:28; see מאס.

מָס m., *wasting, miserable*, Job 6:14.

מַס m., *tribute, tax*; הָיָה לָמַס and הָיָה לְמַס עֹבֵד *became tributary*; שׂוּם לָמַס or נָתַן the same; אֲשֶׁר עַל הַמַּס *who was over the tribute*; pl. שָׂרֵי מִסִּים *chief collectors* (of tribute), Ex. 1:11.

מִסָּה f., const. מִסַּת *tribute, offering*, Deu. 16:10.

תֶּמֶס m., *melting, wasting away*, Ps. 58:9.

מַסַּע, מַסָּע ; see נסע.

מִסְעָד *prop*; see סעד.

מִסְפֵּד *grief*; see ספד.

מִסְפּוֹא *provender*; see ספא.

מִסְפָּחוֹת, מִסְפַּחַת ; see ספח.

מִסְפָּר, מִסְפֶּרֶת *number*; see ספר.

מָסַר, inf. לִמְסָר־ *to stir up, wring out rebellion*, Nu. 31:16. Niph. fut. וַיִּמָּסְרוּ *were extracted, selected*, Nu. 31:5.

מָסֹרֶת f., *fetters, bonds*, Eze. 20:37; from אסר.

מוּסָר *discipline*; see יסר.

מִסְתָּר, מִסְתּוֹר ; see סתר.

מַעְבָּד *work*, see עבד; מַעֲבֶה *deep*, see עבה.

מַעֲבָר, מַעְבָּרָה *passage*; see עבר.

מַעְגָּל, מַעְגָּלָה, מַעְגָּל ; see עגל.

מָעַד *vacillate*. Hiph. *cause to vacillate*. Hoph. *made to vacillate*, Pro. 25:19.

מַעֲדַי p. n. of a man.

מַעַדְיָה, מוֹעַדְיָה p. n. of a man.

מַעֲדַנִּים, מַעֲדַנּוֹת *delicacies*; see עדן.

מָעָה (Arab. *bowels*).

מֵעִים const. מְעֵי m. pl. (with suff. מֵעַי, מֵעֶיךָ).—I. *intestines*.—II. *belly*.—III. *womb*.—IV. *heart, mind*.

מְעִין m. pl. Ch., *belly*.

מָעָה f., מְעוֹתָיו "*its extent*" (Lee), Isa. 48:19.

מָעוֹג *cake*; see עוג.

מָעוֹז, מָעֻזִּים; see עזז.

מָעוֹךְ p.n. of a man, 1 Sa. 27:2.

מָעוֹן, מְעוֹנִים, מְעוֹנָה, מְעוֹנֹתַי ; see עון.

מָעוּף; see עוף.

מָעוֹר *nakedness*; see עור.

מַעַזְיָה, מַעַזְיָהוּ p.n. of a man.

מָעַט *was, became, few, small*. Pi. מִעֵט the same, Ecc. 12:3. Hiph. הִמְעִיט I. *make few*.—II. *give little*.

מְעַט (מְעָט) מְעַט *a little, few*; pl. מְעַטִּים *few*; מְעַט מַיִם *a little water*, Gen. 18:4; מְתֵי מְעָט *few men*, Deu. 26:5; מְעַט מְעַט *by little and little*, Ex. 23:23; בִּמְעַט I. *within a little*.—II. *shortly, soon*.—III. *as a few, as nothing*.

מָעֹט, f. מְעֻטָּה *drawn, naked* (lit. *bald*), of a sword, Eze. 21:20.

מַעֲטֶה *garment*; see עטה.

מַעֲטָפָה; see עטף.

מְעִי; see עוה.

מָעַי p. n. of a man.

מְעִיל *cloak*; see מעל.

מֵעִים *bowels, &c.*; see מעה.

מַעְיָן *well*; see עַיִן.

מָעַךְ, part. מָעוּךְ I. *pressed*, 1 Sa. 26:7.—II. *bruised, injured* (θλαδίας), Lev. 22:24. with בְּ. Pu. מֹעַךְ *pressed*, Eze. 23:3.

מַעֲכָה, מַעֲכַת p. n.—I. of a region and city near Mount Hermon.—II. a name applied both to men and women; מַעֲכָתִי *a Maachathite*.

מָעַל (inf. מְעֹל; fut. יִמְעַל, יִמְעֹל), *do perversely, wickedly, rebel*, with בְּ.

מַעַל m., *perverseness, sin*, Job 21:34; see also in עלה.

מְעִיל m., long *upper garment* worn by persons of rank.

מַעֲלָה, מַעֲלֶה, מֹעַל, מֵעַל; see עלה.
מֵעָלִין, מַעֲלָל, מַעֲלִיל; see עלל.
מָעֳמָד, מַעֲמָד; see עמד.
מַעֲמָסָה; see עמס.
מַעֲמַקִּים *depths;* see עמק.
מַעֲנִית, מַעֲנָה, מַעֲנֶה, (לְמַעַן) מַעַן; see ענה.
מְעֹנָה same as מְעוֹנָה *habitation;* see עון.
מַעַץ p. n. of a man.
מַעֲצֵבָה *labour;* see עצב.
מַעֲצָד *axe;* see עצד.
מַעְצָר, מַעְצוֹר; see עצר.
מַעֲקֶה; see עקה.
מַעֲקַשִּׁים; see עקש.
מַעֲרָת, מַעֲרוֹת, מְעָרָה, מַעֲרֶה, מַעַר; see ערה.
מַעֲרָבָה, מַעֲרָב; see ערב.
מַעֲרֶכֶת, מַעֲרָכָה, מַעֲרָךְ; see ערך.
מַעֲרֻמִּים; see ערם.
מַעֲרָצָה *terror;* see ערץ.
מַעֲשֵׂיָה, מַעֲשַׂי, מַעֲשֶׂה; see עשה.
מַעְשְׂרוֹת, מַעֲשַׂר, מַעֲשֵׂר; see עֶשֶׂר.
מַעֲשַׁקּוֹת; see עשק.
מֹף and **נֹף** p. n., a city of Egypt.
מַפַּח, מַפָּח; see נפח.
מְפִבֹשֶׁת, מְפִיבֹשֶׁת p. n.—I. a son of Saul.—II. a son of Jonathan.
מֵפִיץ; see פוץ.
מַפֶּלֶת, מַפָּלָה, מַפָּל; see נפל.
מִפְלָאָה; see פלא.
מִפְלַגָּה *classes;* see פלג.
מִפְלָט *escape;* see פלט.
מִפְלֶצֶת *idol;* see פלץ.
מִפְלָשׂ *poising;* see פלס.
מִפְעָלָה, מִפְעָל; see פעל.
מֵפַעַת same as מֵיפַעַת.
מַפָּץ, מַפֵּץ; see נפץ.

מִפְקָד; see פקד.
מִפְרָץ; see פרץ.
מַפְרֶקֶת *vertebra;* see פרק.
מִפְרָשׂ; see פרש.
מִפְשָׂעָה *buttocks;* see פשע.
מִפְתָּח, מַפְתֵּחַ; see פתח.
מִפְתָּן *threshold;* see פתן.
מֹץ *chaff,* same as מוֹץ.
מָצָא (fut. יִמְצָא; imp. מְצָא; pl. f. מְצֶאןָ; inf. מְצֹא; with suff. מֹצַאֲכֶם; part. מֹצֵא, מוֹצֵא; f. מוֹצֵאת, מֹצֵאת).—I. *come to, arrive at.*—II. *obtain, acquire.*—III. *find, discover.*—IV. *find,* i. e. meet with, discover.—V. *be enough,* with לְ, עַד. Niph. נִמְצָא (fut. יִמָּצֵא).—I. *was obtained, acquired.*—II. *was found, arrived at.*—III. *was present, at hand,* with לְ. Hiph. הִמְצִיא I. *cause to come, deliver up,* with בְּיַד into the power of any one.—II. *recompense, repay.*—III. *present, offer up.*
מַצֵּבָה, מִצָּבָה, מַצָּבָה, מֻצָּב, מַצֵּב, מַצֶּבֶת; see נצב.
מִצְבָיָה p. n. of an unknown place.
מְצוּדָה, מְצוּדָה, מָצוּד, מָצוֹד, מְצַד; see צוד.
מָצָה *suck, drain, wring out,* with מִן. Niph. נִמְצָה *become sucked, drained, wrung out.*
מַצָּה see in מצץ and נצה.
מִצָּה p. n., a town in the tribe of Benjamin.
מִצְהָלָה *neighing;* see צהל.
מִצְוָה; see צוה.
מְצוֹלָה, מְצוּלָה *depth;* see צול.
מְצוּקָה, מָצוּק, מָצוֹק *restraint;* see צוק.

מָצוֹר p. n., *Egypt*; יְאֹרֵי מ׳ *the river of Egypt*, the Nile; see also מָצוֹר, מְצוּרָה in צור.

מִצְרַיִם p. n.—I. a son of Ham.—II. *Egypt.*—III. *an Egyptian.*

מִצְרִי m.; pl. מִצְרִים; f. מִצְרִית; pl. מִצְרִיּוֹת *an Egyptian.*

מַצּוּת *contention*; see נצה.

מֵצַח m. (with suff. מִצְחוֹ; pl. const. מִצְחוֹת), *forehead.*

מִצְחָה f., *greaves* (guards for the legs), 1 Sa. 17:6.

מְצִלָּה, מְצִלּוֹת, מְצִלְתַּיִם; see צלל.

מִצְנֶפֶת *turban*; צנף.

מַצָּע *bed*; see יצע.

מִצְעָד; see צעד.

מִצְעָר, מִצְעִירָה *little*; see צער.

מִצְפָּה, מִצְפֶּה; see צפה.

מַצְפֻּנִים *hidden places*; see צפן.

מָצַץ *suck* (as an infant), Isa. 66:11.

מַצָּה f., ἄζυμον, pl. מַצּוֹת *pure, unleavened bread, τὰ ἄζυμα*; חַג הַמַּצּוֹת *ἡ ἑορτὴ τῶν ἀζύμων, the feast of unleavened bread*; see also in נָצָה.

מֵצַר, מְצָרִים *trouble*; see צרר.

מִצְרַיִם *Egypt, &c.*; see מָצוֹר.

מַק *rottenness*; see מקק.

מַקֶּבֶת, מַקָּבָה; see נקב.

מַקֵּדָה p.n., a town in the tribe of Judah.

מִקְדָּשׁ; see קדשׁ.

מַקְהֵלוֹת, מַקְהֵלִים *assemblies*; see קהל.

מִקְוָה, מִקְוֶה *hope*; see קוה.

מָקוֹם *place*; see קום.

מָקוֹר *fountain*; see קור.

מַקָּחוֹת, מִקָּח; see לקח.

מִקְטֶרֶת, מִקְטָר; see קטר.

מַקֵּל m. (const. מַקֵּל, מַקַּל; with suff. מַקֶּלְכֶם, מַקְלִי; pl. מַקְלוֹת), *stick.*

מִקְלוֹת p. n. of a man.

מִקְלָט *safety*; see קלט.

מִקְלַעַת *sculpture*; see קלע.

מִקְנֵיָהוּ, מִקְנָה, מִקְנֶה; see קנה.

מָקַץ p. n. of a place.

מַקְצֻעוֹת, מִקְצֹעוֹת, מִקְצוֹעַ; see קצע.

מָקַק. Niph. נָמַק *waste away, consume, fail.* Hiph. הֵמַק *cause to waste*, Zec. 14:12.

מַק m., *rottenness*, Isa. 3:24.

מִקְרָא; see קרא.

מִקְרֶה, מִקָּרֶה; see קרה.

מְקֵרָה *coolness*; see קרר.

מְקַרְקַר Pi. part., from קוּר.

מִקְשָׁה, מִקְשֶׁה; see קשׁה.

מַר, מֹר, מוֹר, מָר־; see מרר.

מָרָא, part. מוֹרְאָה *rebellious*, Zep. 3:1. Hiph. *put forth courage*, Job 39:19; see מָרָה.

מְרִיא m.—I. *fattened.*—II. specially *a fatted calf.*

מָרֵא m. Ch., *Lord.*

מֻרְאָה f., *crop* (of birds), Lev. 1:16.

מַמְרֵא p.n.—I. of a man, *Mamre.*—II. אֵלֹנֵי מַמְרֵא (*oaks of Mamre*), and מַמְרֵא p. n. of a place near Hebron.

מָרָא p. n. of a woman.

בְּרֹאדַךְ בַּ׳, מְרֹאדַךְ בַּלְאֲדָן p. n., one of the kings of Babylon.

מַרְאָה, מַרְאֶה; see ראה.

מַרְאָשׁוֹת, מְרַאֲשׁוֹת, מָרֵשָׁה, מָרֵאשָׁה; see ראשׁ.

מֵרַב p. n., *Merab*, a daughter of Saul

מַרְבַדִּים *coverlets*; see רבד.

מַרְבִּית, מַרְבֶּה, מִרְבָּה; see רבה.

מִרְבָּץ, מַרְבֵּץ; see רבץ.

מַרְבֵּק *stall*; see רבק.

מַרְגֵּעָה, מַרְגּוֹעַ; see רגע.

מַרְגְּלוֹת *at the feet*; see רגל.
מַרְגֵּמָה *heap of stones*; see רגם.

מָרַד *rebelled*, with בְּ, עַל.
מְרַד Ch., *rebellion*, Ezr. 4:19.
מֶרֶד m.—I. the same, Jos. 22:22.—II. p. n. of a man.
מָרָד Ch., f. מָרָדָא *rebellious*, Ezr. 4:12,15.
מַרְדּוּת f., *rebellion*, 1 Sa. 20:30.
מְרֹדַךְ m., perhaps the name of an idol of Babylon, Jer. 50:2.
מָרְדְּכַי p. n., *Mordechai*, a Jew in Persia, Μαρδοχαῖος.

מָרָה *rebelled, rebelled against, disobeyed*, with בְּ; מ׳ אֶת־פִּי יְהוָֹה *they rebelled against the mouth* (i.e. words) *of the Lord*. Hiph. הִמְרָה *fought against, embittered, angered*, with בְּ, עִם.
מוֹרָה m., *razor*.
מְרִי m. (with pause מֶרִי; with suff. מִרְיָם, מֶרְיְךָ).—I. *bitterness*.—II. *rebellion*.—III. *rebellious*.
מְרִיב בַּעַל (מְרִי בַעַל) p. n., the son of Jonathan, called also מְפִיבֹשֶׁת.
מְרָיָה p.n. of a man.
מְרָיוֹת p. n. of a man
מִרְיָם p. n., *Miriam* the sister of Moses, Μαρία.
מְרָתַיִם dual f. (*double rebellion*), a prophetic title of Babylon, Jer. 50:21.
מָרוֹת, מֹרָה, מְרָה, מָרָה; see מרר.
מָרוּד *persecuted*; see רוּד.
מֵרוֹז p. n., a town in the north of Palestine.
מָרוֹחַ; see מרח.
מָרוֹם, מֵרוֹם; see רוּם.
מְרוּצָה מֵרוֹץ; see רוּץ.

מִרְזַח, מַרְזֵחַ; see רזח.

מָרַח *apply* (as a plaster). Isa. 38:21, with עַל.
מְרוֹחַ m., מְרוֹחַ אֶשֶׁךְ *with crushed testicles*, Lev. 21:20.
מֶרְחָב *wide*; see רחב.
מַרְחַקִּים, מֶרְחָק; see רחק.
מַרְחֶשֶׁת *pot*; see רחש.

מָרַט I. *pluck out hair*: hence,—II. *made smooth, polished*. Niph. *became bald*. Pu. *polished*, 1 Ki. 7:45.
מְרַט Ch., *plucked*, Dan. 7:4.
מְרִי, מְרָיָה, מְרָיוֹת, מִרְיָם; see מרה.
מְרִיא *fat*; see מרא.
מְרִיבָה *strife*; see רִיב.
מֹרִיָּה, מוֹרִיָּה f. p. n., *Moriah*, a hill in Jerusalem.
מְרִירִי מְרִירוּת; see מרר.

מֹרֶךְ m., *softness, cowardice*, Lev. 26. 36; LXX. δειλία.
מִרְכֶּבֶת, מֶרְכָּבָה, מֶרְכָּב; see רכב.
מַרְכֹּלֶת *merchandise*; see רכל.
מִרְמָה *deceit*; see רמה.
מְרֵמוֹת p. n. of a man.
מֶרֶם p. n. of a Persian prince.
מַרְסְנָא p. n. of a Persian prince.
מַרְעִית, מִרְעֶה, מֵרֵעַ; see רעה.
מֵרֹנֹתִי m., *a Maronothite*.
מַרְעֲלָה p. n., a town in the tribe of Zebulun.
מַרְפֵּא, מִרְפֶּה; see רפה, רפא.

מָרַץ. Niph. *was, became, unsound, weak, diseased*. Hiph. *urge to folly*, Job 16:3.
מַרְצֵעַ *awl*; see רצע.
מַרְצֶפֶת; see רצף.

מָרַק *rubbed bright, polished*. Pu מֹרַק *was polished*, Lev. 6:21.

מְרוּקִים m. pl., *purifications*, Est. 2: 12.

מָרָק m., *broth*, Jud. 6:19, 20.

תַּמְרוּק m., *purification, cleansing*.

מִרְקַחַת, מֶרְקָחָה, מֶרְקָה; see רקח.

מָרַר ; מַר לִי *it is bitter to me*, with מִן. Niph. נָמַר *was offensive* (an odour), Jer. 48:11. Pi. מֵרֵר (fut. יְמָרֵר) *makes bitter, grieves*; מ' בַּבֶּכִי *was bitter in weeping, wept bitter tears*. Hiph. הֵמַר (inf. הָמֵר) *make bitter*. Hithpalp. הִתְמַרְמַר *was angry*, Dan. 8:7; 11:11.

מַר m.—I. *a drop*, Isa. 40:15.—II. *bitterness*; adj. מַר (pl. מָרִים; f. מָרָה) *bitter, bitterly*.

מֹר, מוֹר, מָר־ m., *myrrh*.

מָרָה f.—I. *bitterness, sorrow*, 2 Sa. 2: 26.—II. p. n., a well in the desert of Sinai.—III. title which Naomi gave herself, Ru. 1:20.

מֶרֶה f., *sorrow*, Pro. 14:10.

מֹרָה f., the same., Gen. 26:35.

מָרוֹת p. n, a town of Judah.

מְרִירִי m., *bitter*, Deu. 32:24.

מְרִירוּת f., *bitter sorrow*, Eze. 21:11.

מְרֹרָה f.—I. *gall*.—II. *bitterness*.

מְרֵרָה f., *gall bladder*, Job 16:13.

מְרֹרִים m. pl., *bitter herbs*.

מְרָרִי p. n., a son of Levi.

מֶמֶר m., *bitterness*, Pro. 17:25.

מְמוֹרָרָה f., *gall bladder*, Job 20:25.

מַמְּרֹרִים m. pl., *bitter things*, Job 9: 18.

תַּמְרוּרִים m. pl., *bitterness, bitter sorrow*; see also תמר.

מַשָּׂאת, מַשְׂאֵת, מַשָּׂא, מַשָּׂאָה, מַשָּׂא, מַשְׂאֹת; see נשא.

מִשְׂגָּב; see שׂגב.

מְשׂוּכָה, see שׂוּךְ; מְשׂוּכָּה, see שׂכך.

מַשּׂוֹר *saw*; see נשׂר.

מְשׂוּרָה; see משׂר.

מָשׂוֹשׂ; see שׂוּשׂ.

מִשְׂחָק *object of laughter*; see שׂחק.

מַשְׂטֵמָה *hatred*; see שׂטם.

מַשְׂכִּיּוֹת, מַשְׂכִּית; see שׂכה.

מַשְׂכֹּרֶת *wages*; see שׂכר.

מַשְׂמְרוֹת *nails*; see סמר.

מִשְׂפָּח; see שׂפח.

מָשַׂר (Arab. *divided*).

מְשׂוּרָה f., *measure for liquids*.

מִשְׂרָה *government*; see שׂרה.

מִשְׂרָפוֹת *burning*; see שׂרף.

מַשְׂרֵקָה p. n., a place in Edom.

מַשְׂרֵת m., *frying-pan*, 2 Sa. 13:9.

מַשׁ p. n., *Mash*, Gen. 10:23, probably the district called Mount Masius, which separates Armenia from Mesopotamia.

מֵשָׁא p. n., *Mesha*, one of the boundaries of the district of the Joktanites, Gen. 10:30, not exactly known.

מַשָּׁא, מַשָּׁאָה, see נשה; מַשָּׁאוֹן, see נשא.

מַשְׁאַבִּים *watering places*; see שׁאב.

מִשְׁאָל, מִשְׁאָלָה; see שׁאל.

מִשְׁאֶרֶת *kneading trough*; see שׁאר.

מִשְׁבְּצוֹת; see שׁבץ.

מַשְׁבֵּר, מִשְׁבָּר *pain*; see שׁבר.

מִשְׁבַּתִּים; see שׁבת.

מִשְׁגֶּה *mistake*; see שׁגה

מָשָׁה *drew* (out of the water), Ex. 2: 10. Hiph. the same.

מֹשֶׁה (*drawn out of water*, Ex. 2:10), p. n., *Moses*, the lawgiver, Μωϋσῆς (Josephus).

מֶשִׁי m. *figured silk*, Eze. 16:10,13.
מַשָּׁה *debt*; see נשה.
מְשׁוֹאָה *desolation*; see שׁוֹא.
מַשְּׁאוֹת, מַשּׁוּאוֹת; see שׁאה.
מְשׁוּבָה, מְשֻׁבָה *apostasy*; see שׁוב.
מְשׁוּגָה *error*; see שׁוג.
מָשׁוֹט, מִשּׁוֹט *oar*; see שׁוט.

מָשַׁח (inf. מְשֹׁחַ, with ה parag. מָשְׁחָה; imp. מְשַׁח; fut. יִמְשַׁח). —I. *anointed.*—II. *anointed to an office.*—III. *set apart to an office*, Isa. 61:1.—IV. *dedicate by anointing.*—V. *anoint oneself for a banquet*, Am. 6:6, const. with בְּ. Niph. נִמְשַׁח *was anointed.*

מָשִׁיחַ m.—I. *anointed.*—II. *the anointed One*, Christ.

מְשַׁח m. Ch., *oil.*

מִשְׁחָה f.—I. *unction.*— II. *portion*, Lev. 7:35.

מָשְׁחָה inf., see מָשַׁח, Nu. 18:8; לְמָ׳ *for a dedication*, i. e. thing set apart for them.

מִמְשַׁח m., *extension, stretching out*, Eze. 28:14.

מִשְׁחָת, מָשְׁחָת, מַשְׁחֵת, מַשְׁחִית; see שׁחת.
מִשְׁחָר *dawn*; see שׁחר.
מְשִׁי; see above משה.
מְשֵׁיזַבְאֵל p. n. of a man.

מָשַׁךְ I. *stretched out the hand*, Hos. 7:5.—II. *took hold of*, Ex. 12:21. —III. *seized as spoil.*—IV. *drew, a bow, yoke, net. &c.*, with בְּ.—V. מָשַׁךְ הַיּוֹבֵל *lengthened the sound of the trumpet*, Ex. 19:13.—VI. *scattered seed*, Am. 9:13.—VII. *continued in a thing.*—VIII. *reckon with* (עִם), Ps. 28:3.—IX. *cheered*, Ecc. 2:3. Niph. *was protracted, delayed.* Pu. I. *spoiled*, Isa. 18:2, 7.—II. *obtained*, Pro. 13:12.

מֶשֶׁךְ m.—I. *acquiring*, Job 28:18. —II. מֶשֶׁךְ הַזָּרַע *scattering of seed*, Ps. 126:6.

מוֹשְׁכוֹת f. pl., *attractions, influences* Job 38:31.

מֶשֶׁךְ p. n.—I. one of the sons of Japhet. —II. the people descended from him, Gen. 10:2. They were probably the Muscovites; LXX. Μοσόχ; Vulg. *Mosoch.*

מִשְׁכָּב, מִשְׁכַּב *bed*; see שׁכב.
מִשְׁכָּן *dwelling*; see שׁכן.

מָשַׁל I. *ruled.*—II. *had power over*, with בְּ.—III. *had power to do*, with לְ.—IV. *assimilated, compared to*, with בְּ, עַל. Niph. *became like*, with כְּ, עִם, אֶל. Pi. *speaking parables*, Eze. 21:5. Hiph. I. *give authority* (inf. הַמְשֵׁל) Dan. 11:39. —II. *made like*, Isa. 46:5. Hith. *become like*, Job 30:19.

מֹשֶׁל m.—I. *authority*, Zec. 9:10.— II. *anything like*, Job 41:25.

מָשָׁל m.—I. *solemn declaration.*—II. *decision, rule, proverb*, *γνώμη.*— III. *bye word, subject of taunt.*

מְשֹׁל m., *taunting proverb*, Job 17:6.

מִמְשָׁל m., *dominion*; pl. *rulers*, 1 Ch. 26:6.

מֶמְשָׁלָה f., *dominion, rule.*

מֶמְשֶׁלֶת f. (pl. מֶמְשְׁלוֹת, מַמְשְׁלוֹת), the same.

מִשְׁלַחַת, מִשְׁלוֹחַ, מִשְׁלַח, מִשְׁלָח; see שׁלח.
מְשֻׁלָּשׁ; see שׁלשׁ.
מְשֻׁלָּם p. n. of a man.

מְשֶׁלֶמְיָה, שֶׁלֶמְיָה p. n. of a man.
מְשִׁלֵּמוֹת, מְשִׁלֵּמִית p. n. of a man.
מְשֻׁלֶּמֶת p. n., *Meshullemeth*, the wife of Manasseh.
מְשַׁמָּה *desolation, &c.*; see שׁמם.
מִשְׁמָן, מַשְׁמַנָּה, מַשְׁמַנִּים; see שׁמן.
מִשְׁמָע, מִשְׁמַעַת; see שׁמע.
מִשְׁמָר, מִשְׁמֶרֶת, מִשְׁמָרוֹת; see שׁמר.
מִשְׁנֶה; see שׁנה.
מְשִׁסָּה *prey*; see שׁסס.
מִשְׁעוֹל *narrow way*; see שׁעל.
מָשַׁע (Arab. *take pains*).
לְמִשְׁעִי *carefully*, Eze. 16:4.
מִשְׁעָם p. n. of a man.
מִשְׁעָן, מַשְׁעֵן, מַשְׁעֵנָה, מִשְׁעֶנֶת; see שׁען.
מִשְׁפָּחָה, מִשְׁפַּחַת *family*; see שׁפח.
מִשְׁפָּט *judgment*; see שׁפט.
מִשְׁפְּתַיִם; see שׁפה.
מֶשֶׁק m., בֶּן־מֶשֶׁק, LXX. υἱὸς Μέσεκ, Gen. 15:2, probably the name of a tribe or district in Syria, whence דַּרְמֶשֶׂק *Damascus*.
מִמְשָׁק m., *overspreading*, Zep. 2:9; but LXX. read Damascus.
מַשָּׁק *running about*; see שׁקק.
מַשְׁקֶה *drink*; see שׁקה.
מִשְׁקוֹל, מִשְׁקָל, מִשְׁקֶלֶת, מִשְׁקֹלֶת; see שׁקל.
מַשְׁקוֹף see שׁקף.
מִשְׁרָה *juice*; see שׁרה.
מַשְׁרוֹקִיתָא *flute*; see שׁרק.
מִשְׁרָעִי p. n. of a man.
מָשַׁשׁ same as מוּשׁ *touch, feel*, Gen. 27:12. Pi. מִשֵּׁשׁ I. *examine by feeling.*—II. *felt his way, groped.* Hiph. (fut. יָמֵשׁ) *that may be felt*, Ex. 10:21; see in מוּשׁ.

מִשְׁתַּחֲוִיתֶם Eze. 8:16. Hith. part. pl with pers. pron., from שׁחה.
מַת or מֵת m., pl. מְתִים, מְתָם, const. מְתֵי *men*.
מֵת, מֵתוּ, מֵתִי, מֵתָה, מַתָּה, מֵתָה, מֵתִים, from מוּת Kal.
מֵתֵא Ch. Pe. inf., from אתה.
מַתְבֵּן *heap of straw*; see תֶּבֶן.
מֶתֶג m. (with suff. מִתְגִּי), *bridle*.
מָתוֹק, מְתוּקָה; see מתק.
מְתוּשָׁאֵל p. n., *Methusael*, one of Cain's descendants.
מְתוּשֶׁלַח p. n., *Methuselah*, the patriarch, the son of Enoch.
מָתַח *stretched out* (as a curtain), Isa. 40:22.
אַמְתַּחַת f. (pl. const. אַמְתְּחוֹת), *sack* or *bag*.
מָתַי pa.—I. *when?*—II. *when*; אַחֲרֵי מָתַי *after how long?* Jer. 13:27; עַד מָתַי *how long?*
מַתְכֹּנֶת; see תכן.
מַתְּלָאָה for מַה־תְּלָאָה *what trouble* see לאה.
מִתְלַהְלֵהַּ Hith. part., from לָהָהּ.
מְתַלְּעוֹת *teeth*; see לתע.
מְתֹם *soundness*; see תמם.
מָתַן root not used; (Arab. *was firm*).
מָתְנַיִם m. dual, *loins*.
אֵמְתָנִי Ch. f., *powerful, mighty*, Dan. 7:7.
מַתָּן, מַתְּנָא, מַתָּנָה, מַתְּנַי, מַתַּנְיָה, מַתַּנְיָהוּ; see נתן.
מִתְנִי p. n. of a man.
מָתַק (fut. יִמְתַּק), *were, became sweet*. Hiph. הִמְתִּיק I. *was sweet*, Job 20:12.—II. *made sweet*, Ps. 55:15

מָתוֹק m. (pl. מְתוּקִים; f. מְתוּקָה).—I. *sweet.*—II. *sweetness.*—III. *pleasant.*

מֶתֶק m., *sweetness.*

מֹתֶק m., the same, Jud. 9:11.

מִתְקָה p.n., a station of the Israelites in the desert.

מַמְתָּק m., pl. מַמְתַּקִּים *sweetness,* Neh. 8:10; Cant. 5:16.

מִתְרְדָת p. n., *Mithridates* the Persian (Μιθριδάτης).

מַתַּת, מַתָּנָה, מַתַּתְיָה, מַתִּתְיָהוּ; see נתן.

מֹתַתִי Pil. pret. 1. pers., from מות.

נ

נָא interj., *I pray!* used,—I. in supplication.—II. in exhortation.—III. in irony or blame; בֹּא־נָא *go I pray!* אִמְרִי־נָא *speak I pray!* אֵלְכָה נָא *let me go, I pray!* אַל־נָא תַעֲבֹר *pass not over, I pray!* יֹאמַר־נָא *let it be told, I pray!* אַל־נָא *do not I pray!* with particles: אִם־נָא *if indeed;* אַל־נָא *not so, I pray!* הִנֵּה־נָא *behold!* אוֹי־נָא *alas!* see also in נִיא.

נֹא, נֹא־אָמוֹן p. n.; Διόσπολις, μερὶς Ἀμμών, perhaps the city of Thebes in Egypt.

נָאַד root not used; (Arab. *poured out water*).

נֹאד (נאוד) m. *skin bottle;* pl. נֹאדוֹת *bottles.*

נָאוָה (pl. const. נָאווּ), *became, was fair,* Ps 93:5; see אָוָה.

נָוָה f., pl. const. נְאוֹת *the best, choice, parts* of any thing; נ׳ דֶשֶׁא *pleasant herbage,* Ps. 23:2; generally translated *habitation,* Ps. 74:20, and elsewhere; but the former appears to give a better sense.

נָאוֶה m., נָאוָה.—I. *becoming, seemly*—II. *fair.*

נָאווּ for נָאֲווּ, from נאה.

נֵאוֹת Niph. fut. pl. 1. pers., from אות.

נָאַם *make a solemn declaration,* Jer. 23:31; part. נְאֻם; נ׳ יְיָ *saith the Lord,* passim: used of Agur, Pro. 30:1.

נָאַף (fut. יִנְאַף).—I. *committed adultery.*—II. *worshipped false gods,* Jer. 3:9; part. נֹאֵף *adulterer,* נֹאֶפֶת *adulteress.* Pi. נִאֵף the same.

נִאֻפִים m. pl.—I. *adulteries.*—II. *acts of idolatry.*

נַאֲפוּפִים m. pl., *repeated acts of adultery,* Hos. 2:4.

נָאַץ (fut. יִנְאַץ *turned away from, despised, rejected.* Pi. נִאֵץ (fut. יְנָאֵץ) the same. Hiph. fut. יָנֵאץ *it is despised,* Ecc. 12:5. Hith. part. מִנֹּאָץ *contemned,* Isa. 52:5.

נְאָצָה f., *reproach, insult,* 2 Ki. 19:3; Isa. 37:3.

נֶאָצָה f., pl. נֶאָצוֹת (נֶאָצוֹתֶיךָ), the same.

נָאַק same as אָנַק *cry out,* Job 24:12.

נְאָקָה const. נַאֲקַת f., *cry of sorrow.*

נָאַר. Pi. נֵאֵר (pret. 2. pers. נֵאַרְתָּה) *rejected as worthless,* Ps. 89:40; Lam. 2:7.

נֶאְשָׁאַר, Eze. 9:8, perhaps comp. of נִשְׁאַר and אֶשְׁאַר; see שאר.

נֹב p. n., a city of the Levites in the

tribe of Benjamin; with ה, נֹבֶה towards Nob.

נָבָא. Niph. נִבָּא *announced as the will of God, prophesied.* Hith. הִתְנַבֵּא, הִנַּבֵּא (inf. הִתְנַבּוֹת).—I. *prophecy.*—II. *be mad.*

נְבָא Ch. Ithp. הִתְנַבִּי *prophesied,* Ezr. 5:1.

נָבִיא m. (with suff. נְבִיאֲכֶם).—I. *a prophet,* one who declares future events.—II. probably one devoted to the study of the revealed will of God; whence בְּנֵי הַנְּבִאִים *the sons,* i.e. *disciples of the prophets* who studied under them.

נְבִיא m. Ch., the same.

נְבִיאָה f.—I. *prophetess.*—II. *prophet's wife.*

נְבוּאָה f.—I. *prediction,* Neh. 6:12. —II. *prophetical book.*

נְבוּאָה f. Ch., the same.

נְבוֹ p. n., *Nebo.*—I. one of the idols of Babylon, Isa. 46:1.—II. a mountain and city in the land of Moab. —III. a town in the tribe of Judah.

נְבוּזַרְאֲדָן p. n., one of Nebuchadnezzar's generals.

נְבוּכַדְנֶאצַּר, נְבוּכַדְנֶצַּר, נְבוּכַדְרֶאצַּר p. n., *Nebuchadnezzar,* the king of Babylon; LXX. Ναβουχοδονόσορ.

נְבוּשַׁזְבָּן p. n., a prince of Assyria.

נָבוּב *proud;* see בּוּב.

נָבוֹת p.n. of a man.

נְבִזְבָּה, נְבָזְבָּה f. Ch., *gift, reward.*

נָבֻזָה, 1 Sa. 14:36, Kal fut. pl. 1. pers. with ה parag. and dag. f. dropped; see בזז.

נָבַח *bark* (as a dog), Isa. 56:10.

נֹבַח p. n. of a man; also of a town in Gilead, Nu. 32:42; Jud. 8:11.

נִבְחַז p. n., an idol of the Avites, 2 Ki. 17:31.

נָבַט. Pi. נִבַּט and Hiph. הִבִּיט.—I. *looked.*—II. *look at, towards,* with לְ, אֶל; *looked after,* with אַחֲרֵי.—III. *looked favourably at,* with בְּ; same as רָאָה *perceived.*—IV. *attended to.*—V. *noticed,* Ps. 10:14.

נְבָט p. n., *Nebat,* the father of Jeroboam.

מַבָּט m., *expectation, hope,* Isa. 20: 5:6.

מֶבָּט m., the same, Zec. 9:5.

נְבִיאָה, נָבִיא; see נבא.

נְבָיוֹת p. n., *Nebaioth,* a people of the race of Ishmael, Gen. 25:13, &c.

נִבֵּאתָ, נִבֵּאתִי, נִבֵּיתִי, נִבֵּית for Niph. pret., from נבא.

נֵבֶךְ "*mazes of the sea*" (Lee), Job 38:16.

נָבֵל (fut. יִבֹּל).—I. *became shrivelled and fell* (as flowers, &c.).—II. *wasted away.*—III. *crumbled to dust.*—IV. *acted foolishly,* Pro. 30: 32. Pi. נִבֵּל *treated as worthless, set at nought.*

נָבָל m., נְבָלָה f.—I. *foolish.*—II. *impious.*—III. p. n. of a man, 1 Sa. c. 25.

נָבֵל, וַנָּבֶל, Isa. 64:5, Hiph. fut. pl. 1. pers. from בלל; or for וַנִּבֹּל Kal fut., from נבל.

נִבְלָה for נָבֹלָה Kal fut. pl. 1. pers., with ה parag.; see בלל.

נְבָלָה f.—I. *disgraceful action.*—II. *punishment of such an action,* Jos

7:15.— III. *impiety*, Isa. 32:6.— IV. *folly*, 1 Sa. 25:25.

נְבֵלָה f. (const. נִבְלַת; with suff. נִבְלָתוֹ, נִבְלָתִי).—I. *carcase of an animal.*— II. *dead body of a man.* —III. *idols*, Jer. 16:18; collect. *carcases.*

נַבְלוּת f., *shame, nakedness*, Hos. 2: 12.

נֵבֶל, נֶבֶל m. (pl. נְבָלִים).—I. *bottle* (of skin).— II. *earthen jar.*— III. *lute, νάβλιον*.

נְבַלָּט p. n., a town in the tribe of Benjamin.

נָבַע, נוֹבֵעַ *springing* (as a fountain), Pro. 18:4. Hiph. הִבִּיעַ.— I. *utters, declares.*—II. *prepares.*

מַבּוּעַ m., *spring, fountain of water.*

נָבְקָה for נָבַקָּה Niph. pret. f., from בקק.

נָבַר Niph., from ברר.

נֶבְרַשְׁתָּא f. Ch., *lamp*, Dan. 5:5.

נִבְשָׁן p. n. of a town in the tribe of Judah.

נִגְאֲלוּ for נִגְאֲלוּ Niph. pret. pl., from II. גאל.

נָגַב (Ch. נְגַב *was dry.*)

נֶגֶב m. — I. the arid desert to the *south* of Judea. — II. *the south*; נֶגְבָּה *towards, on, the south*; לְנֶגְבָּה, בַּנֶּגְבָּה *towards the south*; מִנֶּגֶב *from the south.*

נָגַד. Hiph. הִגִּיד *brought before, told, made known*; with לְ of the person to whom. Hoph. הֻגַּד *was told.*

נְגַד Ch., *proceeding, flowing*, Dan. 7:10.

נֶגֶד subst. *fore pa*
before, in fr
adv. *straight f*
opposite to hi
posite to; גֶד
sight, out of
opposite to, ag

נָגִיד m.—I. *lead*
chief.—IV. *o*
charge.

נָגַהּ *shined.* Hi
shine, Isa. 13:

נֹגַהּ f. (with suff.
— II. *light.* -
David.

נֹגַהּ f. Ch., *daw*

נְגֹהָה f., *light*, Isa

נָגַח (fut. יִגַּח),
Pi. נִגַּח the
entered into c

נַגָּח m., *addicte*
horn, Ex. 21:

נָגַל root not use

מַגָּל m., *sickle*, J

נָגַן and Pi. נִגֵּן *p*

נְגִינָה f.—I. *mus*
subject of a s

מַנְגִּינָה f., *song*
3:63.

נָגַע (inf. נְגֹעַ, ת
imp. גַּע; fut
—I. *touched*,
touched gentl
—III. *touche*
1 Sa. 10:26.-
injure, with
בְּ, Job 1:1
VII. *arrived*
ל, עַד, אֶל, בְּ

en of, with אֶל, Jon. 3:6. Niph. *were beaten in battle*, Jos. 8:15. Pi. נִגַּע *struck with disease.* Pu. *are afflicted*, Ps. 73:5. Hiph. הִגִּיעַ I. *made to touch*, with עַד, לְ, אֶל, עַל.—II. *reached*, with עַד, לְ, אֶל, עַל.—III. *reached the ears of*, with אֶל, Est. 9:26.—IV. *reached its proper time*, with לְ, Est. 9:1.—V. *came near*, with לְ, Ps. 88:4.—VI. *arrived* (of time).—VII. *arrived at*, with עַד, לְ, אֶל.

נֶגַע m. (with suff. נִגְעִי; pl. נְגָעִים, נִגְעֵי).—I. *stroke, blow.*—II. *infliction of evil.*—III. *affliction.*—IV. *mark of a blow, spot.*

נָגַף (fut. יִגֹּף).—I. *struck.*—II. *wounded.* —III. *killed.* — IV. *defeated.* — V. *struck with disease.*—VI. *stumbled.* Niph. נִגַּף (inf. abs. נִגּוֹף), *was defeated, routed* (of an army), with לִפְנֵי *of the enemy.* Hith. *stumble*, Jer. 13:16.

נֶגֶף m.—I. *infliction of disease.*—II. *act of stumbling*, Isa. 8:14.

מַגֵּפָה, const. מַגֵּפַת f.—I. *plague, pestilence.*—II. *defeat.*

נָגַר. Niph. נִגַּר I. *was put forth* (the hand), Ps. 77:3.—II. *overflowed, was spilt.*—III. *was scattered*, as wealth, Job 20:28. Hiph. הִגִּיר I. *dragged away.*—II. *poured out*, Ps. 75:9.—III. *scattered*, Mic. 1:6. Hoph. *poured out*, Mic. 1:4.

נָגַשׂ (fut. יִגֹּשׂ, תִּנְגְּשׂוּ), *exacted a task, debt* or *tax*; part. נוֹגֵשׂ *exactor, taskmaster, slave-driver.* Niph. נִגַּשׂ *was pressed, vexed, fatigued.*

נָגַשׁ (fut. יִגַּשׁ; inf. גֶּשֶׁת; with suff. גִּשְׁתּוֹ; imp. גַּשׁ, גֶּשׁ־, גְּשָׁה) and Niph. נִגַּשׁ I. *came near to, up to, touched*, with עַל, עַד, לְ, בְּ, אֶל.—II. perhaps *depart, go away*, Gen. 19:9. Hiph. הִגִּישׁ I. *brought near.* —II. *offered*, i. e. brought near (an offering). Hoph. הֻגַּשׁ *was brought, placed.* Hith. *approach*, Isa. 45:20.

נֵד *heap*; see נדד.

נָדָא, fut. וַיַּדַּא *drave away*, 2 Ki. 17:21.

נָדַב I. *rendered willing*, with לֵב and רוּחַ.—II. *impelled.* Hith. הִתְנַדֵּב *offered* or *performed willingly.*

נְדַב Ch. Hith. *was willing, gave willingly.*

נָדָב p. n., *Nadab.* — I. the son of Aaron.—II. given also to other men.

נְדָבָה, const. נִדְבַת f.—I. *voluntary offering.* — II. *free-will* (בִּנְדָבָה, נְדָבָה *of his own accord, willingly*), —III. pl. *abundance*; גֶּשֶׁם נְדָבוֹת *plenteous rain*, Ps. 68:10.

נְדַבְיָה p. n. of a man.

נָדִיב m.—I. *willing, liberal.*—II. *noble, distinguished.* — III. Job 21:28; perhaps "*a libertine*" (Lee).

נְדִיבָה f., *liberality.*

הִתְנַדָּבוּת (inf. Hith.) f. Ch., *free-will offerings*, Ezr. 7:16.

נִדְבָּךְ m. Ch., *layer, course of stones*, Ezr. 6:4.

נָדַד (inf. נְדֹד; fut. יִדֹּד, יִדַּד).—I. *fled.* —II. *wandered, walked to and fro.* —III. *flapped the wings*, Isa. 10:14; part. נוֹדֵד. Po. נוֹדַד *was driven away*, Nah. 3:17. Hiph. הֵנֵד *cause to wander*, Job 18:18. Hoph. הֻנַּד *made to wander*, Job

20:8; *driven about*, 2 Sa. 23:6. Hith. *was agitated*.

נְדַד Ch., *fled*, Dan. 6:19.

נְדֻדִים m. pl., *restlessness* (of body or mind), Job 7:4.

נֵד m.—I. *a heap*, Isa. 17:11.—II *a mound*.

נִדָּה f.—I. *legal impurity*.—II. a woman in that state.—III. *moral impurity*.—IV. *that which is impure, worthless*, Eze. 7:19, 20; מֵי הַנִּדָּה *water of impurity*, i. e. for the cleansing of legal impurity

נִידָה f., *impurity*, Lam. 1:8.

מְנַד m., *flight*, Job 7:4.

נָדָה same as נוּד. Pi. נִדָּה *put aside, desired to avoid*, with לְ, Isa. 66:5; Am. 6:3.

נֵדֶה m., *present, gift*, Eze. 16:33.

נָדָן m., the same; see also below.

נָדַח (fut. יִדַּח).—I. *drove an axe*, Deu. 20:19.—II. *drove away*, 2 Sa. 14:14. Hiph. הִדִּיחַ I. *brought with violence*, with עַל.—II. *drove away*.—III. *induced to any thing*, Pro. 7:21. Niph. נִדַּח I. *was impelled*.—II. *was driven away*.—III. *was induced to an action*; part. נִדָּח (with suff. נִדָּחוֹ, נִדַּחֲךָ; f. נִדָּחָה). Pu. part. מְנֻדָּח *driven*, Isa. 8:22. Hoph. part. מֻדָּח *driven astray*, Isa. 13:14.

מַדּוּחִים m. pl., *expulsions, drivings out*, Lam. 2:14.

נָדִיב, נְדִיבָה; see נדב.

נִדְמָה for נִדַּמָּה Niph. fut. pl. 1. pers. with ה parag., from דמם.

נָדָן m., *sheath* (of a sword), 1 Chron. 21:27; see also in נָדָה.

נִדְנֶה m. Ch., "midst," Eng. Ver.; "sheath," Marg., Dan. 7:15.

נָדַף (fut. יִנְדֹּף, יִדֹּף).—I. *scattered, drove about*.—II. *routed, conquered* (an enemy), Job 32:13. Niph. נִדַּף (inf. הִנְדֹּף) *driven away*.

I. נָדַר (fut. יִדֹּר, יִדַּר) *made a vow*.

נֶדֶר, נֵדֶר m. (with suff. נִדְרִי; pl נְדָרִים, נִדְרֵי).—I. *vow*.—II. *thing vowed*.

II. נָדַר root not used; (Arab. *thresh corn*).

אִדַּר Ch., *threshing-floor*, Dan. 2:35; (Arab. the same).

נֹהַּ *lamentation*, Eze. 7:11; see נָהָה.

נָהַג (imp. נְהַג; fut. יִנְהַג).—I. *led, conducted*.—II. *drave cattle, &c.*—III. *guided*.—IV. *commanded an army*. Pi. נִהַג (fut. יְנַהֵג) I. *brought on a wind*: hence—II. נִהֵג *breathed*, Nah. 2:8.—III. *led*.—IV. *drave*.

מִנְהָג m., *driving of horses*, 2 Ki. 9:20.

נָהַד root not used; (Arab. *swelled, grew vigorous*).

הוֹד m.—I. *vigour*, Pro. 5:9.—II. *glory, majesty*.—III. p. n. of a man.

הוֹדַוְיָהוּ, הוֹדַוְיָה p. n.; see ידה.

הוֹדְיָה p. n. of a man.

הוֹדִיָּה p. n. of a man.

נָהָה *lamented*, Mic. 2:4. Niph. fut. וַיִּנָּהוּ *mourn after the Lord*, 1 Sa 7:2.

נְהִי, with pause נֶהִי m., *lamentation*

נְהִי וַנְּהִי fut. apoc. pl. 1. pers., from היה.

נִהְיָה Mic. 2:4; see הָוָה.

נָהַל. Pi. נִהֵל (fut. יְנַהֵל).—I. *led*.—

II. *tended, fed.*—III. *gave rest to,* 2 Chron. 32:22. Hith. *proceed with a flock,* Gen. 33:14.

נַהֲלָל m.—I. *pasture,* Isa. 7:19.—II. p. n., a town in the tribe of Zebulun, called also נַהֲלָל.

נָהַם (fut. יִנְהֹם).—I. *roared,* Isa. 5:29, 30.—II. *groaned.*

נַהַם m., *roaring of a lion.*

נְהָמָה, const. נַהֲמַת f., *roaring of the sea,* Isa. 5:30.—II. *groaning,* Ps. 38:9.

נָהַק (fut. יִנְהַק) *brayed* (as an ass), Job 6:5; 30:7.

נָהַר I. *brighten* (of the face), Isa. 60:5; Ps. 34:6.—II. (fut. יִנְהַר) *flow unto, assemble in.*

נָהָר m. (pl. נְהָרִים, נְהָרוֹת, נַהֲרוֹת).—I. *river, stream.*—II. *current of the sea,* Jonah; הַנָּהָר הַגָּדוֹל, הַנָּהָר same as נְהַר פְּרָת *Euphrates;* אֲרַם נַהֲרַיִם *Aram* (Syria) *of the rivers,* Mesopotamia.

נְהַר m. Ch., *river.*

נְהוֹר (נְהִיר) m. Ch., *light,* Dan. 2:22.

נַהִירוּ f. Ch., *light, wisdom,* Dan. 5:11, 14.

נְהָרָה f., *light of day,* Job 3:4.

מִנְהָרוֹת f. pl., *clefts* in mountains, serving as channels for the rain, Jud. 6:2.

נוא or נוֹא. Hiph. הֵנִיא.—I. *discouraged,* Nu. 32:7.—II. *prohibited.*—III. *frustrated.*

תְּנוּאָה f.—I. *aversion,* Nu. 14:34.—II. *heavy things,* Job 33:10.

נוּב (fut. יָנוּב).—I. *threw out shoots,* Ps. 92:15.—II. *produced fruit,* Pro. 10:31.—III. *increased,* Ps. 62:11. Pi. נוֹבֵב *makes fruitful,* Zec 9:17.

נִיב m., *produce, fruit.*

נֵיבַי p. n. of a man.

תְּנוּבָה f., *produce, fruit.*

נוּגוֹת Niph. part. pl. f. for נוֹגוֹת, from יגה.

נוּגֵי Niph. part. pl. for נוֹגֵי, from יגה.

נוּגִים; see יגה.

נוּד (fut. יָנוּד).—I. *move to and fro.*—II. *wandered as a fugitive;* part. נָד *a fugitive.*—III. *departed.*—IV. *shook the head,* expressing pity, *condoled.* Hiph. הֵנִיד.—I. *moved to and fro.*—II. *drove out.*—III. *disturbed.*—IV. *shake the head* in pity, Jer. 18:16. Hoph. part. מֻנָּד *expelled,* 2 Sa. 23:6. Hithpol. הִתְנוֹדֵד *bemoan himself,* Jer. 31:18.

נוּד Ch., *departs,* Dan. 4:11.

נוֹד m.—I. *wandering,* Ps. 56:9.—II. p. n. (*exile*), the country to which Cain was banished.

נִיד m., *moving of the lips,* Job 16:5.

מָנוֹד m., *shaking the head,* Ps. 44:15.

נוֹדָב p. n., a son of Ishmael.

נָוָה (fut. יִנְוֶה) *dwelt,* Hab. 2:5. Hiph. *prepare a dwelling;* fut. with suff. אַנְוֵהוּ, Ex. 15:2.

נָוֶה m. (const. נְוֵה; with suff. נָוְךָ, נְוֵהֶם, נָוֵהוּ).—I. *fold for cattle.*—II. *dwelling of men.*—III. *habitation of God.*

נָוָה f., *habitation,* Job 8:6; נְוַת בַּיִת *she that remaineth at home;* οἰκουρός, Ps. 68:13.

נָאוָה *dwelt quietly,* Jer. 6:2.

נָיוֹת, Ketib נְוָיוֹת (*habitations*), p. n., a place near Ramah.

נוּחַ (fut. וַיָּנַח, יָנוּחַ).— I. *lay down, rested.*— II. *halted, ceased.*— III. *abode in*, with בְּ.—IV. *alighted on.* — V. *came down and possessed*, with עַל.— VI. *settled on* (as on a shoal, of the ark), Gen. 8:4. Hiph. I. הֵנִיחַ:— 1. *gave rest to.* — 2. *comforted.*— 3. *let fall*, Ex. 17:11.— 4. *caused to rest upon.*— II. הִנִּיחַ and הִנַּח.— 1. *placed.*— 2. *left, forsook, quitted.*—3. *let rest, remain.*— 4. *permitted, gave into the power of.*— 5. *left untouched*, 2 Ki. 23:18, with לְ. Hoph. הוּנַח I. *rest was given*, Lam. 5:5.— II. *was placed, left, remaining.*

נוֹחַ, נֹחַ m. (with suff. נוּחֶךָ).—I. *rest*, Est. 9:16-18.— II. p. n., *Noah*; LXX. Νῶε.

נַחַת f., *being placed*, Job 36:16; see also נחת.

הֲנָחָה (verb. Hiph.) f., *rest, peace*, Est. 2:18.

מָנוֹחַ m. (pl. with suff. מְנוּחָיְכִי).—I. *place of rest.*—II. p. n., *Manoah*, the father of Samson.

מְנֻחָה, מְנוּחָה f.— I. *rest, quiet.*— II. *place of rest*:—III. metaphorically, the land of Canaan.

נִיחֹחַ, נִיחוֹחַ m., *satisfaction, approbation*; רֵיחַ הַנִּיחֹחַ *a sweet* (pleasant) *savour.*

נִיחוֹחַ m. Ch., *offerings to God* or *man.*

נוּט same as מוט *agitate, shake*, Ps. 99:1.

נְוָל root not used; Ch. Pa., *polluted.*

נְוָלִי, נְוָלוּ Ch. f., *dunghill.*

נוּלְּדוּ Niph. pret. pl. with dag. euphon. for נוֹלְדוּ, from ילד.

נוּם *slept.*

נוּמָה f., *sluggishness*, Pro. 23:21.

תְּנוּמָה f., *sleep, slumber.*

נוּן. Niph. fut. יִנּוֹן (Ketib יָנִין Hiph. fut.) *drawn out, perpetuated*, Ps. 72:17.

נוּן p. n., *Nun*, the father of Joshua.

נִין m., *posterity.*

מָנוֹן m., *despiser*, Pro. 29:21.

נוּס I. *fled.*—II. *escaped.*— III. *passed away.* Pol. נוֹסֵס *drive away*, Isa. 59:19. Hiph. הֵנִיס *caused to flee, put to flight*; see נסס.

נָס m., *fugitive*, Jer. 48:44; Kri. נָס.

מָנוֹס m. (with suff. מְנוּסִי).—I. *flight.* —II. *refuge.*

מְנוּסָה, const. מְנֻסַת f., *flight.*

נִוַּסְּרוּ, Eze. 23:48 for נִתְוַסְּרוּ Nith., from יסר.

נוּעַ (fut. יָנוּעַ).—I. *was shaken.*— II. *was disturbed.* — III. *wandered about.*—IV. *varied*, Pro. 5:6.— V. *staggered* (as one drunken).—VI. *moved* (as the lips), 1 Sa. 1:13. Niph. *was shaken*; fut. יִנּוֹעַ. Hiph. הֵנִיעַ.— I. *shook.*— II. *caused to wander*, πλάζειν. — III. *dispersed* (as fugitives), Ps. 59:12.

מְנַעַנְעִים m. pl., *a musical instrument*, allied to the tambourine; Vulg. " sistra."

נוֹעַדְיָה p. n. of men and women.

נוּף *have sprinkled*, Pro. 7:17. Hiph. הֵנִיף I. *cause to sprinkle*, Ps. 68:10.—II. *shake to and fro.*—III.

lifted up the hand, over, and against, with אֶל.—IV. *lifted up an instrument,* with עַל.—V. *presented an offering.* Hoph. הוּנַף *was offered,* Ex. 29:27. Pil. נוֹפֵף *beckons with his hand,* Isa. 10:32.

נוֹן m., *elevated situation;* יְפֵה נ׳ *beautiful for situation,* Ps. 48:3; see also נֹף in מֹף.

נָפָה f.—I. *a sieve,* Isa. 30:28.—II. נָפַת דוֹר p. n. of a city.

נֶפֶר f., *elevated district,* Jos. 17:11.

נֹפֶר f., *dropping liquid, honey.*

תְּנוּפָה f.—I. *lifting up the hand,* Isa. 19:16.—II. *agitation, tumult,* Isa. 30:32.—III. *an offering.*

נו Hiph. הֵנֵץ *blossomed;* see נצץ.

נִיצוֹ m., *a spark,* Isa. 1:31.

נוֹצָ *crest;* see נצה.

נו same as יָנַק. Hiph. fut. with suff. תְּנִיקֵהוּ *gave him suck,* Ex. 2:9.

נו f. Ch., *fire.*

נֵר m.—I. *a light.*—II. *prosperity.*—III. p.n. of a man.

נֵיר same as נֵר.

נִיר m., *a light,* metaph. *prosperity, rank;* see also in נִיר.

נֵרִיָּה p. n. of a man.

מְנוֹרָה f., *the candlestick used in the Jewish ritual.*

נו *be diseased,* Ps. 69:21, same as אָנַשׁ.

נָזָ (fut. יִזֶּה, וַיֵּז, וְיִז), *was sprinkled,* with עַל and מִן. Hiph. הִזָּה (fut. יַזֶּה, וַיַּז), *sprinkled,* specially with blood, with עַל.

נָזִי; see זוד.

נָזִי; see נזר.

נָזַל (fut. יִזַּל).—I. *sank down,* Jud. 5:5.—II. *dropped, dropped down;* part. נוֹזְלִים *flowing streams.* Hiph. הִזִּיל *caused to flow,* Isa. 48:21.

מַזָּלוֹת f. pl., *the planets,* 2 Ki. 23:5.

מַזָּרוֹת *a constellation;* according to some from נָזַר *the northern crown.* Others read מַאֲזָרוֹת *a belt, the belt of Orion.*

נֶזֶם m.—I. *a nose-jewel.*—II. *an earring,* Gen. 35:4.

נְזַק Ch., *suffered loss.* Aph. *caused loss.*

נֵזֶק m., *injury, loss,* Est. 7:4.

נָזַר. Niph. נִזַּר I. *restricted himself.*—II. *devoted him to,* with לְ.—III. *withdrew from.*—IV. *abstained from,* with מִן. Hiph. הִזִּיר I. *set apart to,* with אֶל, אֶת.—II. *restrained from,* with אֶת, מִן.—III. *devoted himself to.*

נָזִיר m.—I. *a Nazarite,* one precluded by a vow from certain things lawful to others.—II. Gen. 49:26, applied to Joseph as separate from his brethren.—III. Lev. 25:5, 11, vines not pruned.

נֵזֶר m. (with suff. נִזְרוֹ, נִזְרֶךָ).—I. state of *separation* and *dedication.*—II. mark of such *separation,* specially the plate of gold in the high priest's mitre.—III. *diadem.*—IV. *sovereignty,* Pro. 27:24.—V. *hair of the head,* as shorn by the Nazarites, Jer. 7:29.

מִנְּזָרִים m. pl., *nobles, princes,* Nah. 3:17.

נַחְבִּי; see חבה.

נָחָה (pret. with suff. נָחָם; imp. נְחֵה; with suff. נְחֵנִי). Hiph. הִנְחָה (fut. with suff. יַנְחֵנִי), *led, conducted, guided.*

נָחוּם same as רְחוּם p. n. of a man.

נָחוּם, נִחוּמִים; see נחם.

נָחוֹר, נְחִירִים; see נחר.

נָחוּשׁ, נְחוּשָׁה; see נחשׁ.

נָחַל (inf. נְחֹל; fut. יִנְחַל).—I. *took possession of.*—II. *possessed.*—III. *took, received, as his portion.*—IV. *apportioned,* Nu. 34:17. Pi. נִחַל *gave settlement to.* Hiph. הִנְחִיל I. *caused to possess.*—II. *left as an inheritance to,* 1 Chron. 28:8. —III. *gave an inheritance,* Eze. 46:18. Hoph. הָנְחַל *was made to possess,* Job 7:3. Hith. הִתְנַחֵל I. *took for himself.*—II. *left as an inheritance,* Lev. 25:46.

נַחֲלָה f.—I. *settlement, dwelling.*—II. *possession.*—III. *assigned portion, share;* נַחֲלַת יְהוָֹה *the Lord's portion,* i. e. Israel, his chosen people. —IV. *inheritance.*

נַחֲלָת f., *portion,* Ps. 16:6.

נְחִילוֹת f. pl. nom., *flutes* (root חָלַל), Ps. 5:1.

נִחַל Niph. pret., from חלל; also Pi. pret., from נחל.

נַחַל m. (dual נַחֲלַיִם; pl. נְחָלִים, נַחֲלֵי; with ה loc. נַחְלָה).—I. *stream;* נַחַל מִצְרַיִם *the stream that divides Egypt* and Palestine.—II. *torrent.*—III. *valley.*

נַחְלָה same as נַחַל *stream,* Ps. 124:4.

נַחֲלִיאֵל p. n., one of the stations of Israel in the wilderness.

נֶחֱלָמִי p. n., *Nehelamite,* a title.

נָחַם. Niph. נִחַם I. *was grieved, repented,* with עַל.—II. *pitied, felt pity,* with עַל, אֶל, לְ, מִן.—III. *pitied and withdrew an infliction,* with עַל, אֶל.—IV. *recovered from his grief,* with אַחֲרֵי, עַל.—V. *avenged, freed himself from one displeasing,* with מִן.—VI. *mourned over,* with אֶל, לְ or עַל.—VII. *changed his purpose,* with עַל. Pi. נִחַם *sympathised with, comforted,* with עַל, מִן. Pu. נֻחַם *comforted, appeased.* Hith. הִתְנַחֵם, הִנַּחֵם I. *comforted himself.*—II. *changed his purpose,* with עַל, Nu. 23:19. —III. *gratified his anger,* with לְ.

נַחַם p. n. of a man.

נֹחַם m., *pity, change of purpose,* Hos. 13:14.

נִחֻמִים, נִחוּמִים m. pl.—I. *consolations.*—II. *pity,* Hos. 11:8.

נַחוּם p. n., *Nahum* the prophet, Ναούμ.

נֶחָמָה f., *consolation.*

נְחֶמְיָה p. n. of a man, *Nehemiah,* Νεεμία.

נַחֲמָנִי p.n. of a man.

תַּנְחוּמִים m.pl., *consolations, comforts.*

תַּנְחוּמוֹת f. pl., the same, Job 15:11; 21:2.

תַּנְחֻמֶת p.n. of a man.

נִחַם pret. Niph. and Pi., from חמם.

נֶחָמִים Niph. part. pl., from חמם.

נַחְנוּ *we;* see אֲנִי.

נֶחֱנַנְתְּ Niph. pret. f. 2. pers. with parag., from חנן.

נָחַץ part. נָחוּץ *urgent,* 1 Sa. 21:9.

נָחַר (Arab. *snorted*).

נַחַר m., *snorting,* Job 39:20.

נַחֲרָה f., the same, Jer. 8:16.

נַחֲרַי, נַחְרַי p. n. of a man.

נָחוֹר p. n., *Nahor*, the brother of Abraham.

נְחִירַיִם m. pl., *nostrils*, Job 41:12.

נָחַר Niph. pret., from חרר.

נָחָשׁ m.—I. *serpent.*— II. p. n. of a man.— III. עִיר נָחָשׁ p. n., a city in the tribe of Judah.

נִחֵשׁ Pi. (denom. from ὀφιομαντεία, *divination by serpents*).—I. *used divination.*—II. *watched, observed.*

נַחַשׁ m., *divination.*

נַחְשׁוֹן p. n., *Naashon*, the son of Amminadab.

נְחָשׁ m. Ch., *brass* or *copper.*

נְחֹשֶׁת com. (with suff. נְחֻשְׁתֵּךְ).— I. *brass.*— II. *chain*, Lam. 3:7; dual נְחֻשְׁתַּיִם *fetters, shackles.*— III. *money*, Eze. 16:36.

נְחֻשְׁתָּא p. n. of a woman.

נְחֻשְׁתָּן m., *the brazen serpent idolized*, 2 Ki. 18:4.

נָחוּשׁ m., *copper* or *brass*, Job 6:12.

נְחוּשָׁה, נְחֻשָׁה f., the same.

נָחַת (fut. יֵחַת, יִנְחַת) same as יָרַד.— I. *came down*, Job 17:16.—II. *came down violently*, with עַל.—III. *penetrated the mind*, with בְּ. Niph. נִחַת *penetrated* (of arrows), with בְּ, Ps. 38:3. Pi. נִחֵת *brought down, levelled* (the bow), Ps. 65:11. Hiph. imp. הַנְחַת *depress*, Joel 4:11.

נְחַת Ch., *came down.* Aph. *placed.* Hoph. *made to descend*, Dan. 5:20.

נַחַת m.— I. *descent, lighting down*, Isa. 30:30.— II. *being placed*, Job 36:16; see also in נוּחַ.

נָחֵת m., pl. נְחִתִּים *coming down* (of an army), 2 Ki. 6:9.

נַחַת p. n. of a man; same as תּוֹחַ.

נִחַת Niph. pret., from חתת.

נָטָה (inf. const. נְטוֹת; fut. יִטֶּה; apoc. וַיֵּט, וַיֵּט, יֵט).— I. *stretch out, extend* (the hand, &c.).— II. *spread out, stretch, pitch a tent.*— III. *bowed, inclined.*—IV. *turn, lead to*, with לְ, אֶל, אַחֲרֵי; or *from*, with מִן.—V. *go, depart*, 1 Sa. 14:7. Niph. נִטָּה *stretched out.* Hiph. הִטָּה (fut. יַטֶּה; apoc. יַט, יֵט; imp. הַטֵּה; apoc. הַט).— I. *stretch out.*— II. *spread out.*—III. *incline, bend down, lower.*—IV. *turn away, put away.* —V. *wrest, pervert.* Hoph. part. מֻטֶּה s., *wresting, perversion.*

מַטֶּה, const. מַטֵּה m. (f., Mic. 6:9).— I. *branch of a tree.*—II. *staff*; שָׁבַר מַטֵּה־לֶחֶם *he brake the staff of bread*, i.e. support, that on which life leans.—III. *rod.*—IV. *sceptre.* —V. *tribe, government*, of which the *sceptre* was a symbol; pl. מַטּוֹת.

מַטָּה *downwards*; לְמַטָּה, מִלְמַטָּה the same.

מִטָּה f.— I. *couch, bed.*— II. *bier* (for the dead), 2 Sa. 3:31.

נְטִיפוֹת *earrings*; see נטף.

נָטַל (fut. יִטּוֹל).—I. *lifted up*, Isa. 40:15.—II. *laid a burden on*, with עַל, Lam. 3:28. Hiph. *took up and removed.*

נְטַל Ch., *lifted up.*

נֵטֶל m., *burden*, Pro. 27:3.

נָטִיל m., *loaded*, Zep. 1:11.

נִטְמֵתֶם for נִטְמֵאתֶם Niph. pl., from טמא.

נָטַע (fut. יִטַּע; inf. נְטוֹעַ, טַעַת).—I. *planted.*—II. *pitched a tent.*—III. *set up an idol temple*, Deut. 16: 21.—IV. *drove a nail.* Niph. *planted*, Isa. 40:24.

נָטִיעַ m., pl. נְטִעִים *planted*, Ps. 144: 12.

נֶטַע m. (with suff נִטְעֲךָ; pl. נְטָעִים, נִטְעֵי).—I. *plant.*—II. *plantation.*

נָטַע const. נְטַע m., *plant*, Isa. 5:7.

מַטָּע m., *planting.*

נָטַף (fut. יִטֹּף).—I. *drop*, Job 29:22.—II. *let drop.* Hiph. הִטִּיף.—I. *let drop* (water), Am. 9:13.—II. *let fall* (sentiments, prophetic declarations).

נָטָף m.—I. *drop*, Job 36:27.—II. *στακτή, myrrh*, Ex. 30:34.

נְטֹפָה p. n., a town near Bethlehem; נְטֹפָתִי *a Netophathite.*

נְטִיפוֹת f. pl., *earrings* or *drops*, Jud. 8:26; Isa. 3:19.

נָטַר (fut. יִנְטוֹר, יִטֹּר) *watched*,—1. *for good.*—2. *for evil*, with לְ, אֵת.

נְטַר Ch., *kept*, Dan. 7:28.

מַטָּרָה (מַטָּרָא, Lam. 3:12) f.—I. *custody, prison.*—II. *mark, object, butt.*

נָטַשׁ (fut. יִטּוֹשׁ).—I. *left.*—II. *forsook*, God, a law, &c.—III. *left.*—IV. *ceased to think of*, 1 Sa. 10:2.—V. *spread, scattered.*—VI. *drew a sword*, Isa. 21:15.—VII. *allowed.* Niph. I. *was forsaken.*—II. *spread itself.*—III. *became loose.* Pu. *was forsaken*, Isa. 32:14.

נְטִישׁוֹת f. pl.—I. *shoots of the vine.*—II. *small towns, shoots of the capital*, Jer. 5:10.

ני׳, נִיהֶם בְּ an error for בְּנֵיהֶם, Eze. 27: 32.

נִיא (Arab *raw*).

נָא m., *raw* (uncooked), Ex 12:9.

נִיב, נֵיבַי; see נוּב.

נִיד, נִידָה; see נוּד.

נָיוֹת; see נוה.

נִיחֹחַ; see נוּחַ.

נִין *posterity*; see נוּן.

נִינְוֵה p.n., *Nineveh*, a city of Assyria; LXX. Νινευΐ.

נִינָם Kal fut. pl. 1. pers. with suff., from ינה.

נִים; see נוּם.

נִיסָן m., the first month of the Hebrew year, called also אָבִיב, which see.

נִיצוֹץ *sparks*; see נוּץ.

נִיר *light*; see נוּר.

נִיר I. *clear ground for cultivation.*—II. *cultivate ground.*

נִיר m., *field newly cultivated*; see also in נוּר.

מָנוֹר m.; מְנוֹר אֹרְגִים *weaver's beam*, 1 Sa. 17:7; 2 Sa. 21:19.

נִירָם, וַנִּירָם Kal fut. pl. 1. pers. with suff., from ירה.

נַךְ, וַנַּךְ Hiph. fut. apoc. pl. 1. pers., from נכה.

נָכָא, נָכֵא, see נכה; **נִכְאוּ**, see כאה.

נְכֹאת f., *storax*, Gen. 37:25; 43:11; LXX. θυμίαμα; Aquila στύραξ.

נֶכֶד m. (with suff. נֶכְדִּי), *posterity*; always with נִין, which see.

נָכָה. Hiph. הִכָּה (imp. הַךְ, הַכֵּה; fut. יַכֶּה, וַיַּךְ; with ה parag. יַכְּכָה).—I. *struck.*—II. *wounded.*—III. *killed.*—IV. *conquered.*—V. *taunted* (struck with the tongue).—VI. *struck the hands together.*—VII

וַיַּךְ לֵב *his heart smote him*, 1 Sa. 24:6. Hoph. הוּכָּה, הֻכָּה *was smitten, &c.*, pass. of Hiph. Niph. נִכָּה *was wounded*, 2 Sa. 11:15. Pi. inf. נַכֵּה־, נַכֵּה *smiting*. Pu. נֻכָּה *smitten*.

נָכֶה m.—I. נְכֵה רַגְלַיִם *lame* (smitten in the feet), 2 Sa. 4:4; 9:3.—II. נ׳ רוּחַ *afflicted in spirit*, Isa. 66:2.

נֵכֶה m., pl. נֵכִים *smiting* (with the tongue), *calumniators*, Ps. 35:15.

נָכֵא m., f. רוּחַ נְכֵאָה *afflicted, broken spirit*, Pro. 15:13, &c.

נָכָא m., pl. נְכָאִים *smitten*, Isa. 16:7.

מַכָּה f. (pl. מַכִּים, מַכּוֹת).—I. *stroke, blow.*—II. *wound.*—III. *slaughter.*—IV. *calamity.*

נְכֹה, נְכוֹ p. n., Pharaoh *Necho*, king of Egypt; LXX. Νεχαώ.

נָכֹן (same as כִּידוֹן), p. n. of a place.

נֹכַח I. *straight forwards.*—II. *opposite, over against.*—III. *in sight of;* אֶל־נֹכַח *towards;* לְנֹכַח *in front of, in behalf of, straight forwards*, עַד־נֹכַח *as far as*.

נֹכַח (with suff. נִכְחוֹ) *opposite to, against.*

נָכֹחַ m. (f. נְכֹחָה; pl. נְכֹחוֹת).—I. *straight forward, upright.*—II. *uprightness*, Isa. 57:2.

נֹכַחַת Niph. part. f., from יכח.

נָכַל *withholding*, Mal. 1:14. Pi. *used artifice*, with לְ, Nu. 25:18. Hith. the same, with בְּ.

נֵכֶל m., pl. נִכְלֵי, נְכָלִים *artifices*, Nu. 25:18.

כֵּלַי, כִּילַי m., *avaricious, oppressive*, Isa. 32:5, 7.

נָכַס root not used; same as כָּנַס.

נֶכֶס m., pl. נְכָסִים *treasures, wealth.*

נְכַס m. Ch., pl. נִכְסִין *treasures, wealth.*

כִּיס m., *purse, bag.*

נִכַּפֵּר Nith., from כפר.

נָכַר. Pi. נִכַּר I. *recognised.*—II. *considered.*—III. *acknowledged.*—IV. *alienated*, Deu. 32:27.—V. *rejected*, with בְּ, 1 Sa. 23:7. Niph. נִכַּר I. *feigned himself unknown*, Pro. 26:24.—II. *was recognised*, Lam. 4:8. 11.—Hiph. הִכִּיר I. *recognised, knew, acknowledged.*—II. *was partial in judgment*, with פָּנִים.—III. *beheld.*—IV. *regarded.*—V. *esteemed, accounted.*—VI. *took judicial cognizance of.* Hith. הִתְנַכֵּר *make one's self strange*, Gen. 42:7.

נֵכָר, const. נֵכַר m., *strange, foreign, a foreigner;* בֶּן־נֵכָר *son of the stranger, foreigner;* אֱלֹהֵי נֵכָר *strange gods.*

נָכְרִי m. (pl. נָכְרִים; f. נָכְרִיָּה, pl. נָכְרִיּוֹת).—I. *foreign.*—II. *a stranger.*—III. *strange, singular.*

נֶכֶר, נֹכֶר m., *treating as a stranger, punishment.*

הַכָּרָה (verb Hiph.) f., *astonishment, consciousness of guilt*, Isa. 3:9.

מַכָּר m., *relative, neighbour*, 2 Ki. 12:6, 8.

נְכֹת, בֵּית נְכֹתֹה 2 Ki. 20:13; Isa. 39:2, *treasury*, γαζοφυλάκιον.

נָלָה root not used; (Arab. *succeeded*). Hiph. inf. with pref. and suff. כַּנְּלֹתְךָ for כְּהַנְלוֹתְךָ *when thou hast accomplished*, Isa. 33:1.

מִנְלֶה *possession, wealth*, Job 15:29.

נִמְבְזָה *despised;* see בזה.

נְמוּאֵל p. n. of a man.

נָמַל (fut. יִמַּל; pl. יִמָּלוּ).—I. *circumcise*, Gen. 17:11.—II. *withered*, Ps. 37:2; Job 14:2. (some derive it from מָלַל same as מוּל). Niph. נִמּוֹל *was circumcised;* part. נִמּוֹלִים (some derive it from מוּל).

נְמָלָה f., *ant*, Pro. 6:6; pl. נְמָלִים, Pro. 30:25.

נָמַר root not used; (Arab. *was spotted*).

נָמֵר m., *a panther*, Jer. 5:6; Hab. 1:8.

נְמַר m. Ch., the same, Dan. 7:6.

נָמַר Niph. pret., from מרר.

נִמְרֹד p. n., *Nimrod*, the builder of Babylon, Νεβρώδης; אֶרֶץ נִמְרֹד *Babylon*.

נִמְרָה, נִמְרִים p. n., same as בֵּית נִמְרָה; see בַּיִת.

נִמְשִׁי p. n., father of Jehu.

נֵס, נִסִּי; see נסס.

נְסַבָּה for נָסַבָּה Niph. pret. fem., from סבב.

נְסִבָּה; see סבב.

נָסַג *recoil, shrink back;* inf. נָסוֹג, Isa. 59:13; fut. יַסֵּג, Mic. 2:6. Hiph. הִסִּיג I. *remove a boundary.*—II. *carry away property*, Mic. 6:14. Hoph. הֻסַּג *was perverted*, Isa. 59:14.

נָסָה imp. נַסֵּה; (see נָשָׂא). Pi. נִסָּה I. *tried.*—II. *proved, made a trial.* —III. *found on trial, experienced.*

מַסָּה f.—I. *trial.*—II. *temptation by trial.*

נְסָה, Ps. 4:7, for נְשָׂא imp., from נשׂא.

נָסַח (fut. יִסַּח) *dispersed, scattered.* Niph. *was dispersed.*

נְסַח Ch. Ith. *was pulled down*, Ezr. 6:11.

מַסָּח m., *disperser, driver away*, 2 Ki. 11:6.

I. נָסַךְ I. *poured out*, Isa. 29:10.—II. *melted.*—III. *anointed*, Ps. 2:6.—IV. *poured out a libation.* Niph נִסַּךְ *was anointed*, Pro. 8:23. Pi. נִסֵּךְ and Hiph. הִסִּיךְ *poured a libation.*—Hoph. *was poured out.*

נְסַךְ Ch., Pa. *made an offering*, Dan. 2:46.

נָסִיךְ m.—I. *libation.*—II. *molten image*, Dan. 11:8.—III. *anointed one, prince.*

נֶסֶךְ, נֵסֶךְ m. (with suff. נִסְכּוֹ, נִסְכֹּה; pl. נְסָכִים).—I. *drink-offering.*—II. *molten image.*

נְסַךְ m. Ch., *drink-offering*, Ezr. 7:17.

מַסֵּכָה I. *fusing;* אֱלֹהֵי מ׳ *molten images.*—II. *libation*, Isa. 30:1.

II. נָסַךְ same as סָכַךְ *covered*, Isa. 25:7.

מַסֵּכָה *covering*, Isa. 25:7; 28:20.

מַסֶּכֶת f. (Arab. *he wove*), *web*, Jud. 16:13, 14.

נָסַס *raised, bore a standard*, Isa. 10:18; 59:19. Hithpo. הִתְנוֹסֵס I. *rally round a standard*, Ps. 60:6. —II. *raise oneself as a standard*, Zec. 9:16.

נֵס m. (with suff. נִסִּי).—I. *banner.*—II. *flag-staff.*—III. *sail.*—IV. *example, warning.*—V. *the leader to whom the banner belongs*, Isa. 11:10.

נָסַע (fut. יִסַּע; inf. נְסֹעַ; imp. pl. סְעוּ) —I. *departed.*—II. *travelled.*—III. *arose* (a wind), Nu. 11:31.—IV. *removed.*—V. *pulled up* or *out.*

Niph. נִסַּע *was pulled up.* Hiph. הִסִּיעַ I. *caused to depart, &c.*—II. *made to blow,* Ps. 78:26. — III. *quarried stone,* 1 Ki. 5:31.

מַסָּע m.—I. *missile weapon,* Job 41: 18. — II. *march, journey;* pl. מַסָּעִים.

נָסַק *go up,* Ps. 139:8.

נְסַק Ch., *go up.* Aph. *lifted up,* Dan. 3:22. Hoph. *was lifted up,* Dan. 6:24.

נִסְרֹךְ p. n., *Nisroch,* an idol of the Ninevites.

נֵעָה p.n., a town in the tribe of Zebulon.

נֹעָה p. n. of a woman.

נֵעוֹר for נָעוֹר Niph. pret., from עוּר.

נְעוּרִים *youth;* see נַעַר.

נְעִיאֵל p. n., a town in the tribe of Naphtali.

נָעִים *pleasant;* see נעם.

נָעַל I. *put on sandals,* Eze. 16:10, lit. *latch them.*—II. *bolted, latched the door.* Hiph. fut. with suff. וַיַּנְעִלוּם *shod them,* 2 Chron. 28:15.

נַעַל f., *shoe, sandal;* dual נַעֲלַיִם *pair of sandals;* pl. נְעָלִים, נְעָלוֹת.

מַנְעוּל m., *bolt, lock of a gate.*

מִנְעָל m., *defence,* Deu. 33:25.

נָעֵם (fut. וּנְעַם) *was pleasant, agreeable,* with לְ.

נָעִים m.—I. *pleasant.*—II. *sweet music.*—III. *amiable.*—IV. *becoming.* —V. *prosperous;* pl. נְעִימִים.

נַעַם p. n. of a man.

נֹעַם m.— I. *pleasantness.*— II. *kindness, grace.*

נַעֲמָה p.n.—I. a town in the tribe of Judah.—II. the daughter of Lamech.—III. the mother of Rehoboam.

נָעֳמִי p. n., *Naomi,* the mother-in-law of Ruth.

נַעֲמִי patron.; see נַעֲמָן.

נַעֲמָן m.—I. *pleasantness,* Isa. 17:10. —II. p.n. of a man.

נַעֲמָתִי p. n., *Naamathite,* a title.

מַנְעַמִּים m. pl., *delicacies,* Ps. 141:4.

נָעַץ (Arab. a *thorny bush* in the Hedjaz).

נַעֲצוּץ m., a species of *thorn bush,* Isa. 7:19; 55:13.

נָעַר I. *roar as a lion,* Jer. 51:38.—II. *shook off, out.* Niph. *was shaken out.* Pi. נִעֵר *threw out.* Hithp. Isa. 52:2, *shake thyself,* with מִן.

נַעַר m., *straying, strayed* (cattle), Zec 11:16; see also below.

נְעֹרֶת f., *tow,* Jud. 16:9; Isa. 1:31.

נַעַר m. (with suff. נַעַרְךָ, נַעֲרוֹ; pl. נְעָרִים, נַעֲרֵי).—I. *infant.*—II. *boy.* —III. *youth.*—IV. *servant.*

נַעֲרָה f.—I. *girl.*—II. *young woman.* —III. *female servant.*—IV. p. n. of a woman.—V. p. n., a town in the tribe of Ephraim, also נַעֲרָן.

נֹעַר m., *childhood, youth.*

נְעוּרִים m. pl., *youth, early life.*

נְעֻרוֹת f. pl., the same.

נְעַרְיָה p.n. of a man.

נַעֲרָן p.n., same as נַעֲרָה.

נֹף same as מֹף.

נֶפֶג p. n. of a man.

נָפָה; see נוּף.

נְפוּסִים, נְפִיסִים, נְפִישְׁסִים p.n. of a m.

נָפַח I. *blew, blew upon,* with בְּ.— II. *blew a fire.*—III. with נֶפֶשׁ *expired;* דּוּד נָפוּחַ *seething pot,* Jer.

15:9. Pu. נֻפַּח *was blown* (of a fire), Job 20:26. Hiph. *puffed at, despised.*

נֹפַח p. n., a town in Moab.

מַפֻּחַ m., *bellows*, Jer. 6:29.

מַפָּח m. מ׳ נֶפֶשׁ, Job 11:20, *expiring*, "giving up the ghost," Eng. Ver.

נְפִילִים; see נפל.

נָפִישׁ p. n., *Naphish*, a son of Ishmael.

נֹפֶךְ m., an unknown precious stone; LXX. ἄνθραξ.

נָפַל (fut. יִפֹּל; inf. נְפֹל; with suff. נָפְלוֹ, נִפְלוֹ).—I. *fell, fell down, was killed, &c.*; (נֹפֵל *one prostrate*).—II. *fell upon*, with עַל.—III. *fell to* (of an inheritance), with לְ.—IV. *fell on his face*, with or without אֶל פָּנָיו, עַל פָּנָיו.—V. *fell on* (was confined to) *his bed*, Ex. 21:18.—VI. *deserted to, joined*, with עַל or אֶל.—VII. *fell into the hand of*, with בְּיַד.—VIII. *perished*, Pro. 11:5, &c.—IX. *fell into a pit, mischief*, with בְּ, לְ.—X. נ׳ בְּעֵינָיו *sank in his own esteem*, Neh. 6:16.—XI. נ׳ בְּנַחֲלָה *obtained an inheritance*, Eze. 47:22.—XII. *sank* (of the heart), 1 Sa. 17:32.—XIII. נ׳ אַרְצָה *perished*. Hiph. הִפִּיל I. *caused to fall*.—II. *killed*.—III. *annihilated*.—IV. *threw down*.—V. *divide* (by lot), Jos. 23:4. with לְ.—VI. *knock out a tooth*, Ex. 21:27.—VII. *overcame*.—VIII. *cause to settle*, Ps. 78:55.—IX. *cast out, forsook*.—X. *threw into the fire*, with עַל or בְּ. Hith. I. *prostrate myself*.—II. *fell upon violently*, with עַל.

נְפַל Ch.—I. *fall, fell down*.—II. *prostrated*.—III. *was thrown down*.—IV. *descended*, Dan. 7:20.—V. *fell* (became needful) to one, Ezr. 7:20.

נֵפֶל, נֶפֶל m., *abortion*.

נְפִילִים m. pl., a tribe of the first inhabitants of Canaan, who were of gigantic stature.

נִפְלְאַתָה Niph. pret. f. with ה parag., from פלא.

נִפְלָל Eze. 28:23, probably an error for נָפַל.

מַפָּל m.—I. *that which falls out of the ear, the worst*, of the corn, Am. 8:6.—II. *pendulous, flaccid parts* (of the flesh), Job 41:15.

מַפֵּלָה, מַפָּלָה f., *ruins* of an edifice, Jeremiah only.

מַפֶּלֶת f.—I. *fall, ruin*.—II. that which falls, *leaf*, Eze. 31:13.—III. *carcase*, Jud. 14:8.

נָפַץ same as פּוּץ.—I. *broke, dashed down*.—II. *dispersed*, Isa. 11:12.—III. *dispersed itself*. Pi. same as Kal I., II. Pu. *was broken down*, Isa. 27:9.

נֶפֶץ m., *breaking forth, bursting*.

מַפֵּץ m., "battle axe," Eng. Ver., Jer. 51:20.

מַפָּץ m., *bruising*, Eze. 9:2.

נְפַק Ch., *came forth*. Aph. *brought out*.

נִפְקָא Ch. f., *outgoings, expence*, Ezr. 6:4,8.

נָפַשׁ. Niph. I. *had breathing time, rest*, Ex. 23:12.—II. *rested*.

נֶפֶשׁ f., seldom m. (with suff. נַפְשִׁי; pl. נְפָשׁוֹת; const. נַפְשׁוֹת; נְפָשִׁים).

—I. *breath.*—II. *an animal* (that which breathes).—III. *a person;* שִׁבְעִים נֶפֶשׁ *seventy souls,* i. e. persons; כָּל נֶפֶשׁ *every one, whosoever.*—IV. *self;* נַפְשִׁי *myself;* נַפְשְׁךָ *thyself.*—V. נֶפֶשׁ מֵת *dead body, carcase;* טָמֵא לָנֶפֶשׁ, טְמֵא נֶפֶשׁ *polluted by a dead body.* —VI. *livelihood,* Deu. 24:6.—VII. *the feelings, desire, inclination.*

נֹפֶת, נָפֶרֶת; see נוּף.

נַפְתּוּלִים; see פתל.

נַפְתֻּחִים p.n. of a people.

נַפְתָּלִי (*my wrestlings,* Gen. 30:8), p.n., *Naphtali,* the son of Jacob and Bilhah.

נֵץ *hawk;* see נצץ.

נָצָא, נָצָה *flew away,* Jer. 48:9; Lam. 4:15.

נָצַב. Niph. נִצַּב I. *stood.*—II. *was placed, appointed,* with עַל; part. נִצָּב *one set over, officer.* Hiph. הִצִּיב I. *placed.*—II. *set up.*—III. *fixed, appointed.*—IV. *set a trap,* Jer. 5:26.—V. *uphold,* Ps. 41:13. Hoph. הֻצַּב *set up,* Gen. 28:12.

נְצִיב m.—I. *pillar,* Gen. 19:26.—II. *garrison.*—III. *chief commander,* 1 Ki. 4:19.—IV. p. n., a town in the tribe of Judah.

נִצָּב m. (part. Niph.), *handle of a knife,* Jud. 3:22.

נִצְבָּא f. Ch., *firmness, strength,* Dan. 2:41.

מַצָּב, const. מַצַּב m.—I. *standing place.*—II. *station, dignity,* Isa. 22:19.—III. *station, column of soldiers.*

מֻצָּב m. (part. Hoph.), the same.

מִצָּבָה, מַצָּבָה f., the same.

מַצֵּבָה, const. מַצְּבַת f.—I. *pillar set up as a memorial.*—II. *image, statue of an idol.*

מַצֶּבֶת f.—I. *pillar.*—II. *monument.*—III. *stem, root,* Isa. 6:13.

נָצַג. Hiph. הִצִּיג *set up, make stand up.* Hoph. הֻצַּג *was stayed,* Ex. 10:24.

נָצָה. Kal *was laid waste;* fut. תִּצֶּינָה, Jer. 4.7. Niph. נִצָּה I. *excited to quarrel.*—II. *was stripped;* (part. pl. נִצִּים). Hiphil הִצָּה *was desolate;* see also נָצָא.

נֹצָה, f. affix נֹצָתָהּ *contents of a bird's crop, entrails,* Lev. 1:16.

נוֹצָה *a feather,* Eze. 17:3.

מַצָּה f., *quarrel, strife,* Pro. 13:10; 17:19; see also in מצץ.

מַצּוּת f., the same, Isa. 41:12.

נִצָּה *blossom;* see נצץ.

נָצַח Kal not used; (Arab. *was innocent*). Pi. נִצַּח *superintend, preside over;* part. מְנַצֵּחַ I. *leader, chief.*—II. *choragus, leader of music.*

נְצַח Ch. Ith. *superior,* with עַל.

נֵצַח, נֶצַח m.—I. a title of God; נ׳ יִשְׂרָאֵל *strength of Israel,* 1 Sa. 15:29.—II. *perpetuity.*—III. *success;* לְנֵצַח לָנֶצַח and נֶצַח I. *according to truth.*—II. *entirely, wholly;* נֶצַח, לָנֶצַח *continually, for ever.*

נֵצַח m., *juice of grapes,* Isa. 63:3, 6; (Arab. *sprinkled*).

נִצַּח (part. Niph.) f. נִצַּחַת *was perfected, finished.*

נִצְטַדָּק Hith. fut. pl. 1. pers., from צדק.

נְצִיב; see נצב.

נָצַל. Pi. נִצֵּל I. *delivered*, Eze. 14:14. —II. *plundered.*—III. *gained spoil*, 2 Chron. 20:25. Hiph. הִצִּיל I. *delivered, rescued.*—II. *took away*, with מִן.—III. *parted*, with בֵּין.—IV. *deliver himself.* Hoph. part. מֻצָּל *rescued.* Niph. נִצַּל I. *was delivered, escaped.*—II. *ran away to*, with אֶל. Hith. *strip themselves*, Ex. 33:6.

נְצַל Ch. Aph. *rescued.*

הַצָּלָה (verb Hiph.) f., *deliverance*, Est. 4:14.

נָצַץ I. *glittering*, Eze. 1:7.—II. *fled.*

נֵץ m. (with suff. נִצָּהּ).—I. *flower*, Gen. 40:10.—II. *hawk.*

נִצָּה f., *blossom.*

נִצָּן m., pl. נִצָּנִים *flowers*, Cant 2:12.

נָצַר (fut. יִנְצֹר, יִצֹּר; inf. abs. נָצוֹר; const. נְצֹר; imp. נְצֹר; with ה parag. נִצְּרָה; with suff. נִצְּרָהּ.—I. *guarded.*—II. *preserved from evil.*—III. *watched.*—IV. *besieged, shut up.*—V. *observed*; נֹצְרִים *keepers.*

נֵצֶר m., *shoot, branch*; (Arab. *shone*).

נָצִיר m., pl. const. נְצִירֵי (נְצוּרֵי) *preserved, liberated.*

נִצְּרָה Kal imp. with ה parag. and dag. euphon., from נצר.

נְקֵא *white*; see נקה.

נָקַב (fut. יִנְקֹב, יִקֹּב).—I. *pierced.*—II. *bored through.*—III. *bored a hole.*—IV. *broke the head with a staff*, Hab. 3:14.—V. *marked.*—VI. *named.*—VII. *pronounced unfortunate.*—VIII. *cursed.* Niph. *were marked by name.*

נֶקֶב m.—I. *holes bored in precious stones*, Eze. 28:13.—II. הַנֶּקֶב p. n., a city in the tribe of Naphtali.

נְקֵבָה f., *female.*

מַקָּבָה f., *hammer*

מַקֶּבֶת f.—I. *hammer.*—II. *hole, shaft of a well*, Isa. 51:1.

נָקַד root not used; (Ch. נְקַד *mark with spots*).

נָקֹד m. (pl. נְקֻדִּים; f. נְקֻדָּה) *spotted sheep or goats*, Gen. 30:32, 33.

נְקֻדָּה f., *studs of silver*, Cant. 1:11.

נֹקֵד m., *shepherd*, 2 Ki. 3:4; Am. 1:1.

נִקֻּדִים m. pl.—I. *bread*, Jos. 9:5, 12—II. *cakes* (probably pricked like Passover cakes), 1 Ki. 14:3.

נְקוֹדָא p. n. of a man.

נָקָה inf. נָקֹה *was pure*, Jer. 49:12. Niph. נִקָּה.—I. *was innocent, clear.*—II. *was made innocent, cleared*, with מִן.—III. *was swept away, devastated.* Pi. נִקָּה I. *cleansed.*—II. *treated as innocent, freed from punishment*, with מִן.

נְקֵא Ch., Pe. part. נְקֵא *pure, white*, Dan. 7:9.

נָקִי m. (pl. נְקִיִּים).—I. *innocent.*—II. *clear from guilt, an oath, &c.*, with מִן.—III. *exempt*, 1 Ki. 15:22.

נָקִיא the same, Joel 4:19; Jonah 1:14.

נִקָּיוֹן m.—I. *innocency.*—II. *cleanness of teeth*, i. e. hunger, Am. 4:6.

מְנַקִּית f., pl. מְנַקִּיּוֹת *bowls for drink-offerings.*

נָקַט same as קוּט *loathe*, Job 10:1.

נָקַל Niph. pret., from קלל.

נָקַם (fut. יִקֹּם).—I. *avenged, took re-*

venge on, with מִיַּד, מֵאֵת, מִן, עַל, לְ.—II. *punished.*—Niph. נִקַּם I. *revenged himself on.*—II. *was punished,* with מִן, בְּ. Pi. נִקֵּם I. *revenged,* with מִן and בְּ. Hoph. fut. יֻקַּם *shall be avenged.* Hith. I. *revenged himself.* — II. part. מִתְנַקֵּם *desired vengeance.*

נָקָם m., נְקָמָה f. (with suff. נִקְמָתִי; pl. נְקָמוֹת).—I. *vengeance taken* or *inflicted;* עָשָׂה, לָקַח, הֵשִׁיב נ׳ *took vengeance;* נָתַן נְקָמוֹת *let vengeance come upon any one.*—II. *punishment.*—III. *thirst for revenge,* Lam. 3:60.

נָקַע (fut. יֵקַע; see יָקַע) *fell away, was estranged from,* Eze. 23:18, 22, 28.

נָקַף; חַגִּים יִנְקֹפוּ "let them kill sacrifices," Eng. Ver., Isa. 29:1. Pi. נִקֵּף I. *cut down,* Isa. 10:34.—II. *pierced,* Job 19:26. Hiph. הִקִּיף I. *fixed, placed around,* with עַל.—II. *surrounded.* — III. *went round a place,* Isa. 15:8.—IV. *came round* (of time), Job 1:5.— V. *shaved the head in a circle,* Lev. 19:27; inf. הַקֵּף, הַקִּיף.

נֹקֶף m., *shaking* of an olive tree to make the fruit fall, Isa. 17:6; 24:13.

נִקְפָּה f., "a rent" (in a garment), Eng. Ver., Isa. 3:24.

נָקַק same as נָקַב.

נָקִיק m., *fissure in a rock.*

נָקַר (fut. יִקֹּר) and Pi. נִקֵּר.—I. *pierced through.*—II. *pecked out* (as a bird). —III. *put out an eye.* Pu. *dug out,* Isa. 51:1.

נִקְרָה f., *cleft* (of a rock).

נָקַשׁ *snared* (as a fowler). Niph. *is ensnared,* Deu. 12:30. Pi. *spread a snare for,* with לְ. Hith. the same, with בְּ.

נְקַשׁ Ch., *struck each other* (of knees), Dan. 5:6.

נֵר, נִר, נֵרָיָה; see נוּר.

נֵרְגַל m., name of an idol, 2 Ki. 17:30.

נֵרְגַל שַׁרְאֶצֶר p. n. of an Assyrian prince, Jer. 39:3, 13.

נִרְגָּן m., *babbler, calumniator.*

נֵרְדְּ m. (with suff. נִרְדִּי; pl. נְרָדִים), *spikenard,* Cant. 1:12; 4:13, 14.

נָשָׂא (fut. יִשָּׂא, יִשְׂאוּ, יִשָּׂאוּ; inf. abs. נָשׂוֹא; const. שְׂאֵת, שֵׂאת, נְשֹׂא, שׂוֹא; imp. שָׂא, נְסָא, נְשָׂא).—I. *lifted up:* (a) *his hand;* (b) with בְּ *against;* (c) *beckoned;* (d) *lifted up his voice;* (e) *lifted up his feet;* (f) *lifted up his face, looked towards,* with אֶל; (g) *lifted up his eyes;* (h) *lifted up his soul* (set his heart on, paid regard, with נֶפֶשׁ), (i) *raised the head, elevated,* with רֹאשׁ; (k) *took the sum of, examined the case of,* with רֹאשׁ.—II. *took, took up:* (a) *took into hand;* (b) *took into the mouth;* (c) *uttered, offered a prayer;* (d) *received a precept;* (e) *took away, took hold of, obtained.*—III. נ׳ פָּנִים *accepted the person, acted with partiality.* —IV. (a) נ׳ עָוֹן *took away iniquity;* (b) *forgave* (without עָוֹן, with לְ of the person).—V. (a) *carried, brought;* (b) *carried away;* (c) *endured;* (d) *bore punishment;* (e) *supported dignity;* (f) *assisted;*

(g) *bore fruit, &c.*; (h) *supported,* with בְּ; (i) *laid upon,* with עַל; (k) *imposed an oath upon,* 1 Ki. 8:31; (l) *removed itself* (of the earth), Nah. 1:5. Niph. נִשָּׂא I. *was lifted up;* part. נִשָּׂא *lifted up.*—II. *raised himself.*—III. *was carried.*—IV. *was carried away.* Pi. נִשֵּׂא, נִשָּׂא I. *took away.*—II. *presented a gift.*—III. *carried.*—IV. *assisted.*—V. *raised in rank,* Est. 3:1.—VI. נ׳ נֶפֶשׁ *set his heart.* Hiph. הִשִּׂיא I. *caused to bear.*—II. *brought,* 2 Sa. 17:13. Hith. הִתְנַשֵּׂא, הִנַּשֵּׂא I. *arose.*—II. *exalted himself.*—III. *was exalted.*

נְשָׂא Ch.—I. *carried away,* Dan. 2:35.—II. *took,* Ezr. 5:15. Ithpa. *exalted himself,* Ezr. 4:19.

נָשִׂיא m.—I. *chief.*—II. *chief of a tribe* among the Israelites.—III. *chief of a subdivision of a tribe.*—IV. *prince.*—V. pl. נְשִׂיאִים *vapours.*

נְשׂוּאָה f., *burden,* Isa. 46:1.

נִשֵּׂאת (Niph. part.) *a gift,* 2 Sa. 19:43.

שִׂיא m., *elevation, dignity,* Job 20:6.

שְׂאֵת inf.—I. *lifting up, elevation,* Gen. 4:7.—II. *swelling in the skin.*—III. *exaltation, dignity.*—IV. *judgment, sentence,* Hab. 1:7.

שֵׂת same as שְׂאֵת *rising,* Job 41:17.

מַשֹּׂא m., מַשֹּׂא פָּנִים *preference of persons,* 2 Chron. 19:7.

מַשָּׂא m.—I. *carrying.*—II. *a burden.*—III. *a load.*—IV. *that which is burdensome.*—V. *a tribute.*—VI. *calamity.*—VII. *lifting up the voice to sing.*—VIII. *solemn declaration.*—IX. *prophecy.*

מַשָּׂאָה f., *rising of flame, burning.* Isa. 30:27.

מַשְׂאֵת f. (const. מַשְׂאַת; pl. מַשְׂאֹת).—I. *the act of lifting up.*—II. *a signal.*—III. *prophecy.*—IV. *gift.*—V. *tribute.*

I. נָשַׂג. Hiph. הִשִּׂיג I. *reached.*—II. *was able to reach.*—III. *attained, obtained, overtook.*—IV. *befel.*

II. נָשַׂג same as סוּג. Hiph. הִשִּׂיג *removed* (land marks), Job 24:2.

נָשַׂק. Hiph. הִשִּׂיק *kindled a fire.* Niph. *was kindled.*

נָשַׂר root not used; (Arab. *saw*).

מַשּׂוֹר m., *a saw,* Isa. 10:15.

I. נָשָׁא. Hiph. הִשִּׁיא I. *caused to err, led astray.*—II. *deceived,* with אֶת, לְ, בְּ.—III. *laid a burden on,* with בְּ. Niph. *was deceived.*

מַשָּׁאוֹן m., *deceit,* Pro. 26:26.

II. נָשָׁא same as נָשָׁה which see.

נָשַׁב *blew,* Isa. 40:7. Hiph. הִשִּׁיב I. *caused to blow.*—II. *dispersed,* as dust.

I. נָשָׁה I. *forgot.*—II. *neglected,* Jer. 23:39. Niph. the same, Isa. 44:21. Pi. *cause to forget.* Gen. 41:51. Hiph. הִשָּׁה *cause to forget,* Job 11:6; 39:17.

II. נָשָׁה, נָשָׁא *lent money,* Jer. 15:10, with בְּ; נֹשֶׁא, נֹשֶׁה *creditor;* נֹשֶׁה *money lender.* Hiph. the same, with בְּ; fut. יַשִּׁיא.

נָשֶׁה m., *the ischiatic nerve,* Gen. 32:33; (Arab. the same).

נְשִׁי m., *a debt*, 2 Ki. 4:7.
נְשִׁיָּה f., *forgetfulness*, Ps. 88:13.
מַשֶּׁה m., *debt*, Deu. 15:2.
מַשָּׁא m., *interest*, Neh. 5:7.
מַשָּׁאָה const. מַשְּׁאַת f., *debt*.
נָשׂוּא, נָשֻׂא for נָשְׂאוּ, from נשׂא.
נְשׂוּי, Ps. 32:1. for נָשׂוּא Kal part. pass., from נשׂא.

נָשִׁים *woman;* see אִשָּׁה in אנשׁ.
נַשִּׁים for נָשִׁים or נְשִׁמֵּם Hiph. fut. pl. 1. pers., from שׁמם.

נָשַׁךְ (fut. יִשֹּׁךְ, יִשַּׁךְ) I. *bit.*—II. *annoyed.*—III. *was lent on interest*, Deu. 23:20. Pi. *bit* (of a serpent). Hiph. *lent on interest*, with לְ, Deu. 23:20, 21.
נֶשֶׁךְ m., *interest.*

נִשְׁכָּה f., (pl. נְשָׁכוֹת for לִשְׁכָּה) *chamber of the temple* (book of Nehemiah only).

נָשַׁל (fut. יִשַּׁל; imp. שַׁל־).—I. *fell off.* —II. *pulled off a shoe.*—III. *drove out.* Pi. *drove out*, 2 Ki. 16:6.

נָשַׁם *snort;* fut. אֶשֹּׁם, Isa. 42:14; see שָׁמַם.
נְשָׁמָה f.—I. *breath.*—II. *life.*—III. *a human being.*—IV. *breath of God:* (a) *his anger;* (b) *the life he gives.* —V. *the wind.*
נִשְׁמָא f. Ch., *breath, life*, Dan. 5:23.
תִּנְשֶׁמֶת f.—I. *an unclean bird* (species uncertain), Lev. 11:18; Deu. 14:16.—II. *an unclean beast*, Lev. 11:30. (species unknown).

נָשַׁף I. *blew.*—II. *blew on*, with בְּ.
נֶשֶׁף m. (with suff. נִשְׁפּוֹ).—I. *dawn.* —II. *evening, twilight.*—III. *darkness.*

יַנְשׁוֹף, יַנְשׁוּף m., *bittern;* LXX. ἶβις.

נָשַׁק (fut. יִשַּׁק ,יִשַּׁק; imp. שַׁק, שְׁקָה). —I. *kissed;* with לְ and אֶל *kissed each other.*—II. *adored*, with לְ.— III. *rule, order*, Gen. 41:40.—IV. *draw up in battle array*, with עַל. Pi. *kissed.* Hiph. *joined, touched*, Eze. 3:13.
נֵשֶׁק, נֶשֶׁק m.—I. *battle*, Ps. 140:8. —II. *battle array*, Job 39:21.—III. *arms.*—IV. *an armoury*
נְשִׁיקָה f., *kiss.*

נָשַׁר (Arab. *eagle*).
נֶשֶׁר m., *an eagle.*
נְשַׁר m. Ch., *an eagle.*

נָשַׁת I. *was parched*, Isa. 41:17.—II. *wasted away*, Jer. 51:30. Niph. *dried up*, Isa. 19:5.
נִשְׁתָּוָה Nith., from שׁוה.

נִשְׁתְּוָן m., *a letter.* Ch. the same (book of Ezra only).

נָתַב (Arab. *was lofty, raised up*).
נָתִיב m., נְתִיבָה f.—I. *path.*—II. *drift of a vein of metal*, Job 28:7. —III. *course of life.*

נָתַח. Pi. נִתַּח *divided, cut in pieces* (a slaughtered animal).
נֵתַח m., *joint, piece of flesh;* pl נְתָחִים.

נָתַךְ (fut. יִתַּךְ) *poured out.* Niph. I. *was poured out.*—II. *was melted.* Hiph. הִתִּיךְ I. *poured out.* — II. *melted.* Hoph. הֻתַּךְ *be melted*, Eze. 22:22.
הִתּוּךְ (verb Hiph.) m., *melting* (metal), Eze. 22:22.

נָתַן (fut. יִתֵּן, יִתֶּן־; pl. יִתְּנוּ; inf. abs. נָתוֹן; const. נְתֹן, תֵּת; with suff. תִּתִּי; imp. תֵּן, תְּנָה).—I. *gave* (as a present, in marriage, &c.).—II. *gave forth* (produced fruit, emitted odour, &c.).—III. *ascribed.*—IV. *sold.*—V. *offered,* Lev. 20:2, 3, with אֵת.—VI. *placed,* with אֶל, בְּ, לְ, עַל.—VII. *appointed.*—VIII. *imposed tribute,* with עַל.—IX. *inflicted.*—X. *wrought miracles.*—XI. *rendered like, considered as,* with כְּ—XII. *made, rendered,* with לְ. מִי יִתֵּן; see מִי. Niph. נִתַּן pass. of Kal.—Hoph. fut. יֻתַּן *shall be given, &c.*

נְתַן Ch., *gave.*

נָתָן p. n.—I. *Nathan,* the prophet.—II. the name also of a son of David and of other men.

נְתַנְאֵל (*gift of God*), p. n. of a man, Ναθαναήλ.

נְתַנְיָה, נְתַנְיָהוּ (*gift of the Lord*), p. n. of a man.

נְתַן־מֶלֶךְ p. n. of king Josiah's chamberlain, 2 Ki. 23:11.

נְתִינִים m. pl., (*devoted*), *Nethinim,* servants of the Temple, waiting upon the Levites; Ch. נְתִינִין.

מַתָּן m. — I. *gift.*— II. p. n. of a man.

מַתָּנָה f.—I. the same.—II. p.n. of a place between Moab and the desert.

מַתְּנָא f. Ch., the same.

מַתְּנַי (for מַתַּנְיָה), p. n. of a man.

מַתַּנְיָה, מַתַּנְיָהוּ p.n. of a man.

מַתַּת f., *a gift.*

מַתִּתְיָה, מַתִּתְיָהוּ p. n. of a man, Ματθαθίας.

מַתַּתָּה p. n. of a man.

נָתַם *break down, cut off,* Job 30:13.

נָתַע. Niph. *broken down, cut off,* Job 4:10, for נָתַץ.

נָתַץ (fut. יִתֹּץ).—I. *broke down, destroyed.*—II. *ruined a person.*—III. *struck out teeth,* Ps. 58:7. Pi. נִתֵּץ *destroyed.* Niph. נִתַּץ, Pu. נֻתַּץ and Hoph. הֻתַּץ *was destroyed.*

נָתַק I. *drew one away from* (a place), Jud. 20:32.—II. *drew off* (a ring), Jer. 22:24.—III. part. נָתוּק *castrated,* Lev. 22:24. Niph. נִתַּק I. *drawn away.*—II. *purged away,* Jer. 6:29.—III. *broken* (of a shoe-string, cord). Pi. נִתֵּק I. *removed took off,* Isa. 58:6.-II. *pulled up, uprooted.* — III. *broke* a cord.—IV. *broke off, frustrated,* Job 17:11, &c. Hiph. הִתִּיק *drew away.* Hoph. הָנְתַּק pass. of Hiph., Jud. 20:31.

נֶתֶק m., *scalled head*; lit. plucking off of hair, Lev. 13:30 — 37; 14:54.

נְתַקְּנוּהוּ Jud. 20:32, Kal pl. 1. pers. with suff. and dag. euphon., from נתק.

נָתַר (fut. יִתַּר), *beat violently* (the heart), Job 37:1. Pi. *leap* (as locusts), Lev. 11:21. Hiph. הִתִּיר I. *loosened,* Ps. 105:20, &c.—II. *stretched out the hand,* Job 6:9.—III. *straightened,* 2 Sa. 22:33.—IV. *made vibrate, caused to tremble,* Hab. 3:6.

נְתַר Ch., *fell off.* Aph. *shake off,* Dan. 4:11.

נֶתֶר m.—I. *nitre, natron,* Pro. 25:20.—II. *soap made of natron and oil,* Jer. 2:22.

נָתַשׁ (fut. יִתּשׁ), with אֶת.—I. *expelled.*—II. *destroyed.* Niph. I. *was expelled, destroyed.*—II. *failed* (of waters). Hoph. הֻתַּשׁ *plucked up* (of trees), Eze. 19:12.

נָתַתִּי, נָתַתְּ, נָתַתָּה, נָתַתָּ Kal pret., from נתן.

ס

סְאָה f., *a dry measure,* containing one third of an ephah, σάτον; dual סָאתַיִם; pl. סְאִים.

סַאסְּאָה f., the same, Isa. 27:8.

סָאַן, part. סֹאֵן *having greaves,* Isa. 9:4.

סְאוֹן m., *greaves* (armour for the legs), Isa. 9:4.

סָבָא *drank wine, became drunk*; part. סוֹבֵא *drinker* (pl. סוֹבְאִים Ketib, סָבָאִים Kri, Eze. 23:42).

סֹבֶא m. (with suff. סָבְאֵךְ).—I. *wine.* —II. *the act of drinking wine,* Nah. 1:10.

סְבָא p. n.—I. the son of Cush, Gen. 10:7.—II. the people descended from him; סְבָאִים *the Sabeans.*

סָבַב (pret. סַבּוּ, סָבְבוּ, סַבֹּתִי; fut. יָסֹב, יִסֹּב; pl. יָסֹבּוּ; inf. סְבֹב, סֹב; imp. סֹב; part. סוֹבֵב, סֹבֵיב). —I. *turned about.*—II. *made a circuit,* with אֶת, בְּ.—III. *reached round.*—IV. *surrounded,* with אֶת, עַל.—V. *ended a circuit at,* with אֶל or לְ.—VI. an act overtaken in its consequences, with אֶת.—VII. *circumvented, entrapped.* — VIII. *went round, examined in succession,* Ecc. 7:25.—IX. *arrived at a conclusion* (after going round), Ecc. 2:20. Niph. נָסַב (fut. יִסֹּב; pl. יִסַּבּוּ). — I. *turn about, make a circle, surround.*—II. *returned.*—III. *came round in turn.*—IV. *was changed, changed, changed his conduct.* Pi. סִבֵּב *brought to pass,* 2 Sa. 14:20. Poel סוֹבֵב I. *made a circuit,* with עַל.—II. *surrounded, with* עַל. Hiph. הֵסֵב (fut. יַסֵּב, יַסֵּבּוּ).—I. *caused to turn about, make a circuit, surround.* — II. *changed his name to.* Hoph. הוּסַב *was turned round, enclosed.*

סָבִיב m.—I. *a circuit*; adv. מִסָּבִיב, סָבִיב סָבִיב *around, from around*; סָבִיב לְ *around.*—II. pl. סְבִיבִים, סְבִיבוֹת *surrounding places, suburbs,* Jer. 17:26; 33:13; with suff. סְבִיבוֹתַי *around me.*

סֹבֵיב for סֹבֵב Kal part., from סבב.

סִבָּה f., *change, turn in affairs,* 1 Ki 12:15.

נְסִבָּה f., the same, 2 Chron. 10:15.

מוּסָב m., *the wall that surrounds a house,* Eze. 41:7.

מֵסַב m. (pl. const. מְסִבֵּי, מְסִבּוֹת). I. *sofas for reclining on* (ranged round), Cant. 1:12.—II. *places surrounding.* — III. adv. *round about,* 1 Ki. 6:29.

סָבַךְ *wrapped, folded, coiled, entangled,* Pu. סֻבַּךְ.

סְבָךְ m., *thicket, tangled place.*

סְבֶךְ m., pl. const. סִבְכֵי; the same.

סֹבֶךְ m., the same; with suff. סֻבְּכוֹ.

סֻבְּכוֹ with dag. euphon. for סֻבְכוֹ, from סֹבֶךְ.

סִבְּכַי p. n., *Sibbechai,* one of David's generals, 2 Sa. 21:18, &c.

שַׂבְּכָא, סַבְּכָא f. Ch., a certain musical instrument, σαμβύκη, of what kind is unknown, Dan. 3:5, 7,10.

סָבַל I. *carried* (a load), Isa. 46:4.—II. *carried* (as a child).—III. *bore consequences of.* Pu. *laden,* Ps. 144:14. Hith. הִסְתַּבֵּל *become a burden.*

סְבַל Ch., the same. Po. *brought,* Ezr. 6:3.

סֵבֶל m., *burden, task.*

סַבָּל m., *porter.*

סֹבֶל m. (with suff. סֻבֳּלוֹ), *burden,* Isaiah only.

סֻבֳּלוֹ; see above.

סִבְלָה f., pl. const. סִבְלוֹת *burdens, labours, tasks,* Exodus only.

סִבֹּלֶת f. (in the dialect of the tribe of Ephraim, for שִׁבֹּלֶת), *ear of corn,* Jud. 12:6.

סְבַר Ch., *hope, propose,* Dan. 7:25.

סִבְרַיִם p.n., a city between Damascus and Hamath.

סַבְתָּא, סַבְתָּה p. n., *Sabtah,* one of the sons of Cush, Gen. 10:7, and the people descended from him.

סַבְתְּכָא, סַבְתְּכָה p. n., *Sabtechah,* one of the sons of Cush, Gen. 10:7.

סִגִּים same as סִינִים; see סוּג.

סָגַד *worshipped,* with לְ.

סְגִד Ch., the same

סָגַל root not used; כְּנַל *bought, acquired.*

סְגֻלָּה f.—I. *collection of valuables.*—II. *an object of special regard.*

סָגָן m., pl. סְגָנִים.—I. *chiefs* among the Babylonians and Persians.—II. *chiefs* among the Jews after the second captivity.

סְגַן m. Ch., pl. סִגְנִין the same.

סָגַר (fut. יִסְגֹּר).—I. *shut a door, shut in.*—II. *closed a breach,* 1 Ki. 11:27, with בְּעַד, עַל; part. סָגוּר *shut up;* זָהָב סָגוּר *pure gold,* lit. such gold as is shut, hoarded up. Niph. נִסְגַּר *was shut.* Pi. סִגַּר, with בְּיַד *delivered up, surrendered.* Pu. סֻגַּר *was shut up.* Hiph. הִסְגִּיר I. *shut up,* with לְ, אֶל, בְּיַד.—II. *delivered up;* part. מַסְגִּיר.

סְגַר Ch., *shut.* Dan. 6:23.

סְגוֹר m.—I. *enclosure,* Hos. 13:8.—II. *refined gold,* Job 28:15.

סוּגַר m., *prison,* Eze. 19:9.

סַגְרִיר m., *rain,* Pro. 27:15.

מַסְגֵּר (part. Hiph.) m.—I. *confinement, prison.*—II. *joiner,* i.e. closer.

מִסְגֶּרֶת f. (pl. מִסְגְּרוֹת).—I. *inclosure.*—II. *border, moulding.*

סָדַד root not used; (Arab. *shut up*).

סַד m., *fetters.*

סְדֹם p.n., *Sodom,* one of the cities of the plain, Σόδομα.

סָדַן root not used; (Arab. *wool, covering*).

סָדִין m.—I. *fine cloth* of Syrian manufacture.—II. a dress made of it, Isa. 3:23.—III. a piece of it used as a sheet, Jud. 14:12, 13.

סָדַר root not used; (Syr. *set in order*).

סֵדֶר m., pl. סְדָרִים *ranks, orderly arrangement,* Job 10:22.

שְׂדֵרָה f., pl. שְׂדֵרוֹת the same.

מִסְדְּרוֹן m., *portico,* Jud. 3:23.

סָהַר root not used (Samar. סהר), *encompassed about, was round.*

סַהַר m., *roundness* (like the full moon), Cant. 7:3.

סֹהַר m., בֵּית הַסֹּהַר *prison*, Gen. 39 & 40, only.

שַׂהֲרֹנִים m. pl., *small moons* (ornaments).

סוֹא p. n., *Serechus* king of Egypt, 2 Ki. 17:4.

I. סוּג *slid back from God.* Niph. נָסוֹג (fut. יִסּוֹג).—I. *driven back.*—II. *induced to go back.*

II. סוּג *fenced*, Cant. 7:3.

סִיג, סוּג m. (pl. סִגִּים, סִינִים), *dross* (of metals).

סוֹד, סוֹדִי; see יסד.

סוּחַ root not used; same as סחה *cleanse.*

סוּחַ p. n. of a man.

סוּחָה f., *filth*, Isa. 5:25.

סוֹטַי (see שׂוּט) p. n. of a man.

סוּךְ same as נָסַךְ.—I. *anoint himself.*—II. *anoint another*, with בְּ. Hiph. *anointed himself*; fut. וַיָּסֶךְ.

אָסוּךְ m., *vessel for anointing oil*, 2 Ki. 4:2.

סוּמְפֹּנְיָה f. Ch., συμφωνία, a musical instrument, *the hautboy*, Ital. *zampogna*, Dan. 3:5, 15.

סְוֵנֵה p. n., *Syene*, a city of Egypt; (hierog. Soun).

סוּס m.—I. *a horse.*—II. *a swallow*, Isa. 38:14; Jer. 8:7.

סוּסָה f., *horses*, Cant. 1:9.

סוּסִי p. n. of a man.

סוּף *come to an end, perish.* Hiph. *cause to perish.*

סוּף Ch., *came to an end, was completed.* Aph. *destroyed.*

סוֹף m.—I. *end, termination, completion, result.*—II. *rear of an army*, Joel 2:20.

סוֹף m. Ch., the same.

סוּפָה f., *whirlwind, tornado*, with ה parag. סוּפָתָה.

סוּף m.—I. *sea weed;* יַם־סוּף *the Red Sea.*—II. p. n. of a man.

סוּר (fut. וַיָּסַר, יָסוּר).—I. *went, turned aside*, with מֵאַחֲרֵי, מֵעַל, מִן, אֶל.—II. *went away*, with מִן.—III. *was removed.*—IV. *ceased.*—V. *rebelled against*, with בְּ. Pil. סוֹרֵר *turned away*, Lam. 3:11. Hiph. הֵסִיר (fut. וַיָּסַר יָסִיר).—I. *removed*, Lev. 1:16.—II. *laid aside, gave up.*—III. *drew off* (a ring).—IV. *set aside.*—V. *destroyed.* ה׳ רֹאשׁ מֵעַל פּ׳ *cut off his head;* ה׳ מֵאַחֲרֵי יְהוָֹה *estranged him from following the Lord.* Hoph. הוּסַר *was removed, taken away.*

סוּר m.—I. *degenerate branch*, Jer. 2:21.—II. p. n., one of the gates of the temple, 2 Ki. 11:6, called יְסוֹד in the parall. pass., 2 Chron. 23:5.

סִיר com.—I. *a thorn;* pl. סִירִים.—II. pl. סִירוֹת *hooks*, Am. 4:2.—III. *pot, vessel;* pl. סִירוֹת.

סָרָה f.—I. *turning from God, rebellion.*—II. ... *from the truth, falsehood*, Deu. 19:16; see סָרַר.

סִרָה p.n. of a well or tank, 2 Sa. 3:26.

סוּת. Hiph. הֵסִית הִסִּית (fut. יָסִית, וַיָּסֶת יַסִּית; part. מַסִּית) *urged, excited, induced*, with אֶת and בְּ.

סוּת, Gen. 49:11, wrong reading for כְּסוּת *covering;* see כסה.

סָחַב I. *drew along the ground*, 2 Sa. 17:13, &c.—II. *tore in pieces and devoured*, Jer. 49:20, &c.

סְחָבָה f., *tearing to pieces*; בְּלוֹיֵ הַסְּחָבוֹת "old cast clouts;" Eng. Ver., Jer. 38:11, 12.

סָחָה. Pi. סִחָה *swept away*, Eze. 26:4.

סְחִי m., *offscouring*, Lam. 3:45.

שָׁחִיס, סָחִישׁ m., *spontaneous produce*, that which comes without sowing, 2 Ki. 19:29; Isa. 37:30; LXX. αὐτόματα; Aquila αὐτοφυῆ.

סָחַף *beat down, crush*, Pro. 28:3. Niph. *beaten down*, Jer. 46:15.

סָחַר *travelled to a place*, with אֶל; *over a country*, with אֵת; part. סֹחֵר (pl. סֹחֲרִים, סֹחֲרֵי) *traveller, merchant*; f. סֹחֶרֶת. Pil. סְחַרְחַר *was agitated* (the heart), Ps. 38:11.

סָחָר m.—I. *commerce.*—II. *wealth acquired by commerce.*—III. *seat of commerce*, Isa. 23:3.

סַחַר m., the same.

סְחֹרָה f., *seat of commerce*, Eze. 27:15.

סֹחֵרָה f., *tower*, Ps. 91:4; (Syr. *tower*).

סֹחֶרֶת f., *black marble* or *tortoise-shell* (uncertain which), Est. 1:6; LXX. πάρινος λίθος.

מִסְחָר m., *traffic*, 1 Ki. 10:15.

סֵטִים *sinners*; same as שֵׂטִים; see שׂוּט.

סִיג *dross*; see סוּג.

סִיוָן m., name of the third month of the Jewish year, Est. 8:9.

סִיחוֹן p. n.—I. *Sihon*, king of the Amorites.—II. the district over which he ruled.

סִין p. n., a city of Egypt, "Pelusium," (Jerome); probably Syene; Eze. 30:15, 16; see סְוֵנֵה.

מִדְבַּר־סִין p. n., the wilderness of *Sin*.

סִינִי p. n.—I. a people of Canaan, Gen. 10:17; 1 Ch. 1:15.—II. אֶרֶץ סִינִים the land of *Sin*.

סִינַי p. n., a mountain on the promontory between Egypt and Canaan; its two summits are called *Sinai* and Horeb.

סִים Jer. 8:7, same as סוּס *a swallow*.

סִיסְרָא p. n., *Sisera*, a Canaanitish leader, and other men.

סִיעָא, סִיעֲהָא p. n. of a man.

סִיר; see סוּר.

סָכַךְ I. *covered.*—II. *protected by covering.*—III. *placed as a covering*, with עַל.—IV. *compacted, put together*, Ps. 139:13; part. סוֹכֵךְ *defence*. Hiph. הֵסֵךְ I. *covered*, with עַל.—II. *protected*, with לְ.—III. *dressed himself*, 2 Sa. 12:20.—IV. *confined*, with בְּעַד. Hoph. הֻסַּךְ *was covered*, with בְּ. Pilp. סִכְסֵךְ *armed*, Isa. 9:10; 19:2.

סָךְ m., *multitude, crowd*, Ps. 42:5.

סֹךְ m. (with suff. סֻכּוֹ, סֻכֹּה), *thicket, hiding-place, dwelling*.

סֻכָּה f.—I. *thicket*, Job 38:40.—II. *hiding-place*, Ps. 31:21.—III. *hut* (of branches or wattles).—IV. *dwelling*; pl. סֻכּוֹת I. *tabernacles*; חַג הַסֻּכּוֹת *feast of tabernacles.*—II. סֻכּוֹת בְּנוֹת, 2 Ki. 17:30, probably a proper name.—III. p. n., a station of the Israelites.— IV. a town of the Gadites.

סֻכּוֹת f., *shrine*, Am. 5:26.

סֻכִּיִּים p. n., *Sukkiims*, 2 Ch. 12:3, some part of the invading army of Shishak; meaning unknown.

סְכָכָה p. n., a town in the tribe of Judah.

מָסָךְ const. מָסַךְ m.—I. *covering* (of tabernacle).— II. (with פָּרֹכֶת) *a veil.*—III. *curtain of a fortress*, Isa. 22:8.

מְסֻכָּה f., *covering*, Eze. 28:13.

מוּסָךְ (מֵיסָךְ) m., *covering, porch*, 2 Ki. 16:18.

סָכַל. Niph. *became foolish, acted foolishly.* Pi. *made foolish.* Hiph. *acted the fool.*

סָכָל m., *a fool, foolish.*

סֶכֶל m., *folly*, Ecc. 10:6.

סִכְלוּת, שִׂכְלוּת f., *folly*, book of Eccles. only.

סָכַן, with לְ, עַל.—I. *was prosperous*, Job 34:9.—II. *was beneficial*, Job 15:3.—III. part. סֹכֵן *a companion, counsellor;* f. סֹכֶנֶת. Hiph. *was familiar with, accustomed to*, with עִם. Pu. part. מְסֻכָּן *poor, needy* (Arab. *was poor*), Isa. 40:20. Niph. נִסְכַּן *exposed himself to danger* (Ch. סְכַן *was in danger*), Ecc. 10:9.

מִסְכֵּן m., *poor.*

מִסְכֵּנֻת f., *poverty*, Deu. 8:9.

מִסְכְּנוֹת f. pl. (same as מִכְנְסוֹת; see כָּנַס), *magazines, treasuries.*

I. **סָכַר.** Niph. *was shut.* Pi. (see סָגַר), *delivered up*, Isa. 19:4.

II **סָכַר** same as שָׂכַר *hired*, Ezr. 4:5.

סָכַת. Hiph. הִסְכִּית *was silent*, Deu 27:9.

סַל, סַלִּים, סִלָּא; see סלל.

סָלָא. Pu. *valued*, Lam. 4:2.

סָלַד. Pi. *harden oneself*, Job 6:10.

סֶלֶד p. n. of a man.

סָלָה *trampled on*, Ps. 119:118. Pi the same, Lam, 1:15. Pu. *valued, estimated*, Job 28:16, 19.

סֶלָה a musical note, in the Psalms and the prayer of Habakkuk.

סָלַח (fut. יִסְלַח), *forgave.* Niph. *was forgiven.*

סַלָּח m., *one who forgives, is placable*, Ps. 86:5.

סְלִיחָה f., *forgiveness.*

סַלְכָה p. n., a town in the land of Bashan.

סָלַל *threw up an embankment, levelled, made a road.* Pilp. סַלְסֵל *exalt*, Pro. 4:8. Hithpo. הִסְתּוֹלֵל *opposing, exalting himself*, with בְּ, Ex. 9:17.

סַל m. (pl. סַלִּים) *basket.*

סִלָּא p.n. of a place.

סַלּוּ p.n. of a man.

סַלּוּא, סַלָּא p. n. of a man.

סָלוּא p. n. of a man.

סַלַּי p. n. of a man.

סִלּוֹן *a thorn*, Eze. 28:24.

סַלּוֹן m., the same; metaph. *wicked man*, Eze. 2:6.

סֹלְלָה f., *a mound.*

סֻלָּם m., *a ladder*, Gen. 28:12.

סַלְסִלּוֹת f. pl., *baskets*, Jer. 6:9.

מְסִלָּה f.—I. *raised highway.*—II. *road, path.*—III. *terraces* (Lee), "steps" (Gesenius), 2 Chron. 9:11.

מַסְלוּל m., *highway*, Isa. 35:8.

סֶלַע m.—I. *cleft in a rock, cavern.*—II. *rock.*—III. p. n. of a city, perhaps *Petra* in Edom.

סָלְעָם m., a kind of *locust*, Lev. 11:22.

סָלַף. Pi. סִלֵּף I. *perverts.*—II. *overthrows.*

סֶלֶף m., *capriciousness, perverseness.*

סְלַק Ch., *came up, grew up.*

סָלַת root not used; (Arab. *shelled grain*).

סֹלֶת com., *shelled grain, fine flour.*

סַם, סַמִּים; see סמם.

סַמְגַּר־נְבוּ p.n., a prince of Babylon.

סְמָדַר m., *flower* (of the grape).

סָמַךְ I. (with אֶת יָדָיו, עַל) *laid his hands on.*— II. *supported.* — III. *pressed, weighed upon,* with עַל, Ps. 88:8.—IV. *advanced towards,* with אֶל, Eze. 24:2. Niph. I. *leaned on.*— II. *trusted in.*— Pi. *support,* Cant. 2:5.

שְׂמִיכָה f., *coverlet,* Jud. 4:18.

סְמַכְיָהוּ p. n. of a man.

סֵמֶל, סֶמֶל m., *figure, form.*

סָמַם (Arab. *exhaled perfume*).

סַם m., pl. סַמִּים *perfumes.*

סָמַן. Niph. part. נִסְמָן "appointed" Eng. Ver. (of barley), Isa. 28:25.

סָמַר *grew hard, rigid,* Ps. 119:120. Pi. the same, Job 4:15.

סָמָר m., *rough, bristly* (of a locust), ὀρθοθριξ, Jer. 51:27.

מַסְמְרִים, מַסְמְרִים m. pl., *nails.*

מַשְׂמְרוֹת, מַסְמְרוֹת, מַסְמְרוֹת f. pl., the same.

סְנָאָה p.n., a town of Judah.

סְנוּאָה p. n., probably of a woman, Neh. 11:9.

סַנְבַלַּט p. n. of a Persian governor of Samaria.

סְנֶה m., *the bush of Sinai,* Ex. 3:2—4; Deu. 33:16.

סֶנֶּה p.n., a rock near Michmash, 1 Sa. 14:4.

סַנְוֵרִים m. pl., *blindness,* Gen. 19:11; 2 Ki. 6:18.

סַנְחֵרִיב p. n., *Sennacherib,* king of Assyria.

סַנְסִנִּים m. pl., *the plume of the palm-tree,* Cant. 7:9.

סַנְסַנָּה p. n., a city of the tribe of Judah.

סְנַפִּיר m., *fin of a fish,* Lev. 11:9; Deu. 14:9.

סָס m., *clothes-moth,* Isa. 51:8.

סִסְמַי p. n. of a man.

סָעַד (fut. יִסְעַד; imp. סְעָד, סְעֹד, סְעָד־; with ה parag. סַעֲדָה).—I. *was prosperous,* Pro. 20:28.— II. *made prosperous,* Ps. 20:3.— III. *supported.*— IV. *cheered, refreshed,* with לֵב.

סְעַד Ch., *assisting,* Ezr. 5:2.

מִסְעָד m., *prop, support,* 1 Ki. 10:12.

סָעָה; רוּחַ סֹעָה *rapid wind,* Ps. 55:9.

סָעַף Kal not used; (Arab. *palm branch*). Pi. סֵעֵף (perhaps from סְעִיף) *cut off branches,* Isa. 10:33.

סְעִיף m.— I. *cleft, cavern.*— II. *sect party,* 1 Ki. 18:21.—III. *a branch.*

סְעַפּוֹת f. pl., *branches,* Eze. 31:6, 8.

סַרְעַפּוֹת f. pl., the same, Eze. 31:5.

סֵעֵף m., pl. סֵעֲפִים *persons of divided minds*, Ps. 119:113.

שְׂעִפִּים *thoughts of the mind* (lit. *branches*).

שַׂרְעַפִּים m. pl., *thoughts*, Ps. 94:19; 139:23.

סָעַר I. *was tempestuous*, Jon. 1:11, 13, &c.—II. *tossed by calamity*, Isa. 54: 11. Niph. *was agitated* (the heart), 2 Ki. 6:11. Pi. סֵעֵר *scattered*, Zec. 7:14. Po. *scattered*, Hos. 13:3; see שָׂעַר·

סַעַר m., *pestilential, violent wind, whirlwind*.

סְעָרָה, const. סַעֲרַת f., the same.

סַף with pause סָף m. (pl. סִפִּים, סִפּוֹת). — I. *dish, bason, goblet, bowl*.—II. *threshold*.— III. p. n. of a man.

הִסְתּוֹפֵף Hith. inf., *remain at the threshold*, Ps. 84:11.

סָפָא (Arab. *filled*).

מִסְפּוֹא m., *provender, fodder*.

סָפַד *lamented, bewailed*, with עַל, לְ, לִפְנֵי· Niph. *was lamented*.

מִסְפֵּד, const. מִסְפַּד m., *lamentation*.

סָפָה I. *came to an end, perished*.—II. *brought to an end, destroyed*; inf. סְפוֹת *increase*, Nu. 32:14. Niph. נִסְפָּה *was perished*. Hiph. הִסְפָּה *heap, accumulate* (trouble), Deu. 23:23.

סִפּוּן; see ספן·

סְפוֹרָה; see ספר·

סָפַח *admitted*, 1 Sa. 2:36. Niph. *was admitted*, Isa. 14:1. Pi. *poured out*, Hab. 2:15. Pu. *scattered*. Job 30:7. Hith. הִסְתַּפֵּחַ *obtained admission*, 1 Sa. 26:19.

סָפִיחַ m.—I. *pouring out of water*. Job 14:19.— II. *spilt, self-sown, grain*; pl. סְפִיחִים·

סַפַּחַת f., *a scar, scald*, Lev. 13:2; 14:56.

מִסְפַּחַת f., *scurf, scab*, Lev. 13:6—8.

מִסְפָּחוֹת f. pl., *cushions, pillows*, Eze. 13:18, 21.

סִפַּי p. n., same as סַף·

סַפִּיר m., *a sapphire*.

סֵפֶל m., *a bowl*, Jud. 5.25; 6:38.

סָפַן I. *covered*.—II. *secured*, Deu. 33: 21.

סִפּוּן m., *ceiling*, 1 Ki. 6:15.

סְפִינָה f., *ship*, Jon. 1:5.

סָפַף, הִסְתּוֹפֵף; see סַף·

סָפַק I. *clapped the hands together*.—II. *smote upon the thigh*.—III. *expressed contempt for*.

סֵפֶק m., *abundance, sufficiency*, with suff. סִפְקוֹ, Job 20:22.

סָפַר (fut. יִסְפֹּר) *numbered, reckoned*; part. סֹפֵר (pl. סֹפְרִים) *writer, scribe*, γραμματεύς. Niph. *was numbered*. Pi. סִפֵּר I. *counted*.— II. *recounted*.—III. *talked*. Pu. סֻפַּר *was related*, &c.

סָפֵר m. Ch., *scribe*.

סְפָר m., *enumeration*, 2 Chron. 2:16.

סֵפֶר m. (with suff. סִפְרְךָ; pl. סְפָרִים, סִפְרֵי).—I. *enumeration*, Gen. 5:1. —II. *register*.—III. *book*.—IV. *letter*.—V. *writing*.

סְפַר m. Ch., *book*.

סִפְרָה f., *book*, Ps. 56:9.

סֹפֶרֶת p.n. of a man.

סְפֹרָה f., *number*, Ps. 71:15

מִסְפָּר m.—I. *number;* אַנְשֵׁי מ׳ or מְתֵי מ׳ *few men.*—II. *narrative,* Jud. 7:15.—III. p. n. of a man; מִסְפֶּרֶת the same.

סְפָר p. n. of a city, Gen. 10:30.

סְפָרַד p. n., a country into which the Jews were carried, Obad. *v.* 20.

סְפַרְוַיִם p. n., *Sepharvaim,* a city of Assyria; סְפַרְוִים *Sepharvites.*

סָקַל *stoned.* Pi.—I. as Kal.—II. *cleared of stones.* Niph. and Pu. *was stoned.*

סָרָב *rebellious,* Eze. 2:6.

סַרְבָּלִין m. pl. Ch., *drawers, trousers,* Dan. 3:21, 27.

סַרְגּוֹן p. n., *Sargon,* king of Assyria.

סֶרֶד p. n. of a man; patron. סַרְדִּי.

סָרָה, סָרָה; see סוּר, סרר.

סָרַח I. *unconfined, loose,* Ex. 26:12, 13, &c.—II. *luxuriant* (of a vine), Eze. 17:6. — III. *loose, dissolute,* Am. 6:4, 7. Niph. *scattered, vanished* (of wisdom), Jer. 49:7.

סֶרַח m., *portion of a thing left loose,* Ex. 26:12.

סִרְיוֹן *corslet,* same as שִׁרְיוֹן; see שׁרה.

סָרִיס m. (const. סְרִיס; pl. סָרִיסִים, const. סָרִיסֵי).—I. *eunuch.*—II. any *chief officer.*

סָרְכִין m. pl. Ch., *superintendants of the whole empire,* Dan. 6:3.

סְרָנִים, const. סַרְנֵי m. pl.—I. *axles,* 1 Ki. 7:30.—II. the name of the five princes of the Philistines.

סַרְעַפּוֹת *branches;* see סעף.

סָרַף same as שָׂרַף. Pi. part. מְסָרֵף *burning, he who burns,* Am. 6:10

סִרְפָּד m., the name of an unknown shrub; LXX. κόνυζα; Vulg. urtica.

סָרַר *was perverse, refractory,* Hos. 4:16; part. סֹרֵר (pl. סוֹרְרִים; f. סוֹרֶרֶת, סוֹרֵרָה) *perverse, rebellious*

סַר m., סָרָה f., *averse, disinclined, sad;* see also another סָרָה in סוּר.

סָתָה root not used; (Arab. *winter*).

סְתָו (סְתָיו) m., *winter,* Cant. 2:11.

סָתַם I. *filled, blocked up.*—II. *repaired.*—III. *shut up, concealed.* Niph. *was repaired,* Neh. 4:1. Pi. *blocked up,* Gen. 26:15, 18.

סָתַר *concealed,* Pro. 22:3. Niph. נִסְתָּר I. *concealed himself.*—II. *was concealed, unknown.*—III. *was sheltered.*—IV. *was distant.*—V. *was excluded;* part. נִסְתָּר *hidden, hidden thing;* pl. נִסְתָּרוֹת *hidden things.* Pi. *hide, shelter,* Isa. 16:3. Pu. *concealed,* Pro. 27:5. Hiph. הִסְתִּיר I. *concealed.*—II. *sheltered* —III. *placed for security,* Isa. 49:2.—IV. *turned his face from.* Hith. הִסְתַּתֵּר I. *concealed, lost.*—II. *hid himself.*

סְתַר Ch. Pa. סַתַּר *put out of sight, destroyed.*

סְתוּר p. n., a prince of Assher.

סֵתֶר m. (with suff. סִתְרִי).—I. *secresy.* —II. *secret place.*—III. בַּסֵּתֶר *secretly.*—IV. *place of concealment.*—V. *place of security.*

סִתְרָה f., *shelter, protection,* Deu. 32:38.

סִתְרִי p. n. of a man.

מִסְתָּר m.—I. *ambush.*—II. *secret place.*

מִסְתּוֹר *hiding place,* Isa. 4:6.

ע

עָב m., *epistyle, frieze* (in architecture), 1 Ki. 7:6; Eze. 41:25, 26; pl. עָבִים; see also עוּב.

עָבַד (inf. and imp. עֲבֹד; fut. יַעֲבֹד). —I. *served* (God or man).—II. *worked, laboured.*—III. *tilled the ground.*—IV. *assented to*, 1 Ki. 12:7.—V. *performed a religious service.*—VI. *made to serve*, with בְּ of the person. Niph. נֶעֱבַד I. *became, was, served*, Ecc. 5:8.—II. *was tilled.* Pu. עֻבַּד *labour was imposed upon*, with בְּ. Hiph. הֶעֱבִיד I. *caused to labour.*—II. *caused to serve.*—III. *wearied*, Isa. 43:23, 24. Hoph. הָעֳבַד *was induced to worship.*

עֲבַד Ch.—I. *made.*—II. *performed, did*, with בְּ, עִם. Ith. *was made.*

עֶבֶד m. (with suff. עַבְדּוֹ; pl. עֲבָדִים). —I. *slave, servant.*—II. *vassal.*—III. עֶבֶד יְהֹוָה *servant of the Lord*, i. e. one who worships and serves him, or executes some special commission for him.—IV. a submissive epithet.—V. p. n. of a man.

עֲבַד m. Ch., the same.

עֹבֵד p.n. of a man.

עַבְדָּא p. n. of a man.

עַבְדְּאֵל p. n. of a man.

עַבְדּוֹן p. n., a city of the Levites in the tribe of Asher.

עַבְדִּי p. n. of a man.

עַבְדִּיאֵל p. n. of a man.

עֹבַדְיָה, עֹבַדְיָהוּ (*servant of the Lord*, 'Αβδίας), p. n., *Obadiah* the prophet and others.

עֶבֶד מֶלֶךְ p.n., an Ethiopian in the service of king Zedekiah, Jer. 38:7, &c.

עֲבֵד (נְגוֹא) נְגוֹ p. n., *Abednego*, one of the three holy children, Dan. chaps. I. II. III.

עֲבָד m., *work*, Ecc. 9:1.

עֲבֹדָה f.—I. *servitude.*—II. *employment.*—III. *tillage.*—IV. *religious service, worship.*—V. *service* required by the king.—VI. לַעֲבֹדַת הָאָדָם *for the service* (use) *of man*, Ps. 104:14.

עֲבֻדָּה f., *slaves, gang of slaves*, Gen 26:14; Job 1:3.

עֲבִידָא f. Ch.—I. *work, building.*—II. *worship, service*, Ezr. 6:18.—III. *business*, Dan. 2:49; 3:12.

עַבְדוּת f., *slavery*, Ezr. 9:8, 9; Neh. 9:17.

מַעְבָּד m. (Heb. and Ch.), pl. מַעְבָּדִים *works, doings*, Job 34:25; Dan. 4:34.

עָבָה *became large, thick, heavy.*

עֲבִי m., *thickness.*

עֳבִי m., the same.

מַעֲבֶה m., *thickness*, 1 Ki. 7:46.

עָבַט *gave a pledge*; fut. יַעֲבֹט. Pi. יְעַבְּטוּן *break ranks*, Joel 2:7. Hiph. הֶעֱבִיט *lent on security*, Deu. 15:6, 8.

עֲבוֹט m., *pledge*, Deu. 24:10-13.

עַבְטִיט m., *accumulation of pledges* in the hands of an unfeeling usurer; "thick clay," Eng. Ver., Hab. 2:6.

עָבַר (inf. and imp. עֲבֹר; fut. יַעֲבֹר). —I. *passed on.*—II. *passed away, ceased.*—III. *passed* a person, place, river, &c.—IV. *passed* a limit.—V. *trespassed, transgressed*; עָבַר

בְּרִית *transgressed a covenant.*—VI. *exceeded, went beyond.*—VII. *overflowed, overwhelmed,* with עַל.—VIII. *passed through,* with עַל, לִפְנֵי, עַל פְּנֵי, מֵעַל.—IX. *passed away, disappeared.*—X. *passed through,* with בְּ.—XI. *entered into,* with בְּ; ע׳ בִּבְרִית *made a covenant.*—XII. *dropped* (as liquid).—XIII. כֶּסֶף עֹבֵר *current money,* Gen. 23:16. Niph. *can be passed,* Eze 47:5. Pi. עִבֵּר I. *conceived,* Job 21:10.—II. *caused to pass,* 1 Ki. 6:21. Hiph. הֶעֱבִיר I. *caused, allowed to pass.*—II. *removed, took,* or *put away.*—III. *removed guilt, &c.*—IV. *destroyed.*—V. *transferred.*—VI. *offered* presents to God or idols; ה׳ לַמֹּלֶךְ *caused to pass through fire to Moloch.*—VII. ה׳ שׁוֹפָר *blew a trumpet,* lit. caused the breath to pass through it. Hith. הִתְעַבֵּר *allowed himself beyond proper limits, was angry,* with עַל, בְּ, עִם.

עֲבוּר (only with pref.), בַּעֲבוּר I. prep. *because of, in return for;* with suff. בַּעֲבוּרִי *on my account;* בַּעֲבוּרֶךָ *because of thee.*—II. conj. 1. *for the purpose that* (לְבַעֲבוּר, בַּ׳ אֲשֶׁר the same).—2. *because, while.*

עָבוּר m., *produce of the ground,* Jos. 5:11, 12.

עֵבֶר m.—I. *ford.*—II. *mountain pass.*—III. *passage over.*—IV. *banks of a river.*—V. *side;* אֶל־עֵבֶר *towards, on the other side;* אֶל־עֶבְרוֹ *separately, alone;* מֵעֵבֶר *beyond, opposite to, across;* מִכָּל־עֲבָרִים *from every side;* עֵבֶר אֶחָד עֵבֶר אֶחָד *on this and on that side;* עַל־עֵבֶר אֶל־פְּנֵי *in front of it,* Ex. 25:37; עֵבֶר פָּנָיו *forwards,* Eze. 1:9, 12.—VI. p. n., *Eber,* the grandson of Shem, Gen. 10:24, 25, and progenitor of Abraham, whose descendants were called from him; עֵבֶר, בְּנֵי עֵבֶר *Hebrews;* הַר or הָרֵי הָעֲבָרִים a range of hills beyond Jordan.

עֲבַר Ch., *beyond.*

עִבְרִי m., *a Hebrew;* pl. עִבְרִים, עִבְרִיִּים; f. עִבְרִיָּה; pl. עִבְרִיּוֹת.

עֲבָרָה f., *raft, passage boat,* 2 Sa. 19:19.

עֶבְרָה f., any unrestrained feeling, specially, *anger.*

מַעֲבָר m.—I. *ford.*—II. *mountain pass.*

מַעְבָּרָה f., pl. מַעְבָּרוֹת the same.

עַבְרוֹנָה p. n., a station of the Israelites.

עָבַשׁ *became shrivelled, worthless,* Joel 1:17.

עָבַת. Pi. *confirm, establish,* Mic. 7:3.

עָבֹת m., עֲבֻתָּה f., *thick, entangled.*

עֲבוֹת m. (pl. עֲבֹתִים, עֲבֹתֹת).—I. *thick branches,* Eze. 31:3, 10, 14.—II. *cord, rope.*—III. *twisted chain.*—IV. *obligation, restraint.*

עָגַב (fut. יַעְגַּב) *loved, fell in love with,* with אֶל, עַל, Eze. *c.* 23.

עֲגָבָה f., *love;* with suff. עֲגָבָתָהּ, Eze. 23:11.

עֲגָבִים m. pl., the same, Eze. 33:31, 32.

עוּגָב, עֻגָּב m., a musical instrument, probably, *the pipe,* Gen. 4:21, &c

עֻגָּה, עֻגָה; see עוג.

עָגוּר m., *crane.*

עָגַל (Syr. *turned round*).
עָגֹל m., **עֲגֻלָּה** f., *round, circular.*
עָגִיל m. *ear-ring.*
עֵגֶל m. (with suff. **עֶגְלְךָ**).— I. *calf.*— — II. *image of one.* — III. **עֶגְלֵי עַמִּים** *princes, leaders, of the people,* Ps. 68:31.
עֶגְלָה f.—I. *she-calf, heifer.*—II. p. n., one of the wives of David.
עֲגָלָה f. (with suff. **עֶגְלָתוֹ**; pl. **עֲגָלוֹת**, **עֶגְלוֹת**).—I. *waggon drawn by two bullocks.*—II. *war chariot,* Ps. 46:10.
עֶגְלוֹן p. n.—I. a city in the tribe of Judah.—II. a king of Moab.
מַעְגָּל or **מַעְגֵּל** m. (pl. **מַעְגָּלִים**, **מַעְגָּלוֹת**).—I *wheel.*—II. *track of a wheel.*— III. *way, path.*— IV. *way, manner.*—V. *waggon.*— VI. *barricade of waggons.*
מַעְגָּלָה f., the same.
עָגַם *despise.* Job. 30:25.
עָגַן. Niph. *prevented from marrying,* Ru. 1:13.
עַד, see **עדה**; **עֹד**, **עֵד**, see **עוּד**.
עָדַד (Arab. *numbered, computed*).
עִדִּים *menstruous,* Isa. 64:5; (Arab. the same).
עִדָּן m. Ch.—I. *time.*—II. *a prophetic period of time.*
עֵדָה; see **יעד**, **עוּד**.
עָדָה (fut. **יַעְדֶּה**).—I. *passed through,* with **עַל**, Job 28:8.—II. *adorned.* — III. *put on as an ornament.* Hiph. *stripped off a garment,* Pro. 25:20.
עֲדָה, **עֲדָא** Ch.—I. *passed upon,* with **בְּ**.—II. *passed away,* with **מִן**.—III. *was altered.* Aph. *removed.*

עַד m.— I. *spoil,* Gen. 49:27; Isa 33:23; Zep. 3:8.—II. *perpetuity, eternity.* — III. *antiquity*; **לָעַד**, **עֲדֵי עַד**, **לְעוֹלָם וָעֶד**, **עוֹלָם וָעֶד** *for ever*; **עַד** (pl. **עֲדֵי**) pa. *unto, as far as, until, before, while, during, still*; **עַד־אִם** *while*; **עַד־אֲשֶׁר** (**שׁ**.) *while*; **עַד־אֲשֶׁר אִם** *until*; **עַד־לֹא**, **עַד־אֲשֶׁר לֹא** *before*; with suff. **עָדַי** *to me*; **עָדֶיךָ**; **עָדָיו**, **עָדֶיהָ**; **עֲדֵיכֶם**.
עַד Ch., *to, as far as, until*; **עַד־דִּי** *while.*
עֲדֶן, Ecc. 4:3, same as **עַד־הֵנָּה** *hitherto, as yet.*
עֲדֶנָּה Ecc. 4:2, the same.
עָדָה p. n., *Adah.*—I. the wife of Lamech.—II. the wife of Esau.
עֲדִי m. (with pause **עֶדִי**; with suff. **עֶדְיֵךְ**, **עֶדְיוֹ**; pl. **עֲדָיִים**).—I. *ornaments.*—II. *trappings of a horse.* —III. *lot, appointment,* Ps. 103:5.
עֲדִיאֵל p. n. of a man.
עֲדָיָהוּ, **עֲדָיָה** p. n. of a man.
עֲדִיתַיִם p. n., a town in the tribe of Judah.
עִדּוֹ, **עִדּוֹא** p. n. of a man.
עֵרוּת; see **עוּד**.
עַדְלַי p. n. of a man.
עֲדֻלָּם p. n., a cave and city of the tribe of Judah; **עֲדֻלָּמִי** *an Adullamite.*
עָדַן. Hith. *live luxuriously,* Neh. 9:25.
עָדִין, f. **עֲדִינָה** *luxurious, delicate,* Isa. 47:8; (s. *smiting,* perhaps), 2 Sa. 23:8; a very difficult place, see Ges. Thes.
עֲדִינָא p. n. of a man.
עֵדֶן m.— I. *pleasure.*— II. *Eden,* the abode of our first parents.

עֶדֶן p. n., a district of Mesopotamia; בֵּית עֶ׳; see בַּיִת.

עֶדְנָה f., *pleasure*, Gen. 18:12.

עַדְנָא p. n. of a man.

עַדְנָה p. n. of a man.

מַעֲדַנּוֹת, מַעֲדַנִּים, מַעֲדַנִּים pl., *delicacies, delights*; adv. *willingly*; מַעֲדַנּוֹת trans. for מַעֲנַדּוֹת *bands*, i.e. *influences*, Job 38:31; see עָנַד.

עִדָּן *time*; see with עַד.

עַדְעָדָה p.n., a town in the tribe of Judah.

עָדַף I. *was superfluous.*—II. *exceeded*, with עַל. Hiph. הֶעְדִּיף *allowed to exceed.*

עָדַר *arranged, set in order.* Niph. נֶעְדַּר I. *was missing, left behind.* —II. *was dilatory, delayed*, Zep. 3:5.—III. *was cleared out.* Pi. עִדֵּר *omitted, neglected*, 1 Ki. 5:7.

עֵדֶר m. (with suff. עֶדְרוֹ; pl. עֲדָרִים, עֶדְרֵי).—I. *flock* or *herd.*—II. p. n., a town in the tribe of Judah.—III. p. n. of a man.

עֶדֶר p. n. of a man.

עַדְרִיאֵל p. n., *Adriel*, son-in-law of Saul, 1 Sa. 18:19, &c.

מַעְדֵּר m., *rake*, Isa. 7:25.

עֲדָשִׁים m. pl., *lentiles.*

עַוָּא, עִוָּה p. n. of an ancient unknown city; עַוִּים *the Avims*, either the inhabitants of this city, or the early settlers in Canaan.

עוּב. Hiph. הֵעִיב *treated as worthless, rejected*, Lam. 2:1.

עָב com. (pl. עָבוֹת, עָבֵי, עָבִים).—I. *cloud.* — II. *covering*, Ex. 19:9 see also עָב in its place.

עֵיבָל, עוֹבָל p. n. of a people descended from Shem.

עוּג *bake cakes*, Eze. 4:12.

עֻגָּה, עֻגָּה f., *cakes*, ἐγκρυφίας.

מָעוֹג m., *round cake of bread.*

עוֹג p. n., *Og*, king of Bashan.

עוּד *testified*, Lam. 2:13, Ketib. Pi. עִוֵּד *surrounded*, Ps. 119:61. Hiph. הֵעִיד I. *called witnesses, to, for*, or *against.*— II. *called as a witness*, with אֶת and בְּ.—III. *made a declaration.* — IV. *enjoined, commanded, reproved*, with בְּ, עַל; הֵעִיד עֵדוֹת בְּ *gave commandment to, &c.* Hoph. הוּעַד *information was given*, Ex. 21:29, with בְּ. Pil. עוֹדֵד *raised up, confirmed*, Ps. 146:9; 147:6. Hithpo. הִתְעוֹדֵד *stood upright*, Ps. 20:9, &c.

עֵד m.—I. *witness.*— II. *testimony.*— III. *proof*, עָנָה עֵד בְּ *gave testimony against.* — IV. *commander*, Isa. 55:4.

עֵדָה f.— I. *eye* or *ear witness* — *proof*; see also in יָעַד.

עֵדוּת, עֵדֻת f. (pl. עֵדוֹת).—I. *covenant.* —II. *the law.*—III. *the book of the law.* — IV. *the decalogue.* — V. *religious ordinance*, Ps. 122:4; אֹהֶל, אֲרוֹן הָעֵדוּת, לֻחֹת הָעֵדוּת הָעֵדוּת *the tables, the ark, the tabernacle of the covenant.*—VI. Ps. 60:1; 80:1, the name of some unknown musical instrument.

עוֹד, עֹד I. *again.*— II. *besides.*— III *still.*—IV. *any longer*; with suff עוֹדֶנִּי *I (am) still*; עוֹדְךָ *thou (art, still;* עוֹדֶנּוּ, עוֹדֶנָּה *he, she (is) still;* עוֹדָם *they (are) still, &c.;* בְּעוֹד בְּעֹד *as yet, while, within;* מֵעוֹד *since;* מֵעוֹדִי *since I (am).*

עוֹדֵד p.n., *Oded.*—I. the father of Azariah the prophet, 2 Chron. 15:1, 8.—II. another prophet, 2 Chron. 28:9.

תְּעוּדָה f.—I. *institution, custom,* Ru. 4:7.—II. *law, oracle,* Isa. 8:16, 20.

עַוִּים, עַוָּה p.n.; see עַוָּא.

עָוָה *was crooked, perverse, did wrong,* Est. 1:16; Dan. 9:5. Niph. נַעֲוָה I. *bent with pain,* Isa. 21:3.—II. *bowed with sorrow,* Ps. 38:7.—III. *perverse in mind,* Pro. 12:8. Pi. עִוָּה I. *made crooked,* Lam. 3:9.—II. *overturned,* Isa. 24:1. Hiph. הֶעֱוָה I. *made crooked,* Jer. 3:21.—II. *perverted,* Job 33:27.—III. *walked perversely.*

עַוָּה f., *being overturned,* Eze. 21:32.

עֲוָיָא f. Ch., *iniquities,* Dan. 4:24.

עוּזָה for עֻזָּה Kal imp. with ה parag., from עזז.

עָוֹן, עָווֹן m. (const. עֲוֹן; with suff. עֲוֹנָהּ; pl. עֲוֹנִים, עֲוֹנוֹת).—I. *sin, iniquity.*—II. *guilt.*—III. *punishment.*

עֲוִית, עֲיוּת p. n., a town of Edom.

עִי m. (pl. עִיִּים).—I. *ruin, heap of ruins, heap.*—II. עִיִּים p. n.—1. a part of Mount Abarim.—2. a town in the tribe of Judah.

עַי, עַיָּא, עַיָּה, עַיָּת p.n., a city of the Canaanites in the tribe of Benjamin.

עִיּוֹן p.n., a strong city in the tribe of Naphtali.

עִוְעִים m. pl., *giddiness;* Vulg. vertigo, Isa. 19:14.

מְעִי m., *heap of ruins,* Isa. 17:1.

עוּז *took refuge with,* Isa. 30:2. Hiph. הֵעִיז I. *took refuge,* Isa. 10:31.—II. *caused to take refuge, collected in a place of safety.*

עוֹז; see עזז.

עוּט (Arab. *dug into any thing).*

עֵט m.—I. *graver.*—II. *pen.*

עוּל part. f. pl. עָלוֹת.—I. *being with young.*—II. *suckling.*

עוּל m., *infant at the breast.*

עֲוִיל m., *suckling,* Job 21:11; see also עֲוִל

עָוַל. Pi. עִוֵּל *acts unjustly.*

עֲוִיל *wicked.*

עַוָּל m., *one habitually unfair, unjust wicked.*

עֶוֶל, עָוֶל m.—I. *unfairness.*—II. *injustice.*—III. *iniquity.*

עַוְלָה f., the same; with ה parag. עַוְלָתָה.

עוֹלָה f., the same; with ה parag. עֲלָתָה; pl. עוֹלוֹת; see also in עָלָה.

עוֹלָלוֹת, עוֹלֵל, עוֹלָל; see עלל.

עוֹלָם; see עלם.

עוֹן (Arab. *to live with).*

עוֹנָה f., *conjugal rites,* Ex. 21:10.

מָעוֹן m.—I. *habitation.*—II. *refuge.*—III. *den of wild beasts.*—IV. p. n.: (a) of a town in the tribe of Judah; (b) of a strange people, Jud. 10:12, &c.; (c) of a man.

מְעֹנָה, מְעוֹנָה f., the same.

מְעוּנִים p.n., the inhabitants of the city of Meon.

מְעוֹנֹתַי p. n. of a man.

עִוְעִים, עָוֹן; see עוה.

1. **עוּף** (fut. יָעוּף).—I. *flew.*—II. *flew*

away.—III *flew upon* (as a bird of prey). Pil. עוֹפֵף I. *flew.* — II. *brandished* (a sword), Eze. 32:10. Hiph. *turned the eyes on*, Pro. 23:5. Hithpo. same as Kal II., Hos. 9:11.

עוֹף m. collect., *birds*. Ch. the same.

II. עוּף (fut. וַיָּעַף) *fainted.*

עֵיפָה f.—I. *darkness*, Am. 4:13. (with ה parag. עֵיפָתָה) *great darkness*, Job 10:22.—II. p. n.: (a) of a son of Midian and the people descended from him; (b) of a man; (c) of a woman.

עַפְעַפַּיִם, const. עַפְעַפֵּי m. dual.—I. *eyelids.*—II. synec. *eyes.*

מָעוּף m., *darkness*, Isa. 8:22.

מוּעָף m., the same, Isa. 8:23.

עוּץ (imp. pl. עֻצוּ) *consult ye*, Jud. 19:30; Isa. 8:10.

עוּץ p.n., a district of Arabia, Αὐσῖτις.

עוּק. Hiph. הֵעִיק *presses, rushes,* Am. 2:13.

עָקָה f., *pressure, oppression,* Ps. 55:4.

מוּעָקָה f., *pressure, pain,* Ps. 66:11.

עוּר *aroused, awoke, arose* (imp. עוּרָה, עוּרִי *arise!*) Niph. נֵעוֹר I. *was awakened.* — II. *was raised to strike* (shoot), Hab. 3:9. Pil. עוֹרֵר.—I. *roused.*—II. *excited, stirred up.*—III. *raised a spear, scourge, cry.* Hiph. הֵעִיר I. *roused, excited.*—II. *awoke*, Ps. 57:9; 108:3. Hith. הִתְעוֹרֵר *awoke.*

עִיר m. Ch., *watcher*, probably an angel, Dan. 4:10, 14, 20.

עוֹר m. (pl. עוֹרוֹת) *the skin of man* or *animals;* עוֹר שִׁנָּיִם *skin of his teeth*, Job 19:20, i.e. *gum.*

מְעָרָה f., *cave;* (Arab. *went under ground*).

מְעוֹרִים m. pl., *nakedness*, Hab. 2:15

עָוַר. Pi. עִוֵּר *blinded.*

עוּר m. Ch., *chaff*, Dan. 2:35.

עִוֵּר m., עִוְרָה f.—I. *blind.*—II. *mentally blind.*

עִוָּרוֹן m., *blindness.*

עַוֶּרֶת f., the same, Lev. 22:22.

עוּשׁ *assemble yourselves*, Joel 4:11.

עוּת *aid, help*, Isa. 50:4.

עָוַת. Pi. עִוֵּת I. *made crooked.*— II. *perverted.*— III. *treated unfairly, unjustly.* Pu. part. מְעֻוָּת *bowed down.* Hith. *bowed himself*, Ecc. 12:3.

עַוָּתָה f., *oppression*, Lam. 3:59.

עוּתַי p.n. of a man.

עֵז f. (pl. עִזִּים).—I. *goat.*—II. *she goat.*—III. pl. *goats' hair.*

עֵז f. Ch., the same, Ezr. 6:17.

עֻזָּא, עֹז, עַז; see עזז.

עֲזָאזֵל m. (lit. *goat of departure;* see אָזַל) *the scape-goat*, Lev. 16:8, 10, 26; LXX. ἀποπομπαῖος.

עָזַב (fut. יַעֲזֹב).— I. *left behind.*—II. *allowed to remain.*—III. *went away from.*—IV. *forsook, neglected.*— V. *failed, allowed to fail.*— VI. *took away.*—VII. *gave loose to.*— VIII. with אֶל, לְ, *entrusted to, left with;* also with עַל. Niph. נֶעֱזַב *was forsaken, entrusted, &c.*, with לְ. Pu. עֻזַּב *was forsaken.*

עֲזוּבָה f.—I. *ruins*, Is. 17:9.—II. p.n. of a woman.

עִזְבוֹנִים I. *merchandise.*—II. *a market*, Eze. c. 27.

עַזְבּוּק p. n. of a man.

עַזְגָּד p. n. of a man.

עָזַז (fut. וַיָּעָז, יָעֹז; inf. עֲזוֹז).—I. *was strong.*— II. *prevailed.*— III. *considered himself strong*, Ps. 52:9.— IV. *showed himself strong*, Ps. 68:29. Hiph. הֵעֵז *made bold;* ה' פָּנָיו or בְּפָנָיו *put on a bold face*, Pro. 7:13; 21:29.

עַז, with pause עָז m. (pl. עַזִּים; f. עַזָּה, pl. עַזּוֹת).—I. *strong.*—II. *harsh.*—III. *strength.*—IV. עַז־פָּנִים *bold.*

עַזָּה p. n., *Gaza*, a city of the Philistines; עַזָּתִי *a Gazathite.*

עֹז, עוֹז, עָז־ m. (with suff. עֻזִּי, עָזִּי, עוּזֵּנוּ).—I. *strength, power, might.*—II. *ascription of power, praise*, Ps. 8:3.— III. *source of strength, refuge.*—IV. עֹז פָּנִים *impudence.*

עֻזָּא, עֻזָּה p.n. of a man.

עֱזוּז m.—I. *might of God.*—II. *might in war*, Isa. 42:25.

עִזּוּז m.— I. *mighty*, Ps. 24:8.— II. *mighty men*, Isa. 43:17.

עָזָז p. n. of a man.

עֲזַזְיָהוּ p.n. of a man.

עֻזִּי p. n. of a man.

עֻזִּיאֵל p. n. of a man.

עֻזִּיאֵל same as יַעֲזִיאֵל.

עֻזִּיָּה, עֻזִּיָּהוּ (*the strength of the Lord*), p.n., *Uzziah*, king of Judah; LXX. Ὀζίας; elsewhere עֲזַרְיָה; applied also to other men.

עֲזִיזָא p.n. of a man.

עַזְמָוֶת p. n. of a man; בֵּית ע' a place in Judah or Benjamin.

מָעוֹז, מָעֹז m. (with suff. מָעֻזִּי, מָעוּזִּי; pl. מָעֻזִּים) *place of strength, munition;* often applied to persons.

עָזְנִיָּה f., *the sea-eagle*, Lev. 11:13; Deu. 14:12.

עָזַק. Pi. עִזֵּק *digged*, Isa. 5:2.

עִזְקָא f. Ch., *engraved ring, seal*, Dan. 6:18.

עֲזֵקָה p.n., *Azekah*, a city in the tribe of Judah.

עָזַר (fut. יַעְזוֹר; pl. יַעְזוֹרוּ; imp. with suff. עָזְרֵנִי; pl. עִזְרוּנִי) *helped, assisted*, with לְ, עִם, אַחֲרֵי; part. עֹזֵר *helper, patron, companion* Niph. נֶעֱזַר *was holpen.* Hiph. *helped*, 2 Ch. 28:23.

עֵזֶר m. (with suff. עֶזְרוֹ).— I. *help.*— II. *helper.*—III. p. n. of a man.

עֶזֶר p.n. of a man.

עֶזְרָה, עֶזְרַת f. (with ה parag. עֶזְרָתָה).— I. *help.*— II. p. n. of a man; same as עֵזֶר.

עֶזְרָא p.n., *Ezra;* LXX. Ἔσδρας.

עַזֻּר, עַזּוּר p. n. of a man.

עֲזַרְאֵל p.n. of a man.

עֲזָרָה f.—I. *court of the temple.*—II. *border, moulding.*

עֶזְרִי p.n. of a man.

עַזְרִיאֵל p.n. of a man.

עֲזַרְיָה, עֲזַרְיָהוּ p.n., *Azariah.*—I. king of Judah; called also עֻזִּיָּה.—II. used also for other men.

עַזְרִיקָם p.n. of a man.

עֵט, see עוּט; עֵטָא, see יעט.

עָטָה I. *put on, wore.* — II. *covered*, with עַל.—III. *invested.*—IV. *took possession of, invested with*, Jer. 43:12. with אֵת. Hiph. הֶעֱטָה *placed as a covering*, Ps. 89:46, with עַל.

מַעֲטֶה m., *garment* (of praise), Isa 61:3.

עֲטַלֵּף m., *bat*. Lev. 11:19; Isa. 2:20.

עָטַן (Arab. *prepared skin*).

עֲטִין m., pl. עֲטִינִים *water* or *milk skin*, Job 21:24.

עָטַף (fut. יַעֲטֹף).—I. *covered*, with לְ.—II. *covered himself*.—III. *covered his face, was exhausted;* part. עָטוּף *worn out, weak*. Niph. *was exhausted*, Lam. 2:11. Hiph. הֶעֱטִיף the same, Gen. 30:42. Hith. הִתְעַטֵּף the same.

מַעֲטָפָה f., *mantle*, Isa. 3:22.

עָטַר I. *surrounded*.— II. *covered*, Ps. 5:13. Pi. עִטֵּר I. *crowned*, Cant. 3:11.— II. *adorned, blessed*, with לְ. Hiph. part. f. מַעֲטִירָה *giving crowns*, Isa. 23:8.

עֲטָרָה (const. עֲטֶרֶת; pl. עֲטָרוֹת) f. —I. *crown, royal diadem*.—II. p.n. of a woman.

עֲטָרוֹת p.n., a city in the tribe of Gad; עֲטָרוֹת and עַטְרוֹת אַדָּר a city in the tribe of Ephraim; ע׳ בֵּית יוֹאָב a place in Judah; ע׳ שׁוֹפָן a place in Gad.

עָטַשׁ (Arab. *sneezed*).

עֲטִישָׁה f., *sneezing*, Job 41:10.

עַי, עִי, עִיִּים, עַיָּה, עַיָּא, עִיּוֹן, עַיּוּת; see עוה.

עֵיבָל p.n.—I. same as עוֹבָל.—II. a rock in the northern range of Mount Ephraim; LXX. Γαιβάλ.

עִיט I. *was angry with*, with בְּ.—II. *rushed on with anger, pounced on*, with אֶל; fut. וַיַּעַט.

עַיִט, const. עֵיט m., *rapacious bird* or *beast*.

עֵיטָם p. n., a town and hill in the tribe of Judah

עֵילוֹם same as עוֹלָם; see עלם.

עִילַי p. n., one of David's generals.

עֵילָם p.n., a people and district, situation uncertain; עֵלְמָיֵא pl. Ch., *the Elamites*.

עָיָם m., *drought*, Isa. 11:15.

עַיִן f. (const. עֵין; with suff. עֵינוֹ; dual עֵינַיִם, עֵינֵי).— I. *an eye*.— II. *the sight*.— III. *the judgment*. — IV. *appearance in the eye*.— V. עֵינַיִם *outward appearance*, 1 Sa. 16:7; לְעֵינֵי פ׳ *in the sight of;* בְּעֵינֵי *in the judgment of;* מֵעֵינֵי *without the knowledge of;* בֵּין עֵינַיִם *between the eyes, on the forehead*, עַיִן בְּעַיִן *eye to eye*.—VI. *fountain, spring*; with ה parag. עַיְנָה *to the fountain;* pl. עֲיָנוֹת, const. עֵינוֹת: hence many p.n.:—I. עַיִן a town of the Levites in the tribe of Simeon. —II. a town in the north of Canaan.— III. עֵינַיִם, עֵינָם a town of Judah. — IV. עֵין גֶּדִי a town of Judah.—V. עֵין גַּנִּים a town of Judah.— VI. a town of Issachar. — VII. עֵין דּוֹר, עֵין דֹּאר a town of the Manassites.—VIII. עֵין חַדָּה a town of Issachar.—IX. עֵין חָצוֹר a town of Naphtali.—X. עֵין חֲרוֹד a *well* near the town of *Charod*. —XI. עֵין מִשְׁפָּט a well in Kadesh. —XII. עֵין עֶגְלַיִם a town of Moab. —XIII. עֵין רֹגֵל a well on the confines of Judah and Benjamin.— XIV. עֵין רִמּוֹן a town in the tribe of Judah.—XV. עֵין שֶׁמֶשׁ a town on the confines of Judah and

Benjamin.—XVI. עֵין תַּנִּים a well near Jerusalem.—XVII. עֵין תַּפּוּחַ a town of Manasseh.

עַיִן com. Ch., *eye.*

עֹיֵן m., *watching with an evil eye,* 1 Sa. 18:9.

עֵינָן p. n. of a man.

מַעְיָן m. (with ו parag. מַעְיְנוֹ; with suff. מַעְיָנוֹ; pl. מַעְיָנִים, מַעְיְנֵי, מַעְיְנוֹת, מַעְיָנוֹת) *fountain, well of water.*

עָיֵף *is weary,* Jer. 4:31; וַיָּעַף, see עוּף.

עָיֵף m., עֲיֵפָה f. — I. *weary.* — II. *parched.*

עֵיפַי p.n. of a man.

עֵיפָה *darkness;* see עוּף.

עַיִר m. (with suff. עִירֹה; pl. עֲיָרִים). —I. *ass.*—II. *young ass.*

עִיר m.—I. *heat, anger, fear,* Ps. 73:20; Jer. 15:8; Hos. 7:4; 11:9; (Ges.)—II. *a city, town, settlement;* עִירָה *towards the city;* pl. עֲיָרִים; see next word.

עָר m.— I. *an enemy.*— II. *city;* pl. עָרִים; עָר, עָר־מוֹאָב *Ar of Moab,* otherwise *Rabbah,* the chief city of Moab.

עָר m. Ch., *an enemy.*

עִיר Ch.; see עוּר.

עִירָא p.n. of a man.

עִירוּ p. n. of a man.

עִירָם p. n., a prince of Edom.

עִירָד p. n. of a man.

עֵירֹם, עֵירֻמִּים; see ערם.

עַיִשׁ; see עָשׁ.

עַיָּה same as עַי; see עוה.

עַכָּבִישׁ m., *a spider.*

עַכְבָּר *the jerboa;* "dipus jaculus" (Linn.)

עַכְבּוֹר p. n. of a man.

עַכּוֹ p. n., a city in the tribe of Asher, Ἀκη, "Ptolemais."

עָכָן (עָכָר) p. n. of a man.

עֶכֶס m.—I. *fetter,* Pro. 7:22.—II. pl. עֲכָסִים *anklets, rings for the feet,* Isa. 3:18.

עִכֵּס, Pi. *wear anklets,* Isa. 3:16.

עַכְסָה p. n., the daughter of Caleb.

עָכַר (fut. with suff. יַעְכָּרְךָ) *caused sorrow, vexation, disgrace.* Niph. נֶעְכַּר *was irritated, excited.*

עָכוֹר p.n., a valley near Jericho.

עָכְרָן p.n. of a man.

עַכְשׁוּב m., *an asp,* Ps. 140:4.

עַל, עַל, עֲלָא; see עלה.

עַל, עֲלָא, עִלָּה; see עלל.

עִלֵּג m., *foreigner, stammerer,* Isa. 32:4.

עָלָה (fut. יַעֲלֶה; apoc. יַעַל) const. with עַל, אֶל, לְ, בְּ.— I. *went up, came up.*—II. *arose* (of the dawn).— III. *grew up, grew.*—IV. *increased.* — V. *produced,* Pro. 24:31.— VI. *was put upon.* Niph. נַעֲלָה I. *is exalted* (God).— II. *was lifted up,* Eze. 9:3.—III. *was led away,* 2 Sa. 2:27.—IV. *was taken up,* Eze. 36:3. Hiph. הֶעֱלָה, הַעֲלָה (pret. הֶעֱלִית, הַעֲלִית; imp. apoc. הַעַל; fut. יַעֲלֶה; apoc. יַעַל).—I. *caused to go up.* — II. *offered a burnt-offering.*— III. *placed a thing on another.*— IV. *placed, set up,* Nu. 8:2. Hoph. הֹעֲלָה I. *was offered,* Jud. 6:28.— II. *was brought up,*

Nah. 2:8.—III. *was placed upon, inscribed*, 2 Chron. 20:34. Hith. fut. apoc. יִתְעַל *lifts up himself*, Jer. 51:3.

עַל m., *the Lofty One, the Most High;* adv. *on high*, 2 Sa. 23:1; מֵעַל I. *from above*, Gen. 27:39; 49:25. —II. *above*, Ps. 50:4, &c.

עַל, עֲלֵי; (with suff. עָלַי; עָלֶיךָ, עָלַיִךְ; עָלָיו, עָלֶיהָ; עֲלֵיכֶם, עֲלֵיהֶם, עָלֵימוֹ) prep. (ὑπέρ, ἐπί).—I. *upon, on.*—II. *above, over.*—III. *beside, near, before.*—IV. *besides, over and above.* —V. *in reference to, towards, against.*—VI. *for, on account of, in behalf of;* עָלַי לָתֵת *it is mine to give* (the kingdom); חָיָה עַל, ζῆν ἐπί, *live by* (bread), Deu. 8:3.

מֵעַל (with suff. מֵעָלָיו, מֵעָלֶיךָ, מֵעֲלֵיכֶם, &c.).—I. *from upon.*—II. *from above.*—III. *above.*

עַל Ch. same as Heb., *upon, above, besides, for.*

עֵלָּא Ch., with מִן *above*, Dan. 6:3.

עָלֶה, const. עֲלֵה m. (with suff. עָלֵהוּ; pl. const. עֲלֵי).—I. *leaf.*—II. *foliage.*

עֹלָה, עוֹלָה f.—I. *a step.*—II. *a burnt-offering.*

עֲלָה, עֲלָתָא f. Ch., *burnt-offering.*

עִלִּי, f. עִלִּית *upper*, Jos. 15:19; Jud. 1:15; pl. עִלִּיּוֹת.

עִלָּי m. Ch.—I. *high, supreme* (of God).—II. *the Most High.*

עִלִּית f. Ch., *upper room, chamber*, Dan. 6:11.

עֵלִי p. n., *Eli*, Ἡλί, the priest.

עֱלִי m., *pestle*, Pro. 27:22.

עֲלִיָּה f.—I. *upper room, chamber.*—II. *ascent, staircase*, 2 Chron. 9:4.

עֶלְיוֹן m., עֶלְיוֹנָה f.—I. *lofty.*—II. *higher, upper* (in place).—III. *high* (in rank).—IV. *the Supreme, the Most High* (of God).

עֶלְיוֹן m. Ch., *the Most High.*

מַעֲלֶה m.—I. *ascent.*—II. *mount.*

מַעַל m., with ה מַעְלָה.—I. *over against, near*, Isa. 6:2, &c.—II. *above;* לְמַעְלָה *upwards, onwards, over, above;* מִלְמַעְלָה *from above, upward;* מִמַּעַל *from above*, with לְ *over, above.*

מֹעַל m., *elevating, lifting up of*, Neh. 8:6.

מַעֲלָה f.—I. *ascent.*—II. *step of stairs.* —III. *graduated face of a sun-dial.*—IV. *mental suggestions*, Ezr. 7:9.—V. an unknown title of some of the Psalms.

תְּעָלָה f.—I. *channel for water.*—II. *recovery from illness*, Jer. 30:13; 46:11.

עַלְוָה f.—I. same as עַוְלָה.—II. p.n., a tribe of the Edomites.

עֲלוּמִים *youth*, see עלם.

עַלְוָן, עַלְיָן p.n. of an Edomite.

עֲלוּקָה f., *a leech*, Pro. 30:15.

עָלַז (fut. יַעֲלֹז; pl. יַעְלְזוּ) *rejoiced, exulted*, with עַל or בְּ (of the subject of joy).

עָלֵז m., *rejoicing*, Isa. 5:14.

עַלִּיז m., *rejoicing, expressing joy.*

עלט (Arab. *was covered with clouds*).

עֲלָטָה f., *darkness.*

עֵלִי, עִלִּית, עֲלִיָּה, עֶלְיוֹן; see עלה.

עֲלִיצוּת; see עלץ.

עָלַל (Syr. *entered*). Po. עוֹלֵל I. *made to enter*, Job 16:15.—II. *treated, acted towards*, with לְ. — III. *affected.* — IV. *gleaned.* — V. part. מְעוֹלֵל *babyish boy*, Isa. 3:12. Poa. *was done, caused*, Lam. 1:12. Hith. I. *exerted himself against.* —II. *insulted.* Hithpo. *practised*, Ps. 141:4

עֲלַל Ch., *entered.* Aph. הַנְעֵל *brought in.* Hoph. הֻעַל *was brought in.*

עֹל, עוֹל m. (with suff. עֻלּוֹ).—I. *yoke*, —II. *servitude.*

עֻלָּא p.n. of a man.

עִלָּה f. Ch., *pretext, ground for complaint*, Dan. 6:5, 6.

עֲלִיל m., *crucible*, Ps. 12:7.

עוֹלֵל, עוֹלָל m. (pl. עוֹלָלִים, עוֹלְלִים) *infant, young child, child.*

עוֹלֵלוֹת, עֹלֵלוֹת f. pl., *gleanings.*

עֲלִילָה f.—I. *action.*—II. *an action* (good or bad).

עֲלִילִיָּה f., *action*, Jer. 32:19.

מֶעָל m. Ch., *setting* (of the sun), Dan. 6:15.

מַעֲלָל m., pl. מַעֲלָלִים *habitual doings* (good or bad).

תַּעֲלוּל m., pl. תַּעֲלוּלִים.— I. *children*, Isa. 3:4.—II. *vexations, calamities*, Isa. 66:4.

עָלַם, part. עֲלֻמִים *hidden things, sins*, Ps. 90:8. Niph. נֶעְלָם *was hidden;* part. נַעֲלָמִים *hidden* (crafty) *men.* Hiph. הֶעְלִים *hide, conceal;* ה׳ עֵינַיִם מִן *turned his eyes away from*, Pro. 28:27. Hith. הִתְעַלֵּם *was hidden*, with מִן.

עוֹלָם, עֹלָם m.— I. *antiquity.* — II. *eternity.*—III. *duration of the earth.* — IV. *whole life.*— V. *unlimited, future time;* מֵעוֹלָם *from of old;* יְמוֹת עוֹלָם *the ancient days;* עוֹלָם, עַד־עוֹלָם, לְעוֹלָם, עוֹלָמִים *for ever;* future duration, unlimited, but not endless.

עֵילוֹם m., *eternity*, 2 Chron. 33:7.

עָלַם m. Ch., *eternity.*

עֶלֶם m., *a young man.*

עַלְמָה f., *damsel, virgin*, ἡ παρθένος.

עֲלוּמִים m. pl., *youth.*

עַלְמוֹן p. n. of a town in the tribe of Benjamin; ע׳ דִּבְלָתָיְמָה p.n., a station of Israel.

עֲלָמוֹת f. pl., an unknown title of Psalm 46.

עַלְמוּת f., the same, Ps. 9:1; 48:15.

עָלֶמֶת p. n. of a man.

עָלֶמֶת p.n., same as עַלְמוֹן.

תַּעֲלֻמָה f., *any thing hidden, secret;* pl. תַּעֲלֻמוֹת.

עֵלְמָיֵא *Elamites;* see עֵילָם.

עָלַס *exult, rejoice*, Job 20:18. Niph. *is exulting*, Job 39:13. Hith. *be exulting*, Pro. 7:18.

עָלַע *gulped, swallowed down*, Job 39:30.

עֲלַע com. Ch., *rib*, Dan. 7:5.

עָלַף. Pu. I. *fainted*, Isa. 51:20.— II. *covered, overlaid*, Cant. 5:14. Hith. *was clothed*, Gen. 38:14, *fainted.*

עֻלְפֶּה m., *languor, fainting*, Eze. 31:15.

עָלַץ (fut. יַעֲלֹץ) *exult, rejoice;* with בְּ *in*, לְ *against*, לִפְנֵי *before.*

עֲלִיצוּת f., *rejoicing*, Hab. 3:14.

עַם, עָם, עִם; see עמם.

עָמַד (fut. יַעֲמֹד).—I. *stood fast, still.* — II. *stood over, overlooked*, with

לִפְנֵי — III. *stood over, presided,* with עַל.—IV. *stood before,* with עַל, אֶת.—V. *ceased,* with מִן.—VI. *stood before,* with מִן, לִפְנֵי, בִּפְנֵי, נֶגֶד.—VII. *persevere, remain in any occupation,* with בְּ.— VIII. *stood against, opposed,* with עַל. Hiph. הֶעֱמִיד I. *cause to stand.*—II. *set up, raise.*—III. *establish.*—IV. *appoint.* — V. *confirm, accomplish.* (הַעֲמַדְתָּ, Eze. 29:7, a wrong reading for הִמְעַדְתָּ *thou madest to tremble.*) Hoph. הָעֳמַד *made to stand.*

עֹמֶד m., *standing-place, station.*

עַמּוּד m., *pillar.*

עֶמְדָּה f., *station, standing.* Mic. 1:11.

מַעֲמָד m.— I. *standing, order.*— II. *station.*

עִמָּד, see עִם, עָמָה; עַמּוֹן, see עמם.

עָמוֹס, see עמם; עָמוֹק, see עמק.

עָמִיר; see עמר.

עָמִית *society, company.*

עָמַל *wrought, laboured.*

עָמֵל m.—I. *working, labouring;* pl. עֲמֵלִים *labourers.* — II. *weary, wretched.*

עָמָל m.—I. *labour.*—II. *sorrow, vexation.*— III. *sorrow brought on by sin.*— IV. *weariness.*— V. *fruit of labour.*—VI. p. n. of a man.

עֲמָלֵק p. n., *Amalek,* a people inhabiting the south of Palestine and the borders of the desert of Sinai; עֲמָלֵקִי *Amalekite;* הַר הָעֲמָלֵקִי *hill of the Amalekites* in the tribe of Ephraim.

עָמַם *concealed,* Eze. 28:3; 31:8. Hoph. הוּעַם *was obscured,* Lam. 4:1.

עַם, עָם com. (with suff. עַמִּי), *people, nation;* בְּנֵי עַמִּי *the children of my people;* pl. עַמִּים, עֲמָמִים.

עַם m. Ch., *people;* pl. עַמְמִין.

עִם prep. (with suff. עִמִּי, עִמָּדִי; עִמְּךָ, עִמָּךְ; עִמּוֹ, עִמָּנוּ; עִמָּכֶם; עִמָּם, עִמָּהֶם) *with, along with;* מֵעִם *from with,* (like the French *de par*).

עִם Ch., the same.

עֻמָּה f.—I. כָּל־עֻמַּת שֶׁ.. *in the same way as;* לְעֻמַּת *near, towards, like, opposite to;* pl. לְעֻמּוֹת *like;* מִלְּעֻמַּת *near.*—II. p. n., a town of Asher.

עַמּוֹן p. n., *Ammon,* the son of Lot's daughter, and his descendants, עַמּוֹנִי; pl. בְּנֵי עַמּוֹן, עַמֹּנִים; f. עַמּוֹנִית; pl. עַמּוֹנִיּוֹת *Ammonites.*

עַמִּיאֵל p. n. of a man.

עַמִּיהוּד p. n. of a man.

עַמִּיזָבָד p. n. of a man.

עַמִּיחוּר p. n. of a man.

עַמִּינָדָב p. n. of a man.

עַמִּישַׁדַּי p. n. of a man.

עַמְעָד p. n., a town in the tribe of Asher.

עַמְרָם p. n. of a man; patron. עַמְרָמִי.

עִמָּנוּאֵל (*God with us*), *Immanuel,* one of our Lord's prophetic titles, Ἐμμανουήλ, Isa. 7:14.

עָמַס, עָמַשׂ (fut. יַעֲמֹס) *load, lay a burden upon.* Hiph. הֶעֱמִיס *caused to be laden,* 1 Ki. 12:11; 2 Chron. 10:11.

עָמוֹס p.n., *Amos,* the prophet.

עֲמַסְיָה p.n. of a man.

מַעֲמָסָה f., *burden,* Zec. 12:3.

עָמַק *was very deep*, Ps. 92:6. Hiph. הֶעֱמִיק *make deep*, Isa. 30:33.
עָמֹק m., עֲמֻקָּה f.—I. *deep.*—II. *subtle, unsearchable.*
עָמֹק or עֵמֶק m., the same; pl. const. עִמְקֵי.
עָמוֹק p. n. of a man.
עֵמֶק m. (with suff. עִמְקְךָ; pl. עֲמָקִים). —I. *deep place.*—II. *unintelligible.*
עֹמֶק m., *depth*, Pro. 25:3.
עֲמִיק m. Ch., *deep, profound thing*, Dan. 2:22.
מַעֲמַקִּים m. pl., *depths.*

עָמַר. Pi. עִמֵּר *binding-sheaves*, Ps. 129:7. Hith. הִתְעַמֵּר *treat as a slave*, with בְּ.
עָמִיר m., *sheaf of corn.*
עֹמֶר m.—I. *sheaf*; pl. עֳמָרִים.—II. *omer*, a dry measure, the tenth part of an ephah.
עֲמֹרָה p. n., *Gomorrah*, one of the cities of the plain; LXX. Γομόῤῥα.
עָמְרִי p. n.—I. *Omri*, king of Israel.—II. of other men.

עֲמַר m. Ch., *wool*, Dan. 7:9.
עַמְרָם p. n.; see עמם.

עָמַשׁ same as עָמַס *carried.*
עֲמָשָׂא p.n. of a man.
עֲמָשַׂי p. n. of a man.
עֲמַשְׁסַי p. n. of a man.

עָנָב (Arab. *grapes*).
עָנָב p. n., a town in the tribe of Judah.
עֵנָב m. (pl. עֲנָבִים, עִנְּבֵי), *grapes.*
עָנוּב p. n. of a man.
עִנְּבֵי pl. const. with dag. euphon., from עֵנָב.

עָנַג Pu. *delicately brought up*, Jer. 6:2. Hith. *delighted himself in*, with עַל, מִן.
עָנֹג m., עֲנֻגָּה f., *delicate, tender.*
עֹנֶג m., *delight, pleasure.*
תַּעֲנוּג m., *delight, pleasure, enjoyment, luxury.*

עָנַד *bound*, Job 31:36; Pro. 6:21.

I. **עָנָה** (fut. וַיַּעַן, אֶעֱנֶה, יַעֲנֶה).—I. *spoke.* —II. *celebrated.*—III. *shout.*—IV. *bellow, bleat.*—V. *answer.* Niph. נַעֲנֶה *was answering, answered.* Pi. עַנָּה *answered, sang in response.* Hiph. *answer favorably*, Ecc. 5:19.
עֲנָה Ch.—I. *answered, spoke, began to speak.*—II. *was afflicted*; see below.

II. **עָנָה** I. *was humbled.*—II. *was afflicted.* Niph. *was humbled, afflicted*, with מִפְּנֵי. Pi. I. *humbled, subdued.*—II. *afflicted*; with אִשָּׁה *had connexion with a woman*; with נֶפֶשׁ *fasted.* Pu. *was afflicted, humbled*; inf. עֻנּוֹתוֹ *his suffering affliction*, Ps. 132:1. Hiph. *oppressed.* Hith. הִתְעַנָּה I. *was afflicted*, 1 Ki. 2:26.—II. *was humbled*, with לִפְנֵי.
עֲנָה p. n.—I. the son of Seir, and his descendants.—II. the son of Zibeon.
עָנָו, עָנָיו m. (pl. עֲנָוִים, עַנְוֵי), *humble, meek, poor, afflicted.*
עֲנָוָה f., *meekness, humility.*
עַנְוָה f., the same.
עֱנוּת f., *affliction of the humble* (Lee), Ps. 22: 25.
עָנִי adj. m. (pl. עֲנִיִּים; f. עֲנִיָּה), *afflicted miserable, poor.*
עֳנִי, with pause עֹנִי m., *misery*
עֻנִּי p. n. of a man.

עֲנָיָה p. n. of a man
עִנְיָן m., *thing, matter.*
עֲנָת p. n. of a man; see בַּיִת.
עֲנָתוֹת p.n.—I. a city of the Levites in Benjamin; עַנְּתֹתִי *inhabitant of Anathoth.*—II. of a man.
עַנְתֹתִיָּה p. n. of a man.
יַעַן pa., *because;* יַעַן כִּי, יַעַן אֲשֶׁר *because, because of;* יַעַן וּבְיַעַן, יַעַן בְּיַעַן the same.
יַעְנַי p. n. of a man.
מַעֲנֶה m.—I. *answer.*— II. *answer to prayer,* Pro. 16:1.
מַעַן, לְמַעַן *intent, purpose.* — I. *because.*—II. *thence, so, accordingly;* לְמַעַן אֲשֶׁר *in order that, because that.*
מַעֲנָה f., *furrow,* Ps. 129:3.
מַעֲנִית Kri, the same.
תַּעֲנִית f., *self-humiliation,* Ezr. 9:5.
עָנִים p.n., a town of Judah.
עָנֵם p.n., a town of Issachar; elsewhere עֵין־גַּנִּים.
עֲנָמִים p.n., a foreign people unknown.
עֲנַמֶּלֶךְ p.n., an idol of the Sepharvites.
עָנַן (part. עֹנֵן; f. עֹנְנָה) and Po. עוֹנֵן (fut. יְעוֹנֵן; part. מְעוֹנֵן) *divined, used auguries,* Isa. 2:6, &c. Pi. (inf. with suff. עַנְנִי) *my bringing on a cloud,* Gen. 9:14; see עָנָן.
עָנָן, const. עֲנַן m.— I. *a cloud.*— II. p. n. of a man.
עֲנָנָה f., *cloud,* Job 3:5.
עֲנָן m. Ch., *cloud,* Dan. 7:13.
עֲנָנִי p.n. of a man.
עֲנַנְיָה ('Ἀνανίας) p.n.—I. of a man. —II. of a place in Benjamin.
עָנָף, const. עֲנַף m. (pl. with suff. עַנְפְּכֶם, עֲנָפֶיהָ) *a branch.*

עֲנַף m. Ch., *a branch.*
עָנֵף, f. עֲנֵפָה *branching out,* Eze. 19 10.
עֲנָק m. (pl. עֲנָקִים, עֲנָקוֹת).—I. *a chain* (collar for the neck).—II. p.n., הָעֲנָק, יְלִידֵי, בְּנֵי עֲנָק (הָעֲנָק), עֲנָקִים, בְּנֵי עֲנָקִים *the Anakims,* the first inhabitants of Canaan, who were giants.
עָנַק *put on a collar,* i.e. exalted, lifted up, Ps. 73:6. Hiph. הֶעֱנִיק *place on the neck* like a collar, Deu. 15:14.
עָנֵר p.n.—I. a man of Canaan, Gen. 14: 13, 24.— II. p.n., 1 Chron. 6:55, probably a wrong reading for תַּעְנַךְ.
עָנַשׁ (fut. יַעֲנשׁ).—I. *taxed.*—II. *fined in money,* with לְ. Niph. *was fined, mulcted.*
עֹנֶשׁ m., *mulct, fine, tax*
עֲנָשׁ m. Ch., *tax.*
עֲנָת, עֲנָתוֹת, עַנְתֹתִיָּה; see ענה.
עֶנֶת, כְּעֶנֶת; see עתת.
עָסַס *tread* (as grapes), Mal. 3:21.
עָסִיס m. — I. *new wine-juice.*— II. *juice of the pomegranate,* Cant. 8:2.
עער, יְעֹעֵרוּ for יְעַרְעֵרוּ *raised a cry,* Isa. 15:5; see עוּר Pil.
עֵפָה, עֵפָתָה; see עֵיפָה in עוּף.
עָפָה root not used; (Syr. *flourished.*)
עֳפִי m., pl. עֳפָאִים *leaves,* Ps. 104:12.
עֳפִי m. Ch., *leaves.*
עָפַל. Pu. *swollen, inflated,* Hab. 2: 4. Hiph. *raised themselves,* Nu. 14:44.
עֹפֶל m. — I. *swelling tumour.*— II *mount, hill.*

a peak of Mount Zion,
.
ast. עֳפָלֵי hæmorrhoids,
ee also טְחוֹרִים.
ity of Benjamin, Jos.

; see עוּף.
lashed with dust, 2 Sa.
בֶּעָפָר.

עָ m.—I. *earth, mould,*
lust.—III. *the earth.*—
f the earth; pl. const.
s, i.e. small dust, mole-

oung goat.
. man.
I. a city of Benjamin.
of Manasseh.—III. of

p.n.—I. a town on the
Ephraim.—II. a moun-
n Judah and Benjamin.
name of a Hittite, Gen.

see עצה.
rieved, thwarted. Niph.
l, grieved, with בְּ, עַל,
bound together, Job 10:
ned, thwarted. Hiph.
hwarted, Ps. 78:40.—II.
er. 44:19; (see Lee).
grieved.
eved.
עֲצַבִּי *idols.*
— I. *tendon, sinew*, Jer.
. *labour.*—III. *pain.*
dol.—II. *pain, grief.*
with suff. (עֲצַבֵּיכֶם) *your*
a. 58:3.

עַצֶּבֶת ,עַצָּבָה f. (const. עַצְּבַת; pl. with suff. עַצְּבוֹתָם).—I. *pain, grief.* —II. "sorrows," Eng. Ver.; perhaps *idols*, Ps. 16:4.

עִצָּבוֹן m., *painful, great, labour*, Gen. 3:16, 17.

מַעֲצֵבָה f., *labour, affliction*, Isa. 50:11.

עצד (Arab. *axe*).

מַעֲצָד m., *axe.*

עצה *close the eyes*, Pro. 16:30.

עֵץ m. (pl. עֵצִים, עֲצֵי).—I. *a tree*, עֵץ פְּרִי *fruit-tree.*—II. *wood.*—III. *gallows.*

עֵצָה f., *wood*, Jer. 6:6; see also in יעץ.

עָצֶה m., *spine of the back*, Lev. 3:9.

עֶצְיוֹן גֶּבֶר p. n., a sea-port, probably on the eastern coast of the Red Sea.

עָצַל. Niph. *be sluggish*, Jud. 18:9.

עָצֵל m., *sluggard*; book of Proverbs only.

עַצְלָה *sloth*, Pro. 19:15, עַצְלוּת f., Pro. 31:27; dual עֲצַלְתַּיִם *great sloth*, Ecc. 10:18.

עָצַם, עָצֵם I. *was numerous.*—II. *was strong.*—III. *was great.* Pi. עִצֵּם I. *bind the eyes*, Isa. 29:10.—II. *break the bones*, Jer. 50:17, from עֶצֶם. Hiph. *strengthens*, Ps. 105:24.

עָצוּם m.—I. *numerous.*—II. *strong.* —III. *great*; pl. עֲצוּמִים *great ones*, Ps. 10:10.

עֶצֶם f. (pl. עֲצָמִים, עֲצָמוֹת).—I. *bone* —II. *body.*—III. *self-same* (never of persons); בְּעֶצֶם הַיּוֹם הַזֶּה *on this very day*—IV. p.n., a city of Judah.

עֹצֶם m., עָצְמָה f.—I. *strength.*—II. *power.*—III. *multitude*, Nah. 3:9.

עַצְמוֹן p. n., a town in the southern borders of Canaan.

עֲצֻמוֹת f. pl., *defence in argument*, Isa. 41:21.

תַּעֲצֻמוֹת f. pl., *strength*, Ps. 68:36.

עֵצֶן m., p.n. of a place, 2 Sa. 23:8.

עָצַר (fut. יַעְצֹר).—I. *shut up, restrain, detain*, with לְ.— II. with כֹּחַ *retain power, reign.* Niph. נֶעֱצַר· *was shut up, detained.*— II. *was assembled.*

עֶצֶר m., *rule, supreme power*, Jud. 18:7.

עֹצֶר m.— I. *shutting up the womb from child-bearing*, Pro. 30:16.— II. *in prison*, Isa. 53:8.

עֲצֶרֶת, עֲצָרָה f.—I. *day of assembly.* —II. *restraint.*

מַעְצָר m., *restraint, hindrance*, Pro. 25:28.

מַעְצוֹר m., the same, 1 Sa. 14:6.

עָקַב (fut. יַעְקֹב).—I. *take by the heel*, Hos. 12:4; see עָקֵב.—II. *circumvent, defraud;* part. עֲקֻבָּה *traced, marked*, Hos. 6:8. Pi. *trace*, Job 37:4.

עָקֵב m.— I. *heel.*— II. *impression of the heel, track;* pl. עֲקֵבִים *heels;* עִקְּבוֹת *footsteps.*—III. *rear of an army*, Gen. 49:19, &c. — IV. עֲוֹן עֲקֵבַי *iniquity of my tracks*, i. e. ways, Ps. 49·6.

עָקֹב m., *steep place*, Isa. 40:4; see above.

עֵקֶב m.—I. *in consequence that, for the sake of.*—II. *consequence, fruit;* ע׳ רָב, Ps. 19:12, "great reward," Eng. Ver.; עֵקֶב, עַל עֵקֶב *in consequence, because, for that reason*, with כִּי ,אֲשֶׁר the same.

עָקְבָה f., *fraud, deceit*, 2 Ki. 10:19.

עַקּוּב p.n. of men.

יַעֲקֹב (*took by the heel*), p. n., *Jacob*, the son of Isaac, afterwards Israel; קְהִלַּת י׳, בֵּית י׳, בְּנֵי יַעֲקֹב, זֶרַע י׳ I. his descendants, the Israelites.—II. the name also of their land and national polity.

יַעֲקֹבָה p. n. of a man.

עָקַד (fut. יַעֲקֹד) *he binds, ties*, Gen. 22:9.

עָקֹד m. (pl. עֲקֻדִּים) *stripe, streak on cattle.*

עָקָה s., *oppression;* see עוּק·

מַעֲקֶה m., *parapet, battlement;* LXX. στεφάνη, Deut. 22:8.

עָקַל. Pu. part. מְעֻקָּל *became perverted*, Hab. 1:4.

עֲקַלָּתוֹן m., *very crooked*, Isa. 27:1.

עֲקַלְקַל m., עֲקַלְקַלּוֹת f. pl., *very crooked, perverted.*

עָקַר *eradicate*, Ecc. 3:2. Niph. *was rooted up, destroyed*, Zep. 2:4. Pi. עִקֵּר *hough, cut the hamstring.*

עֲקַר Ch. Ith. *was rooted*, Dan. 7:8.

עָקָר m., עֲקָרָה, עֲקֶרֶת f., *barren, sterile.*

עֵקֶר m.—I. *root*, i.e. head of a strange family, Lev. 25:47.—II. p. n. of a man.

עִקַּר m. Ch., *nerve, stump*, Dan.4:12

עֶקְרוֹן p. n., one of the five principal cities of the Philistines, Ἀκαρών; עֶקְרֹנִי *an Ekronite.*

עַקְרָב m.—I. *a scorpion.*—II. *some implement of torture.*—III. *a war-*

like engine.—IV. מַעֲלֵה עַקְרַבִּים p. n., a place in the south of Palestine, 'Ακραβίν.

עָקַשׁ *convict of perverseness*, Job 9:20. Niph. *is perverse*, Pro. 28:18. Pi. *made crooked.*

עִקֵּשׁ m.—I. *perverse, tortuous.*—II. p. n. of a man.

עִקְּשׁוּת m., *perverseness.*

מַעֲקָשׁ m., pl. מַעֲקַשִּׁים *unlevel, abrupt places*, Isa. 42:16.

עָר, עָרִים; see עִיר.

עֵר p. n., *Er*, the son of Judah, and other men.

עָרַב I. *was agreeable, sweet.*—II. *agreed, made compact.*—III. *became surety, pledged*, with לְ.—IV. *became dark*; imp. עֲרֹב; fut. יֶעֱרַב. Hith. הִתְעָרֵב I. *intermixed with*, with בְּ, לְ, עִם.—II. *agreed, made compact with*, with אֶת. Hiph. inf. הַעֲרֵב *growing late* (of the day), 1 Sa. 17:16.

עֲרַב Ch., *mixed.* Ith. *was mixed, associated.*

עֲרָב, עֲרַב *Arabia*; עַרְבִי, עֲרָבִי *an Arab*; pl. עַרְבִיאִים, עֲרָבִים *Arabs.*

עֹרֵב m.—I *a raven.*—II. p. n., a prince of Midian.—III. *Oreb*, a rock beyond Jordan.

עָרֵב m., *agreeable, sweet*, Pro. 20:17, &c.

עָרֹב m., *gad-fly*; LXX. κυνόμυια.

עֵרֶב m. (with art. הָעֶרֶב).—I. *foreigner, stranger, mixed multitude.*—II. *woof in weaving.*

עֶרֶב m. (f. 1 Sa. 20:5).—I. *evening*, לָעֶרֶב, עֶרֶב, בָּעֶרֶב *in the evening*; pl. עֲרָבוֹת; dual בֵּין הָעַרְבַּיִם *from evening to evening*, i.e. a whole day.—II. pl. עֲרָבִים, עַרְבֵי *oziers, willows.*—III. נַחַל ע׳ *a stream in Moab*, Isa. 15:7.

עֲרָבָה f.—I. *plain, open country.*—II. *desert.*—III. הָעֲרָבָה the country between Jericho and the gulf of Akabah, called by the Arabs *El Arabah*; יָם הָע׳ *Sea of Arabah*, Dead Sea; נַחַל הָע׳ *brook Kedron.*—IV. p. n., a town in Benjamin; עַרְבָתִי *an Arbite.*

עֲרֻבָּה f., *pledge, surety.*

עֵרָבוֹן m. (ἀῤῥαβών), *security, pledge*, Gen. 38:17, &c.

מַעֲרָב m.—I. *the west.*—II. *merchandise*, Eze. c. 27; מַעֲרָבָה *towards the west.*

מַעֲרָבָה f., *the west.*

תַּעֲרוּבָה f., *security, hostages.*

עָרַג *bleat, cry as an animal from desire*, with אֶל, עַל; fut. יַעֲרֹג.

עֲרוּגָה f., *raised bed in a garden, parterre.*

עָרַד root not used; (Arab. *fled away*)

עָרוֹד m., *wild ass*, Job 39:5.

עֲרָד m. Ch.—I. *wild ass*, Dan. 5:21.—II. p. n., a place in the wilderness of Judah.—III. p.n. of a man.

עָרָה. Pi. עֵרָה (inf. עָרוֹת; fut. apoc. תְּעַר).—I. *make naked.*—II. *empty, pour out.* Hiph. הֶעֱרָה I. *make bare, expose*, Lev. 20:18, 19.—II. *pour out*, Isa. 53:12. Niph. נֶעֱרָה *was poured out*, Isa. 32:15. Hith. הִתְעָרָה I. *was stripped, exposed*, Lam. 4:21.—II. *was spread abroad*, Ps. 37:35.

עָרָה f., pl. עָרוֹת *bare places, pastures,* Isa. 19:7.

עֶרְוָה f.—I. *unfortified country,* Gen. 42:9, 12.—II. *nudity.*—III. *shame, disgrace.*

עַרְוָה f. Ch., *loss,* Ezr. 4:14.

עֶרְיָה f., *nakedness.*

מַעֲרֶה m., *bare place, moor,* Jud. 20:33.

מַעַר m., *nudity.*

מַעֲרוֹת f. pl., *plains, suburbs,* 1 Sa. 17:23.

מַעֲרָת p. n., a town in Judah.

תַּעַר m. (with suff. תַּעְרָהּ).—I. *razor.* — II. *penknife,* Jer. 36:23. — III. *scabbard of a sword.*

עָרוֹם, עֲרוּמִים, עֵרוֹם; see ערם.

עֲרוֹעֵר p. n.; see ערר.

עֵרִי p. n., one of the sons of Gad.

עֲרִיסוֹת *dough;* see ערם.

עֲרִיפִים *nobles;* see ערף.

עָרִיץ; see ערץ.

עֲרִירִים, עֲרִירִי; see ערר.

עָרַךְ (fut. יַעֲרֹךְ).—I. *set in order, arrange, dispose;* with or without מִלְחָמָה *set in battle array;* with or without מִלִּים *prepared an address, speech;* with לְ *to any one;* with אֶל *against any one;* with or without מִשְׁפָּט *prepared a cause for judgment;* ע׳ בְּרִית *prepare a covenant.* — II. *compared together, valued, estimated,* with לְ. Hiph. הֶעֱרִיךְ *valued, set a tax on.*

עֵרֶךְ m.—I. *order, arrangement, system.*—II. *value, estimation.*

מַעֲרָךְ m., *disposings* (of the heart), Pro. 16:1.

מַעֲרָכָה f., *disposition, arrangement.*

מַעֲרֶכֶת f., the same.

עָרַל *esteem profane,* Lev. 19.23. Niph. *appeared uncircumcised,* Hab. 2:16.

עָרֵל, const. עֲרַל, עֲרֵל m., *uncircumcised person;* ע׳ שְׂפָתַיִם *hesitating of speech;* עֲרֵל לֵב *uncircumcised of heart;* לְבָבָם הֶעָרֵל *their heart uncircumcised;* עֲרֵלָה אָזְנָם *uncircumcised of ears.*

עָרְלָה f., *foreskin;* ע׳ לֵב *uncircumcised of heart;* עָרְלָתוֹ פִּרְיוֹ *uncircumcision of its fruits,* i.e. first fruits of a tree, Lev. 19:23; pl. עֲרָלוֹת, const. עָרְלוֹת I. *foreskins.* — II. p. n., a hill not far from Gilgal.

עָרַם *was cunning, subtle.* Hiph. הֶעֱרִים I. *act cunningly.*—II. *act prudently, wisely.* Niph. נֶעֶרַם *became swollen, heaped,* Ex. 15:8.

עָרוּם m.—I. *cunning.*—II. *prudent, cautious.*

עָרוֹם, עָרֹם m. (pl. עֲרוּמִּים; f. עֲרֻמָּה), —I. *naked.*—II. *exposed, spoiled.*

עֵירֹם, עֵרֹם m.—I. *nakedness.*—II. *naked;* adj. pl. עֵירֻמִּים.

עֹרֶם m., *craftiness, cunning,* Job 5:13.

עָרְמָה f.—I. *cunning.*—II. *prudence.*

עֲרֵמָה f., pl. ־ִים—וֹת *heap* (of ruins, of corn, &c.).

עַרְמוֹן m., *the plane tree.*

מַעֲרוֹם m., pl. מַעֲרֻמִּים *nudities,* 2 Chron. 28:15.

עֵרָן p. n. of a man.; patron. עֵרָנִי.

עָרַס root not used; (Ch. עֲרַס *mixed*).

עֲרִיסָה f., pl. עֲרִיסוֹת *dough;* LXX *φύραμα.*

עֲרֹעֵר ,עַרְעָר ,עֲרֹעֵר ,עֲרֹעֵור; see ערר.

עָרַף (fut. יַעֲרֹף).—I. *behead*, Ex. 13:13, &c.—II. *destroy, ruin*, Hos. 10:2.—III. *drop* (as blood from a decapitated bird); applied to speaking.

עֹרֶף m., *neck*; נָתַן עֹרֶף or פָּנָה ע׳ *he turned the back, turned from any one*, with אֶל; הָפַךְ ע׳, פָּנָה ע׳ *turned the back, fled*; נָתַן אוֹיְבִים עֹרֶף *gave him the back of his enemies*, i.e. made them flee before him, Ps. 18:41, with לְ or אֶל.

עָרְפָּה p. n., *Orpah*, a woman of Moab.

עֲרִיפִים m. pl., *clouds*; metaph. nobles, Gen. 37:9.

עֲרָפֶל m., *thick darkness*.

עָרַץ (fut. יַעֲרֹץ).—I. *feared, trembled*.—II. *affrighted, alarmed*.—III. *shook*, with acc. מִפְּנֵי. Niph. part. נַעֲרָץ *terrible*, Ps. 89:8. Hiph. הֶעֱרִיץ *causing to fear*, Isa. 8:13.

עָרוּץ m., *abrupt, fearful place*, Job 30:6.

עָרִיץ m.—I. *strong, mighty*.—II. *violent, cruel*.

מַעֲרִיץ m., *terrible, fearful one*, Isa. 8:13.

מַעֲרָצָה f., *fearfulness, terror*, Isa. 10:33.

עָרַק *fled, escaped*, Job 30:3.

עֹרְקַי *my nerves*, Job 30:17.

עַרְקִי p. n., *the Arkites*, a people of Canaan.

עָרַר (imp. עֹרָה) *was naked*, Isa. 32:11. Po. עוֹרֵר I. *stir up*.—II. *make naked*. Pil. עַרְעֵר and Hithpal הִתְעַרְעֵר *was, became, exposed*.

עֲרִירִי m. (pl. עֲרִירִים) *childless*.

עַרְעָר m., *naked, destitute, poor*.

עֲרֹעֵר ,עֲרוֹעֵר I. perhaps *stump, dead tree*, Jer. 48:6.—II. p. n., *Aroer*, a town on the river Arnon, called also עֲרֹעוֹר.—III. a town near Rabbath Ammon.—IV. p. n., a town in Judah; עֲרֹעֵרִי *an inhabitant of Aroer*.

עֶרֶשׂ f. (pl. עֲרָשׂוֹת) *couch, bed*.

עֵשֶׂב m. (with suff. עֶשְׂבָּם; pl. const. עִשְׂבוֹת) *green herb* (considered as food).

עֲשַׂב m. Ch., the same.

עָשָׂה (fut. יַעֲשֶׂה ,וַיַּעַשׂ; inf. abs. עָשֹׂה, עָשׂוֹ; const. עֲשׂה, עֲשׂוֹת).—I. *wrought, laboured in*, with בְּ.—II. *made, fabricated, produced, constituted, appointed*, with לְ.—III. *did, performed, made, exercised*.—IV. *passed time*, Ecc. 6:12. Niph. נַעֲשָׂה (pret. f. נַעֲשְׂתָה; fut. f. תֵּעָשֶׂה; apoc. תֵּעָשׂ).—I. *was made*.—II. *was done*; יֵעָשֶׂה *to be done*. Pu. עֻשֵּׂיתִי *I was made*, Ps. 139:15. Pi. עִשָּׂה *pressed, injured*, Eze. 23:3, 8.

עֲשָׂהאֵל p. n. of a man.

עֲשִׂיאֵל p. n. of a man.

עֲשָׂיָה p. n. of a man.

מַעֲשֶׂה m. (pl. מַעֲשִׂים).—I. *work* (of an artificer).—II. *labour, business, occupation*.

מַעֲשַׂי p. n. of a man.

מַעֲשֵׂיָהוּ ,מַעֲשֵׂיָה p. n. of a man.

עֵשָׂו (*hairy*), p. n., *Esau*, the son of Isaac; עֵשָׂו ,בֵּית ע׳ ,בְּנֵי עֵשָׂו *the* *sons of Esau, Edomites*; see אֱדֹם; הַר עֵשָׂו *mountains of Edom*.

עָשׂוֹר, עֲשִׂירִי; see עֶשֶׂר.

עָשַׂק. Hithp. *contend with*, Gen. 26:20.

עֵשֶׂק (*strife*), p.n. of a fountain.

עֶשֶׂר f., עֲשָׂרָה, עֲשֶׂרֶת m., *ten*; pl. עֲשָׂרוֹת *tithes*.

עָשָׂר m., עֶשְׂרֵה f. (used only in composition with the other numbers), *ten*; אַחַד עָשָׂר *eleven, the eleventh*; f. אַחַת עֶשְׂרֵה; שִׁשָּׁה עָשָׂר m., שֵׁשׁ עֶשְׂרֵה f., *sixteen*; pl. עֶשְׂרִים *twenty*.

עָשַׂר v. (fut. יַעְשֹׂר) *decimate, tithe*, 1 Sa. 8:15, 17. Pi. עִשֵּׂר *take* or *pay tithe*. Hiph. inf. with pref. לַעְשֵׂר *to pay tithe*.

עָשׂוֹר m., *ten*; בֶּעָשׂוֹר לַחֹדֶשׁ *the tenth* (*day*) *of the month*; נֵבֶל עָשׂוֹר *a lute of ten strings*.

עֲשַׂר f., עַשְׂרָה m. Ch., *ten*; עֶשְׂרִין *twenty*.

עֲשִׂירִי m., *tenth*; f. עֲשִׂירִיָּה, עֲשִׂירִית.

עִשָּׂרוֹן m. (pl. עֶשְׂרֹנִים) *a dry measure*, the tenth part of an ephah.

מַעֲשֵׂר m. (const. מַעְשַׂר; with suff. מַעַשְׂרוֹ; pl. מַעְשְׂרוֹת) *tithe*.

עָשָׂת for עָשְׂתָה Kal pret. f., from עשה.

עָשׁ m., name of a constellation, probably the great bear, Job 9:9; (38:32;) see also עשש.

עַיִשׁ m.; בְּנֵי עַיִשׁ *the three stars in the tail of the bear*, Job. 38 : 32.

עַשְׁוָת p. n. of a man.

עָשֵׁן (fut. יֶעְשַׁן).—I. *smoked*.—II. metaphorically, of the divine wrath.

עָשֵׁן m., *smoking*, Ex. 20:18.

עָשָׁן m. (const. עֲשַׁן; with suff. עֲשָׁנוֹ).—I. *smoke*.—II. *fierce anger*.—III. *cloud*.—IV. p.n. of a town, same as כּוֹר עָשָׁן.

עָשֵׁן m., the same, Ex. 19:18.

עָשַׁק (fut. יַעֲשֹׁק).—I. *oppressed, injured, wronged, defrauded*.—II. *press upon*. Pu. part. f. מְעֻשָּׁקָה *one oppressed*, Isa. 23:12.

עָשׁוֹק m., *fraudulent, oppressive person*, Jer. 22:3.

עֲשׁוּקִים m. pl., *frauds, oppressions*.

עֵשֶׁק p. n. of a man.

עֹשֶׁק m.—I. *oppression, injury*.—II. that which is obtained thereby.

עָשְׁקָה f., *oppresses, ruins me*, Isa. 38:14.

מַעֲשַׁקּוֹת f. pl., *oppressions*.

עָשַׁר (fut. יַעֲשַׁר) *was rich*. Hiph. הֶעֱשִׁיר I. *made rich*.—II. *was, became, rich*. Hith. part. מִתְעַשֵּׁר *becomes rich*, Pro. 13:7.

עָשִׁיר m.—I. *rich*.—II. *proud*.—III. *rich* (in grace), Ecc. 10:6.

עֹשֶׁר m., *riches*.

עָשֵׁשׁ *became old, wasted*.

עָשׁ m., *moth* (that which wastes, eats).

עָשַׁת *was made smooth, shone*, Jer. 5:28. Hith. *remember*, Jon. 1:6.

עֲשַׁת, עֲשִׁית Ch., *thought, designed*, Dan. 6:4.

עֶשֶׁת m.—I. *net-work of ivory*, Cant. 5:14.—II. עַשְׁתֵּי with עָשָׂר, עֶשְׂרֵה (perhaps excess beyond ten) *eleven*.

עַשְׁתּוּת f., *taunting*, Job 12:5.

עֶשְׁתֹּנוֹת f. pl., *devices, machinations*, Ps. 146:4.

עַשְׁתֹּרֶת f., Ἀστάρτη, perhaps the deified planet Venus. It is probably the feminine of אֲשֵׁרָה;

pl. עַשְׁתָּרוֹת *statues of Ashtoreth.* —II. p. n. of a city of Bashan, called also עַשְׁתְּרוֹת קַרְנַיִם *Ashtoreth with horns;* עַשְׁתְּרָתִי *an inhabitant of Ashtoreth;* עַשְׁתְּרוֹת צֹאן *produce of the flock;* LXX. ποιμνία τῶν προβάτων, Deu. 7:13, &c.

עֵת, עֶת־, עֵה com. (with suff. עִתִּי), *time, season,* ὁ καιρός; כָּעֵת הַזֹּאת *about this time;* כָּעֵת מָחָר *about this time to-morrow;* כָּעֵת חַיָּה *this time next year,* or, *as in the times of a vigorous woman* (Lee), Gen. 18:10, 14; כָּעֵת *as at this time;* בָּעֵת הַהוּא *in that time;* בְּעִתּוֹ *in his time;* לְעֵת עֶרֶב *in the evening;* מֵעֵת עַד עֵת *from time to time, always;* עֵת adv. *now, sometimes;* pl. עִתִּים, עִתּוֹת *times, vicissitudes;* רַבּוֹת עִתִּים *many times, on many occasions,* Neh. 9:28.

עַתָּה (with pause עָתָּה adv. νῦν, νύν). —I. *now, shortly, speedily.*—II. *then;* מֵעַתָּה *from this time;* עַד עַתָּה *until this time.*

עִתִּי m., *seasonable,* Lev. 16:21.

עַתַּי p. n. of a man.

עֵת קָצִין p. n. of a man; with ה loc. עִתָּה קָצִין p. n., a city of Zebulon.

עָתַד. Pi. *prepare,* Pro. 24:27. Hith. *have become prepared,* Job 15:28.

עָתִיד m., *prepared, ready.* Pl. עֲתִידוֹת I. *things ready to take place.*—II. *wealth.*

עֲתִיד m. Ch., *ready,* Dan. 3:15.

עַתּוּד m.—I. *he-goat.*—II. *leader, governor.*

עֲתָיָה p. n. of a man.

עֲתָךְ p. n., a town of Judah.

עַתְלַי p. n. of a man.

עֲתַלְיָה, עֲתַלְיָהוּ p. n.—I. *Athaliah,* the wife of Joram.—II. used also for men.

עָתַם. Niph. נֶעְתַּם *is burnt, consumed,* Isa. 9:18.

עָתְנִי p. n. of a man.

עָתְנִיאֵל p. n., *Othniel,* a judge of Israel; LXX. Γοθονιήλ.

עָתַק (fut. יֶעְתַּק).—I. *remove quickly, hurry from,* with מִן.—II. *grow old.* Hiph. הֶעְתִּיק I. *cause to remove.*—II. *transcribe,* Pro. 25:1.—III. *put away, silenced,* Job 32:15.

עָתָק m., *insolent, biting word.*

עָתֵק m., *freedom, liberty,* Pro. 8:18.

עָתִיק m., *freely,* Isa. 23:18.

עַתִּיק m.—I. *ancient,* 1 Chron. 4:22. —II. *removed,* with מִן, Isa. 28:9.

עַתִּיק m. Ch., *ancient,* Dan. 7:9, 13, 22.

עָתַר (fut. יֶעְתַּר), *prayed, supplicated,* with אֶל, לְ. Niph. נֶעְתַּר (inf. נַעְתּוֹר) I. *was prevailed upon by prayer, was made propitious.*—II. נַעְתָּרוֹת *seemingly propitious* (false), Pro. 27:6, with לְ. Hiph. הֶעְתִּיר I. *prayed,* with לְ, בְּעַד.—II. *multiplied,* Eze. 35:13.

עָתָר m.—I. *suppliant,* Zep. 3:10.—II. *abundance,* Eze. 8:1.

עֶתֶר p. n., a town of Simeon.

עֲתֶרֶת f., *riches, abundance,* Jer. 33:6.

פ

פֹּא *here,* Job 38:11, for פֹּה.

פָּאָה. Hiph. fut. with suff. אַפְאֵיהֶם *I will scatter them far and wide,* Deu. 32:26.

פֵּאָה, const. פְּאַת f.—I. *corner, angle* (of a field, table, &c.).—II. קְצוּצֵי פֵאָה *having the hair clipped* or *shaven in angles;* a Canaanitish custom forbidden to the Israelites; פַּאֲתֵי מוֹאָב, Nu. 24:17, *the clipped cornered ones of Moab*, i.e. who trim their hair thus.

פֶּה m. (const. פִּי; with suff. פִּי, פִּיךָ, פִּיו, פִּיהוּ, פִּיהֶם; pl. פִּים, פִּיּוֹת). —I. *mouth;* פֶּה אֶל פֶּה *mouth to mouth, without intervention*, Nu. 12:8; פֶּה אֶחָד *unanimously.*—II. *mouth of a sack, aperture in anything.*— III. *edge of a sword, &c.*— IV. *border of the sea*, Pro. 8:29.—V. פֶּה לָפֶה *from end to end.*—VI. *share, portion;* פִּי שְׁנַיִם *two parts.*— VII. *word, command.* — VIII. *expression, tenor;* with pref. כְּפִי *as, according to;* כְּפִיךָ *as thou (art);* כְּפִי אֲשֶׁר *so as;* לְפִי *according to;* עַל פִּי *according to.*

פֵּיָה f., *edge of a sword;* pl. פֵּיוֹת, Jud. 3:16.

פִּיפִיּוֹת f. pl., *edges, two-edged*, Ps. 149:6; Isa. 41:15.

פִּי־בֶסֶת p.n., a city of Egypt, *Bubastis.*

הַחִירוֹת, פִּי־הַחִירוֹת p.n., a place on the Red Sea.

פִּיכֹל p.n. of a man.

פִּינְחָס p. n. of a man.

פָּאַר. Pi. פֵּאֵר I. *adorned, made beautiful.*—II. *went over the branches accurately*, Deu. 24:20. Hith. הִתְפָּאֵר I. *felt complacency*, with בְּ.—II. *boasted himself*, with עַל.

פְּאֵר m. (pl. פְּאֵרִים, פַּאֲרֵי) *ornamental head-dress.*

פֹּארָה, פֻּארָה f., *a branch.*

פָּארוּר m., *blackness, paleness* (of face) Joel 2:6; Nah. 2:11.

תִּפְאֶרֶת, תִּפְאָרָה f.—I. *beauty, ornament.*—II. *glory.*—III. *boast, subject of glorying.*

פָּארָן p. n., *Paran*, the wilderness between Egypt and Palestine.

פָּגַג (Arab. *unripe fig*).

פַּג m., pl. פַּגִּים *unripe figs*, Cant. 2:13.

פִּגּוּל m., pl. פִּגֻּלִים *impure, disgusting* (thing).

פָּגַע I. *came to a place, reached*, with בְּ.—II. *met, fell in with*, with אֶל, בְּ.— III. *met hostilely, fell upon*, with בְּ.—IV. *waited on in prayer, entreated.*— V. *admitted favourably.* Hiph. הִפְגִּיעַ I. *cause to come, fall in with, wait upon.*—II. *fell upon.*—III. *entreated.*

פֶּגַע m., *occurrence, accident.*

פַּגְעִיאֵל p. n., a prince of Asher.

מִפְגָּע m., *object of attack, butt*, Job 7:20.

פָּגַר. Pi. פִּגֵּר *became languid, unable to proceed*, 1 Sa. 30:10, 21, with מִן.

פֶּגֶר m. (pl. פְּגָרִים, פִּגְרֵי) *dead body of man* or *beast.*

פָּגַשׁ I. *met*, with בְּ.—II. *met hostilely*, Hos. 13:8, &c. Niph. נִפְגַּשׁ *met each other.* Pi. *stumble against*, Job 5:14.

פָּדָה I. *redeemed*, with בְּ (of the price). —II. *delivered.* Niph. נִפְדָּה *was redeemed, delivered.* Hiph. הֶפְדָּה *allowed to be redeemed*, Ex. 21:8.

Hoph. inf. הָפְדֵּה same as Niph., Lev. 19:20.

פְּדַהְאֵל p. n. of a man.

פְּדָהצוּר p.n. of a man.

פְּדוּיִם m. pl., λύτρον.—I. *redemption price, ransom.* — II. *redeemed, delivered persons.*

פָּדוֹן p. n. of a man.

פְּדוּת f.— I. *redemption.* — II. פְּדוּת *separation*, Ex. 8:19.

פְּדָיָה, פְּדָיָהוּ p. n. of a man.

פִּדְיוֹם, פִּדְיוֹן m., *ransom.*

פַּדָּן m., *plain*, Gen. 48:7; פַּדַּן אֲרָם *Padan-Aram;* with ה, פַּדֶּנָה אֲרָם *towards Padan-Aram.*

אַפֶּדֶן Ch., *palace, camp*, Dan. 11:45.

פָּדַע *redeem, deliver*, Job 33:24.

פֶּדֶר m. (with suff. פִּדְרוֹ) *fat.*

פֵּה; see פאה.

פֹּה (פֹּא, פּוֹ).— I. *here.* — II. *hither;* מִפֹּה *hence;* עַד פֹּה *thus far;* אֵיפֹה *where?*

פּוּאָה (פֻּוָה) p. n. of a man.

פּוּג (fut. וַיָּפָג, יָפוּג) *became chilled, languid, ceased to act.* Niph. the same, Ps. 38:9.

פּוּגָה f., *intermission*, Lam. 2:18.

הֲפוּגָה f., *intermission*, Lam. 3:49.

פּוּחַ I. *blew.* — II. *became cool by a breeze.* Hiph. הֵפִיחַ I. *inflamed*, Pro. 29:8.—II. *blew, blew a fire*, with בְּ.—III. *puffed at* (scornfully), with בְּ.—IV. *uttered.*—V. (from פַּח) *ensnared*, Ps. 12:6.

פִּיחַ m., *ashes*, Ex. 9:8, 10.

פּוּט p. n., one of the sons of Ham, and his descendants.

פּוּטִיאֵל p. n. of a man.

פּוֹטִיפַר p. n. (πετεφρη, *he who is devoted to the sun*), an officer in Pharaoh's household.

פּוֹטִי פֶרַע (the same); p. n., Joseph's father-in-law.

פּוּךְ m.—I. *stibium, powdered antimony.*—II. אַבְנֵי פוּךְ; LXX. λίθοι πολυτελεῖς, *a precious stone;* קֶרֶן הַפּוּךְ p. n. of a woman.

פּוֹל m., *beans.*

פּוּל p. n.—I. a people and nation of Africa.—II. a king of Assyria.

פּוּם, פֻּם m. Ch., *mouth, aperture.*

פּוּן, fut. אָפוּנָה; LXX. ἐξηπορήθην; Vulg. conturbatus sum, *I pine away*, Ps. 88:16.

פּוּנֶה p.n., a gate of Jerusalem.

פּוּנִי p.n. of a man.

פּוּנֹן p.n., a town on the borders of the desert.

פּוּעָה p.n. of a woman.

פּוּץ I. *dispersed themselves, were scattered.*—II. *overflowed.* Niph. *were scattered.* Pil. פֹּצֵץ and Pilp. פִּצְפֵּץ *shatter, shake to pieces.* Hiph. הֵפִיץ I. *scattered, confused.* —II. *poured out.*— III. *was scattered.* Hithpo. *are shattered*, Hab. 3:6. Tiphel תְּפוֹצוֹתִיכֶם *I will scatter you*, Jer. 25:34.

מֵפִיץ m.—I. *disperser.*—II. *club*, Pro. 25:18.

I. פּוּק *stagger, stumble*, Isa. 28:7. Hiph. *stagger, stumble*, Jer. 10:4.

II. פּוּק Hiph. הֵפִיק 1. *supplied*, Isa. 58:10.—2 *obtained.*—3. *prospered*, Ps. 140:9.

פּוּקָה f., *cause of stumbling*, 1 Sa. 25:31.

פִּיק m., *staggering*, Nah. 2:11.

I. פּוּר (Arab. *bubbled*); see פָּרַר.

פּוּרָה f., *wine-press*.

פָּרוּר m., *pot for boiling*.

II. פּוּר m., a Persian word.—I. *lot*; pl. פּוּרִים.—II. *the feast of Purim*.

פּוֹרָתָא p.n., a son of Haman.

פּוּשׁ (pret. פִּשְׁתֶּם).—I. *became numerous, flourished*. — II. *spread themselves*, Hab. 1:8. Niph. *were scattered*, Nah. 3:18.

פַּשׁ m., *extent*, Job 35:15.

פִּישׁוֹן p.n., one of the rivers of Paradise.

פּוּת (Arab. *interstice*).

פֹּת m., Isa. 3:17; pl. פֹּתוֹת *hinges*, 1 Ki. 7:50.

פּוּתִי p. n. of a man.

פָּזַז (fut. pl. יָפֹזּוּ) *are strong and active*, Gen. 49:24. Pi. פִּזֵּז *dancing*, 2 Sa. 6:16. Hoph. part. מוּפָז *purified*, 1 Ki. 10:18.

פָּז m.—I. *refined gold*.— II. *refined*, Cant. 5:11.

פָּזַר *dispersed*, Jer. 50:17. Pi. פִּזַּר I. *dispersed*.—II. *distributed liberally*. Niph. and Pu. *was scattered*.

פַּח m. (pl. פַּחִים).—I. *snare, gin*.— II. *any concealed danger*.—III. *plate of metal*, Ex. 39:3; Nu. 17:3.

פָּחַד (fut. יִפְחַד).—I. *feared*, with מִן, מִפְּנֵי. — II. *was agitated*. — III *hastened*. Pi. *feared greatly, continually*. Hiph. *caused to shake, tremble*, Job 4:14.

פַּחַד m. (with suff. פַּחְדְּכֶם; pl. פְּחָדִים).—I. *fear, dread, reverence*. —II. *object of fear*.— III. *thigh*, Job 40:17; פ׳ אֱלֹהִים *fear of God*.

פַּחְדָּה f., *fear*, Jer. 2:19.

פֶּחָה m. (const. פַּחַת; with suff. פֶּחָם, פֶּחָתְךָ; pl. פַּחוֹת; const. פַּחֲווֹת).—I. *governor of a province*. — II. *captain*; Ch. the same; hence the modern word *Pacha*.

פָּחַז (*swelling like boiling water*).—I. *was dissolute*, Jud. 9:4.— II. *was proud*, Zep. 3:4.

פַּחַז m., *wantonness, pride*, Gen. 49:4.

פַּחֲזוּת f., *pride*, Jer. 23:32.

פָּחַם root not used; (Arab. *charcoal*).

פֶּחָם m., *charcoal*.

פָּחַר root not used; (Syr. *he founded*).

פֶּחָר m. Ch., *potter*, Dan. 2:41.

פַּחַת m. (pl. פְּחָתִים).—I. *a pit, well*. —II. *destruction*.

פְּחֶתֶת f., *corrosion, fretting into a garment*, Lev. 13:55.

פַּחַת־מוֹאָב p. n. of a man.

פַּחַת Kal inf., from נפח.

פִּטְדָה f., a precious stone, *topaz* or *emerald*.

פָּטַר (fut. יִפְטַר).—I. *slipped out*, or *away*.—II. *let out* (of water).— III. *expand* (of flowers), 1 Ki. *c*. 6. —IV. *exempt from duty*, 1 Chron. 9:33. Hiph. *open wide* (the mouth), Ps. 22:8.

פָּטִיר Ketib, same as פָּטוּר (part. see פָּטַר), *exempt from duty*, 1 Chron. 9:33.

פֶּטֶר m., *opening, beginning;* פֶּטֶר רֶחֶם *first-born.*

פִּטְרָה f., the same, Nu. 8:16.

פָּטַשׁ root not used; (Arab. *beat out iron with a hammer, spread out*).

פַּטִּישׁ m., *a hammer.*

פַּטִּישׁ m. Ch., *a tunic,* Dan. 3:21.

פִּי with comp. פִּיָה; see פֶּה in פָּאָה.

פִּיד root not used; (Arab. *disappeared, died*).

פִּיד m., *destruction.*

פִּיחַ; see פּוּחַ.

פִּילֶגֶשׁ; see פִּלֶגֶשׁ.

פִּים root not used; (Arab. *was fat*).

פִּימָה f., *fatness, food, strength,* Job 15:27.

פִּינֹן p. n., a prince of Edom.

פִּיפִיּוֹת; see פאה.

פִּיק; see פוק.

פִּישׁוֹן; see פוש.

פִּיתֹן p. n. of a man.

פָּכָה. Pi. *flowing out,* Eze. 47:2

פַּךְ m., *flask, cruse.*

פֹּכֶרֶת הַצְּבָיִים p. n. of a man.

פָּלָא. Niph. נִפְלָא I. *was marvellous.* —II. *appeared marvellous,* with בְּעֵינֵי.—III. *was concealed,* with מִן.—IV. *was struck with wonder;* part. pl. נִפְלָאוֹת, נִפְלָאִים *wonderful things, wonderfully.* Pi. פִּלֵּא *set apart;* פִּלֵּא נֶדֶר *set apart by vow, devoted.* Hiph. הִפְלָא, הִפְלִיא I. *set apart.*—II. *made wonderful.* —III. *acted wonderfully.* Hith. *show one's self wonderful,* with בְּ, Job 10:16.

פֶּלֶא m. (with suff. פִּלְאֲךָ).—I. *separation, peculiarity.*—II. *marvellousness.*—III. *a miracle;* pl. פְּלָאִים adv. *wonderfully;* פְּלָאוֹת *wonderful things.*

פִּלְאִי or פְּלִי m., *wonderful,* Jud. 13:18; Ps. 139:6.

פְּלִיאָה f., or פִּלְאִיָה the same.

פְּלָאיָה p. n. of a man.

פְּלָיָה p. n. of a man.

פַּלּוּא p. n., a son of Reuben; patron. פַּלֻּאִי.

מִפְלָאָה f., *miracle,* Job 37:16.

פָּלַג. Niph. *was divided.* Pi. I. *cut out, formed,* Job 38:25.—II. *divided,* Ps. 55:10.

פְּלַג Ch., *divided,* Dan. 2:41.

פְּלַג m. Ch., *half,* Dan. 7:25.

פֶּלֶג m.—I. *channel, stream.*—II. p. n., a son of Eber.

פְּלַגּוֹת f. pl., *brooks.*

פְּלֻגָּה f., pl. פְּלֻגּוֹת *divisions,* 2 Chron. 35:5.

מִפְלַגָּה f., pl. מִפְלַגּוֹת the same, 2 Chron. 35:12.

פִּלֶגֶשׁ, פִּילֶגֶשׁ f. (pl. פִּלַגְשִׁים, פִּלַגְשֵׁי), *concubine,* παλλακή.

פְּלָדָה f., pl. פְּלָדוֹת *iron of chariots,* perhaps *scythes,* Nah. 2:4.

פִּלְדָּשׁ p. n. of a man.

פָּלָה same as פָּלָא. Niph. *are separated,* Ex. 33:16. Hiph. הִפְלָה I. *separated.*—II. *set apart,* Ps. 4:4.

פְּלֹנִי m.—I. with אַלְמֹנִי ὁ δεῖνα, *a certain one.*—II. p. n. of a man.

פַּלְמוֹנִי m., *this particular one,* Dan. 8:13.

פָּלַח *cut,* Ps. 141:7. Pi. פִּלַּח I. *cut to*

pieces, 2 Ki. 4:39.—II. *disentangle*, Job 39:3. – III. *pierce through*, Pro. 7:23.—IV. *harrow*, Job 16:13.

פֶּלַח m.—I. *piece*, *part*.—II. *millstone*; פֶּלַח רֶכֶב *upper mill-stone*; פ׳ תַּחְתִּית *nether mill-stone*.

פִּלְהָא p. n. of a man.

פְּלַח Ch., *served*, *worshipped*.

פָּלְחָן m. Ch., *service*, *worship*, Ezr. 7:19.

פָּלַט *escaped*, Eze. 7:16. Pi. I. *delivered*.—II. *bring forth safely*, Job 21:10. Hiph. *delivered*.

פָּלִיט, פָּלֵיט m., *fugitive*, *one escaped*.

פְּלֵטָה, פְּלֵיטָה f., *the escaped*, *remnant*.

פַּלֵּט m., *deliverance*.

פֶּלֶט p. n. of a man.

פַּלְטִי p. n. of a man.

פִּלְטַי p. n. of a man.

פְּלַטְיָה p. n. of a man.

פְּלַטְיָהוּ p. n. of a man.

מִפְלָט m., *escape*, *safety*, Ps. 55:9.

פְּלִי, פֶּלִא, פִּלְאָה, פְּלָיָה; see פלא.

פָּלִיל, פְּלִילָה, פְּלִילִי; see פלל.

פָּלַךְ root not used; (Arab. *was round*).

פֶּלֶךְ m.—I. *spinning distaff*.—II. *circuit*, *district*.

פָּלַל. Pi. פִּלֵּל I. *judged*, 1 Sa. 2:25. —II. *adjudged punishment*, with לְ, Eze. 16:52.—III. *inflicted punishment*, Ps. 106:30.—IV. *expected*, Gen. 48:11. Hith. *prayed* (lit. appealed to a judge), with בְּעַד, עַל, לְ, אֶל, לִפְנֵי.

פָּלִיל m., *a judge*; pl. פְּלִילִים.

פְּלִילָה f., *justice*, Isa. 16:3.

פְּלִילִי m., *judicial*, Job 31:28.

פְּלִילִיָּה f., *judgment*, Isa. 28:7.

פָּלָל p. n. of a man.

פְּלַלְיָה p. n. of a man.

תְּפִלָּה f.—I. *prayer*.—II. *intercession*.—III. *hymn*, Ps. 72:20.

פַּלְמֹנִי, פְּלֹנִי; see פלה.

פָּלַס. Pi.—I. *pondered*, Isa. 26:7.—II. *approved*.—III. *planned*.

פֶּלֶס m., *balance*, *steel-yard*.

מִפְלָשׂ m., *poising*, *balancing*, Job 37:16.

פָּלַץ. Hith. *shook*, *trembled*, Job 9:6.

פַּלָּצוּת f., *trembling*, *fear*.

מִפְלֶצֶת f., *idol*, *image*.

תִּפְלֶצֶת f., *terror*, Jer. 49:16.

פָּלַשׁ. Hith. *rolled themselves in dust*.

פְּלֶשֶׁת p. n., *Philistia*, the sea-coast of the south of Palestine; it was divided into five provinces. פְּלִשְׁתִּי *a Philistine*, pl. פְּלִשְׁתִּים; פְּלִשְׁתִּיִּים *Philistines*; LXX. Ἀλλόφυλοι.

פֶּלֶת p. n. of a man.

פְּלֵתִי m., *mercenary soldier*, *Pelethite*.

פֵּן, פִּנָּה, see פנן; פֶּן־, see פנה.

פַּנַּג, perhaps *millet*, in English, *panic*, Eze. 27:17.

פָּנָה (fut. יִפְנֶה, תֵּפֶן, וַיִּפֶן, (עֹרֶף).—I. *turn himself to go away*.—II. *turned towards*.—III. *changed*, *declined*, *began*; לִפְנוֹת בֹּקֶר *at the turn of the morning*, i.e. in the morning; לִפְנוֹת עֶרֶב *in the evening*. Pi. פִּנָּה I. *removed*.—II. *cleared a road* or *house*. Hiph. הִפְנָה (fut. apoc. וַיֵּפֶן).—I. *turned*.—II. *turned himself*. Hoph. *were made to turn themselves*, Jer. 49:8.

פָּנֶה m., pl. פָּנִים; const. פְּנֵי I. *face*

פָּנִים בְּפָנִים ,פָּנִים אֶל־פָּנִים *face to face.*—II. *person, presence;* שׂוּם פָּנִים, with אֶל or עַל *he set his face toward;* נָתַן ,שׂוּם פ׳, with לְ and inf. *he designed to do;* פָּנַי *my person,* i.e. I; פָּנֶיךָ *thy person,* i.e. thou, &c.— III. *surface.*—IV. *front;* פָּנִים *in front;* לְפָנִים *before, formerly;* מִפָּנִים *in, from the presence of;* מִלְּפָנִים *from ancient time;* with prefixes אֶל־פְּנֵי *before, in presence of;* אֶת־פְּנֵי *before;* מֵאֵת פְּנֵי *from before;* בִּפְנֵי *before;* לִפְנֵי *in the sight of, before, preceding, against, in time;* with suff. לְפָנָיו ,לְפָנֶיךָ ,לְפָנַי, לִפְנֵיהֶם ,לִפְנֵיכֶם ;מִלִּפְנֵי *from, because of;* מִפְּנֵי אֲשֶׁר *because of;* עַל־פְּנֵי *in presence of, in preference to, towards;* מֵעַל־פְּנֵי *from before.*

פֶּן־, part. *μή, lest.*

פְּנִיאֵל ,פְּנוּאֵל p.n.—I. a place beyond Jordan.—II. of a man.

פְּנִים m., *within;* פְּנִימָה *to, on, the inside;* לִפְנִימָה *within, on the inside;* מִלִּפְנִים ,מִפְּנִימָה *within.*

פְּנִימִי m., פְּנִימִית f., *inner.*

פְּנִינִים m. pl., *pearls.*

פֵּן m. (with suff. פִּנָּהּ; pl. פִּנִּים) *corner.*

פִּנָּה f.—I. *corner;* אֶבֶן פ׳ ,רֹאשׁ פ׳ *chief corner-stone.*—II. *battlement, parapet.*—III. *dignitary, prince.*

פְּנִנָּה p.n. of a woman.

פָּנַק. Pi. *brought up delicately,* Pro. 29:21.

פַּס ,פַּסִּים ,פִּסָּה; see פסס.

פָּסַג. Pi. *count, observe,* Ps. 48:14.

פִּסְגָּה p.n., a peak on the mountains of Moab.

פָּסַח *passed over for defence, defended, protected.* Niph. *was lamed,* 2 Sa. 4:4. Pi. *leaped about,* 1 Ki. 18: 26.

פָּסֵחַ p.n. of a man.

פֶּסַח m.—I. *feast of the Passover.*—II. *the paschal lamb;* עָשָׂה פ׳ *keep the Passover.*

פִּסֵּחַ m. (pl. פִּסְחִים) *lame.*

תִּפְסַח p.n., a city on the Euphrates, *Thapsacus.*

פָּסַךְ p. n. of a man.

פָּסַל *hewed, carved.*

פָּסִיל m., pl. פְּסִילִים *carved images, idols.*

פֶּסֶל m. (with suff. פִּסְלִי) *an idol.*

פְּסַנְתֵּרִין ,פְּסַנְטֵרִין m. Ch., *ψαλτήριον, a musical instrument.*

פָּסַס *ceased to exist, disappeared,* Ps. 12:2.

פַּס m. כְּתֹנֶת פַּסִּים *coat of many colours,* Gen. 37:3; *long cloak,* covering the hands and feet (Ges. and Lee); but Jacob knew Joseph's coat when torn and dipped in blood; it was the quality or colour of the cloth, therefore, not the shape that distinguished it; LXX. χιτὼν ποικίλος.

פַּס m., *palm of the hand.*

פִּסָּה f., *abundance,* Ps. 72:16.

פַּס דַּמִּים p. n., same as אֶפֶס דַּמִּים.

פִּסְפָּה p.n. of a man

פָּעָה *cry out,* Isa. 42:14

אֶפְעֶה com., *adder, viper*

אֶפַע the same.

פָּעוּ, פָּעִי p.n., a city of Edom.

פְּעוֹר; see פער.

פָּעַל v. (fut. יִפְעֹל יִפְעַל).—I *worked.* —II. *made, formed.*—III. *did, performed.*— IV. *practised,* with לְ or בְּ of the person for whom the action is performed.

פֹּעַל m. (with suff. פָּעֳלוֹ, פָּעָלְךָ, פָּעֳלוֹ; pl. פְּעָלִים).—I. *work, action, practice.*—II. *wages.*—III. *acquisition,* Pro. 21:6.

פְּעֻלָּה f.—I. *work, employment.*— II. *wages,* Lev. 19:13.—III. *reward* or *punishment.*

פָּעֳלוֹ for פָּעֳלוֹ, from פֹּעַל.

פְּעֻלְּתַי p.n. of a man.

מִפְעָל m., } *work, doings.*
מִפְעָלָה f., }

פָּעַם *moved, excited to action,* Jud. 13: 25. Niph. *was moved, disturbed.* Hith. same as Niph., Dan. 2:1.

פַּעַם f. (m. Jud. 16:28).—I. pl. פְּעָמִים *footsteps, feet.*—II. *progress.*—III. *an anvil,* Isa. 41:7. — IV. pl. פְּעָמוֹת *feet of the ark* (Lee).—V. *an act,* and *the time of its performance, a time, once;* dual פַּעֲמַיִם *twice;* שֶׁבַע פְּעָמִים *seven times;* פַּעַם וּשְׁתַּיִם *once or twice,* Neh. 13:20; בַּפַּעַם הַזֹּאת, הַפַּעַם, בַּפַּעַם הַהִיא *now, at the present time;* כְּפַעַם בְּפַעַם *even so as before;* פַּעַם...פַּעַם *sometimes.*

פַּעֲמוֹן m., *bell,* Ex. chapters 38 and 39 only.

פַּעְנֵחַ; see צָפְנַת פ׳.

פָּעַר *open the mouth, gape,* with פֶּה, בְּפֶה.

פְּעוֹר p. n. of a mountain of Moab; בַּעַל-פְּעוֹר and פְּעוֹר an idol of Moab.

פַּעֲרַי p. n., one of David's generals; elsewhere נַעֲרַי.

פָּצָה I. *opened the mouth.*—II. *rescued.*

פָּצַח *broke forth into singing,* with רִנָּה. Pi. *broke to pieces,* Mic. 3:3.

פְּצִירָה; see פצר.

פָּצַל. Pi. פִּצֵּל *peeled,* Gen. 30:37, 38.

פְּצָלוֹת f. pl., *the parts peeled, stripped of bark,* Gen. 30:37.

פָּצַם *broke the earth,* Ps. 60:4.

פָּצַע *wounded;* פְּצוּעַ דַּכָּה *eunuch.*

פֶּצַע m. (with suff. פִּצְעִי; pl. פְּצָעִים), *a wound.*

פָּצַץ Hithpo.; see פּוּץ.

פִּצֵּץ p. n. of a man.

פָּצַר (fut. יִפְצַר).—I. *pressed upon to injure,* Gen. 19:9.—II. *urged to consent,* with בְּ. Hiph. inf. הַפְצַר *was too urgent, obstinate,* 1 Sam. 15:23.

פְּצִירָה f., *a file,* 1 Sam. 13:21.

פָּקַד I. *visited, enquired for.*—II. *enquired for without finding, missed.* —III. *enquired into* or *after, cared for.*—IV. *punished,* with אֶל of the crime, or עַל of the person, and בְּ of the punishment.—V. *examined and arranged*—VI. *numbered, took account of.*—VII. *placed, appointed, set over,* with עַל, אֶת, (פְּקוּדִים *officers*).—VIII. *laid a charge upon any one,* with עַל. Niph. I. *was missed.*—II. *was punished.*—III. *was numbered.*—IV. *punishment was inflicted.*—V. *was visited with evil.* Pi. *ex-*

amined, numbered. Pu. I. *was taken account of*, Ex. 38:21.—II. *was deprived of*, Isa. 38:10. Hiph. I. *placed, appointed*, with עַל or לְ.—II. *committed to some one*, with אֶת, בְּיַד, עַל־יְדֵי. Hoph. I. *was punished*, Jer. 6:6.—II. *placed, appointed;* part. מֻפְקָדִים *officers.* Hith. *was examined, numbered.* Hoth. pl. הָתְפָּקְדוּ the same.

פְּקֻדָּה f.—I. *providence*, Job 10:12.—II. *office.*—III. *government.*—IV. *class*, 1 Chron. 23:11.—V. *treasure*, Isa. 15:7.—VI. *punishment;* בֵּית הַפְּקֻדּוֹת *prison.*

פִּקָּדוֹן m., *deposit.*

פְּקִדוּת f., *captain of the guard*, Jer. 37:13.

פְּקוֹד m.—I. *punishment*, an allegorical name of Babylon, Jer. 50:21.—II. *dominion*, Eze. 23:23.

פִּקּוּדִים m. pl., *precepts of God.*

פָּקִיד m., *officer, chief, superintendent.*

מִפְקָד m.—I. *arrangement*, 2 Chron. 31:13.—II. *census publicly appointed*, 2 Sa. 24:9.—III. שַׁעַר הַמִּפְקָד one of the gates of Jerusalem, Neh. 3:31.

פָּקַח (fut. יִפְקַח) *opened the eyes* or *ears.* Niph. *was opened.*

פֶּקַח p. n., *Pekah*, king of Israel.

פְּקַחְיָה p. n., *Pekahiah*, king of Israel.

פִּקֵּחַ m., *having the eyes opened, able to see.*

פְּקַח־קוֹחַ m., *complete opening, opening of the prison*, Isa. 61:1.

פָּקִיד *officer;* see פקד.

פַּקֻּעֹת f. pl., *the fox-grape*, 2 Ki. 4:39.

פְּקָעִים m. pl., *architectural ornaments of a globular form*, 1 Ki. 6:18; 7:24.

פַּר, פָּר m., *young bull.*

פָּרָה f.—I. *young cow, heifer.*—II. הַפָּרָה p. n., a town in the tribe of Benjamin.

פָּרָא same as פָּרָה Hiph., *propagate*, Hos. 13:15.

פֶּרֶא, פֶּרֶה com. (pl. פְּרָאִים), *wild ass.*

פִּרְאָם p. n., a king of Canaan.

פֹּרָאת same as פֹּארֹת; see פֹּארָה.

פַּרְבָּר, פַּרְוָר m., *suburb.*

פָּרַד *separated, spread* (of wings). Niph. *separated himself*, with מִן, מֵעַל. Pi. *go aside*, Hos. 4:14. Pu. part. מְפֹרָד *separate*, Est. 3:8. Hiph. same as Kal. Hith. same as Niph.

פֶּרֶד m. (with suff. פִּרְדּוֹ; pl. פְּרָדִים), *a mule.*

פִּרְדָּה f., *she-mule.*

פְּרֻדֹת f. pl., *seeds scattered, corn sown*, Joel 1:17.

פַּרְדֵּס m., παράδεισος, *enclosure, park*, Neh. 2:8; Cant. 4:13; Ecc. 2:5.

פָּרָה *heifer;* see פַּר; פֶּרֶה same as פֶּרֶא *wild ass.*

פָּרָה *bore fruit, was fruitful* (of trees, plants, men, animals, &c.); part. f. פֹּרָת, פֹּרִיָּה *fruit tree.* Hiph. הִפְרָה (fut. apoc. וַיֶּפֶר) *made fruitful.*

פְּרִי m. (with pause פֶּרִי; with suff. פִּרְיִי, פֶּרְיְךָ, פִּרְיָם, פֶּרְיְכֶם, פִּרְיהֶם). I. *fruit of a tree;* עֵץ פְּרִי *fruit tree.*—II. *produce of the ground;* אֶרֶץ פְּרִי *a fruitful land.*—III. *fruit of the womb, offspring.*—IV *result of actions, reward or punishment.*

פֶּרֶה p. n. of a man.

פְּרוּדָא ,פְּרִידָא p.n. of a man.

פַּרְוַיִם p. n. of a country, same as סְפַרְוַיִם, which see.

פַּרְוָר *suburb;* see פַּרְבָּר.

פָּרוּר *pot;* see פור.

פָּרַז (Arab. *separated*). see פָּרַץ.

פְּרָז m., *ruler*, Hab. 3:14.

פִּרְזוֹן m., *justice;* with suff. פִּרְזוֹנוֹ, Jud. 5:7, 11.

פְּרָזוֹת f. pl., *unwalled towns, villages.*

פְּרָזִי m., *one living in a village;* pl. פְּרָזִים; Ketib פרוזים.

פְּרִזִּי p. n., *the Perizzite*, a people of Canaan.

פַּרְזֶל m. Ch., *iron;* Heb. בַּרְזֶל.

פָּרַח (fut. יִפְרַח).—I. *budded.*—II. *shot up, flourished.*—III. *spread, extended itself.* Hiph. *caused to bud, budded.*

פֶּרַח m. (with suff. פִּרְחָהּ; pl. פְּרָחִים).—I. *young shoot.*— II. *bud.*—III. *the artificial representation of a bud.*

פָּרוּחַ p.n. of a man.

פִּרְחַח m., *insolent, with insult*, Job 30:12.

אֶפְרֹחַ m., pl. אֶפְרֹחִים *young of birds.*

פָּרַט *abounded* or *sang;* LXX. ἐπικροτοῦντες, Am. 6:5.

פֶּרֶט m., *omission, what is omitted*, Lev. 19:10.

פְּרִי *fruit;* see פרה.

פָּרִיץ *wild beast;* see פרץ.

פֶּרֶךְ m., *harshness, oppression.*

פָּרֹכֶת f., *the veil which separates the holy place from the holy of holies.*

פָּרַם (fut. יִפְרֹם) *rent, torn* (of garments), Leviticus only.

פַּרְמַשְׁתָּא p.n., a son of Haman.

פַּרְנָךְ p.n. of a man.

פָּרַס *broke, distributed, bread.* Hiph. *dividing the hoof;* see פַּרְסָה.

פְּרַס Ch., *divide.*

פֶּרֶס m., *the osprey*, Lev. 11:13; Deu 14:12.

פַּרְסָה f., *a hoof;* pl. const. פַּרְסוֹת, פַּרְסֵי.

פָּרַס *Persia;* פַּרְסִי *a Persian, Parsee.*

פָּרַע I. *uncovered the head.*—II. *placed in a state of disorder*, Ex. 32:25. III. *was disregarded.*— IV. *left a road*, Pro. 4:15. — V. *exempted*, Eze. 24:14.—VI. *avenged*, Jud. 5:2. Niph. *became lawless*, Pro. 29:18. Hiph. I. *made idle*, Ex. 5:4.—II. *brought vengeance on*, 2 Chron. 28:19.

פֶּרַע m., *head of hair;* pl. פְּרָעוֹת, פַּרְעוֹת, *vengeance*, Deu. 32:42; Jud. 5:2.

פִּרְעָתוֹן p.n., a town of Ephraim; פִּרְעָתֹנִי *a Pirathonite.*

פַּרְעֹה title of all monarchs of Egypt. (lit. *φρη the sun*); Φαραώ.

פַּרְעֹשׁ m.—I. *a flea.*—II. p. n. of a man.

פַּרְפַּר p. n., a small river which joins the Amana near Damascus, 2 Ki. 5:12.

פָּרַץ (fut. יִפְרֹץ).—I. *broke down, made a breach in, a wall.*— II. *burst forth, overflowed* (of water).—III. *broke in pieces, afflicted.*—IV. *urged* (a person).—V. *dispersed an enemy*

VI. *distributed* persons, 2 Chron. 11:23. Niph. part. נִפְרָץ *much, frequent* (Lee), 1 Sa. 3:1. Pu. *broken down*, Neh. 1:3. Hith. *breaking loose*, 1 Sa. 25:10.

פָּרִיץ m.—I. *violent, lawless, person.* —II. *wild beast*, Isa. 35:9.

פֶּרֶץ m. (pl. פְּרָצִים, פְּרָצוֹת).—I. *breach in a wall.*—II. *overflowing of water.*—III. *sudden calamity.*—IV. p. n. of a man; patron. פַּרְצִי.

מִפְרָץ m., probably, *creek*, marg. (*breach*, Eng. Ver.), Jud. 5:17.

פָּרַק I. *pulled off*, with מֵעַל, Gen. 27:40.—II. *tore in pieces*, Ps. 7:3.—III. *rescued.* Pi. פֵּרֵק I. *tore in pieces.*—II. *pulled off*, Ex. 32:2. Hith. הִתְפָּרֵק I. *was broken off*, Eze. 19:12.—II. *pulled off from himself.*

פְּרַק Ch., *break off*, Dan. 4:24.

פָּרָק m. (Kri מָרָק without authority), *fragments*, Isa. 65:4.

פֶּרֶק m.—I. *tearing in pieces, prey*, Nah. 3:1.—II. *cross way*, Obad. *v.* 14.

מַפְרֶקֶת f., *vertebræ of the neck*, 1 Sa. 4:18.

פָּרַר *cleft, divided*; inf. abs. פּוֹר. Pil. פּוֹרֵר *cleft*, Ps. 74:13. Hithpo. *was cloven*, Isa. 24:19. Pilp. פִּרְפֵּר *shattered, agitated, the mind*, Job 16:12. Hiph. הֵפֵר, הֵפִיר; with pause הֵפַר I. *broke a covenant* or *command.*—II. *frustrated.* — III. *annulled.* — IV. *withdrew, broke off.* Hoph. הֻפַר *was disannulled.*

פָּרַשׂ (fut. יִפְרֹשׂ). — I. *spread.* — II. *stretched out the hands.*—III. *gave, assisted*, Pro. 31:19. — IV. *seized*, Lam. 1:10. — V. *broke*, like פָּרַס. Niph. *was scattered*, Eze. 17:21. Pi. פֵּרַשׂ, with pause פֵּרֵשׂ I. *spread out the hands.*—II. *scattered.*

מִפְרָשׂ m.—I. *expansions of*, Job 36:29.—II. *sail of a ship*, Eze. 27:7.

פָּרַשׁ *mark distinctly*, Lev. 24:12. Niph. *scattered*, Eze. 34:12; see פרשׂ. Pu. פֹּרַשׁ I. *was marked out distinctly*, Num. 15:34.—II. *made clear*, Neh. 8:8. Hiph. *stung*, Pro. 23:32.

פְּרַשׁ Ch., the same. Pa. part. מְפָרַשׁ *made clear.*

פֶּרֶשׁ m. (with suff. פִּרְשׁוֹ) *dung.*

פָּרָשָׁה f., *distinct account*, Est. 4:7; 10:2.

פָּרָשׁ m., pl. פָּרָשִׁים *horses*; בַּעֲלֵי הַפָּרָשִׁים *horsemen.*

פָּרָשׁ, const. פְּרַשׁ m., *horseman*; pl. פָּרָשִׁים.

פַּרְשֶׁגֶן,(פַּתְשֶׁגֶן)m. Heb. and Ch., *copy of a writing*, Ezra only.

פַּרְשְׁדוֹנָה or פַּרְשְׁדוֹן *dung*, as some render, *podex*, as others, Jud. 3:22.

פַּרְשֵׁז *spreading*, Job 26:9

פַּרְשַׁנְדָּתָא p.n., a son of Haman.

פְּרָת p. n., the river *Euphrates*, Εὐφράτης.

פֹּרָת; see פרה.

פַּרְתְּמִים m. pl., *chiefs, nobles.*

פָּשָׂה *spread itself* (an eruption), Leviticus only.

פָּשַׂע *stepped, trod*, with בְּ, Isa. 27:4.

פֶּשַׂע m., *a step*, 1 Sa. 20:3.
מִפְשָׂעָה f., *buttocks*, 1 Chron. 19:4.

פָּשַׂק *opened, expanded*, Pro. 13:3. Pi. the same, Eze. 16:25.

פַּשׁ *spreading*; see פּוּשׁ.

פָּשַׁח. Pi. *tore to pieces*, Lam. 3:11.

פַּשְׁחוּר p.n. of a man.

פָּשַׁט (fut. יִפְשֹׁט).—I. *stripped off his dress.*— II. *spread, extended itself*, with אֶל, בְּ, עַל. Pi. *stripped another*. Hiph. I. *stripped another*. II. *skinned*, with מֵעַל. Hith. *stripped himself*, 1 Sa. 18:4.

פָּשַׁע I. *rebelled, rebelled against*, with מִתַּחַת and בְּ. — II. *transgressed*. Niph. *transgressed against*, Pro. 18: 19.
פֶּשַׁע m. (with suff. פִּשְׁעִי; pl. פְּשָׁעִים). —I. *rebellion*. — II. *transgression, sin*. — III. *injury* (by loss), Ex. 22:8.

פְּשַׁר Ch., *interpreted, explained*. Pa. the same.
פְּשַׁר m. Ch., *interpretation*.
פֵּשֶׁר m. Heb., the same, Ecc. 8:1.

פִּשְׁתָּה m.—I. *flax*.—II. *linen*.
פִּשְׁתָּה f., *a lamp-wick of flax*, Isa. 42 : 3; 43 : 17; (pl. פִּשְׁתִּים) *linen*, Ex. 9 : 31.

פַּת, פִּתִּים, see פָּתַת; פֹּת, see פּוֹת.
פְּתָאִים; see פְּתִי.
פִּתְאֹם *suddenly*; see פֶּתַע.

פַּתְבָּג m. Heb. and Ch., *portion of food, mess*.

פִּתְגָּם m. Ch.— I. *decree*. — II. *royal letter*.— III. *epistle*; Heb. *decree, sentence*.

פָּתָה *was silly*, Deu. 11:16, Job 31. 27. Niph. *was persuaded, enticed*. Pi. I. *led to folly, persuaded, enticed*.—II. *deceived*.—III. *used fair words to*. Pu. pass. of Pi. Hiph. (fut. apoc. יַפְתְּ) *declared foolish, idolatrous*, with לְ, Gen. 9:27.
פְּתוּאֵל p.n. of a man.
פְּתִי, with pause פֶּתִי m. (pl. פְּתָיִים, פְּתָאִים).—I. *ignorant*.—II. *foolish*. —III. *folly*, Pro. 1:22.
פְּתָי m. Ch., *breadth*.
פְּתַיּוּת f., *folly*, Pro. 9:13.

פְּתוֹר, see פתר; פְּתוֹת, see פתת.

פָּתַח (fut. יִפְתַּח).— I. *opened*.—II. *uttered, opened his mouth*.—III. *opened the ears*, Isa. 50:5.—IV. *cleft a rock*, Ps. 105:41.— V. *loosened, untied*, Isa. 14:17.—VI. *brought out for sale*.—VII. *drew a sword*, Ps. 37:14. Niph. *was opened, unloosed*. Pi. I. *opened, &c.*, as Kal. — II. *carved, engraved*. Pu. *engraven*. Hith. *loose thyself*, Isa. 52:2.
פְּתַח Ch., *opened*.
פֶּתַח m. (with suff. פִּתְחוֹ; pl. פְּתָחִים, פִּתְחֵי). — I. *opening, gateway, entrance*.—II. *door* or *gate*; בְּפֶתַח, הַפֶּתְחָה, פֶּתַח *to the gate*.
פֵּתַח m., *opening, laying open*, Ps. 119:130.
פְּתִיחוֹת f. pl., *drawn swords*, Ps. 55:22.
פִּתּוּחַ m., *engraving, carving*.
פִּתְחוֹן, const. פִּתְחוֹן m., *opening of the mouth*.
פְּתַחְיָה p.n. of a man.
מַפְתֵּחַ m., *key*.

מִפְתָּח m., *opening the lips*, Pro. 8:6.

פְּתִיגִיל m., "stomacher," Eng. Ver., Isa. 3:24, meaning uncertain.

פָּתַל. Niph. *was twisted with, struggled together*, Gen. 30:8. Hith. *struggled against*, Ps. 18:27; תִּתַּפָּל for תִּתְפַּתָּל the same, 2 Sa. 22:27.

פָּתִיל m.—I. *lace, thread, cord.*—II. *string* for a signet-ring.—III. *plate of gold.*—IV. *cloth for a cover*, Nu. 19:15.

פְּתַלְתֹּל m., *perverse*, Deu. 32:5.

נַפְתּוּל m., *struggles*, Gen. 30:8.

פִּתֹם p.n., a city of Egypt in the vicinity of Goshen, probably Damietta.

פֶּתֶן m., *an asp.*

מִפְתָּן m., *threshold of a door, gate, &c.*

פֶּתַע m.—I. *suddenness.*—II. adv. *suddenly*; בְּפֶתַע the same.

פִּתְאֹם adv., *suddenly, immediately*; בְּפִתְאֹם the same; בְּפֶתַע פִּתְאֹם, פ׳ לְפֶתַע and פֶּתַע פ׳ the same; פַּחַד פ׳ *sudden fear.*

פָּתַר (fut. יִפְתֹּר) *interpreted, explained*, Gen. chaps. 40 and 41 only.

פִּתְרוֹן m., *interpretation*, Gen. chaps. 40 and 41 only.

פְּתוֹר p.n., the country of the prophet Balaam, probably *Petra.*

פַּתְרוֹס p. n., some nation bordering upon Egypt; פַּתְרֻסִים its inhabitants.

פַּתְשֶׁגֶן same as פַּרְשֶׁגֶן.

פָּתַת *broke to pieces*, Lev. 2:6.

פַּת f. (with suff. פִּתִּי; pl. פִּתִּים), *a piece, piece of bread.*

פְּתוֹת m., the same, Eze. 13:19.

צ

צֵא, with ה parag. צְאָה Kal imp., from יצא.

צֵאָה *excrement*; see צוֹא.

צֶאֱלִים m. pl., *trees in dry places, shady bushes*, Job 40:21, 22.

צֹאן (צְאוֹן) com. — I. coll. *sheep* or *goats.*—II. *a flock of sheep* or *goats.* —III. *a people* (the flock of God).

צַאֲנָן p. n., a city in the tribe of Judah; called also צְנָן.

צֶאֱצָאִים; see יצא.

צֵאת Kal inf., from יצא.

צַבִּים, צָב; see צבב.

צָבָא I. *assembled for war, fought.*—II. *assembled for a service, performed it.* Hiph. *marshalled an army.*

צָבָא m. (pl. צְבָאִים, צְבָאוֹת Ps. 103:21).—I. *an army.*—II. *any multitude*; אַנְשֵׁי הַצָּבָא *soldiers*; שַׂר הַצָּבָא *commander in chief.*—III *warfare, military service.*—IV. *any appointed service* or *trial.* צְבָא הַשָּׁמַיִם *the host of heaven*, i. e.—1. *the stars.*—2. *the angels*; יְהוָֹה צ׳, אֱלֹהֵי צְבָאוֹת *the Lord of Hosts*, one of the titles of God; see also צְבָאִים, צְבָאוֹת in צְבִי under צָבָה.

צְבוֹיִם, צְבֹאִים p. n., one of the cities of the plain destroyed with Sodom.

צְבָא Ch., *wished, was willing.*

צְבוּ f. Ch., *determination, resolution*, Dan. 6:18.

צָבַב (Arab. *hid, concealed*).

צָב m.—I. *a covered waggon*; pl צַבִּים.—II. *a kind of lizard*, Lev 11:29.

צֹבֵבָה p. n. of a woman.

צָבָה same as צָבָא; part. צֹבֶה I. *waging war.*—II. *burst,* Nu. 5:27. Hiph. *caused to burst,* Nu. 5:22.

צָבֶה m., צָבָה f., *swelling,* Nu. 5:21.

צְבִי m.—I. *beauty, ornament, honour.* — II. *an antelope*; pl. צְבָיִים, צְבָאִים; f. צְבָאוֹת.

צְבִיָּה f., *she antelope.*

צִבְיָה p. n. of a woman.

צִבְיָא p. n. of a man.

צָבַט *took up in his hand,* Ru. 2:14.

צָבַע (Arab. *dyed*).

צְבַע Ch. Pa. *dyed, made wet.* Hith. *was dyed.*

צֶבַע m., *a dyed dress,* Jud. 5:30.

צָבוּעַ m., *hyæna,* Jer. 12:9 (Arab. *hyæna*).

צְבֹעִים p. n., a valley and town of Benjamin.

צִבְעוֹן p. n., a son of Seir.

אֶצְבַּע f. (with suff. אֶצְבָּעוֹ; pl. אֶצְבָּעוֹת).—I. *a finger.*—II. *a toe.* —III. *the hand.*—IV. *a digit.* Ch. the same.

צָבַר (fut. יִצְבֹּר).—I. *heaped up.*—II. *laid up, treasured up.*

צִבֻּרִים m. pl., *heaps,* 2 Ki. 10:8.

צָבַת (Arab. *took in his hand*).

צֶבֶת m., pl. צְבָתִים *handfuls,* Ru. 2:16.

צָדַד (Arab. *turned the face away*).

צַד m. (with suff. צִדָּהּ; pl. צִדִּים). —I. *side,* with ה parag. צִדָּה *to the side;* מִצַּד *at the side;* עַל צַד the same.—II. *adversary,* Jud. 2:3.

צַד m. Ch. *side;* מִצַּד *at the side;* לְצַד *against.*

צְדָד p. n., a town in the north of Palestine.

צִדִּים p. n., a town of Naphtali.

צָדָה *laid wait for,* Ex. 21:13. Niph *was destroyed,* Zep. 3:6.

צְדָא m. Ch., *perverseness,* Dan. 3:14.

צְדִיָּה f., *lying in wait,* Nu. 35:20, 22.

צָדַק (fut. יִצְדַּק).—I. *was righteous, equitable.*—II. *acted justly.*—III. *was in the right.*—IV. *was acknowledged to be just, in the right.* Niph. *was purified, exculpated,* Dan. 8:14. Pi. *justified, cleared, himself* or *another.* Hiph. — I. *did justice.*—II. *gave judgment in favour of, acquitted.*—III *justified before God,* Ex. 23:7. Hith. fut. pl. נִצְטַדָּק *cleared himself,* Gen 44:16.

צֶדֶק m. (with suff. צִדְקוֹ).—I. *truth.* —II. *fairness, equity.*—III. *a just cause.*—IV. *acquittal, justification.* V. *righteousness.*

צְדָקָה f.—I. *truth, equity.*—II. *a just cause* or *claim.*— III. *righteousness.*—IV. *favor, approbation.*

צִדְקָה f. Ch., *equity, righteousness.*

צַדִּיק m.—I. *righteous.*—II. *having a just cause.*—III. *innocent.*—IV. *true,* Isa. 41:26.

צָדוֹק p. n. of a man.

צִדְקִיָּה, צִדְקִיָּהוּ p. n.—I. *Zedekiah* king of Judah.—II. also of other men.

צַדֶּקְתֵּךְ Eze. 16:52. Pi. int., with suff. and f. termination, from צדק.

צָהַב. Hoph. part. מֻצְהָב *of a gold colour,* Ezr. 8:27.

צָהֹב m., *red.*

I. צָהַל 1. *neighed.* — 2. *shouted for joy.* Pi. *shouted for joy* or *sorrow,* with קוֹל.—II. same as זָהַר. Hiph. הִצְהִיל *caused to shine,* Ps. 104: 15.

מִצְהָלָה f., *neighing.*

צָהַר same as זָהַר. Hiph. *made the fine oil called* יִצְהָר, Job 24:11.

צֹהַר m.—I. *a light, window, &c.*—II. *noon.*

יִצְהָר m.—I. *fine olive oil.*—II. p.n. of a man; patron. יִצְהָרִי

צַו, צָו; see צוה.

צוֹא m., *filthy,* Zec. 3:3, 4.

צוֹאָה f., *filth, dung.*

צֵאָה f., *excrement.*

צַוָּאר, צַוָּר, const. צַוַּאר m. (pl. צַוָּארוֹת ; צַוְּארֵי, צַוָּארִים) *neck, shoulder, back;* Ch. the same.

צַוְּרוֹנִים m. pl., *the neck,* Cant. 4:9.

צוֹבָא, צוֹבָה or אֲרַם צ׳ p. n., a city and district of Syria.

צוּד *hunted, pursued, watched for, men or animals.* Pil. צוֹדֵד *ensnare, beguile.* Hith. הִצְטַיֵּד (see צַיִד) *furnished with provisions,* Jos. 9: 12.

צַיִד, const. צֵיד m.—I. *hunting.*—II. *game, prey.* — III. *provisions* (of any kind).

צֵידָה, צֵדָה f., *provisions.*

צַיָּד m., *hunter,* Jer. 16:16.

צִידוֹן p.n., *Zidon,* a city of Phenicia; צִידֹנִי m., צִידֹנִית f., *a Zidonian.*

מְצָד m. (pl. מְצָדוֹת) *fortress, strong place.*

מָצוֹד m. } —I. *prey.*—II. *net.*—III.
מְצוֹדָה f. } *fortress.*

מָצוֹד m., *hunter's net,* Job 19:6.

מְצָדָה, מְצוּדָה f.—I. *prey.*—II. *net* —III. *fortress.*

צָוָה. Pi. צִוָּה (fut. יְצַוֶּה; apoc. יְצַו imp. צַוֵּה ; apoc. צַו). — I. *commanded, gave orders,* with אֶל, עַל, לְ.—II. *appointed.*—III. *caused,* i.e. appointed a thing; צַוֵּה אֶל בֵּיתוֹ *he gave his last orders to his house,* 2 Sa. 17:23. Pu. צֻוָּה *was commanded.*

צַו, צָו m., *precept, command.*

צִיּוּן m.—I. *sepulchral monument.*—II. *waymark,* Jer. 31:21.

מִצְוָה f. (pl. מִצְוֹת) *command, precept.*

צָוַח *shouted for joy,* Isa. 42:11.

צְוָחָה f., *cry of sorrow.*

צוּל (Arab. *lay hid*); see צָלַל *sank.*

צוּלָה f., *the deep,* Isa. 44:27.

מְצוֹלָה, מְצוּלָה f., *depth* (of the sea, &c.)

צוּם *fasted.*

צוֹם m. (pl. צוֹמוֹת) *fasting.*

צוּעַ (Arab. *formed, designed*).

צַעֲצֻעִים m. pl., מַעֲשֵׂה צ׳ *carvings,* 2 Chron. 3:10.

צוֹעַר, צוֹעָר; see צער.

צוּף *flowed,* Lam. 3:54. Hiph. הֵצִיף I. *caused to flow.* — II. *caused to float.*

צוּף m. — I. *honey-comb.* — II. צוּף, צִיף, צוֹפַי p.n., the son of Elkanah.

צָפָה f., *overflowing,* Eze. 32:6.

צַפְצָפָה f., *a willow,* Eze. 17:5.

צוּץ; see ציץ.

I. צוּק same as יָצַק *pour,* Job 28:2; 29:6.

II. צוֹק *was in difficulty*, Dan. 9:25. Hiph. הֵצִיק I. *urged, constrained.* —II. *distressed.*

צוּקָה f., *distress.*

מָצוֹק m., *restraint, difficulty, trouble.*

מָצוּק m.—I. *pillars, supports.*—II. *peaks, projections of rocks*, 1 Sa. 14:5.

מוּצָק with pause מוּצָק m., *constraint;* see also in יָצַק.

מְצוּקָה f., *restraint, difficulty, trouble.*

צוּר I. *formed, fashioned.*—II. *tied up money.*—III. *surrounded.*—IV. *overlaid.*—V. *acted hostilely.*—VI. *besieged*, with אֶל, עַל.

צוּר m. (pl. צֻרִים, צוּרוֹת).—I. *a rock.* —II. *a refuge* (applied to God).—III. *a stone*, Isa. 8:14.—IV. *a sharp stone used as a knife*, Jos. 5:2, 3.—V. *edge of a sword*, Ps. 89:44.—VI. *form, figure*, Ps. 49:15.—VII. p. n. of a man.

צֹר m.—I. *a rock*, Eze. 3:9.—II. *a knife*, Ex. 4:25.

צוֹר, צֹר p. n., *Tyre*, the capital of Phenicia, Τύρος; צֹרִי *a Tyrian.*

צוּרָה f., *form, figure*, Eze. 43:11.

צוּרִיאֵל p.n. of a man.

צוּרִישַׁדַּי (*my rock is the Almighty*), p. n. of a man.

צִיר m.—I. *figure, image*, Isa. 45:16. —II. *hinge*, Pro. 26:14.—III. *pangs of a woman in labour*; see also in loc.

צַר m., צָרָה f., *narrow, small, close;* see also in צרר.

צֵר p.n., a town in the tribe of Naphtali.

מָצוֹר m.—I. *restraint.*—II. *siege.*—III. *mound of besiegers.*—IV. *munition, citadel.*—V. p. n., Egypt, same as מִצְרַיִם, which see.

מְצוּרָה f., *fortress, citadel, mound.*

צַוְּרוֹנִים, צַוָּר; see צַוָּאר.

צוּת: Hiph. הֵצִית *set on fire*, Isa. 27:4; same as יָצַת.

צָחָה root not used; Ch. *thirsted.*

צִחֶה m., *parched*, Isa. 5:13.

צִחָא p. n. of a man.

צָחַח *was white*, Lam. 4:7.

צַח m., צַחָה f.—I. *hot, burning.*—II. *bright, white.*—III. *distinctly, plainly*, Isa. 32:4.

צְחִיחַ m.—I. *dry, bare.*—II. *open, exposed*, Neh. 4:7.

צְחִיחִי m., pl. צְחִחִיִּים *dry places*, Neh. 4:7.

צְחִיחָה f., *a parched land*, Ps. 68:7.

צַחְצָחוֹת f. pl., *dry places*, Isa. 58:11.

צָחַן (Arab. *was hot*).

צַחֲנָה f., *the heat of putrefaction, stench*, Joel 2:20.

צָחַק *laughed*, with לְ. Pi. צִחֵק I. *made laughter, joked.*—II. *laughed at, insulted*, with בְּ.

צְחֹק m., *laughter, ridicule.*

יִצְחָק, יִשְׂחָק p. n., *Isaac*, the son of Abraham and Sarah; LXX. Ισαάκ.

צַחַר m., *whiteness*, Eze. 27:18.

צָחֹר m., *white*, Jud. 10:5.

צֹחַר p. n. of a man.

צִיבָא p. n. of a man.

צַיִד, צֵידָה, צַיָּד, צִידוֹן; see צוּד.

צָיָה root not used; (Arab. *drought*).

צִי m. (see צִיָּה), *a ship*; pl. צִיִּים צִים.

צִיָּה f.—I. *drought*, Job 24:19.—II *parched land, wilderness.*

צִיִּים m. pl., *inhabitants of the desert, men* or *beasts.*

צָיוֹן m., *parched land.*

צִיּוּן; see צוה.

צִיּוֹן f. (*citadel*), p. n., *Zion*, the well known hill on and around which Jerusalem was built.

צִן, צִין p.n., the desert between Canaan and the land of Edom.

צִינֹק *fetters*; see צנק.

צִיעֹר p. n., a town of Judah.

צִיץ (pret. צָץ; fut. יָצִיץ).—I. *flowered.* —II. *flourished.* Hiph. *looked cheerfully*, Cant. 2:9.

צִיץ m.—I. *a flower*; pl. צִצִּים.—II. *anything shining, plate of metal.*—III. *plumage, wings.*—IV. p. n. of a place.

צִיצָה f., *flower*, Isa. 28:4.

צִיצִית f.—I. *lock of hair*, Eze. 8:3.—II. *fringe*, Nu. 15:38, 39.

צִקְלַג, צִיקְלַג, צִיקְלָג p. n., a city of the Philistines in the land of Simeon.

צִיר Kal not used; (Arab. *went*). Hith. הִצְטַיֵּר *prepared for a journey*, Jos. 9:4.

צִיר m., *person sent on a journey, messenger*; see also in צור.

צֵל, צִלָּה, צְלוּל; see צלל.

צְלָא Ch. Pa. *prayed.*

צָלָה *roasted*, Isa. 44:16, 19.

צָלִי m., *roasted.*

צָלַח, צָלֵחַ (fut. יִצְלַח).—I. *crossed a river.*—II. *fell upon, descended*, with עַל, אֶל.—III. *advanced, flourished.*—IV. *was useful, fit*, with לְ. Hiph. הִצְלִיחַ I. *made to prosper*, with לְ.—II. *accomplished.*—III. *was prosperous.*

צְלַח Ch. Aph. הַצְלַח I. *made prosperous.*—II. *was prosperous.*

צְלָחוֹת f. pl., *dishes.*

צְלוֹחִית f., *a dish*, 2 Ki. 2:20.

צַלַּחַת f., the same.

I. צָלַל I. *sank in the water*, Ex. 15:10.—II. *became shaded*, Neh. 13:19. Hiph. part. מֵצַל *giving shade*, Eze. 31:3.

צְלוּל (צְלִיל) m., *a barley cake*, Jud. 7:13.

צֵלֶל m. (with suff. צִלְלוֹ; pl. צְלָלִים, צִלְלֵי), *a shadow.*

צֵל m. (with suff. צִלָּהּ).—I. *a shadow.* —II. *dusk.*—III. *shelter, protection.*

צִלָּה p. n., *Zillah*, the wife of Lamech.

צַלְמָוֶת m., *shadow of death*, applied to any thick darkness.

צַלְמֻנָּע p. n., a king of the Midianites.

צְלֶלְפּוֹנִי (with art.), p. n. of a man.

מְצִלָּה f., *shady place.*

II. צָלַל I. *tingled* (of the ears).—II. *quivered* (of the lips), Hab. 3:16.

צְלָצַל, const. צִלְצַל m.—I. *a cymbal.*—II. *a species of locust*, Deu. 28:42.—III. *tumult of an army* or *shadowing*; see I. צלל Isa. 18:1.—IV. *harpoon*, Job 40:31.

צֶלְצְלִים, pl. const. צִלְצְלֵי *cymbals.*

מְצִלָּה f., pl. מְצִלּוֹת.—I. *cymbals.*—II. *bells.*

מְצֶלֶת f., dual מְצִלְתַּיִם *pair of cymbals.*

צָלַם root not used; (Arab. *was dark*).

צֶלֶם m.—I. *a shadow*, Ps. 39:7.—II *an imagination*, Ps. 73:20.—III *representation, picture, image.*—IV. *resemblance.*

צְלֵם, צֶלֶם m. Ch., *an image.*

צַלְמוֹן (*shady ?*) p. n., a mountain of Ephraim.

צַלְמֹנָה p. n., one of the stations in the wilderness.

צַלְמָוֶת; see in I. צלל.

צָלַע part. צֹלֵעַ; f. צֹלֵעָה *halting, lame.*

צֶלַע m., *limping, falling.*

צֵלָע f. (const. צֶלַע, צֵלַע; with suff. צַלְעוֹ).—I. *a rib.*—II. *a plank for wainscoting.* —III. *a side.*—IV. *side chamber*; pl. צְלָעוֹת; const. צַלְעוֹת *side planks, side chambers; צְלָעִים folding doors.*—V. p. n., the town of Benjamin where Saul was buried.

צֶלֶף p. n. of a man.

צְלָפְחָד p. n. of a man.

צֶלְצַח p. n., a place in Benjamin.

צְלָצַל, צִלְצַל, צֶלְצְלִים; see II. צלל.

צֶלֶק p. n., one of David's captains.

צִלְּתַי p. n. of a man.

צָמֵא, fut. יִצְמָא.—I. *thirsted.*—II. *earnestly desired.*

צָמֵא m., צְמֵאָה f., *thirsty.*

צָמָא m., *thirst.*

צִמְאָה f., *thirst,* Jer. 2:25.

צִמָּאוֹן m., *thirsty land.*

צָמַד. Niph. *was bound, yoked* (to idolatry). Pu. *tied, fastened,* 2 Sa. 20:8. Hiph. *contrived,* Ps. 50:19.

צָמִיד m.—I. *tied, fastened,* Nu. 19:15. —II. *a band, bracelet.*

צֶמֶד m. (with suff. צִמְדּוֹ; pl. צְמָדִים, צִמְדֵי).—I. *a pair, yoke* (of oxen, &c.).—II. the quantity of land ploughed in a day by a *yoke* of oxen.

צִמּוּק; see צמק.

צָמַח (fut. יִצְמַח).—I. *shot, grew up.* —II. *flourished.*—III. *sprang up, arose, began.*—IV. *produced.* Pi. *grew* (of hair). Hiph. (fut. יַצְמִיחַ, וַיַּצְמַח) *caused to grow, produced.*

צֶמַח m. (with suff. צִמְחָהּ).—I. *shooting.*—II. *a shoot.*—III. *plants.*—IV. *the Branch* (a title of Christ).

צְמִיתֻת; see צמת.

צָמַם root not used; (Arab. *tied*); Ch. *covered.*

צַמָּה f., *a woman's veil.*

צַמִּים m.—I. *noose, snare.*—II. *destruction.*

צָמַק *dry* (of the breasts), Hos. 9:14.

צִמּוּק m., *dry grapes*; Ital. *simmuki.*

צֶמֶר m. (with suff. צַמְרִי), *wool.*

צַמֶּרֶת f., *foliage.*

צְמָרִי p. n., an unknown people, Gen. 10:18.

צְמָרַיִם p. n., a town of Benjamin.

צָמַת *silenced, destroyed,* Lam. 3:53. Niph. *was put to silence.* Pi. and Hiph. *put to silence, destroyed.* Pilp. צִמְתֻת the same.

צְמִיתֻת f., *perfect silence;* לִצְמִתֻת, לַצְּמִיתֻת *completely* (without power of redemption), Lev. 25:23, 30.

צִמְּתוּתֻנִי Ps. 88:17. Pil. pret. pl., with suff., from צמת.

צֵן; see צִין.

צֹנֶא, צֹנֶה; see צֹאן.

צִנָּה ,צִנִּים ,צְנִינִים; see צנן.

צִנּוֹר m., *watercourse, cataract.*

צָנַח I. *dismounted.*—II. *went down,* Jud. 4:21.

צָנַם part., f. pl. צְנֻמוֹת "withered," Eng. Ver.; Gen. 41:23 (meaning not very certain).

צִנִּים m. pl., *fence of thorns, thorns.*

צְנִינִים m. pl., *thorns.*

צִנָּה f.—I. *barb of hook,* Am. 4:2.—II. *a shield.*—III. *a shield-shaped vessel* used for snow, Pro. 25:13.

צִנְצֶנֶת f., *a basket,* Ex. 16:33.

צֹנֶן same as צֹאנֶן.

צָנַע *ready, prepared,* Pro. 11:2. Hiph. *being ready,* Mic. 6:8.

צָנַף I. *bound, wrapped round,* Isa. 22:18. — II. *wrapped round the head,* Lev. 16:4.

צָנִיף (צָנוֹף) m., *turban.*

צְנֵפָה f., *wrapping,* Isa. 22:18.

מִצְנֶפֶת f., *turban* worn by the high priest.

צָנַק root not used; (Arab. *fetters*).

צִינֹק m., *fetters,* Jer. 29:26.

צַנְתָּרוֹת f. pl., *pipes, tubes,* Zec. 4:12.

צָעַד (fut. יִצְעַד; inf., with suff. צַעְדְּךָ). —I. *walked, advanced.*—II. *went over a country.*—III. *shot up,* Gen. 49:22. Hiph. *caused to walk, brought over,* Job 18:14.

צַעַד m.—I. *stepping,* Pro. 30:29.—II. *a step,* 2 Sa. 6:13.—III. *progress, action, conduct.*

צְעָדָה f., *marching;* pl. צְעָדוֹת *anklets,* Isa. 3:20.

אֶצְעָדָה f., *bracelet.*

מִצְעָד m., *step, proceeding.*

צָעָה *wandering for plunder, losing one's way, perishing.* Pi. צֵעָה *plundered,* Jer. 48:12.

צָעִיף m., *woman's veil.*

צָעִיר ,צְעִירָה *little;* see צער.

צָעַן *removed,* Isa. 33:20.

צַעֲנַנִּים p. n., a city of the Kenites in Naphtali.

צֹעַן p. n., *Zoan,* a city of Lower Egypt; possibly *Tanis.*

צֶעֱצֻעִים; see צוּעַ.

צָעַק (fut. יִצְעַק) *cried out for help,* with לְ, אֶל. Pi. *cried vehemently,* 2 Ki. 2:12. Hiph. *cause to be summoned,* 1 Sa. 10:17. Niph. I. *were called, summoned.*— II. *assembled themselves.*

צְעָקָה const. צַעֲקַת f., *a cry for help.*

צָעַר *was small, of little importance.*

צֹעַר, צוֹעַר p. n., one of the cities of the plain, formerly בֶּלַע.

צָעִיר m., צְעִירָה f.—I. *small.*—II. *young.*—III. p. n. of a place, 2 Ki. 8:21.

צָעוֹר Ketib, same as צָעִיר, Jer. 14:3; 48:4.

צְעִירָה f., *smallness, inferiority in age.*

מִצְעָר m., *little, small;* לְמִצְעָר *for a little time.*

מִצְעִירָה f., *of a small kind,* Dan. 8:9.

צָפַד *adhered, cleaved to,* Lam. 4:8.

I. **צָפָה** I. *kept watch.*—II. *looked for, expected;* צוֹפֶה *observer, watchman.*—III. *watched, observed,* with בְּ, בֵּין.—IV. *plotted against,* with

לְ. Pi. צִפָּה I. *kept watch.*—II. *looked, expected help.*

צְפִיָּה f., *watch-tower*, Lam. 4:17.

צָפִית f., *watch-tower*, Isa. 21:5.

צְפַת p. n., a town of Canaan, afterwards called חָרְמָה.

צְפָתָה p. n., a valley near Maresha in Judah.

מִצְפֶּה m.—I. *watch-tower.*—II. p. n., a town in Judah.—III. in Moab. —IV. in Gad.—V. in Benjamin.—VI. a valley in the north of Palestine.

מִצְפָּה p. n.—I. a town in Gilead, same as מִצְפֵּה־גִלְעָד.—II. a town in Benjamin, same as מִצְפֶּה.

II. צָפָה *covered, overlaid with wood* or *metal*, with בְּ, אֶל. Pu. *was overlaid.*

צָפָה s. f.; see צוף.

צְפוֹ, צְפִי p. n., a son of Eliphaz.

צִפּוּי m., *covering, coat.*

צְפוֹן, צִפְיוֹן p. n. of a man; patron. צְפֹנִי.

צְפוֹן, צְפוֹנִי; see צפן.

צִפּוֹר, צִפֳּרִים; see צפר.

צפח (Arab. *made broad*).

צוֹפַח, צֹפַח p. n. of a man.

צַפַּחַת f., *a dish, vessel.*

צַפִּיחִית f., *flat cake, cake.*

צָפִיעַ, צְפִיעוֹת; see צפע.

צָפִיר, צְפִירָה; see צפר.

צָפִית; see צפה.

צָפַן I. *hid, concealed.* — II. *excluded*, Job 17:4.—III. *laid up, treasured up.*—IV. *lay hid, lay in wait*, with לְ; part. צָפוּן *a secret, treasure, one hidden* (of God). Niph. I. *was hidden*, with מִן.—II. *was laid up, destined for*, with לְ. Hiph. *hid.*

צָפוֹן com. (*hidden, dark quarter*).—I. *the north.* — II. *the north wind;* מִצָּפוֹן לְ, צָפוֹן לְ *northward of any where;* צָפוֹנָה *towards the north;* לִצְפוֹנָה the same; מִצָּפוֹנָה *from the north;* with לְ *from the north of any where.*—II. p. n., a town of Gad; see also צְפוֹן same as צִפְיוֹן in II. צָפָה; see also in בַּעַל.

צְפוֹנִי m., *northern*, Joel 2:20.

צָפִין (צָפוּן) m., *treasure.*

צְפַנְיָה, צְפַנְיָהוּ (*whom the Lord hath hidden*), p. n.—I. *Zephaniah*, the prophet; LXX. Σοφονίας. — II. other men.

מַצְפּוּן m., *hidden place*, Obad. *v.* 6.

צָפְנַת פַּעְנֵחַ the Egyptian title of Joseph; its meaning altogether unknown, Gen. 41:45.

צֶפַע m., *basilisk*, Isa. 14:29.

צִפְעֹנִי m. (pl. צִפְעֹנִים) the same.

צָפִיעַ m., pl. צְפִיעִים *dung*, Eze. 4:15.

צְפִיעָה f., pl. צְפִיעוֹת, "issue," Eng. Ver., Isa. 22:24.

צָפַף. Pil. צִפְצֵף I. *chirped* (as a bird), Isa. 10:14, &c.—II. *spoke in a low voice.*

צַפְצָפָה; see צוף.

צָפַר *hastened* (fut. יִצְפֹּר), Jud. 7:3.

צָפִיר m., *goat, he-goat.*

צְפִיר m. Ch., the same.

צְפִירָה f.—I. *a crown*, Isa. 28:5.—II. "morning," Eng. Ver., Eze. 7:7, 10; sense uncertain.

צִפּוֹר com. (pl. צִפֳּרִים).—I. *a bird.*—II. specially, *a sparrow.*—III. p. n. the father of Balaam the prophet

צִפַּר com. Ch., *a bird.*

צִפֹּרָה p. n., the wife of Moses.

צְפַרְדֵּעַ com., *a frog.*

צִפֹּרֶן m.—I. *nail of the finger.*—II. *point of the graver.*

צֶפֶת, צְפִתָּה; see צפה.

צֶפֶת f., *capital of a pillar*, 2 Chron. 3:15.

צִצִּים; see צִיץ.

צַק Kal imp., from יצק.

צִקְלַג same as צִיקְלָג.

צִקְלוֹן m., *husk*, 2 Ki. 4:42

צֶקֶת Kal inf., from יצק.

צָר, צַר, צֹר, see צור; צַר, צָרִי, see צרר.

צָרַב. Niph. *was scorched*, Eze. 21:3.

צָרֶבֶת f.—I. *burning*, Pro. 16:27.—II. *inflammation*, Lev. 13:23, 28.

צְרֵדָה p. n., a town of Manasseh; צְרֵרָה, צָרְתָן the same.

צָרָה s. f.; see צרר.

צְרִי, צֳרִי, with pause צֹרִי m., *mastich*, the gum from the pistachia lentiscus.

צְרִי p. n., same as יִצְרִי; see יָצַר.

צְרוּיָה, צְרֻיָה p. n., the mother of Joab.

צְרוֹר same as צְרֹר.

צָרַח *shouted*, Zep. 1:14. Hiph. the same, Isa. 42:13.

צְרִיחַ m., *a high tower.*

צֹרֶךְ m., *need, necessity*, 2 Chron. 2:15.

צָרַע, part. צָרוּעַ and Pu. part. מְצֹרָע m., מְצֹרַעַת f., *struck with leprosy.*

צְרוּעָה p. n., the mother of Jeroboam.

צָרְעָה p. n., a town of the Danites in Judah; צָרְעָתִי, צָרְעִי *a Zarathite.*

צִרְעָה f., coll. *wasps, hornets.*

צָרַעַת f. (with suff. צָרַעְתּוֹ) *the leprosy.*

צָרַף (fut. יִצְרֹף).—I. *refined metals.*—II. *purified a person's character.*—III. *tried a person's character;* part. צֹרֵף *refiner, goldsmith, silversmith;* צָרוּף *purified, pure.* Niph. *shall be purified*, Dan. 12:10. Pi. part. מְצָרֵף *goldsmith*, Mal. 3:2, 3.

צֹרְפִי (with art.), p. n. of a man.

צָרְפַת p. n., a town between Tyre and Zidon; Σάρεπτα, with ה loc. צָרְפָתָה.

מַצְרֵף m., *crucible.*

צָרַר I. *tied or bound up.*—II. *acted hostilely to.*—III. *was straitened;* part. צֹרֵר *an adversary;* impers. צַר לִי *I am distressed, grieved, concerned for some one*, with עַל. Niph. הֵצַר (inf. הָצֵר) *distressed.* Pu. part. מְצֹרָר.

צַר, with pause צָר m.—I. *difficulty, adversity, distress;* f. צָרָה; בַּצַּר לִי *when I am in distress.*—II. *enemy, besieger.*—III. *rival;* with art. הַצָּר; with suff. צָרִי; pl. צָרִים.—IV. *rock;* see צור.

צָרָה f., *enemy, adversary;* with ה parag. בַּצָּרָתָה לִי *when I am in trouble.*

צְרֹר, צְרוֹר m. (pl. צְרוֹרוֹת).—I. *a bundle.*—II. *a bag of money.*—III. *a small stone, a particle, grain.*—IV. p. n. of a man.

מֵצַר m., *restraint, trouble.*

צְרֵרָה; see צְרֵדָה.

צֶרֶת p. n. of a man.

צֶרֶת הַשַּׁחַר p. n., a town of Reuben.
צָרְתָן; see צְרֵדָה.

ק

קִא *vomit;* see קוֹא.
קָאם for קָם Kal pret., from קוּם.
קָאֵם Ch. Pe. part., from קוּם.
קָאַת (with art. הַקָּאָת; const. קְאַת f.), *a pelican* or *heron,* not certain which.
קָבַב *cursed;* imp. with suff. and נ epenth. קָבְנוֹ; with ה parag. קָבָה.
קַב m., a measure, the sixth part of סְאָה, 2 Ki. 6:25.
קֻבָּה f., *alcove, tent,* Nu. 25:8, again in the same verse אֶל קֳבָתָהּ "*in her alcove*" (Lee), generally interpreted of the person of the woman.
קֳבָתָהּ, קֹבָה; see נקב.
קָבָה root not used; (Arab. *stomach*).
קֵבָה f., *the stomach,* Deut. 18:3.
קָבָה (pronounced *kŏbāh*), Kal imp. with ה parag., from קבב.
קָבַל. Pi. קִבֵּל I. *accepted.*—II. *took.* —III. *undertook,* Est. 9:23, 27. Hiph. *taking hold of.*
קַבֵּל Ch. Pa., *received, took.*
קֳבָל prep., *before, the front,* 2 Ki. 15:10.
קֹבֶל m. (with suff. קָבֳלוֹ or קָבָלוֹ), *opposing,* Eze. 26:9.
קֳבֵל, קְבֵל m. Ch., *the front;* לָקֳבֵל 1. *in front of.*—2. *in consideration of;* with דִּי *in consequence of;* כָּל־קֳבֵל דְּנָה *all before that,* i. e. *for this reason, therefore;* כָּל־קֳבֵל דִּי *because.*

קָבְנוֹ Kal imp. with suff. and נ epenth., from קבב.
קָבַע *forsook, neglected.*
קוֹבַע m., *a helmet.*
קֻבַּעַת f., *a drinking cup,* Isa. 51: 17, 22.
קָבַץ *collected, gathered together.* Niph. *were assembled, assembled themselves.* Pi. I. *collected.*—II. *acquired.* Pu. *was gathered together,* Eze. 38:8. Hith. *assembled themselves.*
קְבֻצָה f., *collection, heap,* Eze. 22:20.
קִבּוּץ m., *company, troop,* Isa. 57:13.
קִבְצַיִם (*two heaps*), p. n., a town in Ephraim.
קַבְצְאֵל, יְקַבְצְאֵל p. n., a town of Judah.
קָבַר (fut. יִקְבֹּר) and Pi. קִבֵּר *buried.* Niph. and Pu. *was buried.*
קֶבֶר m., *burial place, sepulchre,* with suff. קִבְרוֹ; pl. קְבָרִים, קִבְרֵי; קְבָרוֹת, קִבְרוֹת.
קִבְרוֹת הַתַּאֲוָה (*the graves of lust*); p. n., a place in the wilderness of Sinai, Nu. 11:34.
קְבוּרָה const. קְבוּרַת, קְבֻרַת f.—I. *burial.*—II. *burial place.*
קָדַד *bowed his head;* fut. יִקֹּד.
קִדָּה f., *cassia.*
קָדְקֹד m. (with suff. קָדְקֳדוֹ), *crown of the head.*
קָדוֹשׁ; see קדשׁ.
קָדַח I. *struck, kindled a fire.*—II. *a fire was kindled.*
קַדַּחַת f., *a fever.*
אֶקְדָּח m., a precious stone, *the carbuncle,* Isa. 54:12.

קָדַם. Pi. קִדֵּם I. *preceded, came before.* — II. *came upon, against.*— III. *hastened, was early*, Ps. 119: 147. Hiph. I. *anticipate*, Job 41:3.—II. *come upon any one* of misfortune, Am. 9:10.

קֶדֶם m. (*that which precedes*).—I. adv., *before, in place.*—II. s., *the east;* אֶרֶץ קֶדֶם and קֶדֶם *the east*, i. e. *eastern country;* קֵדְמָה *towards the east;* מִקֶּדֶם *from the east;* with לְ *from the eastward of any place;* בְּנֵי קֶדֶם *those to the east of Palestine.*—III. *antiquity;* מִקֶּדֶם *from of old;* adv. *formerly;* קַדְמֵי אֶרֶץ *the ancient ones of the earth.*

קָדִים m.—I. *the east.*—II. *the east wind;* קָדִימָה *eastward.*

קְדוּמִים m. pl., *the ancients*, Jud. 5:21.

קֳדָם, קֳדָם Ch.—I. *before.*—II. מִן קֳדָם *from the presence, power of, by order of.*

קַדְמָה f.—I. *former condition.*—II. *origin*, Isa. 23:7. — III. const. קַדְמַת *before* (in time), Ps. 129:6.

קַדְמָה f. Ch., *former state* or *time;* מִן קַדְמַת דְּנָה *before.*

קִדְמָה f., const. קִדְמַת *eastward of any place.*

קֵדְמָה p. n., a son of Ishmael.

קְדֵמוֹת p. n., a town of the Reubenites.

קַדְמַי m. Ch., *first, former.*

קַדְמִיאֵל p. n. of a man.

קַדְמוֹן m., קַדְמוֹנָה f., *eastern*, Eze. 47:8.

קַדְמֹנִי m.—I. *eastern.*—II. *former, ancient;* pl. קַדְמֹנִים *ancestors;* f. קַדְמֹנִיּוֹת *former things.*—III. p. n. of a man.

קָדְקֹד *crown of head;* see קדד.

קָדַר I. *was dark, black, darkened.*— II. *was gloomy, distressed;* קֹדֵר *darkening, mourning.* Hiph. *made dark*, Eze. 31:15; 32:7, 8. Hith *became dark*, 1 Ki. 18:45.

קֵדָר (*blackness*), p. n., *Kedar*, the son of Ishmael and his descendants; בְּנֵי קֵדָר *the sons of Kedar.*

קִדְרוֹן p. n., *Kedron*, a brook which flows by Jerusalem.

קַדְרוּת f., *darkness*, Isa. 50:3.

קְדֹרַנִּית adv., *mournfully*, Mal. 3:14.

קָדֵשׁ, קָדַשׁ (fut. יִקְדַּשׁ).—I. *hallowed, consecrated.*—II. *rendered sacred, set apart from*, Isa. 65:5. Niph. I. *was made holy*, Ex. 29:43.—II. *was reverenced*, with בְּ. Pi. קִדֵּשׁ I. *hallowed, set apart.*—II. *reverenced*, Deu. 32:51.—III. *kept holy.* —IV. *rendered sacred by contact*, Eze. 44:19.—V. *purified by rites.* —VI. *appointed a religious service.* — VII. *prepared*, Mic. 3:5. Pu. *was consecrated, &c.* pass. of Pi. Hiph. I. *hallowed.*— II. *reverenced.*—III. *purified.*—IV. *prepared.* Hith. I. *made himself to be reverenced.*—II. *was celebrated* (a festival).—III. *purified himself.* —IV. *kept himself pure.*

קָדוֹשׁ, קָדֹשׁ m.—I. *holy, pure* (of God, angels, and men).—II. *sacred, set apart to God;* pl. קְדוֹשִׁים.

קַדִּישׁ m. Ch., *holy.*

קֹדֶשׁ, קוֹדֶשׁ m. (with suff. קָדְשִׁי; pl. קֳדָשִׁים or קָדָשִׁים, const. קָדְשֵׁי). —I. *holiness.*—II. *that which is consecrated to God, holy;* קֹדֶשׁ קָדָשִׁים *Holy of Holies* (the place within the vail of the tabernacle and temple).

קָדֵשׁ m. (*one devoted to an idol*).—I. *Sodomite* or, perhaps, priest of Baal-peor.—II. f. קְדֵשָׁה *a harlot.* III. קָדֵשׁ בַּרְנֵעַ ,קָדֵשׁ p. n., a city of the wilderness, between Edom and Egypt.

קֶדֶשׁ p. n.—I. a town of Judah.—II. of Naphtali.—III. of Issachar, called also קִשְׁיוֹן.

מִקְדָּשׁ (מִקְּדָשׁ) m.—I. *sanctuary* (the tabernacle or temple).—II. *sacred thing, part,* Nu. 18:29.—III. *asylum* (place of safety).

קָהָה *were set on edge* (of teeth). Pi. קֵהָה *became blunt* (of an instrument), Ecc. 10:10.

קְהָת p. n., *Kohath,* the son of Levi; patron. קְהָתִי.

קָהַל. Hiph. הִקְהִיל *called together, summoned.* Niph. *assembled themselves.*

קָהָל m.—I. *a meeting.*—II. *assemblage, multitude.*—III. הַקּ׳ *the congregation of Israel.*

קְהֵלָה p. n., a station of Israel in the wilderness.

קְהִלָּה f., *assembly.*

קֹהֶלֶת m. (f., Ecc. 7:27), p n. (*preacher*), applied to Solomon in the book of Ecclesiastes; LXX. ἐκκλησιαστής.

מַקְהֵלִים m. pl., *congregations, assemblies.*

מַקְהֵלוֹת f. pl.—I. the same.—II. p. n., a station in the wilderness.

קַוָּם ,קַו; see קוה.

קוֹא I. *vomited.*—II. *expelled with disgust.* Hiph. הֵקִיא the same.

קֵא m., *a vomit,* Pro. 26:11

קִיא m., the same.

קִיקָלוֹן m., "shameful spewing," Eng. Ver.; Hab. 2:16.

קוֹבַע; see קבע.

קָוָה *hoped in, waited for;* part. קוֹה. Pi. קִוָּה (inf. קַוֵּה ,קַוֹּה; fut. יְקַוֶּה, יְקַו).—I. *trusted in, expected,* with אֶל ,לְ.—II. *watched for evil, plotted against.* Niph. *assembled themselves.*

קָו ,קַו m.—I. *a measuring line.*—II. *a boundary line.*—III. *a limit, rule, direction,* Ps. 19:5; with suff. קַוָּם.

קָוֶה m., 1 Ki. 7:23, Ketib for קַו.

מִקְוֶה m.—I. *expectation, confidence, hope.*—II. *one confided in.*—III. *collection, assemblage.*

מִקְוָה f., *collection, repository,* Isa. 22:11.

תִּקְוָה f.—I. *hope, expectation.*—II. *a cord, thread.*—III. p. n. of a man.

קוֹחַ; see פקח.

I. קוּט (fut. יָקוּט), *was wearied, loathed, scorned,* with בְּ. Niph. *were loathed.* Hith. הִתְקוֹטֵט same as Kal, with בְּ.

II. קוּט (Arab. *was broken*); fut. יָקוּט *will be broken,* Job 8:14.

קוֹל (Arab. *he said*).

קוֹל m. (with suff. קוֹלוֹ ,קֹלְךָ; pl. קֹלוֹת).—I. *voice.*—II. *cry of animals.*—III. *any sound;* קוֹל יְהוָֹה *the voice of the Lord, thunder.*

קוֹלָיָה p. n. of a man.

קָל m. Ch., *voice, sound.*

קוּם (fut. וַיָּקָם ,יָקֻם ,יָקוּם).—I. *rose up.*—II. *arose from bed.*—III. *arose from an ambush.*—IV. with עַל, אֶל, בְּ *arose against in anger* (abs. קָמַי *they that rise up against me*). —V. *stood up.*—VI. *began anything.*—VII. *came into being, appeared.*—VIII. *took place.*—IX. *stood, stood firm.*—X. *was permanent* (an office).—XI. *was fixed* (of the eyes). Pi. קִיֵּם I. *strengthened, supported.*—II. *kept a resolution.*—III. *fixed a time.* Pil. קוֹמֵם I. *set up, restore.*—II. *set himself up,* Mic. 2:8. Hiph. הֵקִים (fut. וַיָּקֶם ,יָקֵם ,יָקִים).—I. *caused to rise up.*—II. *raised up.*—III. *strengthened.*—IV. *set up, fixed.*—V. *raised up, appointed.*—VI. *made* or *confirmed a covenant, or other engagement.*—VII. *put in force.* Hoph. הוּקַם I. *was set up.*—II. *was appointed.*—III. *was confirmed.* Hith. הִתְקוֹמֵם *arose against,* with לְ.

קוּם Ch. I. *arise.*—II. *stand up.*—III. *stand.* Pa. קַיֵּם *confirmed an engagement.* Aph. אֲקִים ,הֲקִים (fut. יְהָקִים ,יְקִים).—I. *set up.*—II. *established.*— III. *appointed.* — IV. *confirmed.* Hoph. הֳקִים *was set up,* Dan. 7:4.

קוֹמָה f., *height, stature.*

קִים *an adversary,* Job 22:20.

קִימָה f., *the act of rising up,* Lam. 3:63.

קְיָם m. Ch., *a decree,* Dan. 6:8, 16.

קַיָּם m., קַיָּמָה f. Ch., *enduring, steadfast.*

קָמָה f. (pl. קָמוֹת), *standing corn,* specially *in the ear.*

קָמוֹן p. n., a town of Gilead.

קוֹמְמִיּוּת adv., *at full height, erect,* Lev. 26:13.

יְקוּם m., *all that lives,* i.e. has been raised up, Gen. 7:4, 23; Deu. 11:6.

מָקוֹם com. (pl. מְקוֹמוֹת).—I. *place.* — II. *habitation, residence.* — III. *room, space.*— IV. *place, country, neighbourhood;* בִּמְקוֹם אֲשֶׁר *in the place where.*

תְּקוּמָה f., *power of resisting,* Lev. 26:37.

תְּקוֹמֵם m., *an adversary,* Ps. 139:21.

קוּן. Pil. קוֹנֵן *uttered a lamentation, lamented,* with אֶל, עַל.

קִינָה f.— I. *lamentation;* pl. קִינִים, קִינוֹת.—II. p. n., a city of Judah.

קוּס or **קָסַס.** Pil. קוֹסֵס *cut off,* Eze. 17:9, same as קצץ.

קוֹעַ m., *prince,* Eze. 23:23; etymon unknown.

קוֹף *ape,* 1 Ki. 10:22; 2 Chron. 9:21.

קוּף *go round,* like נָקַף; not used.

תְּקוּפָה f.— I. *orbit of the sun,* Ps. 19:7.—II. *circle of the year.*

קוּץ I. *loathed,* with בְּ.—II. *feared,* with מִפְּנֵי. — I. Hiph. הֵקִיץ *besieged,* Isa. 7:6.—II. Hiph.— 1. *awoke.*— 2. *arose from the dead, came to life.*—3. *was vigilant, active;* קוּץ from קַיִץ *pass the summer,* Isa. 18:6.

קוֹץ m.—I. *a thorn bush;* pl. קֹצִים, קוֹצִי.—II. p. n. of a man.

קַיִץ m. — I. *summer.* — II. *summer fruits.*

קְוֻצּוֹת f. pl., *locks of hair*, Cant. 5:2.

קוּר *dig a well.* Pil. קַרְקַר I. *dug down*, Num. 24:17.—II. *destroyed a people*, Isa. 22:5. Hiph. הֵקֵר *threw up water* (a well), Jer. 6:7.

קוּר m., *thread*, Isa. 59:5, 6.

קוֹרָה; see קרה.

מָקוֹר I. *spring.*—II. *origin.*—III. *wife.*

קוּשׁ (fut. pl. יְקֹשׁוּן) *ensnared*, Isa. 29:21.

קִישׁ p. n. of a man.

קִישִׁי, קוּשָׁיָהוּ p. n. of a man.

קִישׁוֹן p. n., *Kishon*. — I. a river of Palestine.—II. a town in Issachar.

קֶשֶׁת com. (pl. קַשְּׁתוֹת, קְשָׁתוֹת).—I. *a bow.*—II. *the rainbow.*

קַשָּׁת m., *an archer*, Gen. 21:20.

קַח, in pause קָח, with ה parag. קְחָה Kal imp., from לקח.

קח for לָקַח, Eze. 17:5; with suff. קָחָם for לְקָחָם, Hos. 11:3.

קַחַת, קְחַת Kal inf., from לקח.

קֹטֶב, קֶטֶב m. (with suff. קָטָבְךָ) *cutting down, destruction.*

קָטַט same as קוּט.

קָטַל *slew.*

קְטַל Ch., *slew.* Pa. קַטֵּל the same. Ithpe. and Ithpa. *was slain.*

קֶטֶל m., *slaughter*, Obad. *v.* 9.

קָטֹן (fut. יִקְטַן) *was small, of little importance.* Hiph. *made small*, Am. 8:5.

קָטֹן, קָטָן, קָטֹן m. (pl. קְטַנִּים; f. קְטַנָּה).—I. *small, in size, quantity* or *importance.*— II. *young.*— III. s. *the little finger*; with suff. קָטְנִי or קָטָנִּי.—IV. הַקָּטָן p.n. of a man.

קָטַף *plucked off.* Niph. *was cut off, withered*, Job 8:12.

קָטַר. Pi. קִטֵּר I. *burnt incense.*—II. *fumigated.*—III. *burnt fat*; part. f. pl. מְקַטְּרוֹת *altars of incense.* Pu. part. f. מְקֻטֶּרֶת *was perfumed*, Cant. 3:6. Hiph. הִקְטִיר I. *burnt incense.*—II. *burnt sacrifice.* Hoph. הָקְטַר *was burnt in sacrifice*; part. מֻקְטָר *offering of incense*, Mal. 1:11.

קְטוֹרָה f., *incense*, Deu. 33:10.

קְטוּרָה p. n., *Keturah*, one of Abraham's wives.

קָטֻר, pl. חֲצֵרוֹת קְטֻרוֹת "courts joined," Eng. Ver.; "with chimneys," marg.; *covered* (Ges.), Eze. 46:22.

קְטֹרֶת f., *incense.*

קִיטוֹר m.—I. *smoke.*—II. *vapour*, Ps. 148:8.

מִקְטָר m., *incense*, Ex. 30:1.

מִקְטֶרֶת f., *a censer.*

קְטַר (Syr. *bound*).

קְטַר m. Ch., pl. קִטְרִין.—I. *joints, ligatures.*—II. *difficulties.*

קִטְרוֹן p. n. of a place in Zebulun, called also קַטָּת.

קִיא; see קוֹא.

קָיָה *vomited*; imp. pl. קְיוּ, Jer. 25:27.

קַיִט m. Ch., *summer*, Dan. 2:35.

קִיטוֹר; see קטר.

קִים, קְיָם, קַיָּם, קִימָה; see קוּם.

קִימוֹשׁ same as קִמּוֹשׁ; see קמשׁ.

קין root not used; (Arab. *cane, a spear*).

קַיִן m.—I. *a spear made of cane*, 2 Sa. 21:16.—II. p. n., *Cain*, the son of Adam.—III. p.n., the *Kenites*, a tribe of Canaan.—IV. הַקַּיִן a town of Judah.

קֵינִי ,קִינִי ,קֵינִי the *Kenites*, one of the tribes inhabiting Canaan.

קִינָה; see קוּן.

קֵינָן p. n. of a man.

קַיִץ *summer, &c.*; see קוּץ.

קִיצוֹן ,קִיצוֹנָה; see קצץ.

קִיקָיוֹן m., the shrub *palma Christi, ricinus comm.*, κίκι.

קִיקָלוֹן; see קוא.

קִיר ,קִר com. (pl. קִירוֹת).—I. *a wall.* —II. *side of the altar.*—III. *sides of the heart*, Jer. 4:19.—IV. *city*, Isa. 15:1; 16:7.—V. קִיר מוֹאָב, קִיר חֶרֶשׂ ,קִיר חֲרֶשֶׂת p. n., a city of Moab.—VI. p. n., a part of Assyria.

קֵירֹס ,קֵרֹס p. n. of a man.

קִישׁ ,קִישׁוֹן; see קוּשׁ.

קִיתָרֹס m. Ch., κίθαρις, *a harp.*

קַל ,קַלָּה; see קלל.

קָל Ch., קֹל *voice*; see קוֹל.

I. קָלָה I. *roasted.*—II. *burnt alive*, Jer. 29:22. Niph. part. נִקְלֶה *burning disease*, Ps. 38:8.

קָלִי ,קָלִיא m., *corn roasted in the ear.*

II. קָלָה same as קָלַל. Niph. *was despised*; part. *despised, mean.* Hiph. *despised*, Deu. 27:16.

קָלוֹן m.—I. *worthlessness.*—II. *shame.* —III. *contempt.*—IV. *pudenda.*

קַלַּחַת f., *a caldron.*

קָלַט (Arab. *deformity*); part. קָלוּט *dwarfish.*

מִקְלָט *asylum, place of refuge.*

קֵלָיָה ,קְלִיטָה p.n. of a Levite.

קָלַל (fut. יֵקַל ,יִקַלּוּ).—I. *was diminished, became shallow.*—II. *was swift.*—III. *was worthless, unworthy.* Niph. נָקַל ,נְקַל (fut. יֵקַל, יִקָּלוּ).—I. *was thought a small, easy thing*; impers. נָקֵל מִן *it is a small thing that*; עַל־־נְקַלָּה *lightly, easily.*—II. *was despised.* —III. *lowered himself*, 2 Sa. 6:22. —IV. *became easy*, Pro. 14:6. Pi. קִלֵּל *revile, wished ill to*, with בְּ. Pil. קִלְקֵל I. *shook arrow in divination*, Eze. 21:26 (like the Arab. *removed, shook*). Hiph. הֵקַל I. *slighted.*—II. *lightened, removed a load*, with מִן, מֵעַל. Hithpal. *was shaken*, Jer. 4:24.

קַל m. (pl. קַלִּים; f. קַלָּה).—I. *swift.* —II. *swiftly.*—III. *swift-footed.*

קַלַּי p. n. of a man.

קָלָל m., *polished, shining.*

קְלָלָה, const. קִלְלַת f.—I *reviling.*— —II. *a curse.*—III. *object of reviling.*

קְלֹקֵל m., *worthless food*, Nu. 21:5.

קָלַס. Pi. and Hith. *mocked, scorned.*

קֶלֶס m., *scorn, contempt.*

קַלָּסָה f., the same, Eze. 22:4.

קָלַע I. *cut out, carved.*—II. *slung*, Jud. 20:16.—III. *expelled*, Jer. 10:18; קֹלֵעַ *a slinger.* Pi. *slung a stone.*

קֶלַע m. (with suff. קַלְעוֹ; pl. קְלָעִים) —I. *a sling.*—II. *a curtain*, from its tremulous motion.

קַלָּע m., pl. קַלָּעִים *slingers*, 2 Ki. 3:25

מִקְלַעַת f., *carving, sculpture*, 1 Ki only.

קַלְקֵל; see קלל.

קִלְּשׁוֹן m., שְׁלֹשׁ קִ׳ *three pronged pitch-fork*, 1 Sa. 13:21.

קְמוּאֵל p.n. of a man.

קָמוֹן, see קוּם; קִמּוֹשׂ, see קמשׁ.

קֶמַח m., *flour.*

קָמַט (Arab. *bound with a rope*), *bound as a captive*, Job 16:8. Pu. *was seized and carried off*, Job 22:16.

קָמַל, קָמֵל *withered.*

קָמַץ *grasped, took up in the hand.*

קֹמֶץ m. (with suff. קֻמְצוֹ). — I. *the hand, fist.* — II. *abundance.* — III. pl. קְמָצִים *handfuls.*

קמשׁ root not used.

קִמּוֹשׂ, קִימוֹשׁ, pl. קִמְּשׁוֹנִים m., *nettles.*

קֵן, קַן, קִנִּים; see קנן.

קָנָא. Pi. קִנֵּא I. *was jealous for*, with לְ (ζηλοῦν).—II. *emulated*, with בְּ; *envied*, with לְ, בְּ.—III. *was jealous of*, with בְּ. Hiph. הִקְנִיא *made jealous, angry.*

קַנָּא m., *jealous* (of God against idols only).

קַנּוֹא m., the same.

קִנְאָה f.—I. *jealousy.*—II. *envy.*—III. *anger.*—IV. *zeal.*

קָנָה (fut. apoc. וַיִּקֶן). — I. *make.* — II. *acquire, appropriate to one-self.* Niph. *was acquired, pur-chased*, Jer. 32:15, 43. Hiph. I. *appropriated as a slave*, Zec. 13: 5.—II. *provoked to jealousy*, Eze. 8:3.

קְנָא Ch., *acquired, procured*, Ezr. 7: 17.

קָנָת p. n., a town of Manasseh.

קִנְיָן m., *possession, wealth.*

מִקְנֶה m. (with suff. מִקְנֵהוּ; pl. מִקְנִים) *possession, wealth of land, flocks, cattle;* אַנְשֵׁי מ׳ *possession of cattle;* אֶרֶץ מ׳ *land full of cattle.*

מִקְנָה f., *acquirement, purchase, pos-session.*

מִקְנֵיָהוּ p. n. of a man.

קָנֶה m. (const. קְנֵה; with suff. קָנָהּ, pl. קָנִים קְנוֹת).—I. *reed, cane.*—II. *sweet cane.* — III. *measuring reed of six cubits.*—IV. *beam of the balance.*—V. *stalk of wheat.*—VI. *branch of candlestick.*—VII. *arm-bone above the elbow*, Job 31: 22.—VIII. *a staff to lean upon.*

קָנָה p.n.—I. a place on the borders of Ephraim and Manasseh.—II. a town in Asher.

קַנּוֹא same as קַנָּא; see קנא.

קְנַז p. n.—I. of a man; קְנִזִּי patron. —II. of a people of Canaan.

קֵנִי same as קֵינִי.

קִנָּמוֹן, const. קִנְּמָן־ m., *cinnamon.*

קָנַן. Pi. קִנֵּן *built a nest.* Pu. part. מְקֻנֶּנְתִּי(כ׳) *was built* (of a nest).

קֵן, const. קַן־ m. (with suff. קִנִּי; pl. קִנִּים).—I. *a nest.*—II. *a dwelling.* —III. *a family.*—IV. *cells, cham-bers.*

קִנְצֵי for קִצֵּי, Job 18:2; see קֵץ in קצץ.

קָסַם *divine with arrows, &c.*; part. קֹסֵם *diviner.*

קֶסֶם m. — I. *divination, enchant ment.*— II. *the reward of divina tion.*

מִקְסָם m., *divination*, Eze. 12:24; 13:7.

קָסַם; see קוּם.

קֶסֶת; see קשׁה.

קְעִילָה p.n., a city of Judah.

קַעֲקַע m., *mark, impression*, Lev. 19:28.

קָעַר root not used; (Arab. *being deep*).

קְעָרָה f. (const. קַעֲרַת; pl. קְעָרוֹת, קַעֲרוֹת; with suff. קְעָרֹתָיו) *deep saucer, dish*.

קָפָא I. *congealed* (of waters).— II. *hardened* (of men), Zep. 1:12. Hiph. *condense*, Job 10:10.

קִפָּאוֹן m., *congealing, denseness*, Zec. 14:6.

קָפַד (Arab. *finished his work*). Pi. *finished, cut short*, Isa. 38:12.

קֹפֶד, with ה parag. קְפָדָה m., *destruction*, Eze. 7:25.

קִפּוֹד m., *a hedge-hog*; (Arab. the same).

קָפַז (Arab. *springing serpent*).

קִפּוֹז m., *one of the springing snakes*, Isa. 34:15.

קָפַץ *shut up, close, constrict* (the hand, &c.)— Niph. *are shut up*, Job 24:24. Pi. *leaping*, Cant. 2:8.

קֵץ *end*; see קצץ.

קָצַב I. *cut wood*, 2 Ki. 6:6.—II. *shear sheep*, Cant. 4:2.

קֶצֶב m., *clefts of the mountains*.—II. *form, character*, Jon. 2:7.

קָצָה I. *cut off, destroy*.—II. *cut down*. Pi. *cutting off, down*, 2 Ki. 10:32; Pro. 26:6. Hiph. *cut, scraped, off*; inf. הַקְצוֹת.

קָצֶה m. (const. קְצֵה; with suff. קָצֵהוּ; pl. קְצֵי, קְצָים) *end, extremity, limit*; מִקְּצֵה הָעָם *men from all parts*; מִקְצֵה שְׁלֹשֶׁת יָמִים *at the end of three days*.

קֵצֶה m., the same.

קָצָה f., *extremity, border, limit*; מִקָּצָה *from the extreme parts*; pl. קְצוֹת, with הָעָם *the extremities of the people*, i.e. any of them.

קְצָה f. Ch., *end*.

קֶצֶו m., pl. const. קַצְוֵי *extremities borders*.

קְצָווֹת f. pl., the same.

קְצָת f.—I. *end, limit*; מִקְצָת יָמִים עֲשָׂרָה *at the end of ten days*.— II. Ch. *a part*.

קָצִין m.— I. *judge*.— II. *governor*.— III. *prince*.

מִקְצָת f., *part, limit*.

קֶצַח m., *black pepper*, Isa. 28:25, 27.

קָצִיר *harvest*; see קצר.

קָצַע. Hiph. הִקְצִיעַ *scrapes off*, Lev. 14:41. Pu. part. מְקֻצְעוֹת and Hoph. part. מְהֻקְצָעוֹת *small courts*, Eze. 46:22.

קְצִיעָה f., κασσία.—I. *cassia*, Ps. 45:9. —II. p. n., a daughter of Job, *Keziah*.

מִקְצוֹעַ m., *corner, angle*; pl. מִקְצֹעִים, מִקְצֹעוֹת.

מַקְצוּעָה f., "planes," Eng. Ver., Isa. 44:13.

קָצַף *was angry, wroth, enraged*, with אֶל, עַל. Hiph. *made angry*, with אֶת. Hithp. *became wroth*, Isa. 8:21.

קְצַף Ch., *was angry*.

קֶצֶף m.— I. *a broken branch, stick*,

Hos. 10:7. — II. *anger, wrath of God*, with suff. קִצְפְּךָ, קִצְפִּי.

קְצַף m. Ch., *anger*.

קְצָפָה f., *fracture, wasting*, Joel 1:7.

קָצַץ *cut off*. Pi. קִצֵּץ, קִצֵּץ *cut off*. Pu. part. מְקֻצָּצִים, Jud. 1:7.

קְצַץ Ch. Pa. *cut off*.

קֵץ m. (with suff. קִצּוֹ; pl. קִצִּים, קִצֵּי). —I. *end, limit*.—II. *end, cessation*. —III. *end, ruin*; מִקֵּץ *from the end* (of the earth), *at the end* (of a time); לְקֵץ the same; עֵת קֵץ, קֵץ הַיָּמִים, מוֹעֵד קֵץ *the time of the end*, i.e. of our Lord's first and second advent.

קִיצוֹן m., קִיצוֹנָה f., *the last*, Exodus only.

I. קָצַר (fut. יִקְצֹר), *cut down, reap*; part. *reaper*. Hiph. *reaped*, Job. 24:6.

קָצִיר I. *crop*.— II. *harvest*.— III. *branches*.

II. קָצֵר (fut. יִקְצַר).—1. *short, deficient, unable for*.—2. with רוּחַ or נֶפֶשׁ *unable to bear up, discouraged*. Pi. קִצֵּר *made short*, Ps. 102:24. Hiph. *made short*, Ps. 89:46.

קָצֵר m., *short, cut off*; קְצַר אַפַּיִם, ק׳ רוּחַ *angry*.

קֹצֶר m., with רוּחַ *impatience*, Ex. 6:9.

קַר, קָרִים, קֹר; see קרר.

קִר same as קִיר.

I. קָרָא (inf. קְרֹאות קְרֹא with suff. קָרְאִי; imp. קְרָא; fut. יִקְרָא).— 1. *cried, called, shouted*.—2. *called to* or *for*, with אֶל.—3. *called after*, with אַחֲרֵי.—4. *call upon in prayer*.—5. *celebrate*.—6. *call by name, name*, with לְ.—7. *call together, assemble, invite*, with אֶל, אֶת.—8. *called into question litigation*.—9. *appointed to an office*.—10. *called forth soldiers*, Isa. 13:3. — 11. *proclaim, publish, preach*.—12. *read from a book, read aloud*. Niph. נִקְרָא 1. *called for, summoned*.—2. *called together, assembled*, with בְּ or בְּשֵׁם פ׳ *in the name of some one*.—3. *named*, with שֵׁם פ׳ עַל *the name of some one is upon thee*, with שֵׁם יְהוָֹה עַל *the name of the Lord is named upon thee*, Deu. 28:10. Pu. קֹרָא *called, named*, with לְ.

קְרָא Ch., *read, recited, proclaimed*. Ithp. *was called*, Dan. 5:12.

קֹרֵא m.—I. *partridge*.—II. p. n. of a man.

קָרִיא m., *called, sent*, Numbers only.

קְרִיאָה f., *cry, proclamation*, Jon. 3:2.

מִקְרָא m.—I. *act of assembly*.—II. *convocation*.—III. *reading, reciting*, Neh. 8:8.

II. קָרָא same as קָרָה 1. *approached, met hostilely*.—2. *met*.—3. *happened*; inf. קְרָאָה, לִקְרַאת *to meet, meeting with*; with suff. לִקְרָאתְךָ *over, against thee*; לִקְרַאתְכֶם *over, against you*. Niph. 1. *met, happened to meet*, with עַל.—2. *happened*; fut. יִקָּרֵא; inf. נִקְרֹא. Hiph. *cause to happen to*, Jer. 32:23.

קְרֶאןָ for קְרֶאנָה Kal imp. pl. f., Ex. 2:20, from I. קרא

קְרֹאות Kal inf., with ו quiescent, Jud. 8:1, from I. קרא

קָרַב, קָרֵב (fut. יִקְרַב; inf. קְרֹב, קָרְבָה; imp. קְרַב).—I. *approached*, *drew near*, with לִפְנֵי ,בְּ ,לְ ,אֶל.—II. *attacked*, with אֶל ,עַל.—III. *keep by thyself*, with אֶל, Isa. 65:5. Niph. *should, ought to draw near*. Pi. קֵרֵב *made, caused to draw near*. Hiph. I. *made approach*.— II. *presented*.—III. *removed*, with מִן ,בְּ.

קְרֵב Ch., *came to*. Pa. *offered*. Aph. *brought to, offered*.

קָרֵב m., *approaching, drawing near*.

קָרוֹב m., קְרוֹבָה f., *near, at hand*, with לְ ,אֶל (*of time, place, things, &c.*); מִקָּרוֹב adv., *short, shortly, soon*.

קְרָב m., *contest, battle, war*; pl. קְרָבוֹת.

קְרָב m. Ch., the same.

קֶרֶב m. (with suff. קִרְבִּי; pl. with suff. קְרָבַי).—I. *inward part, entrails*.—II. *amidst, among*, often מִקֶּרֶב ,בְּקֶרֶב the same.

קִרְבָה const. קִרְבַת f., *approach, access*.

קָרְבָּן const. קָרְבַּן m., *offering*.

קֻרְבָּן m., the same.

קָרְבָתָם Kal inf., with ה parag. and suff., from קרב.

קַרְדֹּם (with suff. קַרְדֻּמּוֹ; pl. קַרְדֻּמִּים, קַרְדֻּמּוֹת), *an axe*.

קָרָה s. f.; see קרר.

קָרָה; see קָרָא II. (fut. יִקְרֶה ,וַיִּקֶר), *met, happened*, with לְ. Niph. *met with persons only*, with לִפְנֵי ,אֶל, עַל *met accidentally, dropped in with*. Pi. קֵרָה *framed together, made to join*. Hiph. I. *made, caused to meet with him*, Gen. 27:20.—II. הִקְרָה לוֹ *made convenient for him*, Nu. 35:11.

קָרֶה m., קְרֵה־לָיְלָה *accidental pollution during sleep*, Deu. 23:11.

קוֹרָה f.—I. *a beam*.—II. *a roof*, Gen 19:8.

קְרִי in pause קֶרִי m., *meeting, opposing*; הָלַךְ קְרִי עִם or בְּקֶרִי *he opposed, resisted*.

קִרְיָה f., *a town* or *city*, combined in the names of many cities.—I. קִרְיַת in the tribe of Benjamin.—II. קִרְיַת אַרְבַּע in the tribe of Judah, afterwards Hebron.—III. ק׳ בַּעַל same as ק׳ יְעָרִים.—IV. ק׳ חֻצוֹת in Moab.—V. ק׳ יְעָרִים ,ק׳ עָרִים in Judah.—VI. ק׳ סֵפֶר ,ק׳ סַנָּה in Judah, called also דְּבִיר.— VII. קִרְיָתַיִם 1. in Reuben.—2. in Naphtali, called also קַרְתָּן.—VIII. קְרִיּוֹת in Moab. קִרְיָה ,קִרְיָא Ch.

קֶרֶת f.—I. *a city*.—II. *a pulpit*, Job 29:7.

קַרְתָּה p. n., a town of Zebulun.

מִקְרֶה m.—I. *accident*.—II. *event, result*.

מְקָרֶה m., *building, edifice*, Ecc. 10:18.

קָרַח and Hiph. הִקְרִיחַ *shaved, made bald*. Niph. and Hoph. *have made themselves, become, bald*.

קָרֵחַ p. n. of a man.

קֵרֵחַ m., *bald* (on the crown of the head).

קֶרַח m.—I. *cold*.—II. *frost, ice*.—III. *crystal*, Eze. 1:22.

קֹרַח m.—I. *frost, ice*, Ps. 147:17.—II. p. n., *Korah*, a son of Esau.—III. a son of Eliphaz.—IV. the Levite who conspired against Moses, patron. קָרְחִי.—V. applied to other men.

קָרְחָה ,קָרְחָא f., *baldness*.

קָרַחַת f., *thread bare* (of cloth), Lev. c. 13 only.

קְרִיּוֹת, קִרְיַת, קִרְיָה, קְרִי; see קרה.
קְרִיאָה, קָרִיא; see קרא.

קָרַם *overlaid, cased,* with עַל; fut. יִקְרַם Eze. 37:6, 8.

קֶרֶן f. (dual. קַרְנַיִם, קַרְנַיִם; pl. קְרָנוֹת, קַרְנוֹת).—I. *the horn of an animal.*—II. *used as a vessel for oil.* —III. *used as a trumpet,* Jos. 6:5. —IV. Isa. 5:1, "a very fruitful hill," Eng. Ver.; "a horn, the son of oil;" marg. perhaps Mount Tabor.—V. metaphorically, *power, strength, in men* or *states.*—VI. probably the name of a weapon, 2 Sa. 22:3.—VII. *the ornaments at each corner of the altar.*—VIII. *rays of light,* Hab. 3:4.

קֶרֶן com. Ch., *horn.*

קָרַן *v.* denom., *emitted rays, shone* (the face of Moses), Exodus *c.* 34 only. Hiph. *produced horns,* Ps. 69:32.

קָרַס *became bent, bowed down,* Isa. 46:2.

קֶרֶס m., *hook, link, loop.*

קֵרֹס same as קֵירֹס.

קַרְסֻלַּיִם m. dual, *ankles.*

קָרַע *tore, rent* (as a garment, &c.); once, of the eyes, Jer. 4:30, "*thou rendest* thine eyes with stibium," i. e. givest them an enlarged appearance as if they were torn open; this is the effect of it. Niph. *was torn, rent.*

קְרָעִים m. pl., *rendings, pieces, rags.*

קָרַץ *closed, pressed together* (the lips or eyes, denoting fraud or cunning). Pu. *was cut, hewn out,* Job 33:6.

קֶרֶץ m., *destruction,*

קְרַץ m. Ch., *rending*

קַרְקַע m.—I. *basis, f*
Tabernacle.—II.
Judah.

קַרְקֹר p. n. of a place.

קָרַר (Arab. *was cold,*

קַר or קָר m., *cold w*
cool, quiet, Pro. 1'

קֹר m., *cold* (season),

קָרָה f., *cold, chillines*

מְקֵרָה f., *coolness, re*
20.

קָרַשׁ (Arab. *he cut*).

קֶרֶשׁ m.—I. *plank* or
of a ship, Eze. 27

קַרְתָּן, קַרְתָּה, קֶרֶת; se

קָשָׁה (Arab. *wicker l*

קְשָׂוֹת, קְשׂוֹת f. pl., *s*
ten, phial, or the

קֶסֶת f., *inkhorn carri*
Eze. 9:2, 3, 11.

קַשְׂקֶשֶׂת m., pl. קַשְׂקַשִּׂים
a fish.—II. *scale*
17:5.

קַשְׂקֶשֶׂת f., the same.

קָשַׁט (Arab. *pair of*

קְשִׂיטָה f., *a piece of*
out to pass for a
money.

קַשׁ; see קשׁשׁ.

קִשֻּׁאִים; see קשה.

קָשַׁב (fut. יִקְשַׁב) *att*
32:3. Hiph. *atten*
with בְּ, לְ, עַל, אֶל

קֶשֶׁב m., *attention, h*

קַשָּׁב, f. קַשֶּׁבֶת *atten*
11.

קַשֻּׁב, f. pl. קַשֻּׁבוֹת *attentive.*

קָשָׁה I. *was hard, grievous.*—II. *was difficult*, Deu. 1:17. Niph. part. נִקְשֶׁה *subject to difficulty*, Isa. 8:21. Pi. *hardened* (fut. apoc. וַתְּקַשׁ). Hiph. הִקְשָׁה (fut. apoc. וַיֶּקֶשׁ).—I. *hardened.*—II. *made grievous, difficult.* — III. *made refractory*, Pro. 28:14; Job 9:4.

קָשֶׁה m., קָשָׁה f.—I. *obdurate, unyielding, cruel.* — II. with עֹרֶף *stiff-necked, obstinate.*—III. with פָּנִים *impudent*, Eze. 2:4. — IV. *hard, grievous* (of servitude).—V. with רוּחַ *overwhelmed, depressed*, 1 Sa. 1:15.

קְשִׁי m., *obstinacy*, Deu. 9:27.

קִשְׁיוֹן p.n., a place in Issachar; קֶדֶשׁ the same.

קִשֻּׁאִים m. pl., *cucumbers*, Nu. 11:5.

מִקְשֶׁה m., *wreathed work.*

מִקְשָׁה f.— I. *wreathed work.* — II. *place, garden, of cucumbers*, Isa. 1:8.

קָשַׁח. Hiph.—I. *made obdurate*, Isa. 63:17.—II. *treated hardly*, Job 39:16.

קֹשֶׁט, קְשֹׁט m., *religious truth.*

קְשׁוֹט m. Ch., *truth.*

קָשַׁר (fut. יִקְשֹׁר). — I. *tied, bound*; part. קָשׁוּר *bound, firm.*— II. *conspired against.* Niph. *bound, made firm, sure*, Neh. 3:38; metaph., 1 Sa. 18:1. Pi. I. *bind on* (as ornaments), Isa. 49:18. — II. *secure to thyself*, Job 38:31. Pu. part. f. מְקֻשָּׁרוֹת *compact*, Gen. 30:41. Hith. *conspired.*

קֶשֶׁר m. (with suff. קִשְׁרוֹ) *conspiracy, treason.*

קִשֻּׁרִים m. pl., *bandages, belts.*

קָשַׁשׁ *collect, assemble together*, Zep. 2:1. Po. קֹשֵׁשׁ *collect, gather.* Hithpo. *assemble yourselves*, Zep. 2:1.

קַשׁ m.—I. *stubble.*—II. *chaff.*

קֶשֶׁת, קַשָּׁת; see קוּשׁ.

קַתְרֹס same as קִיתָרֹס.

ר

רָאָה (inf. abs. רָאוֹ, רָאֹה; const. רְאֹה, רְאוֹת; imp. רְאֵה; fut. יִרְאֶה; apoc. וַתֵּרֶא, וַיַּרְא, יֵרֶא).—I. *saw, viewed, observed*, with לְ.—II. *looked out, provided, chose, cared for*, with אֶל, בְּ, עַל.—III. *visited* (a sick person, &c.).—IV. *saw the sun, lived*, Ecc. 7:11.—V. *perceived, found, felt*, with בְּ.—VI. *discern, discriminate* (as a soothsayer). Niph. נִרְאָה (inf. הֵרָאֹה, הֵרָאוֹת; imp. הֵרָאֵה; fut. יֵרָאֶה; apoc. וָאֵרָא).—I. *was seen, apparent, appearing*, with אֶל, לְ, אֶת־פְּנֵי. — II. *was provided.* Pu. רֻאוּ *were seen*, Job 33:21. Hiph. הִרְאָה, הֶרְאָה (fut. יַרְאֶה, וַיַּרְא).—I. *showed.*—II. *see, experience, evil*, with בְּ. Hoph. הָרְאָה. — I. *was seen.*— II. *was shown.* Hith. הִתְרָאָה *looked at each other.*

רָאָה, Deu. 14:13, an incorrect reading for דָּאָה, *a vulture* or *kite.*

רֹאֶה m., *seer, prophet.*

רַאֲוָה, Eze. 28:17, Kal inf., from ראה.

רְאוּת, רְאִית *seeing, viewing*, Ecc. 5:10.

רְאוּבֵן (*behold a son!*), p.n., *Reuben*, Jacob's eldest son; patron. רְאוּבֵנִי *a Reubenite*.

רְאִי m., *mirror*, Job 37:18.

רְאִי with pause רֹאִי m.—I. *vision, revelation*.—II. *appearance, sight*.——III. *monstrosity*, Nah. 3:6.

רְאָיָה p.n. of a man.

רֵו m. Ch., *aspect, appearance*.

מַרְאֶה m.—I. *vision, appearance*.—II. *view, sight*.

מַרְאָה f.—I. *vision* (seen by a seer).—II. *mirror*, Ex. 38:8.

רָאַם *was raised, elevated*, Zec. 14:10.

רְאֵם, רְאֵים, רֵים m. (pl. רְאֵמִים, רְמִים) *buffalo, wild ox*; LXX. *unicorn*, μονόκερως.

רָאמוֹת f. pl.—I. *things high, sublime*, Pro. 24:7.—II. *most precious*.—III. p.n.: (a) a town of Issachar; (b) of Gilead.

רְאוּמָה p. n. of a woman.

רָאמַת נֶגֶב p.n., same as רָמוֹת נֶגֶב.

רֵאשׁ, רָאשׁ; see רוֹשׁ.

רֹאשׁ m. (pl. רָאשִׁים, רָאשֵׁי; with suff. רָאשָׁיו, רָאשֵׁיהֶם).—I. *head of man or beast*.—II. *chief, leader*.—III. *metropolis, chief city*.—IV. *top of a mountain, &c.*—V. *first, chief, principal of any thing*; רֹאשׁ שִׂמְחָה *chief joy*.—VI. *capital, amount, sum* (of numbers, money, &c.).—VII. *source, commencement* (of a river).—VIII. *an unknown poisonous plant, poison*. Phrases: נָשָׂה רֹאשׁ *appointed a chief*; מֵרֹאשׁ *from the beginning*; רֹאשׁ חֳדָשִׁים *the first month* (of the year); ר׳ פִּנָּה *head stone of the corner*; ר׳ דֶּרֶךְ *a cross way*, Eze. 16:25; ר׳ חוּצוֹת *the head of the streets*; רָאשִׁים *sources of rivers*, Gen. 2:10.

רֵאשׁ m. Ch. (pl. רָאשִׁין, רֵאשִׁין).—I. *head*.—II. *chapter, summary*, Dan. 7:1.

רֹאשָׁה f., אֶבֶן הָרֹאשָׁה *head stone*, Zec. 4:7.

רִאשָׁה f., *beginning*, Eze. 36:11.

רַאֲשׁוֹת, pl. const. רַאֲשֹׁתֵי *the part about the head* (of Saul), 1 Sa. 26:12.

רִאשׁוֹן (for רִאישׁוֹן), רִישׁוֹן m.—I. *first, former, foremost* (in time, place, dignity, &c.); pl. רִאשֹׁנִים *ancestors*; מֵרִאשׁוֹן *from the beginning*; f. רִאשֹׁנָה the same.—II. adv. *formerly*; בָּרִאשֹׁנָה *in front*; כְּבָרִאשֹׁנָה *as formerly*, Isa. 1:26; לָרִאשֹׁנָה *formerly*; pl. רִאשֹׁנוֹת *former things*.

רִאשׁוֹנִי, f. רִאשֹׁנִית *first*, Jer. 25:1.

רֵאשִׁית, רֵשִׁית f.—I. *first, former, in state or time*.—II. *firstfruits, firstborn*.—III. *first of way, beginning*.

מַרְאָשׁוֹת f. pl., *places or things where the head is*.

מְרַאֲשׁוֹת f. pl., the same; with suff. מְרַאֲשֹׁתָיו *at his head*.

מָרֵאשָׁה, מָרֵשָׁה p. n.: (a) a fortress of Judah, Μαρισά; (b) of a man.

רֹאשׁ, רוֹשׁ m., *poison*; see רֹאשׁ.

רֹאשׁ p. n., a northern nation: probably the Ῥῶς of the Byzantine authors; now Russia.

רַב same as רִיב.

רָבַב (pret. רַב, inf. רֹב).—I. *became many, numerous*. Pu. see רְבָבָה.

רַב m. (in pause רָב, pl. רַבִּים; f. רַבָּה, pl. רַבּוֹת).—I. *much, many.* — II. *abundant, enough.* — III. *great, vast,* in extent, station, dignity, &c.

רַבָּה (*metropolis*) p. n. — I. the chief city of Ammon.—II. a city of Judah.

רַב m. Ch. (pl. רַבְרְבִין). — I. *great, large.*—II. s., *great men, nobles.*

רֹב, רוֹב, רָב־ m. (with suff. רֻבְּכֶם) *multitude, abundance.* לָרֹב *abundantly.*

רְבָבָה f., *ten thousand, myriad;* pl. רְבָבוֹת, רִבְבוֹת *myriads.* Pu. denom. part. מְרֻבָּבוֹת *increased to myriads,* Ps. 144:13.

רִבּוֹ, רִבּוֹא f., the same; dual רִבּוֹתַיִם *two myriads;* pl. רִבֹּאוֹת, רִבְּאוֹת, רִבּוֹת *myriads.*

רִבּוֹ Ch., the same; pl. רִבְוָן (רִבְבָן).

רְבִיבִים m. pl., *showers.*

רַבִּית p. n., a city of Issachar.

רַבְרְבָן m. Ch., *a prince.*

רַבְשָׁקֵה p. n., *Rabshakeh,* leader of the Assyrians.

II. רָבַב *shot,* as arrows, &c. Pret. pl. רֹבּוּ.

רָבַד *spread, strewed, made up,* Pro. 7:16; (Arab. *tied, bound*).

רָבִיד m., *collar, neck-chain;* (Arab. the same.)

מַרְבַדִּים m. pl., *coverlets.*

רָבָה (fut. יִרְבֶּה, apoc. יִרֶב, יֵרֶב).—I. *became many, multiplied.* — II. *grew.* — III. *was great, powerful.* Pi. רִבָּה *made much,* Ps. 44:13. Hiph. הִרְבָּה (fut. יַרְבֶּה; apoc. יֶרֶב; imp. הֶרֶב; inf. abs. הַרְבָּה, הַרְבֵּה; const. הַרְבּוֹת).—I. *multiplied, increased.*—II. *extended, made large.* — III. *made great.* Inf. הַרְבֵּה, sometimes הַרְבּוֹת adv. *much, very much;* לְהַרְבֵּה *plentifully.*

רְבָה Ch., *grew great,* Dan. 4:8, 19. Pa. *became great,* Dan. 2:48.

רְבִיבִים, רִבּוֹת, רִבּוֹא, רִבּוֹ, רַבָּה, רַבִּית; see רבב.

רִבּוּ, רְבוּת f. Ch., *greatness.*

אַרְבֶּה m., a species of *locust,* so called from the multitudes of them.

מַרְבֶּה m., *greatness, abundance.*

מִרְבָּה f., *much, too much,* Eze. 23:32.

מַרְבִּית, f. — I. *abundance.* — II. *increase, interest.*—III. *offspring.*

תַּרְבּוּת f., *progeny,* Nu. 32:14.

תַּרְבִּית f., *usury.*

רָבִיד; see רבד.

רְבִיעִי, רְבִיעִית; see רבע.

רָבַךְ (Arab. *mixed*). Hoph. part. מֻרְבֶּכֶת *mixed, saturated.*

רִבְלָה p.n., *Riblah,* a city to the north of Palestine.

I. רָבַע *lying with* (carnally). Hiph. *cause to lie with.*

רֶבַע m., *lying down,* with suff. רִבְעִי Ps. 139:3; see also below.

II. רָבַע from אַרְבַּע, רֶבַע; part. רָבוּעַ *four-sided;* pl. רְבֻעִים. Pu. part. מְרֻבָּע m., מְרֻבַּעַת f., *made four-sided.*

רֶבַע I. *fourth part of anything, side of anything square.*—II. p.n., a king of Midian.

רֹבַע m., *fourth part.*

רְבִיעִי m., *the fourth,* רְבִיעִית f., *fourth part;* בְּנֵי רְבִיעִים *children of the fourth generation.*

רְבִיעַי m. Ch., *fourth*.

רִבֵּעִים m. pl., *posterity in the fourth degree*.

אַרְבַּע f., אַרְבָּעָה, אַרְבַּעַת m. — I. *four*; with suff. אַרְבַּעְתָּם *they four*; dual אַרְבַּעְתַּיִם *fourfold*; pl. אַרְבָּעִים *forty*.—II. p. n. of a giant.

אַרְבַּע f., אַרְבְּעָה m. Ch., the same.

רָבַץ (fut. יִרְבַּץ). — I. *lie down* (of beasts, &c.)—II. *lie upon the conscience, soul*, of sin, Gen. 4:7, &c. Hiph. I. *cause to lie down*.—II. *set* (of precious stones), Isa. 54:11.

רֵבֶץ m.—I. *crib, lying place of cattle*. —II. *resting place* (for man), Pro. 24:15.

מַרְבֵּץ m., *a resting place, for cattle* or *wild beasts*, Zep. 2:15.

מִרְבָּץ m., the same, Eze. 25:5.

רָבַק (Arab. *tied up to fatten*.)

רִבְקָה p. n., *Rebecca*, the wife of Isaac, Ῥεβέκκα.

מַרְבֵּק m., *stall for feeding cattle*.

רִבְשָׁקֵה, רַבְרְבָן, רַבְרְבִין; see I. רבב.

רֶגֶב m., pl. רִגְבֵי, רְגָבִים.—I. *clods of earth*, Job 38:38.—II. *stones set up as monuments*, Job 21:33.

רָגַז (imper. רְגָזָה, רְגַז, pl. רִגְזוּ; fut. יִרְגַּז).—I. *shook, trembled*.—II. *became disturbed, agitated*. Hiph. I. *move*.—II. *agitate, disturb*, with לְ. Hith. *thy commotion, excitement*, with אֶל.

רְגַז Ch. Aph., *provoked, excited to anger*.

רֹגֶז m. — I. *vexation, trouble*. — II. *neighing*, Job 39:24. — III. *fury, anger*, Hab. 3:2. — IV. *roar of thunder*, Job 37:2.

רְגַז m. Ch., *anger*, Dan. 3:13.

רַגָּז m., *trembling*, Deu. 28:65.

רָגְזָה f., *perturbation*, Eze. 12:18

אַרְגָּז m., "coffer," Eng. Ver., 1 Sa. 6:8, 11, 15; (Arab. *a panier*, on one side of a camel's pack saddle: also, the sack of stones hung on the other side when but one panier is used.)

רָגַל *go about speaking evil, backbite*, Ps. 15:3. Pi. I. *goes about calumniating*, with בְּ, 2 Sa. 19:28. — II. *explore as a spy*; part. מְרַגְּלִים *spies*, Gen. 42:9. Tiphel תִּרְגֵּל *was near* (*at foot*, i. e., *at hand*), Hos. 11:3.

רֶגֶל com. (dual רַגְלַיִם, רַגְלֵי) *the foot*; בְּרַגְלֵי פ׳ *at the feet of any one*; לְרַגְלֵי פ׳ *on account of any one*. (For many other idiomatic usages of רֶגֶל see Fürst's Concordance.) Pl. רְגָלִים *strokes of the feet, times, repetitions*.

רְגַל, רֶגֶל com. Ch., *foot*.

רַגְלִי m., *foot soldier*; pl. רַגְלִים *infantry*, Jer. 12:5.

רֹגֵל p.n.—I. see עַיִן.—II. pl. רֹגְלִים a place in Gilead.

מַרְגְּלוֹת f. pl., *at the feet, anything at the feet*.

רָגַם *stone to death*, with בְּ, עַל.

רִגְמָה f., *stone of defence*, Ps. 68:28.

מַרְגֵּמָה f., *heap of stones*, Pro. 26:8.

רֶגֶם p.n. of a man.

רֶגֶם מֶלֶךְ p.n. of a man.

רָגַן and Niph. נִרְגָּן *murmuring*; with בְּ *against*.

רָגַע. I. *hastens to decay* (the skin), Job 7:5.—II. *calms* (the sea), Job 26:12. Niph. *rested*, Jer. 47:6. Hiph. I. *rested, found rest.* — II. *give, restore to, make to, rest.*

רָגֵעַ m., *quiet, peaceable*, Ps. 35:20.

רֶגַע m., *instant, moment of time;* רֶגַע, כְּרֶגַע, בְּרֶגַע adv., *in a moment, suddenly;* לִרְגָעִים *moment after moment, incessantly.*

מַרְגּוֹעַ m., *rest, quiet*, Jer. 6:16.

מַרְגֵּעָה f., the same, Isa. 28:12.

רָגַשׁ *are tumultuous, in uproar*, Ps. 2:1.

רְגַשׁ Ch., the same. Aph. *assembled tumultuously.*

רֶגֶשׁ m., *tumult, multitude shouting*, Ps. 55:15.

רִגְשָׁה f., the same, Ps. 64:3.

רַד, Isa. 45:1, Kal inf., from רדד; Jud. 19:11, for יָרַד.

רֵד Kal imp., from ירד.

רָדַד *brings down, subdues*, Ps. 144:2; Isa. 45:1. Hiph. *lays down on*, 1 Ki. 6:32.

רַדַּי p.n. of a man.

רָדִיד m., *loose mantle, veil*, Cant. 5:7; Isa. 3:23.

רָדָה (fut. apoc. יֵרְדְּ; pl. יִרְדּוּ).— I. *subdue, rule, govern*, with בְּ; of fire, Lam. 1:13. — II. *took down*, Jud. 14:9. Hiph. *cause to rule, govern;* fut. apoc. יַרְדְּ, Isa. 41:2.

רְדָה I. in pause רֵדָה Kal imp. with ה parag.—II. Gen. 46:3, inf. with ה parag., from ירד.

רָדַם. Niph. נִרְדַּם *be insensible, as in deep sleep, fast asleep.*

תַּרְדֵּמָה f., *deep sleep, stupor, trance.*

רֹדֵם Kal part. with suff., from רדה.

רֹדָנִים p.n., 1 Chron. 1:7, an unknown people to the west of Canaan.

רָדַף I. *followed after.*—II. *pursued as an enemy*, with אֶל, לְ, אַחֲרֵי. Pi. *followed, pursued.* Hiph. *chased*, Jud. 20:43. Niph. and Pu. I. *was pursued.* — II. *succeeded*, Ecc. 3:15.

מֻרְדָּף m. (Hoph. part.) *pursued, chased*, Isa. 14:6.

רֶדֶת Kal inf., from ירד.

רָהַב I. *deal with as fearing*, Pro. 6:3.—II. *insult*, with בְּ. Hiph. *embolden*, Cant. 6:5.

רַהַב m.—I. *insolence*, Job 9:13; 26:12. — II. a prophetic name for Egypt.

רָהָב m., *insolent*, Ps. 40:5.

רֹהַב m., *pride, insolence*, Ps. 90:10.

רָהְגָה p. n. of a man.

רָהָה, תִּרְהוּ; see יָרֵא.

רָהַט (Syr. *stream;* Arab. *strap, thong, household goods*).

רַהַט m., pl. רְהָטִים. — I. *watering trough.* — II. *thongs*, Cant. 7:6; « *like a king bound in thongs*" (Lee).

רָהִיט m., pl. רָהִיטִים *furniture, furnishing* (of a house), φατνώματα, Cant. 1:17.

רֵו *aspect;* see ראה.

רוֹב *strife;* see רִיב.

רוֹב same as רֹב *many;* see רבב.

רוּד *walked with* (God), Hos. 12:1. Hiph. I. *wander* (mentally), Ps. 55:3.—II. *wander, be a nomade people*, Gen. 27:40.

מָרוּד m., *one persecuted*, Lam. 3:19; מְרוּדִים *persecuted ones*, Lam. 1:7.

רָוָה *was satiated* (with anything), with מִן· Pi. רִוָּה I. *was satiated, filled.* — II. *fill, delight, satisfy.* Hiph. הִרְוָה *satiate, fill.*

רָוֶה m., רָוָה f.—I. *soaked, satiated.*— II. *drunken*, Deu. 29:18.

רִי m., *irrigation*, Job 37:11.

רְוָיָה f., *abundance, plenty of water.*

רָז m. Ch., *a secret.*

רוּחַ, רִיחַ. Hiph. הֵרִיחַ I. *smell* (sweet odour).—II. *was satisfied, appeased.* —III. *was inspired with*, with בְּ, Isa. 11:3.—IV. *feel the fire*, Jud. 16:9. —V. *perceive*, Job 39:25.

רוּחַ com. (pl. רוּחוֹת, רֻחוֹת).—I. *air, breeze, cool breeze.*— II. *breath.*— III. *spirit, soul of man.*—IV. *mind, spirit, disposition.* — V. *spirit of God.*—VI. *the wind.*—VII. *anger, wrath.*— VIII. *vanity, folly* (used idiomatically in many ways; see Concordance).

רוּחַ com. Ch.—I. *the wind.*—II. *spirit, mind.*

רַחַת f., *winnowing fan*, Isa. 30:24.

רֵיחַ m., *odour, smell;* Ch. the same.

רָוַח (fut. יִרְוַח) *there was relief*, with לְ 1 Sa. 16:23; Job 32:20. Pu. part. מְרֻוָּחִים *spacious, ample*, Jer. 22:14.

רֶוַח m.— I. *space, distance.*—II. *deliverance, quiet.*

רְוָחָה, רַוְחָה f., the same.

רוּם (fut. יָרוּם, יָרֹם, וַיָּרָם).— I. *was high, lofty.* — II. *raised himself, was raised.*—III. *was high in rank* or *power.* — IV. *was lifted up, haughty* (fut. וַיָּרֶם); part. רָם m., רָמָה f. — I. *high.*—II. *loud*, Deu. 27:14.— III. *high in rank.* — IV. *haughty;* pl. רָמִים *the heights of heaven.*—V. p.n. of a man.. Pil. רוֹמֵם I. *lifted up, raised.*—II. *made to grow.* — III. *brought up* (children).—IV. *exalted with praise.*— V. *raised a building.* Pul. רוֹמַם *was lifted up, raised, high.* Hiph. הֵרִים I. *lifted up.*—II. *took up.*— III. *took out for an offering.*—IV. *offered.*—V. *removed.*—VI. *set up.* Hoph. הוּרַם I. *was offered.* — II. *was removed.* Hithpal. *raised, exalted himself*, Dan. 11:36.

רוּם Ch., *was lifted up*, Dan. 5:20. Pil. *exalting with praise*, Dan. 4:34. Aph. *exalting in power*, Dan. 5:19. Ithpal. *exaltest thyself*, Dan. 5:23.

רָמָה f.—I. *high place for idolatry*, Eze. c. 16.—II. p.n., *Ramah:* (a) a town of Benjamin; (b) a town of Ephraim, called also רָמָתַיִם צֹפִים; (c) a town of Naphtali; (d) רָמַת הַמִּצְפֶּה a town in Gilead, called also רָאמוֹת, רָמוֹת *Ramoth Gilead;* (e) רָמַת לְחִי same as לְחִי; רָמָתִי *a Ramathite.*

רָמוּת f., *pile, heap of dead bodies*, Eze. 32:5.

רוּם m. — I. *height*, Pro. 25:3.— II. *haughtiness.*

רוּם m. Ch., *height.*

רוֹם m., רוֹמָה f.—I. *height*, Hab. 3:10.— II. *on high, haughtily*, Mic. 2:3.

רוּמָה p.n. of a place.

רוֹמָם m., *extolling praise;* pl. const רוֹמְמוֹת, Ps. 149:6.

רוֹמֵמוּת f., *exaltation, majesty,* with suff. רֹמְמֻתֶךָ, Isa. 33:3.

רֹמַמְתִּי־עֶזֶר p. n. of a man.

רֶמֶת p.n., a town of Issachar.

מָרוֹם m.—I. *high, on high, height.*—II. *a high place.*—III. *haughtiness;* adv. *haughtily.*

מֵי מֵרוֹם p.n., a lake in the north of Canaan, Σαμοχωνῖτις.

תְּרוּמָה f.—I. *contribution, gift.*— II. *offering to God.* — III. *sacrificial gift, heave-offering.*

תְּרוּמִיָּה f., *offering,* Eze. 48:12.

רוּן (Arab. *conquer*). Hithpa. part. מִתְרוֹנֵן *overcome* (of wine), Ps. 78: 65.

רוּעַ. (pret. רָע; inf. רֹעַ) *was evil,* with בְּעֵינֵי *displeased.* Niph. (fut. יֵרוֹעַ).—I. *got worse,* Pro. 13:20.—II. *suffer evil, injury,* Pro. 11:15. Hiph. הֵרַע, הֵרֵעַ I. *did evil.* — II. *did evil to, afflicted;* part. מֵרַע, מֵרֵעַ *evil doer,* with לְ, עַל, עִם, בְּ. Hith. הִתְרוֹעֵעַ *suffered injury,* Pro. 18:24.

רַע in pause רָע m., רָעָה f.—I. *wicked.* II. *fatal, deadly.*—III. *calamitous.* IV. *sad.*—V. *ill-favoured.*—VI. s.: (a) *wickedness;* (b) *harm, injury, calamity.*

רֹעַ, רוֹעַ m.—I. *badness, evil condition.* —II. *sadness of countenance,* Ecc. 7:3.

I. רוּעַ *shout, call together,* רֹעוּ, Isa. 8:9. Hiph. הֵרִיעַ (pl. הֵרֵעוּ).— I. *shouted.*—II. *sounded a trumpet.* Pil. fut. יְרֹעָע *there shall be shouting,* Isa. 16:10. Hithpal. *shouted.*

רֵעַ m., *shouting, crying out;* see also רָעָה.

תְּרוּעָה f.—I. *shout of joy.*—II. *shout of battle.*—III. *sound of a trumpet.*

רוּץ I. *ran, ran to, after.* — II. *rushed upon,* with אֶל, עַל.—III. *ran into for a refuge,* with בְּ.—IV. *hastened.* —V. *did a thing readily,* Hab. 2: 2. Part. pl. רָצִים *runners, couriers.* Pil. רוֹצֵץ *ran swiftly,* Nah. 2:5. Hiph. I. *caused to run.*—II. *brought quickly.*—III. *stretched out his hands quickly,* Ps. 68:32.

מֵרוֹץ m., *a race,* Ecc. 9:11.

מְרוּצָה f.—I. *mode of running.*— II. *course of life.* See also רָצַץ.

רוּק; see רִיק.

רוּר *spat,* Lev. 15:3.

רִיר m.—I. *spittle,* 1 Sa. 21:14.—II. *whey,* Job 6:6.

רוּשׁ; see רֹאשׁ.

רוּשׁ *was poor, in want,* Ps. 34:11; part. רָשׁ, רָאשׁ *poor, a poor man.* Hith. הִתְרֹשֵׁשׁ *feigned himself poor,* Pro. 13:7.

רֵאשׁ, רֵישׁ, רֵישׁ m., *poverty.*

רוּת p. n. of a woman, *Ruth.*

רָזָה *diminished, brought low,* Zep. 2: 11. Niph. *was wasted away,* Isa. 17:4.

רָזֶה m.—I. *lean* (of cattle), Eze. 34: 20.—II. *barren* (of land), Nu. 13: 20.

רָזִי m., *destruction;* רָזִי לִי *woe is me!*

רָזוֹן m., *wasting, destruction.* See also in רָזַן.

רָזַח root not used; (Arab. *cried out*).

מַרְזֵחַ m., *lamentation,* Jer. 16:5.

מִרְזַח *cry of merriment,* Am. 6:7.

רָזַם *laid hold on*, Job 15:12.

רָזַן (Arab. *weighty*); part. רֹזְנִים *chiefs, princes.*

רָזוֹן m., *prince*; see also רָזָה.

רְזוֹן p.n., *Rezon*, king of Damascus.

רָחַב *was widened, enlarged, opened.* Niph. part. *enlarged, extended*, Isa. 30:23. Hiph. הִרְחִיב I. *made broad.*—II. with נֶפֶשׁ *extended his desires, enlarged itself.*—III. *opened the heart, mouth, &c.*—IV. with לְ, *liberated, made room for, gave way.*

I. רָחָב m., רְחָבָה f., *broad, large, extensive, capacious*; with יָדַיִם *broad on both hands, very broad*; with לֵב *of unlimited desires.*

II. רָחָב p. n., *Rahab*, the woman of Jericho.

רַחַב m., *plenty*, Job 36:16; 38:18.

רֹחַב m. (with suff. רָחְבָּהּ).—I. *breadth, width.*—II. *extent, expanse*, Job 37:10.—III. with לֵב *extent of understanding*, 1 K. 5:9.

רְחֹב, רְחוֹב f. (pl. רְחֹבוֹת).—I. *broad, open place in a town, square, street, market-place.*—II. בֵּית רְחֹב and רְחֹב p. n., a town in the north of the tribe of Asher; a Syrian city near it was called אֲרַם בֵּית רְחוֹב and אֲרַם רְחֹב.—III. רְחֹבוֹת p.n., (a) the name of a well; (b) ר׳ עִיר a town in Assyria; (c) ר׳ הַנָּהָר a town on the Euphrates.

רְחַבְיָהוּ p.n. of a man.

רְחַבְעָם p. n., *Rehoboam*, the son of Solomon, king of Judah. LXX. Ῥοβοάμ.

מֶרְחָב m.—I. *wide places.*—II *prosperity*, considered as freedom.

רַחִיק, רָחוֹק; see רחק.

רָחִיטִים Ketib for רָהִיטִים; see רהט.

רֵחַיִם m. dual, *pair of millstones.*

רָחֵל f.—I. *a ewe.*—II. *any sheep.*—III. p. n., *Rachel*, the wife of Jacob; LXX. Ῥαχήλ.

רָחַם or **רָחֵם** *loved*, Ps. 18:2. Pi. רִחַם *loved, pitied, had mercy on*, with accus. עַל. Pu. רֻחַם *obtained mercy.*

רָחָם, רָחָמָה m., *the aquiline vulture*; vultur percnopterus (Linn.), Lev. 11:18; Deu. 14:17.

רַחוּם m., *merciful* (of God only).

רְחוּם p. n. of a man.

רֶחֶם, רַחַם m. (f. Jer. 20:17).—I. *the womb.*—II. *a girl*; dual רַחֲמָתַיִם.—III. רַחַם p. n. of a man.

רַחֲמִים m. pl.—I. *the viscera.*—II. *pity, mercy.*

רַחֲמִין m. pl. Ch., *mercy.*

רַחְמָנִי m., f. pl. רַחְמָנִיּוֹת *tender, merciful*, Lam. 4:10.

רָחַף *shook, trembled*, Jer. 23:9. Pi. רִחֵף *fluttered, hovered*, Deu. 32:11; part. מְרַחֶפֶת *hovering, brooding* (of the Spirit of God), Gen. 1:2.

רָחַץ (fut. יִרְחַץ; imp. רְחַץ, pl. רַחֲצוּ; inf. רְחֹץ, רָחְצָה) *washed himself* or *another*; *washed away.* Pu. *was washed.* Hith. *washed himself*, Job 9:30.

רַחַץ m., *washing*, Ps. 60:10.

רַחְצָה f., *washing-place for sheep*, Cant. 4:2; 6:6.

רְחַץ Ch. Ith. *depend on, trust to,* Dan. 3:28.

רָחַק (fut. יִרְחַק; inf. רָחֳקָה) I. *was distant.*—II. *kept at a distance, withdrew himself.* Pi. רִחַק *placed at a distance, forsook.* Hiph. הִרְחִיק I. *caused to be distant.*—II. *went to a distance;* inf. הַרְחֵק adv., *afar off.*

רָחֵק m., *one who forsakes,* Ps. 73:27.

רָחוֹק m., רְחוֹקָה f. — I. *a distance, interval.*—II. *distant.*—III. *out of reach.* — IV. *difficult,* Pro. 31:10 (i.e., *brought from afar, precious*); בְּרָחוֹק *afar off;* מֵרָחוֹק *from, at a distance* (of time or space); לְמֵרָחוֹק *at a distance* (time or space); עַד־רָחוֹק *to a distance.*

רַחִיק m. Ch., *distant,* Ezr. 6:6.

מֶרְחָק m. (pl. מֶרְחַקִּים), *distance, distant part.*

מַרְחָק m., the same; pl. מַרְחַקִּים.

רָחַשׁ *threw up, bubbled up* (as a spring), Ps. 45:2.

מַרְחֶשֶׁת f., *pot for boiling.*

רַחַת; see רוּחַ.

רָטַב (fut. יִרְטַב) *was wet* (with rain), Job 24:8.

רָטֹב m., *moist, fresh,* Job. 8:16. (Arab. the same).

רָטָה, יִרְטֵנוּ; see יָרַט.

רָטַט root not used; Ch. *trembled;* Syr. the same.

רֶטֶט m., *trembling,* Jer. 49:24.

רֻטֲפַשׁ *grew fresh, moist,* Job 33:25.

רָטַשׁ. Pi. רִטֵּשׁ *smote, killed.* Pu. *were killed.*

רִי; see רָוָה.

רִיב (pret. רָב, רַבְתָּ, רִיבוֹתָ; inf. abs. רֹב; inf. const. and imp. רִיב; fut. יָרִיב).—I. *disputed, quarrelled with,* with עִם, אֶת, אֶל, בְּ.—II. *defended,* with לְ.—III. *opposed,* with עַל.—IV. *decided a cause favourably.* Hith. part. מֵרִיב *opposed, contended with.*

רִיב, רִב m. (pl. רִיבִים, רִיבוֹת). — I. *controversy, suit.* — II. *quarrel, strife.*

רִיבַי p. n. of a man.

יָרֵב m., *an adversary,* Hos. 5:13; 10:6.

יָרִיב m.—I. the same.—II. p.n. of a man.

יְרִיבַי p.n. of a man.

יְרֻבַּעַל, יְרֻבֶּשֶׁת p.n., titles of Gideon.

מְרִיבָה f.—I. *strife, contention.* — II. p.n., a spring in the desert of Sinai.

רֵיחַ, הֵרִיחַ, רֵיחַ; see רוּחַ.

רֵים same as רְאֵם.

רֵיעַ, הֵרִיעַ, see רוּעַ; רֵיעַ, see רָעָה.

רִיפוֹת f. pl., *grain.*

רִיפַת p. n., one of Japhet's sons, and his descendants.

רִיק. Hiph. הֵרִיק — I. *emptied.* — II. *made empty, poured out.*—III. *drew a sword, made ready for war,* Gen. 14:14. Hoph. הוּרַק *was poured out.*

רִיק m.—I. *empty.*—II. *an empty, vain thing.*—III. *in vain.*—IV. adv. רִיק, לָרִיק *in vain.*

רֵיק, רֵק m., רֵקָה f.—I. *empty.* — II. *hungry, poor.* — III. *unimportant,* Deu. 32:47. — IV. *worthless in character.*

רֵיקָם adv. — I. *emptily.* — II. *empty*

handed.—III. *without cause.*—IV. *without effect.*

רִיר *ran;* see רוּר.

רֵישׁ, רֵישׁ *poverty;* see רוּשׁ.

רִישׁוֹן, Job 8:8; same as רִאשׁוֹן *first.*

רֹךְ, רַךְ; see רכך.

רָכַב (fut. יִרְכַּב; inf. רְכֹב).—I. *rode on a horse, ass,* or *camel.*—II. metaph. of God on the clouds or wind, with עַל, בְּ, accus.; part. רֹכֵב *a horseman.* Hiph. I. *caused to ride.*—II. *carried in a chariot.*—III. *placed upon.* — IV. *caused to be ridden,* Hos. 10:11.

רֶכֶב m. (f. Nah. 2:5). — I. *riding, a rider.* — II. *the upper millstone* (that which rides).—III. *a chariot, chariots.*

רֵכָב p. n. — I. *Rechab,* the father of Jonadab, from whom the Rechabites (רֵכָבִים) were descended. — II. used also of other men.

רְכוּב m., *vehicle, chariot,* Ps. 104:3.

רַכָּב m.—I. *horseman.*—II. *charioteer.*

מֶרְכָּב m.—I. *any carriage to ride in,* Lev. 15:9.—II. *chariots,* 1 K. 5:6.

מֶרְכָּבָה f. (with suff. מֶרְכַּבְתּוֹ; pl. מַרְכְּבוֹת, מַרְכָּבוֹת), *a chariot.*

מִרְכֶּבֶת f., the same.

רֵכָה p. n. of a place unknown.

רְכוּשׁ *wealth;* see רכשׁ.

רָכִיל *slander;* see רכל.

רָכַךְ *was timid, gentle.* Niph. *was timid;* fut. יֵרַךְ. Pu. *was softened,* Isa. 1:6. Hiph. הֵרַךְ *rendered timid,* Job 23:16.

רַךְ m., רַכָּה f.—I. *tender, young.*—II. *object of care.*—III. *effeminate.* —IV. *weak, timid, gentle.* — V. *tender-eyed,* i.e. having sore eyes, Gen. 29:17.

רֹךְ f., *effeminacy,* Deu. 28:56.

רָכַל *went to and fro, travelled as a merchant;* part. רֹכֵל, f. רֹכֶלֶת *a merchant, dealer.*

רָכָל p. n., a town of Judah.

רָכִיל m.—I. *a busy body.*—II. *slander;* הָלַךְ רָכִיל *he went about tale bearing.*

רְכֻלָּה f., *merchandise* (Ezekiel only).

מַרְכֹּלֶת f., *merchandise,* Eze. 27:24.

רָכַס *tied, fastened.* Ex. 28:28; 39:21.

רֹכֶס m., רִכְסֵי אִישׁ *combinations, artifices,* Ps. 31:21.

רֶכֶס m., pl. רְכָסִים *rugged places,* Isa. 40:4.

רָכַשׁ *acquired, gained* (Genesis only).

רְכוּשׁ, רְכֻשׁ m., *property, wealth.*

רֶכֶשׁ m., *swift species of horse.*

רָם, רָמָה, see רוּם; רֵם same as רְאֵם

רָמָה I. *threw.*—II. *shot with a bow* Pi. רִמָּה *deceived,* lit. threw down.

רְמָה, רְמָא Ch. — I. *threw.*—II. *imposed tribute.* Ithpe. *were thrown placed.*

רִמָּה, רִמּוֹן; see רמם.

רָמוֹת, רָמוּת; see רוּם.

רְמִיָּה f.—I. *deceit.*—II. *negligence.*

רְמַיָה p.n. of a man.

מִרְמָה f.—I. *deceit, artifice.*—II. p.n. of a man.

תָּרְמָה f., *deceit, craft,* Jud. 9:31.

תַּרְמִית (תַּרְמוּת) f., the same.

רֹמַח m. (pl. רְמָחִים; with suff. רָמְחֵיהֶם) *a spear.*

רַמִּי, pl. הָרַמִּים same as הָאֲרַמִּים *the Syrians.*

רַמָּךְ f., *a mare*, Est. 8:10.

רְמַלְיָהוּ p. n., *Remaliah*, the father of Pekah, king of Israel.

רָמַם (pret. pl. רֹמּוּ, רַמּוּ) *was high, lofty*; part. f. רוֹמֵמָה *high*. Niph. (imp. pl. הֵרֹמּוּ; fut. pl. יֵרֹמּוּ) *was raised*, Eze. 10:15, 17, 19.

רִמָּה f., *a worm, worms*.

רִמּוֹן m.—I. *a pomegranate fruit* or *tree*.—II. *an artificial imitation of the fruit*.—III. p. n.: (a) a city of Simeon; (b) a city near Gibeah; (c) an idol of the Syrians; (d) רִמּוֹן הַמְּתֹאָר a town of Zebulun; (e) רִמּוֹן פֶּרֶץ one of the stations of the Israelites.

רָמַס I. *trampled on, trod on*. — II. *walked in*; part. רֹמֵס *an oppressor*, Isa. 16:4. Niph. *was trodden down*, Isa. 28:3.

מִרְמָס m., *that which is trampled under foot*.

רָמַשׂ I. *move* (as a quadruped).—II. *creep* (as a reptile).

רֶמֶשׂ m. collec.—I. *reptiles*.—II. *small land animals*.— III. *sea creatures*, perhaps *seals*, Ps. 104:25.

רֶמֶת; see רוּם.

רָנָה *rang, rattled*, Job 39:23.

רָנַן (fut. יָרֹן).—I. *sung*.—II. *shouted*.— III. *invited*.— IV. *called for help*. Pi. רִנֵּן I. *sung, rejoiced*, with בְּ, עַל. —II. *sung of, celebrated*, with לְ, אֶל. Pu. fut. יְרֻנַּן *there shall be singing*, Isa. 16:10. Hiph. הִרְנִין I. *caused to sing*. — II. *rejoiced*. Hith. see in רוּן.

רְנָנִים m., pl. רְנָנִים *ostriches*, Job 39:13.

רְנָנָה f., *singing, rejoicing*.

רֹן m., pl. רָנִּים *songs*, Ps. 32:7.

רִנָּה f.—I. *singing, shout of joy*.—II. *a shout* or *cry* of any kind.—III. *a cry for help*.—IV. p. n. of a man.

רֶסֶן m.—I. *bridle, halter*.—II. p. n. a city of Assyria.

רָסַס *sprinkled*, Eze. 46:14.

רִסָּה p.n., one of the stations in the wilderness.

רְסִיסִים m. pl. — I. *sprinkling, drop*, Cant. 5:2.—II. *fractures*, Am. 6:11.

רָע, רַע, רֹעַ, see רוּעַ; **רֵעַ**, see רוּעַ, רָעָה.

רָעֵב (fut. יִרְעַב).—I. *was hungry*.—II. *hungered for, was famished*.—III. *suffered from famine*, with לְ. Hiph. הִרְעִיב *allowed, caused to suffer hunger*.

רָעֵב m., רְעֵבָה f., *hungry, famishing*.

רָעָב m.—I. *hunger*.—II. *famine*.

רְעָבוֹן, const. רַעֲבוֹן m., the same.

רָעַד (fut. יִרְעַד) *trembled*, Ps. 104:32. Hiph. the same.

רַעַד m., } *trembling, awe*.
רְעָדָה f., }

רָעָה (fut. יִרְעֶה; apoc. יֵרַע).— I. *fed*. — II. *consumed*. — III. *devastated*. — IV. *fed on, delighted in*. — V. *associated with*.—VI. *fed cattle*.— VII. *governed a people*. — VIII. *nourished*. — IX. for רָעַע *injured, oppressed*; part. רֹעֶה *a shepherd*. Pi. רֵעָה *became a companion*, Jud. 14:20. Hiph. pres. aff. יַרְעֵם *ruled them*, Ps. 78:72. Hith. הִתְרָעָה *was intimate with, became a companion*, with אֵת.

רֵעַ, רֵעֶה, רֵיעַ m. (pl. with suff. רֵעֵהוּ

for רֵעֵיהוּ)—I. *a friend, neighbour, companion, lover;* אִישׁ...רֵעַ *one... the other.*—II. *thought, will,* Ps. 139:2, 17; see also רוּעַ.

רֵעָה f., pl. רֵעוֹת *female friend, companion.*

רָעָה f., *evil, &c.;* see רַע in רוּעַ.

רֹעָה *breaking;* see רעע.

רְעוּת f.—I. *friend, neighbour.*—II. with רוּחַ *feeding on the wind.*

רְעוּת f. Ch., *wish, will.*

רְעוּ p.n. of a man.

רְעוּאֵל p.n. of a man.

רְעִי m., *pasture.* 1 Ki. 5:3.

רֹעִי m., *a shepherd.*

רֵעִי p.n. of a man.

רַעְיָה f., *female companion, friend.*

רַעְיוֹן m., *desire, pursuit.*

רַעְיוֹן m. Ch., *desire, purpose, thought.*

מֵרֵעַ m. (with suff. מֵרֵעֵהוּ; pl. מֵרֵעִים) *desire, purpose, thought.*

מִרְעֶה m., *pasture.*

מַרְעִית f.—I. *pasturing, feeding cattle.*—II. *a flock.*

רָעַל. Hoph. הָרְעַל *were thrown* (of javelins), Nah. 2:4.

רַעַל m.—I. *trembling, giddiness,* Zec. 12:2.—II. pl. רְעָלוֹת *veils,* Isa. 3:19.

רְעֵלָיָה p. n. of a man.

תַּרְעֵלָה f., *trembling, staggering.*

רָעַם (fut. יִרְעַם).—I. *resounded, roared* (of the sea).—II. *was excited,* Eze. 27:35. Hiph. הִרְעִים I. *thundered.*—II. *caused anger, vexation.*

רַעַם m.—I. *thunder.*—II. *tumult, rage,* Job 39:25.

רַעְמָה f.—I. *rage,* Job 39:19.—II. p. n. of a city of Cush.

רַעַמְסֵס, רַעְמְסֵס (*born of the sun*), p. n.—I. the district which forms the eastern boundary of Egypt, called also Goshen.—II. a city built there by the Israelites.

רָעַן. Pil. רַעֲנַן *was green.*

רַעֲנָן m.—I. *green, flourishing.*—II. *prosperous.*—III. *surrounded with foliage,* Cant. 1:16.—IV. *anointed,* Ps. 92:11.

רַעֲנַן m. Ch., *green, flourishing.*

רָעַע (fut. יָרֹעַ; inf. רֹעָה).—I. *broke, broke to pieces.*—II. *crushed.* Niph. fut. יֵרוֹעַ and Hiph. הֵרַע; see in רוּעַ. Hith. הִתְרוֹעֵעַ *was broken to pieces, ruined.*

רְעַע Ch. (fut. f. תֵּרֹעַ), *broke.* Pa. the same.

רֹעָה f., *breaking;* שֵׁן רֹעָה *a broken tooth.*

רָעַף and Hiph. הִרְעִיף *flowed, let drop.*

רָעַץ *crushed, overpowered, oppressed.*

רָעַשׁ (fut. יִרְעַשׁ), *was shaken, trembled.* Niph. *quaked* (of the earth), Jer. 50:46. Hiph. I. *shook.*—II. *filled with eagerness* (of a horse), Job 39:20.

רַעַשׁ m.—I. *shaking.*—II. *an earthquake.*—III. *rumbling of wheels.*—IV. *rattling of a horse's hoofs,* Job 39:24.—V. *any tumult,* Job 41:21.—VI. *the rattling of a spear.*

רָפָא (imp. רְפָא, רְפָה; fut. יִרְפָּא; pl. f. תִּרְפֶּינָה).—I. *healed.*—II. *restored to prosperity, delivered from calamity.*—III. *healed,* i. e., *removed transgressions;* part. רֹפֵא *a physician.* Niph. נִרְפָּא (pret. f. נִרְפָּתָה; inf. הֵרָפֵא, הֵרָפֵה; fut.

pl.יִרָּפוּ).—I. *was repaired* (a vessel). — II. *was healed* (a person or wound).—III. *was rendered wholesome* (water), Eze. *c.* 47.—IV. *was restored to prosperity*, Isa. 53:5. Pi. רִפֵּא (fut. pl. יְרַפּוּ). — I. *repaired*, 1 Ki. 18:30.—II. *healed.*—III. *caused to be cured*, Ex. 21:19. —IV. *made wholesome*, 2 Ki. 2:21. Hith. *get himself cured.*

רְפָאֵל p. n. of a man.

רְפָיָה p. n. of a man.

רְפָאִים p. n., the name of a people inhabiting the country on the east of the Dead Sea, supposed to have been giants; called also יְלִידֵי הָרָפָה. עֵמֶק רְפָאִים *the valley of the Rephaims*, close to mount Moriah.

רִפְאוּת f., *health*, Pro. 3:8.

רְפֻאוֹת f. pl., *bandages, remedies.*

רָפוּא p.n. of a man.

מַרְפֵּה, מַרְפֵּא m.—I. *remedy.*— II. *healing.*—III. *soundness.* See also in רָפָה.

תְּרוּפָה f., *healing*, Eze. 47:12.

רָפַד *supported himself*, Job 41:22; fut. יִרְפַּד. Pi. I. *constructed a couch*, Job 17:13. — II. *refreshed*, Cant. 2.5.

רְפִידָה f., *a throne;* Vulg. reclinatorium, Cant. 3:10.

רְפִידִים p.n., *Rephidim*, a station in the wilderness.

רָפָה (fut. יִרֶף ,יִרְפֶּה).—I. *hung down* (the hands).—II. *declined* (the day). —III. *sank down* (fuel in the fire), Isa. 5:24.—IV. *gave way* (to anger), Jud. 8:3; with מִן. — V. *became weak*, Jer. 49:24. — VI. *desisted.* Niph. part. נִרְפִּים *became, were idle*, Ex. 5:8, 17, &c. Pi. רִפָּה I. *allowed to hang down*, Eze. 1:24, 25. — II. *weakened* (part. מְרַפֵּא). Hiph. הִרְפָּה (imp. apoc. הֶרֶף; fut. apoc. יֶרֶף) I. *ceased from*, with מִן.—II. *withheld.*—III. *gave up.*—IV. *let go.*—V. *ceased.* Hith. *relaxed himself, was slothful.*

רָפֶה m. (pl. f. רָפוֹת), *weak.*

רָפָה p. n.; see in רפא.

רִפְיוֹן m., *weakness*, Jer. 47:3.

מַרְפֵּא m., *yielding*, Ecc. 10:4; see also in רפא.

רֶפַח p. n. of a man.

רָפַס, רָפַשׂ *trampled down.* Niph. part. נִרְפָּשׂ *disturbed by trampling.* Hith. הִתְרַפֵּס *submitted, humbled himself.*

רְפַס Ch., the same.

מִרְפָּשׂ *water made muddy by trampling*, Eze. 34:19.

רַפְסֹדוֹת f. pl., *floats, rafts*, 2 Ch. 2:15.

רָפַף. Po. רוֹפַף *trembled.*

רָפַק. Hith. *trembled*, Cant. 8:5.

רָפַשׂ; see רפס.

רֶפֶשׁ m., *mud*, Isa. 57:20.

רְפָתִים m. pl., *stalls for oxen*, Hab. 3:17.

רַץ, רַצֵּי, see רצץ; רָצִים, see רוץ.

רָצָא, Eze. 1:14; same as רוּץ *he ran.*

רָצַד. Pi. *he laid wait for*, Ps. 68:17.

רָצָה (fut. יִרְצֶה, וַתֶּרֶץ).—I. *approved of, took pleasure in*, with בְּ.—II. *received favourably.*—III. *loved.*—IV. *fulfilled.*—V. *associated with*,

17

with עִם.—VI. *was received favourably*; (part. רָצוּי *accepted*). Niph. נִרְצָה I. *was received favourably*.—II. *was fulfilled*, Isa. 40:2. Pi. *satisfied by restitution*, Job 20:10. Hiph. *fulfilled*, Lev. 26:34. Hith. *made himself acceptable*, 1 Sa. 29:4.

רָצוֹן m. — I. *approbation, favour* (עַל ר׳, לְרָצוֹן *acceptable, well-pleasing*).—II. *object of approbation*.—III. *will, pleasure, choice*.—IV. *uncontrolled will, violence*, Gen. 49:6.—V. *enjoyment*.

רָצַח (fut. יִרְצַח) *struck fatally, killed*; with or without נֶפֶשׁ; part. רֹצֵחַ *homicide*. Niph. *was killed*. Pi. *killed habitually, was a murderer by profession*. Pu. *be killed*, Ps. 62:4. תְּרָצְּחוּ for תְּרָצְחוּ, תְּרֻצְּחוּ.

רֶצַח m. — I. *crushing*, Ps. 42:11. — II. *slaughter*, Eze. 21:27.

רִצְיָא p. n. of a man.

רְצִין p.n., *Rezin*, king of Syria.

רָצַע *pierced, bored*, Ex. 21:6.

מַרְצֵעַ m., *an awl*.

רָצַף *covered, overlaid*, Cant. 3:10.

רֶצֶף m.—I. *burning coals*, 1 Ki. 19:6. —II. p. n., a city of some country subdued by the Assyrians.

רִצְפָּה f.—I. *burning coal*, Isa. 6:6. — II. *an inlaid pavement*. — III. p. n., *Rizpah*, the concubine of Saul.

מַרְצֶפֶת f., *the pavement on which the brasen sea stood*, 2 Ki. 16:17.

רָצַץ (fut. יָרוּץ, תָּרֹץ). — I. *bruised, broke, crushed*.—II. *oppressed*.—III. *became broken, burst*.—IV. *relaxed himself*, Isa. 42:3. Niph. נָרוֹץ *was bruised*. Pi. רִצַּץ I. *bruised*. — II. *oppressed*. Po. רוֹצֵץ the same; see also in רוץ. Hiph. *bruised*; fut. וַתָּרִץ. Hithpo. *struggled together*, Gen. 25:22.

רַץ m. (pl. const. רַצֵּי), *small piece of silver*, Ps. 68:31.

מְרוּצָה f., *oppression*, Jer. 22:17; see also in רוץ.

רַק, רֹק, רָקִי; see רקק.

רֵק; see רִיק.

רָקַב (fut. יִרְקַב) *became rotten, decayed*.

רָקָב m, *decay, rottenness*.

רִקָּבוֹן m., the same, Job 41:19.

רָקַד *leaped, danced*. Pi. the same. Hiph. *made to leap*, Ps. 29:6.

רַקּוֹן, רַקָּה; see רקק.

רָקַח (fut. יִרְקַח) *compounded, prepared*, Ex. 30:33; part. רֹקֵחַ *a compounder of drugs and aromatics*. Pu. part. מְרֻקָּחִים *compound, ointment*, 2 Chron. 16:14. Hiph. *threw in spices*, Eze. 24:10.

רֶקַח m., *perfuming, the preparing of perfumes*, Cant. 8:2.

רֹקַח m., *ointment*, Ex. 30:25, 35.

רַקָּח m., *apothecary, perfumer*; f. pl. רַקָּחוֹת.

רִקֻּחִים m. pl., *perfumes*, Isa. 57:9.

מֶרְקָח m., pl. מֶרְקָחִים *perfumes*, Cant. 5:13.

מֶרְקָחָה f.—I. *a pot of ointment*, Job 41:23.—II. *spices eaten as condiments*, Eze. 24:10.

מִרְקַחַת f., *perfumery*.

רָקִיעַ, see רקע; רָקִיק, see רקק.

רָקַם *streaked*; part. רֹקֵם s. *an embroid-*

erer. Pu. *wrought with art* (met. of Christ's mystical body), Ps. 139:15.

רִקְמָה f.—I. *embroidery*.—II. *variety of colours*, Eze. 17:3; dual רִקְמָתַיִם *embroidered on both sides*, Jud. 5:30.

רֶקֶם p. n.—I. a town of Benjamin.—II. of a man.

רָקַע I. *stretched out* (of God in creation). — II. *stamped on*, 2 Sa. 22:43. — III. *stamped with the feet*, Eze. 6:11. Pi. I. *beat into thin plates*. — II. *covered with a thin plate of gold*, Isa. 40:19. Pu. part. *overlaid*, Jer. 10:9. Hiph. *stretched out*, Job 37:18.

רָקִיעַ m.—I. *the expanse of heaven, atmosphere, sky*, Vulg. firmamentum.—II. *a canopy* (Ezekiel only).

רִקֻּעִים m. pl., *plates of metal*, Nu. 17:3.

רָקַק same as יָרַק *spit*, with בְּ; fut. יָרֹק, Lev. 15:8.

רָקִיק m., *a thin cake*.

רֹק m. (with suff. רֻקִּי) *spittle*.

רַק m., רַקָּה f. (Arab. *was thin*) *thin, lean*, Gen. *c*. 41.

רַק adv.—I. *only*.—II. *certainly*, i. e. this only.—III. *except*, with a negative.

רַקָּה f.—I. *the temple* (of the head), Jud. 4:21, 22; 5:26.—II. *the cheek*, Cant. 4:3; 6:7.

רַקּוֹן p. n., a town of Dan.

רַקַּת p. n., a town of Naphtali.

רָשׁ; see רוּשׁ.

רֵשׁ, רָשׁ Kal imp., from ירשׁ.

רָשָׁה root not used; (Syr. *he gave*).

רִשְׁיוֹן m., *grant, permission*, Ezr. 3:7.

רֵשִׁית *beginning*; see רֵאשִׁית in ראשׁ.

רָשַׁם *wrote, decreed*, Dan. 10:21.

רְשַׁם Ch., the same.

רָשַׁע *was, acted, wickedly, unjustly, impiously*. Hiph. הִרְשִׁיעַ I. *condemned*. — II. *declared, proved guilty*.—III. *acted wickedly*.

רָשָׁע m., רְשָׁעָה f.—I. *wicked*.—II. *guilty, faulty*.

רֶשַׁע m. (with suff. רִשְׁעוֹ) *wickedness, impiety, injustice*; pl. רְשָׁעִים.

רִשְׁעָה f.—I. *wickedness*. — II. *fault*, Deu. 25:2.

רִשְׁעָתַיִם p. n.; see כּוּשַׁן.

מִרְשַׁעַת f., *wickedness*, 2 Chron. 24:7.

רֶשֶׁף m. (pl. const. רִשְׁפֵּי).—I. *a burning coal*, Cant. 8:6.—II. *lightning*. III. בְּנֵי ר׳ *burning arrows*, Job 5:7; רִשְׁפֵי קָשֶׁת the same, Ps. 76:4.—IV. *burning disease*, Deu. 32:24.—V. *lust*, Cant. 8:6.—VI. p. n. of a man.

רָשַׁשׁ. Po. רשֵׁשׁ *reduced, subdued*, Jer. 5:17. Pu. רֻשַּׁשׁ *was subdued*, Mal. 1:4.

תַּרְשִׁישׁ I. p.n., *Tarshish*, some country far distant from Canaan; אֳנִיּוֹת ת׳ probably *merchant ships*.—II. *a precious stone*, probably *the topaz*.—III. p. n. of a man.

רֶשֶׁת Kal inf., from יָרַשׁ.

רָתַח. Pi. and Hiph. *boil, caused to boil*. Pu. *was boiled, agitated*, Job 30:27.

רֶתַח m., *boiling*, Eze. 24:5.

רָתַם *bind, yoke*, Mic. 1:13.

רֹתֶם m. (pl. רְתָמִים), *the broom;* in Spanish, *retama.*

רִתְמָה p. n., one of the stations in the wilderness.

רָתַק (Arab. *joined*). Niph. *was bound,* Ecc. 12:6, Kri. Pu. the same, Nah. 3:10.

רַתּוֹק m., *a chain,* Eze. 7:23.

רַתּוּקוֹת (רַתִּיקוֹת) f. pl., *chains,* 1 Ki. 6:21.

רְתֻקוֹת f. pl., the same, Isa. 40:19.

רָתַת (Syr. *he trembled*); see רטט.

רְתֵת m., *trembling,* Hos. 13:1.

שׂ

שְׂא Kal imp. and inf. from נשא.

שְׂאֹר m., *leaven.*

שְׂאֵת from נשא.

שָׂבַךְ same as סָבַךְ, *twist.*

שׂוֹבֶךְ m., *entangled branch,* 2 Sa. 18:9.

שְׂבָךְ m., pl. שְׂבָכִים *ornaments of wreathing,* 1 Ki. 7:17.

שְׂבָכָה f.—I. *network* on the capitals of pillars.—II. *lattice,* 2 Ki. 1:2.—III. *a net,* Job 18:8.

שַׂבְּכָא same as סַבְּכָא.

שְׂבָם, שִׂבְמָה p. n., a city of the Reubenites.

שָׂבַע, שָׂבֵעַ was full, satisfied, surfeited, with בְּ, מִן. Pi. *satisfied.* Hiph. *filled,* with לְ *of the person;* with בְּ, מִן *of the thing.*

שָׂבֵעַ m., שְׂבֵעָה f., *full, satisfied, surfeited.*

שָׂבָע m., *abundance.*

שֹׂבַע m., the same; לָשֹׂבַע *to the full.*

שָׂבְעָה, שִׂבְעָה f., the same, Eze. 16:49.

שָׂבַר *looked at, examined,* Neh. 2 13, 15; with בְּ. Pi. *looked to, hoped for* or *in,* with אֶל, לְ.

שֶׂבֶר m. (with suff. שִׂבְרִי), *hope.*

שָׂגָא same as שָׂגָה. Hiph. I. *increased,* Job 12:23. — II. *magnified,* Job 36:24.

שְׂגָא Ch., *increased, became great.*

שַׂגִּיא m., *the Great One* (of God), Job 36:26; 37:23.

שַׂגִּיא m., שַׂגִּיאָה f. Ch.—I. *great.*—II. *much, many.*—III. *greatly.*

שָׂגַב *was exalted.* Niph. I. *was lofty, exalted.*— II. *was secure,* Pro. 18:10. Pi. I. *raised, placed in security.* —II. *made powerful,* Isa. 9:10. Pu. pass. of Pih., Pro. 29:25. Hiph. *was lofty,* Job 36:22.

שְׂגִיב, שְׂגוּב p. n. of a man.

מִשְׂגָּב m. (with suff. מִשְׂגַּבִּי). — I. *a hill, strong place.*—II. *refuge* (of God).

שָׂגַג same as שָׂגָא. Pil. שִׂגְשֵׂג *cause to grow;* according to others, from סוג *he fences,* Isa. 17:11.

שָׂגָה *increased, became great.* Hiph. *increased,* Ps. 73:12.

שָׂדַד. Pi. *harrowed.*

שִׂדִּים p. n., the valley of the Dead Sea, *Siddim.*

שָׂדֶה m. (with suff. שָׂדֵהוּ; pl. שָׂדוֹת; const. שְׂדֵי, שְׂדוֹת).—I. *a field.*— II. *the country.*—III. any *country;* אִישׁ שָׂדֶה *husbandman;* חַיַּת הַשָּׂדֶה *the beasts of the field;* שְׂדֵה מוֹאָב *the land of Moab;* שְׂדֵה אֲרָם *Mesopotamia.*

שָׂדַי sing., the same.

שְׂדֵרוֹת; see סדר.
שֶׂר same as שֶׂיָה.
שָׂהֵד (Syr. and Ch. סְהַד *bare witness*).
שָׂהֵד m., *eye witness*, Job 16:19.
שָׂהֲדוּת f. Ch., *testimony*, Gen. 31:47.
שַׂהֲרֹנִים *crescents*; see סהר.
שׂוֹא Kal inf., from נשׂא.
שׂוּב; see שִׂיב.
שׂוֹבֶךְ; see שׂבך.
שׂוּג same as סוּג *drove back*, 2 Sa. 1: 22.
שׂוּחַ same as שִׂיחַ *to meditate*, Gen. 24:63.
שׂוּט *turn aside*, Ps. 40:5.
סֵטִים, שֵׂטִים m. pl., *they who turn aside to*, Ps. 101:3; Hos. 5:2.
שׂוּךְ *hedged with thorns*. Pil. שׂוֹכֵךְ the same, Job 10:11.
שׂוֹךְ m., שׂוֹכָה f., } *a bough*, Jud. 9:48, 49.
שׂוֹכֹה p. n., a town of Judah.
שׂוֹכָתִי *a Succothite*.
מְסוּכָה, מְשׂוּכָה f., *a thorn hedge*.
שִׂים, שׂוּם (fut. יָשׂוּם, יָשִׂים; apoc. וַיָּשֶׂם, יָשֵׂם; inf. abs. שׂוֹם; const. שִׂים, שׂוּם; imp. שִׂימָה, שִׂים).—I. *placed, set*.—II. *set up*.—III. *set in array*.—IV. *placed aside*.—V. with עַל, *set over*.—VI. with עַל, *place upon*.—VII. with עַל, בְּ, לְ, *impute to any one*.—VIII. with שֵׂם לְ *named*.—IX. with שְׁמוֹ *placed His name* (of the Lord), i. e. the true worship.—X. with or without לְבוֹ *set his heart, considered, regarded*, with לְ, אֶל, עַל.—XI. with עַל לֵב or אֶל לֵב or בְּלֵב *considered, laid to heart*.—XII. שׂוּם עַל לֵב *he considered*.—XIII. with לְנֶגְדּוֹ *considered, set before him*.—XIV. with שׂוּם בְּאָזְנֵי פ׳ *he told*.—XV. שׂוּם אַף *heaped up wrath*. (For other idiomatic usages of שׂוּם see concordance.) Hiph. (imp. הָשִׂימִי; part. מֵשִׂים) *place, set*. Hoph. *was placed*; fut. יוּשַׂם.
שׂוּם Ch.—I. *appointed*.—II. with טְעֵם *made a decree*.—III. with טְעֵם עַל, לְ, *regarded*. — IV. with בָּל לְ *endeavoured*. — V. שֵׂם דִּי פ׳ *named*. Ithpe. אִתְּשָׂם I. *was made, placed*. —II. with טְעֵם *was decreed*.
תְּשׂוּמֶת f., with יָד *a deposit*, Lev. 5: 21; [6:2.]
שׂוּר I. *governed*; fut. וַיָּשַׂר, Jud. 9: 22. Hiph. הֵשִׂיר *appointed princes*, Hos. 8:4.—II. same as שָׂרָה *strove, contended*, Hos. 12:5.—III. same as סוּר *departed*. — IV. same as Ch. נְסַר *he sawed*, 1 Chron. 20:3; fut. וַיָּשַׂר.
שׂוֹרָה f., *a row, in rows*, Isa. 28:25; (Arab. the same).
שִׂישׂ, שׂוּשׂ (fut. יָשׂוּשׂ, יָשִׂישׂ; inf. abs. שׂוֹשׂ; const. שׂוּשׂ; imp. שִׂישׂ) *rejoiced, exulted in*, with בְּ, עַל.
שָׂשׂוֹן m., *joy, rejoicing*.
מָשׂוֹשׂ m., *joy*.
שַׂחַ; see שִׂיחַ.
שָׂחָה *swam*, Isa. 25:11. Hiph. *overflowed*, Ps. 6:7.
שָׂחוּ m., *swimming*, Eze. 47:5.
שָׂחַט *squeezed, crushed*, Gen. 40:11.
שָׂחַק I. *laughed*.—II. with אֶל *approved*.—III. with עַל *laughed at*.—IV.

with לְ *despised.*—V. *caused laughter.* Pi. שִׂחֵק (inf. שַׂחֵק; fut. יְשַׂחֵק). —I. *rejoiced, sported.*—II. *played on an instrument,* 2 Sa. 6:21.—III. *made sport,* Jud. 16:25.—IV. *skirmished,* 2 Sa. 2:14. Hiph. *derided,* with עַל, 2 Chron. 30:10.

שְׂחֹק, שְׂחוֹק m.—I. *laughter.*—II. *subject* or *object of laughter.*

מִשְׂחָק m., *object of laughter,* Hab. 1:10.

שָׂטָה (fut. יִשְׂטֶה; apoc. יֵשְׂטְ). —I. *went aside,* Pro. 7:25.—II. *went astray,* Nu. c. 5.

שֵׂטִים; see שׂוּט.

שָׂטַם *acted fiercely, hardly towards, was hated.*

מַשְׂטֵמָה f., *hatred,* Hos. 9:7, 8.

שָׂטַן *was an adversary to, opposed;* part. שֹׂטֵן *an adversary,* Ps. 71:13.

שָׂטָן m.—I. *an adversary.*—II. הַשָּׂטָן *the devil, the great adversary.*

שִׂטְנָה f.—I. *accusation,* Ezr. 4:6.—II. p. n. of a well.

שִׂיא; see נשׂא.

שִׂיאוֹן p. n., one of the peaks of Hermon.

שִׂיב *was grey-headed.* Part. שָׂב, Job 15:10; Ch. the same.

שֵׂיב m., *grey hairs, old age,* 1 K. 14:4.

שֵׂיבָה f., the same.

שִׂיג m., *retirement,* 1 K. 18:27

שִׂיד *plastered,* Deu. 27:2, 4.

שִׂיד m., *plaster.*

שֶׂה, שֵׂיָה com. (const. שֵׂה, with suff. שֵׂיוֹ, שֵׂיֵהוּ), *a sheep* or *goat.*

שִׂיחַ I. *meditated,* with בְּ.—II. *spoke,* with לְ *with,* or בְּ *of.*—III. *composed a psalm, sung,* with בְּ. Pil. I. *uttered,* Isa. 55:8.—II. *meditated,* Ps. 143:5.

שַׂחַ m., *purpose, design,* Am. 4:13.

שִׂיחַ m.—I. *a plant, bush.*—II. *speech, message.*—III. *a complaint.*—IV. *sorrow,* Job 7:13.

שִׂיחָה f., *complaint, prayer, meditation.*

שִׂים; see שׂוּם.

שְׂכוֹת, שַׂךְ, שִׂכִּים, שֹׂךְ; see שׂכך.

שָׂכָה root not used; (Syr. *expected*).

שְׂכוּ p. n., a place near Ramah.

שֶׂכְוִי m., "*a thunderstorm*" (Lee), Job 38:36.

שְׂכִיָּה f., *objects* (of sight or thought), Isa. 2:16.

מַשְׂכִּית f. (pl. מַשְׂכִּיּוֹת). — I. *figure, external image.*—II. *imagination, internal image.*

שַׂכִּין m., *a knife,* Pro. 23:2; (Arab. the same).

שְׂכִירָה, שָׂכִיר; see שׂכר.

שָׂכַךְ *placed as a covering,* Ex. 33:22.

שַׂךְ m., pl. שִׂכִּים *thorns,* Nu. 33:55.

שֹׂךְ m. (with suff. שֻׂכּוֹ), *a fence,* Lam. 2:6.

שֻׂכָּה f., pl. שֻׂכּוֹת *spears,* Job 40:31.

מְשׂוּכָה f., *a fence,* Pro. 15:19; Isa. 5:5; see שׂוּךְ.

שָׂכַל *was wise, careful, skilful,* 1 Sa. 18:30. Pi. *acted wisely, designedly,* Gen. 48:14. Hiph. I. *looked at.*—II. *reflected.*—III. *cared for*—IV. *acted wisely, was wise.*—V *prospered.*—VI. *made wise, taught* with אֶל, עַל, בְּ; part. מַשְׂכִּיל I *thoughtful, prudent.*—II. *a didacti* *poem* (title of Psalms); inf. הַשְׂכֵּל, הַשְׂכִּיל *understanding, wisdom,* with accus. לְ.

שְׂכַל Ch. Ith. part. מִשְׂתַּכַּל *considered, looked at,* with בְּ.

שֶׂכֶל, שֵׂכֶל m. (with suff. שִׂכְלוֹ).—I. *understanding, skill.* — II. *estimation, esteem,* Pro. 3:4. — III. *signification,* Neh. 8:8.

שִׂכְלוּת; see סכל.

שָׂכְלְתָנוּ f. Ch., *understanding, skill,* Dan. 5:11, 12, 14.

שָׂכַר I. *hired.* — II. *bribed.* Niph. *hired himself,* 1 Sa. 2:5. Hith. הִשְׂתַּכֵּר the same, Hag. 1:6.

שָׂכָר m.—I. *reward, hire.*—II. p. n. of a man.

שֶׂכֶר m., *hire.*

שָׂכִיר m., *hired person* or *thing.*

שְׂכִירָה f., *the act of hiring,* τὸ μισθοῦν, Isa. 7:20.

מַשְׂכֹּרֶת f. (with suff. מַשְׂכֻּרְתִּי).—I. *wages.*—II. *reward,* Ru. 2:12.

שְׂלָו f. (pl. שַׂלְוִים), *a quail.*

שַׂלְמָה trans. for שִׂמְלָה f. (pl. שְׂלָמוֹת). —I. *a garment.*—II. *any cloth.*—III. *clothing.*—IV. p.n., the father of Boaz, who was called also שַׂלְמוֹן.—V. p.n. of a man.

שַׂלְמַי p. n. of a man.

שְׂמֹאל, שְׂמֹאוֹל m., *the left hand* or *side*; מִשְּׂמֹאל *on the left* or *north*; שְׂמֹאל or עַל שְׂ׳ *on* or *to the left* or *north.*

הִשְׂמִיל, הִשְׂמְאִיל, הַשְׂמְאִיל Hiph.—I. *went to the left.* — II. *used the left hand.*

שְׂמָאלִי, שְׂמָלִי m., **שְׂמָאלִית** f., *belonging to the left, on the left.*

שָׂמַח, שָׂמֵחַ I. *was glad.* — II. *expressed joy.*—III. *burned brightly,* with לְ, עַל, בְּ. Pi. שִׂמַּח *made to rejoice,* with עַל, לְ, מִן. Hiph. the same.

שָׂמֵחַ m. (pl. const. שְׂמֵחֵי, שִׂמְחֵי; f. שְׂמֵחָה).—I. *joyful.*—II. *expressing joy.*—III. *rejoicing in* or *at,* with לְ.

שִׂמְחָה f. (pl. שְׂמָחוֹת).—I. *joy.*—II. *a festival.*—III. *merriment.*

שְׂמִיכָה; see סמך.

הִשְׂמִיל; see in שְׂמֹאל.

שִׂמְלָה f. (pl. שְׂמָלוֹת), *garment*; see שַׂלְמָה I.

שַׂמְלָה p. n., a king of Edom.

שְׂמָמִית f., a species of lizard, Pro. 30:28.

שָׂנֵא (fut. יִשְׂנָא; inf. abs. שָׂנֹא, const. שְׂנֹא, שִׂנְאַת, שִׂנְאָה) *hated,* with לְ; part. שֹׂנֵא *hater, enemy.* Niph. *was hated.* Pi. part. מְשַׂנֵּא *an enemy.*

שְׂנֵא Ch. part. שָׂנְאַיִן, *haters.*

שִׂנְאָה f., *hatred.*

שָׂנִיא m., שְׂנִיאָה f., *hated,* Deu. 21:15.

שְׂנִיר p. n., the name of mount Hermon among the Amorites.

שְׂעִפִּים; see סעף.

שָׂעַר I. *shuddered.* — II. *feared,* Deu. 32:17, with עַל.—III. *swept, tore away as a tempest,* Ps. 58:10. Niph. *a tempest raged,* Ps. 50:3. Pi. *swept away with a tempest,* Job 27:21. Hith. *raged like a tempest,* Dan. 11:40.

שָׂעִיר m., שְׂעִירָה f.—I. *hairy,* Gen. 27:11, 23. — II. *a goat* (always with עִזִּים). Pl. שְׂעִירִים I. probably *wild goats*, Isa. 13:21; 34:14.—II. *showers*, Deu. 32:2.

שֵׂעִיר p.n., *Seir.*—I. the district between the Dead Sea and the gulf of Akabah.—II. a mountain of Judah.

שְׂעִירָה p. n., a district unknown.

שֵׂעָר const. שְׂעַר m., *the hair.*

שְׂעַר m. Ch., *the hair.*

שַׂעַר m.—I. *a storm, tempest.*—II. *shuddering, horror*; same as סַעַר.

שְׂעָרָה f., *a tempest.*

שַׂעֲרָה f.—I. *a hair.*—II. *the hair.*

שְׂעֹרָה f., *barley* (the plant); pl. שְׂעֹרִים *barley* (the grain).

שְׂעֹרִים p.n. of a man.

שָׂפָה f. (dual שְׂפָתַיִם, שִׂפְתֵי; with suff. שְׂפָתָיו; pl. const. שִׂפְתוֹת).—I. *a lip.*—II. *a language.*—III. *words.*—IV. *brim of a vessel.*—V. *shore of the sea, bank of a river.*—VI. *edge, edging.*—VII. *border of a country*, Jud. 7:22.

שָׂפַח. Pi. *struck with baldness*, Isa. 3:17.

מִשְׂפָּח "oppression," Eng. Ver., Isa. 5:7.

שָׂפָם m., *the chin, the beard.*

שָׂפַן *hid, concealed*, Deu. 33:19.

שָׂפַק I. *clapped the hands*, Job 27:23.—II. *sufficed*, 1 Ki. 20:10. Hiph. *bargained with*, Isa. 2:6; with בְּ.

שֶׂפֶק m., *contempt*, Job 36:18.

שַׂק m. (with suff. שַׂקּוֹ; pl. שַׂקִּים).—I. *sack-cloth.*—II. *a sack.*

שָׂקַד. Niph. *was bound, tied*, Lam. 1:14.

שָׂקַר. Pi. *painted the eyes with stibium* (a black powder), Isa, 3:16.

שַׂר; see שׂרר.

שָׂרַג. Pu. *was interwoven*, Job 40. 17. Hith. the same, Lam. 1:14.

שְׂרוּג p.n. of a man.

שָׂרִיגִים m. pl., *branches of a vine.*

שָׂרַד *fled, escaped*, Jos. 10:20; (Arab. the same.)

שָׂרִיד m., *one that escapes.*—II. *a remnant*, Isa. 1:9.

שְׂרָד m., *colour*; בִּגְדֵי שׂ׳ *coloured garments* (Exodus only).

שֶׂרֶד m., *only.*

שָׂרָה *was a prince, prevailed*, with אֵת, עִם; see שָׂרַר.

שָׂרָה s. f.; see שָׂרַר.

שָׂרַי p. n., *Sarai* (afterwards *Sarah*), the wife of Abraham..

שְׂרָיָה, שְׂרָיָהוּ p.n. of a man.

מִשְׂרָה f., *government*, Isa. 9:5, 6.

שֶׂרַח p. n. of a man.

שָׂרַט *cut, made incisions.* Niph. *was crushed*, Zec. 12:3.

שֶׂרֶט m., *an incision*, Lev. 19:28.

שָׂרֶטֶת f., the same, Lev. 21:5.

שָׂרִיגִים, see שׂרג; שָׂרִיד, see שׂרד.

שָׂרַךְ. Pi. part. f. מְשָׂרֶכֶת *twisting its course, wandering in all directions*, Jer. 2:23.

שְׂרוֹךְ m., *shoe latchet.*

שַׂרְסְכִים p. n. of an Assyrian eunuch.

שָׂרַע, part. שָׂרוּעַ *stretched out, monstrously prolonged* (of a limb). Hith. *stretched himself out*, Isa. 28:20.

שַׂרְעַפִּים *thoughts*; see סעף.

שָׂרַף I. *burned, consumed.*—II. *burned spices at a funeral.*—III. *baked* *bricks*, Gen. 11:3. Niph. and Pu. *was burnt*.

שָׂרָף m.—I. *a venomous serpent*, probably the coluber cerastes.—II. p. n. of a man.

שְׂרָפִים m. pl., *seraphim, six-winged spirits*, Isa. 6:2, 6.

שְׂרֵפָה f.—I. *burning fire*.—II. *a funeral burning*.

מִשְׂרָפוֹת f. pl. — I. *burning*. — II. מִשְׂרְפוֹת מַיִם p. n., a place near Sidon.

שָׂרַק *combed, hackled flax*, Isa. 19:9.

שֹׂרֵק m., שֹׂרֵקָה f. — I. a vine of a choice quality.—II. שֹׂרֵק p. n., a valley between Askelon and Gaza.

שְׂרוּקִים m. pl., *shoots of the vine*, Isa. 16:8.

שָׂרֹק m., pl. שְׂרֻקִּים *bay* (colour of a horse), Zec. 1:8.

שָׂרַר *acted as a prince*. Hith. הִשְׂתָּרֵר *made himself a prince*.

שַׂר m. (pl. שָׂרִים), *prince, ruler, chief, captain*.

שָׂרָה f.—I. *a princess, a woman of rank*. — II. p.n., *Sarah*, the wife of Abraham; see שָׂרַי.

שָׂשׂוֹן; see שׂוּשׂ.

שֵׂת for שְׂאֵת; see נשׂא.

שָׂתַם *shut out*, Lam. 3:8.

שָׂתַר. Niph. *were concealed*, 1 Sa. 5:9.

שׁ

שֶׁ...שַׁ...שֶׁ.. an abbreviation of אֲשֶׁר, prefixed to every part of speech.

שָׁאַב (fut. יִשְׁאַב) *drew water*.

מַשְׁאָב m., pl. מַשְׁאַבִּים *watering places*, Jud. 5:11.

שָׁאַג (fut. יִשְׁאַג).—I. *roared as a lion* —II. *shrieked for anguish*, Ps. 38:9.

שְׁאָגָה const. שַׁאֲגַת f.— I. *roar of a lion*. — II. *groan, shriek of anguish*.

שָׁאָה *was desolate* (a city), Isa. 6:11. Niph. I. *was desolate* (a city), Isa. 6:11. — II. *were dashed together*, Isa. 17:12, 13. Hiph. *lay waste*, Isa. 37:26. Hith. הִשְׁתָּאָה *wondered, was in astonishment*, with לְ.

שַׁאֲוָה f., Pro. 1:27, Ketib *a storm*; same as שׁוֹאָה.

שְׁאִיהֶם; see שׁוֹא.

שְׁאִיָּה f., *crash, destruction*, Isa. 24:12.

שְׁאֵת f., *desolation*, Lam. 3:47.

שֵׁת f., *noise, tumult of war*, Num. 24:17.

שָׁאוֹן m. — I. *shouting, the noise of waves*.— II. *desolation, ruin*.

מַשָּׁאוֹת, מַשּׁוּאוֹת f. pl., *desolation, a desolate place*.

שְׁאָט, שְׁאָטְךָ *contempt*; see שׁוּט.

שָׁאט part. from II. שׁוּט.

שָׁאַל, שָׁאֵל (fut. יִשְׁאַל). — I. *questioned, enquired*. — II. *requested, prayed for*. — III. *borrowed*, with שָׁאַל; לְ, or מִן, מֵאֵת, מֵעִם, לְשָׁלוֹם לְ *enquired of his welfare, saluted*; שָׁאַל בֵּאלֹהִים *enquired of God*. Niph. *requested for himself*. Pi. שִׁאֵל *asked earnestly*, with בְּ. Hiph. *gave in answer to a request, gave*.

שְׁאֵל Ch., *asked, enquired*.

שְׁאָל p. n. of a man.

שָׁאוּל p. n. of a man, *Saul*. Patron. שָׁאוּלִי.

שְׁאוֹל, שְׁאֹל com., *the abode of the*

soul after death (see אֲבַדּוֹן), with ה loc. שְׁאֹלָה.

שְׁאֵלָה f. (with suff. שְׁאֵלָתִי, שְׁלֵתֵךְ, שְׁאֶלָתְכֶם), *asking, a request.*

שֵׁלָה I. same as שְׁאֵלָה. — II. p. n., one of the sons of Judah; patron. שֵׁלָנִי.

שְׁאֵלָא f. Ch., *demand*, Dan. 4:14.

שַׁלְתִּיאֵל, שְׁאַלְתִּיאֵל p. n. of a man.

מִשְׁאָל p. n., a town of the Levites in the tribe of Asher.

מִשְׁאָלָה f., *prayers.*

שָׁאַן. Pil. שַׁאֲנַן *was quiet, secure, wanton.*

שַׁאֲנָן m., שַׁאֲנַנָּה f. — I. *quiet.* — II. *wanton, luxurious.* — III. *wantonness, pride.*

שְׁאָט, שְׁאָטֵךְ; see שסם.

שָׁאַף I. *panted, gasped*, Ps. 119:131. — II. *panted for, desired eagerly.* —III. *swallowed up, destroyed.*

שָׁאַר *was left*, 1 Sa. 16:11. Niph. the same. Hiph. *left, had left.*

שְׁאָר m., *the remainder, remnant.*

שְׁאָר m. Ch., the same.

שְׁאָר יָשׁוּב (*a remnant shall return*). Prophetic name of the son of Isaiah, Isa. 7:3.

שְׁאֵר m. — I. *flesh.* — II. *any near relation.*—III. *a right arising from marriage*, Ex. 21:10.

שַׁאֲרָה f., *near, relation, relationship*, Lev. 18:17.

שֶׁאֱרָה p. n. of a woman.

שְׁאֵרִית, שֵׁרִית f., *remainder, remnant.*

מִשְׁאֶרֶת f., *kneading trough.*

שְׂאֵת; see שאה.

שֵׁב, with ה parag. שְׁבָה Kal imp. from ישב.

שְׁבָא p. n. of a country, probably Arabia Felix.

שָׁבַב (Arab. *kindled*).

שָׁבִיב m., *flame*, Job 18:5.

שְׁבִיב m. Ch., the same.

שְׁבָבִים m. pl., *fragments*, Hos. 8:6.

שָׁבָה (imp. וּשֲׁבֵה; fut. apoc. וַיִּשְׁבְּ), *carried captive, took prisoners, carried off*; part. שֹׁבִים m., שֹׁבִיּוֹת f., *captives.* Niph. *was led captive.*

שְׁבוּאֵל p. n. of a man; written also שׁוּבָאֵל.

שְׁבִי, with pause שֶׁבִי m. (with suff. שִׁבְיוֹ, שֶׁבְיְךָ, שִׁבְיְכֶם); f. שִׁבְיָה I. *captive.* — II. *troop of captives.* — III. *captivity.*

שִׁבְיָה f. — I. *troop of captives, spoil.* —II. *captivity.*

שְׁבוּת, שְׁבִית f. — I. *captivity.* — II. *captives.* שׁוּב שׁ׳ I. *turned from captivity.* — II. *restored to prosperity.*

שְׁבוֹ m., *an agate*; LXX. ἀχάτης.

שָׁבַח. Pi. שִׁבַּח I. *praised, commended* —II. *quieted, restrained, kept back.* Hiph. *quieted*, Ps. 65:8. Hith. *boast of, glory in*, with בְּ.

שַׁבַּח Ch. Pa. *praised.*

שֵׁבֶט, שֶׁבֶט com. (with suff. שִׁבְטִי). —I. *staff.*—II. *rod* (for punishment). — III. *sceptre.* — IV. *dart, short spear.*—V. *tribe.*

שְׁבַט com. Ch., *a tribe*, Ezr. 6:17.

שְׁבָט m., the eleventh month of the Jewish year, corresponding to our February and March.

שַׁרְבִיט m., *a sceptre* (Esther only).

שְׁבִי, שִׁבְיָה *captive, &c.*; see שבה.

שְׁבִי and שֹׁבִי p. n. of a man.

שְׁבִיסִים m. pl., "*sun-like ornaments of the neck*," (Schrœder); "cauls," Eng. Ver., Isa. 3:18; sense uncertain.

שְׁבִיעִי, שְׁבִיעִית; see שבע.

שְׁבִית; see שבה.

שְׁבִיל m., *a path, mode of conduct;* (Arab. the same).

שֹׁבֶל m., "locks" (of hair), Eng. Ver., Isa. 47:2.

שִׁבֹּל or שִׁבֹּל f., pl. const. שִׁבֲּלֵי *a branch*, Zec. 4:12.

שִׁבֹּלֶת f. (pl. שִׁבֳּלִים).—I. *a stream of water.*—II. *an ear of corn.*

שַׁבְּלוּל m., *a snail*, Ps. 58:9.

שֶׁבְנָא, שֶׁבְנָה p. n., *Shebna*, the scribe.

שְׁבַנְיָה p. n. of a man.

I. שֶׁבַע, const. שְׁבַע, f. שִׁבְעָה, const. שִׁבְעַת m., *seven, the seventh;* adv. *seventh, sevenfold;* שִׁבְעָה שִׁבְעָה *by sevens;* שִׁבְעָה עָשָׂר m., שְׁבַע עֶשְׂרֵה f., *seventeen;* dual שִׁבְעָתַיִם I. *sevenfold.* — II. *seventimes.* Pl. שִׁבְעִים *seventy.*

שִׁבְעָנָה m., *seven*, Job 42:13.

שָׁבוּעַ m. (dual שְׁבֻעַיִם; pl. שָׁבֻעִים, שָׁבֻעוֹת).—I. *a week;* חַג שָׁבֻעוֹת *the feast of weeks.*—II. *a week of years*, Dan. c. 9 & 10.

שְׁבִיעִי m., שְׁבִיעִית f., *seventh.*

II. שֶׁבַע p. n., (a) a town of Simeon; (b) of a man; (c) שִׁבְעָה name of a well.

שָׁבַע *bound by oaths*, Eze. 21:28. Niph. נִשְׁבַּע *swore*, with לְ; *swore to*, with בְּ; *swore by.* Hiph. I. *caused to swear.*—II. *adjured.*

שְׁבֻעָה, שְׁבוּעָה f., *an oath.*

שָׁבַץ. Pi. "embroider," Eng. Ver., Ex. 28:39; sense doubtful. Pu. *set* (of a precious stone), Ex. 28:20.

שָׁבָץ m., *perplexity*, 2 Sa. 1:9.

מִשְׁבְּצוֹת f. pl.—I. *gold settings* (for stones).—II. *cloth of gold*, Ps. 45:14.

תַּשְׁבֵּץ m., *embroidery*, Ex. 28:4.

שְׁבַק Ch., *left.* Ith. *was left.*

שָׁבַר (fut. יִשְׁבֹּר).—I. *broke to pieces.*—II. *tore* (as a wild beast).—III. *broke the heart.*—IV. *broke the power of, destroyed.*—V. *quenched thirst.*—VI. *assigned*, with חֹק.—VII. from שֶׁבֶר *sold corn*, Gen. 41:56.—VIII. *bought corn.* Niph. I. *was broken.*—II. *was torn.*—III *was broken* (the heart). —IV. *was destroyed.* Pi. שִׁבַּר, שִׁבֵּר *broke with violence.* Hiph. I. *caused to suffer labour pains*, Isa. 66:9. — II. *sold corn.* Hoph. *was broken-hearted*, Jer. 8:21.

שֶׁבֶר, שֵׁבֶר (with suff. שִׁבְרוֹ) I. *breaking, fracture.* — II. *vexation, sorrow.* — III. *calamity, ruin.* — IV. *provision, corn.*—V. *interpretation*, Jud. 7:15.—VI. p. n., a place near Ai.

שִׁבָּרוֹן m.—I. *breaking*, i. e. pain, sorrow, Eze. 21:11. — II. *calamity, ruin*, Jer. 17:18.

מַשְׁבֵּר m.—I. *pains of childbirth.*—II. *violent pains* (of any kind), 2 Sa. 22:5.—III. *breakers* (of the sea).

מִשְׁבָּר m., the same.

שְׁבַשׁ Ch. Ith., *perplexed*, Dan. 5:9.

שָׁבַת (fut. יִשְׁבַּת, יִשְׁבֹּת).—I. *ceased.*—II. *rested;* with מִן *from.*—III. *was interrupted,* Neh. 6:3.—IV. *ceased to exist, came to an end.*—V. with שַׁבָּת *kept the sabbath.* Niph. *came to an end.* Hiph. I. *caused to cease.* — II. *interrupted.* — III. *brought to an end.*

שֶׁבֶת m.—I. *ceasing.* — II. *intermission;* see also in יָשַׁב.

שַׁבָּת com. (with suff. שַׁבַּתּוֹ; pl. שַׁבָּתוֹת; const. שַׁבְּתוֹת) *cessation, time of rest, sabbath;* שַׁבַּת שָׁנִים *a sabbath of years.*

שַׁבָּתוֹן m., *rest, a time of rest.*

שַׁבְּתַי p. n. of a man.

מִשְׁבָּת m., pl. מִשְׁבַּתִּים *cessations,* Lam. 1:7.

שֶׁבֶת Kal inf., from יָשַׁב.

שָׁבַת Ch. Kal pret. f., from שׁוּב.

שָׁגָא same as שׁנה.

שָׁגַג *erred, committed an error,* Lev. 5:18; inf. בְּשַׁגָּם *because of their sin.*

שְׁגָגָה f., *error, unintentional fault.*

שָׁגָה *erred, went astray,* with מִן. Hiph. I. *allowed to err,* Ps. 119:10.—II. *caused to go astray.*

שָׁגֵא p. n. of a man.

שְׁגִיאָה f., *error,* Ps. 19:13.

שִׁגָּיוֹן m. (pl. שִׁגְיוֹנוֹת) *a doleful song, lament,* Ps. 7:1; Hab. 3:1.

מִשְׁגֶּה m., *mistake, inadvertency,* Gen. 43:12.

שָׁגַח. Hiph. *looked to.*

שָׁגַל *lay with a woman;* fut. יִשְׁגַּל. Niph. and Pu. pass. of Kal.

שֵׁגָל f., *a queen.*

שֵׁגָל f. Ch., the same.

שַׁגָּם Kal inf. with suff., from שׁגג.

שָׁגַע. Pu. part. מְשֻׁגָּע *maddened, mad.* Hith. *acted like a madman.*

שִׁגָּעוֹן m., *madness, impetuosity.*

שֶׁגֶר, שָׁגָר m., *offspring, progeny* Exod. 13:12.

שַׁד, see שָׂדֶה; שֵׁד, see שׁוּד; שֹׁד see שָׂדָה, שָׁדַד.

שָׁדַד (fut. with suff. יְשָׁדְּדֵם, יְשָׁדֵּם).—I. *attacked, invaded.*—II. *plundered, laid waste, ruined;* part. שֹׁדֵד *invader, plunderer;* שָׁדוּד *destroyed.* Niph. *was laid waste.* Pi. *laid waste, ruined utterly.* Pu. שֻׁדַּד, שֻׁדַּד *was laid waste.* Po. *laid waste.* Hoph. הוּשַׁד *was laid waste.*

שֹׁד, שׁוֹד m.—I. *destruction, ruin.*—II. *violence, oppression.*—III. *extorted property,* Am. 3:10.

שַׁדַּי m., *the Almighty* (the name of God as revealed to the Patriarchs); LXX. παντοκράτωρ.

שָׂדָה root not used; (Arab. *was well watered*).

שַׁד m.—I. *teats of an animal.* — II. *breast of a woman;* dual שָׁדַיִם, שְׁדֵי *the breasts.*

שֹׁד m., the same.

שִׁדָּה f., שִׁדָּה וְשִׁדּוֹת, Ecc. 2:8, "musical instruments and that of all sorts," Eng. Ver.—*pleasures of every kind* (Ges. and Lee).

שְׁדֵיאוּר p. n. of a man.

שְׁדֵמָה f., *blighted corn;* pl. שְׁדֵמוֹת, שַׁדְמוֹת.—I. *fields.*—II. *corn fields.* Hab. 3:17.—III. *vineyards.*

שָׁדַף *blighted.*

שִׁדָּפוֹן f., *blight in corn*, 2 Ki. 19: 26.

שְׁדֵף m., the same.

שׁ Ch. Ithp. *exerting himself*, Dan. 6:15.

שׁ p.n., *Shadrach*, one of the three holy children.

שׁ m.—I. *onyx* or *sardonyx*.—II. p. n. of a man.

שׁ m. (pl. with suff. שְׁאִיהֶם) *ragings*, Ps. 35:17.

שָׁו m.—I. *guilt*.-II. *calamity*.-III. *worthlessness, vanity*.—IV. *falsehood*.

same as שָׁוְא.

שׁוֹ f.—I. *a storm*.—II. *destruction*. —III. *a desolate place*.

מְשׁוֹ f., *desolation, a desolate place*.

תְּשׁוּ f., pl. תְּשֻׁאוֹת *tumult, shouting*.

, Jer. 42:10, for יָשׁוֹב Kal inf., from ישב.

ׁ (fut. יָשׁוּב ,יָשֹׁב ,יָשֵׁב ,וַיָּשָׁב).—I. *went or came back*; with מִן *from*; *turned to, returned*, with עַל ,לְ ,אֶל, עַד *to*.—II. *turned himself about*, 1 Chron. 21:20.—III. *changed his course of life*. (For many uses with other words which slightly modify these primary meanings, see Concordance.) Pil. שׁוֹבֵב I. *led back*.—II. *restored*.—III. *led astray*, Isa. 47:10.—IV. *refreshed*, Ps. 23:3. Pul. שׁוֹבַב *was brought back*. Hiph. הֵשִׁיב (fut. יָשִׁיב ,יָשֵׁב ,וַיָּשֶׁב).—I. *brought back*.—II. *restored*.—III. *requited*. —IV. *brought upon a person*.—V. *sent as a tribute* or *atonement*.—VI. *distributed, assigned*.—VII. *moved away, put aside*.—VIII. *repelled, hindered*.—IX. *recalled, revoked a declaration*.—X. *caused to turn from sin*.—XI. *withheld, withdrew*.—XII. *brought down, reduced*.—XIII. *caused to answer*, Job 20:2. With דָּבָר *answered*; with פָּנָיו *turned away his anger*; with (עַל) אֶל-לֵב *laid to heart, considered*; with פְּנֵי פ׳ *turned away, refused*. Hoph. הוּשַׁב *was returned, brought back*.

שׁוּבָה f., *returning*, Isa. 30:15.

שִׁיבָה f., *returning*, Ps. 126:1; see another meaning in ישב.

שׁוֹבָב m.—I. *a rebellious person*.—II. p.n. of a man.

שׁוֹבֵב m., שׁוֹבְבָה f., *a rebel*.

שׁוּבָאֵל p. n., same as שְׁבוּאֵל.

מְשׁוֹבָב p.n. of a man.

מְשֻׁבָה ,מְשׁוּבָה f.—I. *turning away* (from God).—II. *rebellious, backsliding*.

תְּשׁוּבָה f.—I. *return*.—II. *an answer*.

שׁוֹבָךְ p. n. of a man.

שׁוֹבָל p. n. of a man.

שׁוֹבֵק p. n. of a man.

שׁוּג same as שָׁגַג ,שָׁגָה.

מְשׁוּגָה f., *error*, Job 19:4.

שׁוּד same as שָׁדַד *laid waste*; fut. יָשׁוּד, Ps. 91:6.

שׁוּד same as שׁד; see שָׁדַד.

שֵׁד m., pl. שֵׁדִים *idols*, Deu. 32:17; Ps. 106:37; LXX. δαιμόνια.

שָׁוָה I. *was equal to, resembled*.—II. *was of equal value* or *importance*. —III. *was fitting, proper*, Est. 3:8. —IV. *was sufficient*, Est. 7:4. With

·אֶל ,לְ ,בְּ Pi. שִׁוָּה I. *made level, smoothed*, Isa. 28:25. — II. *made similar*, Ps. 131:2. — III. *made himself like*, Isa. 38:13. — IV. *placed, proposed*. — V. *produced fruit*, Hos. 10:1. Hiph. *made like, compared*. Nithpa. נִשְׁתַּוָּה *being made like*, Pro. 27:15.

שְׁוָא Ch. Pa., *placed, made equal*, Dan. 5:21, with עִם. Ithpa. *was made into*, Dan. 3:29.

שָׁוָה f., *equity*, Job 33:27.

שָׁוֵה p.n., a plain to the north of Jerusalem; שָׁוֵה קִרְיָתַיִם a city of Moab.

שׁוּחַ *went down, sank*.

שׁוּחַ p. n. of one of Abraham's sons; patron. שׁוּחִי.

שׁוּחָה f.—I. *a pit, pitfall*.—II. p.n. of a man.

שִׁיחָה f., *a pit*, Ps. 119:85.

שׁוּחָם p. n. of a man.

שַׁחַת f.—I. *a pit*.— II. *a dungeon*.— III. *a grave*; see also in שָׁחַת.

I. **שׁוּט** 1. *spread like water, went to and fro*.—2. *struck, struck into the water*, i.e. rowed. Pil. שׁוֹטֵט *ran far and wide*. Hithpal. הִתְשׁוֹטֵט same as Pil.

שׁוֹט m.—I. *a whip, scourge*.—II. *calamity*.

שַׁיִט m., *an oar, oars*, Isa. 33:21.

שֹׁטֵט m., *a whip, scourge*, Jos. 23:13.

מָשׁוֹט m., *an oar, rudder*, Eze. 27:29.

מִשּׁוֹט m., the same, Eze. 27:6.

II. **שׁוּט** (Syr. *despised*); part. שָׁאט *despised* (Ezekiel only).

שְׁאָט m. (with suff. שָׁאטְךָ), *contempt* (of another), Ezekiel only.

שׁוּל m., *skirt* (of a garment), *train*

שׁוֹלָל *spoil*; see שלל.

שׁוּלַמִּית; see שלם.

שׁוּם m., *garlick*, Nu. 11:5.

שׁוּנִי p. n., a son of Gad.

שׁוּנֵם p. n., a town of Issachar; שׁוּנַמִּי m., שׁוּנַמִּית f., *a Shunemite*.

שׁוּעַ, שָׁוַע. Pi. שִׁוַּע *cried out for help, implored*, with אֶל. Pil. and Hiph. see in יָשַׁע.

שֶׁוַע m. (with suff. שַׁוְעִי), *a cry for help*, Ps. 5:3.

שׁוֹעַ m.—I. *affluent*, Job 34:19.—II. *liberal*, Isa. 32:5.

שׁוּעַ m. —I. *safety*, Job 30:24. — II. *affluence*, Job 36:19.—III. p.n. of a man.

שַׁוְעָה f., *cry for help*.

שׁוּעָא p. n. of a man.

תְּשֻׁעָה ,תְּשׁוּעָה f., *freedom, safety, salvation, deliverance*.

שׁוּעָל; see שׁעל.

שׁוֹעֵר; see שׁער.

שׁוּף (fut. יְשׁוּף).—I. *bruised, shattered*, Gen. 3:15; Job 9:17. — II. *concealed*, Ps. 139:11.

שׁוֹפָךְ p. n., same as שׁוֹבָךְ.

שׁוּפַמִי p. n. of a man.

שׁוֹפָר *trumpet*; see שׁפר.

שׁוּק same as שָׁקַק. Hiph. הֵשִׁיק I. *caused to run over*, Joel 2:24. — II. *overflowed*, Joel 4:13. Pil. שׁוֹקֵק *cause to overflow*, Ps. 65:10.

שׁוּק m. (pl. שְׁוָקִים), *a street*.

שׁוֹק com. (dual שֹׁקַיִם), *leg* (of a man or animal); trop. שׁוֹקֵי הָאִישׁ perhaps *infantry*, Ps. 147:10.

שָׁק m. Ch., *leg*.

תְּשׁוּקָה f., *desire*

שׁוּר (fut. יָשׁוּר). — I. *viewed, beheld, perceived.* — II. *watched* (for good or evil). — III. *went*, Is. 57:9; part. f. pl. שָׁרוֹת *travellers*, Eze. 27:25. See also in שִׁיר.

שׁוּר m. — I. *an enemy* (one who watches for evil), Ps. 92:12. — II. *a wall*; pl. שׁוּרוֹת. — III. p. n., a place in the wilderness; מִדְבַּר שׁוּר *the wilderness of Shur*, between Egypt and Palestine.

שׁוּר m. Ch., *a wall*.

שָׁרוֹת f. pl., *walls*, Jer. 5:10.

שׁוֹר m. (pl. שְׁוָרִים).—I. *an ox*.—II. *a herd of oxen*.

תְּשׁוּרָה f., *a present*, 1 Sa. 9:7.

שׁוּשׁ root not used; (Syr. *alabaster*).

שַׁיִשׁ m., *white marble*, 1 Ch. 29:2.

שֵׁשׁ m.—I. *white marble*, Est. 1:6.—II. *very fine linen*. (See also in its place.)

שׁוּשַׁן m.—I. *a lily*.—II. *an artificial lily*.—III. שׁוּשַׁן עֵדוּת probably the name of a musical instrument.—IV. שׁוּשָׁן p. n.: (a) the city of *Susa* in Persia; (b) a place unknown.

שׁוֹשָׁן m., *a lily*; pl. שׁוֹשַׁנִּים. — I. *lilies*.—II. *musical instruments*.

שׁוֹשַׁנָּה f., the same.

שׁוּשַׁנְכָיֵא Ch., an inhabitant of Susa.

שׁוֹשֵׁתִי Po. pret. from שׁשׁה; same as שׁסה.

שׁוּת; see שִׁית.

שׁוּתֶלַח p. n. of a man. Patron. שׁוּתַלְחִי.

שֵׁזַב Ch. Pe. שֵׁיזִב, שֵׁיזֵב *delivered, rescued*.

שָׁזַף *beheld, saw*. (See also in שָׁדַף.)

שָׁזַר Hoph. part. שֵׁשׁ מָשְׁזָר *fine twined linen* (probably wrung out for the purpose of bleaching it).

שַׁח; see שחח.

שָׁחַד *bribed*.

שֹׁחַד m.—I. *a present*.—II. *a bribe*.—III. *bribery*, Job 15:34.

שָׁחָה *bowed himself*, Isa. 51:23. Hiph. הִשְׁחָה *bowed down*, Pro. 12:25. Hith. הִשְׁתַּחֲוָה (inf. הִשְׁתַּחֲוֹת; Ch. הִשְׁתַּחֲוָיָה; imp. f. הִשְׁתַּחֲוִי; fut. יִשְׁתַּחֲוֶה; apoc. יִשְׁתַּחוּ) I. *prostrated himself*; with לִפְנֵי, לְ *before*.—II. *worshipped*.

שׁוּחָה f., *a pit*, Pro. 28:10.

שְׁחִית f., the same.

שָׁחוֹר same as שִׁיחוֹר; see שחר.

שָׁחַח (pret. שַׁח, שָׁחֲחוּ; fut. יָשֹׁחַ). — I. *bowed himself, stooped*. — II. *was brought low, humbled*. Niph. the same. Hiph. הֵשַׁח *brought low, humbled*. Hithp. הִשְׁתּוֹחַח *brought low, broke*.

שַׁח m., *having downcast eyes, meek*, Job 22:29.

שָׁחַט (fut. יִשְׁחַט; inf. שַׁחֲטָה). — I. *slaughtered* (an animal).—II. *slew* (a person).—III. זָהָב שָׁחוּט "*alloyed gold*" (Lee). Niph. *was slaughtered*.

שְׁחִיטָה f., *slaughtering, sacrifice*, 2 Ch. 30:17.

שְׁחִין; see שחן.

שָׁחִים *spontaneous*; see סָחִישׁ.

שְׁחִית, see שחח; שְׁחִיתָה, see שחת.

שַׁחַל m., *a lion*.

שְׁחֵלֶת f., some kind of perfume, or pastil; LXX. ὄνυξ, Ex. 30:34.

שַׁחַן (Arab. *fever*).

שְׁחִין m., *inflammation, any burning disease*; שׁ׳ מִצְרַיִם *the ulcer of Egypt*.

שָׁחַף root not used; (Arab. *was thin*).

שְׁחִיף m., *thin covering of wood*, Eze. 41:16.

שַׁחַף m. LXX. λάρος; *a sea gull*, Lev. 11:16; Deu. 14:15.

שַׁחֶפֶת f., *consumption*.

שָׁחַץ (Arab. *was lifted up*).

שַׁחַץ m., *mightiness, fierceness*.

שַׁחֲצִים p. n., a place in the tribe of Issachar.

שָׁחַק *reduced to dust, crushed, wasted away*.

שַׁחַק m.—I. *dust*, Isa. 40:15.—II. *a cloud*; pl. שְׁחָקִים *clouds*.—III. *the sky*.

שָׁחַר I. *was black*, Job 30:30.—II. *did a thing early, sought early*. Pi. שִׁחֵר *sought early*, with אֶל.

שָׁחֹר, שָׁחוֹר m., שְׁחוֹרָה f., *black*.

שְׁחוֹר m., *blackness*, Lam. 4:8.

שַׁחַר m.—I. *the dawn*; בֶּן שַׁחַר *lucifer*, "the morning star." — II. adv. *in the morning*. — III. *rise, origin*, Isa. 47:11.

שַׁחֲרוּת f., *dawn of life, youth*, Ecc. 11:10.

שְׁחַרְחֹרֶת f., *very black*, Cant. 1:6.

שְׁחַרְיָה p. n. of a man.

שַׁחֲרַיִם p. n. of a man.

מִשְׁחָר m., *the dawn*, Ps. 110:3.

שִׁיחוֹר, שִׁחוֹר, שִׁחֹר m.—I. the name of a river of Egypt, probably the *Nile*. —II. שִׁיחוֹר לִבְנָת a river in Asher.

שָׁחַת. Niph. I. *was spoilt*.—II. *was corrupted*, Gen. 6:11, 12. — III. *was destroyed*, Ex. 8:20. Pi. שִׁחֵת I. *acted corruptly*. — II. *destroyed*. — III. *broke a covenant*, Mal 2:8. — IV. *laid aside* (of pity), Am. 1:11. Hiph. הִשְׁחִית same as Pi.; with or without דַּרְכּוֹ *corrupted his way*. Hoph. הָשְׁחַת; part. מָשְׁחָת I. *injured*, Mal. 1:14. —II. *polluted*, Pro. 25:26.

שְׁחַת Ch., part. שְׁחִיתָה *a fault*.

שַׁחַת m.—I. *corruption*.—II. *destruction*; see also שׁוּחַ.

מַשְׁחִית m. (Hiph. part.).—I. *destroyer*, Ex. 12:23—II. *plunderer*,

מָשְׁחָת m., *defilement*, Lev. 22:25.

מַשְׁחֵת m., *destruction*, Eze. 9:1.

מִשְׁחַת m., *disfigured*, Isa. 52:14.

שִׁטָּה f. — I. *the pea-thorn*; (Arab. שׁנט; Egypt. *shont*); pl. שִׁטִּים *shittim wood, the wood of the pea-thorn*.—II. p. n., a valley of Moab.

שָׁטַח *spread abroad, strewed*. Pi. שִׁטַּח *spread abroad* (the hands in prayer), Ps. 88:10.

מִשְׁטוֹחַ, מִשְׁטָח m., *place for spreading nets*, Eze. 26:5, 14; 47:10.

שֹׁטֵט; see שׁוּט.

שָׁטַף I. *washed off* or *away*.—II. *cleansed by washing*. —III. *swept away* (of a torrent). Niph. I. *was cleansed*, Lev. 15:12. — II. *was swept away*, Dan. 11:22. Pu. *was cleansed*, Lev. 6:21.

שֶׁטֶף, שֵׁטֶף m., *washing away, overflowing, inundation*.

שָׁטַר; part. שֹׁטֵר *magistrate, ruler*, Ex. 5:10, 14; Deu. 1:15.

שִׁטְרַי p. n. of a man.

מִשְׁטָר m., *authority, influence*, Job 38:33.

שְׁטַר m. Ch., *sovereignty* (if the reading be correct; some suppose an error for שְׂטַר *side*), Dan. 7:5.

שַׁי m., *offering, present* (always with יוֹבִילוּ *bring ye*).

שִׂיאוֹן p. n., a name of Hermon.

שִׁיבָה; see יָשַׁב, שׁוּב.

שָׁיָה, fut. apoc. תֶּשִׁי *thou forgettest*; LXX. ἐγκατέλιπες, Deu. 32:18; see נָשָׁה.

שִׁיזָא p. n. of a man

שֵׁיזִיב; see שׁזב.

שַׂיִט; see שׁוּט.

שִׁיחָה; see שׁוּחַ.

שִׁילֹנִי, שִׁילֹה; see שׁלה.

שׁוּן, שִׁין (Syr. *minxit*).

שַׁיִן or שִׁין m., pl. שֵׁינִים *urine*.

שֵׁיצָא Ch.; see יצא.

שׁוּר, שִׁיר (fut. יָשִׁיר, וַיָּשַׁר, יָשֹׁר).—I. *sung*; with לְ *to*.—II. *sung of*; part. שָׁרִים, שָׁרוֹת *singers*. Pil. שׁוֹרֵר *sounded*, Zep. 2:14; part. *a singer*. Hoph. הוּשַׁר *was sung*.

שִׁיר m.—I. *singing*.—II. *a song*.—III. *instrumental music*; כְּלֵי שִׁיר *musical instruments*.

שִׁירָה f., *a song*.

שַׁיִשׁ; see שׁוּשׁ.

שִׁישַׁק p. n., *Shishak*, king of Egypt; LXX. Σεσογχις·

שׁוּת, שִׁית (fut. יָשִׁית, יָשֵׁת, וַיָּשֶׁת; inf. abs. שׁוֹת; inf. const. and imp. שִׁית) same as שׂוּם.—I. *placed, laid*; with לְ, עַל *upon*; with עָלָיו *decorated himself*:—also II. *set over, appointed*.—III. *set together, compared*, with עִם.—IV. שׁ׳ פָּנָיו אֶל *looked towards*.—V. שׁ׳ עֵינָיו *looked out after*, Ps. 17:11.—VI. שׁ׳ לֵב *set his heart upon, regarded*, with לְ, אֶל.—VII. שׁ׳ יָד עִם *assisted*.—VIII. שׁ׳ לְנֶגְדּוֹ *looked at, examined*, Ps. 90:8.—IX. *laid up treasure*.—X. *rendered*. Hoph. הוּשַׁת *was required*, with עַל, Ex. 21:30.

שַׁיִת m. (with suff. שִׁיתוֹ) *thorns* (Isaiah only).

שִׁית m., *putting on a dress*.

שָׁתוֹת m. pl., *foundations*.

שֵׁת p. n.—I. *Seth*, the son of Adam.—II. an epithet of the Moabites, Nu. 24:17.

שַׁךְ, שֵׁךְ Kal inf., from שׁכך.

שָׁכַב (fut. יִשְׁכַּב; inf. שְׁכַב, שְׁכֹב; imp. שְׁכַב, שִׁכְבָה).—I. *lay down*.—II. *slept*.—III. *kept his bed*.—IV. *slept with his fathers, died*.—V. *rested* (of the head).—VI. *lay with* (carnally). Pu. *to be laid, to lie*. Niph. I. *placed*.—II. *caused to rest, stopped*. Hoph. *was placed, laid*.

שְׁכָבָה, const. שִׁכְבַת f.—I. *the act of lying with*.—II. *covering of dew*, Ex. 16:13, 14.

שְׁכֹבֶת f., *act of lying with*.

מִשְׁכָּב m. (pl. מִשְׁכָּבִים, מִשְׁכָּבוֹת).—I. *a bed*.—II. *a bier*, 2 Chron. 16:14.—III. *lying in bed*.—IV. *lying with*.

מִשְׁכַּב m. Ch., *a bed*.

שָׁכָה. Hiph. part. מַשְׁכִּים *wandering about lasciviously*, Jer. 5:8.

שָׁכוֹל, שַׁכּוּל; see שׁכל.

שִׁכּוֹר; see שׁכר.

שָׁכַח, שָׁכֵחַ (fut. יִשְׁכַּח) *forgot, disregarded, neglected*, with מִן. Niph. *was forgotten, neglected*. Pi. and

Hiph. *cause to forget.* Hithpa. same as Niph., Ecc. 8:10.

שָׁכֵחַ m. (pl. const. שְׁכֵחֵי) *forgetting, neglecting.*

שְׁכַח Ch. Ithp. הִשְׁתְּכַח *was found, was.* Aph. הַשְׁכַּח *found, discovered.*

שְׁכַנְיָה p.n. of a man.

שָׁכַךְ (inf. שֹׁךְ, שַׁךְ; fut. pl. וַיָּשֹׁכּוּ). I. *stooped.* — II. *abated.* Hiph. הֵשַׁךְ I. *placed.*—II. *emptied.*

שָׁכֹל (fut. יִשְׁכַּל) *lost children, became childless.* Pi. I. *made childless.*—II. *stripped of inhabitants.*—III. *destroyed* (of a sword), Deu. 32:25.—IV. *produced an abortion.*—V. *lost fruit, &c., was barren;* part. מְשַׁכֶּלֶת *an abortion.* Hiph. *lost its inhabitants* (a land).

שְׁכוֹל m.—I. *privation of children.*—II. *destitution.*

שַׁכּוּל m., שַׁכֻּלָה f.—I. *childless.*—II. *deprived of, without young.*

שִׁכֻּלִים m. pl., *loss of children,* Isa. 49:20.

אֶשְׁכֹּל m. (pl. const. אֶשְׁכְּלוֹת, אַשְׁכְּלֹת).—I. *a cluster, bunch of grapes* or *flowers;* (Arab. *bound*). —II. p. n.: (a) of a valley in the south of Palestine; (b) of a man.

שַׁכְלֵל; see כָּלַל.

שָׁכַם. Hiph. הִשְׁכִּים I. *arose in the morning.*—II. *as soon as he arose.* —III. *came in the morning.*

שְׁכֶם with pause שֶׁכֶם m. (with suff. שִׁכְמוֹ).—I. *shoulder, shoulders.*—II. *a load, portion,* Gen. 48:22.—III. p. n., *Shechem,* a city of the Levites in Ephraim; with ה loc. שְׁכֶמָה, with pause שֶׁכְמָה.—IV p.n. of a man.

שֶׁכֶם p. n. of a man; patron. שִׁכְמִי.

שִׁכְמָה f., *the shoulder-blade,* Job 31:22.

שָׁכֵן, שָׁכַן (fut. יִשְׁכֹּן).—I. *lay down to rest, rested.*—II. *continued*—III. *dwelt.*— IV. *inhabited, was inhabited;* part. שָׁכוּן *inhabiting.* Pi. I. *caused to dwell.* — II. *placed;* שִׁכֵּן שְׁמוֹ *placed his name.* Hiph. I. *caused to dwell.*—II. *fixed.*

שְׁכַן Ch. Pa., same as Pi. Heb.

שָׁכֵן, const. שְׁכַן m., שְׁכֵנָה, שְׁכֶנֶת f. —I. *inhabitant.* — II. *neighbour, neighbouring people.*

שֶׁכֶן m., *a dwelling;* with suff. שִׁכְנוֹ, Deu. 12:5.

שְׁכַנְיָה p.n. of a man.

שְׁכַנְיָהוּ p.n. of a man.

מִשְׁכָּן m.—I. *habitation, dwelling.*—II. *the Tabernacle and Temple.*—III. *lair of beasts.*

מִשְׁכַּן m. Ch., *habitation.*

שָׁכַר (fut. יִשְׁכַּר). — I. *drank wine* or *strong drink.*—II. *was exhilarated, intoxicated.* — III. *became giddy.* Pi. and Hiph. *made drunken.* Hith. *made himself drunken,* 1 Sa. 1:14.

שִׁכּוֹר, שִׁכֹּר m., שִׁכֹּרָה f., *drunken, a drunkard.*

שֵׁכָר m.—I. *strong drink* (not wine). —II. *wine,* Nu. 28:7.

שִׁכָּרוֹן m., *drunkenness* (Ezekiel only)

שִׁכְּרוֹן p.n., a place of Judah.

אֶשְׁכָּר m., *rich gift, present.*

שֶׁל; see אֲשֶׁר.

שַׁל, שַׁלְאֲנַן; see שלה.

שָׁלַב. Pu. part. מְשֻׁלָּבוֹת *joined together* (Ex. 26 : 17 ; 36 : 22).
שְׁלַבִּים m. pl., *edges, borders*, 1 Ki. 7: 28, 29.

שֶׁלֶג m., *snow*.
הִשְׁלִיג Hiph. "was white as snow," Eng. Ver., Ps. 68:15.

שָׁלָה ,שָׁלַו (pret. שָׁלַוְתִּי ,שָׁלוּ ; fut. יִשְׁלָיוּ ; fut. apoc. יֵשֶׁל). — I. *was prosperous, at ease.*—II. *made prosperous, gave ease to.* Niph. *became negligent,* 2 Ch. 29:11. Hiph. *flattered, deceived,* 2 K. 4:28.
שְׁלָה Ch., *was at rest,* Dan. 4:1.
שַׁל m., *fault, error,* 2 Sa. 6:7.
שָׁלָה f. Ch., *error;* same as שָׁלוּת, Dan. 3:29. Ketib.
שֵׁלָה, 1 Sa. 1:17, same as שְׁאֵלָה; see שאל.
שָׁלֵו m. (pl. const. שַׁלְוֵי) שְׁלֵוָה f. — I. *prosperous, at ease.* — II. *unmindful of God,* Eze. 23:42.
שְׁלֵיו ,שָׁלֵיו m. — I. *prosperous.* — II. *prosperity.*
שֶׁלֶו m. (with suff. שַׁלְוִי), *prosperity,* Ps. 30:7.
שַׁלְוָה f.—I. *prosperity, ease.*—II. *negligence of God.*
שְׁלֵוָה f. Ch., *prosperity,* Dan. 4:24.
שָׁלוּת ,שָׁלוּ f. Ch., *error, fault, trespass.*
שְׁלִי m. בַּשֶּׁלִי *quietly, privately,* 2 Sa. 3:27.
שִׁלְיָה f., *the after-birth,* Deu. 28:57.
שַׁלְאֲנָן (from שַׁאֲנָן and שָׁלָה) m., *wholly at rest,* Job 21:23.
שִׁילֹה ,שִׁלֹה, Gen. 49:10; *quasi* אֲשֶׁר לוֹ, i. e., *he whose it is ;* "Shiloh," Eng. Ver.

שִׁילֹה ,שִׁלֹה ,שִׁילוֹ ,שִׁלוֹ p. n., a city of Ephraim, where the tabernacle stood; שִׁילֹנִי *a native of Shiloh.*
שַׁלְהֶבֶת *flame ;* see להב.
שָׁלוֹם ,שְׁלוּם ,שַׁלֻּם; see שלם.
שַׁלּוּן p. n. of a man.
שָׁלוֹשׁ ; same as שָׁלֹשׁ.

שָׁלַח (fut. יִשְׁלַח ; inf. שְׁלֹחַ ,שְׁלֹחַ, שְׁלֹחַ ; imp. שַׁלַּח ,שְׁלְחָה).—I. *sent* (a person or thing), with לְ, or אֶל, sometimes עַל. — II. *sent word, charge ;* with לְ *to ;* and בְּיַד *by, by the hand of.*—III. *sent a message to,* with or without דָּבָר.—IV. יָד or בְּ *put forth his hand* (to injure), *laid his hand on,* with אֶל. It has the same meaning without יָד, 2 Sa. 6:6. — V. *shoot out arrows.* (For other modifications of the primary senses, see Concordance.) Niph. inf. נִשְׁלוֹחַ *to be sent,* Est. 3:13. Pi. שִׁלַּח I. *sent.*—II. *sent away.*—III. *allowed to depart, dismissed.* — IV. *set at liberty.* — V. *gave in marriage.*—VI. *sent away, divorced* (a wife). — VII. *put in a place.*—VIII. *put forth* (his hand). —IX. with בָּאֵשׁ *set on fire.* — X. *inflicted a calamity.*—XI. *caused,* Pro. 16:28.—XII. *threw, threw off.* —XIII. *cast out, shoot forth.* (See also Concordance.) Pu. שֻׁלַּח *was sent, dismissed, set at liberty, divorced, thrown.* Hiph. with בְּ I. *sent.*—II. *inflicted a calamity.*
שְׁלַח Ch.—I. *sent word, orders.*—II. *put forth* (his hand).
שִׁלּוּחִים m. pl., *divorce* (of a wife), Ex. 18:2. — II. *renunciation* (of a

claim), Mic. 1:14. — III. *presents, dowry,* 1 Ki. 9:16.

שֶׁלַח m. (with suff. שִׁלְחוֹ).—I. *missile.* —II. *rejection, contempt.*—III. pl., *shoots, produce.*—IV. p. n. of a man. —V. p. n., *Siloah,* a stream which ran through Jerusalem; called also שִׁלֹחַ.

שְׁלֻחוֹת f. pl., *shoots,* Isa. 16:8.

שִׁלְחִי p. n. of a man.

שִׁלְחִים p. n., a town of Judah.

שֻׁלְחָן m. (pl. שֻׁלְחָנוֹת), *table*; עָרַךְ שֻׁלְחָן *spread, provided, a table*; שׁ׳ הַמַּעֲרֶכֶת, שׁ׳ הַפָּנִים *the table of shew-bread.*

מִשְׁלָח m.—I. *the sending forth of cattle* (to graze).—II. (with יָד) *the putting out the hand.*

מִשְׁלֹחַ, מִשְׁלוֹחַ m., the same; I. and II.

מִשְׁלַחַת f., the same as II.

שָׁלַט (fut. יִשְׁלַט) *ruled, had power over,* with בְּ, עַל. Hiph. I. *allowed to rule.*—II. *gave authority to, permitted,* with בְּ and לְ.

שְׁלֵט Ch., with בְּ.—I. *ruled.*—II. *had power over.* — III. *seized.* Aph. *caused to rule.*

שֶׁלֶט m., pl. שְׁלָטִים, שִׁלְטֵי *shields.*

שַׁלִּיט m., שַׁלֶּטֶת f.—I. *ruler, prince.*— II. *violent,* Eze. 16:30.

שַׁלִּיט m. Ch.—I. *a ruler.*—II. *that which is permitted, lawful*; לָא שַׁלִּיט *it is not lawful,* Ezr. 7:24.

שִׁלְטוֹן m., *power, authority,* Ecc. 8: 4, 8.

שִׁלְטוֹן m. Ch., *authority, ruler,* Dan. 3:2, 3.

שָׁלְטָן m. Ch., *authority, empire.*

שַׁל, שִׁלְיָה, שָׁלֵיו; see שלה.

שָׁלִישׁ, שְׁלִישִׁי, שְׁלִישִׁית; see שלשׁ.

שָׁלַךְ. Hiph. הִשְׁלִיךְ I. *threw into,* אֶל; *on,* בְּ, עַל; *to,* לְ; *from,* מִן. — II. *threw down, out, away.*—III. *cast off* (as a plant its leaves).—IV. *expelled* (a people).—V. with אַחֲרָיו, אַחֲרֵי גֵוּוֹ *cast behind him, despised.* — VI. with עַל יְהוָֹה *committed to the Lord.* Hoph. הֻשְׁלַךְ, הָשְׁלַךְ I. *was thrown down, out.*—II. *was thrown upon the Lord* (for help), with עַל

שָׁלָךְ m., *the gannet*; LXX. καταράκτης, Lev. 11:17; Deu. 14:16.

שַׁלֶּכֶת f.—I. *felling a tree,* Isa. 6:13. II. p. n., a gate of the temple.

שָׁלַל (pret. שָׁלוּתִי, שָׁלְלוּ; inf. שֹׁל, שָׁלֹל; fut. תָּשֹׁלּוּ, with suff. יִשָׁלוּךָ).—I. *plundered, spoiled.*—II. *carried off spoil.* — III. *scattered,* Ru. 2:16. Hith. אֶשְׁתּוֹלֵל (Ch. for הִשְׁתּוֹלֵל) *spoiled.*

שָׁלָל m.—I. *spoil, plunder.*—II. *gain,* Pro. 31:11.

שׁוֹלָל m., (spoiled) *a captive, captives.*

שָׁלַם (fut. יִשְׁלַם). — I. *was at peace,* Job 9:4.—II. *was completed.* Part. שֹׁלְמִי *one at peace with me,* Ps. 7:5; שְׁלוּם *peaceable,* 2 Sa. 20:19. Pi. שִׁלֵּם, שַׁלֵּם I. *completed.* — II. *restored.*—III. *gave in return, requited.*—IV. *performed a vow.* Pu. I. *was requited.*—II. *was performed* (a vow). Part. *made perfect,* Isa. 42:19. Hiph. I. *made peace with* — II. *made at peace with,* with אֶל, עִם, אֵת. — III. *completed.* — IV. *brought to an end.* Hoph. *was made at peace,* Job 5:23.

שְׁלַם Ch., *completed.* Aph. I. *terminated*, Dan. 5:26.—II. *restored*, Ezr. 7:19.

שָׁלֵם m, שְׁלֵמָה f.—I. *perfect, complete, full.* — II. אֲבָנִים שְׁלֵמוֹת *rough, unhewn stones.* — III. אֶבֶן שְׁלֵמָה *hewn, prepared stone,* 1 Ki. 6:7.—IV. *peaceable, at peace,* with עִם. —V. *at peace with God,* with עִם יְהוָֹה. — VI. p. n. of a place, Gen. 33:18.—VII. p. n., *Jerusalem,* Σόλυμα.

שָׁלוֹם m.—I. *peace.*—II. *public quiet.* —III. *prosperity.*—IV. *safety.*—V. *soundness of body.*—VI. *friendship.* Phrases: הֲשָׁלוֹם לְ *is he well?* שָׁאַל לְשָׁלוֹם לְ *enquired after their welfare;* שָׁלוֹם *farewell!* עָשָׂה שׁ׳ לְ *made peace with them;* קָרָא לְשָׁלוֹם לְ *named peaceable proposals;* עָנָה שָׁלוֹם אֵת *gave a peaceable answer.*

שְׁלָם m. Ch., *peace, safety.*

שֶׁלֶם and pl. שְׁלָמִים m. — I. *peace offering.*—II. *thank offering.*—III. *offering in completion of a vow.*

שִׁלֵּם m. — I. *retribution,* Deu. 32:35. —II. p. n., a son of Naphtali; patron. שִׁלֵּמִי.

שִׁלֻּם, שִׁלּוּם m., *retribution.*

שִׁלְמָה f., the same, Ps. 91:8.

שַׁלֻּם, שַׁלּוּם p. n.—I. *Shallum,* king of Israel.—II. used for other men.

שְׁלֹמֹה p. n, *Solomon,* king of Israel; LXX. Σαλωμών.

שַׁלְמַי p.n. of a man.

שְׁלֻמִיאֵל p.n. of a man.

שֶׁלֶמְיָהוּ p. n., same as מְשֶׁלֶמְיָה.

שְׁלֹמִית p. n. of a man.

שׁוּלַמִּית p. n. of a woman.

שַׁלְמֹן m., pl. שַׁלְמֹנִים *bribes, penalties,* Isa. 1:23.

שַׁלְמַנְאֶסֶר, שַׁלְמַן p.n., a king of Assyria.

שָׁלַף I. *drew a sword.*—II. *took off a shoe,* Ru. 4:7, 8.— III. *plucked up grass,* Ps. 129:6; אִישׁ שֹׁלֵף חֶרֶב *a man drawing the sword;* i. e., *armed.*

שֶׁלֶף p. n. of some foreign nation; perhaps Σαλαπηνοί.

שָׁלֹשׁ, שָׁלוֹשׁ const. שְׁלֹשׁ, שְׁלָשׁ־; f. שְׁלֹשָׁה, const. שְׁלֹשֶׁת m., *the numeral three;* with suff. שְׁלָשְׁתְּכֶם *ye three;* שְׁלָשְׁתָּם *they three;* שְׁלֹשׁ עֶשְׂרֵה *thirteen;* pl. שְׁלֹשִׁים *thirty, thirtieth.*

שִׁלֵּשׁ Pi. I. *divided into three parts.*— II. *did a thing the third time.*— III. *did a thing on the third day.* Pu. part. I. *threefold.* — II. *three years old,* Gen. 15:9.

שֵׁלֶשׁ p.n. of a man.

שְׁלִישִׁי m., שְׁלִישִׁיָּה, שְׁלִישִׁית f., pl. שְׁלִישִׁים I. *third parts.*—II. *chambers third in order, third stories;* f. *a third part;* בַּשְּׁלִישִׁית, שְׁלִישִׁיתָה *the third, on the third;* הַשְּׁלִישִׁית; see מָחָר.

שָׁלִשׁ, שָׁלִישׁ m.—I. *a measure,* probably *the third part of an Ephah.* —II. *abundantly;* pl. שָׁלִישִׁים.— III. *a musical instrument, a trichord* (either harp or lute).— IV. *officers of high rank.*— V. *a peculiar class of soldiers,* LXX. ἀναβάται τριστάται; their commander was called רֹאשׁ הַשָּׁלִישִׁים, הַשָּׁלִישׁ and רֹאשׁ הַשָּׁלִשִׁי.

שִׁלֵּשִׁים m. pl., *descendants of the*

third generation, great grandchildren.

שָׁלִשָׁה p.n., a region of Palestine.

שִׁלְשָׁה p.n. of a man.

שִׁלְשׁוֹם, שִׁלְשֹׁם adv. *three days ago;* תְּמוֹל שִׁלְשׁוֹם *yesterday and the day before,* i.e. formerly; כִּתְמוֹל שׁ׳ *as before;* מִתְּמוֹל שׁ׳ *heretofore, previously.*

מִשְׁלֹשׁ m., *a triad;* כְּמִשְׁלֹשׁ חֳדָשִׁים *a triplicity of,* i.e. three *months,* Gen. 38:24.

שֵׁלָתֵךְ 1 Sa. 1:17, for שְׁאֵלָתֵךְ; see שְׁאֵלָה in שאל.

שָׁם adv., *there, thither;* אֲשֶׁר...שָׁם *where;* שָׁם...שָׁם *here...there;* אֲשֶׁר..שָׁמָּה *thither, there;* שָׁמָּה *whither...where;* מִשָּׁם *thence;* אֲשֶׁר...מִשָּׁם *whence.*

שֵׁם, שֶׁם־ m. (with suff. שְׁמִי, שִׁמְךָ; pl. שֵׁמוֹת).—I. *a name;* בְּשֵׁם פּ׳ *in the name of any one.*—II. *fame, reputation* (good or bad).—III. *memory.*—IV. p. n., *Shem* the son of Noah.

שֻׁם m. Ch. (with suff. שְׁמֵהּ; pl. שְׁמָהָן), *a name.*

שֶׁמְאֵבֶר p. n., a king of Zeboim.

שְׁמוּאֵל (perhaps for שְׁמוּעָאֵל *heard of God*), p. n.—I. *Samuel,* the judge of Israel.—II. used also of other men.

שְׁמִידָע p. n., a son of Gilead; patron. שְׁמִידָעִי.

שַׁמָּא p. n. of a man.

שִׁמְאָה p. n. of a man; שִׁמְאָם the same.

שַׁמְגַּר p. n., *Shamgar,* a judge of Israel.

שָׁמַד. Hiph. *destroyed;* inf. *destruction.* Niph. *was destroyed.*

שְׁמַד Ch. Aph. *to destroy.*

שָׁמָה root not used; (Arab. *heaven*)

שָׁמַיִם, const. שְׁמֵי m. pl.—I. *heaven, the sky.*—II. *toward heaven, the sky.*

שְׁמַיִן emph. state, שְׁמַיָּא m. pl. Ch., *heaven.*

שַׁמָּה, שַׁמְּהוּת; see שמם.

שַׁמּוּעַ p. n., same as שִׁמְעָא.

שְׁמוּעָה; see שמע.

שַׁמּוֹת Eze. 36:3, Kal inf., from שמם.

שָׁמַט I. *gave up a debt.*—II. *left the land to itself.*—III. *threw down.*—IV. *stuck fast.* Niph. *was thrown down,* Ps. 141:6. Hiph. *gave up, forgave,* Deu. 15:3.

שְׁמִטָּה f., *release, acquittal;* שְׁנַת הַשְּׁמִטָּה *year of release.*

שָׁמַיִם *heavens;* see שמה.

שְׁמִינִי, שְׁמִינִית; see שְׁמֹנֶה.

שָׁמִיר; see שמר.

שְׁמִירָמוֹת p. n. of a man.

שַׁמְלַי p. n. of a man.

שָׁמֵם (fut. יֵשֹׁם; pl. יָשֹׁמּוּ; imp. שֹׁם). I. *was desolate, laid waste.*—II. *was astonished;* part. שׁוֹמֵם *desolate, solitary;* שׁוֹמֵמוֹת *desolate places.* Niph. נָשַׁם *was desolate, astonished.* Po. part. מְשׁוֹמֵם I. *a desolator.*—II. *astonished,* Ezr. 9:3, 4. Hiph. הֵשַׁם (fut. יַשִּׁים; inf. הַשְׁמֵם; part. מַשְׁמִים) I. *made desolate, laid waste.*—II. *astonished.*—III. *was astonished.* Hoph. הָשַׁם or הֻשַּׁם (pl. הָשַׁמּוּ) *was made desolate.* Hith. הִשְׁתּוֹמֵם (fut. יִשְׁתּוֹמֵם, תִּשׁוֹמֵם) I. *was dis-*

consolate (of the heart).—II. *wondered.*—III. *destroyed himself*, Ecc. 7:16.

שְׁמַם Ch. Ith., *was astonished*, Dan. 4:16.

שָׁמֵם m., שְׁמֵמָה f., *desolate.*

שְׁמָמָה f.—I. *desolation.*—II. *astonishment.*—III. *a desolate place.*

שִׁמֲמָה f.—I. *desolation*, Eze. 35:7, 9.

שַׁמָּה f.—I. *desolation* (pl. שַׁמּוֹת).—II. *astonishment.*—III. p.n.: (a) a brother of David, called also שִׁמְעָא שִׁמְעָה; (b) used also for other men.

שַׁמְּהוּת, שַׁמּוֹת p. n.; same as שַׁמָּה.

שִׁמָּמוֹן m., *astonishment, terrors*, Eze. 4:16; 12:19.

מְשַׁמָּה f.—I. *astonishment*, Eze. 5:15. —II. *desolation.*

שָׁמַן or שָׁמֵן (fut. יִשְׁמַן) *was fat, prosperous.* Hiph. I. *became fat*, Neh. 9:25. — II. *made fat*, Isa. 6:10.

שָׁמֵן m., שְׁמֵנָה f.— I. *plump* (of an animal). — II. *robust, stout* (of a man).—III. *nourishing* (of food). —IV. *rich, fertile, abundant.*

שֶׁמֶן m.—I. *oil.*—II. *ointment.*— III. *richness, delicacy of food*, Isa. 25:6. — IV. *fertility.*—V. *prosperity*, Isa. 10:27. (עֵץ שֶׁמֶן *any resinous tree.*)

שְׁמַנִּים m. pl., *fatness*, Gen. 27:28, 39.

אַשְׁמַנִּים m. pl., "desolate places," Eng. Ver., Isa. 59:10.

מִשְׁמָן m., *fatness*; pl. מִשְׁמַנִּים *fertile places.*

מַשְׁמַנִּים m. pl., *rich food*, Neh. 8:10.

מִשְׁמַנָּה p. n. of a man.

שְׁמֹנֶה f., שְׁמוֹנָה const. שְׁמֹנַת m., *eight*; pl. שְׁמֹנִים *eighty.*

שְׁמִינִי m., *eighth*; שְׁמִינִית a musical instrument, probably *with eight strings.*

שָׁמֵעַ, שָׁמַע (fut. יִשְׁמַע; inf. שָׁמֹעַ; const. שְׁמֹעַ, with ה parag. שָׁמְעָה, with suff. שָׁמְעוֹ; imp. שְׁמַע, with ה parag. שִׁמְעָה).—I. *heard.*—II. *hearkened*, with בְּ, אֶל, לְ.—III. *understood.* Niph. I. *was heard.*—II. *was hearkened to.* Pi. I. *caused to hear, summoned.* Hiph. הִשְׁמִיעַ (fut. apoc. תַּשְׁמַע).— I. *caused to hear, be heard.*—II. *proclaimed.*—III. *summoned.*

שְׁמַע Ch., *he heard.* Ith. *he obeyed.*

שָׁמָע p. n. of a man.

שֵׁמַע, שֶׁמַע m. (with suff. שִׁמְעִי, שִׁמְעֲךָ).—I. *the act of hearing.*— II. *report, fame.*—III. *sound.*

שֶׁמַע p.n. of a man.

שְׁמָע p. n., a town of Judah.

שֹׁמַע m. (with suff. שָׁמְעוֹ), *fame.*

שִׁמְעָא p. n. of a man; see שַׁמָּה.

שִׁמְעָה p n., same as שַׁמָּה; patron שִׁמְעָתִי.

הַשְּׁמָעָה (with art.) p. n. of a man.

שִׁמְעוֹן p. n.—I. *Simeon*, the son of Jacob and Leah (LXX. Συμεών). —II. used also of his descendants; שִׁמְעֹנִי *a Simeonite.*

שִׁמְעִי p. n. of a man, *Shimei.*

שְׁמַעְיָה, שְׁמַעְיָהוּ p. n. of a man.

שְׁמַעַן Kal imp. pl. f. for שְׁמַעְנָה from שמע.

שִׁמְעַת p. n. of a woman.

שְׁמֻעָה, שְׁמוּעָה f.—I. *a report.*—II. *a message.*

הַשְׁמָעוּת f., *a hearing*, Eze. 24:26.

מִשְׁמָע m.—I. *act of hearing*, Isa. 11:3. —II. p. n. of a man.

מִשְׁמַעַת f. — I. *court of hearing, council.*—II. *subjects,* Isa. 11:14.

שָׁמַץ root not used; (Arab. *hastened*).

שֶׁמֶץ m., *a small portion, a hint,* Job 4:12; 26:14.

שִׁמְצָה f., *defeat,* Ex. 32:25.

שָׁמַר (fut. יִשְׁמֹר).—I. *kept watch over, watched.*—II. *guarded, preserved.* —III. *kept in mind.*—IV. *attended to an office.*—V. *took heed.*—VI. *observed, remembered.*—VII. *regarded, reverenced.*—VIII. *guarded against, avoided.* Niph. I. *noticed, was aware of, perceived.*—II. *was preserved, delivered.*—III. *took heed.*—IV. *guarded himself, abstained,* with מִן and מִפְּנֵי; imp. הִשָּׁמֵר, הִשָּׁמֶר. Pi. *regarded,* Jon. 2:9. Hith. הִשְׁתַּמֵּר *kept, guarded himself.*—II. *was observed.*

שָׁמִיר m.—I. *a thorny shrub,* "spina Egyptiaca."—II. *a diamond.*—III. p.n.: (a) a town of Judah; (b) a town of Ephraim; (c) of a man.

שֶׁמֶר m., pl. שְׁמָרִים.—I. *sediment, lees, dregs.*—II. שְׁ׳ מְזֻקָּקִים *clear wine.*—III. p. n. of a man.

שֹׁמֵר p. n. of a man, and of a woman.

שָׁמְרָה f., *a watch,* Ps. 141:3.

שְׁמֻרוֹת f. pl., the same, Ps. 77:5.

שִׁמֻּרִים m. pl., *observance of a festival,* Ex. 12:42.

שִׁמְרוֹן p. n.—I. a town of Zebulun. —II. a son of Issachar. Patron. שִׁמְרֹנִי.

שֹׁמְרוֹן p.n.—I. *Samaria* (Σεβάστη). —II. the land of Israel; שֹׁמְרֹנִי *a Samaritan.*

שָׁמְרַיִן Ch., p. n., *Samaria.*

שִׁמְרִי p. n. of a man.

שְׁמַרְיָה p. n. of a man

שְׁמַרְיָהוּ p. n. of a man.

שִׁמְרִית p. n. of a woman; same as שֹׁמֵר.

שִׁמְרָת p. n. of a man.

אַשְׁמוּרָה f., *night-watch;* const. אַשְׁמֹרֶת; pl. אַשְׁמֻרוֹת.

מִשְׁמָר m. — I. *the act of guarding, watching.* — II. *keeping guard.*— III. *imprisonment.*—IV. *a prison.* —V. *an appointed duty.*

מִשְׁמֶרֶת f. (pl. מִשְׁמָרוֹת).—I. *guarding, watching.*—II. *imprisonment.*

שְׁמַשׁ Ch. Pa., *attended, served,* Dan. 7:10.

שֶׁמֶשׁ com. (with suff. שִׁמְשֵׁךְ), *the sun,* pl. שִׁמְשׁוֹת *thy pinnacles,* Isa. 54:12; עִיר שֶׁמֶשׁ a city of Dan.

שִׁמְשׁוֹן p. n., *Samson.* (LXX. Σαμψών.)

שִׁמְשַׁי p. n. of a man.

שַׁמְשְׁרַי p. n. of a man.

שֻׁמָתִי p. n. of a man.

שִׁנְאָב, שִׁנּוֹ, שֵׁן; see שנן.

שִׁנְאָן, שָׁנָא; see שנה.

שֵׁנָא *sleep,* Ps. 127:2; see יָשֵׁן.

שֶׁנְאַצַּר p. n. of a man.

שָׁנַב (Arab. *had a cool mouth*).

אֶשְׁנָב m., *a latticed window.*

שָׁנָה (fut. יִשְׁנֶה, יִשְׁנָא).—I. *repeated an action.*—II. *was different,* with מִן.—III. *was changed.*—IV. *was disobedient* (part. שֹׁנִים *rebellious*). Niph. *being repeated,* Gen. 41:32. Pi. שִׁנָּא, שִׁנָּה I. *changed.* — II. *violated a promise.*—III. *removed a person to another place,* Est. 2:9;

with אֶת־טַעְמוֹ *changed his mind, feigned himself mad.* Pu. fut. יְשֻׁנֶּא *was changed,* Ecc. 8:1. Hith. *changed, disguised himself,* 1 Ki. 14:2.

שְׁנָא Ch —I. *was changed.*— II. *was different from,* with מִן. Pa. I. *changed.*—II. *made different;* part. pass. *different.* Ith. *was changed.* Aph. *changed.*

שָׁנָה f. (pl. שָׁנִים, שְׁנֵי, שָׁנוֹת, שְׁנוֹת). —I. *a year.*—II. *the produce of a year;* מִדֵּי, שָׁנָה בְּשָׁנָה, שָׁנָה שָׁנָה בִּשְׁנַת שְׁתַּיִם *yearly;* שָׁנָה בְּשָׁנָה לְיוֹאָשׁ *in the second year of Joash;* בִּשְׁנַת שֵׁשׁ מֵאוֹת שָׁנָה *in the six hundredth year.* Dual שְׁנָתַיִם *two years;* שְׁנָתַיִם יָמִים *for two years.*

שְׁנָה, שְׁנָא f. Ch., *year;* pl. שְׁנִין.

שְׁנָה, שֵׁנָה *sleep;* see יָשֵׁן.

שֶׁנְהַבִּים *ivory;* see שנן.

שָׁנִי m., *bright, scarlet colour;* pl. שָׁנִים.

שְׁנַיִם const. שְׁנֵי m., שְׁתַּיִם const. שְׁתֵּי f. dual, *the numeral two;* שְׁנַיִם שְׁנַיִם *apiece;* with suff. שְׁנֵיהֶם *both of them;* f., *twice, again;* בִּשְׁתַּיִם *again.* שְׁנֵים עָשָׂר m., שְׁתֵּים עֶשְׂרֵה f., *twelve.*

שֵׁנִי m., שֵׁנִית f., *second;* f., *again.* Pl. שְׁנִיִּים.

שִׁנְאָן m., "angels," Eng. Ver.; אַלְפֵי שִׁ׳ *thousands repeated* (Ges.), Ps. 68:18.

מִשְׁנֶה const. מִשְׁנֵה m.—I. *second.*— II. *the second rank, second in rank.* III. *double.*—IV. *a copy.*—V. *of an inferior kind,* 1 Sa. 15:9. — VI. *a division of Jerusalem.*

שָׁנַן (pret. שַׁנּוֹתִי, שָׁנְנוּ).—I. *sharpened a sword, &c.*— II. *sharpened the tongue* (of slanderers), Ps. 64:4; 140:4. Pi. *taught assiduously,* with לְ, Deu. 6:7. Hithpo. הִשְׁתּוֹנֵן *was pained acutely,* Ps. 73:21.

שֵׁן, שֶׁן־ com. (with suff. שִׁנִּי; dual שִׁנַּיִם, שִׁנֵּי).—I. *a tooth.*—II. *ivory.* —III. *the ridge of a rock;* שֵׁן סֶלַע. — IV. *the prong of a fork.* — V. p.n. of a place.

שֶׁנְהַבִּים m. pl., *elephant's tooth, ivory.* (The word is probably a compound of שֵׁן *a tooth,* and הָב *an elephant;* from the Sanscrit *ibha.*)

שְׁנִינָה f., *pointed saying, taunt;* הָיָה לִשְׁנִינָה *he was for a taunt.*

שִׁנְאָב p. n. of a king.

שָׁנַס. Pi. שִׁנֵּס *girded his loins,* 1 Ki. 18:46.

שִׁנְעָר p. n., one of the names of Babylon and its vicinity.

שָׁסָה *plundered;* part. שֹׁסִים *spoilers.* Po. שׁוֹשָׂה the same, Isa. 10:13.

שָׁסַס (fut. יָשֹׁס) the same; part. שֹׁאֵס, with suff. שֹׁאֲסַיִךְ. Niph. נָשַׁס *was plundered.*

מְשִׁסָּה f., *prey.*

שָׁסַע *having a division;* שֹׁסַע שֶׁסַע פַּרְסָה or שֹׁסַעַת *having divided hoofs;* פַּרְסָה הַשְּׁסוּעָה *having a divided hoof.* Pi. I. *clove,* Lev. 1:17. — II. *tore asunder,* Jud. 14:6, &c.—III. *withheld,* 1 Sa. 24:8.

שֶׁסַע m., *division in a hoof.*

שָׁסַף. Pi. שִׁסֵּף *cut down,* 1 Sa. 15:33.

I. שָׁעָה (fut. apoc. וַיִּשַׁע) *looked at favourably, approved,* with אֶל.—II *looked at with attention,* with בְּ

—III. *looked to for help*, with אֶל, עַל. — IV. *looked away from, respited*, with מִן, Job 7:19. Hiph. imp. הָשַׁע 1. *looked away from*, with מִן, Ps. 39:14.—II. *turn away the eyes*, Isa. 6:10. See also in שָׁעַע. Hith. fut. apoc. תִּשְׁתַּע *look about with alarm*, Isa. 41:10; pl. with ה parag. נִשְׁתָּעָה *we may look with alarm, be dismayed*, Isa. 41:23.

II. שָׁעָה same as שָׁעַע; imp. שֹׁעוּ *be blinded* (Ges.); "cry," from שׁוּעַ, Eng. Ver., Is. 29:9.

שָׁעָה f. Ch., *an hour*; בַּהּ שַׁעֲתָא *immediately*.

שַׁעֲטָה f., *stamping of hoofs*, Jer. 47:3. (Arab. *pounded*.)

שַׁעַטְנֵז m., *cloth of a mixture of wool and flax*, Lev. 19:19; Deu. 22:11.

שַׁעַל, שֹׁעַל (with suff. שָׁעֳלוֹ; pl. שַׁעֲלֵי, שְׁעָלִים). — I. *palm of the hand*, Isa. 40:12.—II. *a handful*.

שׁוּעָל m.—I. *a fox*. — II. p. n. of a man.

שַׁעֲלִים p. n. of a district.

שַׁעַלְבִּין, שַׁעַלְבִים p. n., a town of the Danites; שַׁעַלְבֹנִי *a Shaalbonite*.

מִשְׁעוֹל m., *a narrow way*, Nu. 22:24.

שָׁעַן. Niph. נִשְׁעַן 1. *leaned on*, with עַל.—II. *reclined*.—III. *touched a boundary* with לְ, Nu. 21:15.—IV. *depended on*, with עַל, אֶל, בְּ.

מִשְׁעָן m., *a support*.

מַשְׁעֵן m., מַשְׁעֵנָה f., the same, Isa. 3:1.

מִשְׁעֶנֶת f. (pl. מִשְׁעֲנוֹת), *walking stick, staff*.

שָׁעַע Pil. שִׁעֲשַׁע 1. *delighted*. — II. *played*, Isa. 11:8. Pul. שֳׁעֲשַׁע *was fondled*, Isa. 66:12. Hiph. imp הָשַׁע *cover the eyes, make blind*, Isa. 6:10; see in שָׁעָה. Hithpal. הִשְׁתַּעֲשַׁע *delighted himself*, with בְּ.

שַׁעֲשׁוּעִים m. pl., *delights, source of delight*.

שַׁעַף p. n. of a man.

שָׁעַר Pro. 23:7, "thinketh," Eng. Ver.; meaning uncertain.

שַׁעַר m.—I. *value, measure*, Gen. 26:12. — II. m. (f. Isa. 14:31). — 1. *opening, gate of a city*. — 2. *the people assembled at the gate*, Ru. 3:11. — 3. *the city itself*; with ה loc. שַׁעְרָה; pl. שְׁעָרִים, שַׁעֲרֵי.

שַׁעֲרַיִם p. n., a town of Judah.

שׁוֹעֵר m., *a porter*.

שׁוֹעָר m., pl. שֹׁעָרִים *blighted figs*, Jer 29:17.

שַׁעֲרוּר m., f. שַׁעֲרוּרָה *causing to shudder, horrible*.

שַׁעֲרוּרִי m., f. שַׁעֲרוּרִיָּה, שַׁעֲרֻרִית *horrible*, Jer. 18:13.

שְׁעַרְיָה p. n. of a man.

שַׁעַשְׁגַּז p. n. of a man.

שַׁעֲשֻׁעִים, שְׁעָשַׁע; see שעע.

שָׁפָה (Arab. *became visible*). Niph. הַר נִשְׁפֶּה *a lofty, conspicuous mountain*, Isa. 13:2. Pu. שֻׁפּוּ *became prominent* (the bones), Job 33:21.

שְׁפָה or שָׁפָה f., *cheese*; pl. const. שְׁפוֹת, 2 Sa. 17:29.

שְׁפִי in pause שֶׁפִי m. (pl. שְׁפָיִים, שְׁפָיִם) *elevated, conspicuous place*

שְׁפִי, שְׁפוֹ p. n. of a man.

שִׁפְחָה f. (pl. שְׁפָחוֹת) *female servant* or *slave.*

מִשְׁפָּחָה const. מִשְׁפַּחַת f. (with suff. מִשְׁפַּחְתִּי; pl. מִשְׁפָּחוֹת). — I. *a household.* — II. *a family* or *clan.* —III. *a race* or *kind.*

שָׁפַט I. *judged.*—II. *decided a cause.* —III. *defended the right of.*—IV. *decided between,* with בֵּין...וּבֵין, בֵּין...לְ.—V. *punished.*—VI. *ruled;* part. שֹׁפֵט *a judge, ruler.* Niph. נִשְׁפַּט I. *was judged,* Ps. 9:20.—II. *reasoned with another, disputed,* with אֶת, עִם, לְ, עַל. Po. part. מְשֹׁפְטִי *my judge.*

שְׁפַט Ch. part. שָׁפֵט *judge,* Ezr. 7:25.

שְׁפוֹט m. (pl. שְׁפוּטִים) *judgments.*

שָׁפָט p. n. of a man.

שֶׁפֶט m., pl. שְׁפָטִים *judgments, punishments.*

שְׁפַטְיָה p. n. of a man.

שְׁפַטְיָהוּ p.n. of a man

שִׁפְטָן p.n. of a man.

מִשְׁפָּט m.—I. *deciding, decision, sentence.* — II. *punishment.* — III. *a court of justice.*— IV. *a cause for trial.* — V. *justice, equity.* — VI. *any positive institution; the right claimed upon such institution.*— VII. *custom.* — VIII. *manner, appearance.*

שְׁפִי, שֶׁפִי, שְׁפָיִם; see שפה.

שְׁפִים, שְׁפִיפוֹן; see שפף.

שָׁפִיר, שַׁפִּיר; see שפר.

שָׁפַךְ I. *poured out.*—II. *shed blood.*— III. *threw up a mound.* — IV. *uttered a prayer.* — V. metaph. *poured out his soul, his heart, his anger.* — VI. *gave abundantly* Niph. trop. *was poured out, was shed.* Pu. I. *was poured out.*—II. *slipped.* Hith. הִשְׁתַּפֵּךְ *was shed.*

שֶׁפֶךְ m., *the place of pouring out,* Lev. 4:12.

שָׁפְכָה f., *membrum virile,* Deu. 23:2.

שָׁפֵל (fut. יִשְׁפַּל; inf. שְׁפַל).—I. *was low, was lowered.*—II. *was humbled.* Hiph. I. *brought low.*—II. *sent down,* Isa. 57:9.—III. *cast down, humbled;* שׁ׳ רוּחַ *humble in spirit.*

שְׁפַל Ch. Aph. *humbled, brought low.*

שָׁפָל m., שְׁפָלָה f.—I. *low.*—II. *low in rank* or *importance.*—III. *humble.*

שְׁפַל m. Ch., *low in rank,* Dan. 4:14.

שֵׁפֶל m. (with suff. שִׁפְלֵנוּ), *lowly place, condition.*

שִׁפְלָה f., the same, Isa. 32:19.

שְׁפֵלָה f., *low country;* הַשְּׁפֵלָה *the low country,* i. e. the plain between Joppa and Egypt.

שִׁפְלוּת f., *lowness of the hands, inactivity,* Ecc. 10:18.

שָׁפָם p.n. of a man.

שְׁפָם, שִׁפְמוֹת p.n., a town of Judah; שִׁפְמִי *a Shiphmite.*

שָׁפָן m.—I. *the jerboa;* LXX. χοιρογρύλλιος, Lev. 11:5; Deu. 14:7. —II. p.n. of a man.

שָׁפַע (Syr. *inundated*).

שֶׁפַע m., *overflowing, abundance,* Deu. 33:19.

שִׁפְעָה f.—I. *inundation.*—II. *multitude.*

שִׁפְעִי p.n. of a man.

שָׁפַף (Syr. *he crept;* Arab. *a speckled snake*).

שְׁפִיפוֹן m., *a species of serpent*, Gen. 49:17.
שְׁפוּפָם p.n., a son of Benjamin.
שְׁפוּפָן p.n. of a man.
שֻׁפִּים p.n. of a man.

שָׁפַר *was pleasing*, with עַל, Ps. 16:6.
שִׁפְרָה f., *beauty*, Job 26:13.
שְׁפַר Ch., *was fair, pleasing*, with עַל, קֳדָם.
שׁוֹפָר m. (pl. שׁוֹפָרוֹת), *trumpet, curved horn*.
שֶׁפֶר m. — I. *pleasantness, beauty*, Gen. 49:21. — II. p.n., a mountain in the wilderness.
שִׁפְרָה p.n. of a woman.
שָׁפִיר p.n., an unknown place.
שַׁפִּיר m. Ch., *pleasing, fine*.
שַׁפְרִיר (שַׁפְרוּר) m., *royal canopy*, Jer. 43:10.
שְׁפַרְפָּרָא m. Ch., *the dawn*, Dan. 6:20.

שָׁפַת *fixed, placed*.
שְׁפַתַּיִם m. dual, *cooking vessels*.
מִשְׁפְּתַיִם dual, the same.

שֶׁצֶף m., *overflowing*, Isa. 54:8.
שָׁק Ch., *leg*, same as שׁוֹק.

שָׁקַד I. *was sleepless, awake*. — II. *watched, kept watch for*, with עַל. Pu. see next word.

שָׁקֵד I. *almond tree*. — II. *almond*. Hence denom. Pu. part. מְשֻׁקָּדִים *formed like almonds*.

שָׁקָה. Niph. *was overflown* (see שָׁקַע), Am. 8:8. Hiph. הִשְׁקָה (fut. apoc. וַיַּשְׁקְ) I. *gave drink to any one*. — II. *watered the ground*; part. מַשְׁקֶה *giving water*, Ps. 104:13. Pu. *watered, refreshed*, Job 21:24.

שֹׁקֶת f., *drinking-trough*; pl. const. שִׁקֲתוֹת.
שִׁקּוּי m. (pl. with suff. שִׁקּוּיַי). — I. *refreshment*. — II. *drink*.
שִׁקּוּ or שִׁקֻּו m. (pl. with suff. שִׁקֻּוָי), *drink*.
מַשְׁקֶה m. — I. *cup-bearer*. — II. *drink*. — III. *a watered country*.
שְׁקָה Kal imp. with ה parag., from נשק
שִׁקּוּץ; see שקץ.

שָׁקַט I. *was quiet, undisturbed*. — II. *ceased*. — III. *remained inactive*. — IV. *was silent*. Hiph. I. *caused to cease*. — II. *was quiet, ceased*, with לְ and מִן; inf. הַשְׁקֵט *rest, tranquillity*.
שֶׁקֶט m., *rest, quiet*, 1 Chron. 22:9.

שָׁקַל I. *weighed*. — II. *weighed in payment, paid*. — III. *estimated, judged*. — Niph. I. *was paid*. — II. *was judged*.
שֶׁקֶל m. (pl. שְׁקָלִים, שִׁקְלֵי). — I. a certain standard weight, *the shekel*. — II. a silver coin of that weight.
מִשְׁקָל m., *act of weighing, weight*.
מִשְׁקוֹל m., *weight*, Eze. 4:10.
מִשְׁקֶלֶת f., *balance*, Isa. 28:17.
מִשְׁקֹלֶת f., the same, 2 Ki. 21:13.

שִׁקְמָה f., pl. שִׁקְמִים, שִׁקְמוֹת *sycamore tree, a species of fig*.

שָׁקַע I. *sank*. — II. *was overflown*. — III. *abated* (of fire). Niph. *was overflown*, Am. 8:8 (Ketib נִשְׁקָה) which see in שָׁקָה.
מִשְׁקָע m., *a pond*, Eze. 34:18.
שְׁקַעֲרוּרוֹת f. pl., *hollows, parts corroded*, κοίλαδες, Lev. 14:37.

שָׁקַף. Niph. and Hiph. I. *looked*. —

II. *looked down, through, towards.* —III. *threatened.*

שֶׁקֶף m., *covering, coping,* 1 Ki. 7:5.

שְׁקֻפִים m. pl., *coped, having copings,* 1 Ki. 6:4.

מַשְׁקוֹף m., *lintel, beam over a doorway.*

שָׁקַץ. Pi. I. *regarded with disgust.* —II. *loathed,* Ps. 22:25.—III. *polluted.*

שֶׁקֶץ m., *abominable thing.*

שִׁקּוּץ m., *an abomination.*

שָׁקַק (fut. יָשֹׁק).—I. *ran to and fro.*— II. *was eager.* Hithpal. *run to and fro;* fut. pl. יִשְׁתַּקְשְׁקוּן, Nah. 2:5.

מַשָּׁק m., *running to and fro,* Isa. 33:4.

שָׁקַר (fut. יִשְׁקֹר) *acted falsely towards,* with לְ. Pi. שִׁקֵּר with בְּ.—I. *uttered a falsehood.*—II. *acted falsely.*

שֶׁקֶר m. — I. *falsehood.* — II. *a deceitful thing.* — III. עֵד שׁ׳ *false witness;* לַשֶּׁקֶר *in vain, falsely;* בַּשֶּׁקֶר, בְּשֶׁקֶר *falsely;* שֶׁקֶר adv. *in vain.*

שִׁקֻתוֹת, שֹׁקֶת; see שקה.

שֹׁר, שָׁרֵךְ; see שרר.

שְׁרָא; see שרה.

שַׂרְאֶצֶר p. n. of an Assyrian prince; see נֵרְגַל שׁ׳.

שָׁרָב m.—I. *drought,* Isa. 49:10.—II. *the mirage,* Isa. 35:7 (Arab. the same).

שֵׁרֵבְיָה p. n. of a man.

שַׁרְבִיט same as שֵׁבֶט *a sceptre* (Esther only).

שָׁרָה *set at liberty,* Job 37:3. Pi. שָׁרָה the same, Jer. 15:11.

שְׁרָא Ch.—I. *untied.*—II. *solved.*—III *halted, dwelt.* Pa. I. *untied.*—II. *began.* Ithpa. *was loose.*

שָׁרָה, שָׁרוֹת *walls;* see שׁוּר.

שָׁרַי p. n. of a man.

שִׁרְיָה f., *coat of mail,* Job 41:18.

שִׁרְיָן m., the same.

שִׁרְיוֹן, סִרְיוֹן m. (pl. שִׁרְיֹנוֹת, שִׁרְיֹנִים, סִרְיֹנוֹת).—I. *a coat of mail.*—II.

שִׂרְיוֹן p.n., a part of Mount Hermon.

מִשְׁרָה f., *juice;* מִשְׁרַת־עֲנָבִים *juice of grapes,* Nu. 6:3.

שֵׁרָה, שֵׁרוֹת; see שרר.

שָׁרוּחֶן p. n., a city of the tribe of Simeon.

שָׁרוֹן p. n., the plain between Joppa and Cesarea.

שְׁרִיקוֹת; see שרק.

שָׁרִיר, שְׁרִירוּת; see שרר.

שֵׁרִית same as שְׁאֵרִית; see שאר.

שָׁרַץ (fut. יִשְׁרֹץ). — I. *became numerous.* — II. *produce in great numbers, swarm.*—III. *creep, crawl,* Eze. 47:9.

שֶׁרֶץ m. col., *small creatures,* whether insects, reptiles, or fishes.

שָׁרַק (fut. יִשְׁרֹק).—I. *whistle,* or *hiss for, call by whistling,* with לְ.—II. *hiss at in contempt,* with עַל.

שְׁרֵקָה f., *derision, scorn.*

שְׁרִיקוֹת f., *hissing, derision,* Jer. 18:16. —II. *whistling, piping,* Jud. 5:16.

מַשְׁרֹקִית m. Ch., "flute," Eng. Ver.; LXX. σύριγγος, Dan. 3:5—15.

I. **שָׁרַר** (Arab. *made wicked*); part. שֹׁרֵר *adversary.*

שָׁרָר p. n. of a man.

II. **שָׁרַר** (Syr. *was firm*).

שֹׁר m. (with suff. שָׁרֵךְ), *the navel*, Cant. 7:3.

שֹׁר m. (with suff. שָׁרֵּךְ), the same.

שָׁרִיר m., pl. שְׁרִירִים *firm, solid parts*, Job 40:16.

שְׁרִירוּת f. with לֵב, *firmness, obstinacy of heart.*

שֵׁרָה f., pl. שֵׁרוֹת *chains, bracelets*, Isa. 3:19.

שַׁרְשְׁרָה f., *a chain.*

שַׁרְשָׁה f., pl. const. שַׁרְשׁוֹת *chains, small bracelets*, Ex. 28:22.

שֹׁרֶשׁ m. (with suff. שָׁרְשָׁם; pl. שָׁרְשֵׁי, שָׁרָשִׁים).—I. *a root.*—II. *shoot, suckers*, Isa. 11:10; 53:2. —III. *lowest part of any thing*; e. g., *sole of the foot, bottom of the sea, &c.*—IV. *foundation, groundwork*; שֹׁ׳ דָּבָר *ground of complaint*, Job 19:28.

שֵׁרֵשׁ Pi. denom. *rooted up.* Pu. שֹׁרַשׁ *was rooted up.* Poel שֹׁרֵשׁ and Poal שֹׁרַשׁ *took root.* Hiph. הִשְׁרִישׁ the same.

שֹׁרֶשׁ m. Ch., *a root.*

שֶׁרֶשׁ p. n. of a man.

שְׁרשׁוּ, (שְׁרשִׁי) f. Ch., *rooting up, banishment*, Ezr. 7:26.

שַׁרְשְׁרוֹת, שַׁרְשׁוֹת; see שרר.

שָׁרַת. Pi. שֵׁרֵת.—I. *waited on*, with אֶת.—II. *attended to*, with accus., לְ.—III. שׁ׳ בְּשֵׁם יְהוָֹה or שׁ׳ אֶת־יְהוָֹה *performed the service of the sanctuary.*—IV. *worshipped*, Eze. 20:32. Part. מְשָׁרֵת m., מְשָׁרֶת f., *minister.*

שָׁשָׂה, Po. שׁוֹשָׂה; see שָׁסָה.

שֵׁשׁ f., שִׁשָּׁה const., שֵׁשֶׁת m., *six*; pl. שִׁשִּׁים *sixty*, see also in שׁוּשׁ.

שִׁשָּׁה Pi. *gave a sixth part of*, Eze 45:13.

שִׁשִּׁי m., שִׁשִּׁית f., *the sixth*; in f. *a sixth part.*

שָׁשָׁא. Pi. שִׁשֵּׁא *caused to walk, led*, Eze. 39:2.

שֵׁשְׁבַּצַּר p. n., the Persian name of Zerubbabel.

שָׁשַׁי p. n. of a man.

שֵׁשַׁי p. n. of a man.

שֵׁשַׁךְ p. n., a prophetic title of Babylon.

שֵׁשָׁן p. n. of a man.

שָׁשַׁק p. n. of a man.

שָׁשֵׁר with pause שָׁשַׁר m., *red ochre* or *red lead*; LXX. μίλτος.

שַׁת, שַׁתָּה, שַׁתִּי pret. from שׁוּת.

שֵׁת *tumult*, see שאה.

שֵׁת p. n., שָׁתוֹת, see שִׁית.

שֵׁת, שְׁתוֹת, see שתת.

שֵׁת Ch., *six*; pl. שִׁתִּין *sixty.*

שָׁתָה (inf. שְׁתֹה, שָׁתוֹ, שָׁתוֹת; fut. יִשְׁתֶּה; apoc. יֵשְׁתְּ).—I. *he drank.* —II. *sat at table, banqueted*, Est. 7:1.—III. met., *experienced.*—IV. *consumed.* Niph. fut. יִשָּׁתֶה, *was drunk*, Lev. 11:34.

שְׁתָה, שְׁתָא Ch., *he drank*; pret. with א pros. אִשְׁתִּיו.

שְׁתִי m.—I. *drinking.*—II. *the warp of a well.*

שְׁתִיָּה f., *drinking*, Est. 1:8.

מִשְׁתֶּה m.—I. *the act of drinking.*—II. *a banquet.*—III. *the drink itself.*

מִשְׁתֵּה emph. מִשְׁתְּיָא m. Ch., the same.

שַׁתּוּ Ps. 73:9, pret. pl., from שתת.

שְׁתַּיִם; see שְׁנַיִם.

שָׁתַל *planted a tree.*

שְׁתִלֵי זֵיתִי *olive shoots*,
s. 128:3.

c close); שְׁתֻם הָעָיִן
es were opened," Eng.
1:3, 15.

de water; מַשְׁתִּין בְּקִיר
inst the wall; i. e., a
nan.

e still, was at rest.—
of strife), Pro. 26:20.
ince of Persia.
of a Persian.

שִׁית *placed.*
h suff. שְׁתוֹתֵיהֶם), *the*

ת

or *chamber;* pl. תָּאִים,
ab. *habitation*).

, *longed for*, with לְ,
174.
e, Ps. 119:20.

as תָּעַב. Pi. part.
orring, Am 6:8.

rk, mark out; fut. pl.
34:7, 8.

תְּאֶהֱבוּ Kal fut. pl.,

the Egyptian antelope;
yx (Linn.).
ee אוה.

with suff. for תְּאַכְּלֵהוּ,
with suff. for תֹּאכְלֵהוּ,

see אלה.

le; part. תֹּאֲמִים *twins.*
ced twins.

תְּאוֹם m., pl. תְּאוֹמִים, תּוֹמִים *twins;* pl. const. תְּאֳמֵי.

תַּאֲנִיָּה, תְּאֵנָה, תַּאֲנָה; see אנה.

תְּאָנִים, תְּאֵנָה; see און.

תַּאֲנַת שִׁלֹה p. n., a town of Ephraim.

תָּאַר I. *turned, made a circuit.*—II. *was formed, drawn*, used in both senses of a boundary only. Pi. *delineated, marked the form of.*

מְתֹאָר p. n. of a place, Jos. 19:13.

תֹּאַר m. (with suff. תָּאֳרוֹ, תֹּאֲרוֹ).—I. *form, personal appearance.*—II. *beauty.*

תַּאְרֵעַ p.n. of a man.

תְּאַשּׁוּר; see אשר.

תֹּבֵא for תָּבֹא, תֹּאבֶה Kal fut. 2. pers., from אבה.

תְּבֹאֶינָה Kal fut. pl. f., from בּוֹא.

תֵּבָה const. תֵּבַת f. (Coptic *an ark, chest;* Hierog. the same).—I. *Noah's ark.*—II. *the basket in which Moses was exposed.*

תְּבוּאָה; see בּוֹא.

תָּבֹאתִי, תָּבֹאתָה, תְּבוֹאָה for תָּבוֹא; for תָּבֹאִי Kal fut. with ה parag., and with suff. תְּבוֹאֲתְךָ for תְּבוֹאֶךָ, from בּוֹא.

תְּבוּנָה, תָּבוּן; see בִּין.

תְּבוּסָה; see בּוּס.

תָּבוֹר p. n.—I. a mountain of Galilee on the borders of Zebulun and Naphtali.—II. a city of the Levites in Zebulun.—III. a grove of oaks in Benjamin.

תֵּבְךְּ, וַתֵּבְךְּ Kal fut. apoc., from בכה.

תֵּבֵל, see יבל; תֶּבֶל, see בלל.

תֻּבַל same as תּוּבַל.

תַּבְלִית; see בלה.

תְּבַלֵּל; see בלל.

תֶּבֶן m., *straw.*

תִּבְנִי p. n. of a man.

מַתְבֵּן m., *heap of straw*, Isa. 25:10.

תַּבְנִית; see בנה.

תִּבְעָיוּן Kal fut. pl. with נ parag. from בעה.

תַּבְעֵרָה; see בער.

תֵּבֵץ p. n., a place not far from Sichem.

תְּבַר Ch. part., f. תְּבִירָה *brittle*, Dan. 2:42.

תִּגְבְּהֶינָה for תִּגְבַּהְנָה Kal fut. pl. f. from גָּבַהּ.

תְּגִיוּן Hiph. fut. pl. with נ parag. from יגה.

תִּגָּל Niph. fut. apoc. from גלה.

תִּגְלַת פִּלְאֶסֶר, תִּלְגַּת פִּלְנֶסֶר, תִּגְלַת פִּלְאֶסֶר, תִּ׳ פִּלְנֶאסֶר, תִּ׳ פִּלְנֶסֶר p.n., a king of Assyria.

תַּגְמוּל; see גמל.

תִּגְרָה; see גרה.

תּוֹגַרְמָה, תֹּגַרְמָה p. n., some country to the north of Palestine.

תִּדְהָר; see דהר.

תְּדִירָא; see דור.

תְּדַמְּיוּנִי Pi. fut. pl. with suff. from דמה.

תַּדְמֹר p. n., a city in the Syrian desert, *Palmyra.*

תִּדְעָל p. n. of a king, Gen. *c.* 14.

תָּהָה (Arab. *a desert*).

תֹּהוּ m. — I. *emptiness.* — II. *a vain thing, nothing.*—III. *desolation.*— IV. *a desert, wilderness.* — V. adv. *in vain.*

תְּהוֹם *the deep;* see הום.

תְּהִי, וַתְּהִי, in pause תֶּהִי, fut. apoc., from היה.

תְּהִימֶנָּה for תְּהִימֶינָה Hiph. fut., from הום.

תְּהִלָּה, תְּהִלָּה; see הלל.

תְּהִלָּתֵיךְ for תְּהִלָּתֵךְ; see תְּהִלָּה in הלל.

תַּהֲלוּכָה *procession;* see הלך.

תַּהְפֻּכוֹת, תַּהְפּוּכָה; see הפך.

תְּהַתֵּלּוּ Pi. fut. pl. with dag. euphon., from התל.

תָּו; see תָּוָה.

תּוֹא same as תְּאוֹ.

תּוּב Ch., *returned.* Aph. הֲתִיב I. *returned, carried back.* — II. *answered*, with פִּתְגָם.

תֻּבַל, תּוּבַל p.n. of some northern nation, perhaps *the Tibarenes.*

תּוּבַל קַיִן p. n., a son of Lamech, the first artificer in iron.

תּוּגָה; see יגה.

תּוֹדָה; see ידה.

תְּוַהּ Ch., *was amazed*, Dan. 3:24.

תָּוָה. Pi. תִּוָּה *made marks, scrabbled*, 1 Sa. 21:14. Hiph. I. with תָּו *made a mark*, Eze. 9:4. — II. metaph. *provoked*, i. e. made a painful mark, scratch, wound, Ps. 78:41; Vulg. exacerbaverunt.

תָּו m., *a mark* or *sign*, Eze. 9:4; (Arab. *a mark in the form of a cross*, put upon the necks of camels; hence the Phœnician and Greek letters τ *tau*).

תּוֹחַ p.n. of a man.

תּוֹחֶלֶת; see יחל.

תָּוֶךְ, const. תּוֹךְ m., *the middle;* בְּתוֹךְ *in the middle, among, within, through;* מִתּוֹךְ *from the midst of;* אֶל־תּוֹךְ *into the midst of;* תּוֹךְ *oppression;* see in תָּכַךְ.

תִּיכוֹן m., תִּיכוֹנָה f., *middle.*

תּוֹכֵחָה, תּוֹכַחַת; see יכח.

תּוֹלָד, תּוֹלְדֹת; see ילד.

תּוֹלָל; see ילל.

תּוֹלָע, תּוֹלֵעָה, תּוֹלַעַת; see תלע.

תּוֹמִים same as תְּאוֹמִים; see תאם.

תּוֹמִיךְ for תּוֹמֵךְ Kal part., from תמך.

תּוֹעֵבָה, תּוֹעֵבַת; see תעב.

תּוֹעָה; see תעה.

תּוֹעָפוֹת; see יעף.

תּוּף (Arab. *spit through detestation*).

תֹּפֶת f.—I. תּ׳ לְפָנִים *object of detestation* (one in whose face they spit), Job 17:6.—II. תֹּפֶת, with ה parag. תָּפְתֶּה p.n., a place in the valley of Hinnom, near Jerusalem.

תּוֹצָאוֹת; see יצא.

תּוּר I. *go about as a spy, spy out.*—II. *search out, explore.*—III. *travel about*, 1 Ki. 10:15.—IV. *seek after the heart, go astray*, Nu. 15:39, with אַחֲרֵי. Hiph. I. *send spies*, Jud. 1:23.—II. *direct aright*, Pro. 12:26.

תּוֹר m.—I. *turn, order*, Est. 2:12, 15.—II. *row, string of beads*, Cant. 1:10, 11.—III. *a turtle dove.*—IV. same as תּוֹרָה *way, manner*, 1 Chron. 17:17.

יְתוּר m., "*that which one discovers*" (Ges.); "*abundance*," see יֶתֶר (Lee); "range," Eng. Ver., Job 39:8.

תּוֹרָה; see ירה

תּוֹר m. Ch., *an ox.*

תּוֹשָׁב; see ישב.

תּוּשִׁיָּה f.—I. *abundance, wealth.*—II. *abundantly, entirely*, Job 30:22.—III. *security.*—IV. *wisdom.*

תּוֹתָח; see יתח.

הֶתַּז, תָּזַז; see תיז.

תֵּזְלִי for תֶּאֱזְלִי, תֵּאזְלִי Kal fut. 2. pers from אזל.

תַּזְנוּת; see זנה.

תַּזְרֵנִי for תְּאַזְּרֵנִי Pi. fut. with suff. from אזר.

תַּחְבֻּלוֹת, תַּחְבּוּלוֹת; see חבל.

תֹּחוּ p.n., same as תּוֹחַ.

תֶּחֱז Kal fut. apoc. from חזה.

תֹּחֵז for תֹּאחֵז Kal fut. from אחז.

תְּחִי fut. apoc. from חיה.

תַּחְכְּמֹנִי p.n. of a man.

תֵּחֵל for תֵּחַל Niph. fut. from חלל.

תְּחִלָּה; see חלל.

תַּחֲלוּאִים; see חלה.

תַּחְמָס; see חמס.

תַּחַן, תַּחֲנוֹת; see חנה.

תְּחִנָּה, תַּחֲנוּנִים, תַּחֲנוּנוֹת; see חנן.

תַּחְפַּנְחֵס, תְּחַפְנְחֵס (תַּחְפְּנֵס), p. n.—I. a city of Egypt.—II. תַּחְפְּנֵיס a queen of Egypt.

תַּחֲרָא, תַּחֲרָה; see חרה.

תַּחְרֵעַ p. n. of a man.

תַּחַשׁ m. עוֹר תַּחַשׁ, עוֹרֹת תְּחָשִׁים.—I. a colour of which skins were dyed, probably *blue*; "badgers' skins," Eng. Ver. — II. p. n. of a man.

תַּחַשׁ, וַתַּחַשׁ, Job 31:5; Kal fut. apoc. (חָשָׁה); see חוש.

תָּחַת root not used; (Ethiop. "cast down").

תַּחַת m., *that which is under, below.* Adv. *below*; prep. ὑπό.—I. *under.*—II. *instead of.*—III. *in return for*; תַּחַת אֲשֶׁר *whereas, because that*; תּ׳ כִּי *because*; (also without כִּי) With suff. תַּחְתַּי (תַּחְתֵּנִי); תַּחְתֶּיךָ; תַּחְתֵּינוּ; (תַּחְתֶּנָּה) תַּחְתֶּיהָ, תַּחְתָּיו;

תַּחְתֵּיהֶם, תַּחְתֵּיכֶם, תַּחְתָּם. Comp. מִתַּחַת *from under, under;* מִתַּחַת לְ *under, beyond;* אֶל־תַּחַת *under.*

תַּחַת p. n.—I. one of the stations of Israel in the wilderness.—II. name of a man.

תְּחֵת Ch., } *under.*
תְּחוֹת Ch., }

תַּחְתִּי m., תַּחְתִּיָּה, תַּחְתִּית f., *lower, lowest;* pl. m. תַּחְתִּיִּים, f. תַּחְתִּיּוֹת *lowest parts* or *places.*

תַּחְתּוֹן m., תַּחְתּוֹנָה f., *lower, lowest.*

תַּחֵת Ch. Aph. fut. from נחת.

תֵּחַת Kal fut. f. from נחת.

תֵּט Kal fut. apoc. from נטה.

תִּיז. Hiph. הֵתַז, with pause הֵתַז *cut off.*

תִּיכוֹן; see תָּוֶךְ.

תִּילוֹן, תּוּלוֹן p. n. of a man.

תֵּימָא, תֵּמָא p. n. of a people of Arabia, and of their country.

תֵּימָן; see ימן.

תִּימְרוֹת; see תמר.

תֵּיעָשֶׂה, Ex. 25:31, for תֵּעָשֶׂה Niph. fut. from עשׂה.

תִּירוֹשׁ, תִּירשׁ; see ירשׁ.

תִּירְיָא p. n. of a man.

תִּירָס p. n., one of the sons of Japhet.

תַּיִשׁ m. (pl. תְּיָשִׁים), *he-goat* or *ram.*

תָּכָה. Pu. תֻּכּוּ *were seated, sat down,* Deu. 33:3.

תֵּכֶהּ, וַתֵּכֶה, תֵּכֶהּ Kal fut. apoc. from כהה.

תְּכוּנָה; see כּוּן, תכן.

תּוּכִּיִּים, תֻּכִּיִּים m. pl., probably *peacocks,* 1 Ki. 10:22; 2 Ch. 9:21.

תְּכַךְ Ch., *injured, hurt.*

תֹּךְ, תּוֹךְ m., *craft, oppression;* see also תּוֹךְ in תָּוֶךְ.

תְּכָכִים m. pl., *oppressions, injuries,* Pro. 29:13.

תַּכְלִית, תִּכְלָה; see כלה.

תְּכֵלֶת f., *violet blue.*

תָּכַן I. *weighed.* — II. *pondered, examined.* Niph. I. *was measured, examined.*—II. *was of just measure, fair, equal.* Pi. תִּכֵּן I. *measured.* —II. *fixed,* Ps. 75:4.—III. *directed,* Isa. 40:13. Pu. *measured, reckoned,* 2 Ki. 12:12.

תֹּכֶן m.—I. *fixed quantity,* Ex. 5:18. —II. *measure, standard,* Eze. 45:11. —III. p. n., a town of the Simeonites.

תְּכוּנָה f. — I. *arrangement, order, structure.* — II. *costly thing,* Nah. 2:10; see also in כּוּן.

תָּכְנִית f., *measure, standard.*

מַתְכֹּנֶת f. (with suff. מַתְכֻּנְתּוֹ), *measure, proportion.*

תְּכַס Pi. fut. apoc. from כסה.

תִּכַּסֶּה Hith. fut. from כסה.

תְּבָרֵיךְ; see ברך.

תֵּל, תִּלָּה; see תלל.

תָּלָא, תְּלָאִים; see תלה.

תְּלָאָה; see לאה.

תַּלְאֻבוֹת, תַּלְאוּבָה; see לאב.

תְּלַאשָּׂר, תְּלַשָּׂר p. n., a city of Syria or Mesopotamia.

תִּלְבֹּשֶׁת; see לבשׁ.

תְּלַג m. Ch., *snow.*

תִּלְגַּת; see תגלת.

תָּלָה (part. תָּלוּי; pl. תְּלוּיִם, תְּלוּאִים, תְּלָאִים).—I. *hung,* with בְּ, עַל *upon* (a tree). — II. *"made dependent,"* Job 26:7 (Lee).—III. *placed in sus-*

pense. Niph. *was hanged.* Pi. *hung*, Eze. 27:10, 11.

תְּלֶה, וַתֵּלֶה Kal fut. apoc., from להה.

תְּלִי m. (with suff. תֶּלְיְךָ) *quiver* (that which is suspended), Gen. 27:3.

תְּלוּנּוֹת; see לון.

תֶּלַח p. n. of a man.

תָּלַל *raised a mound;* part. תָּלוּל *elevated, thrown up*, Eze. 17:22; (הָתֵל, see הֵתֵל).

תֵּל m. (with suff. תִּלָּהּ, תִּלָּם).—I. *heap of ruins.*—II. *hill, mound.*—III. תֵּל אָבִיב p. n. of a town of Babylonia. —IV. תֵּל חַרְשָׁא p.n.; see חֶרֶשׁ. —V. תֵּל מֶלַח (*hill of salt*), p.n., a place in Babylonia.

תֶּלֶם m., *furrow.*

תַּלְמַי p. n. of a man.

תַּלְמִיד; see למד.

תָּלֵן Kal fut. apoc., from לון.

תָּלַע. Pu. part. מְתֻלָּעִים *clothed in scarlet*, Nah. 2:4.

תּוֹלָע m. (pl. תּוֹלָעִים) — I. *worm* of any kind. — II. *the worm used in dying scarlet.* — III. *scarlet cloth.* — IV. p.n., *Tolah:* (a) a son of Issachar; patron. תּוֹלָעִי. — (b) a judge of Israel.

תּוֹלֵעָה f., *a worm.*

תּוֹלַעַת f. (with suff. תּוֹלַעְתָּם) *a worm;* שְׁנִי ת׳, ת׳ שָׁנִי I. *scarlet* or *crimson.*—II. *the kermes insect whence it was dyed.*

תַּלְפִּיּוֹת f. pl., "an armoury," Eng. Ver., Cant. 4:4; meaning uncertain.

תְּלַשַּׂר same as תְּלַאשַּׂר.

תְּלָת f., תְּלָתָה, תְּלָתָא m. Ch., *three;* pl. תְּלָתִין *thirty.*

תְּלַת m. Ch., the same; שַׁלִּיט תַּלְתָּא and תַּלְתָּא *prince third in rank.*

תְּלִתַי m. Ch., *third.*

תְּלִיתַי Ch., f. תְּלִיתָאָה the same.

תַּלְתַּלִּים m. pl., *hanging, flowing of hair;* LXX. ἐλάται, Cant. 5:11.

תַּם Ch., with ה parag. תַּמָּה *there.*

תָּמָּה, תֹּם, תַּמָּה, תָּם; see תמם.

תֵּמָא same as תֵּימָא.

תָּמַהּ *wondered, was amazed.* Hith. imp. הִתַּמְּהוּ *be astonished*, Hab. 1:5.

תְּמַהּ m. Ch., *wonder, miracle.*

תִּמָּהוֹן m., *astonishment, terror.*

תַּמּוּז p. n a Syrian idol, perhaps *Adoni*

תְּמוֹל adv., *yesterday;* אֶתְמוֹל, אִתְמוֹל, אֶתְמוּל the same.

תְּמוּנָה; see מין.

תְּמוּרָה; see מור.

תְּמוּתָה; see מות.

תֶּמַח p. n. of a man.

תֶּמַח Hiph. fut. apoc., with י parag תֶּמְחִי, from מחה.

תָּמִיד; see מוד.

תָּמִים; see תמם.

תָּמַךְ I. *took hold of*, with בְּ.—II. *held, held up, supported.*—III. *obtained.* —IV. *apprehended.*—V. *arrived at, reached.* Niph. *was holden*, Pro. 5:22.

תָּמַם (fut. יִתֹּם, יִתּוֹם, תִּתַּם; pl. יִתַּמּוּ, with pause יִתָּמּוּ). — I. *was completed, ended.*—II. *was perfect in character, upright.*—III. *ceased, came to an end, finished.* — IV. *wasted away, consumed, destroyed;* עַד תֻּמָּם *until they were destroyed.*

Niph. (fut. pl. יִתַּמּוּ).—I. *was finished.*—II. *was consumed.* Hiph. הֵתֵם (fut. יַתֵּם; inf. with suff. הֲתִימְךָ).—I. *finished, consumed.*—II. *declared perfect.*—III. *took the sum of, counted,* 2 Ki. 22:4.—IV. *cause to cease, remove,* with מִן, Eze. 22:15. Hithpa. *showed himself perfect;* fut. תִּתַּמָּם, 2 Sa. 22:26; Ps. 18:26.

תָּמִים m., תְּמִימָה f.—I. *complete.*—II. *whole, entire.*—III. *free from fault, defect.*—IV. *integrity.*

תָּם m., תַּמָּה f., *blameless, honest, virtuous, pious.*

תֹּם, תּוֹם, תָּם־ m. (with suff. תֻּמּוֹ).—I. *completeness.*—II. *security, peace, prosperity.*—III. *innocence, integrity;* pl. תֻּמִּים probably *truth;* see אוּרִים.

תֻּמָּה f., *innocence, integrity.*

תַּמִּים *double,* contr. for תְּאֳמִים.

מְתֹם m., *unhurt, sound, soundness.*

תִּמְנָה p. n., a city of Judah.

תִּמְנָתָה p. n., a town of the Philistines; תִּמְנִי *a Timnite.*

תִּמְנַת חֶרֶס, תִּ׳ סֶרַח p. n., a town in Mount Ephraim.

תִּמְנָע p. n.—I. of a woman.—II. of one of the tribes of Edom.

תֶּמֶס; see מסס.

תֶּמֶס, וַתֶּמֶס Hiph. fut. apoc., from מסה.

תָּמָר m.—I. *a palm tree;* pl. תְּמָרִים.—II. p. n. of a woman.—III. p. n. of a town in south Palestine.—IV. p. n., same as תַּדְמֹר.—V. עִיר הַתְּמָרִים (*city of pa.ms*), a name of Jericho.

תֹּמֶר m. *palm-tree,* Jer. 10:5.

תִּמֹּרָה f. (pl. תִּמֹּרִים, תִּמֹּרוֹת), *artificial palm tree.*

תַּמְרוּרִים m. pl., *columns,* Jer. 31:21; see also in מָרַר.

תִּימָרָה f., pl. const. תִּמְרוֹת *pillars of smoke.*

תַּמֵּר Ex. 23:21, for תָּמֵר Hiph. fut., from מרר (same as מרה).

תֹּמְרוּ for תֹּאמְרוּ Kal fut. pl., from אמר.

תַּמְרוּק; see מרק.

תַּן, תַּנִּים; see תנן.

תֵּן, תְּנָה Kal imp., from נתן.

תִּנְדַּע Ch. Pe. fut., from ידע.

תָּנָה *hired,* Hos. 8:10. Pi. I. *ascribed praise to,* Jud. 5:11.—II. *celebrated an action,* Jud. 11:40. Hiph. same as Kal, Hos. 8:9.

תַּנּוֹת f. pl., *habitations,* Mal. 1:3; see also in תַּנִּים.

אֶתְנָה f., *gift, wages of prostitution,* Hos. 2:14.

אֶתְנִי p. n. of a man.

אֶתְנָן m. (with suff. אֶתְנַנָּהּ).—I. *fee, gift, wages of prostitution.*—II. p. n. of a man.

תִּנְיָן m. Ch., *the second:* f. תִּנְיָנָה, Dan. 7:5.

תִּנְיָנוּת Ch. adv., *a second time, again,* Dan. 2:7.

תְּנוּאָה; see נוא.

תְּנוּבָה; see נוב.

תְּנוּךְ; see תנך.

תְּנוּמָה; see נום.

תְּנוּפָה; see נוף.

תַּנּוּר m., *a furnace, oven.*

תַּנְחֻמוֹת, תַּנְחוּמוֹת, תַּנְחוּמִים; see נחם.

תְּנוּךְ m., with אֹזֶן *the lower part of the ear.*

תַּן or תָּן m., pl. תַּנִּים, תַּנִּין *jackals, or*

other wild animals of the desert; the precise meaning unknown.

תַּנִּים m. sing., for תַּנִּין Eze. 29:3; 32:2.

תַּנִּין m. (pl. תַּנִּינִים).—I. *a serpent.*—II. *any large marine animal.*—III. *a crocodile.*

תִּנְשֶׁמֶת; see נשם.

תֹּסֵף for תֹּאסֵף Kal fut., from אסף.

תָּעַב. Pi. תִּעֵב I. *abhorred.* — II. *rendered loathsome.* — III. *was abominable.* Hiph. הִתְעִיב I. *acted abominably.*—II. adv. *abominably.* Niph. נִתְעַב *was abhorred.*

תּוֹעֵבָה const. תּוֹעֲבַת f.—I. *abomination.*—II. *impure detestable action.* —III. *anything polluting.*—IV. *an idol.*

תְּעֻגְּנָה for תְּעָנֵגְנָה Niph. fut. pl., from ענן.

תָּעָה (fut. apoc. תֵּתַע).—I. *wandered, went astray.*—II. *staggered through drunkenness.* — III. *was in confusion, disorder.*—IV. with מֵעַל, מִן, מֵאַחֲרֵי *departed from the true worship.* Niph. נִתְעָה I. *was led astray.*—II. *was made to stagger.* Hiph. הִתְעָה (fut. apoc. יֵתַע) I. *caused to wander, go astray.*—II. *deceived, led astray.*—III. *acted deceitfully.*

תּוֹעָה f.—I. *apostacy,* Isa. 32:6.—II. *hurt, injury,* Neh. 4:2, 8.

תֹּעוּ, תֹּעִי p. n. of a man.

תְּעוּדָה; see עוד.

תְּעָלָה, תְּעָלַת; see עלה.

תַּעֲלוּלִים; see עלל.

תַּעֲלֻמָה; see עלם.

תַּעֲנוּג; see ענג.

תַּעֲנִית; see ענה.

תַּעְנַךְ, תַּעֲנָךְ p. n., a city of the Manassites in the tribe of Issachar.

תָּעַע. Pil. part. מְתַעְתֵּעַ *mocking,* Gen. 27:12. Hith. part. pl. מִתַּעְתְּעִים *mocked,* 2 Chron. 36:16.

תַּעְתֻּעִים m. pl., *mockeries, deceptions,* Jer. 10:15; 51:18.

תַּעֲצֻמוֹת; see עצם.

תַּעַר; see ערה.

תַּעֲרוּבָה; see ערב.

תֹּף, תֻּפִּים; see תפף.

תִּפְאָרָה, תִּפְאֶרֶת; see פאר.

תַּפּוּחַ m.—I. *apple-tree.*—II. *apple.*—III. p. n.: (a) a town of Judah; (b) a town of Ephraim; (c) a town between Ephraim and Manasseh; (d) the name of a man.

תְּפוֹצוֹתֵיכֶם Thiphel 1. pers. with suff., from פּוּץ.

תֹּפֵהוּ, וַתֹּפֵהוּ for תֹּאפֵהוּ Kal fut. with suff., from אפה.

תֻּפִינֵי; see אפן.

תָּפַל (Arab. *was unseasoned*).

תָּפֵל m.—I. *that which is insipid, unsavoury,* Job 6:6. — II. *insipid, foolish,* Lam. 2:14. — III. *lime, lime-wash for walls* (Eze. only).

תֹּפֶל p. n., a place in the wilderness.

תִּפְלָה f., *insipidity, folly.*

תְּפִלָּה; see פלל.

תִּפְלֶצֶת; see פלץ.

תִּפְסַח; see פסח.

תָּפַף, part. f. pl. תּוֹפְפוֹת *beat the tambourine or drum,* Ps. 68:26. Pi. *smite the bosom,* Nah. 2:8.

תֹּף m. (pl. תֻּפִּים), *tambourine, drum*

תָּפַר *sew, join together.* Pi. the same, Eze. 13:18.

תָּפַשׂ I. *laid hold of, seized,* with בְּ.

—II. *took in war.*—III. *handle, manage the bow, &c.*—IV. *carry on war.*—V. *set, enchase,* Hab. 2:19.—VI. *administer the law,* Jer. 2:8.—VII. *used the name of God irreverently, perjured himself,* Pro. 30:9. Niph. *was taken, caught.* Pi. *took hold,* Pro. 30: 28.

תֹּפֶת, תָּפְתֶּה; see תּוּף.

תִּפְתָּיֵא Ch. m. pl. emph. *lawyers* or *judges,* Dan. 3:2, 3.

תְּצִלֶּנָה for תְּצַלֶּינָה Kal fut. pl., from צלל.

תִּקְוָה; see קוה.

תְּקוּמָה, תְּקוֹמֵם; see קום.

תְּקוֹעַ; see תקע.

תְּקוּפָה, see קוף; תַּקִּיף, see תקף.

תְּקַל Ch., *weighed;* part. pass. תְּקִל; *weighed;* pret. תְּקִלְתָּ *thou art weighed.*

תָּקַן *was arranged, straight.* Pi. I. *set in order.*—II. *made straight* (Ecclesiastes only).

תְּקַן Ch., the same. Hoph. הָתְקַן *was set in order, established.*

תָּקַע I. *smote the hands together* (for joy, &c.).—II. *thrust in, stabbed* (of a weapon).—III. *fixed, fastened.*—IV. *pitched a tent.*—V. *threw into the sea,* Ex. 10:19.—VI. with שׁוֹפָר, בַּשּׁוֹפָר *blew a trumpet;* with תְּרוּעָה *blew a horn.* Niph. I. with לְיָד *strikes hands, becomes a surety,* Job 17:3.—II. with שׁוֹפָר *a trumpet is blown.*

תָּקוֹעַ m., *blast with a trumpet,* Eze. 7:14.

תֵּקַע m., the same, Ps. 150·3.

תְּקוֹעַ p. n., *Tekoa,* a town of Judah, whence the name מִדְבַּר תְּקוֹעַ *the wilderness of Tekoa;* m. תְּקֹעִי, f. תְּקֹעִית *a Tekoite.*

תָּקַף *overpower, prevail over.*

תְּקֵף Ch.—I. *was strong.*—II. *was violent.* Pa. *made strong.*

תֹּקֶף m., *might, power.*

תְּקֹף m. Ch., the same.

תְּקוּפָה *circuit;* see קוּף.

תַּקִּיף m., *strong, powerful,* Ecc. 6:10.

תַּקִּיף m. Ch., *strong, powerful.*

תַּרְאֲלָה p. n., a town of Benjamin.

תֵּרֶב, וַתֵּרֶב Kal fut. apoc., from רבה.

תַּרְבּוּת, תַּרְבִּית; see רבה.

תִּרְגַּל; see רֶגֶל.

תַּרְגֵּם Ch. quadrilitt., *interpreted, translated;* part. pass. מְתֻרְגָּם, Ezr. 4:7.

תַּרְדֵּמָה; see רדם

תִּרְהָקָה p. n., *Tirhakah,* king of Egypt and Ethiopia

תְּרוּמָה, תְּרוּמִיָּה; see רום.

תְּרוּעָה; see רוּעַ.

תְּרוּפָה; see רפא.

תֵּרוֹץ Niph. fut., from רצץ.

תִּרְזָה f., name of a tree, *the holly.*

תֶּרַח p. n.—I. a station of Israel in the wilderness.—II. the father of Abraham.

תִּרְחֲנָה p. n. of a man.

תְּרֵין const. תְּרֵי m., תַּרְתֵּין f. Ch., *two.*

תָּרְמָה, תַּרְמִית; see רמה.

תֹּרֶן I. *mast of a ship.*—II. *flag* or *banner.*

תְּרַע m. Ch.—I. *entrance, door.*—II *palace* (the porte).

תָּרָע m. Ch., *door keeper.*

תַּרְעֵלָה; see רעל.

תִּרְעָתִי p.n. of a man.

תְּרָפִים m. pl., *Teraphim;* idols of some kind.

תְּרַפֶּינָה, Job 5:18, Kal fut. pl., from רפה.

תִּרְצָה p.n.—I. one of the royal cities of Israel.—II. the name of a woman.

תֶּרֶשׁ p.n. of a Persian.

תַּרְשִׁישׁ; see רָשַׁשׁ.

תִּרְשָׁתָא, with art., a title of Nehemiah.

תַּרְתָּן p.n., a chief of the Assyrians.

תַּרְתָּק p.n., an idol of the Arvadites.

תִּשֶּׂאינָה, תִּשֶּׂנָּא for תִּשֶּׂאנָה Kal fut. pl., from נשא.

תְּשׂוּמֶת; see שׂים.

תְּשֻׁאוֹת; see שׁוא.

תִּשְׁבִּי p. n. of a man.

תַּשְׁבֵּץ; see שׁבץ.

תְּשׁוּבָה; see שׁוּב.

תְּשׁוּעָה; see שׁוּעַ.

תְּשׁוּקָה; see שׁוּק.

תְּשׁוּרָה; see שׁוּר.

תֶּשִׁי, Deu. 32:18, fut. apoc., from שׁיה.

תֵּשַׁם fut., from ישׁם.

תֵּשַׁע const. תְּשַׁע, f. תִּשְׁעָה const. תִּשְׁעַת m., *nine, the ninth;* pl תִּשְׁעִים *ninety.*

תְּשִׁיעִי m., תְּשִׁיעִית f., *the ninth.*

תֵּשְׁתְּ Kal fut. apoc., from שׁתה.

תִּשְׁתַּחוּ Hith. fut. apoc. sing. for תִּשְׁתַּחֲוֶה, from שׁחה.

תִּשְׁתָּע Hith. fut. apoc. for תִּשְׁתָּעֶה, from שׁעה.

תֵּת, with suff. תִּתִּי Kal inf., from נתן.

תִּתְבָּר for תִּתְבָּרַר Hith. fut., from ברר.

תַּתָּה for נָתַתָּה Kal pret., from נתן.

תִּתְחַר Hith. fut. apoc., from חרר.

תִּתֹּם, תִּתֹּם, תִּתֹּם Kal fut., from תמם.

תַּתְּנַי p.n., a Persian noble.

וַתֵּתַע, תֵּתַע Kal fut. apoc., from תעה

תִּתַּפָּל, 2 Sa. 22:27, transpos. for תִּתְפַּתָּל Hith. fut., from פתל.

תֵּתַצַּב, Ex. 2:4, for תִּתְיַצֵּב Hith. fut., from יצב.

וַתֹּתַר, תֹּתָר Hiph. fut. in pause from יתר.

AIDS TO THE STUDY OF THE SCRIPTURES IN THE ORIGINAL LANGUAGES.

THE POLYMICRIAN GREEK NEW TESTAMENT. With References. 32mo, cloth, red edges, 1s. 6d. Bound with a Lexicon, price 2s. Various styles up to 10s.

SCHMIDT'S GREEK CONCORDANCE TO THE NEW TESTAMENT SCRIPTURES. Pocket volume, price 2s. 6d.

The Greek New Testament binds conveniently with this Concordance and with a Lexicon. The three works constitute a pocket companion of the highest value.

THE GREEK STUDENT'S MANUAL: containing a Practical Guide to the Greek Testament, designed for those who have no knowledge of the Greek language. The New Testament, Greek and English, and a Greek and English Lexicon to the New Testament. Foolscap 8vo, cloth, 7s.

THE STUDENT'S ANALYTICAL GREEK TESTAMENT: presenting at one view the Text of Scholz, and a Grammatical Analysis of the Verbs, in which every occurring Inflexion of Verb or Participle is minutely described and traced to its proper Root. With the Readings, Textual and Marginal, of Griesbach; and the Variations of Stephens, 1550; Beza, 1598; the Elzevir, 1633. Square 16mo. Cloth, 5s. 6d.

THE TRAVELLER'S NEW TESTAMENT: a pocket volume, containing the Critical Greek and English New Testament, with a Lexicon and a Concordance. In cloth, 7s. 6d., or bound in limp morocco, with projecting morocco edges, and an elastic band, £1.

TEXTUAL CRITICISM OF THE NEW TESTAMENT, for English Bible Students. Being a succinct comparison of the Authorised Version with the Critical Texts of Griesbach, Scholz, Lachmann, Tischendorf, Tregelles, and Alford, and Uncial MSS. By C. E. STUART, Esq. Third Edition. Revised and Corrected. Foolscap 8vo, cloth, 2s. 6d.

THE HEBREW STUDENT'S MANUAL. *Contents:*—Preface, Recommendations to the Learner. I. A Hebrew Grammar. II. A Series of Hebrew Reading Lessons, Analysed. III. The Book of Psalms, with Interlineary Translation, the Construction of every Hebrew Word being clearly indicated, and the Root of each distinguished by the Use of Hollow and other Types; to which is added an Article on Pronunciation, with Portions of Texts Transliterated and Translated. IV. A Hebrew and English Lexicon, containing all the Hebrew and Chaldee Words in the Old Testament Scriptures. Fcap. 8vo, cloth. 6s.

A CRITICAL GREEK AND ENGLISH CONCORDANCE OF THE NEW TESTAMENT. Prepared by CHARLES F. HUDSON, A.M. Revised and completed by EZRA ABBOTT, D.D., LL.D. Fifth Thousand. Crown 8vo, cloth, pp. 530. Price 7s. 6d.

Highly commended by Drs. LIGHTFOOT, WESTCOTT, ANGUS, and many others.

GESENIUS'S HEBREW GRAMMAR: Enlarged and Improved by Professor E. RODIGER. With a Hebrew Reading Book. 4to, cloth, 5s. 6d.

THE POCKET HEBREW LEXICON. Price, cloth, 2s. 6d.

The arrangement of this manual Lexicon combines two things—the etymological order of Roots, and the alphabetical order of words. This arrangement tends to lead the learner onward; for, as he becomes more at home with roots and derivatives, he learns to turn at once to the root, without first searching for the particular word in its alphabetical order.

"This is the most beautiful and, at the same time, the most correct and perfect Manual Hebrew Lexicon we have ever used."—*Eclectic Review.*

S. BAGSTER & SONS, Limited, 15, Paternoster Row, London.

REVIEW NOTICES AND OPINIONS OF EMINENT MEN.

Letter from the Bishop of Derry.—PALACE, DERRY, *Jan. 1886.*

"I can safely say that my attention was throughout stimulated, and that my interest never flagged from the first page to the last. There are few scholars who may not learn from Mr. Smyth."

WILLIAM, DERRY AND RAPHOE.

"It gives much interesting information with admirable simplicity."

ARCHDEACON FARRAR.

"This little volume is indispensable to the Bible reader who wishes to have in small compass an account of ancient manuscripts and early versions. It supplies a felt need."—*The Christian.*

"We have seldom met with a better written digest of the history of our English Bible. It might honestly have been presented to the public as a five-shilling volume."—*Sword and Trowel.*

"In these pages a flood of light is thrown on the sources of our English version, most valuable in answer to questions raised by the new revision."—*Word and Work.*

"This volume is partly historical, partly bibliographical, and partly critical. . . . Anybody can understand it, and everybody would be better for the thoughtful study of it."—*Christian Advocate.*

"Gives an excellent and comprehensive account for popular reading of the ancient manuscripts of the Bible."—*The Christian World.*

"It ought to find its way into our Training Colleges, Bible Classes, and Upper Classes in Schools."—*Ecclesiastical Gazette.*

"This little book deserves the attention of the large number of professing Christians who cannot devote the time to the larger histories of our English Bible."—*Presbyterian Churchman.*

"The book is a fine study of the history of the Bible, and should be read attentively and with profit."—*Publishers' Circular.*

"This very interesting little work cannot fail to be highly appreciated."—*Northern Whig.*

"This is a capital little hand-book on the history of the Bible, which should be in the hands of every teacher and preacher."—*The Primitive Methodist World.*

"The author has done good service by this most interesting and instructive little book."—*The Messenger.*

"Mr. Smyth possesses the true teaching instinct. . . . We have never before seen so much valuable information on the subject conveyed in so portable a form, and in such clear and interesting style."—*Dublin Daily Express.*

"This book supplies a real need."—*Christian Commonwealth.*

"This is altogether an admirable little book."—*Dublin Evg. Mail.*

ENGLISH VERSIONS OF THE BIBLE

A HANDBOOK.

With Copious Examples illustrating the Ancestry and Relationship of the several Versions, and Comparative Tables.

By the Rev. J. I. MOMBERT, D.D.

This volume, on which the Author has spent years of laborious research and study, presents an exhaustive view of the English Versions from Anglo-Saxon times to the Revision of 1881, brings together information not contained in any single work extant, and is an indispensable work of reference to all readers of the Bible.

508 pp. crown 8vo, cloth, 3*s*. 6*d*.

NOTICES OF THE PRESS.

"Several works on the different English versions of the Scriptures have from time to time appeared. This is the most complete which has come into our possession."—*Presbyterian Journal.*

"This is a most valuable historical work, which has required great research."—*Herald and Presbyter.*

"The thanks of all who love the Bible are due to Dr. Mombert. . . . The author seems to be specially fitted, by his extensive learning and painstaking industry, for the task he has so successfully accomplished."—*Messenger.*

"The book can be recommended to readers and students alike."—*Literary World.*

"A book crowded with facts and replete with interest, and one that is likely to live and to become a standard book of reference. . . . This book will give new and deeper impressions of the value of the English Bible, for it will show how great a cost of time, labour, and learning the world owes to it."—*The Churchman.*

"Dr. Mombert has thoroughly understood the subject . . . and he has produced a book as correct in information, as clear in style, and as conclusive in result, as either scholar or Christian could desire."—*The Scotsman.*

"Information is here given with great correctness, which can be had only by repeating the difficult labours of the industrious author, a task impossible to pastors, who can draw rich material from this treasury of information."—*Christian Advocate.*

"Dr. Mombert . . . has given us in this beautifully printed volume . . . by far the most complete account of the origin of our English Bible that is to be found anywhere. . . . We doubt not such a volume will have many purchasers."—*Southern Churchman.*

"This valuable and timely contribution to Biblical Literature tells the story of The Book, as it has passed through various versions, in a very graphic style. It invests what is generally regarded a dry subject with exceeding interest; and without any parade of learning, exhibits on every page the fruits of mature scholarship. . . . It will strengthen our love for the Bible, as the Word of God."—*Episcopal Register.*

"There is enough of keen and thorough research and its results in these pages to render them useful to Biblical students; but it is so put before the reader, in a pleasant, narrative style, enlivened by many graphic and suggestive extracts, that no intelligent person, even if he be not learned in such matters, can help enjoying it."—*The Congregationalist.*

"A clearer and more comprehensive collation of the copious materials on the history of the English Bible does not exist."—*Good Literature.*

"This is the latest addition to the large literature called forth by the English Bible. Many works, both English and American, are in existence, treating of the Authorized Version with its predecessors and successors, but this one is more complete and full than any other."—*Christian Intelligencer.*

"A characteristic of this work is its mingling the internal with the external history of the descent of our English versions. Crowded as the volume is, it is readable throughout, and, in some of its sections, intensely interesting."—*Sunday School Times.*

"The latest, and, in some respects, the most complete of the various histories of the English Bible."—*Bible Society Record.*

S. BAGSTER & SONS, LTD., 15, PATERNOSTER ROW, LONDON.

www.ingramcontent.com/pod-product-compliance
Lightning Source LLC
Chambersburg PA
CBHW031405270326
41929CB00010BA/1335

* 9 7 8 3 3 3 7 2 2 6 0 9 1 *